Perspectives on Argument

Nancy V. Wood

Professor and Department Chair
English Department
The University of Texas at Arlington

PRENTICE HALL
Englewood Cliffs, New Jersey 07632

Library of Congress Cataloging-in-Publication Data

Wood, Nancy V.
    Perspectives on argument / Nancy V. Wood.
      p. cm.
    Includes index.
    ISBN 0–13–010745–X
    1. English language—Rhetoric.   2. Persuasion (Rhetoric)
  3. College readers. I. Title.
  PE1431.W66 1995
  808'.0427—dc20
                           94–33423
                           CIP

Acquisitions editor: Alison Reeves
Editorial assistant: David Schecter
Editorial/production supervision: Susan Finkelstein
Interior design: Doug Smock
Copy editor: Peter Reinhart
Cover design: Sue Behnke
Buyer: Lynn Pearlman

Credits

Bernard Adelsberger. "Survey Says?...Don't Lift Gay Ban." Reprinted courtesy of *Navy Times*. Copyright by Army Times Publishing Co., Springfield, VA.
Lois Agnew. "Special Education's Best Intentions." Reprinted by permission of the author.
Drummond B. Ayres, Jr. "Shadow of Pessimism Eclipses a Dream." Copyright © 1992 by The New York Times Company. Reprinted by permission.
Sandy Banisky. "Adversaries on Abortion Begin Reaching for Common Ground." The *Baltimore Sun*, January 14, 1992. Reprinted with permission.
Stephen Bates. "The Textbook Wars." Copyright © 1993 by Stephen Bates. Reprinted by permission of Pocket Books, a division of Simon & Schuster, Inc. Originally appeared in *The National Review*, September 28, 1993.
Nilesh Bhakta. "Argument in Zimbabwe." Reprinted by permission of the author.
"The Birds and the Trees." From *Newsweek*, April 5, 1993. © 1993, Newsweek, Inc. All rights reserved. Reprinted by permission.
Roberta F. Borkat. "A Liberating Curriculum." © Roberta F. Borkat. Originally appeared in *Newsweek*, April 12, 1993. Reprinted by permission.

Credits continue on page 615, which constitutes an extension of the copyright page.

© 1995 by Prentice-Hall, Inc.
A Simon & Schuster Company
Englewood Cliffs, New Jersey 07632

Printed in the United States of America
10 9 8 7 6 5 4 3 2 1

ISBN 0-13-010745-X

Prentice-Hall International (UK) Limited, *London*
Prentice-Hall of Australia Pty. Limited, *Sydney*
Prentice-Hall Canada Inc., *Toronto*
Prentice-Hall Hispanoamericana, S. A., *Mexico*
Prentice-Hall of India Private Limited, *New Delhi*
Prentice-Hall of Japan, Inc., *Tokyo*
Simon & Schuster Asia Pte. Ltd., *Singapore*
Editora Prentice-Hall do Brasil, Ltda., *Rio de Janeiro*

Brief Contents

PART FOUR   The Reader   **361**

Contents

7 Types of Claims 214

PART THREE Writing a Research Paper That Presents an Argument 259

10 Organizing, Writing, and Revising 311

Synthesis of Chapters 1–10: Summary Charts 349

Section IV: Freedom of Speech Issues 476

Section V: Environmental Issues 505

Preface

Purpose

English departments across the country, in increasing numbers, are devoting a semester of English composition to argument. This is at least partly in response to the general perception that critical thinking should have a more central place in the curriculum. Argument classes encourage critical thinking, since it is there that students learn to identify controversial topics that are "at issue," to read and form reactions and opinions of their own, and to write argument papers that express their individual views and perspectives.

Modern argument classes are motivated by the notion that good citizens should be able to understand and participate in public argument. Such participation is critical not only in a democratic society, but also in a global society in which issues become more and more complex each year. This text teaches students to develop and value their own viewpoints, perspectives, and styles of argument. It also teaches students to acknowledge perspectives and argument styles that are different from their own. Students learn to take a variety of approaches to argument, such as taking a position and defending it, adapting to the context of an argument, seeking common ground, withholding opinion at times, negotiating when necessary, and even changing their original beliefs when they can no longer make a case for them. The perspectives and abilities taught here are those that an educated populace in a world community needs to coexist cooperatively and without constant destructive conflict.

A pervasive idea in this text is that argument exists everywhere and that students will encounter it in their other classes, at home, on the job, and in the national and international spheres. A student who test-read this book saw these applications immediately and asked the teacher early in the semester if it was all right for him to use what he was learning outside of class. He was told, of course, that it was exactly what he should expect to do with his new knowledge of argument.

Special Features

Both instructors and students who pick up this book have the right to ask how it differs from some of the other argument texts that are presently available. They deserve to know why they might want to use this book instead of another. This text, which is targeted for freshmen and sophomores enrolled in argument classes in two-year and four-year colleges, is both a reader and a rhetoric. Within this reader and rhetoric format are a number of special features that, taken together, make the book unique.

- **Reading, critical thinking**, and **writing** are taught as integrated and interdependent processes. More instruction in critical reading is provided in this book than in any other book of its kind.
- **Cross-gender** and **cross-cultural communication styles** are presented in a unique chapter that provides for a classroom in which every student can find a voice. Also included are international students' perspectives on argument. Many readings are by authors of different cultural, international, and ethnic backgrounds.
- **Multiple perspectives on issues are stressed in favor of pro and con positions** that polarize issues and invite the declaration of "winners." A strong emphasis is placed on finding common ground and reaching consensus. Rogerian argument is presented in a special section.
- **Theory includes the Toulmin model of argument**, classical types of claims and proofs, the rhetorical situation, and cross-cultural and cross-gender argument styles. Theory is integrated and translated into language that students can easily understand and apply. Students, for example, use theory to recognize and analyze the parts of an argument while reading and to develop and structure their own ideas while writing.
- **Audience analysis** includes the concepts of the familiar and the unfamiliar audience as well as Chaim Perelman's concept of the universal audience.
- **Productive invention strategies** help students develop ideas for papers. **Additional strategies** are presented for each stage of the reading/writing process and are formatted so that students will be able to remember and use them.
- **Important topics are highlighted in boxes and charts** throughout to make them more accessible for students.
- **Classroom-tested exercises at the ends of the chapters invite individual, small group, and whole class participation**. The collaborative exercises and writing assignments in particular have been tested by students repeatedly and revised until they work. Nearly one hundred students, in fact, test-read this book while it was in manuscript form. Worksheets at the end of Chapters 1, 8, and 9 are products of this testing. They can be used repeatedly to help students develop papers.
- **Major writing assignments include an exploratory paper,** which teaches students to explore several different perspectives on an issue, **the critical analysis paper,** which teaches students to analyze and evaluate a written argument, and the **research paper**, which teaches students to take a position on an issue and defend it. All are models for writing assignments that students are likely to encounter in their other college classes. An optional writing project that begins in the first chapter and ends with the last allows the student to consolidate and integrate the theory and explanations presented in the first ten

chapters. Other writing assignments are provided throughout. A variety of both reading and writing assignments, in fact, accompanies every chapter.

- **Research is presented as a creative activity** that students are invited to enjoy. Workable strategies for research and note taking are provided.
- **Summary charts at the end of the rhetoric section present the main points of argument** in a handy format. They also integrate the reading and writing processes for argument by placing strategies for both side by side and showing the interconnections.
- **A total of 118 different readings** in the rhetoric section and "The Reader" provide students with multiple perspectives on the many issues presented throughout the book.
- **Examples of student papers are provided** for each major type of paper. MLA and APA formats are provided for research papers.
- **The readings in "The Reader" are clustered under subissues** that are related to the seven major general issue areas that organize "The Reader." This helps students focus and narrow broad issues. Furthermore, the readings in each subissue group "talk" to each other, and questions invite students to join the conversation.
- **Topics and formats for class debates and symposia** are provided at the end of "The Reader." Classes can thus experiment both with pro and con and with multiple-perspective formats of argument.

Organization

The text is organized into four parts and, as much as possible, chapters have been written so that they stand alone. Instructors may thus assign them either in sequence or in a more preferred order to supplement their own course organization.

Part One: Engaging with Argument for Reading and Writing. This part introduces students to issues and the characteristics of argument in Chapter 1, helps them begin to develop a personal style of argument in Chapter 2, and provides them with processes for reading and writing argument in Chapters 3 and 4. Part One ends with the exploratory paper.

Part Two: Understanding the Nature of Argument for Reading and Writing. This part identifies and explains the parts of an argument according to Stephen Toulmin's model of argument in Chapter 5, presents the types of proofs along with clear examples and tests for validity in Chapter 6, and explains the types of claims and purposes for argument in Chapter 7. Proofs are discussed before claims because certain types of proofs are particularly appropriate for developing different kinds of claims, and an initial understanding of proofs helps students understand and use the claims. Part Two ends with the critical analysis paper.

Part Three: Writing a Research Paper That Presents an Argument. This part teaches students to write a claim, clarify purpose, and analyze the audience in

Chapter 8; to use various creative strategies for inventing ideas and gathering research materials in Chapter 9; and to organize, write, revise, and prepare the final manuscript in Chapter 10. Methods for locating and using resource materials in the library are presented in Chapters 9 and 10.

Part Four: The Reader. This part is organized around the broad issues of men's and women's roles, education, crime and the treatment of criminals, freedom of speech, the environment, racism in America, modern technology, and one deliberately inflammatory issue, abortion. The development of common ground is presented as a key strategy for arguing this last issue. Strategies and questions to help students explore issues and move from reading and discussion to writing are also included.

The Instructor's Manual

In preparing the Instructor's Manual, my coauthors of the manual, Leslie Snow and Corri Wells, and I have included chapter-by-chapter suggestions for using the book. We have also included a sample syllabus that shows how the book can be used in a one-semester class on argument. The instructor who class-tested the book during two different semesters has written a day-by-day teaching journal in which she details how she worked with this book in class and how the students responded. Also included in the manual are strategies for teaching this material in the computer classroom and strategies for teaching students to use the electronic data bases and other resources for research in the library. A set of class handouts ready for photocopying is also included. Copies of this manual may be obtained from your Prentice Hall representative.

N.V.W.

Acknowledgments

My greatest debt is to my husband, James A. Wood, who has also taught and written about argument. He helped me work out my approach to argument mainly by listening, but also by asking questions and discussing ideas. The process renewed my faith in peer groups and writing conferences. Most writers, I am convinced, profit from talking through their ideas with someone else. I was lucky to find someone so knowledgeable and generous with his time and insights.

I also owe a debt to the freshman English program at The University of Texas at Arlington. In the 1980s an NEH grant provided considerable creative energy for this program, and when I joined the program a few years later, I found myself caught up in its ideas and controversies. It provided me with much of the interest and motivation to write this book.

For the past several years, I have trained the graduate teaching assistants in our department who teach argument. An exceptionally alert group of these students read an early draft of this book and recommended changes. I am very grateful to them. Five other seasoned graduate students provided additional help. Leslie Snow and Robb Pocklington helped me organize "The Reader." Leslie Snow also classroom-tested the book in two classes and, with Corri Wells, provided material for the Instructor's Manual. Joanna Johnson formatted and typed the Instructor's Manual.

I am also indebted to other colleagues and friends who contributed ideas, favorite articles, and encouragement. James Kinneavy is the originator of the exploratory paper as it is taught in this book. Audrey Wick, Jan Swearingen, Judith McDowell, Sam Wood, Elizabeth Conquest, Joe Wood, Simone Turbeville, and David Wood contributed articles and ideas. DeAnn Coffin provided expert assistance with the manuscript. I wish I had the space to acknowledge by name the many undergraduate students who read the manuscript and made recommendations for improvements. I paid particularly close attention to their comments, and I know their efforts have made this a better book for other undergraduates throughout the country.

At Prentice Hall, my greatest debt is to Phil Miller, President, Humanities and Social Sciences, who got me started with this project. I also thank Alison Reeves,

English editor, Julie Williams, developmental editor, and Susan Finkelstein, production editor at P. M. Gordon Associates, for seeing the book through all phases of production. Other colleagues around the country provided additional ideas and recommended changes that have helped improve the book. They include Margaret W. Batschelet, University of Texas at San Antonio; Linda D. Bensel-Meyers, University of Tennessee; Gregory Clark, Brigham Young University; Alexander Friedlander, Drexel University; William S. Hochman, University of Southern Colorado; James Kinneavy, University of Texas at Austin; Elizabeth Metzger, University of South Florida; Margaret Dietz Meyer, Ithaca College; Randall L. Popken, Tarleton State University; William E. Sheidley, United States Air Force Academy; Diane M. Thiel, Florida International University; and Jennifer Welsh, University of Southern California. I am grateful to them for the time and care they took reviewing the manuscript.

This book has been a genuinely collaborative effort. I hope students will profit from the example and learn to draw on the expertise of their instructors and classmates to help them write their papers. Most writing is more fun and more successful when it is, at least partly, a social process.

PART ONE

Engaging with Argument for Reading and Writing

The strategy in these first four chapters is to introduce you to issues and the special characteristics of argument in Chapter 1, to help you begin to develop a personal style of argument in Chapter 2, and to help you develop your processes for reading and writing argument in Chapters 3 and 4. The focus in these chapters is on you and how you will engage with argument both as a reader and as a writer. When you finish reading Part One:

- You will understand what argument is and why it is important in a democratic society.
- You will have found some issues (topics) to read and write about.
- You will have analyzed your present style of argument and considered ways to adapt it for special contexts.
- You will have new strategies and ideas to help you read argument critically.
- You will have adapted your present writing process to help you think critically and write argument papers.
- You will have experience with two major types of argument papers: the Rogerian argument paper and the exploratory argument paper.

CHAPTER 1

A Perspective on Argument

You engage in argument, whether you realize it or not, nearly every day. Argument deals with *issues*, or the topics that have not yet been settled, topics that invite two or more differing opinions and that are, consequently, subject to question, debate, or negotiation. Pick up today's newspaper and read the headlines to find some current examples. Here are some issues that have been raised by headlines of the past: Should one country intervene in the affairs of another? What is the best way to slow population growth in Third World countries? Should politicians be more ethical than everyone else? What should be done about the latest crime wave? Or, think of examples of issues that may be closer to your daily experience: Should one "eat, drink, and be merry," or exercise daily and avoid fatty foods? Which is the more important consideration in selecting a major: finding a job or enjoying the subject? How can one minimize the frustrations caused by limited campus parking?

All of these issues, whether they seem remote or close to you, are related to the big issues that have engaged human thought for centuries. In fact, all of the really important issues—those that deal with life and death, the quality of life, ways and means, war and peace, the individual and society, the environment—these and others like them are discussed, debated, and negotiated somewhere in the world on a regular basis. There are usually no simple or obvious positions to take on such important issues. Still, the positions we do take on them and, ultimately, the decisions and actions we take in regard to them can affect our lives in significant ways. In democratic societies individuals are expected to engage in effective argument on issues of broad concern. They are also expected to make moral judgments and to evaluate the decisions and ideas that emerge from argument.

The purpose of this book is to help you participate in two types of activities: evaluating other people's arguments and creating arguments of your own. The book has been organized in parts, and each part will help you become a more effective participant in the arguments that affect your life. Part One will help you engage with argument personally as you begin to identify the issues, the argument styles, and the processes for reading and writing that will work best for you; Part Two will help you understand the nature of argument as you learn more about its essential parts and how they operate in argument to convince an audience; Part Three will provide you with a process for thinking critically and writing an argument paper that requires both critical thought and research; Part Four will provide you with many good examples of effective argument to analyze and draw on as you create original arguments of your own.

WHAT IS YOUR CURRENT PERSPECTIVE ON ARGUMENT?

You may never have been in an argument class before. If that is the case, as it is with most students, you will have a few ideas about argument, but you will not have a totally clear idea about what you will be studying in this class. It is best to begin the study of any new subject by thinking about what you already know. Then you can use what you know to learn more, which is the way all of us acquire new knowledge.

What does the word "argument" make you think about? The following list contains some common student responses to that question. Place a check next to those that match your own. Or, do other ideas come to your mind? Add them to the list.

_____ 1. It is important to include both sides in argument.
_____ 2. Argument is "an argument," with people mad and yelling at each other.
_____ 3. Argument is a debate in front of a judge; one side wins.
_____ 4. Argument takes place in courtrooms before judges and juries.
_____ 5. Argument is what I'd like to be able to do better at home, at work, with my friends so that I'd win more, get my way more often.
_____ 6. Argument is standing up for your ideas, defending them, and minimizing the opposition by being persuasive.
_____ 7. Argument requires one to keep an "open mind."
_____ 8. Argument papers are difficult to write because they require more than a collection of personal feelings and opinions about a subject.
_____ 9. Argument, to me, is like beating a dead horse. I have done papers in high school about subjects I'm supposed to care about, like abortion, homosexuality, drugs, capital punishment. They're old news. They no longer spark my imagination.
_____ 10. Argument is something I like to avoid. I see no reason for it. It makes things unpleasant and difficult. And nothing gets settled anyway.
_____ 11. _____
_____ 12. _____

Whether your present views of argument are positive, negative, or just vague, it's best to acknowledge them so that you can now begin to expand on them or even modify some of them in order to develop a broad perspective on argument.

A definition of argument at this point should help clarify the broad perspective we are seeking for this word. There are many approaches and views of argument, and consequently various definitions have been suggested by argument theorists. Some focus on identifying opposing views, providing evidence, and declaring winners. Others emphasize reasoning, understanding, agreement, and consensus. Both types of definition are useful depending on the context and the purpose of the argument. Chaim Perelman, a respected modern argument theorist, provides the definition that we will use in this book. Perelman suggests that the goal of argument "is to create or increase the adherence of minds to the theses presented for their [the audience's] assent."[1] This definition is broad enough to include both argument that focuses on opposing views and the declaration of winners and argument that emphasizes understanding and results in consensus. This definition further invites argument participants either to agree to the best position on a matter of dispute or to create a new position that all participants can agree on. Using this definition as a starting point, we can now add to it and consider argument in its broadest sense.

DEVELOPING A BROAD PERSPECTIVE ON ARGUMENT

Think about the implications of this idea: *Argument is everywhere.*[2] It is not only found in obvious places such as courts of law, legislative assemblies, or organized debates. Indeed, it is a part of all human enterprise, whether at home, at school, at work, or on the national or international scene. Home argument, for example, might center on spending money, dividing the household work, raising the children, and planning for the future. School argument might include such issues as increasing student fees, finding parking, understanding grades, or selecting classes and professors. Work argument might focus on making hiring decisions, delegating responsibility, or establishing long-term goals. National argument might deal with providing health care, abolishing crime, or electing leaders. International argument might deal with protecting human rights, abolishing hunger, or negotiating international trade agreements. Thus argument appears in virtually any context in which human beings interact and hold divergent views about topics that are at issue. Furthermore, argument is a perspective, a point of view that people adopt to identify, interpret, analyze, communicate, and try to reach settlements or conclusions about subjects that are at issue.

If we accept the idea that argument can, indeed, be found anywhere, then we discover that it can also appear in several different forms and involve varying numbers of people. Argument can take eight different forms, as in the fol-

---

[1]Chaim Perelman and L. Olbrechts-Tyteca, *The New Rhetoric: A Treatise on Argumentation* (Notre Dame, IN: Notre Dame Press, 1969), p. 45.

[2]I am indebted to Wayne Brockriede for this observation and for some of the other ideas in this chapter. See his article "Where Is Argument?" Journal of the American Forensic Association, Spring 1975, pp. 179–182.

lowing list. Some, like organized debate and courts of law, will not surprise you. Others may.

Forms of Argument

1. *Debate, with participants on both sides trying to win.* In a debate, people take sides on a controversial issue that is usually stated as a proposition. For example, the proposition "Resolved that capital punishment be implemented in all 50 states" might be debated by an affirmative debater who would argue in favor of this idea and a negative debater who would argue against it. A judge, who listens to the debate, usually selects one of the debaters as the winner. The debaters do not try to convince one another, but instead they try to convince the judge who is supposed to be impartial. Debates are useful for exploring and sometimes resolving issues that have distinct pro and con sides. Debates on television often feature people who hold conflicting views. The judge for these programs is the viewing public who may or may not pick a winner. Certainly the participants give the impression that they hope viewers will side with one or the other of them.

2. *Courtroom argument, with lawyers pleading before a judge and jury.* As in a debate, lawyers take opposing sides and argue to convince a judge and jury of the guilt or innocence of a defendant. Lawyers do not try to convince one another. Also as in debate, someone is designated the winner. Television provides opportunities to witness courtroom argument, particularly on cable channels devoted exclusively to televising real trials. You can also visit court, since trials are open to the public.

3. *Dialectic, with people taking opposing views and finally resolving the conflict.* In dialectic, two or more people argue as equals to try to discover what seems to be the best position. A questioning strategy is often used to test the validity of each of the opposing views. The ancient philosopher Plato used this form of argument in his dialogues to examine such questions as what is truth, what is the ideal type of government, and what is more important: honesty and justice or political power. Dialectic is used by some professors to help students think about and finally arrive at positions that can be generally accepted by most of the class. For example, dialectic might be used to ascertain students' views on academic honesty or political action. Participants explain and justify their own positions and test others' positions. The object is to discover a common bedrock of ideas that everyone can agree on. There are no winners. There is, instead, a consensual discovery of a new position on the issue that is agreeable to everyone.

4. *Single-perspective argument, with one person arguing to convince a mass audience.* We encounter argument in single-perspective form constantly on television and in newspapers, journals, books, and public speeches. It is usually clear what the issue is and what position is being taken. Other opposing views, if referred to at all, are usually refuted. Specific examples of such argument range from a politician trying to influence voters to change their ideas about taxes, to an environmentalist trying to influence management to eliminate toxic waste,

to an advertiser trying to sell blue jeans. The arguer does not usually know what immediate effect the message has had on the audience unless a poll or vote is taken, unless there is an opportunity for the readers to write letters to the editor, or unless there is a publicized change in policy or behavior. It is not clear, in other words, whether anyone "wins."

5. *One-on-one, everyday argument, with one person trying to convince another.* Convincing another person, one on one, is very different from convincing an impartial outside judge or a large unspecified audience. In the one-on-one situation, one person has to focus on and identify with the other person, think about what he or she wants and values, and be conciliatory if necessary. Each person either wins, loses, or is partially successful in winning. Examples of this form of argument might include convincing a partner to sell the business, convincing an employment officer to hire a favored candidate, or convincing a potential customer to buy a car.

6. *Academic inquiry, with one or more people examining a complicated issue.* The purpose of academic argument is to discover new views, new knowledge, and new truths about a complex issue. For example, physicists engage in academic inquiry about the nature of gravity, historians about the causes of major wars, or political scientists about the benefits of a strong state government. There are no clear-cut pro and con positions, no judges, and no emphasis on winning. Instead, anyone can participate, and there are potentially as many views as there are participants. Inquiry is a common form of argument that you will encounter in many of your college classes, where you will also be assigned to write inquiry papers. Virtually every discipline includes matters that are still open to inquiry, matters that people are still thinking and arguing about. Many professors expect their students to be able to identify the issues for inquiry in an academic discipline and also to participate in the ongoing search for answers. Imagine, for example, people reasoning together in a sociology class about whether war is ever justified, or in a psychology class about whether discrimination can ever be eliminated from society. These are not simple questions with yes or no answers. Inquiry can, however, produce insight into very difficult questions, with each new participant contributing a new reason, a new example, or a new angle that the others may not have considered. As the conversation progresses, participants achieve better understanding through mutual feedback, and some may even change their minds in order to bring their ideas in line with those of other participants. The inquiry form of argument is appropriate for the complex issues that one can find in every area of study and in every field of human endeavor. Like other forms of argument, it focuses on an issue and examines evidence. It is conducted through a cooperative search for knowledge, however, rather than on finding a winning position at the expense of others. Its result, ideally, is a consensus theory of truth, even though it may take some time to reach it.

7. *Negotiation, with two or more people working to reach consensus.* This is an important form of argument that is used to create the plans of action that solve problems. Both the Palestinians and the Israelis, for example, could not claim ownership

of the same land, so a joint plan for separate states had to be negotiated. One country could not kill sea life that another country depended on, so rights to the sea had to be negotiated. Closer to home, people negotiate who gets the car, who picks up the check, or who takes out the newspapers. Negotiation most often takes place between two people, one on one, or in group meetings. It involves both competition and cooperation, and in order for it to be successful, everyone must state his or her favored position and support it. Everyone must also be willing to listen to alternative views and reasons and modify original views in order to reach consensus.

8. *Internal argument, or working to convince yourself.* Internal argument is used by all of us for individual decision making and also to increase our own levels of motivation. New Year's resolutions are one example of internal argument and decision making. As in other forms of argument, different possibilities are identified, reasons both for and against are considered, and conclusions are finally reached.

Now reconsider some of the student perspectives on argument that are listed at the beginning of this chapter. Most of those ideas fit into one of the eight forms of argument just described. The exception is item 2, argument defined as "an argument," with people mad and yelling at each other. No argument can be effective when people stop listening, stop thinking, and engage in vocal fighting, so "an argument" is not part of the broad perspective on argument defined in this chapter. Look back also at item 8 (argument is difficult to write because it requires more than opinion), item 9 (I'm tired of some of the topics for argument), and item 10 (argument makes me uncomfortable). If you found yourself initially in sympathy with those responses, you may now have discovered forms of argument that could be acceptable vehicles for your ideas. Here is the list again: debate, courtroom argument, dialectic, single-perspective argument, one-on-one argument, academic inquiry, negotiation, and internal argument. Which have been successful forms for you in the past? Which others are you drawn to? Why?

These examples and explanations of forms of argument demonstrate that effective argument does not take place automatically. Special conditions are necessary, in fact, if argument is to be effective. Let's look at some of those conditions to further expand our perspective on argument.

UNDER WHAT CONDITIONS DOES ARGUMENT WORK BEST?

To work best, argument requires (1) an arguable issue, (2) a person who will argue, (3) an audience that will listen, (4) some common ground between the arguer and the audience, (5) a forum in which the argument can take place, and (6) some changes in the audience. Let's look at some optimal requirements for each of these important elements.

1. *An issue.* An argument needs to have as its central focus an issue that has not yet been settled. Furthermore, there must be the potential for at least two or more views on that issue. For example, some people seem to think that the hand-

gun issue has only two sides—that is, everyone should, by constitutional right, be allowed to own handguns, or no one should be allowed to own them. Between these two extreme views, however, people can and do take a variety of positions, including the view that owning and using handguns may be acceptable under certain conditions but not others.

2. *An arguer.* Every argument requires an arguer who is willing, interested, and motivated to take a position on an issue, get information and think about it, and communicate it to others. This person needs to develop expertise on an issue and be willing to take the risk to express his or her own ideas about it. Furthermore, the arguer should be willing to go beyond the "current wisdom" about an issue and give fresh perspectives and approaches that will suggest original insights to the audience. For example, an individual arguing for tougher handgun laws needs to present fresh reasons and evidence to get people's attention and agreement.

3. *An audience.* Every argument needs an audience that is willing to listen or read and consider new views or perspectives. The audience should also be capable of understanding, thinking, questioning, discussing, and answering. It may be composed of one or more people who are personally known to the arguer, or it may be unknown, in which case the arguer must imagine and invoke its background, motives, and values. The arguer should want to communicate with this audience. It should not be composed of people who are usually ignored or who are not respected by the arguer. It is a compliment to draw someone into discussion on an issue, so the audience should be valued, and, to be effective, the arguer must show that he or she cares about the audience, its interests, and its state of mind. This approach will assure a willing audience that listens and does not shut the arguer out or otherwise try to escape. Receptive audiences are potentially willing to change their minds, a desirable outcome of argument.[3] Consider, for example, an audience member who favors handgun ownership, who is a parent of schoolchildren, and who is willing to listen to an opposing view because a respectful fellow parent has described the number of children who own handguns in their children's school.

4. *Common ground.* Effective argument requires a community of minds that is achieved through common language and the establishment of some common ground that is relevant to the issue. People from different countries obviously need a common language, but they also need an understanding and respect for one another's cultural differences in order to argue effectively. People from different disciplines must be able to understand and respect one another's technical jargon and other words and concepts central to the understanding of a particular field of study. In addition, they need to share some background, values, and views to make communication possible. Three situations are possible when one works to establish common ground in argument. First, if two parties agree totally, they do not argue. For example, two parents who agree that their child should go to college do not argue about that part of the child's future. Second, if two parties are too far apart, they

---

[3]Some of the observations in this chapter about the special conditions for argument, especially for the audience, are derived from Perelman and Olbrechts-Tyteca, *The New Rhetoric*, Part 1.

usually do not understand one another well enough to argue. The United States did not have enough common ground with Iraq in 1991 to work out differences, and the two countries went to war. There were several causes for this war. Iraq had invaded Kuwait, and the United States was committed to help this country maintain its independence. Kuwait's independence was important to the United States because Kuwait was a major source of U.S. oil. Finally, Iraq was developing a powerful military with nuclear potential, so it seemed important to the United States to stop that military growth. Common ground in this situation virtually did not exist, and, as a result, reasoned argument gave way to "an argument," and many people were killed. The third possible situation for establishing common ground creates more effective conditions for argument than do the first two. Common ground may be established through the discovery of common interests—common ideas, motives, or values—or even through recognizing common friends or enemies. As soon as two parties realize they have something in common, they can more easily achieve identification, even if it is minimal, and engage in constructive argument. Imagine, once again, two parties who disagree on handgun ownership. One party believes handgun ownership should be forbidden to stop random killing. The other party believes people should own handguns to protect themselves from random killers. Both agree that random killing is bad and must be stopped, and this basic agreement provides the common ground they need to begin to engage in constructive argument about handgun ownership. Figure 1.1 provides a diagram of these three possible situations for establishing common ground in argument.

5. *A forum.* People need safe forums for argument where they can feel creative and know they will be heard. Such widely available forums include magazines and journals, newspapers, books, letters and reports, television programs of all sorts, courtrooms, legislative assemblies, motion pictures, art, drama, fiction, poetry, advertisements, and music. College is another safe forum for arguments. Professors and students argue in class, at meals, and in dorms and apartments. Outside speakers present argument. The argument class, with its discussions, papers, and other assignments, can be a safe forum for practicing argument, particularly if both the students and the instructor work to create an environment in which all students participate and are respected.

6. *Audience outcomes.* Successful arguments should produce changes in the audience. These changes will vary with the audience and situation. At times the audience becomes convinced and decides to change its mind. Or a successful negotiation is achieved, people find themselves in consensus, a decision is reached, and a plan of action is proposed. Other arguments may not have such clear-cut results. A hostile audience may be brought to a neutral point of view. A neutral audience may decide to take a stand. Sometimes, it is a significant accomplishment to get the audience's attention and to raise its level of consciousness. This success can lay the groundwork for a possible future change of mind. As the world prepared to send its leaders to the first Earth Summit in the summer of 1992, *Newsweek* magazine reported that some people were already discouraged because they were afraid that too little would be decided and that there would not be enough com-

THE ISSUE: WAS HUMAN LIFE CREATED OR DID IT EVOLVE

Possibility 1: Complete agreement and not argument. Two creationists believe the biblical language about the six days of creation literally, agree totally, and share the same common ground.

Possibility 2: Total disagreement, no common ground, and no argument. A creationist literally believes the biblical six days of creation, and an evolutionist believes that human life evolved from a single cell over eons of time. They disagree totally, and there is no common ground.

Possibility 3: Two parties discover something in common and there is a possibility of argument. Another creationist allows that biblical language may be metaphorical and therefore that creation may have occurred over eons of time. An evolutionist also believes humans took eons to evolve. They share common ground on that point, but disagree on other points.

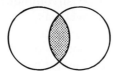

Figure 1.1 Establishing Common Ground

mitment to act. Not so, said the *Newsweek* reporter; any action on the environment, no matter how minimal, should always be welcomed.[4] He pointed out that getting anything on paper is a vital first step, that progress may be agonizingly slow, but that first steps are necessary for future initiatives.

Some students in argument class wonder if they are required to convince their teachers of their point of view in every paper they write if they are to get good grades. This demand may be too great, since audiences and the outcomes of argument vary so much. Convincing the teacher that the argument paper is effective with a particular audience is probably the best possible outcome in argument class.

UNDER WHAT CONDITIONS DOES ARGUMENT FAIL?

We have just examined the optimal conditions for argument. Now let's look at the conditions that can cause it to flounder or fail. No argument, we have seen,

---

[4]Gregg Easterbrook, "A House of Cards," *Newsweek*, June 1, 1992, p. 33.

can take place when there is no real disagreement, no uncertainty, or no possibility for two or more views. Also, neutral people who do not have enough interest in an issue to form an opinion do not argue. For example, some young people do not want to argue about possible retirement plans because they are neutral on this issue. Argument also cannot take place unless people perceive an issue as a subject for argument. An example might be a college orientation session where various department representatives argue in favor of their areas as majors. This is not an issue for students who have already decided, and thus they will not identify issues or perceive this session as a forum for argument.

Big problems or risky problems that may require radical change are difficult for some people to argue about. Finding a new career or dissolving a longtime relationship may fit into this category, and many people, wisely or not, tend to leave such difficult issues alone rather than argue about them. Religious issues or issues that threaten global disaster are also sometimes too big, too emotional, or too scary for many people to argue about. At the other extreme, some issues may be perceived as low risk, trivial, boring, or even ridiculous. Some family arguments fall into this category, like what to eat for dinner. One person may care, but the rest do not.

Arguments that lack common ground among participants do not work well. It is sometimes difficult to establish common ground and argue constructively with "true believers," for example, who have made up their minds on certain issues and will not listen, budge, or change. Racial bigots fall into this category. It is also difficult to argue with some religious people who take certain issues on faith and do not perceive them as subjects for argument. In fact, argument often fails when one participant perceives a topic as an issue and the other does not. Again, there is no common ground. Finally, argument cannot take place when one party is not motivated to argue. "Don't bring that up again" or "I don't want to discuss that" puts an end to most argument. The "Calvin and Hobbes" cartoon in Figure 1.2 provides a similar example.

We have already described the audience outcomes of effective argument. When argument is not working, as in the situations just described, the outcomes

CALVIN AND HOBBS

Figure 1.2   When Argument Fails

are negative also. Sometimes poor argument results in a standoff: both parties agree to keep their original views and not to cross the line. Or emotions run strong, verbal fighting breaks out, and extreme views are expressed. No one agrees with anyone else. People shake their heads and walk away, or they become hurt and upset. Some individuals may become strident, wanting to debate everyone to demonstrate that they are right. When classroom argument results in such negative outcomes, some students drop the class, others become silent and refuse to participate, and everyone becomes confused.

One important aim of this book is to provide you with the insight and skill to manage these negative situations so that more constructive argument can take place. Students are in an excellent position to overcome some of the fear, resistance, and aversion associated with difficult issues and, by using evidence and good sense, get to work and face some of them. Understanding audience members, especially their attitudes, needs, and values, is an important first step. Another useful idea to keep in mind is that most arguers have more success with some audiences than with others depending upon the amount of common ground. Even in the most difficult situations, some common ground can usually be found among people who seem to disagree on almost everything else. Recent research suggests that one vehicle for establishing common ground is through narratives, with each side relating personal experiences and stories. Even the most hostile adversaries can usually relate to one another's personal experiences and find some unity in the common villains, heroines, or themes in their stories. What sometimes also happens in this process is that the issues themselves change or are transformed in ways that make them easier for both parties to argue.[5]

Arguing effectively in difficult situations requires a conscious effort to avoid both stereotypical reactions and entrenched behavioral patterns. Past habits must be replaced with new strategies that work better. It is sometimes difficult to make such changes because habits can be strong, but it is possible to do so, and the stakes are often high, especially when the choice is constructive argument or verbal fighting and standoffs.

ENGAGING WITH ISSUES

The most easily arguable issues, to summarize, are those that invite two or more views, that are perceived by all parties as issues, that are interesting and motivating to all participants, and that inspire research, information gathering, and original thought. They also promise common ground among participants, and they do not appear too big, too risky, too trivial, too confusing, too scary, or too specialized to discuss profitably. But you may also find yourself drawn to some of the more difficult issues that do not meet all of these criteria, and you should not nec-

---

[5] Linda Putnam in the keynote speech at the Texas Speech Communication Association Conference, October 1993, reported these results from her study of negotiations between teachers and labor union leaders.

essarily shun them just because they are difficult. You will need to work with your audience in creative ways and consider the entire context for argument, regardless of the nature of the issues you select. Most important is that you now identify some issues that are arguable and important to you and to your classroom audience. Identifying issues will help you keep a high level of motivation and receive the maximum instructional benefits from argument class. Finding your own arguable issues is much better than accepting assigned issues as writing topics.

So now the search begins. What will help you find your arguable issues? Issues exist in contexts, and the issues most engaging to you will probably emerge from those parts of your life that demand your greatest attention and energy. For example, people who are compellingly engaged with their professions think about work issues, new parents think about child-rearing issues, dedicated students think about the issues raised in class, and many teenagers think about peer-group issues. To begin the search for your issues, examine those parts of your life that demand your most concentrated time and attention right now. Also, think about some of the special characteristics of issues in general. Here are a few of them:

Issues Are Compelling.   People get excited about issues, and they usually identify with a few in particular. In fact, most people can quickly name one or more issues that are so important to them that they think about them often. Some people even build careers or change careers because of issues that are vital to them. People who devote large amounts of time and study to particular issues become the "experts" on those issues. Can you think of some issues of your own that are particularly compelling to you?

Issues Often Originate in Dramatic Life Situations.   Things happen— teenagers get shot at school, the ozone layer begins to disappear, riots break out in an inner city, a person who took fertility pills gives birth to five deformed babies. To understand these occurrences better, people react to them intellectually, and then issues emerge. Should teenagers, or should anyone, be allowed to purchase guns? Should the ozone layer be protected by law, and if so, when, and how? Should new social programs be installed in inner cities? Should people take fertility pills? Because of their dramatic origins, many issues are intensely interesting to many people. Pay attention to the stories that are newsworthy this week and begin to identify the issues that are associated with them. Select the ones that interest you the most.

Current Issues Are Related to Enduring Issues.   Current issues can be linked to enduring issues, those that have engaged people for many ages. For example, the current issues about military spending have their roots in the age-old issues that are associated with war. Is war ever justified? Should a country constantly be prepared for war? The abortion issue has its roots in the enduring issues about life. Should life be protected at all costs? Should the individual or a social agency have the greater control over one's life? Think about the enduring issues that engage you. They may help you find your arguable issues.

Issues Go Underground and Then Resurface.   Public concern with particular issues is not constant. Experts may think about their issues continuously, but the public usually only thinks about an issue when something happens that brings it to public attention. How to deal with increasing population is an example of such an issue. Experts on that issue may think about it daily, but the general public may think about it only when census figures are released or when an international meeting on the subject commands media attention. Such issues are, of course, always lurking in the background, always important. But we do not think about all of them all of the time. Think back. Are there some issues that used to concern you that you have neither thought about nor read about for a long time? What are they?

Issues Sometimes Get Solved, but Then New Ones Emerge.   Some issues command so much public attention that the people who can do something about them finally perceive them as problems and pass laws or take other measures to solve them. As soon as an issue is solved, however, other, related issues spring up in its place. For example, for a long time, people argued about what to do about the ozone layer. As soon as legislation was passed to prohibit the use of the harmful chemicals that destroy it, new issues emerged that focused on agendas and deadlines for abolishing the use of these chemicals. Another issue that emerged was a consideration of the best ways to profit economically from the change to new technologies. Are there any new issues of this type that might interest you? Think of problems that now seem solved but probably aren't fully solved.

Issues Seem to Be Getting More Complex.   The world's issues seem to become more and more complex as the world becomes more complex. In an interview, the actress Susan Sarandon, who has always been engaged with social issues, stated that in the mid- to late 1960s, when she was in college, the issues seemed simpler, more black and white. The issues at that time, for example, centered on civil rights and the Vietnam war. "We were blessed with clear-cut issues," she says. "We were blessed with clear-cut grievances. Things were not as gray as they are now."[6]

Because issues are now more complex, people need to learn to engage with them in more complex ways. The word "perspectives" as used in this book refers not only to a broader perspective on issues and argument itself, but also to the variety of different perspectives that individuals can take on particular issues. Few issues are black and white or can be viewed as pro or con anymore. Most invite several different ways of looking at them.

As you develop your own perspectives on the complex issues that engage you, keep in mind that it takes many years to become an expert. You will want to look at what the experts say. But you will not have the background and information to write as comprehensively as they do. When you write your own argument,

---

[6]Ovid Demaris, "Most of All, the Children Matter," *Parade*, March 1, 1992, pp. 4, 5.

you will want to write on a limited aspect of your issue, one that you can learn enough about. Limiting your topic will permit you to get the information and gain the perspective to be convincing. Suggestions to help you limit your approach to a complex issue will be made in future chapters.

Some Examples of Arguable Issues

Looking at examples of some of the issues that typically engage people should help you select the ones that will interest you. Date rape, political correctness, hate language, the treatment of criminals, environmental protection, gay rights, men's and women's roles and responsibilities, and censorship are issues that often interest students. In the 1992 presidential campaign, a number of public issues, such as reducing unemployment, providing health care, improving the quality of inner-city life, and establishing family values, commanded fairly constant attention from the candidates. Campaign issues do not change radically from one election to the next, although some may receive more attention some years than others. In Box 1.1 some contemporary public issues have been linked with enduring issues to demonstrate the timeless quality of most of them. See if you can add additional examples of your own as you read through those in the "current" column.

Box 1.2 illustrates some of the issues you are likely to encounter in your other classes in college. These are examples of issues that your professors argue about, the subjects for academic inquiry. You may be expected to take positions and develop arguments yourself on these or similar issues if you take classes in some of these subjects. As you read, try to add additional examples from your own classes.

HOW SHOULD YOU ENGAGE WITH ISSUES?

Boxes 1.1 and 1.2 represent only a sampling of issues. When you begin to focus on issues, you will identify many more. Here are some final suggestions to help you engage with issues:

- Listen for issues in all of your classes and identify them with a circled *I* in the margins of your lecture notes. Ask your professors to identify the major issues in their fields.
- Read a newspaper daily, if possible, or at least three or four times a week. If you do not take a newspaper, read one or more of them in the library or set up a newspaper recycling system in class. You will find stories about issues throughout the paper. The opinion and editorial pages, however, are the best source.
- Read a news magazine, like *Time* or *Newsweek*, on a regular basis, and look for issues.
- Concentrate your television viewing on programs where issues are discussed: news programs and programs that focus on interviews about issues, like "The MacNeil/Lehrer News Hour," "Crosscurrents," "Larry King Live," "Firing

What Are Some Public Issues?

CURRENT ISSUES	ENDURING ISSUES

Ways and Means Issues

Should everyone pay taxes and in what proportion to their income?

Where should a government get money, and how should it spend it?

Should free trade be limited?

How much business profit can be sacrificed to keep the environment clean and safe?

Should scholarships and fellowships be taxed?

Quality of Life Issues

Should more resources be directed to protecting the environment?

What is a minimum quality of life, and how do we achieve it?

Are inner cities or rural areas better places to live?

Personal Rights Versus Social Rights Issues

Should individuals, the government, or private business be responsible for
  health care?
  day care?
  the homeless?
  the recovery of drug addicts?
  race problems?
  minority problems?
  the punishment or rehabilitation of criminals?
  worker safety?
  deciding who should buy guns?

Can individuals be responsible for their own destinies, or should social institutions be responsible?

Can individuals be trusted to do what is best for society?

War and Peace Issues

How much should the government spend on the military?

Is war justified, and should countries stay prepared for war?

Should the United States remain prepared for a major world war?

Should you, your friends, or your family be required to register for the draft?

continued

BOX 1.1 Examples of Current and Enduring Public Issues

Self-Development Issues

What opportunities for education
and training should be available
to everyone?

Should the welfare system be
revised to include opportunities
for self-development?

Should gays be allowed the same
opportunities to participate
as other people?

What opportunities for self-development should societies make
available to individuals?

Human Life Issues

Should abortions be permitted?

Should capital punishment be
permitted?

Is mercy killing ever justifiable?

Should human life be protected
under any conditions?

Foreign Affairs Issues

Which is wiser, to support an
American economy or a global
economy?

How much foreign aid should we
provide, and to which countries?

Should college graduates be
provided with opportunities for
foreign service?

In world politics, how do we balance
the rights of smaller countries
and different ethnic groups
against the needs of larger
countries and international
organizations?

Law and Order Issues

Is the judicial system effective?

Does the punishment always
fit the crime?

Is police brutality a problem in
your community?

What is an appropriate balance
between the welfare and
protection of society as a whole
and the rights of the individual?

BOX 1.1 Examples of Current and Enduring Public Issues (*continued*)

Line," "This Week with David Brinkley," "Meet the Press," "60 Minutes," or
"PrimeTime Live." Many of these programs focus mainly on debate and pro
and con argument.

- Browse at the newsstand or in the current periodicals in the library and look
  for issues.
- Browse in the new-books section of the library and look for books that address issues.
- Listen for issues in conversations and discussions with other students. If you
  get confused, ask, "What is at issue here?" to help focus an argumentative
  discussion.

What Are Some Academic Issues?

In Physics—Is there a unifying force in the universe? Is there enough matter in the universe to cause it eventually to stop expanding and then to collapse? What is the nature of this matter?

In Astronomy—What elements can be found in interstellar gas? What is the nature of the asteroids?

In Biology—What limits, if any, should be placed on genetic engineering?

In Chemistry—How can toxic wastes best be managed?

In Sociology—Is the cause of crime social or individual? Does television have a significant negative effect on society?

In Psychology—Which is the best approach for understanding human behavior, nature or nurture? Can artificial intelligence ever duplicate human thought?

In Anthropology—Which is more reliable in dating evolutionary stages, DNA or fossils?

In Business—Can small privately owned businesses still compete with giant conglomerate companies? Are chief executive officers paid too much?

In Engineering—How important should environmental concerns be in determining engineering processes? To what extent, if any, are engineers responsible for the social use of what they produce? How aggressive should we be in seeking and implementing alternative sources of energy? Should the government be involved in funding the development of consumer-oriented technology to the same extent that it funds military-oriented technology?

In History—Have historians been too restrictive in their perspective? Does history need to be retold, and, if so, how? Is the course of history influenced more by unusual individuals or socioeconomic forces?

In Political Science—Where should ultimate authority to govern reside, with the individual, the church, the state, or social institutions? Is power properly divided among the three branches of government in the United States?

In Communication—How can the best balance be struck between the needs of society and freedom of expression in the mass media? How much impact, if any, do mass media have on the behavior of individuals in society?

In English—Is the concept of traditional literature too narrowly focused in English departments? If yes, what else should be considered literature?

BOX 1.2   Examples of Academic Issues across the Disciplines

- Study the table of contents of this book and sample some of the issues in the various readings at the ends of chapters and in "The Reader." Notice that "The Reader" is organized around broad issue areas and specific issues that are related to them. The articles have been selected to provide various perspectives, both historic and modern, on many specific current and enduring issues.

DEVELOPING A PERSONAL STYLE OF ARGUMENT

Some students feel resistant about the idea of finding issues and participating in argument because they think they will be required to take an opposing view, to debate, or to be contentious or aggressive in class, and they feel that they do not do these things well. A major idea that will be developed in the next chapter, is that everyone can and should participate in argument, but that not everyone may participate in the same way. You already have developed your own personal style of argument, and it has probably been influenced by several forces in your background. Some people think, for example, that men argue differently from women, that Asians argue differently from Europeans and Americans, and that blacks and Hispanics may argue differently from everyone else. Individuals can develop distinctive styles that use their best talents and abilities. Finding your style and developing it should become a major goal for you in the coming weeks.

The consequence of all people knowing how to argue effectively to resolve differences in personal, national, and international relationships is potentially a very powerful idea. Think of a country and a world where major problems are resolved through profitable argument instead of through confrontation, shouting orders, having arguments, fighting, or even going to war. You will often be in fervent disagreement with other people. In fact, life would be boring if you never disagreed. Yet, even when you disagree, even when you decide to enter an ongoing argument, you can learn to use a style that is comfortable and natural for you. And that approach is preferable to the alternatives: either remaining silent or becoming involved in destructive arguments that solve nothing and that may even cause harm.

EXERCISES AND ACTIVITIES

1. CLASS DISCUSSION: "ARGUMENT IS EVERYWHERE"
Jot down and discuss some examples from your experience that illustrate the statement "Argument is everywhere." Think about television shows, motion pictures, college classes, and other contexts for argument.

2. GROUP WORK AND CLASS DISCUSSION: CRITERIA FOR EFFECTIVE ARGUMENT
Both of the following arguments were submitted to and accepted by the *New York Times* for publication. The first was written by a college student and the second by

a married couple. Why do you think these arguments were selected to be published? Write the title "Characteristics of Effective Argument" at the top of a sheet of paper and divide the sheet into two columns by drawing a line down the middle. List the subtitles "Argument 1" and "Argument 2" at the top of the two columns. Now list the conditions, special characteristics, and qualities of each of these arguments that contribute to their success as arguments. At the bottom of each column you might also list any weaknesses. Use what you have learned from this chapter and your own past experience with argument to do this critique and evaluation. Now discuss the results. Compile a class list of the best argumentative features of each essay, as well as a list of the weaknesses. Keep a copy of this class list. It is a starting point. You will add to it as you learn more about what it takes to make a good argument. Establishing these characteristics will help you recognize good argument when you read and also help you write better argument yourself.

ARGUMENT 1

SOME COLLEGE COSTS SHOULD BE TAX DEDUCTIBLE

Davidson Goldin

Ithaca, N.Y.

As the Government spends increasingly less on student financial aid, many leading colleges and universities are using a greater percentage of tuition revenues for scholarships. Just as income tax breaks are given for charitable contributions, this portion of tuition should be tax deductible.

Statistics compiled by the Consortium on Financing Higher Education, which does research and analysis for 32 member colleges, show the growing importance of tuition for scholarships. In 1980, the consortium schools spent an average 9.8 percent of tuition revenues on financial aid; last year, that figure rose to 15.9 percent. It will continue to rise as Federal and state financing drops further.

The median tuition at the consortium schools in 1991 was approximately $15,000 per year. These schools devoted an average of $2,400 from each student's tuition to discounts for students with financial need.

Of the consortium schools, the University of Chicago spent the largest portion of tuition on aid in 1991: 30.7 percent of its $15,135 tuition. Brown, Cornell, Columbia, Johns Hopkins, Stanford, Wesleyan and Williams spent 14 percent to 16 percent. Princeton spent the least, 1.4 percent, but it finances an unusually large portion of student aid from its permanent endowment. Other schools include Rochester (28.6 percent), Harvard (8.6 percent) and Pennsylvania (19.5 percent).

After four years, families paying full tuition often provide more than $10,000 for easing the economic burden of others but do not receive any tax relief for this contribution to society. Scholarships based on financial need promote a socioeconomically diverse student body, and they enable economically strapped students to attend top schools.

Many tax-deductible contributions enhance the quality of life in a community or promote social, cultural and educational programs—gifts to orchestras, churches, social welfare agencies and libraries, and so on. All donations to colleges are tax deductible, whether the money is used for scholarships, an endowed professorship or a new building.

Tuition, unlike these voluntary contributions, is obligatory. Yet the portion of tuition that directly finances scholarships is in effect a charitable contribution, so it deserves the same tax treatment. In the tuition bill, schools should disclose the percentage of tuition set aside specifically for financial aid. Unlike the portions of tuition that pay for the educational enterprise—faculty and administration salaries, security and maintenance—the amount allotted for aid does not directly benefit those who provide the money.

Many families considered able to afford exorbitant tuition fees are hard-pressed to pay the bill. Many parents have refinanced their homes, incurred long-term debt and forfeited countless purchases and opportunities to pay for a college education.

All students benefit from the social and economic diversity that would be impossible without scholarships. Our society, which similarly thrives on diversity, should reward those who pay extra to make it possible.[7]

ARGUMENT 2

WE'RE GOOD REPUBLICANS—AND PRO-CHOICE

Beverly G. Hudnut and William H. Hudnut 3d

Indianapolis

An open letter to the Republican National Committee:

Last year, during the 18th week of Beverly's pregnancy, we discovered through testing that our baby suffered from grave defects that would have prevented him from becoming a healthy human being. Anencephaly was just one problem. Ultrasound and, later, an autopsy revealed several more.

After talking with our families, physicians and pastors, we decided to terminate the pregnancy. It was a heart-wrenching decision, because we wanted our baby very badly and already loved him dearly. But we felt that our decision was the only good one to make, grounded as it was in sound professional advice, the love of family and friends, and our faith.

At the time, Bill was in his 16th year as Republican Mayor of Indianapolis. So ours was a public decision as well as a private one. We issued a news release, and tried to be upfront with the press. The outpouring of love and support from all over the country—mostly from people who had struggled with the same decision—was heartwarming.

-----

[7]*New York Times*, April 18, 1992, Sec. A, p. 5.

We would have been terribly upset if an outside force, namely government, had prevented us from following the dictates of our conscience in this matter. Granted, our case represents a small fraction of the total number of abortions performed in the U.S., but nonetheless we feel constrained to ask: Why should political parties, our party in particular, stake out a position on abortion? Why borrow trouble on a matter on which people are so seriously divided?

It seems to us that under traditional minimalist Republican policy, government would choose *not* to interfere with a woman's right to make her own decision about whether or not to bear a child. We consider ourselves to be good members of the Republican team. It has been fairly easy to keep quiet about the abortion issue in the past and vote for candidates in spite of their position on abortion. It was perhaps easy because we felt protected by the *Roe* v. *Wade* decision. Following the same logic, it is now easy to speak up publicly because our party leaders are encouraging the Supreme Court to reverse *Roe* v. *Wade*.

If the Court takes steps this year to dilute laws determining whether or not a woman has control over her choice about bearing a child, we fear for our party in this year's election and those in the future. Pro-choice Republicans can no longer afford to keep their opinions to themselves. There are many of us with different political beliefs who find ourselves in the middle. Our voices are not being heard, primarily because we have kept quiet, and no forum of discussion has existed to date to learn from one another. Surely we are mature enough as a country to be able to talk civilly about abortion without yelling or screaming or trying to force our viewpoint on others.

When Beverly applied to testify at Tuesday's party platform meeting in Salt Lake City, she was told that the Republican National Committee had already selected its speakers on "both sides" of the abortion issue. The response perplexed us, because this complex subject has more sides than two. How about a third side? Granted, we are pro-choice, but why not simply leave abortion out of the platform, which has opposed abortion in recent years. As soon as a party or politician or citizen takes a stand on abortion, an "us against them" situation is set in place, leaving little room for dialogue or diversity of opinion.

In his book, *Life Itself*, Roger Rosenblatt wrote that we have to "learn to live on 'uncommon ground' in the matter of abortion; that we must not only accept but embrace a state of tension that requires a tolerance of ambivalent feelings, respect for different values and sensibilities, and no small amount of compassion." We call on our party leadership to take a stand on that "uncommon ground" by not taking a stand on abortion.[8]

3. WRITING ASSIGNMENT: UNCOMMON GROUND

Write a one-page explanation and evaluation of the perspective of "uncommon ground" in "We're Good Republicans—and Pro-Choice" and apply it to some additional difficult issues where it might facilitate constructive argument.

---

[8]*New York Times*, May 29, 1992, Sec. A, p. 15.

4. READING AND WRITING ASSIGNMENT: COMPELLING ISSUES

The following interview is included as an illustration of one man's lifelong engagement with issues. Note that his issues have influenced both his career choice and what he has chosen to write about. Complete one of the following writing assignments when you have read the essay. The first requires critical reading and a personal reaction. The second requires critical thinking and an argument of your own. Notice that both require reading and writing.

Assignment 1. Reading critically and writing about other people's argument. Write a two-page paper and include the following information:
a. Identify the two issues that have dominated Hardin's thought and describe his position on them.
b. Write a personal reaction. Which, in your opinion, are his best and his weakest reasons for his point of view? Was he justified in changing his mind about one of the issues? Why? What is your own present position on these issues?

Assignment 2. Thinking critically and writing your own argument.
a. Select any passage that is significant or striking to you in this essay.
b. Quickly write some ideas and responses that come to your mind as a result of reading it.
c. Write a two-page paper in which you develop an argument of your own that your reading has generated.
d. Use the two examples of argument in exercise 2 as possible models of argumentative strategy.

AN INTERVIEW WITH GARRETT HARDIN

Cathy Spencer

"Every time we send food to save lives in the present, we are destroying lives in the future," says a biologist whose ideas may be shocking, but just might preserve the planet.

As high winds whipping along the Pacific coast bounced and shook the small propeller plane, I tried to concentrate on my reason for flying to Santa Barbara. I was on my way to interview Garrett Hardin, microbiologist and human ecologist, most widely known—notorious even—for his 1968 essay, "The Tragedy of the Commons," in which he describes the follies of overpopulation.

I was five months pregnant, and given Hardin's views on population control and prophecies concerning the fate of the environment, I dreaded his response to my condition. To my surprise, the reputed harshly opinionated and fiery aspects of his personality had been greatly exaggerated—I suspect by his many critics. Instead, I found a gentle man suffused with a love of nature, family, and classical music. Despite his 77 years and a polio handicap, Hardin swims laps daily at his

Santa Barbara home, which has become a haven surrounded by giant eucalyptus and dense chaparral.

Stronger than his determination to exercise vigorously, however, is his relentless 40-year challenge—in many books, papers, and lectures—to conventional social ideals. His latest book, *Living Within Limits,* . . . further explores the concept that unrestrained reproductive growth throughout the world threatens to wreak widespread social disorder.

Born in 1915, Hardin grew up in the Midwest where his father's job with the Illinois Central Railroad moved the family from one town to another. Even though they never settled in one place, he found a sense of constancy at his grandfather's farm near Butler, Missouri. Hardin got his degree in zoology in 1936 at the University of Chicago, where he studied under W. A. Allee. At the time, the birthrate in the United States was declining. Books and articles prophesied the end of civilization, the extinction of the human race. But Allee, a professor of ecology, was virtually alone in insisting that the decline was temporary, a mere blip in the population curve. The birthrate, he maintained, would soon start going up again. "So early in my training," explains Hardin, "I was influenced by an unpopular theory. Alone with a small group of biologists, I was concerned about future population growth."

After completing a Ph.D. in microbiology at Stanford, during World War II, Hardin worked for the Carnegie Institution of Washington's Division of Plant Biology on the Stanford Campus, investigating how algae might be used for antibiotics and as a possible human food source. In 1946, he left the project. "The more I thought about producing algae for food," he remarks, "the less use I saw in the research." Developing new food sources would only encourage continued population growth.

Hardin was also influenced by Thomas Malthus, who in 1798 wrote that food would be the limiting factor of population size. When food resources were depleted, Malthus claimed, chaos and massive suffering would ensue, halting population growth. "Malthus was correct when he said there will be limits to increasing population, but wrong about what the limits would be," says Hardin. Since Malthus' prediction, per-capita production of food has increased dramatically in the world. "Overpopulation causes other obstacles," adds Hardin. "We've plenty of food, but we're wasting an awful lot of time trying to go anywhere." Hardin, like Malthus, suspects that if population growth continues at its current rate, chaos will ultimately ensue.

The same year Hardin left the algae project at Stanford, he accepted a teaching position at what is now the University of California at Santa Barbara to teach biology, genetics, evolution, and later human ecology. Retired in 1978, Hardin continues to stimulate debate and provoke controversy with his far-reaching ideas about the human condition.

SPENCER: In your 1972 book, *Exploring New Ethics for Survival*, you said you feel as if you are "living in the eye of a hurricane waiting." What did you mean?

HARDIN: I'm impressed with the reluctance of society to confront certain issues, and the ingenuity people show in developing a rhetorical defense against controversial concerns. We don't budge from our positions. Everyone has a computer in his head that does a lot of work on its own. Many difficult conflicts are worked out at a subconscious level. When we run into a roadblock, the conflict is intercepted by the in-house computer and prevented from coming to the conscious level. Any thought brought to the surface is in a censored form. We look only for certain answers, closing our eyes to the possibility of others. This is the roadblock for all discussions of population.

Our censored view about population is reflected in the widely accepted "child-survival hypothesis." In a primitive community where couples have too many children and large numbers of them are dying, supporters of the child-survival thesis believe we can reduce infant mortality by sending these people the best modern medicine. Obviously, the first effect of reduced infant mortality is an increase in the rate of population growth. But, according to this theory, couples in Third World countries have so many children because so many die. A high birthrate is a safety measure to ensure some children's survival. So if child mortality is reduced, these people will supposedly eventually reduce their fertility.

The hypothesis is true in a sense: People do diminish their fertility somewhat. But the result is nevertheless an increase in the number of people that reach age 20. Fewer are born, but more reach adulthood, providing the next generation of breeders. So the population does not decrease and the hypothesis isn't really true.

Why do we continue to practice the child-hypothesis theory? Because we are tenderhearted. We'd feel terrible if we didn't let others know there are ways to prevent infant mortality. So international Planned Parenthood generally provides medical assistance to reduce infant mortality in Third World countries. We think if we do the right thing—save babies—population control will happen spontaneously.

SPENCER: In 1967, Paul Ehrlich's *Population Bomb* prompted the formation of the organization Zero Population Growth (ZPG). Was this an effective move toward better understanding of population problems?

HARDIN: The policy of ZPG has a fundamental weakness. Like the founders of Planned Parenthood, the members of ZPG were determined to enable women to have the number of children they wanted when they wanted. They believe if women are made aware of the importance of reducing population, ultimately they will want fewer of them. But women who want large families will have them—there's no way to tie their individual wants to national needs without some sort of coercion. I saw ZPG headed for failure. But still, it was a step in the right direction for helping to change the climate for population control.

ZPG also had another problem. To put it exceedingly bluntly and in prejudicial terms: In general, people who go to college are more intelligent than those who don't. It would be better to encourage the breeding of more intelligent people rather than the less intelligent. ZPG's entire attraction has been among the college population. So in effect, ZPG is encouraging college-educated people to have fewer children instead of encouraging reduced fertility among the less intelligent.

SPENCER: Writing "The Tragedy of the Commons" was very difficult, you've said, because "I was reaching conclusions that repelled me and tried desperately to avoid them."

HARDIN: The basic concept of that essay was first published in 1833 by the mathematician William Foster Lloyd. He wrote that if a community purse is made available to the public, someone will spend a crown more quickly without thinking than if the crown comes from that person's own purse. Lloyd also said that public land is like a public purse: If everyone can dip into a common pasture, then that land will be abused. The pasture on private land will be protected by the owner and not overgrazed, so it can be used year after year. Rather than focusing primarily on a common purse, I concentrated on a common land, common pasture, and developed my essay from there. I tried to show how reproductive freedom, like a common pasture or community purse, is abused. People are allowed to have as many children as they choose without complete responsibility for their care. Society carries the extra burden parents can't undertake.

I kept coming up against a conflict with the idea of individual freedom—that each should do whatever he or she wants and everything will be all right. This is widely believed in Western civilization where individualism has been successful in so many other areas, particularly free enterprise. Laissez-faire economics permits an entrepreneur to price his goods any way he wishes. On the free market, the person pricing his products too high will go broke because he doesn't sell enough; the person selling too low will also go broke because he doesn't make a decent profit. Eventually prices balance out. By and large, this is the way the free market works, and it's a good system.

In writing "The Tragedy of the Commons" I resisted giving up the idea of applying the principle of laissez-faire economics to population control. Can a free market be applied to how many children a couple raises? Unfortunately, because some of the expense of having children is born by society, there is not sufficient pressure on the couple to have only the number of children they can take care of. So unlike the equilibrium obtained in the free financial market, a laissez-faire system of parentage yields too many children, too poorly taken care of. I finally gave up the idea that free-market principles could be used to control population.

SPENCER: Haven't a number of people criticized the validity of the concept embraced in "The Tragedy"?

HARDIN: Sure. One argument claims that a community of lobster fishermen who fish off the coast of Maine functions as a successful commons. "Therefore Hardin is wrong!" my critics say. What these skeptics miss is that this commons of lobster fishermen has only a few members. They take as much lobster as they want, but the commons is not depleted. A commons only works successfully when a restricted number of people dip into its resources. Numbers become very important.

The example I frequently cite is a successful communistic group of religious farmers, the Hutterites, in the northwestern U.S. and Canada. They are disciples of the Marxist principle, "To each according to his needs," where a general pot is provided for the entire populace. The Hutterite society has found from practical experience, however, that the Marxist concept doesn't work if the community grows beyond 150 people. People start going astray, stop doing their share of the work.

To resolve this problem, when a new community of Hutterites forms, its members immediately lay plans for splitting into two separate groups. They buy another farm as soon as they can; when the community grows over 150, they divide into two villages with the same number of old, young, and workers. The Hutterites can't make a commons work over 150. So to my critics I say, "A commons doesn't work if it's made up of too many people, even if they are good." With today's growing populations, the possibility for a successful commons becomes less and less likely.

SPENCER: Yet you've also frequently argued that there is no such beast as a global population problem.

HARDIN: True. Roads all over the world have potholes. Now suppose that people suddenly become concerned with "the world pothole problem" and as a result set up the World Pothole Commission to fix the widespread potholes. Would you get the pothole in front of your house fixed faster by a local county agency or a world agency? We'd never get those potholes filled if we depended on a world authority to do it. Potholes are not a global problem and should not be considered globally. Population isn't a global problem either. It is produced in each bedroom; a very local activity produces it, and so the control of it needs to be local.

Many of my critics believe people of Third World countries can't handle these issues and need outside help. Certainly they can be given information about birth control from other countries, but to give them food or money is a mistake. This is the commons again: If they don't have to pay for it themselves, they won't use it wisely.

Sending food to Ethiopia, for instance, does more harm than good. Each year the production obtained from Ethiopian land declines. The lands are used beyond their carrying capacity because there are far more people than renewable resources. Overproduction occurs. Eventually the soil loses its nutritional value and forests are stripped bare, causing soil erosion and severe floods. The more we encourage population growth by sending more and more food, the more damage is done to the production system. Every time we send food to save lives in the present, we are destroying lives in the future.

Most conventional ethics, such as "I am my brother's keeper," work only where small numbers of people are involved. Those who initially formulated these ethics I suspect never conceived of a time when people in the U.S. could see others starving to death on TV in "real time" on the opposite side of the world. We must realize our ability to know what's going on in other parts of the world far exceeds our ability to do anything about it. Conventional ethics sound good but don't work when the scale is enlarged. It works in the village, not in the whole world.

Our best chance of solving these problems is to let each country produce as many babies as the government decides is appropriate. This means each country must take care of the babies it produces. No rich country should be an escape hatch for a poor country.

But then no nation is really poor. If it has a small enough population, it can be rich. Bangladesh, for instance, is a rich country. It's the same size as Iowa. But 115 million people live in Bangladesh, while Iowa supports 3 million. If Bangladesh had 3 million citizens, its people would be living in the lap of luxury. Only one crop can be grown annually in Iowa, whereas in Bangladesh, two or three can grow each year. There's no reason for starvation to occur in Bangladesh. It's a much richer country than Iowa, but not with 115 million people.

SPENCER: What form of population control do you favor?

HARDIN: Well, the one that sounds the nicest was raised by Charles Darwin's grandson, Charles Galton Darwin. He said increase people's expectations so they don't think they're living the good life unless they have a motorcar. Use the automobile as the symbol for personal luxury. Reduce fertility by pointing out advantages of not having such large families.

The quickest, easiest, and most effective form of population control in the U.S., that I support wholeheartedly, is to end immigration. Our population growth would be spontaneously controlled. The U.S. accepts more immigrants each year than the other 179 nations of the world combined.

Economist Kenneth Boulding suggested that at birth, every female in the country be endowed with a certain number of green stamps giving her the right to have a certain number of children when she reaches child-bearing age. Depending on the population, the value of these stamps may vary from year to year. Let's say one year each woman is entitled to one and eight-tenths green stamps. If a woman wants to have one child she can sell the eight-tenths to somebody else. If she wants two children, she has to enter the market and buy two-tenths more stamps. This could work in any country.

SPENCER: What is your opinion of China's population policy, which prohibits couples from having more than one child?

HARDIN: I give the Chinese credit for officially recognizing that they have a problem and for having the nerve to propose the single-child program. China is the only country in the world that recognizes it has too many people. They have failed, however, by not making this directive universal throughout the country. The one-child policy is only enforced in congested urban areas. People in rural regions continue to have too many children. So the Chinese haven't solved their problems at all.

SPENCER: Will population control cause other problems in Chinese society? Might a single child truly become what they call "a little emperor"?

HARDIN: The Chinese admit their children are being spoiled, but this is natural behavior. I don't see any particular difficulty developing because less babies are born there. On the contrary, a smaller population should contribute to a better quality of life in China.

As for too many old people, the existence of a dominant elderly populace is not a serious danger anywhere. If an excess of young people exist, the older members of society are encouraged to retire early. When a deficiency of young develops, the elderly will be urged to work longer. This process automatically adjusts itself. How much and for how long a person works before retiring depends on the community.

SPENCER: Infanticide as a form of population control is hard to accept, yet you support it in its historical context.

HARDIN: Yes. Looking at history with an open mind you'll see that infanticide has been used as an effective population control. In writings about the South Seas, Robert Louis Stevenson expresses astonishment that island peoples practiced infanticide and yet were unusually loving towards children. Stevenson came from Calvinistic Scotland where, by God, children were treated severely. The Scots would never think of killing a child, but they'd never pamper it either. In the South Seas, the reverse occurred. In all societies practicing infanticide, the child is killed within minutes after birth, before bonding can occur. The mother never nurses the child. The South Pacific peoples must have easily seen the problems associated with overpopulation. When you live on an island, you know you live in a limited world.

Through most of history there's been no need for concern about population control. Nature would come along with epidemic diseases and take care of the matter for us. Disease has been the primary population controller in the past. Because widespread disease and famine no longer exist, we have to find another means to stop population increases.

SPENCER: What scenarios will unfold if world population growth continues at its current rate?

HARDIN: Some organizations have done the proper demographic analyses and have the best answers for the future. Usually I quote one of these projections. Now having said that, I'll go a step further and say that I don't have confidence in these projections. The pressures from expanding populations will become so great that trends will change. I suspect disasters such as widespread famine will prevent us from reaching the projected numbers.

I reluctantly make this statement because people say, "Oh you cruel man, you want to kill people." I don't want to kill anyone; but clearly, crippling conditions already exist in parts of the world due to escalating populations. People in central Africa suffer greatly from the effects of overpopulation; the land has been stripped of vegetation, causing erosion and flooding, leaving little hope for new crops. These countries may yet face a worse disaster, perhaps, in the spread of AIDS.

SPENCER: In the early Sixties you stopped writing and lecturing about population and decided to speak out in favor of abortion. Why?

HARDIN: First, I didn't want to fight two battles at once. I didn't want people to oppose population control if they were not in favor of abortion. It's quite possible to be against abortion and still be in favor of population control. Until the mid Fifties, I strongly opposed abortion. Then in 1958, I read *Abortion in the United States*, an account of a conference of doctors and Planned Parenthood professionals.

I'd always thought abortion was an extremely dangerous operation. Reading this book, I discovered abortions, when performed by competent medical professionals, were only one-fourth as dangerous as normal childbirth. (Today a normal childbirth is ten times more dangerous.) Other evidence presented at this conference suggested that having an abortion was a psychologically sound procedure, less harmful mentally for a woman than being compelled to have a child she didn't want. By 1962, I'd moved around to the other side and became a strong supporter of legalized abortion. By spring 1963, I was ready to go public with my ideas. Certainly the time was right for me to speak out on legalized abortion.

SPENCER: The Supreme Court decision legalizing abortion in 1973 stated, "The unborn have never been recognized in the law as persons in the whole sense." Why is this significant?

HARDIN: The argument for and against abortion today encompasses this very issue. Is a fetus a person? Are all lives equally valuable? Biologists don't believe all life has the same worth. In many instances, qualification is important. Evidence is clear in nature. About 50 percent of all conceptions in mammals perish before birth. By having fewer offspring, mammals are able to take better care of their young. The conceptions that perish are virtually without value; if they persisted, the continued existence of the species might be jeopardized.

This happens with humans as well. About half of all pregnancies are lost the first few days after conception. If people say that an embryo is a human being from the moment the sperm enters the egg, then all laws applying to humans must apply to this tiny embryo. This fertilized egg has to be buried with all the expenses applied to a person who dies. Suppose a woman thinks she's pregnant because she's missed her period. A week later she gets it and says, "I guess I was just late." Maybe she wasn't late; maybe she was pregnant and had a spontaneous abortion. In such cases—if the conception might be "life"—whenever a woman is late with her period, the menstrual products will have to be collected and given a proper burial. If people want to change the law and declare that a human is present from the time the sperm enters the egg, they must face these consequences.

A fetus is of so little value, there's no point in worrying about it in a society where over- not underpopulation is a problem. We don't need to chase after every last one of these embryos. Like the blueprint of a house, a fetus doesn't have the same value as the house itself; it is not a human being. Just like 10,000 acorns; the loss of these seeds would not be considered the loss of 10,000 oak trees, or deforestation. If a woman wants an abortion, either because of poverty, poor health, or because she doesn't think she will be a good mother—whatever reason—it's not in society's interest to urge her to have the child. We have enough poorly taken care of children already; we don't need any more. If a woman says she doesn't want a baby, that should be final.

SPENCER: What might happen if *Roe* v. *Wade* is reversed?

HARDIN: It's difficult to predict history, but I can see no good resulting from forcing women to have babies they don't want. Many who oppose legal abortion condemn women who have them as selfish and immoral. I urge people to forget about the problems these women may face and instead consider how reversing the right to have an abortion might affect them. The cost of raising these children will sooner or later reach the general public. As taxpayers, do they really want to support an unwanted child? Studies conducted in Europe show unwanted children have more psychological, educational, and health-related problems than children born to women who want them. It is paradoxical that people who call themselves conservatives oppose abortion. Conservatives usually strive to avoid taxes and high expenses. And yet, by opposing abortion, they ultimately ensure higher taxes. They should be the last to condemn abortion.

SPENCER: After the 1973 Supreme Court decision, why did you stop lecturing on this topic?

HARDIN: We had essentially won the battle, or so we thought at the time. I decided I could go back to talking about population and its effects. When I first started lecturing on abortion, so few people were talking about it, I figured I was needed even though I was a man. But I was relaying secondhand information. By the early Seventies, women were speaking out on their own. If anything needed to be said about abortion, women could say it better.

SPENCER: Might you start speaking out regularly again?

HARDIN: It's possible. Whether I start defending *Roe* v. *Wade* depends on what happens—on whether I get riled up enough, so irritated that I can't stand being silent.[9]

5. INDIVIDUAL ONGOING PROJECT: SELECT AN ISSUE, TEST IT, WRITE AN ISSUE PROPOSAL

Find an issue that you can research during this class that can be a topic for both short and longer argument papers of your own. Identify one that you care about, that you have not yet made up your mind about, and that you would like to study. To help you find your issue, look through the table of contents for possibilities, and also use the other suggestions in this chapter. When you have selected your issue, apply the tests on the next page to make certain that it is arguable.

Now write a one-page issue proposal.

a. Write the issue in question form.
b. Explain why it is compelling to you.
c. Describe what you already know about it.
d. Explain what more you need to learn.

6. UNDERSTANDING THE CHAPTER: WHOLE CLASS, GROUPS, OR INDIVIDUALS

Summarize the major ideas in the chapter by completing the following sentences briefly and in your own words:

a. Some implications of the statement "Argument is everywhere" are . . .
b. Some forms of argument are debate and courtroom drama, but also academic inquiry and negotiation. Some differences in these forms are . . .
c. Some conditions under which argument works best are . . .
d. Some conditions that may cause argument to fail are . . .

---

[9]*Omni,* June 1992, pp. 55–63.

Twelve Tests of an Arguable Issue

Your issue (write as a question): _____

Yes ——— No ——— 1. Is this an issue that has not been resolved or settled?

Yes ——— No ——— 2. Does this issue potentially inspire two or more views?

Yes ——— No ——— 3. Are you interested and engaged with this issue, and do you want to communicate with an audience about it?

Yes ——— No ——— 4. Can you inspire your audience to be sufficiently interested to pay attention?

Yes ——— No ——— 5. Do other people, besides you, perceive this as an issue?

Yes ——— No ——— 6. Is this issue significant enough to be worth your time?

Yes ——— No ——— 7. Is this a safe issue for you? Not too risky? Scary? Will you be willing to express your ideas?

Yes ——— No ——— 8. Will you be able to establish common ground with your audience on this issue, that is, a common set of terms, some common background and values?

Yes ——— No ——— 9. Can you get information and come up with convincing insights on this issue?

Yes ——— No ———10. Can you eventually get a clear and limited focus on this issue, even if it is a complicated one?

Yes ——— No ———11. Is it an enduring issue, or can you build perspective by linking it to an enduring issue?

Yes ——— No ———12. Can you predict some audience outcomes? (Think of your classmates as the audience. Will they be convinced? Hostile? Neutral? Attentive? Remember, any outcomes at all can be regarded as significant in argument.)

e. Some characteristics of issues are as follows: they are compelling, . . .

f. Some examples of enduring issues are . . .

g. Some examples of contemporary issues are . . .

h. Some issues I will probably encounter in my other classes this semester are . . .

CHAPTER 2

Joining the Conversation

This chapter develops the idea that not all people think about argument or participate in it in the same way. Individuals' personalities certainly affect their styles of argument. Many people believe that a person's gender, ethnic background, race, and country of origin all have an effect on argument style as well.

Before this book was published, it was test-read in manuscript form by nearly one hundred college students in four different classes. These students critiqued the book, chapter by chapter, to help make it clear and useful for future student readers, and, when they read this chapter, "Joining the Conversation," several of them added their own voices and examples to provide further evidence for the idea that styles of argument differ among individuals. These students did not always agree on the causes for these differences, however, and you may not either. This chapter invites differing views on the issues it raises.

The final purpose of this chapter is to encourage you and your classmates to become aware at the outset of how each of you argues best. Thus you will learn to recognize, rely on, and perhaps even improve your existing style of argument. You will also learn from others how to modify or change to another style in certain situations when your preferred style may not be working well. This process will help you learn flexibility. Finally, you will learn to recognize and adapt to other people's styles, and you will therefore become a more sensitive and persuasive arguer, more likely to establish the common ground essential for the give and take of argument.

Individual tendencies and preferences in argument are present in many but not all argumentative situations. If you discover, for example, that you prefer reaching consensus in most instances over winning the argument, this discovery does not mean that you should always argue for consensus. Furthermore, if you discover that you are reluctant to participate in argument, your reluctance does not mean that you cannot find a way to participate. An awareness of individuals' predominant styles should reduce the dissonance and discomfort experienced by some people in argument classes where a single argument style or perspective may seem to dominate. By acknowledging instead that individualistic and preferred perspectives and styles not only exist but also are valued, everyone in class should feel empowered to join the ongoing conversation about issues with confidence and skill. The goal is to create and maintain an inclusive classroom where everyone has a voice and where every approach and style is tolerated and understood. This is a worthy "real-life" goal as well for a world in which cultural, racial, and gender diversity often influence the nature and special characteristics of the ongoing conversations about issues.

INDIVIDUAL STYLES OF ARGUMENT

Most contemporary argument classes are composed of varied groups of male and female students who represent several races and cultural backgrounds from various parts of the world. In fact, when students are asked to describe their styles of argument—that is, what they do when they have to be convincing—individual differences in style and strategy surface right away. Some of these differences seem to be related to gender, others to the background and experience provided by different races and cultures. Men and women, for instance, often describe different approaches to argument. African-American, Asian-American, Hispanic-American, and Native American students may also describe distinctive styles and approaches. Finally, international students, particularly those from non-Western cultures, sometimes describe approaches that are distinctive and particularly unique, especially when compared to others.

These differences among styles are usually neither consistent nor strong enough for typecasting. In fact, in some studies, a sizable minority of men indicate they prefer the styles that researchers have identified as predominantly female.[1] Also, a particular style may be more convincing in some contexts than in others, so that students who have a preferred style find that they vary it at times to meet the demands of particular argumentative situations. Thus no single style emerges as best for all occasions for anyone. For example, one student in the group that test-read this book reported that when he argues with close friends about baseball players he always wants to be right, and he expects to win. On the job, however, where he has low status in an office of four women, he never argues to win. Another student said she argues most aggressively when she is secure in her knowledge about the subject. She is tentative or even silent when she is not sure of her facts. Students also point out that there is a difference between home or "kitchen" argument and argument that takes place in school or on the job. Home argument may be more emotional and less controlled, especially in some cultures, than the reasoned discourse that is carried on at school or on the job.

Students also often identify their early home training as an influence on their style. Some students from military families, for example, say that argument was not encouraged at home. Instead, orders were given in military fashion, and opposing views were not encouraged. Other students, such as those whose parents

---

[1]Carol S. Pearson, "Women as Learners: Diversity and Educational Quality," *Journal of Developmental Education*, Winter 1992, p. 10.

were teachers or lawyers, have reported that arguing about issues occurred frequently in their households. In spite of these special influences, many students still are immediately aware that their gender, their culture, and their race have influenced their personal development and style as arguers. In fact, students tend to identify the well-known arguers who are most like themselves as the role models they like to imitate as they develop their own styles. Now, let us look at some of the special characteristics associated with gender, race, and culture that may be influencing the ways in which you prefer to argue.

DO MEN AND WOMEN ARGUE DIFFERENTLY?

Some people think there are differences in the ways that men and women argue, and that the basis for these differences lies in the power relationships that exist between the sexes in certain situations. That is, men may often be better able to dominate an argument, while women may tend to remain silent. Men are thus perceived to have more personal power in these situations. In an essay entitled "The Classroom Climate: Still a Chilly One for Women," Bernice Sander describes the results of some unequal male-female power relationships. Even though most people think that women talk more than men in everyday situations, she says, a number of studies show that in formal situations, such as a class, a meeting, or a formal group discussion where argument is conducted, the stereotype of women talking the most does not hold up. In these situations men often talk more than women. Men, Sander claims, talk for longer periods, take more turns, exert more control over what is said, and interrupt more often. Furthermore, their interruptions of women tend to be trivial or personal, and thus they often get women off the track and cause the focus of the discussion to change.[2]

Sociolinguist Deborah Tannen in her best-selling book *You Just Don't Understand: Women and Men in Conversation* also provides detailed descriptions of some differences between men and women arguing.[3] Tannen asserts that many men make connections with one another primarily through conflict. (She qualifies this assertion because she realizes that she cannot generalize about *all* men.) Men see the world as competitive, and the competition can be either friendly and involved or unfriendly. Men, furthermore, like self-display and achieve it often by reporting what they see and what they know. Typical male behavior is centered on "the idea of contest, including combat, struggle, conflict, competition, and contention." As evidence, Tannen quotes Walter Ong, a scholar of cultural linguistics, who reminds us that many men enjoy ritual combat such as rough play and sports. Friendship among men often takes the form of friendly aggression. Ong also asserts, according to Tannen, that in daily argument men expect the discussion to

---

[2]See *Educating Men and Women Together*, ed. Carol Lasser (Urbana and Chicago: University of Illinois Press, 1987), p. 188.

[3]Deborah Tannen, *You Just Don't Understand: Women and Men in Conversation* (New York: Ballantine Books, 1990). See Chapter 6, "Community and Context."

stick to the rules of logic. They expect argument to be adversative, to include clash, to take the form of debate, and to rely primarily on logic.

Most women, on the other hand, Tannen says, do not like ritualized combat. They do not like conflict, either, and will often try to avoid it at all costs. Women, according to Tannen, tend to be the peacemakers and to want to work for the general good. They are as interested in making connections with other people as men are in competing. Making connections and keeping the peace are such strong tendencies in women's argument that even when women are being competitive and critical, they often mask their actual intentions with apparent cooperation and affiliation. Women, in fact, are often less direct than men in argumentative situations, and their indirect style sometimes causes men to think that women are trying to be devious and to manipulate them.

To summarize Tannen, men's power comes from acting in opposition to others and to natural forces. Women's power comes from their place in a community. For women, in fact, life is often a struggle to keep from being cut off from the group and to stay connected with the community.

TENDENCIES OF WOMEN	TENDENCIES OF MEN
—— To be indirect	—— To be direct and open
—— To give reasons	—— To give orders and make demands
—— To prefer cooperation	—— To prefer competition
—— To favor group consensus	—— To favor individual opinions
—— To like affiliation	—— To like conflict
—— To hate to fight	—— To like to fight
—— To avoid confrontation	—— To like confrontration
—— To avoid argument	—— To like argument
—— To dislike combat	—— To enjoy the rough and tumble of combat
—— To be nonaggressive	—— To be aggressive
—— To solicit many views on an issue	—— To tend to see issues as two-sided, pro and con, black and white
—— To be both logical and emotional	—— To be primarily logical
—— To try to make connections	—— To be adversarial
—— To prefer negotiating	—— To prefer winning
—— To favor the personal example, story, anecdote	—— To favor abstract ideas
—— To want to keep the community strong	—— To want to keep the individual strong

BOX 2.1 Women's and Men's Styles of Argument

Box 2.1 provides a summary of male and female qualities that may influence the way both groups approach argument. As you read the lists, check the items that are most typical of you. Does one list describe your style of argument better than the other? Or can your style best be described by items derived from both lists?

Recent studies of the leadership styles of men and women confirm some of the generalizations made by Tannen and others. Women leaders, for instance, are usually described as being more democratic and affiliative, and men as more authoritarian and hierarchical. One study, for example, surveyed more than 1,000 male and female leaders from a variety of cultures and backgrounds. Women, it was discovered, were most interested in creating a sense of social equality in their groups and in building a consensus of opinion among members of the group. Men, on the other hand, were more interested in competing for rank and status in the groups.[4]

Another effort to study some of the possible differences between men and women identifies additional characteristics that could affect their argument styles. Mary Belenky and her associates conducted in-depth interviews of 135 women who were either students in universities or who were clients in social service agencies.[5] Interviewees were asked about preferred types of classrooms for the exchange of ideas. These researchers discovered that debate—the style of argument that has dominated Western education and that is typically associated with the "masculine adversary style of discourse"—was never selected by women as a classroom forum for exchange and discussion. Instead, women students more typically gravitated toward the class in which there was a sense of community as opposed to a sense of hierarchy. In hierarchical groups some people possess more power and, consequently, more ability to be heard than others. In groups that favor community, equality is favored and power relationships become less important.

Belenky finally recommends "connected" classrooms for women students. Women learn better, she claims, in classrooms that minimize the power relationships and hierarchies that are often associated with the traditional "adversarial doubting" classroom model favored by male professors. Box 2.2 provides a list of the characteristics of both types of classrooms. Imagine the types of argumentative exchanges that would occur in each of them. Imagine also the possible outcomes of these argumentative exchanges. Check the items that best describe the climate in which you prefer to argue. Does one list describe you better than the other? Or would you prefer a climate that combines items from both lists?

You have now checked items on two lists that identify factors that are typically associated with predominantly male or female styles of argument. Do not be disturbed if your preferences do not reflect your gender. Many males find they prefer connection and consensus over contention and winning, and many females like the excitement and energy that are associated with winning debates. One

---

[4]William F. Allman, "Political Chemistry," *U.S. News & World Report*, November 2, 1992, p. 65.

[5]See Mary Field Belenky, Blythe McVicker Clinchy, Nancy Rule Goldberger, and Jill Mattluck Tarule, *Women's Ways of Knowing: The Development of Self, Voice, and Mind* (New York: Basic Books, 1986), especially Chapter 10, "Connected Teaching."

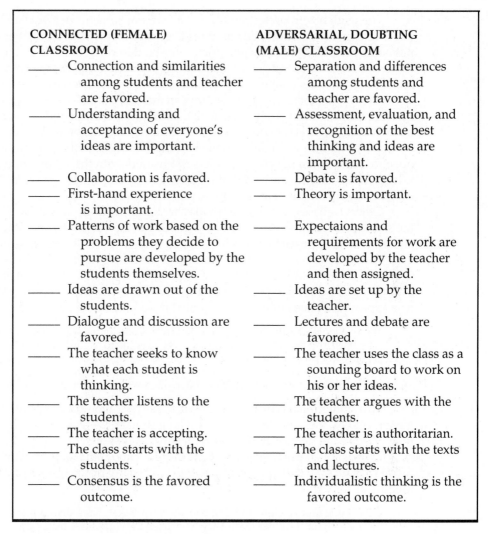

CONNECTED (FEMALE) CLASSROOM	ADVERSARIAL, DOUBTING (MALE) CLASSROOM
_____ Connection and similarities among students and teacher are favored.	_____ Separation and differences among students and teacher are favored.
_____ Understanding and acceptance of everyone's ideas are important.	_____ Assessment, evaluation, and recognition of the best thinking and ideas are important.
_____ Collaboration is favored.	_____ Debate is favored.
_____ First-hand experience is important.	_____ Theory is important.
_____ Patterns of work based on the problems they decide to pursue are developed by the students themselves.	_____ Expectaions and requirements for work are developed by the teacher and then assigned.
_____ Ideas are drawn out of the students.	_____ Ideas are set up by the teacher.
_____ Dialogue and discussion are favored.	_____ Lectures and debate are favored.
_____ The teacher seeks to know what each student is thinking.	_____ The teacher uses the class as a sounding board to work on his or her ideas.
_____ The teacher listens to the students.	_____ The teacher argues with the students.
_____ The teacher is accepting.	_____ The teacher is authoritarian.
_____ The class starts with the students.	_____ The class starts with the texts and lectures.
_____ Consensus is the favored outcome.	_____ Individualistic thinking is the favored outcome.

BOX 2.2 Classroom Climates for Argument

young male student, for example, when asked to describe his style of argument, said that it was important to him to keep the peace, to negotiate, to work things out, and to gain consensus in argument. When he discovered that some of these qualities were on the female lists, he quickly changed his description of himself, saying, instead, that he liked to win at any cost. This young man did not want his classmates to question his masculinity, so he switched his description of himself to one less accurate. Actually, when questioned, a number of the male students in class admitted to preferring negotiation over winning at any cost. And the women in the class, even those who preferred to think of themselves as winners, still strongly supported the idea of men as negotiators rather than aggressive winners.

The tendency to prefer the style of argument sometimes associated with females is often evident among "real-world" groups of men, including those in business and politics. One manager, for example, describes himself in the *Harvard Business Review* as a "soft" manager. He explains that this description does not mean he is a weak manager. As a soft manager, he welcomes argument and criticism from subordinates, is often tentative in making difficult decisions, admits his own human weaknesses, and tries to listen to employees and understand them. In other words, he stresses connection over conflict, and negotiation over winning. He believes that these qualities make him more human, more credible, and more open to change than the classic leaders of business with their "towering self-confidence, their tenacity and resolution, their autocratic decision making, and their invulnerable lonely lives at the top."[6]

Other examples of male and female characteristics in argument can be found in the language of politics. Maureen Dowd, writing in the *New York Times Magazine*, analyzes the language used by politicians in a recent election. "Politicians and their strategists," she claims, "have long been entranced by the image of themselves as warriors. Certainly, it is more romantic for a politician to think of himself as a warrior than as a bureaucrat, hack, pencil-pusher, or blowhard."[7] The very next day after Dowd's article appeared, a male politician was quoted in another newspaper as saying,

> Today it looks as if the Indians are about to overwhelm the wagon train. The wagons are circled and the arrows are flying. . . . We're going to begin a cavalry charge, which is going to bring us into the battle. . . . We've waited to get out on the playing field. The last three weeks has reminded me of a locker room before a big game—everybody nervous, everybody ready—tomorrow, we go charging down the chute.[8]

This quotation, according to Dowd's analysis, would be typical of the language used by many male politicians who gravitate toward male styles of argument. Notice the images associated with battle and sports.

Dowd, in her article, also contrasts the old "blood-and-guts" politicians with the new "touchy-feely" politicians who exhibit many of the traits some theorists identify as female:

> Bill Clinton and Al Gore, the first baby-boomer ticket, have shared intimacies about their search for the inner man. They have used the sort of feel-better jargon never before heard in the manly arena of politics. They talk about confronting problems, connecting with people, shattering emotional barriers, embracing the pain and working it out with counseling and self-examination.

Personally, Dowd says, she is thrilled with this new approach and sees it as a "welcome respite from the war talk that usually drives politics."[9] She does not

---

[6]William H. Peace, "The Hard Work of Being a Soft Manager," *Harvard Business Review*, November–December 1991, pp. 40–42, 46–47.

[7]Maureen Dowd, "Guns and Poses," *New York Times Magazine*, August 16, 1992, pp. 10, 12.

[8]Karen Potter, "Gramm Gets 'Em Going with a Little Pre-Speechmaking," *Fort Worth Star-Telegram*, August 17, 1992, Sec. A, p. 6.

[9]Dowd, "Guns and Poses," p. 10.

see it as a weakness or as a feminization of style, but as a new style that can also be strong and effective.

As you continue to analyze the argument styles of men and women, and yourself and your classmates, you may discover that the people who break the male-female stereotypes are some of the most effective arguers in class. Deborah Tannen makes a plea for the flexibility that can come from adapting features of both male and female styles. Both men and women, she says, could benefit from being flexible enough to borrow one another's best qualities: "Women who avoid conflict at all costs," she suggests, "would be better off if they learned that a little conflict won't kill them. And men who habitually take oppositional stances would be better off if they broke their addiction to conflict." Such flexibility has other advantages as well. It is also useful to realize that what may sometimes seem like an unfair or irrational approach to argument may simply be a manifestation of a particular individual's style. Such realization makes it less frustrating, usually, to argue with such an individual.[10]

DO RACE AND CULTURE INFLUENCE ARGUMENT STYLE?

Now consider the possibility that members of different racial or cultural groups in America may exhibit distinctive styles of argument, and that individuals learn these styles through affiliation with their groups. Here are some differences that may be influenced by either racial or cultural identity, as well as by experience.

Some people think that many African-Americans tend to focus strongly on issues and that, even though they make effective use of logical and ethical appeal, they sometimes also make superior use of emotional appeal. Many African-Americans have regular access to two distinctly black forums for argument: rap music, which is relatively new, and the black church, which is old and traditional. Both provide members of the black race with the opportunity to observe and imitate distinctive black styles of argument.

Contemporary issues, presented forcefully and emotionally, form the main content of much rap music, as Sister Souljah, the New York rapper, recognizes. "I think it would be a good idea," she says, "for members of Congress and the Senate and all people who consider themselves policy makers to listen to the call of help that is generated by rap artists." She sees rap music as a deliberate effort to organize black people to think about issues and to engage in social action. She and other rap artists have, in fact, organized a ten-point program to engage African-Americans in such issues as African life, economics, education, spirituality, defense, and how not to support racism.[11] Reviews of rap music also sometimes stress the argumentative slant of some of this music. Rap has been described as "so top-

---

[10]Tannen, *You Just Don't Understand*, p. 187

[11]Sheila Rule, "Rappers' Words Foretold Depth of Blacks' Anger," *New York Times*, May 26, 1992, Living Arts Section, pp. B1–B2.

ical that it'll probably leave newsprint on your ears" and as a "checklist of intractable Big Issues set to a metal soundtrack."[12]

The black church has also been regarded by many as another potent forum for argument. In an article describing a protest against a questionable court decision, the author observes that the African-American church was at the forefront of the protest, "stepping into its time-honored role in politics and advocacy for social change."[13]

Some of the most influential African-American leaders who have addressed black issues have also been preachers in black churches. Included in this group are Martin Luther King, Jr., Malcolm X, and Jesse Jackson. These three leaders are masters of the use of emotional appeal. Notice, for example, Martin Luther King's use of emotional language, examples, and analogies, both figurative and literal, in "Letter from Birmingham Jail," which begins on page 246. If you tend to favor emotional appeal in your argument, this essay provides some excellent examples and models of effective and convincing emotional appeal.

The following description of his argument style was provided by a black student in an argument class. As you can see, he attributes some of his preferences and characteristics as an arguer to the fact that he is young, black, and male.

> What influences my style of argument the most is the fact that I am a young black male. The fact that I am young makes me want to be fair and direct with my opponent. That is, I attempt to be free of vagueness, ambiguity, and fallacies. Also, the fact that I am black affects the way I approach my audience. For instance, I tend to use emotional language, and my language is sometimes racially manipulative. I think that blacks tend to see people's race before they see people's attitudes and feelings. Finally, the fact that I am a male probably influences my argument. I think that males tend to be a bit more harsh in their argument. They tend to want to "rock the boat" and stir some emotions. I think that this is a strong tendency in my argument style. The use of facts, emotions, fairness, and strong language is very typical of black argument.[14]

Some Asian-American students, according to recent researchers, may be more reluctant than other students to participate in argument because of their cultural background. Students who have spent a portion of their school years in Japan, China, or other Far Eastern Asian countries or whose parents or grandparents come from these countries may regard argument class as an odd environment that has little to do with them. This statement may be particularly true if they view these classes as places where pro and con issues are debated and winners are declared. The reason is that argumentation and debate are not traditionally practiced in the Asian countries in the Far East. Carl Becker, a professor of Asian curriculum research and development, explains some of the reasons for the lack of argumentation in the Far East. For these Asians, sympathetic understanding and intuition are a more important means of communication than are logic and debate. Furthermore,

---

[12]John Austin, "Noize from the 'Hood,' " *Fort Worth Star-Telegram*, Arts and Entertainment, March 2, 1993, p. 1.

[13]Gracie Bonds Staples and Anjetta McQueen, "Ministers Lead Prayers in Call for Awakening," *Fort Worth Star-Telegram*, March 27, 1993, p. 1.

[14]Provided by Kelvin Jenkins, with permission.

Asians do not like to take opposite sides in an argument because they do not like becoming personal rivals of those who represent the other side. They value harmony and peace, and argument, as they perceive it, has the potential of disturbing the peace.[15] A friend who taught for a brief period in Japan reported that he could not get his Japanese students to take pro and con sides on an issue and debate it. Instead, they all insisted on taking the same side.[16] A book recently published in Japan teaches Japanese how to say "no" to Americans. Taking an opposing stance and defending it is a skill that must be learned in Japan. It is not part of the traditional culture. Read the short article provided in exercise 3 at the end of this chapter for some examples of what Japanese really mean when they say "yes" to people outside their culture.

Here is the self-reported argument style of a young male Asian-American in an argument class. This account was written at the beginning of the semester.

> My style of argument is to avoid argument as much as possible. I think that I argue more with other men than I do with women. I think the reason I don't argue a lot is because I analyze the situation a bit too much, and I can pretty much tell what the outcome is going to be. During argument I usually blank out what the other person is saying and think about when they are going to stop talking.[17]

He was more comfortable and skilled with argument at semester's end. He credited argument class, finally, with teaching him to listen more, argue more, and be less self-centered.

An Asian international student who petitioned to be excused from argument class said that, for her, the idea of such a class was very confusing because she could not understand why she or any other student should spend time arguing and trying to convince others to agree with their points of view. She associated such activity with advertising and selling and could not envision it as useful in other contexts. Ironically, this student went on to write a convincing argument about why she should not have to take an argument class. This was an important issue for her, and she wrote a good argument in spite of her reluctance to participate in it.

The Asian students who test-read this book warned that not all Asian cultures are the same, and that the reluctance to argue may be stronger in some Asian cultures than others. For example, a Sri Lankan student pointed out that in her country, as well as in India and Bangladesh, argument is encouraged. Students also observed that there is a tradition of lively, contentious, and even combative "kitchen" argument among close family members in some Asian cultures. This, they say, is typical of the Korean culture. Amy Tan, in her books about her childhood in a Chinese immigrant household, gives examples of the lively home argument in that culture as well. Outside of the home, however, Asians may be reluctant

---

[15]Carl B. Becker, "Reasons for the Lack of Argumentation and Debate in the Far East," *International Journal of Intercultural Relations*, vol. 10 (1986): 75–92.

[16]Interview with Clyde Moneyhun.

[17]Jim Lui. Quoted with permission.

to enter into argument. In exercise 2, at the end of this chapter, Judy Ching-Chia Wong argues that Asian-Americans must learn to speak out. Argument class is a safe place for practicing that special ability.

Since the Hispanic culture promotes strong family ties and group values, many Hispanic students seem to favor connection over contention, and negotiation over winning. Here is a female Hispanic student describing her style of argument.

> What I like best about my current style of argument is the fact that I listen and try to understand others' points of view. I also like the fact that I can express my feelings without hurting other people. A negotiated solution eventually comes through. I would like to be more assertive. The ideal arguer, for me, is the one who can accept it if she is wrong.

The three descriptions of argument style that you just read were written by students enrolled in argument classes who were responding to an assignment that asked them to describe their current argument styles. These students, along with more than 600 additional students, also completed a questionnaire about their argument styles, and, in addition, they were asked to identify their gender and race. The idea was to see if the links between style and the gender and race characteristics already discussed in this chapter seemed to have any validity.

The students were questioned in three areas. First, they were asked how they viewed the outcomes of argument. Then they were asked to report on their personal participation in argument. Finally, they were asked about their present style of argument. Several possible answers were provided for each of the three items, and students were asked to identify one item under each question that best described them, and then to identify two others that also described them, but perhaps not quite so forcefully. The questions appear in Box 2.3. As you read them, answer them yourself. Under each question identify the item you agree with most as number 1. Then number as 2 and 3 the additional items that also describe your opinions and practices.

You may now want to compare your own answers to the questions with those reported by other students. The 647 argument-class students who completed this questionnaire one week after classes started also identified themselves as male or female and as Euro-American, black, Hispanic, or Asian. Sixty-nine percent of them were second-semester freshmen, 19 percent were sophomores, and 12 percent were juniors and seniors. Figures 2.1–2.3 provide summaries of their answers in graph form. The numbers of students who responded in each group are indicated in parentheses. The base used for computing percentages was the possible number of total weighted points for each answer. Thus the percentages indicate the relative strength of preference for each group as compared with the others.

One of the most interesting results of this study was that no items on the questionnaire were rejected by all students. Every item on the questionnaire was marked by at least a few students as being typical or somewhat typical of themselves. These students' responses suggest the wide diversity of attitudes and preferences among them.

Although no Native American students participated in this study, research concerning Native American culture and values suggests that Native American students

---

Question 1. How would you describe the usual outcomes of argument?

—— Argument helps people understand each other's points of view.
—— Argument separates and alienates people.
—— Argument causes conflict and hard feelings.
—— Argument resolves conflict and solves problems.
—— Argument can change people's minds.
—— Argument rarely changes other people's minds.

Question 2. How would you describe your personal participation in argument?

—— Argument makes me feel energized, and I like to participate.
—— Argument makes me uncomfortable, and I dislike participating.
—— I participate a lot.
—— I participate sometimes.
—— I never participate.
—— I think it is fun to argue.
—— I think it is rude to argue.

Question 3. What is your style of argument at present?

—— I am contentious and enjoy conflict.
—— I am a peacekeeper, and I value conflict resolution.
—— I try to win and show people I am right.
—— I try to listen, understand, make connections, negotiate solutions.
—— I tend to use reason and facts more than emotion.
—— I tend to use emotion more than reason and facts.

BOX 2.3   Student Questionnaire on Attitudes and Style in Argument

value community and cooperation more than rivalry and competition. Furthermore, in traditional Native American culture young people are expected to agree with authority figures, especially with those seen as older and wiser. Native American students are often, as a consequence, reluctant to debate, particularly with the teacher.[18]

We concluded that the differences among these groups of students are certainly not great enough to create stereotypes. College students, in fact, often break stereotypes because of their close association with one another, which often results in greater flexibility, adaptability, and increased tolerance, and because of their common goal to become educated. There are interesting tendencies, however, among these students that seem to confirm the notion that gender and racial groups may have special characteristics as arguers that are unique to them. For instance, Asian students were less enthusiastic about argument than the others, the white

---

[18]B. C. Howard, *Learning to Persist/Persisting to Learn* (Washington, DC: Mid-Atlantic Center for Race Equity, American University, 1987). Quoted in Pearson "Women as Learners," p. 6.

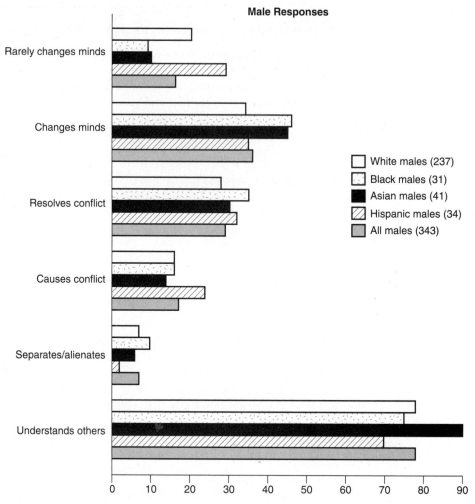

Figure 2.1 Question 1: Describe Argument Outcomes

males liked to win more than any of the other groups, more females than males said they typically try to listen and connect, and so on.

Some findings, however, are not typical of some of the tendencies described by recent researchers. For instance, listening, understanding, making connections, and negotiating solutions was a preferred style for nearly as many men as for women, and the contentious, conflictive style was less popular with both groups. Also, it seems clear that these students as a group value knowing the facts, are suspicious of too much emotion particularly if it results in anger and loss of control, and have positive opinions about the outcomes and uses of argument.

The study mainly emphasized the many differences in argument style that can be found in argument classrooms. The study confirms the importance of the goals for

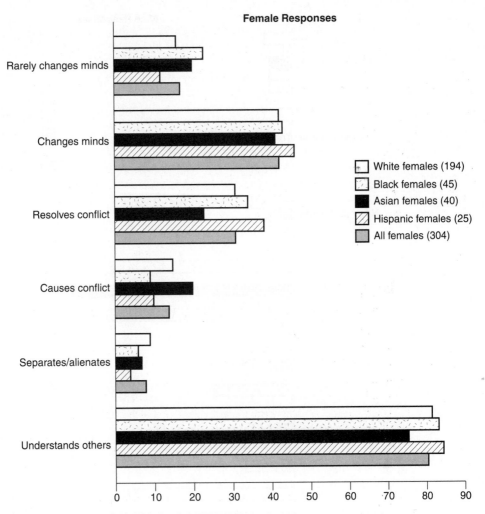

Figure 2.1 *(continued)*

argument class listed at the beginning of this chapter: students need to learn to value one another's styles, to develop flexibility by extending their own styles and learning to borrow from others, and to become adaptable to styles other than their own.

DO DIFFERENT COUNTRIES HAVE DIFFERENT STYLES OF ARGUMENT?

Argument class can often be thought of as a microcosm of the larger world, particularly when the students in it represent a variety of different countries and cultures. Cultural backgrounds exert a powerful influence over the way in which

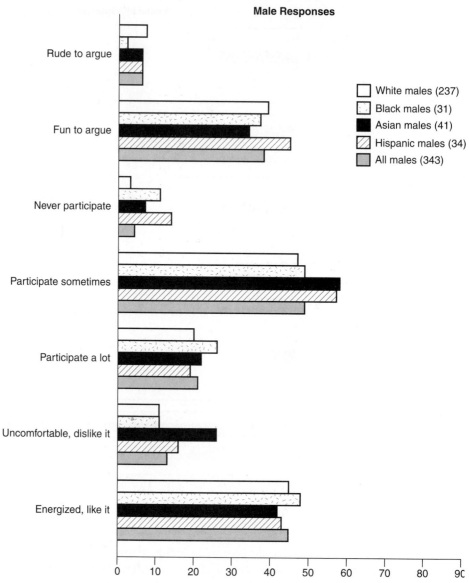

Figure 2.2 Question 2: Describe Your Participation

individual people view and practice argument. Studying argument across cultures is a complicated field, and most of its findings are tentative because of the vast individual differences in people from culture to culture. Still, even tentative findings are important for the argument classroom. Hypothesizing about how argument differs according to nationality helps students focus on the preferences in argument styles that may be typical of certain groups and cultures. Developing an awareness

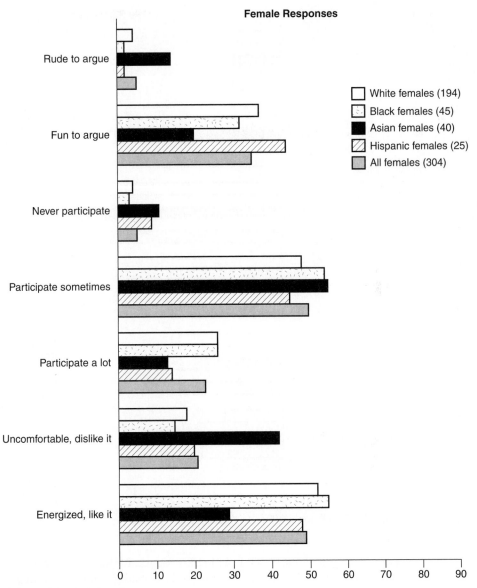

Figure 2.2 *(continued)*

of these characteristics and preferences and learning to adapt to them not only helps students achieve the goals of the inclusive argument classroom, but also helps prepare students for life long communicating and negotiating with people from other countries and cultures.

Here are some examples of some possible differences. Deborah Tannen claims that argument in some societies is a way of coming together, a pleasurable sign of

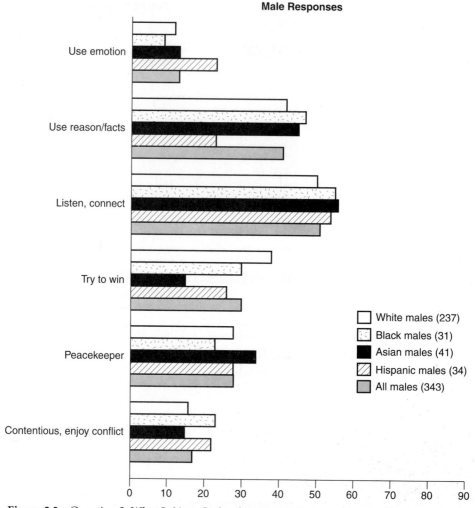

Figure 2.3 Question 3: What Is Your Style of Argument?

intimacy, a kind of game that people play together. This observation is particularly true of Italy, Greece, and Eastern Europe. To outsiders, the argument in these countries may seem to be contentious, "an argument," rather than reasoned inquiry into issues. Italian *discussione* strikes outsiders as loud, contentious arguing, but to Italians it is a friendly game. Greeks and East Europeans may appear bossy and overbearing. In their view, however, they are showing friendly caring.[19]

In the following essay, Nilesh Bhakta, a student from Zimbabwe, describes a different attitude and style of argument in his country.

---

[19]Tannen, *You Just Don't Understand*, pp. 160–162.

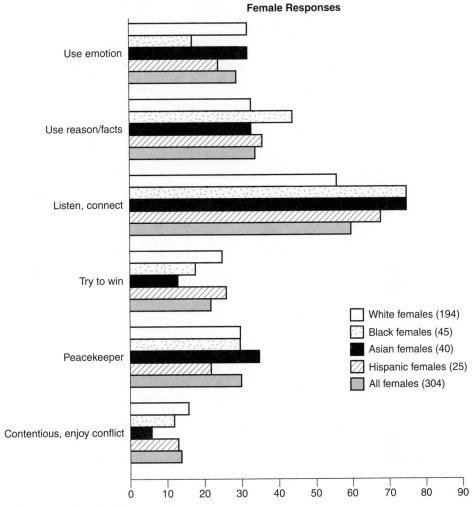

Figure 2.3 *(continued)*

ARGUMENT IN ZIMBABWE

Nilesh Bhakta

Zimbabwe is located in central Africa, south of the equator. It is a landlocked country surrounded by South Africa to the south, Mozambique to the east, and Zambia to the north and northwest. The argument styles used in Zimbabwe are somewhat different from those used here in the

United States. Very, very rarely are arguments based upon emotional appeals or ethical virtues.

From a very young age, children are taught to respect their elders (mainly grandparents) who are considered to be wise and knowledgeable. As a result, children and everyone else are not allowed to argue with them, since it shows their lack of respect. With parents, however, it is somewhat relaxed. Most children are allowed to question or bring up their own perspectives on an issue. *But* whatever are the parents' view, that is what the whole family adapts to. This view is then readily accepted (with no arguments to preserve respect) among family members, thus creating a sense of unity within the family. This unity symbolizes the "traditional closely knit" meaning of family.

There are three general races widespread in Zimbabwe--the natives (blacks), Europeans (whites), and the Asians. Because of the colonial class system imposed by the colonial power (whites at the top, Asians in the middle, and blacks at the bottom), there tends to be very little argument across the different races. The main reason for this avoidance of argument is the fear that it may spark violence. Thirteen years after independence, this situation still exists. Maybe the new generation that has grown up after independence will overcome this barrier.

The logical approach seems to be the dominant style among people of similar age groups and races. They tend to favor direct relationships, like stating a problem and a solution. With this approach it is easier to follow and understand the problem at hand. And since most of the population is uneducated, the logical approach is the widely used style, since it makes the issue easier to grasp.[20]

International students in your class may be able to provide additional examples that represent predominant styles of argument in their countries and cultures.

Some researchers have speculated about the reasons for the differences in argument styles among different cultures. *Preferred cultural values* and *preferred patterns of thinking* may be the two major factors that differentiate argument styles across cultures.[21] Differences in value systems from culture to culture are often particularly obvious. For example, Americans who relocate to Saudi Arabia are some-

---

[20]Used with permission.

[21]Gregg B. Walker, "Assessing Multicultural Argument in the Law of the Sea Negotiations: A Rationale and Analytical Framework," *Spheres of Argument: Proceedings of the Sixth SCA/AFA Conference on Argumentation,* ed. Bruce E. Gronbeck (Annandale, VA: Speech Communication Association, October 1989), pp. 600–603.

times surprised when they receive copies of newspapers from outside the country. Before the newspapers are delivered, the Saudi censors use wide felt-tipped ink pens to obliterate visual material that is offensive to their cultural values. Pictures of a ballerina's legs and arms may be colored over, as well as other parts of the female anatomy usually kept covered in Arab countries.

Boxes 2.4 and 2.5 list some of the preferred cultural values and preferred patterns of reasoning that recent researchers have identified as typical of cultures in certain countries or areas of the world.[22] As you look at these very brief lists, remember that they represent generalizations based on specific instances and examples, and that they are, thus, only probably true rather than certainly or always true. Test these lists against your experience and the experience of the international students in your classroom. Add items to the lists if you can. Also, as you read, remember that shared values and shared ways of thinking are critical for building common ground and thus have significant implications for cross-cultural argument.

These partial lists suggest some significant differences among cultures that can affect the outcomes of argument. Certainly problems can arise in cross-cultural argument if participants do not identify the values and preferred patterns of thinking that each party brings to the argument. As you read newspaper accounts of intercultural communication and argument, watch for the problems and misun-

---

Americans value individual achievement, hard work, independence.

Russians value security, patience, collective freedom.

Arabs value honor, dignity, nationalism, unity.

Indians value discipline, tact, openness to experience, courage.

Greeks value patience, willpower.

Mexicans value community, family.

Japanese value achievement, concern with being right, serenity, self-confidence.

English value independence.

Asians in general value interdependence, sharing.

South Americans in general value interdependence, group values, sharing.

Africans in general value interpersonal relationships.

Europeans in general value individual and personal status gained through education and making money.

BOX 2.4 The Preferred Values of Selected Countries and Cultures That Affect Common Ground in Argument

---

[22]See Walker, "Assessing Multicultural Argument," pp. 600–601. Walker summarizes the results of considerable cross-cultural research into the values and patterns of thought preferred by different cultures. See his article for additional sources and information. Pearson, "Women as Learners," p. 6, also summarizes some of the cultural values included here.

Americans prefer inductive reasoning: generalizations based on facts, examples, and cases. They trust experience as grounds, and action as outcomes. They are skeptical of pure reason, or of generalizations without grounds or backing.

Russians prefer deductive reasoning, that is, starting with a general principle, applying it to cases, and reasoning to a conclusion. They consider generalizations and truths as adequate by themselves. They trust pure reason and the notion of absolute truth. They also like to establish who is right.

French prefer relativism, that is, the concept that truth varies according to individual reasoning and experience. They distrust the idea of absolute truth.

Chinese prefer individualistic thinking. They have difficulty in thinking collectively. People are not often asked to think critically in China. They trust prior wisdom from ancient texts which are favored far more as grounds than are logical reasoning or hypothetical cases. They also like contentious argument.[23]

Mexicans prefer contemplation, intuition, group thinking. They dislike competition, and they dislike contention and debate.

Arabs prefer intuition and the affective or emotional dimensions of argument.

Japanese prefer intuition, making suggestions, giving hints, communicating indirectly. They like ambiguity, or saying one thing and meaning something else. They often use understatement. Their communication can seem incomplete to outsiders because they often omit logical links, expecting others to infer them. They dislike contention and debate.[24]

Italians prefer debate, contention, and clash. They trust logical thinking, including giving reasons and providing evidence.

BOX 2.5 The Preferred Patterns of Reasoning of Selected Countries and Cultures That Influence Argument Styles

derstandings that can arise from an absence of shared values and shared ways of thinking. Here are two recent examples:

1. **A Japanese Example.** In an article concerning deliberations in Japan about whether or not that country should have a permanent seat on the United Nations Security Council, David Sanger wrote in the *New York Times*:

> The Tokyo Government has not wanted to appear to be openly seeking the Security Council seat, even though countries with far less economic power sit there today. But

---

[23]Joel Bloch, "The Tradition of Chinese Rhetoric: Its Implications for the Chinese ESL Student," paper delivered at the Conference on College Composition and Communication, Cincinnati, March 18–21, 1992.

[24]Michael David Hazen, "The Role of Argument, Reasoning and Logic in Tacit, Incomplete and Indirect Communication: The Case of Japan," in *Spheres of Argument. Proceedings of the Sixth SCA/AFA Conference on Argumentation*, ed. Bruce E. Gronbeck (Annandale, VA: Speech Communication Association, 1989).

there is also an underlying fear that Japan, if given a bully pulpit, may have little to say. "We might be ashamed to raise our hand," Seiki Nishihiro, a former Deputy Defense Minister, said during a recent conference.[25]

Nishihiro's comment is puzzling unless one recalls the Japanese reluctance to participate in contentious debate, which is a regular feature of the Security Council.

2. **A Russian Example.** A human interest story about an international student from Russia says she was confident she would do well on her first exam. She studied hard, memorized the material, and wrote it well in the exam booklet. She was surprised, however, when she received a D grade. Her professor had penalized her for writing only what the book said and for not including her own opinions.[26]

This incident can be puzzling unless one realizes that not all countries and cultures encourage critical thinking, evaluative opinion, and argument. Totalitarian governments like the former Soviet Union, in fact, discouraged or even forbade diverse opinion in public forums.

Argument is fundamental to democracy, and it flourishes in democratic societies. In totalitarian societies, however, if it exists at all, it usually must go underground. Thus, the argument in such countries may be found in the secret meetings of opposition political groups or in private meetings of citizens. Written argument may appear in underground newspapers or in material written by dissidents or political exiles. Forums for argument in such societies are severely limited compared to those in democratic societies. Some international students from such countries may, at first, find it difficult to participate in argument.

The following account was written by a Russian student describing Soviet and post-Soviet argument in her country. Notice that the Soviet Communist government was never completely successful in eliminating argument among Russian citizens.

FROM SHOES AND FISTS TO GLASNOST: ARGUMENT IN RUSSIA

Nadejda Michoustina

<u>First Dog</u>: How are things different under Yeltsin?

<u>Second Dog</u>: Well, the chain is still too short and the food dish is still too far away to reach, but they let you bark as loud as you want.

<u>A post-Soviet political anecdote</u>

---

[25]*New York Times*, May 5, 1992, Sec. A, p. 1.
[26]David Wallechinsky, "This Land of Ours," *Parade*, July 5, 1992, p. 4.

When in the early 1960s Nikita Khrushchev shook his fist and threatened the United Nations with a shoe, the former Soviet leader was regarded as comical rather than convincing, ridiculous rather than persuasive. When in the early 1990s the debates in the Russian Parliament moved from words to blows, the diagnosis became obvious: the Parliament lacked argumentation skills, and the causes were many.

Russians historically have been influenced by the habits and traditions of authoritarian rule which provides a belief system to live by, whether it is Communism or Russian Orthodoxy. Five centuries of absolutism from Ivan the Terrible to Leonid Brezhnev have left the Russian people uncomfortable with the Western notion of the democratic process.

Most Russians through habit have looked to the state, the ruler, the parent, or the teacher as the authority figures that provide ideology and purpose, law and order, age and status, and the indisputable truths to live by. To take an opposing side on issues in most cases has meant also to become a personal rival of authorities or even to risk becoming a political prisoner. The Communist Party line kept the Russians numb, choked their public voices, denied them the means of communication and civilized argumentation, drowned them in the foam of the Party press, kept them impotent and powerless politically, and suspicious and frightened socially.

Fear, however, did not make all Russians totally submissive or silent. Even under Communist rule they distrusted the media, questioned the authorities; and were suspicious and skeptical. Cynical jokes, political anecdotes, and personal opinions, however, were voiced in the private spaces of kitchens rather than in public forums. The kitchen became a free speech arena, a hot line for political debates, and a tribune for personal opinions. Russians by nature love to argue, and they argue in order to grasp a notion of what they consider truth. To most Russians truth is not merely a matter of testing the accuracy of a proposition; instead, it is a human virtue, an indicator of human "goodness."

History has taught Russians to be skeptical and distrustful, but it has not provided them with the tools and techniques of argumentation. Argument in Russia is bare, straightforward, and at times crude. Because for centuries argumentation and rhetoric have neither been taught nor publicly practiced, Russians tend to believe that actions speak louder than words, and that loud words speak for themselves. Russian argument is almost always contentious and presupposes "winners" and "losers." It usually is not settled until one side is willing to yield to the other.

It was not until the late 1980s that the huge army of in-kitchen debaters were given a public microphone. Even though the word <u>glasnost</u> does not correspond to the American freedom of speech, it comes from the Russian word <u>glas</u>, voice, and literally means voiceness or speaking out. Along with <u>glasnost</u>, words like "pluralism" and "compromise" now have entered the pages of Russian newspapers and are also a part of the vocabulary of Russian political leaders. Modern Russians are gradually realizing that the Parliament is not that far removed from the kitchen and that pounding shoes do not speak so eloquently as words.

All participants in argument, whether they come from democratic or totalitarian societies, need to work to establish common ground if argument across cultural, racial, and gender boundaries is to be successful. This effort can be difficult and time-consuming. An issue that historically has been argued and debated through the ages is the fishing, navigation, and territorial rights to the oceans of the world. In the 1970s the United Nations Conference on the Law of the Sea was charged with the task of reaching agreement among nations on access to and use of the seas. This group spent nine years engaged in intercultural argument and negotiation, finally reaching agreement on some but not all of the issues raised by this subject.[27]

President Boris Yeltsin of Russia made an effective attempt to achieve common ground on his visit to Japan in late 1993 when there was considerable tension between the two countries. Unlike some of his predecessors, Yeltsin is accomplished in building common ground. Soon after arriving in Japan he apologized for Russia's treatment of thousands of Japanese prisoners of war who were sent to Siberia after World War II. More than 60,000 of them died, and many Japanese believed an apology was long overdue. Later, Yeltsin repeated this apology to the Japanese prime minister and, at the same time, bowed deeply to express his remorse, a gesture that is valued in the Japanese culture.[28] His efforts, according to reports, relieved a considerable amount of tension between the two countries because of the common ground he was able to establish. When common ground is not established, the consequences can be devastating. Wars are a frequent alternative to productive argument and successful negotiations, especially when the differences among the arguing parties are extreme.

---

[27]Walker, "Assessing Multicultural Argument," pp. 599–600.
[28]David E. Sanger, "Yeltsin, in Tokyo, Avoids Islands Issue," *New York Times*, October 14, 1993, Sec. A, p. 5.

In fact, when value systems and habits of reasoning vary widely among arguing parties, special techniques must sometimes be used to establish common ground. You will learn a number of special strategies that can be used for this purpose in future chapters. Rogerian argument is one such technique, however, that is particularly useful for reducing conflict and establishing common ground among parties who hold extreme or hostile positions on an issue. The following description of Rogerian argument will suggest at least one way of bringing hostile parties closer together, and it may also provide you with additional insight into your own argument style. Rogerian argument can be difficult for individuals who favor contention and agonistic debate because the emphasis is on making connections and reducing hostility. Rogerian argument can be learned, however, even if it is not your preferred style. It can be useful in some situations.

ROGERIAN ARGUMENT AS ONE MEANS FOR ACHIEVING COMMON GROUND

"Where Are Men and Women Now?" was the title of a public performance staged in New York City in 1991 by Deborah Tannen, author of *You Just Don't Understand*, linguistics professor, and expert in male-female communication, and Robert Bly, author of *Iron John: A Book about Men* and leader of many "men's movement" workshops. The press publicized this exchange as a "face-to-face, word-to-word confrontation." An all-out "battle of the sexes" was predicted. The program was sold out to 1,000 people, half of whom were men and half women.

The audience and press expectations of open conflict between these two were not realized, however. Instead, Bly and Tannen began the program with the reading of a poem by Emily Dickenson. Tannen read while Bly played a stringed instrument. Next, Bly read from Tannen's book, who, in turn, read from his book. Then the dialogue began as follows:

> ROBERT BLY: The first time I came in contact with your book, my wife and I were having dinner up in northern Minnesota, and someone started to read out of it. We both fell off our chairs laughing, because it illuminated every mistake we had made, including every misunderstanding. . . .

He continued by explaining how Tannen's book had helped him and his wife gain insight and communicate better. Bly explained how he had learned from Tannen to build rapport.

Tannen then replied.

> DEBORAH TANNEN: There's another side to this. You're assuming that it's good for men to learn to talk this way. And I always stop short of saying that because it's very important for me as a woman to say that men's styles are okay too.[29]

---

[29] Robert Bly and Deborah Tannen, "Where Are Men and Women Today?" transcript printed in *New Age Journal*, January/February 1992, pp. 28–33, 92–97.

These two, meeting for the first time at this special program, were determined not to fulfill the predictions of the press by providing a traditional war-between-the-sexes debate complete with the audience functioning as judge and trying to declare winners. Instead, they resorted to Rogerian argument, a special strategy that can be used at any time in argument to cool emotions, reduce conflict, and create sympathetic understanding. In their case their strategy involved demonstrating at the outset that they both understood and valued one another's ideas.

Carl Rogers was a psychotherapist who was well known for the empathetic listening techniques he used in psychological counseling. He later became interested in how these same techniques could be used to improve communication in other difficult, emotionally charged situations. Richard Young and his co-authors Alton Becker and Kenneth Pike built on Rogers's ideas to formulate Rogerian argument,[30] a method for helping people in difficult situations connect and understand one another. The object was to avoid undue conflict or, even worse, a mutual standoff.

According to Young, Becker, and Pike, written Rogerian argument reduces the reader's sense of threat and conflict with the writer so that alternatives can be considered. Three things are accomplished by this strategy:

1. **Writers let readers know they have been understood.** To accomplish this purpose, the writer restates the opponent's position in summary form by using dispassionate, neutral language. Thus the writer demonstrates that the reader has been heard and that the writer understands the issue exactly as the reader does. Note how Tannen and Bly begin their special presentation by reading from one another's works to demonstrate that they are hearing one another.

2. **Writers show how reader's positions are valid in certain contexts and under certain conditions.** The writer thus demonstrates to the reader that at least part of the reader's position is acceptable, and thereby makes it easier for the reader to reciprocate and accept part of the writer's position. Notice how Bly says at the outset that Tannen's observations are valid and can be applied to conversations he has actually had with his wife. Tannen then points out that males' preferences in communicating are also okay. Thus they validate one another's positions.

3. **Writers get readers to believe that both of them share the same values, types of experience, attitudes, and perceptions, and are thus similar in significant ways.** Tannen and Bly accomplish this end by borrowing one another's theories and applying them to their own personal experiences. They make it clear that they both share the same values and types of experience.

The most important feature of Rogerian argument is listening empathetically and nonjudgmentally. Rogers says that people usually listen judgmentally and evaluatively. They are eager to jump in, point out what is right or wrong, and make corrections or refutations. Rogerian listening puts the writer in the reader's place by requiring the writer to provide neutral summaries of the reader's position that show sympathetic understanding. Thus the writer encourages a continued and

[30]Richard Young, Alton Becker, and Kenneth Pike, *Rhetoric: Discovery and Change* (New York: Harcourt Brace and World, 1970), pp. 7–8, 274–290.

open exchange of ideas with the reader. In Rogers's words, the writer "listens with" as opposed to "evaluating about."

Table 2.1 is a chart that contrasts Rogerian argument, as explained by Young, Becker, and Pike, with the traditional pro-and-con model of argument associated with debate.

In Chapter 5 you will learn about the Toulmin model for argument. The Toulmin model and Rogerian argument have one extremely important feature in

TABLE 2.1   Traditional Pro-and-Con Debate Model and Rogerian Argument Compared

	TRADITIONAL PRO-AND-CON DEBATE MODEL OF ARGUMENT	ROGERIAN ARGUMENT
Basic Strategy	Writer states the claim and gives reasons to prove it. Writer refutes the opponent by showing what is wrong or invalid.	Writer states the opponent's claim and points out what is sound about the reasons used to prove it.
Ethos	Writer builds own character (ethos) by citing past experience and expertise.	Writer builds opponent's character perhaps at expense of his or her own.
Logos	Writer uses logic (all the proofs) as tools for presenting a case and refuting the opponent's case.	Writer proceeds in an explanatory fashion to analyze the conditions under which the position of either side is valid.
Pathos	Writer uses emotional language to strengthen the claim.	Writer uses descriptive, dispassionate language to cool emotions on both sides.
Goal	Writer tries to change opponent's mind and thereby win the argument.	Writer creates cooperation, the possibility that both sides might change, and a mutually advantageous outcome.
Use of Argumentative Techniques	Writer draws on the conventional structures and techniques taught in Chapters 5–7 of this book.	Writer throws out conventional structures and techniques because they may be threatening. Writer focuses, instead, on connecting empathetically.

common. They both provide for the creation of common ground. It is created by the warrant in the Toulmin model (see pages 146–162) and the shared values and assumptions established through summary and restatement in Rogerian argument.

In order to write Rogerian argument, according to Young, Becker, and Pike, the writer proceeds in phases rather than following set organizational patterns or argumentative strategies. These phases are as follows:

1. The writer introduces the issue and shows that the opponent's position is understood by restating it.
2. The writer shows in which contexts and under what conditions the opponent's position may be valid. Note that the opponent is never made to feel completely wrong.
3. The writer then states his or her own position, including the contexts in which it is valid.
4. The writer states how the opponent's position would benefit if the opponent were to adopt elements of the writer's position. An attempt is finally made to show that the two positions complement each other and that each supplies what the other lacks.

The advantages of Rogerian argument are clear. Such an approach helps release tension and disagreement and encourages negotiation and cooperation when values and aims are in conflict. Also, Rogerian argument has the potential of leveling or at least controlling uneven power relationships that may interfere with the peaceful resolution of conflicting issues.

There are also perceived disadvantages of Rogerian argument. It is sometimes difficult for the writer to understand and restate the reader's position, particularly when the reader/opponent is not present and no written material is available to explain the opposing position. Also, connecting with the reader/opponent by restating the opposing position may be extremely difficult if the writer is emotionally involved and strongly dislikes the opposing ideas. It takes courage, Rogers says, to listen and restate ideas that are strongly antithetical to your own. One has to want to make connections to succeed.

Rogerian argument has also been criticized as annoying to women. Some researchers claim that women have always been expected to understand others, sometimes even at the expense of understanding themselves. As one female critic puts it, Rogerian argument "feels too much like giving in."[31] Another critic finds the advice that the writer should always use unemotional, dispassionate language to restate the opponent's argument unrealistic and constraining. Avoiding rude or insulting language is necessary, a matter of common sense. But to avoid all emotionally connotative language may be impossible.[32]

---

[31]See Catherine Lamb, "Beyond Argument in Feminist Composition," *College Composition and Communication*, February 1991, pp. 11–24. See also Phyllis Lassner, "Feminist Response to Rogerian Rhetoric," *Rhetoric Review*, 8 (1990): 220–232.

[32]Doug Brent, "Young, Becker, and Pike's 'Rogerian' Rhetoric: A Twenty-Year Reassessment," *College English*, 53 (April 1991): 452–446.

Rogerian argument persists as a viable model, however, in spite of some of its shortcomings. Its central notion, that it is important to understand and see some validity in other people's opposing positions, is sometimes the only way to create common ground in difficult situations.

EXERCISES AND ACTIVITIES

1. CLASS DISCUSSION: ANALYZE YOUR STYLE AND THE CLASSROOM ENVIRONMENT

a. Prepare for class discussion by freewriting, that is, by writing rapidly what first comes to mind without worrying about exact phrasing. Think about the last time you had to be convincing and argue for a certain point of view. Write for *ten minutes* in response to the following questions:

When you argued, what was the issue that you were arguing about?

What were you trying to achieve?

What did you do to achieve it?

Was that typical of your usual style of argument?

If yes, say why.

If no, say why and describe your usual style.

b. Now take *five more minutes* to list some influences on your style of argument. Consider role models, home training, gender, race, culture, nationality, national heritage, or any other life experience that has influenced you. Now write a brief story about something that happened in your past that has influenced the way you argue today.

c. Discuss the results of your freewriting. As your individual classmates report on their individual styles, try to develop a sense of the distinctive styles of argument that exist in your classroom. What are some of the strongest influences on these styles?

d. Now discuss the environment that you need to create in your classroom to accommodate all of these different styles. To get you started, Jürgen Habermas, a modern European rhetorician, describes his version of an ideal environment for argument.[33] Read each item and decide whether you agree or disagree and say why. What would you eliminate? Why? What would you add? Why?

(1) Each person should have the freedom to express ideas and critique other's ideas directly, openly, and honestly.

(2) The use of force and personal power that tend to inhibit some participants are to be eliminated.

(3) Arguments based on an appeal to the past and tradition are to be exposed. These arguments superimpose the past on the present, and everyone does not share the same past.

---

[33] Habermas's ideas are summarized by James L. Golden, Goodwin F. Berquist, and William E. Coleman in *The Rhetoric of Western Thought*, 4th ed. (Dubuque, IA: Kendall Hunt, 1989), p. 438.

(4) The aim of argument is to arrive at truth through consensus and an adherence of minds.

(5) _____

(6) _____

(7) _____

   e. Write a page and a half, double-spaced, explaining your plan for developing flexibility in your present argument style.
What do you like best about your current style of argument?
What would you like to change?
How would you describe an ideal arguer?

2. GROUP WORK AND CLASS DISCUSSION: ANALYZE STYLES AS INFLUENCED BY GENDER AND RACE

Read the following two articles, written, respectively, by a female African-American and a female Asian-American. Read also excerpts from the "Letter from Birmingham Jail" written by the black male author Martin Luther King, Jr. It begins on page 246. Then discuss them in small groups of four or five students each. Appoint a scribe to record your findings and report them to the class. The following will help organize your discussion:
   a. Identify some of the effective argument strategies in each of the essays.
   b. Do you think that the author's race, culture, or gender could have influenced the argumentative strategies used by each author? Discuss how.
   c. Answer the bottom-line question: Could this article have been written as convincingly by a member of another race or of the opposite gender? Why or why not?

STOLEN PROMISE

Patricia Raybon

It is cruel, like a bad joke. Spring has come, and soon the season of love and weddings will enter nicely in—but not for my daughter.

She is smart and beautiful. But she is black.

And all the men are gone.

Gone to jail. Gone to drugs. Gone to graves.

I exaggerate, I suppose, but I am a mother. I know about logic. But I dream of the unlikely. Of romance and Champagne and sugary cake. Of bouquets and white dresses and silky veils. Instead I get the evening news and the morning papers, and the reports have not been good: more black men in jail than in college. More dropping out of some schools than dropping in. Hundreds killed on mean streets every year. It is a war, but nobody with power is fighting it. It is the news, but no one with clout will explain it.

I put down the papers and telephone my daughter, for a chat that ends with a question I shouldn't ask.

"So do you have a date this weekend?" My daughter, listening 2,500 miles away at an all-black university in Atlanta, answers first with a pause.

"A date?" she finally says. "Mom, with *who?*"

I clear my throat, primed for the logic I want to believe. Surely, I say, there are some nice young men on the campus.

"Mom," she says with a voice all mothers know. "We're talking supply and demand here, and the supply is low." She knows the numbers. "Seven to one, Mom. That's the ratio of women to men on this campus. Bad odds," she tells me.

So bad I want to blame somebody. Or better, I want somebody to fix it—to take away the bad juju stealing the virility and pride and promise from black American life and leaving in its place crowded jail cells and dead boys and too many girls without husbands or Saturday night dates.

I want somebody to fix the look on the face of a friend whose daughter is getting married—to a man the girl would not have chosen in the past. "Too few black men to choose from," my friend explains, tapping a truth I can't deny.

The inner city's chaos and the neglect that causes it aren't somebody else's problems, they're mine. And I am surprised. Stupidly so. Have I been blind? Dumb? Indifferent? No, but I live a comfortable life. Privilege and advantage have blessed three generations of my family, and I will admit this: Comfort is a dangerous drug. It dulls one's sense of the scope of disarray in America. It makes the 6 o'clock news seem like another world—certainly not a threat to one's own—certainly not a worry for us in the charmed circle: handsome, vibrant people living our rewarding, productive lives and rearing our beautiful, talented children.

But no woman is an island. What pulls at one tugs at another. It is a circle unbroken. When mother after mother bury their sons, daughters remain to shoulder the grief. Daughters, like my own, whose phones rarely ring, whose friends are now rivals, whose quiet weekends force them to wonder where the boys are.

The boys are all gone. Far too many of them anyway.

Pain has caught up with them and turned them against one another and even against themselves. They live lives of danger, lives too cheap and too quick for the leisure and tenderness of romance and dreams of hope.

Too hazardous to look at a pretty girl like mine and want to make a long life together, because what's life? A struggle, unfair, a stacked deck with the other guy holding all the aces.

That is frustration talking, because it conjures up nagging demons I try to resist: envy when somebody else's daughter meets a wonderful boy and falls in love. Fear that my own "educated" girl will have to "marry down." And shame for thinking it. Anger when accomplished black men choose white women for their wives. Rage that history and indifference have let segments of black America unhinge and implode. Hate for forces that allow it.

These are "race" feelings, of course, so they churn up from some unfathomable well that holds hurts and hidden memories. Mix in romance. The feelings and images get hot and combustible. One floats out of nowhere: my father, now dead, is sitting at our kitchen table at the "new" house in the suburbs—not the "old" house in the city—and he is shyly and painfully spelling out a new and curious rule: no daughter of his will be allowed to date white boys.

"Yes?" I say, waiting for more. To live near them and attend their schools and take advantage of the opportunities that their neighborhoods provide is one thing. To go on dates with them, not to mention marry them, is something else again—and it is forbidden. "Yes," I say.

Not bigotry, but deep pain and long history—and the chance, innocent phone call from a white male schoolmate—give birth to this American moment: a father's feverish dictate against race and sex and all that the combination can mean.

But during that summer, his anxiousness seems overwrought, and his rule—replete with his pain—doesn't matter much anyway.

Because handsome *black* suitors are around every corner, on every dance floor, across every crowded room.

Brown, beautiful, smart young men with "possibility" still part of their vocabulary—they are everywhere, and they pursue black womanhood as moths chase down flame.

Something hopeful and lovely propels them to our doorsteps, where they offer flowers and candy and marriage and happiness ever after. And it is magic. We are alive and desirable, and their boldness, their *maleness*—in their soft white shirts and creased trousers and heady aftershave scents and Saturday-night haircuts—prove it.

That was then.

This is now:

My porch is empty. Rarely is it graced by the footfall of brave and earnest young men seeking the company of someone to watch over and love.

Last month in Denver, where I live, three young black men were gunned down for something to do with anger and macho and maybe crack cocaine—fuzzy reasons for dying, little consolation when a coffin lid closes for good.

On the evening news, I recognize the mother of one of the dead boys. She went to my junior high school many years ago. She was a high flame then, a bright spirit with dancing eyes and frosted lipstick and laughter and sass. But the pretty girl I remember is now a grieving mother, chanting the litany for our sad season. "A senseless act," she says. Nobody argues that she is wrong.

In another time, her son might have met my daughter and danced off with her into the night—their laughter following them in the dark like a sweet essence, a prelude to all the things that they could be, a melody they could call their song, through these long, dark years of death without meaning and dying without love.

A mother's dream is a hopeful thing. One day perhaps it won't be folly.[34]

---

[34]*New York Times Magazine*, May 3, 1992, pp. 20, 22.

VICTIMS OF BOTH RACES

Judy Ching-Chia Wong

During the Los Angeles riots, Asian-Americans across the country found themselves in a media spotlight that they most probably found unpleasant. This was hardly new. Beginning with the flood of articles during the 80's on the "model minority," in which Asian-Americans were reported to resent preferential treatment given to black and Hispanic students, and continuing to the TV images of Korean-American storekeepers waving pistols at looters in Los Angeles, Asian-Americans have found themselves pushed into a racial conflict not of their making.

Many have little knowledge of the anti-Asian riots in the 1800s that closed off Asian immigration until 1965. They have even less understanding of the institutionalized racism that plagued African-Americans through most of America's history and continues today in subtler but no less invidious forms.

Yet Asian-Americans have become pawns in America's racial battles. Their pursuit of achievement has been used insensitively by whites as a model for blacks and Hispanics, enabling whites to attack welfare and affirmative action. Many African-Americans think Asians use their business skills to exploit the black community.

Yet for Korean-Americans, blacks' targeting of their stores amounted to lawless destruction by those jealous of their hard work and relative success. The unwillingness of the police to involve themselves in what they apparently considered an "inter-ethnic" way to protect Korean-American businesses was a breach of the social contract.

Asian-Americans must learn to speak out. After the riots, we heard Korean-American shop owners admonishing President Bush for not responding fast enough to their plight. Yet the shop owners cannot just protest to the Government. They must reopen their stores and attempt to reconcile themselves with the community they depend on.

The public response of other Asian-Americans has been tepid. As a Chinese-American, I know that my family and friends have strong sympathy for the Koreans. Yet as a group, Chinese-Americans have been silent, though they too have been affected by the events. A friend of my father warns his son daily to avoid arguments with blacks and to say he is not Korean if harassed. Not only is this not helpful to Korean-Americans, it reinforces stereotypes and fears.

Some Asians continue to say that by using the term "Asian-American" we are implying an affinity among Asians that many do not feel, drawing attention to ourselves and making the racial climate even more hostile. Yet as the debate over the riots has shown, we risk having our role defined for ourselves by others.

Asian-Americans have an uneasy relationship with white America, upon whom our dreams of success depend. Yet society will never fully accept Asians as white. Asian-Americans, on the personal and community level, must begin to address issues that stem directly from racism: Japan-bashing and anti-Asian violence, stereotyping in the media and the problems of immigrants who have not made it and who instead stock the sweatshops or turn to crime.

Dialogue between African-Americans and Asian-Americans must begin across America. One paradox of racism is that a lack of opportunities has forced Korean-Americans into small businesses in neighborhoods where they are seen as invaders, as white suburbia looks on from a safe distance, shocked at the violence.

Most importantly, by speaking out we can try to force the media to stop viewing America in biracial terms. The problems and experiences of Asian-Americans, African-Americans, Hispanics, etc., while sometimes similar, are not the same. Unless Asian-Americans learn to think and speak out as a group, we will continue to be caught in the middle, misunderstood and pummeled by both sides.[35]

3. CLASS DISCUSSION AND WRITING ASSIGNMENT: INTERNATIONAL ARGUMENT

Read the following article by the novelist and author Reiko Hatsumi in which he explains what "yes" (*hai*) means in Japanese. Are there other examples of words, customs, beliefs, or values like this one that could create confusion or distrust among people from different cultures? Draw on the experiences of international students both in and outside of class and on international news reports. Write a paper in which you explain one of the differences you have identified, along with what would be required to achieve common ground and better understanding.

A SIMPLE "HAI" WON'T DO

Reiko Hatsumi

Tokyo

When a TV announcer here reported Bill Clinton's comment to Boris Yeltsin that when the Japanese say yes they often mean no, he gave the news with an expression of mild disbelief.

Having spent my life between East and West, I can sympathize with those who find the Japanese yes unfathomable. However, the fact that it sometimes fails to correspond precisely with the Occidental yes does not necessarily signal intended deception. This was probably why the announcer looked bewildered, and it marks a cultural gap that can have serious repercussions.

I once knew an American who worked in Tokyo. He was a very nice man, but he suffered a nervous breakdown and went back to the U.S. tearing his hair and exclaiming. "All Japanese businessmen are liars." I hope this is not true. If it were, all Japanese businessmen would be driving each other mad, which does not seem to be the case. Nevertheless, since tragedies often arise from misunderstandings, an attempt at some explanation might not be amiss.

A Japanese yes in its primary context simply means the other person has heard you and is contemplating a reply. This is because it would be rude to keep someone waiting for an answer without supplying him with an immediate response.

---

[35]*New York Times*, Op-Ed, May 28, 1992.

For example: a feudal warlord marries his sister to another warlord. (I am back to TV.) Then he decides to destroy his newly acquired brother-in-law and besieges his castle. Being human, though, the attacking warlord worries about his sister and sends a spy to look around. The spy returns and the lord inquires eagerly, "Well, is she safe?" The spy bows and answers "Hai," which means yes. We sigh with relief thinking. "Ah, the fair lady is still alive!" But then the spy continues, "To my regret she has fallen on her sword together with her husband."

Hai is also an expression of our willingness to comply with your intent even if your request is worded in the negative. This can cause complications. When I was at school, our English teacher, a British nun, would say, "Now children, you won't forget to do your homework, will you?" And we would all dutifully chorus, "Yes, mother," much to her consternation.

A variation of hai may mean, "I understand your wish and would like to make you happy but unfortunately . . ." Japanese being a language of implication, the latter part of this estimable thought is often left unsaid.

Is there, then, a Japanese yes that corresponds to the Western one? I think so, particularly when it is accompanied by phrases such as "sodesu" (It is so) and "soshi-masu" (I will do so). A word of caution against the statement, "I will think about it." Though in Tokyo this can mean a willingness to give one's proposal serious thought, in Osaka, another business center, it means a definite no. This attitude probably stems from the belief that a straightforward no would sound too brusque.

When talking to a Japanese person it is perhaps best to remember that although he may be speaking English, he is reasoning in Japanese. And if he says "I will think about it," you should inquire as to which district of Japan he hails from before going on with your negotiations.[36]

4. GROUP WORK AND CLASS DISCUSSION: ROGERIAN ARGUMENT AND ESTABLISHING COMMON GROUND

Read the following historic statements by President George Bush of the United States and President Boris Yeltsin of Russia that officially ended the cold war between the two countries. What attempts were made by both men to establish common ground? How successful were they? What more could they have done? Write a two-page paper in response to these questions.

STATEMENTS BY PRESIDENTS BUSH AND YELTSIN

BY PRESIDENT BUSH

Well, today for the first time an American President and the democratically elected President of an independent Russia have met. And we did so not as adversaries,

---

[36]*New York Times*, April 15, 1992, Sec. A, p. 12.

but as friends. And this historic meeting was yet another confirmation of the end of the cold war and the dawn of a new era. Russia and the United States are charting a new relationship, and it's based on trust, based on a commitment to economic and political freedom; it's based on a strong hope for true partnership.

So we agreed here that we're going to pull closer together economically and politically. I invited President Yeltsin to come to the States for a state visit. He accepted, and he in turn asked me to come to the Soviet Union, and I accepted. That will be later in the year, and he will be coming in the first half of the year, the date to be determined later on. We agreed to cooperate in the safe handling of nuclear weapons, arms reductions and a wide array of other subjects.

So from my standpoint, and the standpoint of the United States, our first meeting here, we felt it was a very good visit. The only problem was it was very short. But we'll have a chance to follow up at the state visit. And, Mr. President, the floor is yours. And welcome once again, even though you're heading off now down the hill to see, meet some members of Congress.

BY PRESIDENT YELTSIN

President Bush, ladies and gentlemen. I am very grateful to my friend, George, for the words which he has just spoken in terms of our meeting and aimed at Russia and towards me. I feel that the meeting was exceptionally positive, necessary and historic.

We discussed a whole range of issues—as a matter of fact, those kinds of issues that have never been exposed and open many, many years and many, many decades: issues of economic reform in Russia, as well as cooperation and assistance, so that this reform not die on the vine: and issues having to do with the Commonwealth of Independent Nations; economic issues having to do with the military condition now, the condition of the military; and on the initiative of President Bush and Russia, also, we talked about reduction of strategic and tactical arsenals, down to the minimal of, say, two and a half thousand warheads for either side, and in this issue we will now begin very specific and concrete negotiations; the issue of arms sales; of non-proliferation of nuclear weapons, issues of the so-called brain drain, well, and a whole series of others.

Now, maybe some very specific and personal issues, but I think having to do with a relationship which really has a great importance. I'm very satisfied that today one might say that there has been written and drawn a new line, and crossed out all of the things that have been associated with the cold war. Today we are going to sign a statement or declaration on a new nature or character of the relationship between the United States of America and Russia. From now on, we do not consider ourselves to be potential enemies, as it had been previously in our military doctrine. This is the historic value of this meeting.

And another very important factor in our relationship, right away, today, it's already been pointed out that in the future there will be full frankness, full openness, full honesty in our relationship. And we, both of us, value very, very much. Thank you so much.

JOINT DECLARATION

At the conclusion of this meeting between an American President and the President of a new and democratic Russia, we, the leaders of two great peoples and nations, are agreed that a number of principles should guide relations between Russia and America.

1. Russia and the United States do not regard each other as potential adversaries. From now on, the relationship will be characterized by friendship and partnership founded on mutual trust and respect and a common commitment to democracy and economic freedom.

2. We will work to remove any remnants of cold war hostility, including taking steps to reduce our strategic arsenals.

3. We will do all we can to promote a mutual well-being of our peoples and to expand as widely as possible the ties that now bind our peoples. Openness and tolerance should be the hallmark of relations between our peoples and governments.

4. We will actively promote free trade, investment and economic cooperation between our two countries.

5. We will make every effort to support the promotion of our shared values of democracy, the rule of law, respect for human rights, including minority rights, respect for borders and peaceful change around the globe.

6. We will work actively together to:
   - Prevent the proliferation of weapons of mass destruction and associated technology, and curb the spread of advanced conventional arms on the basis of principles to be agreed upon.
   - Settle regional conflicts peacefully.
   - Counter terrorism, halt drug trafficking and forestall environmental degradation.

In adopting these principles, the United States and Russia today launch a new era in our relationship. In this new era, we seek a peace, an enduring peace that rests on lasting common values. This can be an era of peace and friendship that offers hope not only to our peoples but to the peoples of the world.

For a while our conflicts helped divide the world for a generation. Now, working with others and with each other, we can help unite the globe through our friendship—a new alliance of partners working against the common dangers we face.[37]

5. WRITING ASSIGNMENT: ROGERIAN ARGUMENT

Write a three-page double-spaced Rogerian argument on an issue of your choice. Select one that you have strong feelings about. You should also have strong negative feelings about the opposing viewpoint. Include all of the following parts in your paper:

   a. Introduce the issue and restate the opposing position to show you understand it.

---

[37] *New York Times*, February 2, 1992, p. 6.

b. Show in which contexts and under what conditions the opposing position may be valid. State it so that it is acceptable to the opposition.
c. State your own position and describe the context in which it is valid.
d. Show how the opposing position would be strengthened if it added elements of your position.

Here are two models of Rogerian argument written by students. The first, "Capitalism Today: Understanding Our World," was written by a student who is hostile to capitalism. He sees it as a system that is destructive both to individuals and to the environment. He had a difficult time writing this argument paper because, in the first part, he had to think of an audience extremely unlike himself and write to them from their point of view. Stating this opposing position was a frustrating experience for him because he felt he was giving up a lot of the power of his own argument. Notice, however, how he eventually introduces his own views and works to make them acceptable to his audience. Even though this student felt he was giving in, he finally wrote an argument that his audience might accept. He and the rest of the class, at least, believed it would be more successful than an argument that only attempted to prove that the audience was wrong.

The second model, "Special Education's Best Intentions," was written by a student who had returned to school after several years and whose handicapped child required special education. The issue of how handicapped children are educated in the public schools was, understandably, a particularly compelling issue for her. She had often been frustrated by school officials who seemed more interested in procedures than in her child. Even though she felt hostility for some of these individuals, she still managed to state their point of view in a way that should be acceptable to them before she introduced her own. When she finished writing this paper, she commented that she usually feels powerless when talking with school officials. The approach taken here, she thought, would probably achieve better results than a confrontational argument that accused her audience of wrongdoing and neglect.

CAPITALISM TODAY: UNDERSTANDING OUR WORLD

Joshua Kretchmar

Capitalism, specifically late capitalism, is the driving force behind our modern world. Destroying the capitalist system is tantamount to destroying the world. That is, our technology, sciences, art, even our basic liberties are a direct result of the systems and concepts behind the word "capitalism" as many understand it. Even, indeed especially, our material standard of living is a product of this system. If there is any doubt about it in anyone's mind, simply point to any government system which stifles capitalism. The worse the impediments to capitalism, the worse the material qualities of life (and in most cases the worse the social and political liberties). Take the most obvious example, the late Soviet Union: We have all seen the pictures of Soviet citizens queuing up in incomprehensibly long lines for such basic necessities as bread and toilet paper. And we know that speaking out against the injustices of such deprivations was not tolerated. This last scenario and its consequences are not part of conceivable reality for people raised under the capitalist system, people like you and me.

Late capitalism produces major improvements in society through subtle methods we may not even be aware of. Women, to the extent that they have been liberated, have been liberated because capitalism opened up the job market to them. New technologies, the shift to service-oriented enterprise, and the continued rise of big business have created uncounted opportunities for women and minorities. Such positions would be closed to people in societies driven by other political systems. In these systems people who are part of unfavored political parties, troublesome minorities, or unpopular religions do not get jobs. Examples of such places include Iran, China, and the former Soviet Union, Cuba, etc. In contrast, the only prerequisite to participate in our system is the willingness to participate.

Having said all of this, I believe we must recognize that capitalism, like everything else, has its limits. This is not to deprecate its achievements. On the contrary, perhaps by recognizing its current limits, we can expand those limits. In other words, perhaps we can make our great system even greater by recognizing its flaws and eliminating them or at least improving on them.

So what are capitalism's limits? One limit is that capitalism and capitalists see everything in terms of *commodities*. Please understand, I am not putting a value judgment on this way of seeing. I am not saying: "This is bad" or, "This is good." I am saying only that this is the "delineating" characteristic of late capitalism. When we look at an object through our capitalist glasses we do not ask what its aesthetic or poetic qualities are. We do not ask about how we are liberating people and why we are liberating them. Instead, we consider objects in terms of production and consumption, in terms of desire for those objects. And that desire itself is produced or at least influenced by capitalism and its system of values.

Just as some of the greatest benefits of capitalism are not apparent or obvious, neither are its limits. Ironically, the limits and the benefits are often two sides of the same coin. Consider the example of women's liberation cited earlier. From a strictly legal standpoint women and men are equal before the law, and women should have equal opportunities. However, in a system which ultimately measures value in terms of production and consumption, we have now produced women who are expected to be producers at home and producers in the workplace. Statistics show clearly that women are still the primary home managers in our society. They are still responsible for most of our cooking, cleaning, and child care. When they leave the home, again generally speaking, it is not to replace one type of production with another; it is to double their production by doing a second job on top of their role as home managers.

Late capitalism never replaces one type of production for another. We always seek to produce more. This has several implications: It means that people who fill a niche in the market are not released from that role even when we want them to occupy other roles, and so these people end up exploited. Because we seek to always produce more and better things and systems, we encourage consumption with equal vigor. We consume material goods in inordinate quantities and seek to consume even more. The resultant effects on the environment have been made plain to us all.

There are other problems with consumption. As we switch from production of material goods to production of services and information technologies, these are what we then also consume. The results of service and information technology consumption are showing up in our children most visibly. As they passively consume more and more manufactured information, they lose track of their own cognitive abilities. In more succinct terms, they cannot think.

My objective here is not to solve any of these particular problems or the countless other problems produced as part of late capitalism. I simply want to examine a system which is unquestionably the best there is. I want to start a process of inquiry. I want to acknowledge that the system has problems inherent in its structure. If we can acknowledge both the merits of our system and its faults, we can work on both merits and faults alike. We need to do this before the problems overwhelm the system, before we become like our children and lose our ability to think, and before we thereby also lose our ability to cure.[38]

SPECIAL EDUCATION'S BEST INTENTIONS
Lois Agnew

The American public's growing recognition of the educational rights of handicapped children culminated in the 1975 enactment of the Education for All Handicapped Children Act, Public Law 94-142. Once the need to provide quality education for all students was clearly established as a matter of public record, it also became a need that would demand immediate action on the part of parents and educators; the issue at hand shifted from a question of whether it should be done to how it could be done.

It is natural in the midst of such change to turn to experts for guidance about how to face the challenges that lie ahead. In the years following the passage of PL 94-142, educators attempted to develop methods for identifying the needs of handicapped students in a way which would allow for the development of educational programs designed to serve their individual needs. As time went on, the methods for addressing students' goals became more carefully prescribed and were im-

---

[38]Used with permission.

plemented primarily through the agency of designated professionals who were specially trained for dealing with such matters.

Of course developing a system for helping students whose needs are out of the ordinary has been a necessary step in assimilating those students into the world of public education. Hurling handicapped students into a regular education classroom without careful assessment of their needs would unquestionably lead to frustration on all sides. The need to determine the level of each student's skills clearly indicates the need for some type of testing program, and demands the presence of individuals trained to administer and interpret those tests. The entire process is obviously a crucial element in meeting the educational needs of handicapped students.

However, the challenge of efficiently offering help to massive numbers of students inevitably has resulted in the evolution of a bureaucratic network with all of the disadvantages inherent in such a system. State education agencies and local school districts alike have carefully allocated tremendous resources to carrying out the letter of PL 94-142; the assurance they have provided anxious parents lies in their promise to find appropriate educational placement in the least restrictive environment possible for each child. The means for attempting such a mammoth task involves the use of a standard process of evaluation and diagnosis that will enable the experts assigned to the task to assess not only each child's present levels of performance educationally, but ultimately to make judgments about the child's potential for classroom performance in the future.

It is in this respect that the bureaucratic nature of the special education program falters in meeting the needs of the individual child. As necessary as such a system may be to guarantee the efficient handling of large volumes of work, it becomes difficult in practice to maintain a focus on evaluation as the necessary means to the worthwhile end of providing children with new educational opportunities; too often it becomes and end in itself, a source of a convenient label which in turn is used to predict where a child's limits will lie. It is a tragedy of our educational system that, in spite of the good intentions that have led us to emphasize test results and diagnosis for children with special needs, the machinelike efficiency of our program has achieved most of its goals without acknowledging that which is most important, addressing the needs of students as individuals. The idea of trained diagnosticians administering objective tests to students to determine their educational placement must be appealing to a society that values scientific method to the degree ours does; however, few real live children fall neatly into the categories that represent the conclusion of the process. Once their futures have been charted by the system, it becomes increasingly difficult for them to prove that they have potential beyond that which has been predicted by the experts.

I am the parent of such a child, and have on many occasions experienced the frustration of watching well-meaning educators become so absorbed with finding an appropriate label for my son that they have apparently lost sight of the final goal of educating him. Although I share the interest they have in finding an appropriate educational placement for him, I have in the meantime grown weary of the process. I have seen my child through the ordeal of psychological, neurological, language, and educational evaluations, all conducted by authorities in their fields with an impressive assortment of credentials, and can state with certainty that the ability to help him is unrelated to the specialized training the system values most. Those who have made a significant difference in my son's life have been those rare people who have encountered him as an individual and have devoted their energies to bringing out his potential without reservation, and have been willing in the process to stop worrying about how he should be labeled. My contact with other parents of children with special needs tells me that my reaction to the process is quite common.

There is no question about the fact that the special education bureaucracy serves a useful purpose in helping students find the classrooms and programs most suited to their needs. At the same time, it often appears to be a tendency for any bureaucratic system to become so absorbed with its own structure, so convinced of the infallibility of the experts it employs, that it fails to devote adequate attention to

each person it attempts to serve. Because special education involves so
many thousands of unique students, it seems almost impossible to find a
balance between the efficiency that benefits everyone and the personal
attention that is a crucial part of the process. Yet with children's
lives at stake, it is critical that we never give up the effort to do
so.[39]

6. **INDIVIDUAL ONGOING PROJECT: ROGERIAN ARGUMENT**
   Write a Rogerian argument, as described in exercise 5, on your issue. Imagine
   the position that is most unlike or most opposed to your own, and write in response to it.

7. **GROUPS OR INDIVIDUALS**
   Summarize the major ideas in the chapter by completing the following sentences
   briefly and in your own words:

   a. This chapter is called "Joining the Conversation" because its focus is . . .
   b. Individual styles of argument may be influenced by . . .
   c. In argument, women, in general, seem to favor . . . . Men seem to favor . . .
   d. Racial and cultural groups may show tendencies to argue in characteristic
      ways. Some examples are . . .
   e. It is important to be aware of different styles in international or cross-cultural
      argument because . . .
   f. Rogerian argument helps reduce conflict and build common ground by . . .
   g. Some values of understanding different styles of argument are . . .

---

[39]Used with permission.

CHAPTER 3

A Process for Reading Argument

This chapter will focus on how to identify an argumentative purpose in a text and also on how to employ active reading strategies to help you read argument. The next chapter will help you employ active writing strategies to help you write argument. You will need a variety of strategies to help you do this reading and writing, and they will be most useful to you if they are perceived as processes.

You will usually adapt your reading process to the relative level of difficulty and to your purpose for reading specific materials. At times, when the reading material is easy or you only want to get the gist, you will "just read," without employing conscious strategies. Other times, when the material is complex and unfamiliar and your purpose is to understand, analyze, evaluate, and perhaps even write about it, you will need a strategic reading process to help you meet the requirements of this more demanding task. Actively employing a process for reading will help you connect with the text, draw on what you know to understand it, and use it to generate ideas of your own.

Before we look at process, however, let us first consider how you can recognize an argumentative purpose in the material you read.

RECOGNIZING WRITTEN ARGUMENT

Some texts are obviously intended as argument, and others conceal their argumentative purpose and make it more difficult to recognize. You will recognize an argumentative purpose more easily if you think of a continuum of six types of writing that ranges from obvious argument on one end through objective writing on the other. Each of the six types exhibits not only a different authorial intention but also a different relationship between the author and the audience.

1. **Exploratory Argument.** The author's purpose in exploratory articles, which are commonly found in newspapers and magazines, is to lay out and explain all of the major positions on a controversial issue but not to favor one par-

ticular position. The audience thus is invited to view an issue from several perspectives and to understand all of them better.

2. **Single Perspective Argument.** The author's purpose is clearly and obviously to change minds or to convince others. The author's point of view and purpose are clearly expressed along with reasons and supporting details that appeal to a wide audience. This is a pure form of argumentative writing.

3. **Extremist Argument.** Authors who are "true believers" and who write about causes or special projects sometimes use strong values and emotional language to appeal to narrow audiences who already share their views. Imagine a labor union leader, for example, who is writing to workers to convince them to go on strike.

4. **Hidden Argument.** Some ostensibly objective texts, on close examination, actually favor one position over another, but not in an obvious, overt manner. One sign that the text is not totally objective is selected and stacked supporting material that favors a particular point of view. Also, the presence of emotional language, vivid description, or emotional examples can be another sign that an author has strong opinions and intends not only to inform but also to convince the audience. For example, an author who actually favors reducing student financial aid writes an "objective" report about students who have received aid. However, all the students described in the article either left college early or defaulted on their loans, and they are described as dropouts and parasites on society. No examples of successful students are reported. Even though the author does not state a position or write this article as an obvious argument, it is still clear that the author has a position and that it manifests itself in biased reporting. The intention, even though concealed, is to convince.

5. **Unconscious Argument.** Sometimes an author who is trying to write an objective report is influenced unconsciously by strong personal opinions about the subject, and the result is an unconscious intent to change people's minds. Imagine, for example, a strong prolife newspaper reporter who is sent to write an objective expository article about an abortion clinic. It would be difficult for this individual to describe and explain the clinic without allowing negative perceptions to influence the way the facts are presented. Again, stacked or selected evidence, emotional language, quotes from authorities with well-known positions, or even pictures that establish a point of view may attest to an argumentative purpose while the author is unaware of it.

6. **Objective Reporting.** Sometimes authors simply describe, explain, or report facts and ideas that everyone would accept without controversy. The author's own point of view, opinions, or interpretations are deliberately omitted. This type is a pure form of expository writing. Examples include almanacs, data lists, weather reports, some news stories, and government, business, science, and technical reports. The audience reads such material to get information.

When you read and analyze argument, you will be studying and interpreting all these types of material with the exception of the last, objective reporting, and sometimes even there opinion creeps in. Now let's examine what you do at present when you read argument.

HOW DO YOU READ NOW?

You already have a reading process, but you may not have consciously adapted it to reading argument. You can improve your present reading process by analyzing what you do now and then acknowledging present habits that you will not want to give up. To that base you can add additional information and strategies to build further reader expertise. Analyze your present reading process by answering the following questions. At this point, think about reading in general rather than about reading argument.

What do you do . . .

- before you read?
- while you read?
- when the material is hard?
- when you finish reading?

Now change the focus to reading argument.

What do you do . . .

- before you read argument?
- while you read argument?
- when the argumentative material is hard?
- when you finish reading argument?

Many students answer that they do nothing before they read, that they then just read, that they reread when the material is hard, and that they do nothing when they finish reading. That is a typical profile for students beginning an argument course. In answering the second question, "What do you do while you read argument," students new to argument class typically add one or more additional strategies to their usual reading process: They try to identify both sides of the issue, they try to keep an open mind, they decide whether to agree or disagree with the author, and they decide what stand to take.

What can you add to your present process to improve your reading of argument? Your goal is to become an active reader who concentrates and uses existing knowledge to construct new knowledge. Critical reading and thinking strategies will help you accomplish that. But first, consider a simple idea that can have a huge impact on your reading.

WRITE WHILE YOU READ

You will probably be willing to admit, along with most students, that you sometimes read without thinking. You perhaps count the pages of your assignment and then go back and stare at the words until you reach the end, or you may stare at the computer screen, and even change screens, but your mind is blank or focused elsewhere. The best and quickest way to change this blank reading pattern is to *write while you read.* As soon as you begin to read with a pencil or pen in hand—underlining, annotating (see the example on pages 92–93), summarizing, writing out ideas and responses—everything changes. You *have* to think to write. Furthermore, writing while you read helps you with two types of thinking.

First, you will *think about* the material you read and perhaps even rephrase it so that it makes better sense to you. Second, you will *think beyond* the material you read and use it to help you generate ideas for your own writing. Your reading, in other words, will become a springboard for your original thoughts and ideas. So, pick up a pencil now and begin to write as you read. This process may take a little more time, but you will end up knowing far more than you would otherwise, and your book with your own annotations and ideas in it will be a valuable addition to your personal library.

HOW CAN YOU ORGANIZE A PROCESS FOR READING ARGUMENT?

The following version of the reading process for argument integrates prereading, reading, and postreading strategies and incorporates writing at every stage. Before you examine this process, however, here are three cautionary notes:

1. Use your own reading process for most reading and add strategies either when you are not getting enough meaning or when your comprehension is breaking down altogether.
2. Be advised that no one uses all of the reading strategies described here all of the time. Instead, you should select those that are appropriate to the task, that is, appropriate for a particular type of material and for your reading purpose. You will need to practice all of the strategies so that you will be familiar with them, and you will be given an opportunity to do so in the exercises and activities. This is an artificial situation, however. Later, in real-life reading, you will be selective and use only those that apply to a particular situation.
3. There is no set order for employing active reading strategies even though the strategies will be laid out in an apparent order under the headings of prereading, reading, and postreading. In actuality, you may find yourself stopping to do some prereading in the middle of a difficult text, or you may stop to summarize a section of material, a postreading strategy, before you continue reading. The order here is simply to make these strategies easier to explain and use.

Special Note: Many of the strategies are explained in more detail later in the chapter.

PREREADING STRATEGIES

You will use what you already know to learn new material. It is all you have. To read better, learn to access what you know about a subject to help you interpret new, incoming material. If you know nothing about a subject, you will need to take

A Reading Process for Argument

PREREADING STRATEGIES

Read the title and first paragraph. Ask "What is at issue?"

Background the issue. Free-associate and write words and phrases that the issue brings to mind.

Evaluate your background. Do you know enough? If not, read or discuss to get background. Look up a key word or two.

Jot down your present position.

Survey the material. Locate the claim (the main assertion) and some of the subclaims (the ideas that support it); notice how they are organized. Do not slow down and read.

Analyze and make some guesses about the **rhetorical situation:** text, reader, author, constraints, exigence.

Assess the common ground between you and the author.

Predict and jot down two or three ideas that you think the author may discuss.

Write one big question that you would like answered.

READING STRATEGIES

Anticipate and **read** the information in the **introduction, body**, and **conclusion**.

Identify **claim, subclaims**, and **support**. Box the **transitions** to highlight relationships between ideas and changes of subject.

Discover the organization and **jot down a simplified outline**.

Continue to analyze the **rhetorical situation**.

Underline and annotate the ideas that seem important.

Circle key words that represent major concepts and jot down meanings if necessary.

Monitor your comprehension with brief summaries and notes.

Check the accuracy of your predictions and change any that are wrong.

POSTREADING STRATEGIES

Write a **summary** or **make a map** of the ideas.

Reflect and write an answer to your big question.

Write out all **original ideas** inspired by your reading.

Write a comparison of the **author's position** with your **own**.

Compare your present position with your original position.

Evaluate the argument and decide whether it is convincing or not.

Decide what value this material has for you and **how you will use it**.

special steps to learn more. Otherwise the new material will seem too difficult to read. The following sections present seven prereading strategies to help you organize your prior knowledge about a subject, build background when you need it, and begin to analyze the material and make some predictions.

Background the Issue.   Read the title and the first paragraph quickly to find out what is at issue. If you do not discover the issue there, read the last paragraph, where it is often stated, or read rapidly through the essay until you discover it. Then, access your background on the issue by writing, in phrases only, everything that comes to mind when you think of that issue. This process is called *backgrounding*. Here is an example: Suppose you read "Some College Costs Should Be Tax Deductible," the argument on page 21 in Chapter 1, and you have a negative initial reaction. You learn from the first paragraph that the issue is *tuition and tax deductions*. Your backgrounding might include

charity deductible
religious income deductible
tuition—not deductible
no college costs are deductible
students even pay taxes on scholarships
IRS reaction?

Here is a second example that refers back to the short argument entitled "We're Good Republicans—and Pro-Choice" that appears on page 22 in Chapter 1. The issue is *abortion*. Here is backgrounding by two different students who have different backgrounds and views:

Republicans	prochoice
against abortion	permit abortion
prolife	individual
abortion wrong	not political
conflict	Democrats

Evaluate Your Background Information.   When attempts to background an issue are unsuccessful and it is clear that you lack information, use some special strategies to help you build background. Read a text that is difficult for you once, to the end, without stopping. You will understand some of it, but not all. Then, write brief summary notes on what you do understand. Also, list a few words and topics to indicate what you do not understand. Now, locate and read other material on the subject that you can understand easily. An encyclopedia or an easier book may be good sources of such information. Or you can talk with someone who understands the material, like a professor or fellow student. Also, identify the key words that you do not know that are used repeatedly to represent major concepts. Look up their meanings in the glossary or dictionary and analyze how they are used in context. Finally, reread the material, using active reading strategies to help you get meaning. Your comprehension will still be imperfect, but it will improve as you build background and learn the vocabulary.

Write Out Your Current Position on the Issue. When you have finished backgrounding, jot down your own current ideas and position on the issue. This strategy will help guarantee your active interest as you read and will also promote an interaction between your ideas and the author's. Here are examples of such initial position statements; the first, on college costs, continues the initial negative reaction:

> There are too many tax breaks as it is—especially for the rich. Tuition does not fall into a tax-exempt category. The IRS would never allow this.

On the prochoice issue the two students might write:

> I'm prolife. Abortions are wrong. There should be some limits, laws, punishments against abortion. I'm not sure what or how to mandate them.

> I'm prochoice. Abortions are an individual not a political issue, and they should be readily available.

Suppose you now begin to read the article on abortion that argues in favor of abortions in certain circumstances. Consider some unfortunately typical responses that readers of argument sometimes make at this point. Suppose you disagree strongly with the article, because you believe abortion is always wrong. You may be tempted not to read at all or to read hastily and carelessly, dismissing the author as a crackpot. Or, if your initial reaction has been different and you happen to agree with these authors' ideas, you might read carefully, marking the best passages and insisting on reading them aloud to someone else. If you are neutral on this issue, without opinions on either side, you might read with less interest and even permit your mind to wander. Your reading of the article about financial aid could be influenced in similar ways, depending on your perspective on that issue. These responses, as you can see, will distract you and interfere in very negative ways with your understanding of the article. Once you become aware of such unproductive responses, however, you can compensate for them by analyzing the common ground between you and the author and using this information to help you read more receptively.

Survey the Material. You can survey a book or an article before you read for an introduction to the major ideas and a few of the supporting details. Surveying also provides you with a context for reading later.

Books. To survey a book (not a novel), follow these six steps in this order:

1. Read the *title* and focus on what it tells you about the contents of the book.
2. Read the *table of contents*. Notice how the content has been divided into chapters and organized.
3. Read the *introduction*. Look for background information about the subject and author and also for information to help you read the book.
4. Examine the special *features* of the book. Are there headings and subheadings in boldface type to highlight major ideas? Is there a glossary? An index? Charts? Other visuals? A bibliography?

5. Read the title and first paragraph of the *first* and *last chapters* to see how the book begins and ends.
6. Read the title and first paragraph of the *other chapters* to get a sense of the flow of ideas.

This procedure should take about half an hour. It will introduce you to the main issue and approaches in a book, and reading now will be much easier.

Articles and Chapters.   To survey an article or chapter in a book, follow these six steps in this order:

1. Read the *title* and focus on the information in it.
2. Read the *introduction*, which is usually the first paragraph but can be several paragraphs long. Look for a claim and any forecasts of what is to come.
3. Read the *last paragraph* and look for the claim.
4. Read the *headings and subheadings*, if there are any, to get a sense of the ideas and their sequence. Read the first sentence of each paragraph, if there are no headings, to accomplish the same goal.
5. Study the *visuals:* pictures, charts, graphs. Read their captions. They often illustrate major ideas.
6. Identify the *key words* that represent the main concepts.

Surveying an article or chapter takes 10–15 minutes. It introduces you to the issue, the claim, and some of the subclaims and support. Survey before you read to make reading easier; survey when you do research to get a context for the material you quote; and survey when you review to help you refocus on the important ideas.

Analyze the Rhetorical Situation.   "Rhetorical situation" is a term coined by Professor Lloyd Bitzer to describe the elements that combine to constitute a communication situation.[1] To understand these elements as they apply to argument helps us understand what motivates or causes the argument in the first place, who the author is, who the audience is, how they might react to it, and how we as readers might also respond. By analyzing and understanding the rhetorical situation, we gain critical insight into the entire context as well as the parts of an argument, and this insight ultimately helps us evaluate its final success or failure. Analyzing the rhetorical situation is an important critical reading strategy that can be initiated during the prereading stages but that should continue to be used as a tool for analysis throughout the reading process.

According to Bitzer, a rhetorical situation has five elements: the *exigence*, the *audience*, the *constraints*, the *author*, and the *text*. Let's look at these elements to see how they can help us understand and evaluate argumentative writing.

Exigence is the real-life, dramatic situation that signals individuals that something controversial has occurred and that they should try to make some sense of it.

---

[1] Lloyd Bitzer, "The Rhetorical Situation," *Philosophy and Rhetoric*, 1 (January 1968): 1–14.

Exigence is a problem to be solved, a situation that requires some modifying response from an audience. Here are some examples of exigence for argument: Some scientists think they have discovered a new source of cheap energy but others cannot replicate it; a president is shot; the new medicine for AIDS doesn't seem to be working; too many homeless people are living in the streets and subways; several women's breast implants either collapse or make them ill; a presidential candidate, it is revealed, tried long ago to avoid the draft; a well-known athlete commits rape; the ozone layer is disappearing. To bring the idea of exigence closer, here are some examples that might provide you with the exigence to engage in argument: You get a parking ticket, your registration is canceled for lack of payment but you know you paid, or you and the person you live with are having trouble deciding who should do the household chores. In all cases, something is wrong, imperfect, defective, or in conflict. Exigence invites analysis and discussion, and sometimes also a written response to encourage both individual public awareness and discourse about problematic situations.

The *audience* or *reader* is the second element in the rhetorical situation. For argument to work, a potential audience must care enough to listen, read, and pay attention, to change its perceptions as a result of the argument, and, hopefully, even have the ability to mediate change or act in a new way. A rhetorical situation invites these special types of audience responses and outcomes. Most authors have a targeted or intended audience in mind, and, as you read a text, you may discover that your analysis and response vary considerably from the targeted audience's probable response, particularly if different cultures or periods of time are involved. When you read, compare your perceptions of the argument with the perceptions you imagine the targeted or intended reading audience might have had. More information about audience is provided in Chapter 8.

Constraints make up the third element of the rhetorical situation. They include the existing people, events, values, beliefs, and traditions that constrain or limit the targeted audience and cause it to analyze the situation and react to it in a particular way. They also include the character, background, and style of the author that limit or influence him or her to write in a certain way. Constraints may bring people together or they may drive them apart. They certainly influence the amount of common ground that will be established between an author and an audience. Here are some examples of constraints: An audience feels constrained to mistrust the media because it thinks reporters exaggerate or lie; reporters believe it is their responsibility to expose character flaws in candidates running for office, so they feel constrained to do so at every opportunity; candidates think voters want to hear rousing platitudes, so they deliver rousing platitudes; voters have lost their faith in public leaders, so they do not want to vote; an audience is too disturbed by the severity of the environmental crisis to want to listen to information about it, so it shuts it out. Or, to continue with the closer examples, you parked your car in a no-parking zone because you were late to class, but the police feel constrained by law to give you a ticket; you are angry because your college has made errors with your tuition payments before; and you believe both men and women should share the household chores but your partner disagrees. These constraining circumstances will influence the way you react to the issues and address the targeted audiences.

The exigence, audience, and constraints are in place before the author becomes a part of the rhetorical situation.

The *author* writes an argument in response to the exigence of the situation and usually with a particular audience in mind. The author ideally should consider any constraining circumstances or values as well.

The *text* is the written argument that has unique characteristics of its own that can be analyzed, such as the format, organization, argumentative strategies, language, style, and so on.

The following set of questions will help you analyze the rhetorical situation and get insight into its component parts. Note that *you as the reader* have been differentiated from the *original reader* to help with analysis.

1. **Exigence.** What happened to cause this argument? Why is it perceived as a defect or problem? Is it new or recurring?

2. **Targeted Reader/Audience.** Who thinks this is a problem? What is the nature of this group? Can they be convinced? What are the anticipated outcomes?

3. **Constraints.** What special constraining circumstances will influence the audience's and author's responses to the subject? What beliefs, attitudes, people, habits, events, or traditions are already in place that will limit or constrain their perceptions?

4. **Author.** Who is the author? Consider background, experience, education, affiliations, and values. What is motivating the author to write?

5. **The Text.** What kind of a text is it? What are its special qualities and features?

6. **You as Reader.** How do you, as a potential audience member, compare with the targeted audience? What are your constraints? How much common ground do you share with the author? What is your initial position? Are you motivated to change your mind or modify the situation?

Here is a mnemonic to help you remember the five elements in the rhetorical situation. They have been arranged in a different order so that their first letters form a word: text; reader; author; constraints; exigence. Remember that there is a TRACE of the rhetorical situation in every argument that you read. Now, let's analyze the rhetorical situations of the two essays we have been using as examples in this chapter.

EXAMPLES OF ANALYSIS

Example 1: "Some College Costs Should Be Tax Deductible"

Exigence. The described situation is occurring in many colleges. Less government money is available for scholarships, so tuition money is being diverted to scholarships by the colleges. People who pay full tuition are helping to fund scholarship students but without the tax break they would get if they donated money directly to scholarship funds.

Reader/Audience. Taxpayers and tuition payers who also can understand tax-deductible charitable contributions are potential audience members.

Constraints.   Some readers might feel constrained by tradition. Tax breaks for tuition are not usually given, and the IRS might balk. Also, changes in the tax structure would be required, and making such changes might be a lot of trouble. Readers might be constrained by the knowledge that tuition payments are required and charitable contributions are voluntary.

Author.   He advocates this change as a benefit to both scholarship and nonscholarship families. It is not clear which type of family he represents or what his personal stake is.

Type of Text.   This is a short newspaper opinion piece.

You as Reader.   What is your reaction? Where did you stand on this issue before you read? Where do you stand now? Why?

Example 2: "We're Good Republicans—and Pro-Choice"

Exigence.   Many Republicans across the country are by tradition prolife, and they support reversal of the *Roe* v. *Wade* Supreme Court ruling that protects abortion. The authors had an abortion and are in conflict because they are also Republicans.

Reader/Audience.   Both Republicans and Democrats with many different views on abortion are the potential audience. The authors want to modify the audience's perceptions of the issue.

Constraints.   The issue is perceived as black or white, with two sides only, by many people. The Republican party is prolife, and many of its members feel constrained to take a prolife position. The *Roe* v. *Wade* decision is in jeopardy. The authors hold a respected position in their community that influences the way they write. Some audience members may be "true believers" and hold extreme views on this issue.

Authors.   These are high-profile people who announced their abortion in the newspaper. They seem to want to be role models for others. They need to reconcile their decision and values with their party loyalty. They hope to convince others that there are more than two potential positions on the abortion issue.

Type of Text.   This is a short opinion piece in the newspaper.

You as Reader.   Where did you stand before? Where do you stand now? Why?

Assess the Common Ground between You and the Author

As you begin to analyze the rhetorical situation, you can also make an initial assessment of the common ground you think you will share with the author and use written symbols to indicate how much or how little of it may exist: ◯ can mean you and the author are basically alike in your views and share common ground; ◯◯ can mean you are alike on some ideas but not on others and share some common ground; ◯◯ can mean your ideas are so different from the author's that there is no common ground; and ✕ can mean that you are neutral in regard to the subject, that you consequently have little or no interest in it, and that you are not likely to agree, disagree, or establish common ground with the author. To avoid reading problems, you will now need to compensate for common-ground differences that might interfere with comprehension. The symbols ○○, for disagreement and no common ground, and ✕, for neutral and no common ground should signal that you will have to use all of the active strategies for reading that you can muster to give these authors a fair hearing. Try to generate interest or suspend major critical judgment until you have finished reading. Then, reassess your original position to determine whether you now have reason to modify or change your perspective on the issue.

Make Some Predictions, and Write One Big Question

Reading is a constant process of looking back at what you know and looking ahead to predict what you think may come next. Facilitate this natural process by linking what you know with what you predict will be in the text. Write your predictions and one big question to help focus your attention. Change your predictions as you read if they are off target and also stay open to the new ideas you did not predict. Finally, try to answer your big question when you finish reading.

> Here are examples of predictions you might write about the tuition article:
> Will say that tuition is an unusual expense
> Will say that tuition is a sacrifice
> Will say tuition benefits society by educating people
> Will say tuition should be tax deductible

> Here is an example of a big question you might ask before you read: How will the author justify a tax deduction for tuition?

> Here are some predictions you might make about the abortion article:
> Will say own experience causes them to be prochoice
> Will need to reconcile that position with being Republicans

> Here is a big question you might ask: How will these authors reconcile their politics with their experience?

READING AND POSTREADING STRATEGIES

> ***Anticipate and Read the Information in the Introduction, Body, and Conclusion.*** The organization of ideas in argumentative texts is not very different from other texts. Much of what you read, for example, follows the easily recognizable introduction, main body, and conclusion format. The introduction may provide background information about the issue and the author, get attention, state the main point, or forecast some of the ideas to be developed in the main body. The main body will explain and develop the author's main point by giving reasons and

support to prove it. The end or conclusion either summarizes by restating important points or concludes by stating the most important point, that is, what the author wants you to believe. Not all texts follow this pattern exactly, but enough of them do to justify your checking what you read against it.

Identify Claims, Subclaims, Support, and Transitions.   All arguments have the structural components you are familiar with from other kinds of discourse. The main difference is their names. The special characteristics of the components will be described when the Toulmin model is discussed in Chapter 5. We start using Toulmin's terms here, however, to help you get used to them. The thesis of an argument, which shapes the thinking of the entire text and states what the author finally expects you to accept or believe, is called the *claim. Subclaims* are assertions or reasons that develop the claim. They are, however, almost meaningless without further explanation. *Support* in the form of facts, opinions, evidence, and examples is the most specific material that provides additional information and further explanation. Support makes the claim and subclaims clear, vivid, memorable, and, above all else, believable. *Transitions* lead the reader from one idea to another and also sometimes state the relationships among ideas. Furthermore, there is a constant movement between general and specific material in all texts, including argumentative texts, and this movement becomes apparent when the ideas are presented in various types of outline form.

Discover the Organization, and Write Simplified Outlines and Summaries. We will now present simplified outlines and summaries of the two essays we are using as examples. The outlines lay out the ideas in these essays according to their levels of generality and specificity. Study these outlines to help you develop the ability to locate the most important ideas and understand their relationship to each other in any written text. Notice that the material is restated and condensed to a briefer form. The claim, the most general idea, is written at the left-hand margin, the subclaims are indented from the claim, and the support—the specific facts, opinions, examples, illustrations, and other data and statistics that ground the claim and subclaims in reality, the most specific material—is indented even further. Internalize the idea of a simplified outline and use it to help you find the claim and understand the ideas that support and develop it in the arguments you read.

Two types of summaries are illustrated: one written in paragraph form with complete sentences and the other written in phrases only. Use whichever form works best for you.

A Summary Written in Paragraph Form

The portion of tuition costs diverted to pay for scholarships for needy students should be tax deductible, like charitable contributions. Government funding for scholarships has diminished. Colleges are forced to use part of the tuition money for scholarships. Families who pay tuition sacrifice to do so. This plan would give them a break, and it would keep needy students in college.

A Summary Written in Phrases

Government funding for scholarships down—colleges using tuition money for scholarships—make part of tuition bill diverted to scholarships tax deductible—like charitable contributions—help those who pay full tuition—help those who need aid.

EXAMPLES OF ANALYSIS

Example 1: A Simplified Outline and Summaries for "Some College Costs Should Be Tax Deductible"

Claim	Tuition should be tax deductible like contributions to charities.
Support: statistics data, facts	32 colleges use tuition for scholarships. Increase from 9.8% in 1980 to 15.9% in 1990. Median: $2,400 of $15,000 average tuition costs used for scholarships. Chicago most (30.7%); Princeton least (1.4%). Some families contribute $10,000 in 4 years and no tax relief.
Subclaims	Scholarships good: create diversity. Tax-deductible contributions voluntary and good: improve quality of life. Tuition obligatory but improves life and is a charitable contribution when used for scholarships. Should have same tax treatment. Benefits people who pay full tuition and students on scholarship.

A Summary Written in Paragraph Form

Authors are Republicans and prochoice. They had an abortion because the baby was deformed. Now the Republican party is favoring prolife, no abortions. It is trying to reverse the ruling that protects abortions, *Roe* v. *Wade*. Prochoice Republicans have to speak out. There are more than two positions on this. Two extreme positions cannot develop common ground. There is a need to embrace "uncommon ground" on this one and tolerate many views even when we do not agree.

A Summary Written in Phrases

Prochoice Republicans—need to speak out—party supporting prolife—trying to change legislation—party should not be pro or con but adopt third position—"uncommon ground"—tolerate many views because no simple solution.

Example 2: A Simplified Outline and Summaries for "We're Good Republicans—and Pro-Choice"

Support: personal example | Bad pregnancy problems with baby.
Decided on abortion.
Public decision—news release.
People symphathetic, understanding.

Subclaim | Individual decision—no business of government or Republican party.

Support: example of law | *Roe* v. *Wade* protects this right.

Subclaims | Prochoice Republicans need to speak out. Not just two sides.

Claim | Look at from third side: uncommon ground that permits different perspectives.

Look back at the shape of the two simplified outlines. In the first, the claim is at the beginning, and in the second it is at the end. Now notice the types of support used by the authors. The first author relies on statistics and data, and the second on a personal example. The rhetorical situations for these essays are very different. The first deals with a relatively neutral issue, tuition and taxes, and most people will probably favor the claim, so it is placed first and supported with facts and data. The second deals with the difficult issue of abortion, so a story is told to create common ground, and the claim is deferred to the end, where more people will be likely to accept it. The positioning of the main points and the decision to use certain types of support are argumentative strategies. The authors have good reasons for using these strategies as they have. Chapters 5–7 will go into more detail about the special strategies of argument.

Underline and Annotate Important Ideas. Underlining or highlighting helps keep your mind on the material as you read, and it also reduces the material so that you can review and find information more easily later. The key to successful marking is to do it very selectively. Do not color an entire paragraph with a yellow highlighter. Instead, highlight or underline only the words and phrases that help you reduce the content so that you can later reread only those parts to help you get a sense of the whole. To further reduce the text and make it even more useful, jot the major ideas in the margins, or summarize them at the end of sections. Write the big ideas along with your personal reactions on the flyleaves of a book or at the ends of chapters or articles. If you do not own the book, write on separate sheets of paper and keep them organized in a folder or in a section of your notebook that is set aside for reading notes.

Here is an example of the first two paragraphs of the essay about tuition and scholarships underlined and annotated as recommended. Note that this material is now easier to understand and review:

Tax breaks: tuition for scholarships

As the government spends increasingly less on financial aid, many leading colleges and universities are using a greater percentage of tuition revenues for scholarships. Just as income tax breaks are given for charitable contributions, this portion of tuition should be tax deductible.

Tuition for Scholarships increasing

Statistics compiled by the Consortium on Financing Higher Education, which does research and analysis for 32 member colleges, show the growing importance of tuition for scholarships. In 1980, the consortium schools spent an average of 9.8 percent of tuition revenues on financial aid; last year, that figure rose to 15.9 percent. It will continue to rise as federal and state financing drops further.

Understand the Key Words. Sometimes figuring out the meaning of one word in a difficult passage will suddenly make the whole passage easier to understand. Most of us, unfortunately, do not even see many of the words we do not know unless we make the effort to look for them. Instead, our eyes slide over unfamiliar words because there is nothing in our background to help us make sense of them.

When reading material suddenly seems hard, go back and look for words you do not understand. Try to identify the key words, those that represent major concepts. In this chapter, "backgrounding" and "rhetorical situation" are examples of key words. First, read the context in which you find the word to help you understand it. A word may be defined in a sentence, a paragraph, or even several paragraphs. Major concepts in argument are often defined at length, and understanding their meaning will be essential to an understanding of the entire argument. If the context does not give you enough information, try the glossary, the dictionary, or another book on the subject. Remember that major concepts require longer explanations than a single synonym. Synonyms are useful for other minor words that are less critical to the understanding of the entire passage.

Monitor Your Comprehension.   The results of reading are very much a private product that belongs to you and no one else. Consequently, only you can monitor and check your understanding as you go along. Stop periodically and either recite to yourself or write a few notes about what you have just read. If you cannot, you have not understood well enough. Reread, actively using reading strategies, and try again. Periodic comprehension checks will help you concentrate and understand.

Make a Map.   As an alternative to summaries, make a map of the ideas in a text. For many students, maps are the preferred way to reduce and reorganize the material they read. To make a map, write the most important idea, the claim, in a circle or on a line, and then attach major subclaims and support to it. Make your map in very brief form. Figures 3.1 and 3.2 are possible maps of the two essays we have been using as examples. You can be creative with map formats. Use whatever layout will give you a quick picture of the major ideas.

The reading strategies described in this chapter, such as backgrounding, predicting, asking questions, surveying, analyzing the rhetorical situation, abstracting the organizational scheme, making maps, and summarizing, all work because they help you access what you already know, relate it to new material, see the parts as well as the whole, rephrase the material in your own words, and reduce it to a manageable size. Research studies have demonstrated that these activities help readers understand, analyze, and remember the material they read.

The reading strategies described in this chapter, such as backgrounding, predicting, asking questions, surveying, analyzing the rhetorical situation, abstracting the organizational scheme, making maps, and summarizing, all work because they help you access what you already know, relate it to new material, see the parts

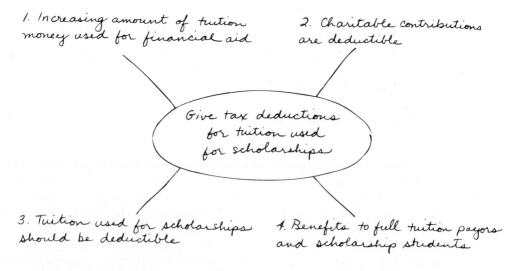

Figure 3.1   Map of Ideas for "Some College Costs Should Be Tax Deductible"

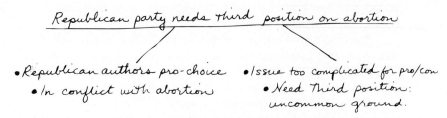

Figure 3.2 Map of Ideas for "We're Good Republicans—and Pro-Choice"

as well as the whole, rephrase the material in your own words, and reduce it to a manageable size. Research studies have demonstrated that these activities help readers understand, analyze, and remember the material they read.

EXERCISES AND ACTIVITIES

1. CLASS DISCUSSION: RECOGNIZING WRITTEN ARGUMENT

The following newspaper article was published on the front page of the *New York Times* as an objective story about some people in Los Angeles after the riots in 1991. First, identify what seems to be at issue in this article. It is not directly stated. Then, read the article carefully to see if you can recognize the author's attitudes, feelings, and opinions toward the subject at issue. What is the author's intention in this article? To explain? To convince? Or both? Justify your answer with specific examples from the article.

JOBS ILLUMINATE WHAT RIOTS HID: YOUNG IDEALS

Sara Rimer

When Disneyland came two weeks ago to the First A.M.E. Church in South-Central Los Angeles to hold interviews for 200 summer jobs, it was a good-will gesture born of the riots.

When more than 600 young men and women, many in coats and ties or dresses showed up, the Disney officials were taken aback.

America has been bombarded with television images of the youth of South-Central Los Angeles: throwing bricks, looting stores, beating up innocent motorists. The Disneyland staff who interviewed the applicants, ages 17 to 22, found a different neighborhood.

"They were wonderful kids, outstanding kids," said Greg Albrecht, a spokesman for Disneyland. "We didn't know they were there." Nor, Mr. Albrecht added, had they known that the young people of South-Central Los Angeles would be so eager to work at Disneyland.

Joe Fox, a spokesman for the First A.M.E. Church, said that had there been time to better publicize the Disneyland jobs, thousands would have applied. "People just want to work, period," he said. With hundreds of small businesses destroyed during the riots, jobs are harder to find than ever.

One of the 600 who wanted to work at Disneyland was Olivia Miles, at 18 the youngest of seven children of a nurse's aide and a disabled roofer. "My friend Lakesha's mother told us Disneyland was hiring," said Miss Miles, who has worked at McDonald's and Popeye's since she was 15. "I said: 'Disneyland! C'mon, let's go!' "

Miss Miles will graduate on June 30 from one of South-Central Los Angeles's public high schools, Washington Preparatory, where she has earned mostly A's and B's and was the co-captain of the drill team. Next fall, she will attend Grambling University in Louisiana.

Washington has 2,600 students; 70 percent are black, 30 percent are Hispanic. The principal, Marguerite LaMotte, says that as impressive as Olivia Miles is, she is not exceptional. "I have a lot of Olivia's," she said. Indeed, 118 seniors plan to attend four-year colleges and 131 will go to two-year colleges.

The world knows about the gang members; estimates put the number at 100,000 across Los Angeles County, and last year there were 771 gang-related homicides. No one has tried to count the young people like Olivia Miles. They are among the invisible people of South-Central Los Angeles.

In some ways, Miss Miles is just another high school senior. One of her favorite shows is "Beverly Hills 90210." She admires Bill Cosby and Oprah Winfrey. She enjoys reading books by Maya Angelou. And shopping. She loves soft-spoken, 17-year-old Damon Sewell, the defensive football captain at nearby Hawthorne High School. He will go on to Grambling with her.

Miss Miles and Mr. Sewell and their friends who live in the neighborhood pay a terrible price because of geography. They have to worry about simply staying alive. They have friends who have been shot and killed. They can't even get dressed in the morning without thinking, red and blue are gang colors; wearing them is dangerous. Then they have to confront the stigma that comes with being young and black and from Los Angeles.

"The neighborhood is famous now," Miss Miles said on Saturday as she and Mr. Sewell gave a tour of the devastation. They were just 15 minutes away from Beverly Hills and Hollywood. Miss Miles's tone was plaintive. "Why did it have to be famous for a riot? Why couldn't it be famous for people getting up in the world, or making money, or being actors?"

Getting ahead, despite enormous obstacles, is the story of the Miles family. Her parents, Aubrey and Willie Mae Miles, grew up in the South and migrated to Los Angeles. They started their lives together in an apartment in Watts and eventually bought a two-bedroom on 65th Street, in the heart of South-Central Los Angeles.

Olivia remembers playing softball on the block with another little girl, LaRonda Jones, who became her best friend and who will attend Santa Monica Community College next year. She also remembers how scared she was at night.

"I would lie in bed and hear the police helicopters overhead," she said.

Her four sisters and two brothers are all high school graduates. Except for 22-year-old Tracy, who is home with a 2-year-old daughter, they are all working. Shirley has a job in a school cafeteria. Cynthia is a mail carrier. Jacqueline is a cashier at Dodger Stadium. William is a custodian at police headquarters. Masad drives a school bus. Olivia visited Disneyland once, when she was 8. Jacqueline took her.

Mrs. Miles said she had never been there. Admission is $28.75 for adults, $23 for children 3 to 11. "Disneyland's a little high for me," she said.

Olivia Miles is tall and slim and walks with her head held high. "My mama tells me: 'Be the best of everything; be proud, be black, be beautiful,' " she said.

Miss Miles knew some white people when her family lived briefly in Long Beach, but that was years ago. She says she wishes there were white students at her high school. "I want to learn about different cultures," she said. She believes a job at Disneyland will give her that chance.

Aubrey Miles, who is 45, says he has taken pains to tell his daughter that there are good white people. They saved his life, he told her. He was putting a roof on an office building seven years ago when a vat of hot tar exploded. He was severely burned.

"The guys on the job, who were white, helped me," he said. "I was on the ground, on fire. They put the fire out. One guy sat me up and put his back against my back. I could feel the connection. Then, afterward in the hospital, it was the same thing with the doctors."

Mr. Miles was speaking by telephone from Gautier, Miss. He and his wife moved there last year to care for Mrs. Miles's mother. Olivia remained in Los Angeles with her sister Shirley so she could graduate with her friends.

By last September, she and Mr. Sewell were already talking about the prom. It was set for May 1 in Long Beach. To save money for the big night, Mr. Sewell, whose father was recently laid off from his machinist's job at McDonnell-Douglas, worked as many hours at McDonald's as he could get.

Two days before the prom, Miss Miles still needed shoes. After school, she caught the bus to the Payless store at Crenshaw Plaza. It was April 29, the day the four policemen who beat Rodney G. King were acquitted.

"This lady on the bus told me, 'Baby, you better hurry up and get in the house,' " she said. "I said, 'Why what's going on?' She said, 'The verdict was not guilty.' "

Miss Miles bought her shoes—"two pairs for $24.99"—and went home. The prom was postponed because of the riots. Watching the images of fire and violence engulfing her neighborhood on television, she wept. "It hurt me when they beat that man in the truck up," she said. "I didn't know people could be that mean."

Her parents kept telephoning. "I was asking my Daddy, 'Why did this happen, why are they doing this?' " Miss Miles said. "He told me some people were just using it as an excuse, and some people were hurt that those cops didn't get any time."

Mr. Miles said the acquittal shattered his daughter. "She was about to lose it," he said. "She kept saying: 'Why am I working so hard? Why have you been telling me that I can achieve?' She had been sheltered. This was reality."

Mr. Miles, who grew up in a segregated Louisiana, said he had agonized over how to comfort her. "I didn't want her to just use it to sit on the curb and say, 'I'm black so I can't achieve,' " he said. "I told her: 'Don't let this stop you. You're going to college. Keep going on, even though you will be met with discrimination.'"

"I was praying, and talking to her," he said. "I was worried. I'm still worried. The summer's not over. . . ."

His daughter plans to be a lawyer. So does Mr. Sewell.

The riots presented Olivia Miles with the biggest ethical quandary of her life. "I saw people on television coming out with boxes of shoes and pretty furniture," she said. Her smile was embarrassed. "It was like Christmas. I wanted to get some. I was asking my sister if we could go. She said, 'No, you can't go out.' I thought: 'She's going to go to work. Should I get it, or shouldn't I get it? It's not fair that I can't. Everyone else is going to get stuff.' "

This, too, her father had foreseen. "I told her, 'There are going to be a lot of opportunities for you to get things, so just stay in the house,' " Mr. Miles said. "She knew automatically that stealing was a no-no. . . ."

That Sunday, Olivia was in her regular pew at the Mt. Sinai Baptist Church. "The pastor was saying, 'If you took something, shame on you. That's a sin,' " she said. She looked relieved all over again. "I was so happy."

Three weeks later, she and Mr. Sewell went to the prom in Long Beach. "We loved it," Mr. Sewell said. "We loved it." He was surprised, he said, when his classmates voted him prom king.

"I felt like a queen," Miss Miles said. Last Friday, Disneyland telephoned: She got the job. This summer, she will be selling balloons and popcorn at the amusement park, about 30 miles from her home, that calls itself "the happiest place on earth."

The job, which includes transportation furnished by Disneyland, will also be hers on holidays during the year. The pay is $5.25 an hour.

Miss Miles has made herself familiar with Disneyland's grooming code. "Good-bye, nails," she said exuberantly, holding out her long, manicured ones. "A job's a job! Disneyland's Disneyland. It's not like Popeye's or McDonald's. It's like 'Hey, girl, how'd you get that job at Disneyland?' "[2]

2. CLASS DISCUSSIONS: THE READING PROCESS

Make a composite of the current reading strategies used by class members. On the board, record answers to the questions, How do you read? and, How do you read argument? Organize the answers under the headings *prereading, reading, reading when it is hard,* and *postreading.* Discuss, in addition, what strategies various class members may be willing to add to their present processes.

3. GROUP WORK: PRACTICE THE READING PROCESS

Practice the active reading strategies described in this chapter on the essay, "Reading, Writing, Rehabilitation," starting on page 100. The strategies are listed below to help you remember them. Appoint a group leader to keep your group moving through these strategies. Some strategies will take less than a minute. Others will take 5–10 minutes.

---

[2]*New York Times,* June 18, 1992, Sec. A, pp. 1, 12.

You will be reading as a group, so try to get consensus on your responses. Experiment with using all of the strategies. Appoint a scribe to write the group responses to strategies 1, 4, 6, 7, 9, 15, 18, and 22. The scribe can then use these written notes later to report out to the class. The report should include information only on the starred strategies.

Active Reading Strategies

Prereading

*1. What is at issue?
 2. Background the issue.
 3. Do you know enough? Pool information.
*4. What is your present position?
 5. Survey (title, introduction, summary headings or first sentences, visuals, words).
*6. Analyze the rhetorical situation (text, reader, author, constraints, exigence).
*7. Assess common ground.
 8. Predict three ideas.
*9. Write one big question.

Reading

10. Pay special attention to introduction, body, and conclusion.
11. Identify the claim, subclaims, support, and transitions.
12. Discover the organization, and jot down a simple outline.
13. Add information on the rhetorical situation.
14. Underline and annotate.
*15. Identify key words that represent the major concepts.
16. Monitor your comprehension.
17. Check the accuracy of your predictions.

Postreading

*18. Summarize or make a map.
19. Write an answer to your big question.
20. Write out your original ideas.
21. Write what the author thinks and what you now think. Any change?
*22. Evaluate the argument. Is it effective?
23. How will you use it? What value does it have for you?

4. **READING AND WRITING ASSIGNMENT: WRITE A SUMMARY AND A REACTION TO THE FOLLOWING ESSAY ABOUT PRISON LITERACY**
    a. Underline and annotate the essay, and then write a one-paragraph summary of it.
    b. Write your reaction to the ideas in the essay. Show why you agree or disagree with the author. Propose, finally, what you consider to be the best solution to the problem.

READING, WRITING, REHABILITATION

Richard C. Wade

In our efforts to combat escalating crime, we have failed to acknowledge an elementary fact: one out of every five adult Americans is functionally illiterate.

A substantial number of violent criminals are in prison for good reasons and should remain there. Yet many can be returned to society without jeopardizing the public's safety—they can even learn to lead useful and productive lives. A renewed emphasis on literacy in prisons would enhance this prospect.

The functionally illiterate cannot read want ads or fill out job applications; they cannot do elementary banking, read their children's report cards or their own indictments.

The cost of illiteracy is up to $200 billion annually, if we take into account unemployment, health, welfare and incarceration. New York State's bill alone is about $20 billion, in large part the result of an overburdened criminal justice system. Each inmate costs the state $150 a day, more than $50,000 a year. By every estimate, the majority of the 60,000 prisoners in New York State and the 21,000 in New York City are functionally illiterate. They enter illiterate, leave illiterate and more often than not return illiterate.

A literacy program not only has the value of introducing prisoners to a world they never knew, it also gives them a chance for gainful employment. If they lack these skills and face diminished opportunities, should we be surprised that they revert to crime and wind up back in prison?

This has been the experience of the last two decades, during which more than 40 percent returned to jail within three years, and 20 percent more within five years. In Japan, by contrast, convicts cannot get out of prison until they can read and write. The recidivism rate there is 5 percent. Of course, in this country we cannot condone such compulsion, but we can make literacy an attractive option for the incarcerated.

Almost all maximum- and medium-security institutions have some library resources programs to encourage inmates to use such materials and volunteers to help. Support for this effort, however, is erratic and modest. More disconcerting is the fact that participation is voluntary and requires the inmate to request the service, a procedure that generally filters out functional illiterates.

This has to change. The Governor's Commission on Libraries is expected to recommend to Mario Cuomo next month that literacy be placed into the sentencing system for convicted criminals. Currently, a period of inquiry between the guilty verdict and sentencing produces a profile of the prisoner for the judge to use in determining the terms of imprisonment. The question on education now establishes the length of schooling, not the ability to read and write. The commission will suggest that a literacy test be given to prisoners before sentencing.

To take literacy into account, the judge could declare that if the prisoner goes into a literacy program and successfully completes it, the sentence will be reduced.

This proposal requires no new legislation because it falls within present judicial discretion. We reduce sentences for good behavior and community service; there is no reason why the acquisition of literacy should not yield the same reward.

In addition, this incentive can be extended to prisoners who already read and write well. There is no reason why a highly literate inmate cannot get a reduced sentence for teaching fellow prisoners basic literacy skills. Educated white collar criminals also cost the system $50,000 a year.

This proposal assumes that libraries play a central role. Every corrections institution holding prisoners sentenced to three years or more should have adequate facilities to operate a literacy program. It would also mean attracting additional staff and volunteers to teach and assist in instruction.

For such a small investment, it is hard to see where the public could get a larger return. It takes $2,000 to teach an adult to read and write: it costs $8,000 to put him on welfare and $50,000 to put him in jail. What should a prudent society do?[3]

5. GROUP WORK ON INDIVIDUAL ONGOING PROJECT: FOCUS YOUR ISSUE BY MAKING CLASS MAPS

Work with other members who are planning to write about issues that are related to the broad issue area in "The Reader" that you are interested in. Prepare for this exercise by surveying the related essays in "The Reader." (If your issue is not related to others in the class, you will have to work alone.)

Make a group map of the issue area. One of you will do the writing. The purpose is to help you see all of the different prongs of the issue. This procedure should focus your issue and also provide ideas for developing it. Proceed as follows:

Write the broad issue area in the center circle, and attach your issue, those of your classmates, and all of the other related issues that your group can discover.

When you have completed the map, check to see if your issue can now be narrowed, modified, changed, or enlarged as a result of seeing it in this larger perspective.

Example: Figure 3.3 is a map of the issue area *race* that was made by some of the students who test-read this book. They made this map after they had surveyed the articles about race in "The Reader." The map answers the question, What are the issues related to race?

6. UNDERSTANDING THE CHAPTER: WHOLE CLASS, GROUP, OR INDIVIDUALS

Summarize the major ideas in Chapter 3 by completing the following sentences:

a. Argumentative purpose is sometimes open and obvious but also sometimes hidden. The signs of a hidden purpose include . . .

---

[3] *New York Times*, May 29, 1993, Sec A, p. 10.

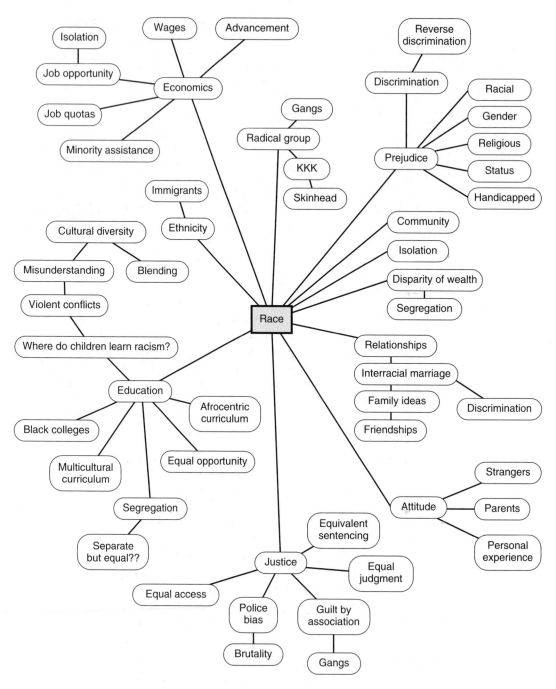

Figure 3.3 A Map That Answers the Question, What Are the Issues Related to Race? Use this map to discover specific related issues for paper topics. (By Eric West, Patricia Pulido, Ruby Chan, and Sharon Young. Used with permission.)

b. The key elements in the rhetorical situation (TRACE) are. . . . Questions to help you analyze these elements are . . .

c. Some prereading strategies I like to use are . . .

d. Some reading strategies I like to use are . . .

e. Some postreading strategies I like to use are . . .

CHAPTER 4

A Process for Writing Argument

The purpose of this chapter is to provide you with the expertise, confidence, and motivation that you will need to write arguments of your own on issues that are compellingly important to you. This chapter parallels Chapter 3, which covers the reading process, except that here the focus is on the writing process. First, you will be invited to analyze and describe your present individualistic writing process and adapt it for writing argument. Then, a possible process for writing argument will be laid out for your consideration. Next, you will think how you can incorporate elements of this process into your own present process while making it flexible and workable for you. Finally, you will practice the process by writing an exploratory paper in which you describe several perspectives on a single issue.

You will usually adapt your writing process to the specific writing task at hand. Sometimes, when you know a great deal about the issue and you are close to the audience, you will "just write," without consciously employing very many elements of your writing process. Other times, however, when you are expected to write longer, more complicated papers, particularly those that rely on research in outside sources, you will need a well-developed writing process that is composed of a variety of thinking and writing strategies. Such a process makes the most difficult writing task seem less difficult. It also helps you avoid procrastination and the discomforts of writer's block.

HOW DO YOU WRITE NOW?

You already have a writing process and, to make it useful for writing argument, you will need to adapt it to that purpose. Begin by thinking first about what you do when you write various other types of papers: lab reports, term papers, book reports, summaries of research, and so on.

What do you do . . .

- before you write the draft?
- while you are writing the draft?
- when you get stuck?
- when you finish writing the draft?

Many beginning college students, including those who test-read this book and who were asked to describe their writing processes during the first days of class, say they do nothing before they write unless the paper is long or difficult. They simply get some ideas, mentally organize them, and write the paper. When the paper is long or complicated, most students read, make some sort of outline, write what they can, read some more, and continue to add information until their paper is long enough to meet the requirements of the assignment.

Now change the focus of your writing process to describe how you would write argument.

What do you do . . .

- before you write the draft of an argument paper?
- while you are writing the draft of an argument paper?
- when you get stuck?
- when you finish writing the draft of an argument paper?

What can you add to your present process to improve your ability to write argument? Additional critical thinking strategies, research methods, and writing strategies will help you improve your present process. First, consider some simple ideas that can have a huge impact on your writing.

USE THE READING-THINKING-WRITING CONNECTIONS AS PART OF YOUR PROCESS

Did you include various reading and thinking activities as parts of your writing process? All writing comes from what you know and what you think. Your mind must be full of information and ideas in order for you to write. If you find that you cannot think of anything to write, you will need to read and think more. Reading and thinking are essential for writing.

Read While You Write

In Chapter 3 the suggestion was made that the best way to convert blank reading to thoughtful reading is to *write while you read*. This strategy helps you *think about* the text and *think beyond* the text to develop ideas of your own.

Now consider the possibility that you may at times "write" without thinking very much. That is, you find an idea, write something "off the top of your

continued

head," and turn it in without reading it yourself. One of the best ways to convert this blank writing to thoughtful writing is to *read while you write*. Reading while you write will provide you with background on your subject, new ideas to write about, fresh perspectives on your issue, and evidence and supporting details for your paper. It will at the same time suggest ways to solve writing problems as you read to understand how other writers have solved them.

The following are examples of questions that will help you use the material you read to help you think and write argument:

- How does my position on this issue compare with the author's?
- Do I agree, disagree, or am I neutral?
- If I were writing this myself, what would I add or write differently? Why?
- Which specific ideas do I agree with and which do I disagree with? Why?
- How can I answer those I disagree with?
- What original ideas are occurring to me as I read this material?
- What can I use from this reading: What do I want to quote and what do I want to paraphrase?
- Have any of my ideas been changed by what I have just read? If yes, what are they? If no, why not?
- Are there any effective argument strategies here that I might want to use in my own paper?

Here is a second idea that can improve your writing process dramatically:

Write at All Stages of the Process

Writing helps you learn about your subject, and it also helps you think. Start writing ideas as soon as you begin to think about your issue. Most people are especially creative and insightful during the early stages of a new writing project. Continue to write at all stages of the process, including while you are thinking and gathering materials, organizing your ideas, and writing, rewriting, and revising your final copy. Notes and ideas on sheets of paper, on cards, and in notebooks are useful, as are lists, maps, various types of outlines, responses to research, drafts, and rewrites. You need also to be prepared to jot down ideas at any time during the process. Once your reading and thinking are under way, your subconscious mind takes over. At odd times you may suddenly see new connections or think of a new example, a new idea, a beginning sentence, or a good organizational sequence for the main ideas. Insights like these often come to writers when they first wake up. Plan to keep paper and pencil available so that you can take notes when good ideas occur to you.

HOW CAN YOU ORGANIZE A PROCESS FOR WRITING ARGUMENT?

The following version of the writing process for argument integrates reading and writing at every phase. Also, similar to the reading process in Chapter 3, the strategies are laid out here as prewriting, writing, and postwriting strategies. A fourth category, strategies to use when you get stuck, is added. As you think about how you can adapt and use some of these ideas for writing argument, remember to keep the process flexible. That is, use your own present process, but add selected strategies as needed. It is unlikely that you will ever use all these strategies for one paper. Also, even though these strategies are explained here in an apparent order, you will not necessarily follow them in this order. You might write an entire section of your paper during the prewriting stage, or do some rewriting and revising while you are working on the initial draft. The strategies are not steps. They are suggestions to help you complete your paper. Integrate them with your present writing process and develop a way of writing argument papers that is uniquely yours.

The bare bones of the process can be stated simply. You need to

- select an issue, narrow it, take a tentative position, and write a claim
- do some reading and research
- create a structure
- write a draft
- revise and edit it

Special Note: Many of the strategies are explained in more detail later in the chapter.

A Writing Process for Argument

PREWRITING STRATEGIES

Get organized to write. Set up a place with materials. Create motivation to write.

Understand the writing assignment and schedule time. Break a complicated writing task into manageable parts and find the time to complete them.

Identify an issue area and an issue within it. Do some initial reading. Map or list aspects of the issue. Narrow it if necessary. State the issue in question form, and apply the twelve tests of an arguable issue (p. 33). Take a position on it and write a tentative claim.

Generate some initial ideas (use any or all of the following).

Analyze the rhetorical situation. Pay particular attention to the exigence, audience, and constraints at this point. Chapter 8 will provide more information on audience analysis.

continued

Focus on your issue and freewrite.

Brainstorm, make lists, map ideas.

Talk it through with a friend, your instructor, or members of a peer editing group.

Keep a journal, notebook, or folder of ideas.

Mentally visualize.

Read to get a sense of the different perspectives on the issue. Jot them down. Further narrow and limit the issue to one aspect or approach if necessary.

Think of an original perspective or approach, a new way of looking at the issue—for example, the idea of "uncommon ground" and a personal example in "We're Good Republicans—and Pro-Choice" (p. 22).

Clarify your position on the issue; revise your claim. Write the word "because" and list some reasons. Or list some reasons, write the word "therefore," and write the claim. Decide for now whether your paper would be stronger with the claim at the beginning or at the end. Decide which words in the claim need defining.

Plan research tasks.

Decide on your argumentative purpose. Chapters 7 and 8 will help you with this task. Decide on your main purpose and also on secondary purposes.

Write a guide to research: a list of ideas and what you need to find and read.

Read and take notes to fill in places on the outline where you need more information.

Use argument strategies. Employ the Toulmin model, the lists of proofs, and the types of claims to help you discover ideas and plan supporting evidence for your paper. You will learn how in the next three chapters.

Use reading strategies to help you plan structure, read, and revise.

Use critical thinking strategies to further explain your ideas.

Make an expanded list or outline to guide your writing. Cross-reference ideas and research notes. Think about what to put at the beginning and the end.

WRITING STRATEGIES

Write the first draft. Get your ideas on paper so that you can work with them. Use your outline and notes to help you. Either write and rewrite as you go, or write the draft quickly without rereading or rewriting along the way.

STRATEGIES TO USE WHEN YOU GET STUCK

Read more and take more notes. Write ideas and insights that come to you as you read.

Read your outline, rearrange parts, or add more information to it.

continued

Freewrite on the issue. If you cannot do so, read some more about your issue, and then freewrite.

Talk about your ideas to get fresh insights and solve problems.

Lower your expectations for your first draft. It does not have to be perfect.

POSTWRITING STRATEGIES

Read your draft critically. Try putting it aside for 24 hours to develop the perspective to read and improve it.

Evaluate your paper to see if it meets the criteria of a good argument paper. Apply the Toulmin model, as taught in the next chapter.

Make changes and additions until you think your paper is ready for other people to read. Move sections, cross out material, add other material, or rephrase, as necessary.

Read it aloud to yourself or someone else, or have someone read and critique it for you. Make final changes.

Write a title.

Check your paper for final mechanical and spelling errors, type or print it, and submit it.

Prewriting Strategies

Prewriting is creative, and creativity is delicate to teach because it is individual. Still, like most writers, you will need directed prewriting strategies from time to time, either to help you get started on writing or to help you break through writer's blocks. Here are some suggestions to help you get organized, access what you already know, think about it, and plan what more you need to learn. You will not use all of these suggestions. Some, however, may become your favorite prewriting strategies.

Get Organized to Write. Some people develop elaborate rituals like cleaning the house, sharpening the pencils, buying some special pens, putting on comfortable clothes, chewing a special flavor of gum, or making a cup of coffee to help them get ready to write. These rituals help them get their minds on the writing task, improve their motivation to write, and help them avoid procrastination and writer's block. A professional writer, describing what she does, says she takes a few moments before she writes to imagine her work as a completed and successful project. She visualizes it as finished, and she thinks about how she will feel at that time.[1]

---

[1] Barbara Neely, "Tools for the Part-Time Novelist," *The Writer*, June 1993, p. 17.

Creating a place to write is an essential part of getting organized to write. A desk and a quiet place at home or in the library work best for most students. Still, if ideal conditions are not available, you can develop alternative places like a parked car on a quiet street, an empty classroom, the kitchen or dining room table, or a card table in an out-of-the-way corner of a room.

Writing projects usually require stacks of books and papers that, ideally, one can leave out and come back to at any time. If you cannot leave them out, however, use a folder, briefcase, or box to keep everything in one safe place. You can then quickly spread your work out again when it is time to write. You will need a system to keep these writing materials organized. You may have idea notes, research notes, lists and outlines, and drafts at various stages of completion to keep track of. Categorize this material, keep it in stacks, and arrange the material in each stack in the order in which you will probably use it.

Finally, make a decision about the writing equipment you will use. The major choices will be the computer, the typewriter, paper and pens or pencils, or some combination of these. Experiment with different methods and decide which is best for you. Most students prefer computers for the same reasons that many professional writers like them: writing is faster, and the copy is easier to read and revise. A disadvantage of computers is that some people write too much. They literally write everything that occurs to them, and some of it is undeveloped, poorly organized, or off the subject. If you tend to write too much, you can solve your problem by cutting ferociously when you revise.

Understand the Assignment and Schedule Time.   You will need to analyze the writing assignment and find time to do it. Divide the assignment into small, manageable parts, assign a sufficient amount of time for each part, set deadlines for completing each part, and use the time when it becomes available. Below is an example.

Assignment.   Write a five- to six-page, typed, double-spaced argument paper in which you identify an issue of your choice, take a position, make a claim, and support it so that it is convincing to an audience of your peers. Do as much reading as you need to do, but plan to draw material from at least five sources when you write your paper. Use MLA style (explained in Chapter 10) to document your sources and prepare your bibliography.

Analysis of Assignment

Week One

Read in "The Reader," get an issue, and write down some ideas.	2 hours Tuesday night.
Do some initial library research, including background reading, thinking, and note taking; write a first draft.	3 hours Thursday night.
Read the draft to a peer group in class	Friday's class.

and get ideas for additional research.
Do research to fill in the needs of the first draft.   3 hours Saturday.

Week Two

Incorporate research and write a   3 hours Thursday night.
second draft.
Read it to the peer editing group   Friday's class.
in class.

Week Three

Rewrite, revise, and prepare final copy.   4 hours Tuesday night.
                                                             Hand in on Wednesday.

Notice that the work on this paper has been spread out over two and a half weeks and that it is also broken down into manageable units. A student would be able to complete this paper successfully, on time, and without panic and discomfort if this schedule were followed. Notice that 15 hours have been set aside and protected for the various stages. The time is available even though the student may not need all of it. The student's focus should now be on finishing the paper as quickly as possible, and not on simply using all of this time.

Here is a professional writer who cautions about the importance of working to finish rather than working to put in time: "Don't set your goal as minutes or hours spent working; it's too easy to waste that time looking up one last fact, changing your margins, or, when desperate, searching for a new pen." Instead, she advises, set a realistic writing goal for each day and work until you complete it.[2] Another author advises that you avoid creating units of work that are so large or unmanageable that you won't want to do them, such as writing an entire paper in one day. It may sound good on the surface to write a whole paper in one day or one night, "but you'll soon feel overwhelmed," and "you'll start avoiding the work and won't get *anything* done." Remember, she says, "it's persistence that counts" in completing writing projects.[3]

Analyze the Rhetorical Situation.   In Chapter 3 you learned to apply the elements of the rhetorical situation to help you read critically and analyze other authors' arguments. As a writer, you can now use the rhetorical situation to help you think critically and make decisions about your own writing.

All five elements of the rhetorical situation are important considerations for writers. Recall that three elements of the rhetorical situation are in place before you begin to write. They are the *exigence*, the *audience*, and the *constraints*. When you begin to write, two additional elements are added: you the *author*, and the *text* that

---

[2]Peggy Rynk, "Waiting for Inspiration," *The Writer*, September 1992, p. 10.
[3]Sue Grafton, "How to Find Time to Write When You Don't Have Time to Write," *The Writer's Handbook*, ed. Sylvia K. Burack (Boston: The Writer, 1991), p. 22.

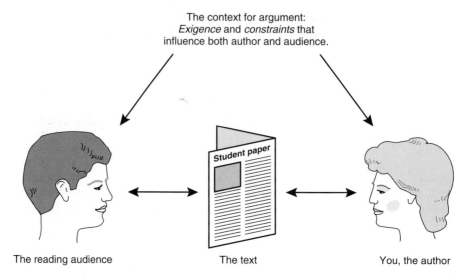

The context for argument:
Exigence and *constraints* that
influence both author and audience.

Student paper

The reading audience   The text   You, the author

Figure 4.1   The Five Elements of the Rhetorical Situation That the Writer Considers While Planning and Writing Argument

you create. Figure 4.1 provides a diagram of these five elements to suggest some of the relationships among them.

Now consider the five elements from the writer's point of view:

Exigence.   The exigence of the situation provides the motivation to write about the issue in the first place. Issues often emerge from real-life events that signal something is wrong. One student found a topic when a local jury appeared to have made a mistake because it assigned probation to a murderer instead of prison time. Another student developed an exigence to write when she visited a national forest and discovered that acres and acres of trees had been cut down since the last time she was there. Yet another student discovered an exigence when he read a newspaper article about the assisted death of an old woman who was very ill, and he began to compare her situation with his grandmother's. Such occurrences can cause the writer to ask the questions associated with exigence: What issue is associated with each of these incidents? Are these new or recurring issues? Do they represent problems or defects? How and why?

Audience.   Now think about how potential reading audiences might regard the issues that emerge from these situations. Who are these people? Would they perceive these situations as problems or defects, as you do? Would they agree or disagree with you on the issues, or would they be neutral? What do they believe in? What are their values? Will you need to make a special effort with them to achieve common ground, or will you already share common ground? What audience outcomes can you anticipate? Will you be able to get the audience to agree and reach consensus, to take action, to agree on some points but not on others, or to agree to disagree? Or will they probably remain unconvinced and possibly even hostile?

Constraints.   Remember that constraints influence the ways in which both you and your audience think about the issues. What background, events, experiences, traditions, values, or associations are influencing both you and them? If you decide to write for an audience of lawyers to convince them to change the nature of jury trials, for instance, what are the constraints likely to be? How hard will it be to change the system? Or, if you are writing for forest service employees whose job it is to cut down trees, what constraints will you encounter with this group? If you are writing for a group of doctors who have been trained to preserve human life as long as possible, what constraints will you encounter with them? And how about you? What are your own constraints? How are your training, background, affiliations, and values either in harmony or in conflict with your audience? In other words, will your respective constraints drive you and your audience apart or will they bring you together and help you achieve common ground?

Author.   Other questions will help you think like an author of argument. Why am I interested in this issue? Why do I perceive it as a defect or problem? Is it a new or old issue for me? What is my personal background or experience with this issue? What makes me qualified to write about it? Which of my personal values are involved? How can I get more information? Refer to your direct experience if you you have some. You may, for instance, be planning to go to law school, and you are interested in trial results, or you may have spent many happy childhood vacations camping in the forests, or maybe one of your relatives suffered many years before she died. Or you may have no direct experience, just an interest.

Text.   At this point, you can begin to plan your paper (the text). What strategies should you use? Should you employ Rogerian argument to build common ground? What types of support will work best? Should you state your claim right away or build up to it? What will your argumentative purpose be? What will your original approach or perspective be?

As you can see, the rhetorical situation can be employed to help you get ideas and plan, and you should actually keep it in mind throughout the writing process. It will be useful to you at every stage.

Focus and Freewrite.   Focus your attention, write a tentative title for your paper, and then freewrite for 10 or 15 minutes without stopping. Write about anything that occurs to you that is relevant to your title and your issue. Freewriting must be done quickly to capture the flow of thought. It may also be done sloppily, in incomplete sentences, with abbreviated words, even with errors.

Go back through your freewriting and find a phrase or sentence that you can turn into a claim. This freewriting is also your first partial manuscript. Later, you may use some or none of it in your paper. Its main value is to preserve the first creative ideas that flood your mind when you begin to work on a paper. Its other value is to focus and preserve your ideas so that they won't get lost when you later read the thoughts and opinions of others. If you start to freewrite and you find you do not have very many ideas, do some background reading in your issue area, and then try to freewrite again.

Brainstorm, Make Lists, Map Ideas.   Brainstorming is another way to get ideas down on paper in a hurry. The rules for brainstorming are to commit to a time limit, to write phrases only, to write quickly, and to make no judgments about what you or other members of a group are writing. Later you may go back to decide what is good or bad, useful or not useful. Brainstorming is like freewriting since it helps you get some ideas on paper quickly. It is also different from freewriting, since it usually produces only words and phrases, and it is often practiced as a group activity.

Listing is related to outlining. Insights may come at any time about how to divide a subject into parts, or how to set up three or four major headings for your paper. Write these ideas in list form. Or map your ideas to get a better sense of what they are and how they relate to each other (review Chapter 3, p. 94). You may also use a flowchart. Flowcharts are good for laying out processes or ideas and events that occur chronologically, over a period of time.

Talk It Through.   Many people find it easier to speak the first words than to write them. Typical audiences for an initial talk-through may include a peer editing group which is a small group of students in your class who will listen and read your paper at all stages; your instructor who, in conference, may ask a few questions and then just listen to you explore your ideas; or a writing center tutor who has been trained to ask questions and then listen. Friends or family members can also become valued listeners. Some people like to tape-record the ideas they get from such sessions. Others prefer to end them with some rapid freewriting, listing, or brainstorming to preserve the good ideas that surfaced. If you do not tape-record or write, your good ideas may become lost forever. Security is writing your paper with a stack of notes and ideas already at hand and ready to use.

Keep a Journal, Notebook, or Folder of Ideas.   Instead of talking to others, some authors talk to themselves on a regular basis by writing in a journal or notebook or simply by writing on pieces of paper and sticking them in a folder. To help you gather material for an argument paper, you may clip articles, write summaries, and write out ideas and observations about your issue as they come to you. These materials will provide you with an excellent source of information for your paper when it is time to write it.

A professional writer describes this type of writing as a tool that helps one think. This author sets out some suggestions that could be particularly useful for the writer of argument:

> Write quickly, so you don't know what's coming next.
> Turn off the censor in your head.

Write from different points of view to broaden your sympathies.

Collect quotations that inspire you and jot down a few notes on why they do.

Write with a nonjudgmental friend in mind to listen to your angry or confused thoughts.

When words won't come, draw something—anything.

Don't worry about being nice, fair, or objective. Be selfish and biased; give your side of the story from the heart.

Write even what frightens you, *especially* what frightens you. It is the thought denied that is dangerous.

Don't worry about being consistent. You are large; you contain multitudes.[4]

You can write entire sections of material, ready to incorporate later into your paper. Or you can jot down phrases or examples to help you remember sudden insights. The object is to think and write on a regular basis while a paper is taking shape. Writing at all stages helps you discover what you know and learn about what you think.

Mentally Visualize.   Create mental pictures related to your issue, and later describe what you see in your "mind's eye." For example, if you are writing about preserving forests, visualize them before any cutting has been done and then later after clear-cutting, which removes all trees in an area. Use these descriptions later in your paper to make your ideas more vivid and compelling.

Use Argument Strategies.   You will learn more about these in future chapters. The Toulmin model (Chapter 5) will help you plan the essential parts of your paper. Later, when you are revising, you can employ the Toulmin model to read and check the effectiveness of your argument. The list of proofs from Chapter 6 will provide you with a variety of ways to develop your paper. They can also be used to guide research. The claim questions in Chapter 7 will help you discover and write claims to focus your purpose for argument.

Use Reading Strategies.   Use what you know about analyzing the organization of other authors' essays to help you organize your own paper. For example, you can plan an introduction, main body, and conclusion. You can make an outline composed of a claim, subclaims, support, and transitions. You can write a simplified outline to help you visualize the structure of your paper. When you have finished your draft, you can try to summarize it to test its unity and completeness. Or you can survey it. If you have problems with summarizing or surveying, you will probably need to revise more. Much of what you learned about reading in Chapter 3 can now be used not only to help you write argument of your own but also to read and evaluate it.

Use Critical Thinking Prompts.   You can get additional insight and ideas about your issue by using some well-established lines of thought that stimulate critical think-

---

[4]Marjorie Pellegrino, "Keeping a Writer's Journal," *The Writer*, June 1992, p. 27.

ing. The following list provides some prompts that will cause you to think in a variety of ways. First, write out your issue, and then write your responses. You will be pleased by the quantity of new information these questions will generate for your paper.

Critical Thinking Prompts

1. **Associate it.** Consider other, related issues, big issues, or enduring issues. Also associate your issue with familiar subjects and ideas.
2. **Describe it.** Use detail. Make the description visual if you can.
3. **Compare it.** Think about items in the same or different categories. Compare it with things you know or understand well. Compare what you used to think about the issue and what you think now. Give reasons for your change of mind.
4. **Apply it.** Show practical uses or applications. Show how it can be used in a specific setting.
5. **Divide it.** Get insight into your issue by dividing it into related issues or into parts of the issue.
6. **Agree and disagree with it.** Identify the extreme pro and con positions and reasons for holding them. List other approaches and perspectives. Say why each position, including your own, might be plausible and in what circumstances.
7. **Consider it as it is, right now.** Think about your issue as it exists, right now, in contemporary time. What is its nature? What are its special characteristics?
8. **Consider it over a period of time.** Think about it in the past and how it might present itself in the future. Does it change? How? Why?
9. **Decide what it is a part of.** Put it in a larger category and consider the insights you gain as a result.
10. **Analyze it.** Break it into parts and get insight into each of its parts.
11. **Synthesize it.** Put it back together in new ways so that the new whole is different, and perhaps clearer and better, than the old whole.
12. **Evaluate it.** Decide whether it is good or bad, valuable or not valuable, moral or immoral. Give evidence to support your evaluation.
13. **Elaborate on it.** Add and continue to add explanation until you can understand it more easily. Give some examples to provide further elaboration.
14. **Project and predict.** Answer the question, "What would happen if. . . ?" Think about further possibilities.
15. **Ask why, and keep on asking why.** Examine every aspect of your issue by asking why.

Write an Outline.   A written outline helps many people see the organization of ideas before they begin to write. Other people seem to be able to make a list or even work from a mental outline. Still others "just write" and move ideas around later to create order. There is, however, an implicit outline in most good writing.

The outline is often referred to metaphorically as the skeleton or bare bones of the paper because it provides the internal structure that holds the paper together. An outline can be simple, a list of words written on a piece of scrap paper, or it can be elaborate, with essentially all major ideas, supporting details, major transitions, and even some of the sections written out in full. Some outlines actually end up looking like partial, sketchy manuscripts.

If you have never made outlines, try making one. Outlining requires intensive thinking and decision making. When it is finished, however, you will be able to turn your full attention to writing, and you will never have to stop to try to figure out what to write about next. Your outline will tell you what to do, and it will ultimately save you time and reduce much of the difficulty and frustration you would experience without it.

Talk It Through Again. When you have completed your outline and are fairly satisfied with it, you can sharpen and improve it even more by reading it aloud and explaining its rationale to some good listeners. It is more and more common to organize peer editing groups in writing classes to give students the opportunity to talk through outlines and to read drafts to fellow students who then act as critics who make recommendations for improvement. Reading and talking about your outline in the early stages helps clarify ideas, and it is easier to write about them later. At this stage, your student critics should explain to you what is clear and unclear and also what is convincing and not convincing.

Writing and Rewriting Strategies

Write the First Draft. The objective of writing the first draft is to get your ideas in some kind of written form so that you can see them and work with them. Here is how a professional writer explains the drafting process:

> Writing a first draft should be easy because, in a sense, you can't get it wrong. You are bringing something completely new and strange into the world, something that did not exist before. You have nothing to prove in the first draft, nothing to defend, everything to imagine. And the first draft is yours alone, no one else sees it. You are not writing for an audience. Not yet. You write the draft in order to read what you have written and to determine what you still have to say.[5]

This author advises further that you "not even consider technical problems at this early stage." Nor should you "let your critical self sit at your desk with your creative self. The critic will stifle the writer within." The purpose, he says, is "not to get it right, but to get it written."[6]

Here is another writer, Stephen King, who advises putting aside reference books and dictionaries to concentrate on writing the first draft:

> Put away your dictionary. . . . You think you might have misspelled a word? O.K., so here is your choice: either look it up in the dictionary, thereby making sure you have it right—

---

[5]John Dufresne, "That Crucial First Draft," *The Writer*, October 1992, p. 9.
[6]Ibid., pp. 10–11.
[7]Stephen King, "Everything You Need to Know about Writing Successfully—in Ten Minutes," *The Writer's Handbook*, ed. Sylvia K. Burack (Boston: The Writer, 1991), p. 33.

and breaking your train of thought and the writer's trance in the bargain—or just spell it phonetically and correct it later. Why not? Did you think it was going to go somewhere? And if you need to know the largest city in Brazil and you find you don't have it in your head, why not write in Miami or Cleveland? You can check it . . . but *later*. When you sit down to write, *write*. Don't do anything else except go to the bathroom, and only do that if it absolutely cannot be put off.[7]

You will be able to follow this advice if your outline and notes are available to guide you and keep you on track. If you occasionally get stuck, you can write some phrases, freewrite, or even skip a section that you cannot easily put into words. You will have another chance at your draft later. Right now, work only to capture the flow of ideas that is on the outline. You will discover, as you write, that many of the ideas that were only half formed on your outline will now become clear and complete as you get insight from writing.

Have Someone Read It.   When you have drafted your paper and done some initial revision, you can seek the opinion of other students once more. The usual procedure for a peer editing session on a draft is to read the paper aloud to the group, or to do a round-robin reading session, where group members read all of the papers silently and make some notes before they discuss them one by one.

Peer groups make the writing task more sociable and provide you with immediate reactions from a real audience. They also help you become a more sensitive critic both of your own and of others' work. Most professional writers rely heavily upon other people's opinions at various stages of writing. Look at the prefaces of some of the books you are using this semester. Most authors acknowledge the help of several people who read their manuscript and made suggestions for improvement. Many individuals recommended improvements for this book. Some of these people were teachers, some were editors, some were friends and family members, some were colleagues, and many were students. The students who test-read this book have already been described. They wrote many good suggestions for improvement. In fact, these students were responsible for several of the major changes and special features in the book that make it easier to read and use. One student commented that she liked being a part of the writing process for this textbook because it helped her read her other textbooks more critically. If peer review groups are not part of your writing class, try to find someone else to read your draft. You need someone to make suggestions and give you ideas for improvement.

Rewrite and Revise.   Working with a rough draft is easier than outlining or drafting. It is, in fact, creative and fun to revise because you begin to see your work take shape and become readable. Skillfully revised material, incidentally, makes a good impression on the reader. It is worthwhile to finish your draft early enough so that you will have several hours to read and revise before you submit it in its final form to a reader.

Most writers have some ideas and rules about writing that come to their aid, from an inner voice, when it is time to revise. Listen to your inner voice so that you will know what to look for and what to change. If you do not have a strongly developed inner voice, you can strengthen it by learning to ask the following questions. Notice that these questions direct your attention to global revisions for improved clarity and organization, as well as to surface revisions for details.

1. **Is it clear?** If you cannot understand your own writing, other people won't be able to, either. Be very critical of your own understanding as you read your draft. Make your writing clearer by establishing some key terms and using them throughout. Add transitions as well. Use those that are associated with the organizational patterns you have used. There is more information about these in Chapter 10. Or write a transitional paragraph to summarize one major part of your paper and introduce the next. If you stumble over a bad sentence, begin again and rewrite it in a new way. There are a dozen possible ways to write one sentence. Also, change all words that do not clearly communicate to you exactly what you want to say. This is no time to risk using words from the thesaurus that you are not sure about. Finally, apply this test: Can you state the claim or the main point of your paper and list the parts that develop it? Take a good look at these parts and rearrange them if necessary.

2. **What should I add?** Sometimes in writing the first draft you will write such a sketchy version of an idea that it does not explain what you want to say. Add fuller explanations and examples, or do some extra research to improve the skimpy parts of your paper.

3. **What should I cut?** Extra words, repeated ideas, and unnecessary material find their way into a typical first draft. Every writer cuts during revision. Stephen King, who made $7,000,000 in one year as a professional writer, describes how he learned to cut the extra words. His teacher was the newspaper editor John Gould who dealt with his first feature article as follows:

> He started in on the feature piece with a large black pen and taught me all I ever needed to know about my craft. I wish I still had the piece—it deserves to be framed, editorial corrections and all—but I can remember pretty well how it looked when he had finished with it. Here's an example:

Last night, in the well-loved gymnasium of Lisbon High School, partisans and Jay Hills fans alike were stunned by an athletic performance unequalled in school history: Bob Ransom, known as "Bullet Bob" for both his size and accuracy, scored thirty-seven points. He did it with grace and speed...and he did it with an odd courtesy as well, committing only two personal fouls in his knight-like quest for a record which has eluded Lisbon thinclads since 1953...

When Gould finished marking up my copy in the manner I have indicated above, he looked up and must have seen something on my face. I think *he* must have thought it was horror, but it was not: it was revelation.

"I only took out the bad parts, you know," he said. "Most of it's pretty good."

"I know," I said, meaning both things: yes, most of it was good, and yes, he had only taken out the bad parts. "I won't do it again."

"If that's true," he said, "you'll never have to work again. You can do *this* for a living." Then he threw back his head and laughed.

And he was right: I *am* doing this for a living, and as long as I can keep on, I don't expect ever to have to work again.[8]

4. **Are the language and style consistent and appropriate throughout?** Edit out all words that create a conversational or informal tone in your paper. For example,

> *Change:* And as for target shooting, well go purchase a BB gun or a set of darts.[9]
>
> *To read:* A BB gun or set of darts serve as well for target shooting as a handgun.

Also, edit out all cheerleading, slogans, clichés, needless repetition, and exhortations. You are not writing a political speech. For example,

> *Change:* Violence! Why should we put up with it? Violence breeds violence, they say. America would be a better place if there were less violence.
>
> *To read:* Violent crime has begun to take over the United States, affecting everyone's life. Every day another story of tragedy unfolds where a man, a woman, or a child is senselessly killed by someone with a gun. Under the tremendous stress of this modern society, tempers flare at the drop of a hat, and people reach for a gun that was bought only for defense or safety. Then they make rash, deadly decisions.[10]

You will learn more about language and style in Chapter 6. In general, use formal, rational style in an argument paper unless you have a good reason to do otherwise. Use emotional language and examples that arouse feelings only where appropriate to back up logical argument.

5. **Is there enough variety?** Use some variety in the way you write sentences by beginning some with clauses and others with a subject or even a verb. Vary the length of your sentences as well. Try to write not only simple sentences, but also compound and complex sentences. You can also vary the length of your paragraphs. The general rule is to begin a new paragraph every time you change the subject. Variety in sentences and paragraphs makes your writing more interesting to read. Do not sacrifice clarity for variety, however, by writing odd or unclear sentences.

6. **Have I used the active voice most of the time?** The active voice is more

---

[8]Ibid., pp. 30–31.
[9]From a student paper by Blake Decker.
[10]Ibid.

direct, energetic, and interesting than the passive voice. Try to use it most of the time. Here is a sentence written in the active voice; it starts with the subject:

> Virtual reality is an exciting new technology that will enhance nearly every aspect of our lives.[11]

Notice how it loses its directness and punch when it is written in the passive voice:

> Nearly every aspect of our lives will be enhanced by virtual reality, an exciting new technology.

7. **Have I avoided sexist language?** Try to avoid referring to all people in your paper as though they were either all male or all female. You can create as big a problem, however, by referring to everyone as "he or she" or "himself or herself." One way to solve this problem is to use plural pronouns, *they* or *them*, or occasionally rewrite a sentence in the passive voice. It is better to write, "The pressure-sensitive glove is used in virtual reality," than to write, "He or she puts on a pressure-sensitive glove to enter the world of virtual reality."

8. **Have I followed the rules?** Learn the rules for grammar, usage, and punctuation, and follow them. No one can read a paper that is full of errors of this type. Make the following rules a part of that inner voice that guides your revision, and you will avoid the most common errors made by student writers:

- Write similar items in a *series*, separated by commas, and finally connected by *and*. **Example:** "The National Rifle Association, firearms manufacturers, and common citizens are all interested in gun control."[12]
- Use *parallel construction* for longer, more complicated elements that have a similar function in the sentence. **Example:** "Parents who fear for their children's safety at school, passengers who ride on urban public transit systems, clerks who work at convenience stores and gas stations, and policemen who try to carry out their jobs safely are all affected by national policy on gun control."
- Keep everything in the same *tense* throughout. Use the present tense to introduce quotes. **Example:** "As Sherrill *states*, 'The United States is said to be the greatest gun-toting nation in the world.' Millions of guns create problems in this country."
- Observe *sentence boundaries*. Start sentences with a capital letter and end them with a period or question mark. Make certain they express complete thoughts.
- Make *subjects agree with verbs*. **Example:** "*Restrictions* on gun control *interfere* (not *interferes*) with people's rights."
- Use *clear and appropriate pronoun referents*. **Example:** "The *group* is strongly in favor of gun control, and little is needed to convince *it* (not *them*) of the importance of this issue."
- Use commas to set off long initial clauses that are seven or more words long, to separate two independent clauses, to introduce quotes, and to separate words in

---

[11]From a student essay by Greg Mathios.

[12]The examples in this list are drawn from a student paper by Blake Decker. I have revised his sentences for the sake of illustration.

a series. **Example:** "When one realizes that the authors of the Constitution could not look into the future and imagine current events, then one can see how irrational and irresponsible it is to believe that the right to bear arms should in these times still be considered a constitutional right, and, according to Smith, the groups that do so, 'are short-sighted, mistaken, and ignorant.' "

- Check the spelling of every word you are not absolutely sure about. If spelling is a problem for you, buy a small spelling dictionary that contains only words and no meanings, or use the spell checker on the computer.
- Correct all typographical errors.
- Add a title if you haven't already.
- Complete your revision process by reading your paper aloud. Read slowly and listen. You will be surprised by the number of problems that bother your ears but that were not noticeable to your eyes.

Your paper should be ready now to submit for evaluation. Either type it or print it out on a word processor.

PRACTICE THE PROCESS BY WRITING THE EXPLORATORY PAPER

The exploratory paper[13] is an extended version of Rogerian argument (see pages 58–62). In writing the exploratory paper, the arguer identifies not just one opposing position, as in Rogerian argument, but as many of the major positions on an issue as possible, both past and present, and explains them through summaries and an analysis of the total rhetorical situation for the issue. The analysis of the rhetorical situation in these papers explains what caused the issue and what prompted past and present interest and concern with it, identifies who is interested in it and why, and examines the constraints of the inquiry and debate associated with it. The summaries of the positions not only explain each of the different perspectives on the issue, but also provide the usual reasons cited to establish the validity of each perspective. The writer's own opinions are not expressed at all, or are withheld until later in the paper.

There are a number of advantages of writing and reading exploratory papers. When writers and readers view an issue from many perspectives, they acquire a greater depth of understanding of it. They also acquire information and facts as well as opinion on all the various views. All these are beneficial because both the arguer and the reader become better educated and more fluent in their discussions of the issue. Exploratory papers also help establish common ground between writers and readers. Writers, by restating all opposing positions along with the usual reasons for accepting them, are forced to understand all opposing views in the best Rogerian sense. The reader is also interested because the exploratory paper explains all views, which usually includes the reader's as well. The reader feels that he or she has been heard and, consequently, is more willing to read and get information about the other positions on

---

[13]I am indebted to Professor James Kinneavy of the University of Texas at Austin for the basic notion of the exploratory paper.

the issue. Exploratory papers provide the mutual understanding and common ground essential for the next stage in argument, the presentation of the writer's position and reasons for holding it. The exploratory paper thus paves the way for the writer to enter the conversation on an issue with a single-perspective argument.

Exploratory papers are a common genre in argumentative writing. You will encounter them in newspapers, news magazines, other popular magazines of opinion, and scholarly journals. They are easy to recognize because they take a broad view of an issue, and they explain multiple perspectives, instead of just one.

The following extract is an example of a short exploratory paper about the recent problems associated with the logging industry in the northwestern United States. The main problem is that the environmentalists are intent on saving forests and the spotted owl that lives in them, and loggers and mill workers make their living by cutting down the forests and destroying the owl's habitat. The author of this article summarizes the different positions associated with this issue and explains enough of the rhetorical situation to provide a context for it, but does not take sides or express personal opinions. The reader gets a sense of the complexity of the issue and also of some new perspectives on it.

THE BIRDS AND THE TREES

What is the rhetorical situation?

The "forest summit" will let timber-industry officials and environmentalists square off in the infamous "jobs vs. owls" debate. . . . The summit is intended to inspire a compromise that would save jobs *and* birds, as well as cool tempers. . . . And cool is sorely needed. For three years the spotted owl has been a cat's-paw in the battle over national forests, which lumber companies are allowed to log. Some of that public land is what's known as old-growth forest. Owls need these ancient forests to survive, so under the Endangered Species Act, the government must protect the birds' habitat. Since 1991, the courts have banned logging on millions of acres in 17 national forests and five Bureau of Land Management parcels in northern California, Oregon and Washington. Faster than you could say "whoo," SAVE A LOGGER, SHOOT AN OWL bumper stickers became as common as flannel shirts in the timber towns. And a few diehard, out-of-work loggers would just as soon replace "owl" with "environmentalist."

What is the environmentalist's position?

But beneath the din of the professional railing, quieter voices, those of the battered timber workers, are changing the terms of the debate and shaking up old allegiances. Many rank-and-file forest and millworkers still fume at "extreme" environmentalists and harbor a lingering hatred of greens who drove spikes into trees to prevent cutting. But they've come to believe they were victims of the industry as much as they were of the spotted owl. Environmentalists would not have gotten such a foothold, says Bill Rodgers, a former millworker who is now a peer counselor for a retraining program, "if the industry had started policing itself

What is the traditional logger's position?

in 1970 instead of clear-cutting every hillside." Workers complain bitterly that they've been betrayed by an industry that uses loss of jobs as an argument against closing national forests to logging, but then turns around and exports raw logs to Japan, which eliminates U.S. mill jobs.

What is the Sierra Club's position?

The timber industry blames environmentalists for the loss of at least 30,000 jobs since 1990 and for the dive in timber sales from federal lands to roughly 10 percent of their 1991 levels. The Sierra Club countered last week with a report reiterating that "timber exports and robotization of the timber industry, not environmental regulations, are the principal causes for a poor Northwest economy." But many workers have moved

What is the new, revised logger's position?

beyond finger-pointing and fry-the-owl rhetoric. Whether they become unemployed because forests are placed off-limits to logging, or because trees are fewer and mills are automating, a lost job is a lost job. Men who started logging at the age of 7, carrying tools for their fathers in the cathedral-like forests, know that a way of life is vanishing, and nothing will

How are loggers dealing with the changes?

bring it back. "Three years ago people were in denial," says Dave Schmidt, commissioner of Linn County, Ore. "Now we know we are just not going to have what we had before."[14]

Now, practice the process explained in this chapter by writing an exploratory paper of your own. Exercises at the end of this chapter will set up the assignment and help you complete it.

EXERCISES AND ACTIVITIES

1. CLASS DISCUSSION: THE WRITING PROCESS

Make a composite of the writing strategies used by class members. On the board, record answers to the questions, How do you write? and, How do you write argument? Organize the answers under the headings *prewriting, writing, writing when you get stuck,* and *rewriting.* In addition, discuss strategies that various class members may be willing to add to their present processes.

2. CLASS DISCUSSION, READING, AND WRITING: THE EXPLORATORY PAPER

All members of the class should first read the six articles about gays in the military that follow. Then, the class should plan an exploratory paper by discussing the following items. A scribe should jot down information about each item on the board:

a. Explain the different perspectives on the issue of gays in the military and describe the rhetorical situation for it. What caused it? What has prompted interest and concern? Who is interested and why? What are the constraints?

---

[14]"The Birds and the Trees," *Newsweek*, April 5, 1993, p. 53.

b. Map all of the specific issues that have emerged within the context of the larger issue. Do this by writing the big issue, "Gays in the military," and drawing a circle around it. Write the specific related issues, such as housing problems and morale problems, and attach them to the large circle.

c. Use the critical thinking prompts on p. 116 to help you get additional ideas. They are especially effective prewriting strategies for exploratory papers. Write down your ideas.

d. Summarize the different positions on the issue.

e. You now have the materials for an exploratory paper. Make an outline or list to organize your ideas. Then write a three-page paper in which you first explain the issue and the rhetorical situation. Next, summarize the various positions on the issue. Finally, state your position on the issue and indicate briefly why you hold it. Use "The Birds and the Trees" on p. 123 as a model to help you organize and write your paper.

BACKGROUND INFORMATION ON THE RHETORICAL SITUATION FOR THE ISSUE OF GAYS IN THE MILITARY

Whether gays and lesbians should be allowed to serve in the military is a modern civil rights issue that surfaced when Bill Clinton became president. One of his campaign promises was to eliminate an existing ban on homosexuals in the armed services. This situation provided a strong exigence for argument on the subject. Those who favored this policy wanted access to military service and equal treatment for gays. Those who opposed it wanted gays to be banned from the military. Clinton established a compromise policy in 1993 that was known as "don't ask, don't tell, don't pursue," which essentially meant that gays and lesbians could serve in the military only if they kept their sexual orientation secret and private. Late in 1993 the Pentagon set up rules for homosexual conduct in the military. These became controversial immediately with gays and lesbians because they perceived them as a retreat from Clinton's original promise that they be allowed to serve openly. At that time it appeared that the issue was far from settled and that gays would be challenging these rules in the courts for some time to come. What is the current status of this issue as you read this book? What is the current status of the larger issue of gay civil rights?

READING 1

SHOULD THE MILITARY BAR HOMOSEXUALS?

IS THERE A BETTER WAY TO DESTROY MILITARY READINESS?

Sailors and Marines are an executive order away from having homosexuals serving in the same foxhole, in the same boiler room, in the same berthing area.

President Clinton's pledge to eliminate the ban on homosexuals in the armed services has created an uproar in the military and has rekindled the debate over the military's right to bar homosexuals.

"It is a very big problem for us," Gen. Colin Powell said, "and it is not just the generals and admirals who are saying this. We're hearing it throughout the force." Powell and other leaders have advised Clinton that the morale, good order, and discipline of the services would be undermined if heterosexual personnel were forced to share barracks, bathrooms, and showers with homosexuals.

Homosexual activists contend that the military's exclusion policy is a violation of their civil rights. During the past 20 years, however, federal courts have rejected this argument and ruled that military service is a duty and a privilege, not a right. Based on the needs of the armed forces, the military lawfully bars whole segments of the population from entering the service: those over 35 years of age, high school dropouts, drug users, convicted felons, and many others.

The public debate has been clouded by flawed research, misinformation, and assertions that equate the homosexual cause with the Black civil rights movement. To argue that DOD's homosexual exclusion policy is similar to racial segregation ignores the facts and diminishes our nation's civil rights struggle. You can't change your race or ethnic origin, but the existence of more than 100 nationwide counseling groups for "former homosexuals" presents a strong argument that individuals can choose to change homosexual behavior. Recent studies indicate that barely 2% of the nation's population is homosexual.

Prominent lawmakers have cautioned the President not to hastily lift the ban on homosexuals. Sen. Sam Nunn (D-GA), the Chairman of the Senate Armed Services Committee, has endorsed DOD's policy and stated, "We have to consider not only the rights of homosexuals but also the rights of those who are not homosexual and who give up a great deal of their privacy when they go in the military."

Individual rights are important, but the real issue is military readiness. Lifting the homosexual ban would adversely affect the morale and combat effectiveness of our volunteer force with no apparent gain to the Sea Services.

HOW THE HOMOSEXUAL ISSUE COULD AFFECT MILITARY FAMILIES

In addition to hurting morale, discipline, and readiness, legalizing homosexuality in the military would also impact the military family. Here are some of the possible effects excerpted from "In Focus," published by the Family Research Council:

HOUSING

Following the pattern already established in cities that have homosexual rights ordinances, it is reasonable to foresee that homosexual couples would press for equal access to base housing without regard for the impact that their open embrace of homosexuality might have on children.

Once sexual orientation is eliminated as a selective factor, marriage itself will be redefined or suffer reduced status in the consideration of on-base housing assignments. For example, in the wake of the adopting of specials rights for homosexuals at Stanford University, the campus now extends housing privileges to same-sex couples. Objections by families with children were brushed aside as "bigotry." The campus already has a waiting list for family housing, so mothers and fathers with children now face additional competition from homosexual couples.

ENVIRONMENTAL FACTORS

Most people recognize that some homosexuals are already in the military but keep their sexual orientation and practices private. If, however, open homosexuals are permitted in the military, parents will find it difficult to shield their children from public displays of homosexual affection. Older children who may be struggling with their budding sexual identities are not prepared to deal with homosexuals as potential role models.

BENEFIT DEMANDS

Military medical facilities are already hard-pressed to meet the needs of families. Lifting the ban on homosexuals would add to the burden on medical facilities in disproportionate numbers. Because of their higher incidence of sexually-transmitted diseases, homosexuals as a group will compete disproportionately for services with other participants in the military's medical system. Families may find one of their children, suffering from chicken pox, standing in waiting room lines behind homosexuals suffering from diseases they incurred during homosexual activity.

The military attempts to provide for the co-location of spouses when a husband and wife both serve in the military. If the ban is lifted, homosexual couples would press for the same benefits, and compete with these families.

Military families already face a number of unique and difficult challenges in their service to our country. A relatively low pay scale, frequent relocations and long deployments away from home make the military family especially vulnerable. Undermining military families by placing homosexual behavior on a par with marital fidelity would provide devastating evidence that our government no longer recognizes the importance of strong families in cultivating the virtues that enable us to be a free, self-governing people.[15]

READING 2

KITTY HAWK CREW MULLS END TO GAY BAN

ABOARD THE USS KITTY HAWK—There's a lot of green ink going into Lt. Fred Drummond's log book these days.

To pilots and air crew members the green entries highlight the combat missions they've flown. Many who fly for a living in the military, wait their whole careers for just one.

---

[15]*Naval Affairs*, February 1993, p. 4.

But while Drummond and his shipmates aboard the aircraft carrier Kitty Hawk were flying into the antiaircraft fire of Saddam Hussein's forces in southern Iraq last month, another battle was being waged in Washington: The battle of the gay ban.

Ironically, it is people like those in Kitty Hawk's crew who, among others, will be most affected by any change to the ban that now bars homosexuals from service.

"It's us and guys in units like the Marines and Army infantry who are going to get hit the hardest if the gay ban is lifted," said one Navy chief.

Drummond, a veteran of the 1986 raid on Libya, the '88 Praying Mantis operation, Operation Just Cause in '89, Operations Desert Shield and Desert Storm and even the latest strikes against Iraq, already has more green ink in his book than most. He's been through a lot. He and his 5,000-plus shipmates say they've got more important things to worry about than the gay ban, he says.

Every two days, Drummond, a naval flight officer, boards his EA-6B Prowler with three other crew members, and is catapulted to 180 mph in two seconds from this 1,065-foot aircraft carrier. For the next four hours, he patrols the airspace of southern Iraq below the 32nd parallel. Antiaircraft artillery follows his flight path across the sky.

"Yes," he says, even as the missions begin to slip into routine, "the adrenaline still pumps every time we go up."

"UNPLEASANT"

His words echo those of sailors and aviators across the ship. Whether vehemently opposed to lifting the ban or part of the minority who say they feel comfortable with the idea, all agree: Any change is heightened tenfold when induced under the tight confines of a ship at sea.

"The acceptance [levels] of that element within the Navy and in confines of the Kitty Hawk are going to be very unpleasant," predicts Capt. James Maslowsky, the skipper.

The major issue, he explains, is not whether homosexuals will be able to perform the various jobs aboard ship, but rather, "where we're going to berth them."

Maslowsky says if confronted with the issue tomorrow, he would try to put all self-proclaimed homosexuals in separate berthing from the heterosexuals.

"It's the only answer I can come up with," he says.

With the approval of allowing women to serve aboard combatant ships beginning to appear over the distant horizon, the skipper concedes he may be working himself into a hole.

But if you separate homosexuals and heterosexuals in berthing, he said, "then you have to protract that out between male and female and the traditional rank separation we have in the Navy—officers, chief petty officer, enlisted. It would be a manager's nightmare" with at least 12 different berthing arrangements. And what would be done, he wondered, with people who consider themselves bi-sexual?

"DOESN'T MATTER TO ME"

On the bridge, Quartermaster Second Class Gerald Drayton plots and logs the ship's course.

"Personally, it doesn't really matter to me," he says on the ban being lifted, but, he adds, "I don't think it would be very healthy."

Drayton homes into the core of his captain's dilemma.

It all comes down to a matter of privacy, he says, "You just don't have any."

Drayton explains he wouldn't have any problem with the man standing next to him on the bridge being a homosexual. But when their duty for the day was over and it came time to undress in front of him and perhaps take a shower, "I'd start feeling very uncomfortable."

Drayton adds, however, that the "Navy teaches us to adapt to whatever environment they set for us—it can be done." The bottom line, he says, "is that it won't change anything at all," in terms of getting the job done.

THE MARINE VIEW

Down five stories below the flight deck, the ship's contingent of 60 Marines think otherwise.

"It would wipe away everything I joined the Marines for," says Cpl. Tony Nitto. "You have to have faith in your fellow Marines. You want him thinking about the job, not something—I don't know—personal, I guess, between him and you."

LCpl. Mike Stocker paints a bleak picture of what life would be like for any self-proclaimed homosexual deployed with them.

"It would be hell for him. The harassment would be intolerable," he says. "There would be some way to get him out." A way in which, he says, "that nothing would come of it."

Nitto agrees.

"He'd be virtually tortured," he says, "verbally and probably physically. Nobody would want him aboard."

The two Marines' NCO doesn't offer much sympathy either.

"The sad thing is we'd have to protect this guy," explains Sgt. Dallas Jacobs of his duties as a leader if the ban is lifted.

Of his subordinates, he says they would be out of control. "They won't care what happens to them."

PRACTICAL, NOT SPIRITUAL

One of the Kitty Hawk chaplains, Lt. Cmdr. William Shuppert says he is uncomfortable with lifting the ban more on a practical level than on a spiritual level.

"I couldn't imagine a gay person wanting to be in this situation." The level of frustration and temptation, he thinks, would be overwhelming.

As far as Shuppert is concerned, "I would treat a gay person like any other. With as much compassion and understanding as anyone else." Shuppert notes, however, that compassion and understanding do not constitute endorsement.

"Jesus says hate the sin, not the sinner."

The real challenge, as a chaplain, he says, would be to get that message through to the rest of the crew. "It's not always easy for me to be compassionate and understanding," he says, "and I'm a priest."

The fact that the majority of chaplains do consider homosexuality a sin raised valid questions on counseling services. With chaplains providing the only on-ship professional counseling, it remains dubious, considering the overriding influence of the theological issue, that homosexuals would feel comfortable seeking advice or counseling from them.

"EMOTIONAL LAND MINE"

Lt. Larry Dishong, the assistant maintenance officer for the ship's F-14 squadron, agrees with his captain that if the ban is lifted, homosexuals should be berthed together. He worries, though, that putting them all together will provide too much of a symbolic, if not actual, target place for hate crimes.

"This is an emotional land mine," he says. "Racism, women in the military, drug and alcohol abuse are all emotional issues, but this tears at the moral fabric."

Working with, or even for, a gay person, he says, is not an issue. "It wouldn't bother me, as long as he was professional and didn't cross any lines."

As a matter of fact, Dishong feels confident any gay person could do his job just as well, or even possibly better, than he could. "You're talking about human talents, which doesn't have anything to do with sexual preference."

But where technical ability ends and the leadership responsibilities of an officer begin, "a gay person is going to have problems commanding authority—just like a woman, or black person or a Jew—anyone who is the target of discrimination."

Even though he thinks the ban does amount to discrimination, Dishong hopes the ban will remain in force. "This has nothing to do with my professional opinion. It has everything to do with my personal opinion. I think it's sinful behavior."

Over in the ship's five channel TV station control room, where entertainment videos, training tapes and the daily news are broadcast, Interior Communications Electrician First Class Tony Woods wonders why this needs to be brought up now.

"We have bigger problems," he says. "It just seems a little esoteric to me."

Like many on board, Woods suspects there are plenty of gays in the Navy already. Lifting the ban, he says, will just make it legal.

The core of the issue, however, he says he can identify with. An African-American, Woods has been named Kitty Hawk's Sailor of the Year.

"This is about equal rights," he says. "It's about a certain minority of people being able to serve freely in the military."

In principle, he agrees completely with lifting the ban. But like so many others, "it's the practical application that bothers me."

In the officer's mess, Airman Josh Black counts the days until he's through with mandatory temporarily assigned duty and is up on the flight deck buckling pilots into their planes and doing what he joined the Navy for.

In the few weeks he's been aboard the Kitty Hawk, Black has been amazed at how fast he's grown up. "It's a hard life. I never thought I'd appreciate my Mom and Dad so much," he says.

"THEY CAN LIVE THEIR LIFE"

The gay issue doesn't bother him at all though. "They can live their life" he says. "As long as they don't bother me, I'm fine with it. People are different. That's what life is all about."

He concedes, though, that he is in the minority with his level of acceptance. "What can I say? There are a lot of rednecks in the Navy."

Back in the squadron's ready room, Drummond is preparing for another late-night mission over Iraq. "You know, sometimes this job really sucks," he says with a half smile, "but for some reason we just keep coming back to it."

When it's all said and done, it's just a matter of "saluting smartly and saying 'aye, aye.' And if it ever gets to the point where I don't like my job anymore," he adds, "I'll just quit."[16]

READING 3

SURVEY SAYS? . . . DON'T LIFT GAY BAN

Bernard Adelsberger

WASHINGTON—Two researchers are trying to inject science into the debate over gays in the military: The pair are surveying military people to gauge how they would feel about a change in the current policy, which bars homosexuals from serving in the U.S. armed forces.

Nearly 1,000 Army soldiers took part in the survey at two posts in December, and their response was not surprising.

Roughly eight in 10 men and almost half the women surveyed opposed lifting the gay ban.

The survey was conducted by Charles Moskos and Laura Miller, sociologists at Northwestern University in Evanston, Ill.

The total negative response—those who disagreed or strongly disagreed with lifting the ban on gays—was 78 percent of the men and 47 percent of the women. About two-thirds of the men and one-third of the women were strongly opposed to lifting the ban.

"The basic finding is that opposition, especially among men, is quite widespread and strong," Moskos said.

Agreeing or strongly agreeing with lifting the ban were 43 percent of the women and 17 percent of the men.

---

[16]*Navy Times*, March 8, 1993, p. 8.

The soldiers were not selected randomly, Moskos said. However, they were representative in race, age and rank. Men and women were represented equally, although women make up about 12 percent of the Army.

There were some surprises in the results, Moskos said. For one, more senior soldiers were less likely to oppose lifting the ban. "There was greater [negative] reaction at the E-4 level [corporal and specialist] than at the senior NCO and officer end," Moskos said.

The differences between men and women and between junior enlisteds and more senior service members could be due to how those populations would have to interact with gays if the ban were lifted, Moskos said. Women don't serve in combat arms units, which involve close contact between soldiers. And junior enlisted soldiers are much more likely than senior members to live in barracks.

Another surprise: Military people appear to be far less accepting of homosexuals now than they were of accepting blacks in 1948, when the Army was integrated. An Army survey during the Korean War found only 33 percent of 195 white infantrymen objected strongly to serving in a racially integrated platoon.

"There is more opposition to gays in the liberated '90s than there was to blacks in the 1950s," Moskos said.[17]

READING 4

GAYS AND THE MILITARY

Ellen Goodman

If you want a hint of what the military is going to face when it lifts the ban on gays in the military, follow me. Come on over here and reach into my mailbag.

What They Think

In a survey by Northwestern University sociologists, 474 male and 472 female soldiers were asked for their reaction to the statement, "Lesbians and gays should be allowed to enter and remain in the military." Their response:

	Men	Women
Strongly agree	7%	17%
Agree	10%	26%
Not sure	5%	10%
Disagree	11%	12%
Strongly disagree	67%	35%

---

[17]*Navy Times*, March 8, 1993, p. 9.

First, may I suggest that you put on a glove. Or grab a set of tongs. Some of the letters I've gotten about gays are too slimy for the naked touch.

But put aside those wonderful missiles which come regularly to every journalist from that far-flung family of foul-mouthed misanthropes who share the same name—Anonymous. There's still some pretty interesting reading. "Interesting" is putting it mildly, and neutrally.

For openers, nine out of every 10 letters I received on this subject when I last wrote about it came from men. Virtually all of the letters *from* men were *about* men. Relatively few people who wrote about gay women worried that they would get too high, but the legions who opposed gay men wanted to keep them from getting too close.

The specter of showers and barracks came up so often in my correspondence that I suspect the Army spends more time in the sack than in the trenches, more time under the water than under the gun.

A military man from Cape Coral, Fla., wrote, "This tells me as a straight man showering in the barracks, that I have no choice but to expose myself to any gay men present."

A man from Apache Junction, Ariz., who spent three years overseas in World War II, remembers sleeping 40 men to a barracks. "Now suppose," he writes, "that neighbor was a man with the sexual inclinations of a woman, i.e., a homosexual."

Yet another man, this one from Tobyhanna, Pa., asked us to "imagine putting a homosexual in a community shower with 60 or so naked men."

The fascinating thing to this—female—reader was that nearly all the letter writers shared the same perspective: that of straight men worrying about being victims of sexual assault, harassment, lusting or just plain ogling. This garden variety homophobia—fear of homosexuals—was fear of becoming the object of unwanted sexual attention. Being the oglee instead of, say, the ogler.

It's the closest that most men may come to imagining the everyday real-life experiences of women. The closest they may come to imagining a trip past a construction site, unease in a fraternity house, fear that a date could become date rape. In short, the closest men come to worrying about male sexual aggression.

A writer from Idaho put it in this rather charming vernacular, "Some of the gays are not little pansy guys but big hulking guys, and if a small man said no, what is to stop him?"

I am sure that gay men and women do make some wrong passes at Mr. or Ms. Straight. I suspect this happens more often in a closeted atmosphere when communication is reduced to a secretive system of readings and misreadings.

There are instances of assault and harassment by homosexuals. There are also daily assaults of homosexuals. Consider the alleged gay-bashing-to-death of Seaman Allen Schindler a month after he told the Navy he was gay.

But—back to the barracks—if showers are such a charged venue, barracks such a threatening situation, how come the problem hasn't already wrecked morale and created dissension in the ranks? How come it's come up so rarely?

After all, between 5 percent and 10 percent of the military is estimated to be gay right now. The lifting of the 10-year-old ban on homosexuality would allow these men and women to acknowledge that they are homosexual without being dismissed.

It wouldn't mean that a straight man would be showering with a gay for the first time. It might mean that he would *know* for the first time.

Finally, the military has every right to make rules about sexual behavior. It can enforce any sort of sexual prohibition or aggression, from a shipmate's "incest taboo" to harassment to ogling in the shower. There is and should be a clear distinction between sexual behavior and sexual orientation. A difference between what we do and what we are:

And by the way, dear writers, wouldn't it be something if the military finally cracked down on sexual misbehavior because men were worrying about men?[18]

READING 5

"OUTED" BY THE ARMY: ONE SOLDIER'S STORY

Zsa Zsa Gershick

Austin

Captain Brenda Hammer was everything the Army could want in a soldier. Assertive, confident, and capable, the 30-year-old company commander loved the spit and polish of the service and considered herself a "lifer." Then the Army heard a rumor that she was a lesbian. Tipped off by a disgruntled enlistee to whom Hammer had given a less-than-favorable work evaluation, agents of the Army's Central Intelligence Division (CID) arrested Hammer in full view of her troops and led her away in handcuffs. Without so much as a photograph, a letter or an eyewitness account to support their suspicions, CID agents charged her with lewd and lascivious acts, conduct unbecoming an officer and fraternization. They threatened to send her to Fort Leavenworth Prison if she didn't supply the names of other lesbians.

No matter how they sweated her, she wouldn't name names. Four months later, a spotless service record notwithstanding, Hammer was out of the Army. "I felt lower than life," said Hammer, now 40 and a counselor with the Austin Independent School District. "I was very angry at the world, at life, at myself. I was angry the most because I didn't come out. And I've lived with this for the last 10 years. Why didn't I have the guts to stand up and say, 'Yes, I am gay, and there's nothing wrong with me!' I still have nightmares. I'll wake up and I'll have been dreaming that I was back in the military, back in Germany, living through the humiliation again," she said. Hammer's tale of harassment and intimidation is not an unusual one. Over the last decade, the armed forces have investigated, identified and dismissed nearly 17,000 gays and lesbians. According to Department of Defense regulations, gay men and lesbians are prohibited from serving in the military. This rule, which President Clinton has promised to rescind with an executive order, is backed by Article 125 of the Uniform Code of Military Justice. Article 125 expressly prohibits homosexuals from serving in the military and can be struck down only with the approval of Congress.

---

[18]*Dallas Morning News*, January 26, 1993, p. 11-A.

Hammer got her first taste of the Army in 1975, when a Women's Army Corps (WAC) recruiter visited Ball State University in Muncie, Ind., looking for officer candidates. After completing a summer-long boot camp, Hammer qualified for officer training, and when she graduated from college with a bachelor's degree in physical education, she was sent to Fort McClellan, Alabama, for three months of Officer's Basic Training. "I fell in love with the WAC," said Hammer, whose voice still has the strident ring of a platoon leader. "I knew I was gay at the time, but I didn't know there were other gay women in the Army. It wasn't until much later that I learned that. I was deeply in the closet, and so was everybody else. We didn't talk about it because we were afraid. We liked the Army so much. We wanted to stay in, and we didn't want to take a chance on anything spoiling it." Oddly enough, it is not inefficiency, insubordination or inequity that spoils the careers of many lesbians in the Army. Instead, the problem is very often softball. Yes, softball. Settling into her first duty assignment as a recreation services officer at Fort Hood in 1976, Hammer, then a second lieutenant, said she was first investigated by CID because she played slow-pitch softball. "CID investigates every woman who plays softball. They reason that you're obviously a lesbian if you're athletic," said Hammer. "The minute I signed up someone told me, 'You're going to be investigated now!' I heard that a number of times at Fort Hood, but I was never confronted by CID." After the years at Fort Hood, Hammer was sent to Germany in 1979 and became the personnel officer for the Army's Eighth Infantry Division. She was later promoted to captain and became the company commander of the regional personnel center.

Although she had earned numerous citations including the Army Com-mendation Medal, she was well-respected by superiors and subordinates alike, Hammer's athletic activities continued to arouse the suspicions of CID agents. "I was coaching women's softball, and we were under scrutiny a lot. CID was always watching us, investigating everyone on the team," said Hammer. "It was all very secretive. You could never turn your back; you were always afraid that someone was out looking at who you were with and taking notes." Then in 1982 Hammer learned that she was about to be investigated for more than coaching the softball team. She had been alerted by a friend in CID—a closet lesbian—that her name had been given with four other lesbians under investigation. One, striking a vindictive blow, had turned Hammer in because Hammer, as company commander had given her an unsatisfactory evaluation. And then it happened. Early one morning, three burly CID men marched into Hammer's office and arrested her in front of her staff. Hammer was mortified. "They wanted to handcuff me to take me out to the car. Here are these three big men, and they want to handcuff me because I'm a lesbian. I'm going to do something terrible, you know," said Hammer. "CID went through all my papers, and when they went through my desk, I kept thinking, 'I hope they don't go through the trunk of my car!' They would have really hit the jackpot. I was hiding a copy of *The Joy of Lesbian Sex* for a friend of mine who was afraid to keep it in the barracks," she added. Hammer was then whisked off to CID headquarters where she was placed beneath a bright light and asked repeatedly about her sexuality. She was warned that she was facing prison time, and she was asked to name other lesbians. Hammer refused to give them anything.

"It was the classic 'Let's See How Much Stress We Can Put On This Woman' situation," said Hammer. They'd say, 'We have information that you're a lesbian.' I'd say, 'Oh, that's interesting.' I refused to answer their questions. They had a light in my face, and I was seated in a little room with a chair and a table and nothing else. It was just like the movies, and I felt so damned isolated," she said. Hammer's unwillingness to name names was appreciated by her friends, many of whom were spared guilt-by-association investigations. But according to Tanya Domi, legislative director of the Gay, Lesbian, Bisexual Veteran's Association (GLBVA) in Washington, D.C., such resolve is uncommon. "When witch hunts start, people freak out. Sometimes there's a rush to confess and point fingers," said Domi, a former Army captain who, as a company commander at Schofield Barracks, Hawaii, was investigated as a lesbian after a male officer she refused to date gave her name to CID. "Investigators need very little proof to drag someone in," said Domi, who was en route to West Point and a coveted teaching position when she elected to leave the Army in 1990. "They don't need photos or letters. It can be strictly hearsay. I was a single woman, nearly a nun. There was nothing going on, and I was getting into this kind of trouble? I began to re-evaluate my life. Being in the Army just wasn't worth enduring that kind of homophobia."

According to the General Accounting Office (GAO), the Congressional auditing agency, . . . training replacements for dismissed lesbians and gay men annually costs taxpayers at least $27 million. While she was being investigated, Hammer was relieved of her command and forced to undergo psychiatric examinations. One month prior to the inquisition, Hammer had received an officer evaluation report that listed her work, conduct, and leadership as "excellent." That evaluation was rescinded and replaced with a report that rated her below average. "I had a copy of the original and a copy of the one they later redid," said Hammer, who holds a master's degree in counseling from Indiana's Ball State University. "They rewrote the report as a way to justify their actions." In the end, on the advice of her lawyer, Hammer wrote a 10-page statement admitting that she'd had a lesbian affair prior to her military service, but conceding to nothing after that. CID had dug up hotel and airfare receipts showing that Hammer had flown in her lover, an Army sergeant, to Germany and had gone on holiday with her. Hammer's lover was called in for questioning, but managed to stay in the service. Hammer was not so lucky. In November 1982 she received a less-than-honorable discharge and Uncle Sam showed her the door. One of the things that hurt her most, said Hammer, was the way that colleagues and friends failed to support her during the four-month ordeal. "The people I worked with said, 'Brenda, we're so sorry that this is happening to you. You don't deserve this. But on the other hand, this is CID and this is what they think should happen.' The commanding general even went along with it, even though we knew each other and he thought that I was a good soldier. He didn't want to put his neck on the line," said Hammer. "One special friend, a woman I had once been in a relationship with, told me to stay the hell away from her, that she never wanted to see me again. I know that she was worried about guilt by association, but that hurt a lot," she added.

According to a report the GAO issued last June, women in the service are more likely than men to be investigated for homosexuality. Though women made up just 10 percent of the armed services (200,000 out of two million troops), nearly a quarter of the people discharged for homosexuality during the 1980s were female. "I had male troops who were gay and had come out to me, and they never got harassed. Never. But the women would," said Hammer, recalling the Army dictum that the women in its ranks are either queers or whores. "Even the really nelly men got teased occasionally, but they never came under investigation like the women did. I mean, if you were a woman and you even looked butch, you were under investigation," added Hammer. "It was like the only job CID had was to investigate and purge the military of all the lesbians."

Domi concurred. "The stereotype of what a good soldier is, is what lesbians are: Assertive, aggressive, confident, commanding. Most of the lesbians I knew were terrific soldiers," said Domi. "We're everything the Army wants in terms of a leader, and yet they don't want you to be that really because then that means you're a lesbian. It's the Catch-22 that women are always in."

Returning to the States embarrassed and embittered in November 1982, Hammer stayed with Army friends in Killeen before finding work as an elementary school teacher in neighboring Copperas Cove. When people asked why she'd left the service, she'd lie and say that she'd grown tired of the travel. She envied her friends who were still on active duty, and she feared that the whole ugly business of her investigation would haunt her stateside. "When I got my first teaching job there were a lot of military kids in my class, and I was really scared that I would have the child of one of my former people," said Hammer. "I was afraid they'd march into my classroom, raise hell, and say: 'I don't want that lesbian teaching my children!' I never had that experience. I did have some former soldiers who had their kids there, and they respected me and treated me very well."

Hammer is circumspect about her experiences in the service. The passage of a decade's time has done much to soften the blow that being booted out of the service was to a young gung-ho trooper. Therapy and a renewed spirituality have helped Hammer to accept what happened to her. "I was happy with my job, but I wasn't happy about being closeted all the time, worrying about what was going to happen," said Hammer. "I had thought about getting out, but then I'd think, no, this is my security base. I've done this for eight years, just stay in. What's another 12 years; you've got retirement. And I think my higher power was saying, okay Brenda, it's time to go. This may not be the best way to take it, but this is going to be your lesson. . . ."

Hammer is not optimistic about the fate of gay men and lesbians in the service. Even if Clinton succeeds in fulfilling his campaign promise to rescind DOD regulations banning homosexuals from the military, she said, fear and loathing of lesbians and gay men is deeply entrenched. "I think Clinton's move to lift the ban is outstanding, and it's about time," said Hammer. "But at the same time, I don't think it's going to be safe to come out immediately. This is something that's going to take time."[19]

---

[19]*Texas Observer*, February 12, 1993, pp. 10–11.

READING 6

MILITARY DOCTOR DISPUTES ONE REASON FOR GAY BAN

Eric Schmitt

Dismissing an argument used by those who oppose homosexuals in the military, the Pentagon's senior medical official says that sexual orientation is not a health issue that should be considered in the debate about gay men and lesbians in the armed services.

The official, Dr. Edward D. Martin, the Acting Assistant Secretary of Defense for Health Affairs, said in an internal memorandum that "homosexuality, per se, cannot scientifically be characterized as a medical issue," so Pentagon policies on homosexual or heterosexual behavior should be based on "mission concerns and considerations."

If senior Pentagon policy makers adopt Dr. Martin's views, it would be a significant setback to supporters of the military's ban on homosexuals. The supporters contend that lifting the ban would increase the risk of sexually transmitted diseases, including AIDS, to heterosexual troops.

For example, the Commandant of the Marine Corps, Gen. Carl E. Mundy, Jr., last year endorsed a position paper written by a senior Marine chaplain that said, "One does not need a medical degree to recognize that admitting homosexuals into the military would bring about an increase in the number of AIDS cases and would put additional financial and personnel strains on military medicine."

Gay-rights groups say the medical fears are a bogus argument. They point out that recruits who test positive for H.I.V., the virus that causes AIDS, are barred from serving. Active duty personnel are tested annually or semi-annually for H.I.V. and are removed from combat units if they test positive.

In his March 30 memorandum to the civilian service secretaries, which was reported today by the *Washington Times*, Dr. Martin said his five-paragraph statement was an official response to requests about the health implications of allowing acknowledged homosexuals to serve in the military.

"We are not aware of any scientific evidence that individual sexual preferences, in and by themselves, be they homosexual, heterosexual or bisexual, affect work productivity, scholastic aptitude, disease incidence, medical costs or crime rate in the population at large," Dr. Martin said.

DEBATE AMONG COLLEAGUES

The remarks by Dr. Martin, a career Public Health Service official whose specialty is pediatrics, have stirred debate within the military's medical ranks, Pentagon officials said today.

"It's divided over here," one Navy medical official said. "Some people sympathize with his views, but a lot of medical people here think he's wrong. People were surprised he came out with that statement."

Dr. Martin declined through a Pentagon spokeswoman to be interviewed today, saying his statement spoke for itself.

Several months after President Clinton said he wanted to allow homosexuals in the military, the Defense Department recently formed a high-level panel, headed by Lieut. Gen. Robert M. Alexander of the Air Force, to study the practical effects of doing so. The panel is expected to examine several issues, including privacy considerations, housing arrangements, potential health risks and morale.[20]

3. READING AND WRITING ASSIGNMENT: READ TO WRITE

Read the essay "Gays and the Military" by Ellen Goodman on p. 133. Freewrite for five minutes in response to what you have just read. Do not summarize the article. Instead write what you are thinking as a result of having read it. Are there ideas in this freewriting that you could use in a single-perspective argument paper in which you state your position on this issue and defend it? Underline two or three possibilities for a claim in your freewrite.

4. WRITING ASSIGNMENT: YOUR WRITING PROCESS

Write a description and self-evaluation of your present process for writing argument. What strategies from this chapter might you add? What might you reject? Why? Limit yourself to two pages or 500–600 words.

5. INDIVIDUAL ONGOING PROJECT: EXPLORATORY PAPER AND PAPER PROPOSAL ON YOUR ISSUE

a. Review all of the material you have gathered about your issue, and also read the articles that pertain to it in "The Reader." Do additional library research for this paper if you need to. Read pages 291–299 in Chapter 9 to help you with library research.

b. Identify and summarize the different positions and perspectives on your issue. Include at least three positions: for, against, in the middle. Include more positions and perspectives than these three if you can.

c. Write a three-page double-spaced exploratory paper in which you explain your issue, describe its rhetorical situation, and summarize the different positions on it along with some reasons for the validity of each position.

d. Conclude by explaining your interest in the issue. Then make a claim and indicate how you will develop it in a single-perspective argument paper.

e. The following is an example of an exploratory paper with a proposal for a single-perspective paper at the end. It was written by a student in an argument class, Tanya Pierce. Her single-perspective argument paper on the same subject appears at the end of Chapter 10 on pages 338–342.

---

[20]*New York Times*, National, April 10, 1993.

EXPLORATORY PAPER

TRIAL BY JURY, A FUNDAMENTAL RIGHT AND A FLAWED SYSTEM

Tanya Pierce

The right to a trial by jury is a fundamental part of the United States legal system. It is a right firmly entrenched in our democratic tradition. The jury system provides a buffer between the complex and often inflexible legal system and the average citizen on trial. The right to be judged by a jury of one's peers is a right that most Americans feel very strongly about. However, due to recent jury decisions, some critics are questioning the value of this institution.

Our jury system is by no means flawless. It is subject to constant scrutiny and debate concerning its merit and its downfalls. As is true in all institutions, juries are capable of making mistakes. Psychological studies have been done on many aspects of jury behavior. Political scientists are also intrigued by juries and the manner in which they arrive at important decisions. Although I believe most Americans believe in the jury system, there has been considerable controversy surrounding it lately. The public has become even more concerned about this institution recently. The outcome of the Rodney King trial in Los Angeles and the destructive outrage that followed the jury's decision is just one example of an instance when the effectiveness of the jury system has come under fierce attack. From the public reaction to that decision and others like it, it is very clear that the way in which juries reach their decisions is often as important to the American people as it is to the specific person on trial. Many people feel that the average jurist is not equipped to make the kinds of decisions they are faced with. These critics' suggestions range from restructuring the system to totally eliminating it.

Most average Americans, I believe, feel that the right to a jury trial is a fundamental one, and its guarantees should be honored. These people would argue that laws are inflexible. Statutes cannot deal with the individual circumstances in each case, but juries can take these

into account. Still others believe that juries are favorable because
they reflect the morals and values of the community they come from.
Indeed, many proponents of the jury support the system because of a
particular kind of jury bias, the tendency for jurors to place justice
above the law (Goldberg 457).

Opponents of the system argue that juries are uneducated in legal
procedures and should not be given the type of responsibility they have
traditionally had. These people also argue that juries are biased. In
fact, the psychological literature provides many examples of this bias.
Jurors are less likely to punish a sad or distressed defendant, as opposed to a joyful one, apparently because the defendant is already
being punished emotionally (Upshaw and Romer 162). Some opponents say
that although juries are instructed not to pay attention to the media,
they are more easily influenced by the news than judges. Critics of the
jury system also point out that juries are expensive and are often unable to reach a consensus. They argue that the decision making should
be left up to the people who know the law, judges and lawyers.

In between these two extremes are those people who agree with the
jury system as a whole, but feel that some changes need to be implemented
to improve its effectiveness. These people suggest that juries receive
instruction prior to hearing testimony as well as before they begin deliberations. They argue that this would improve the system by providing
some working legal knowledge for the jury as well as giving them an idea
of what they are to listen for. Research has shown that in laboratory
mock jury situations, exposing jurors to the laws involved in their decision making resulted in significantly fewer verdicts of guilty compared
to not exposing jurors to the relevant laws (Cruse and Browne 131). This
finding suggests that lawyers and judges should have the responsibility
of insuring that the jury is adequately informed of the legal issues at
hand and the laws and statutes available to handle those issues.

As a prospective law student, I am fascinated by this topic. I think
it is incredible that juries, made up of ordinary citizens, make some of
the most profound legal decisions in the world. I decided to write on
this particular issue because of recent events such as the Rodney King

verdict and the verdict in the Broskey case in Fort Worth. These examples force me to evaluate the positive and negative aspects of jury trials. The rise in crime in this country and the question of what to do with the offenders makes the role of juries even more interesting. As a whole, though, I feel that the American guarantee of trial by jury is a valuable one. I do feel, however, that in order to improve its utility, judges and attorneys need to accept the responsibility for educating the jury on relevant legal issues. That is my claim. I will define the problem in detail and then explain how my solution of jury training can be implemented.[21]

Works Cited

Cruse, Donna, and Beverly A. Brown. "Reasoning in a Jury Trial: The Influence of Instructions." <u>Journal of General Psychology</u> 114 (1987): 129–133.

Goldberg, Janice C. "Memory, Magic, and Myth: The Timing of Jury Instructions." <u>Oregon Law Review</u> 59 (1981): 451–475.

Upshaw, Harry S., and Daniel Romer. "Punishments of One's Misdeeds as a Function of Having Suffered from Them." <u>Personality and Social Psychology Bulletin</u> 2 (1976): 162–169.

6. UNDERSTANDING THE CHAPTER: WHOLE CLASS, GROUP, OR INDIVIDUALS

Summarize the major ideas in the chapter by completing the following sentences briefly and in your own words:

a. Some benefits of including reading as part of the writing process are . . .
b. When writers get organized to write, they make decisions about . . .
c. The rhetorical situation can be used by a writer to help analyze . . .
d. Some prewriting strategies I like to use are . . .
e. I like to write my first draft by . . .
f. When I get stuck with my writing, I . . .
g. To rewrite and prepare my paper for a reader, I . . .

---

[21]Used by permission.

PART TWO

Understanding the Nature of Argument for Reading and Writing

Chapter 5 identifies and explains the parts of an argument, Chapter 6, presents the proofs for argument, and Chapter 7 describes the types of claims and purposes in argument. Proofs are discussed before claims because certain types of proofs are particularly appropriate for developing certain types of claims, and an initial understanding of proofs helps you understand the claims. Part Two ends with an assignment that synthesizes the critical reading and writing strategies taught in Chapters 1–7. When you finish reading Part Two:

- You will understand and be able to identify the essential parts of an argument.
- You will understand how argument can appeal to your reason, your emotion, and your sense of values about people's character in order to be convincing.
- You will know the major ways for developing the ideas in an argument and for making them convincing.
- You will know the key questions that arguments attempt to answer.
- You will be able to identify types of claims and purpose in argument.
- You will have acquired additional strategies for reading and writing argument.
- You will have experience with another major type of argument paper: the critical analysis paper.

CHAPTER 5

The Essential Parts of an Argument

The purpose of this and the next two chapters is to present some ideas from argument theory that will help you add additional strategies for reading and writing argument with confidence and expertise. Because people have been analyzing argument and writing theories of argument for 2,500 years, there is a considerable tradition of theory to draw on to help with this task. A theoretical background is useful because theory describes argument, and once you possess good descriptions, argument will be more familiar and consequently easier for you to read and write yourself.

As you work to acquire new understanding of argument, you will be adding to what you already know and gradually building a stronger and larger body of knowledge and understanding. Eventually, you will achieve "all-at-onceness," a quality Ann E. Berthoff describes in her book *The Sense of Learning* to describe the use of many ideas, bits of information, and strategies about reading and writing that finally come together so that you are able to use them unconsciously, simultaneously, and automatically.[1]

For now, however, you are still expanding your knowledge. Your goals in this chapter will be to get a better understanding of the usual anticipated outcomes of argument and to identify its component parts as they are identified by Stephen Toulmin in his model for argument.

THE OUTCOMES OF ARGUMENT: PROBABILITY VERSUS CERTAINTY

In Chapter 1 you learned that arguable issues require the possibility of at least two different views. It is the nature of argument to invite differing views and perspectives on issues. Outcomes can include achieving a closer agreement with a friendly

---

[1] Ann E. Berthoff, *The Sense of Learning* (Portsmouth, NH: Boynton/Cook, 1990), pp. 86–91.

audience or getting the attention and even perhaps some consensus from a neutral or hostile audience. Notice that these outcomes of argument are usually not described as establishing certainty or truth in the same sense that mathematics and science seek to establish certainty and truth. We do not argue about the fact that $2 + 3 = 5$ or that the area of a circle is πr^2. Mathematical proofs seek to establish such truths. Argument seeks to establish what is probably true as well as what might be expedient or desirable for the future. Arguers tell you what they think for now along with what they think should be done, given their present information. On that basis, you decide what you think for now, given your present information.

Throughout history, some thinkers have been drawn more to the idea of establishing truth and some have been drawn more to the idea of establishing probabilities. In ancient times the Greek philosopher Plato was interested in establishing truth. He employed dialectic, the question-and-answer method used in his dialogues, to help participants discover the Platonic ideas about truth. Aristotle, another Greek philosopher, was interested in probabilities. His *Rhetoric*, written somewhere between 360 and 334 B.C., is a key book in the history of argument theory, and its purpose is to train persuasive speakers to be convincing to audiences. Aristotle observed the orators of his time and described what they did. He noted that they were mainly concerned with matters and views concerning both the present and the future that were probably true instead of certainly true. The reason for their perspective lay in the audience. The ancient audience, like modern audiences, would disagree with many views that were stated as absolutely true. Those audiences could think of exceptions and reasons why certain views might not be true. Responsible persuaders, to communicate effectively, had to modify and qualify their views in order to make them acceptable to their audiences. They had to present probabilities instead of absolute truths. Thus views that are probably true comprise the realm of argument. To understand that realm better, it is useful to understand the parts that contribute to the whole argument.

THE PARTS OF AN ARGUMENT ACCORDING TO THE TOULMIN MODEL

Stephen Toulmin, a modern English philosopher, developed a six-part model of argument in his book *The Uses of Argument*, and this model has been useful to many people for explaining the essential parts of an argument.[2] At the time Toulmin wrote his book, his colleagues were logicians who were interested in discovering truth rather than probabilities. Toulmin tells us that his book had a chilly welcome among those English colleagues. His graduate adviser at Cambridge, he tells us, "was deeply pained by the book, and barely spoke to me for twenty years." Another colleague described it as "Toulmin's *anti*-logic book."[3] After that, Toulmin expected

---

[2]Stephen Toulmin, *The Uses of Argument* (Cambridge: Cambridge University Press, 1958). I have adapted and added applications of the model to make it more useful for reading and writing.

[3]"Logic and the Criticism of Arguments," in James L. Golden, Goodwin F. Berquist, and William E. Coleman, *The Rhetoric of Western Thought*, 4th ed. (Dubuque, IA: Kendall Hunt, 1989), p. 375.

his book to be a failure. But his editors assured him that people were buying it, and Toulmin found out who many of these people were when he visited the United States some time later. Professors in speech departments and departments of communication all over the United States were using his book to teach students to become better argumentative speakers. If you have ever taken a speech class, you may have already encountered the Toulmin model of argument. As time went by, the model was picked up by English departments to help students improve their reading and writing of argument. The Toulmin model has also been used in schools of law to help students learn to present legal argument. The Toulmin model is a very natural and practical model because it follows normal human thought processes. You will find that you have had experience with all its parts either in the everyday argument you carry on with your friends and family or in the arguments that you see on television.

The Toulmin model has six parts. The first three parts are essential to all argument. They include (1) the *claim*, (2) the *data* (which we are calling *support*), and (3) the *warrant*. Arguments may also contain one or more of three additional elements: (4) the *backing*, (5) the *rebuttal*, and (6) the *qualifier*. Figure 5.1 shows Toulmin's diagram of these three essential parts along with the three optional parts of the model.

Here is an example to illustrate how these parts work together in an actual argument: The narrator of a television program makes the *claim* that critical thinking is more important now than it was 60 years ago. This is followed by *support* that includes pictures of modern scientists launching space shuttles and air traffic controllers directing airplanes to land. These individuals seem intent and busy. It appears to be clear that if they do not think critically, there will be trouble. Then the camera switches to children riding on an old-fashioned school bus of 60 years ago. One is saying that he wants to grow up and be a farmer like his dad. This youngster is relaxed and bouncing along on the bus. He doesn't look like he is thinking critically or that he will ever need to. The unspoken part of this argument, the assumption that the author of this program hopes the audience will share, is the *warrant*. The author hopes the audience will agree, even though it is not explicitly stated, that farmers of 60 years ago did not have to think critically, that modern scientists

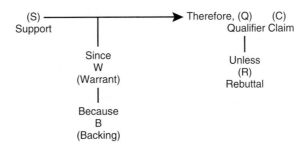

Figure 5.1 A Diagram of the Three Essential Parts of Toulmin's Model of Argument: Claim, Support, and Warrant; and the Three Optional Parts: Backing, Rebuttal, and Qualifier. From Stephen Toulmin, *The Uses of Argument* (Cambridge: Cambridge University Press, 1958), p. 104.

and engineers do have to think critically, and that critical thinking was not so important then as now. The author hopes that the audience will look at the two bits of support, the scientist and the farmer's son, and make the leap necessary to accept the claim. That's right, the audience will think, those scientists and that young boy don't seem to share the same demands for critical thinking. Times have changed. Critical thinking *is* more important now than it was 60 years ago. Those three parts, the *claim*, the *support* and the *warrant*, are the three essential parts of an argument.

The other three parts, if present, might go like this: Suppose the camera then shifts to an old man who says, "Wait a minute. What makes you assume farmers didn't think? My daddy was a farmer, and he was the best critical thinker I ever knew. He had to think about weather, crops, growing seasons, fertilizer, finances, harvesting, and selling the crops. The thinking he had to do was as sophisticated as that of any modern scientist." This old fellow is indicating that he does not share the unstated warrant that farmers of 60 years ago had fewer demands on their thinking processes than modern scientists. In response to this rejoinder, the author, to make the argument convincing, provides *backing for the warrant*. This backing takes the form of additional support. The camera cuts to the narrator of the program: "At least two out of three of the farmers of 60 years ago had small farms. They grew food for their families and traded or sold the rest for whatever else they needed. The thinking and decision making required of them was not as complicated and demanding as that required by modern scientists. Your father was an exception." Notice that this backing takes the form of a smaller unit of argument within the argument. It is linked to the main argument, and it is used to back up the weakest part of the main argument. Furthermore, this smaller argument has a claim–support–warrant structure of its own: (1) the *claim* is that most farmers did not have to think; (2) the *support* is that two out of three did not have to think and that the old man's father was an exception; and (3) the *warrant*, again unstated, is that the old man will believe the statistics and accept the idea that his father was an exception. If he accepts this backing, the argument is on solid ground again. If he does not, if he asks for more backing for the new warrant by asking, "Hey, where did you get those statistics? They're not like any I ever heard," then another argument would need to be developed to cite the source of the figures and to convince the old man of their reliability. As you can see, the requests for backing, for more information to serve as further proof, can go on and on. But let's leave the old man and the narrator and look at what else might appear in this argument.

Suppose the camera now shifts to a modern science professor who wants to take exception with the claim itself by making a *rebuttal*. She makes her own claim, "The critical thinking required 60 years ago was demanding and sophisticated. Critical thinkers of that time had to figure out how to get the country out of a severe recession, and they had to develop the technology to win the Second World War." These opinions are then supported with factual evidence that includes pictures of individuals thinking.

After all of these challenges, exceptions, and requests for more information, the author at this point finds it necessary to *qualify* the original claim in order to make it acceptable to more of the audience members. He restates the qualified claim, "Critical

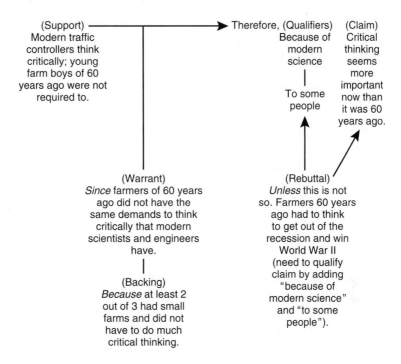

Figure 5.2 A Diagram of the Six Elements in the Toulmin Model

thinking, because of modern science, seems to some people to be more important now than it was 60 years ago." Compare this with the original claim that critical thinking is more important now than it was 60 years ago. Figure 5.2 provides a diagram of this argument laid out according to the Toulmin model. You have probably never systematically used this or any other model to read or write argument. The model can serve as a kind of guide for reading and analyzing arguments and also for writing them. Authors do not usually use the model as an exact formula for writing, however. Rather, it describes what can be but not necessarily always is present in an argument. Consequently, when you read argument, you will at times easily locate some parts of the model and at other times you will not. Some arguments, in fact, may not contain one or more of the parts at all, like a rebuttal, for example. You are not getting it wrong if you read and do not find all of the parts. When you write, you do not need to make all parts explicit either. The following sections provide some details about each of the six parts that will help you understand them better.

Claim

Discover the claim of an argument by asking the question, What is this author trying to prove? Or plan a claim of your own by asking, What do I want to prove? The claim is the main point of the argument. Locating or identifying the claim as soon as possible helps you focus on what the argument is all about.

Synonyms for *claim* are *thesis*, *proposition*, *conclusion*, and *main point*. Sometimes an author of an argument in a newspaper or magazine will refer to "the proposition," or an individual arguing on television will ask, "What is your point?" They both are referring to the claim. When someone refers to the claim as the conclusion, don't confuse it with the conclusion, or final idea at the end of an argument. The claim can appear at the end, but it can also appear other places in the argument. The claim is sometimes stated in a sentence or sentences called the *statement of claim*. This sentence can also be called the *thesis statement*, the *purpose sentence*, the *statement of focus*, or the *statement of proposition*.

The terms used in this text to describe the main elements in argument along with some of their synonyms appear in Table 5.1. Become familiar with them so that you will understand other writers on the subject who may vary the terminology.

To locate the claim, what should you look for? The claim may be explicitly stated at the beginning of an argument, at the end, or even somewhere in the middle. Or, it may not be stated anywhere. It may sometimes be *implied*, in which case you will be expected to *infer* it. To infer an implicit claim, you will need to use what you already know about the subject along with what you have just read to formulate your own statement of it. In this case, the author is paying you a kind of compliment. The assumption is that you are smart enough to figure out the claim for yourself. You should probably make your own claims in your written arguments clear and explicit, however, at least at first.

Another interesting variation on the claim occurs in the case of irony. In irony the author says one thing but means something else. Usually the stated claim in irony is exaggerated, outrageous, or odd in some way. You may read it and think to yourself, "Surely the author doesn't *mean* this." The questions to ask at this point are "What does the author say?" and "What does the author really mean?" Again, you are expected to use your background and judgment to figure out what the author really means. Roberta Borkat in her essay "A Liberating Curriculum" (p. 421 in "The Reader") claims that she has decided to give all of her college students A's, but this assertion is not what she actually means. She uses this exaggerated ironic claim to get her audience's attention in hopes that they will pay more attention to the problems of grade inflation. This author says one thing but means something else.

The claim, whether implied or explicitly stated, organizes the entire argument, and everything else in the argument is related to it. The best way to identify it, if it is not obvious or easy to locate, is to complete the following statement as soon as you have finished reading: "This author wants to convince me to think that . . ." When you have finished that statement, you have the claim. As a writer, you can check your own claim during revision by completing this statement: "I have convinced my audience to think that . . ."

Authors often make conscious decisions about where to place a claim and whether to make it explicit or implicit. Their decisions are related to their notions about the audience. A claim at the beginning is straightforward and draws the reader in right away, like the claim in "Some College Costs Should Be Tax Deductible" (p. 21). Both parties are thinking along the same lines, together, from

TABLE 5.1   Argument Terms Used in This Book and Some of Their Synonyms

CLAIM	STATEMENT OF CLAIM	SUBCLAIMS	SUPPORT	WARRANTS
Thesis	Thesis statement	Reasons	Evidence	Assumptions
Proposition	Purpose sentence	Main ideas	Opinions	General principles
Conclusion	Statement of focus	Micro-arguments	Reasons	Widely held values
Main point	Statement of proposition	Arguments	Examples	Commonly accepted beliefs
Macro-argument		Lines of argument	Facts	Appeals to human motives
Controlling idea		Supporting arguments	Data	Cultural values
		Specific issues	Grounds	Presuppositions
			Proof	Unstated premises
			Premise	Generally accepted truths
			Statistics	
			Explanations	
			Information	
			Personal narratives	

the outset. Or an author may decide to lead up to the claim, in which case it may appear either in the middle or at the end. A delayed claim pulls the audience in even more and increases interest and attention, as in "We're Good Republicans—and Pro-Choice" (p. 22). "What is this author after?" the audience wonders, and reads to find out. The end of an essay is the most emphatic and memorable place for a claim. Many authors prefer to put the claim there to give it as much force as possible. There is some risk involved in putting the claim at the end. Students who use this strategy must be careful to cue their readers so that they understand where the argument is headed and do not feel they are being led through a random chain of topics. Both the unstated claim and the ironic claim require special attention on the part of the reader because, in these cases, the reader has to make an inference to figure them out. As a result of this effort, the reader may find an inferred claim especially convincing and memorable.

Argument, like any other discourse, has main ideas and ideas that support them, as was shown in Chapter 3. The claim is the main point of the entire piece, and the subclaims are the shorter supporting arguments or reasons for the claim. We will present two examples that illustrate the relationships among the issues, related issues, claims, and subclaims in argument. Included are the following:

1. **Two issue areas,** *racism* and the *environment*, that are at the most general level in these examples.
2. **Two of many possible specific related issues** in these issue areas that represent ideas *about* the general issue areas.
3. **Examples of claims** made in response to the specific related issues that are even more specific.
4. **Examples of some subclaims** used to support the claims. The subclaims are at the most specific level in this example because they represent ideas about the claims.

Example 1

Issue Area: Racism
Specific Related Issue: Where do racist attitudes come from?
  Claim: People are not born with racist attitudes; they have to be taught them.
    Subclaims: 1. Some parents transmit racist attitudes.
          2. The press can reinforce racist attitudes.
          3. Peer groups can also strengthen racist attitudes.
          4. Segregated schools and neighborhoods contribute to racist attitudes.

Example 2

Issue Area: The Environment
Specific Related Issue: How serious are the world's environmental problems?
  Claim: The environment is the single most serious problem the world faces today.

Subclaims: 1. The rain forests are being destroyed, causing global warming.
2. Increasing population is depleting resources in some parts of the world.
3. Many important water sources are being polluted by industry.
4. The ozone layer, which protects us from harmful sun rays, is being destroyed by chemicals.

Think for a moment about the two essays at the end of Chapter 1 that we have used as examples, "Some College Costs Should Be Tax Deductible" (p. 21) and "We're Good Republicans—and Pro-Choice" (p. 22). What are their claims? Complete these sentences: "The author of the essay about abortion wants me to believe that . . .," and, "The author of the essay about tuition and taxes wants me to believe that . . ." Can you do it? If you can, you understand the concept of the claim, and you will be able to recognize the main controlling idea in the arguments you read and also use one to develop your own arguments.

Support

Discover the support in an argument by asking, What additional information does the author supply to convince me of this claim? Or, if you are the author, ask, What information do I need to supply to convince my audience? You can summarize the most essential elements of an argument as a *claim with support*. Aristotle wrote in his textbook the *Rhetoric* that the only necessary parts of an argument are the statement of proposition (the claim) and the proof (the support). There has been general agreement about those two essential parts of an argument for more than 2,300 years.

Support provides the evidence, opinions, reasoning, examples, and factual information about a claim that make it possible for us to accept it. Look back at the claims and subclaims on page 152. If you are to take these claims seriously, you will want some support to make them convincing.

The synonyms that Toulmin uses for support are *data* and *grounds*, the English equivalents. In the United States you will often read arguments in which the author says he is "grounding" a claim with particular support, and "data" is sometimes used as a synonym for facts and figures. Other synonyms for support are *proof, evidence,* and *reasons.* Sometimes authors refer to major evidence as *premises.* When you encounter that term in your reading, remember that premises lead to and support a conclusion (a claim). Don't confuse premises with the claim.

To locate support, what should you look for? One bit of good news: support is always explicitly stated, so you will not have to infer it as you sometimes have to infer the claim. Thus an understanding of the types of support is all you really need to help you recognize it. Here are some of the most common types:

Facts. In a court of law, factual support (the murder weapon, for example) is laid out on the table. In written argument it must be described. Factual support can include detailed reports of *observed events*; specific *examples* of real happenings; references to *events*, either *historical* or *recent*; and *statistical reports*. Factual support is vivid, real, and verifiable. Two people looking at it together would agree on its existence and what it looks like. They might not agree on what it *means* to each of them. That is, they might interpret it differently, but essentially they would agree on the facts themselves.

Opinions.   When people start interpreting the facts, opinion enters the picture. The following quotation is an example of some statistics that have been interpreted. The author is a wildlife scientist who has studied wolves and other wild animals in Alaska for many years, and he is arguing against a plan by the state of Alaska to shoot wolves in order to protect herds of caribou.

> The state is portraying the wolf kill as an emergency measure to boost the size of what is called the "Delta caribou herd," which ranges east of Denali. But the herd's population decrease since 1989—from 11,000 to 4,000—represents little more than a return to the numbers that prevailed for decades until the mid-80's. The short-lived increase to 11,000 probably resulted largely from a temporary shift of caribou from a neighboring herd.
>
> The Delta herd didn't even exist until about 60 years ago; it is probably an offshoot of a much larger herd farther to the east. There is no major caribou-hunting tradition in this area, so the plan is not a matter of restoring something that hunters had enjoyed for generations. Over the past 12 months, most of the Delta herd has spent most of its time well outside the wolf-control area.
>
> In fact, the state's view that this and other caribou herds should be managed at stable or minimum sizes is a mistake. Virtually all of Alaska's caribou belong to a single population within which, over the span of decades, there are shifting centers of abundance. Thousands of caribou may abandon a range they have inhabited for decades and move to an area where numbers have traditionally been low. Despite recent declines in the Delta herd and in several nearby areas, other herds have increased dramatically. Statewide, the number of caribou has more than tripled over the past 15 years to about a million animals and is continuing to increase rapidly.[4]

Note that the raw data, the herd's decrease in numbers from 11,000 to 4,000, have been interpreted and explained. The author says the decrease in the caribou population has been caused by the herds moving around, and that actually there are now more caribou statewide than 15 years ago. Thus there is no need to slaughter wolves to protect caribou. State officials had interpreted the same data to indicate that wolves should be killed to save the caribou. You need to distinguish between facts everyone would agree on and interpret in the same way and facts that are open to interpretation and opinion. We do not argue with the facts, as the saying goes, unless of course they are lies or they omit important information. We do, however, argue with interpretation and opinion.

Opinions may be those of the author or those of an expert the author selects to quote. The quotes may be direct quotes, set off in quotation marks, or they may be summaries or paraphrases of what someone else thinks or has said. Furthermore, opinions may be informed, based on considerable knowledge and excellent judgment, or they may be ill-founded, based on hearsay and gossip. The most convincing opinions are those of experts, whether they be those of the author or of

---

[4]Excerpt from Gordon C. Haber, "The Great Alaska Wolf Kill," *New York Times*, October 2, 1993, Op-Ed. The entire text appears on page 165.

another person. Experts possess superior background, education, and experience on an issue. Contrast in your own mind the opinions of experts with the opinions of people on the evening news who are frequently cornered in the streets by reporters to give their opinions. The opinions of experts can be more interesting and convincing than the facts themselves. Ill-founded, baseless opinion, on the other hand, is boring and rarely convincing.

Examples. Examples can be real or made up, long or short. They are used to clarify, to make material more memorable and interesting, and, in argument particularly, to prove. Examples that are real, such as instances of actual events or references to particular individuals, function in the same way that fact does in an argument. They are convincing because they are grounded in reality. Made-up or hypothetical examples are invented by the writer and, like opinions, can only demonstrate probabilities. Personal experience is one type of example that is frequently used in argument. Writers often go into considerable detail about the experiences that have influenced them to think and behave as they do. A combination of personal experience and the opinions and reasoning that have resulted from it is a common way to develop a claim.

There are no set rules about the placement of support in an argument. Support can appear *before* the claim, as in the following example: "The caribou have moved around and are alive (the support); *therefore*, we do not need a wolf-kill policy (claim)." Or support can appear *after* the claim: "The wolf-kill policy should be abandoned (claim) *because* the caribou have moved around, and there are three times as many of them as 15 years ago (support)."

Different authors manage support in different ways depending on the requirements of the subject, their purpose, and their audience. When the issue is an abstract idea and the audience is informed, the author may present mainly opinions and few, if any, facts or examples. Such arguments include a claim and blocks of logical reasoning organized around subclaims to develop and prove the claim. If you were to outline the argument, you might not need more than two levels, as in the claim and subclaim examples on page 152. When the subject requires more specific support or the audience needs more information to be convinced, specific materials at lower levels on an outline are required to ground the subclaims in facts, figures, quotations from others, or author opinions.

Here is an example that illustrates these levels. It includes (1) a general issue area, (2) one of many specific issues that could be generated by it, (3) a claim, (4) some subclaims, and (5) some support.

Example

Issue Area: Cities

Specific Related Issue: How should cities be planned so that people will live happily in them?

   Claim: Inner cities can be made more inhabitable.

   Subclaim: One way is to omit automobiles and encourage walking.

Support: With no cars, people are forced to walk and interact, and inter-
acting is pleasant. (opinion)
Subclaim: Another way is to eliminate public housing projects.
Support: More than half the poor are often in public housing. (fact)
Support: Warehousing the poor is destructive to the neighborhood and
occupants. (opinion)[5]

To summarize, support comprises all the explicitly stated explanations, information, facts, opinions, personal narratives, and examples that authors use to
make their claims and subclaims convincing and believable. Notice that support
may be true, as in the case of facts and real examples, or probable, as in the case of
opinions and made-up stories and examples.

Readers and writers of argument should require that the support in an argument be acceptable and convincing. Factual evidence needs to be true and verifiable. All evidence needs to be clear, relevant, and understandable. It also should
represent all of the significant information available; it must, in other words, be an
adequate sample. The experts whose opinions are quoted should be experts, and
their credentials should when necessary be identified by the author to show their
degree of expertise. Personal opinion to be convincing should be original, impressive, interesting, and backed by factual knowledge, experience, good reasoning,
and judgment. Support that meets these requirements is not only accepted but is
often shared by the audience because they have had similar experiences and ideas
themselves. Such quality support helps build common ground between the arguer
and the audience. Rantings, unfounded personal opinions that no one else accepts,
or feeble reasons like "because I said so" or "because everyone does it" are not effective support. Audiences usually do not believe such statements, they do not
share experiences or ideas suggested by them, and they lose common ground with
the arguer when they read or hear them.

When reading argument, to help you focus on and recognize the support,
complete this sentence as soon as you finish. "The *author wants me to believe that* . . .
(the claim) *because* . . . (list the support)." Now, try to complete this sentence as applied to "Some College Costs Should Be Tax Deductible" and "We're Good
Republicans—and Pro-Choice" (Chapter 1): "The authors of the essay about abortion want me to believe that we need to consider more than two views on abortion
because . . .," and, "The author of the essay about tuition and taxes wants me to believe that the parts of tuition diverted for financial aid should be tax deductible
because . . ." If you can list and summarize the support in these essays, you understand it. When you read to revise your own writing, you can complete this statement: "I have convinced my audience to believe (the claim) because (list your
support)."

---

[5] Witold Rybczynski, "How to Rebuild Los Angeles," *New York Times*, June 6, 1992, Sec. A, p. 15.

Warrants

Warrants are the assumptions, general principles, widely held values, commonly accepted beliefs, and appeals to human motives that are an important part of any argument. Even though they can be spelled out as part of the written argument, they usually are not. In many instances, it would be redundant and boring if they were. For example, an argument might go as follows: *Claim:* The president of the United States is doing a poor job. *Support:* The unemployment rate is the highest it has been in ten years. The unstated *warrants* in this argument might include the following generally accepted beliefs: The president is responsible for creating jobs; when unemployment is high, it is a sign that the president is doing a poor job; or, even though the president may be doing well in other areas, creating jobs is the main index to how well he is doing. You may be able to think of some other ways of expressing the warrants in this argument. Since individual audience members vary in their backgrounds and perspectives, not everyone will state the warrants in exactly the same way.

Warrants originate with the arguer. Note, however, that the warrants also exist in the minds of the audience. Furthermore, if the audience shares the warrants with the arguer, the audience will accept them, and the argument is convincing. If the audience does not accept them (they believe the president is not responsible for solving unemployment problems), then the argument is not convincing to them.

Here is another example. A politician arguing that crimes are caused by a lack of family values expects the audience to supply the warrant that people with family values do not commit crime. The argument is strong and convincing for audiences who happen to share those same values and who thus share the warrant. It is not so convincing for audience members who believe there are other causes for crime that have nothing to do with family values.

Warrants are also culture-bound. They represent the values, beliefs, and training typical of individual cultures, and so they differ from culture to culture. Some tension between Japan and the United States was caused by a Japanese official's claim that American workers are lazy and do not work hard enough. American workers were angry and countered with a rebuttal about how hard they think they work. Japanese and American workers have different work schedules, attitudes, and experience with leisure and work time. Consequently, the part of both arguments that was unstated, the warrant, described hard work in different ways for each culture. The lack of a shared warrant caused the tension. Furthermore, neither side was convinced by the other's argument.

You may be thinking at this point, How am I going to be able to understand warrants when they usually are not printed on the page, they exist in the minds of the author and the audience, and they may even differ from one individual or culture to another? You will not have the difficulty with warrants that you may be anticipating because you already know a great deal about people and the opinions and beliefs they are likely to hold. You may have never noticed warrants before. But, once you become aware of them, you will recognize them in every argument you read. Warrants are one of the most interesting features of argument. They represent the psychology of an argument in the sense that they reveal unspoken beliefs and values of the author and invite you to examine your own beliefs and make comparisons.

Finding warrants is not very different from "psyching people out," or trying to discover their "real reasons for saying things." Here is an example that might make finding warrants easier: Suppose your wife/husband/roommate makes the claim that you really should start sleeping at night, instead of staying up to study, because it is more beneficial to study in the daytime. As support, you are reminded that sunshine keeps people from getting depressed, that people sleep more soundly at night than in the day, and that you need to build daytime work habits because you probably will not get a nighttime job when you graduate.

To understand the warrants in this argument, you have to try to figure out what else your roommate believes, values, and wants but has not said directly. The warrants might include these: Daytime people are better than nighttime people; you should be like other people and change your work habits to conform; you will get more done in the daytime because other people do; and you will have trouble switching from night to day if you ever have to. You might go a step further and ask, Why else is my roommate trying to change my work habits? What is the hidden agenda? Maybe it is because you leave the lights on and music playing all night. We figure out the subtexts or hidden agendas in our conversations with other people all the time. Warrants and hidden agendas are not the same, as you can see from these examples, but they are similar in the sense that neither are usually spelled out and that discovering them requires looking for what is left unstated in our communications with other people.

Some of the synonyms for warrants are *unstated assumptions, presuppositions of the author*, and *unstated premises*. Warrants are also sometimes described as generally accepted truths that the audience also will accept as true.

Warrants provide critical links in argument. For instance, they link the support to the claim by enabling an audience to accept particular support as proof of a particular claim. Without the linking warrant, the support may not be convincing. Here is an example:

The claim:	We no longer value human life.
The support:	Because we have legalized abortion.
The expected warrants:	Abortion destroys the fetus, which is human life. The author makes this assumption and expects you to also. If you do, the argument is convincing.
An alternative warrant:	Another individual believes the fetus is not a human life. This audience member does not share the author's warrant. The argument is not convincing for that individual.

Here is another example:

The claim:	The appeal process for criminals should be shortened.
The support:	Because the appeals for criminals on death row can cost more than two million dollars per criminal.
The expected warrants:	Spending more than two million dollars to keep a convicted criminal alive a little longer is a waste of money. This individual shares the author's warrant, and the argument is convincing.
An alternative warrant:	We are dealing with human life here, and we should spend whatever is necessary to make certain we have a fair conviction. This individual supplies an opposing warrant, and the argument is not convincing.

Supply your own warrant in the following argument:

The claim:	The government should abolish loan funds for college students.
The support:	Because many students default on their loans, and the government cannot tolerate these bad debts.
The warrants:	Do you believe that evidence supports that claim? If yes, why? If no, why? Your answer provides the warrant. Is the argument convincing for you?

These examples demonstrate that the warrant links the evidence and the claim by justifying particular evidence as support for a particular claim. Notice also, however, how the warrant establishes or fails to establish a link between the author and the audience as well. Shared warrants result in successful arguments. When the warrant is not shared, the audience will question or disagree with the claim. When American workers argued with the Japanese about whether they are lazy or hardworking, a shared warrant was missing.

The Japanese claim:	American workers are lazy.
The support:	Because they only work 40 hours a week.
The Japanese warrant:	People who only work 40 hours a week are lazy.
The American rebuttal:	American workers are hardworking.
The support:	Because they work 40 hours a week.
The American warrant:	People who put in 40 hours a week are industrious and hardworking.

Perhaps now you can begin to appreciate the importance of shared warrants in argument. Shared warrants are critical to the success of an argument because they provide the most significant way that common ground is established between reader and writer in argument. Shared warrants and common ground, as you can imagine, are particularly important in international negotiations. Skillful negotiators take time to analyze warrants and to determine whether or not both parties are on common ground. If they are not, communication breaks down and argument fails.

At this point, you may wonder why authors do not spell out the warrants, since they are so critical to the success of the argument. There are two reasons for usually leaving warrants implicit, or unstated, so that the audience has to supply them. First, an audience who supplies the warrant is more likely to buy into the argument through a sense of participation. If there is potential for agreement and common ground, it will be strengthened by the audience supplying the warrant. Second, remember that audiences differ and that their views of the warrant also vary somewhat, depending on their past experiences and present perceptions. A stated warrant negates the rich and varied perceptions and responses of the audience by providing only the author's interpretation and articulation of the warrant. Less active participation is then required from the audience, and the argument is less powerful and convincing to them.

To help you discover warrants, ask questions like the following:

What is left out here?
Where is this author coming from?
What is causing this author to say these things?
Where am I coming from?
Do I believe that this evidence supports this claim? Why or why not?

As the author of argument, you should consider your audience and whether or not they will accept your warrants. More information will be provided in Chapter 8 to help you do so. Now let's look at the other three parts of the Toulmin model. Recall that these are optional. All or none might appear in a written argument.

Backing

You should have a sense by now that warrants, themselves, may require their own support to make them more acceptable to an audience, particularly if the audience does not happen to share them with the author. An author may provide backing, or additional evidence to "back up" a warrant, whenever the audience is in danger of rejecting it. When you are the author, you should provide backing also. In exchanges like debates or rebuttal letters to the editor, the author is sometimes asked to prove the warrant with additional support. Or the author may analyze the beliefs and values of the audience, anticipate a lack of common ground, and back the warrant with additional support explicitly in the text, just in case. For example, in the criminal appeals argument, the author might back the warrant that it is a waste of time to spend two million dollars on a criminal appeal with additional statistical evidence that shows these appeals rarely result in a changed verdict. This additional backing would improve the likelihood that the audience would accept the claim.

Here is another example of backing for a warrant:

The claim: All immigrants should be allowed to come into the United States.
The support: Because immigration has benefited the U.S. economy in the past.
The warrant: Current economic conditions are similar to past conditions.
Backing for the warrant: Now, as in the past, immigrants are willing to perform neces sary low-paying jobs that American citizens do not want, particularly in the service areas. Statistics could be supplied to show how many jobs of this type are available.

Look for backing in an argument by identifying the warrant and then determining whether or not you accept it. If you do not, try to anticipate additional information that would make it more acceptable. Then look to see if the author supplied that or similar additional support. For example, the author who assumed that a fetus is a human being would need to provide convincing backing for people not inclined to believe that it is.

Rebuttal

A rebuttal establishes what is wrong, invalid, or unacceptable about an argument and may also present counterarguments, or new arguments that represent entirely different perspectives or points of view on the issue. To attack the validity of the claim, an author may demonstrate that the support is faulty or that the warrants are faulty or unbelievable. Counterarguments start all over again, with a new set of claims, support, and warrants.

Here is an example of a rebuttal for the argument about immigration:

Rebuttal 1: Immigrants actually drain more resources in schooling, medical care, and other social services than they contribute in taxes and productivity.

Rebuttal 2: Modern immigrants are not so willing to perform menial, low-skilled jobs as they were in past generations.

Here is an example of a counterargument for the immigration argument:

The claim: Laws should be passed to limit immigration.

The support: Because we have our own unskilled laborers who need those jobs.

The warrant: These laborers are willing to hold these jobs.

Rebuttals may appear as answers to arguments that have already been stated, or the author may anticipate the reader's rebuttal and include answers to possible objections that might be raised. Thus an author might write a rebuttal to the claim that we should censor television by saying such a practice would violate the first amendment. Or, if no claim has been made, the arguer could anticipate what the objections to television violence *might* be (violence breeds violence, children become frightened, etc.) and refute them, usually early in the essay, before spelling out the reasons for leaving television alone.

Look for a rebuttal or plan for it in your own writing, by asking, What are the other possible views on this issue? When reading, ask, Are they represented here along with reasons? Or when writing, ask, How can I answer them? Phrases that might introduce refutation include, "some may disagree," "others may think," or "other commonly held opinions are," followed by opposing ideas.

Qualifiers

Remember that argument is not expected to demonstrate certainties. Instead, it usually only establishes probabilities. Consequently, the language of certainty (*always*, *never, the best, the worst,* and so on) promises too much when used in claims or in other parts of the argument. It is not an uncommon experience for an author to make a claim, and in the midst of writing, to begin to revise and qualify it to meet the anticipated objections of an audience. Thus words like *always* and *never* change to *sometimes; is* or *are* change to *maybe* or *might; all* changes to *many* or *some; none* changes to a *few;* and *absolutely* changes to *probably* or *possibly*. Qualified language is safer for demonstrating the probabilities of an argument. Look to see if the author has stated the claim in other parts of the argument in probable or absolute terms, and then read the entire argument to figure out why.

The following is a qualified version of the claim that all immigrants should be allowed to come into the United States. These qualifications would make the original claim more acceptable to the people who offered the rebuttals and counterargument.

> Immigrants should be allowed to enter the United States only if they can prove that they already have jobs yielding sufficient income to offset social services and that no American citizens are currently available to perform these jobs.

WHY IS THE TOULMIN MODEL VALUABLE FOR ANALYZING ARGUMENT?

The Toulmin model has some advantages that make it an excellent model for both reading and writing argument. Its most essential advantage is that it invites common ground and audience participation in the form of shared warrants, increasing the possibility of interaction between author and audience. The optional three parts of the Toulmin model also encourage an exchange of views and common ground because they require an arguer both to anticipate other perspectives and views and, at times, to acknowledge and answer them directly. The backing, for instance, requires additional evidence to satisfy audience concerns. The rebuttal requires answers to different or opposing views. The qualifier requires a modification of the claim to gain audience acceptance. The backing, rebuttal, and qualifier in the Toulmin model invite audience participation. They encourage dialogue, understanding, and agreement as argument outcomes. These features make it valuable for examining the multiple perspectives likely to be expressed in response to complex modern issues.

Thus the model works for reading or writing, not only in debate and single-perspective argument, but also in academic inquiry, negotiation, dialectic, or any other form of argument that requires exchange and attempts to reach agreement. It can even be a useful tool for one-on-one argument or personal decision making. In other words, the Toulmin model accommodates all the various forms of argument. It is versatile and useful because it can be used to describe and analyze what takes place in all types of argumentative situations, including those that aim at consensus and those that aim at the establishment of winners.

WHAT STRATEGIES CAN YOU NOW ADD TO IMPROVE YOUR PROCESS FOR READING AND WRITING ARGUMENT?

You can now begin to put the theory in this chapter into practice. Here are some additional reading and writing strategies that suggest practical applications. Add them to your present list of strategies to futher improve your ability to read and write argument.

Reading Strategies

1. **Find the claim.** Look for the claim at the beginning and at the end before you read. Infer it, if it is not stated, by answering the question "What does this author want me to believe?"

2. **Summarize the core of an argument:** (1) state the claim; (2) add the word *because*; and (3) list the support. Example: "The author wants me to believe that increased population is a problem *because* . . ." (list support, including subclaims, facts, and opinions).

3. **Discover the warrants.** Ask, Where is this author coming from? What is causing this author to say this? What does this author believe? What is left out? Where am I coming from? Do I accept this support as convincing for this claim? Why, or why not?

4. **Participate in the argument.** Decide whether the warrants need backing to make them convincing to you, think of rebuttal arguments, and determine whether or not the claim would be more acceptable if it were qualified.

5. **Decide what you believe is *probably* the best position to take** on an issue, given the existing information. Stay open to new information and developments.

Writing Strategies

1. **Write a claim.** Identify an issue area, test it with the 12 tests (page 33), and write a claim about it early in the writing process. Decide eventually where to locate the claim in your paper.

2. **Plan the core of your argument.** Add the word *because* to your claim and list some subclaims and specific support. Or determine what specific support you will need to find in other sources.

3. **Discover your warrants.** Make sure your warrants link or establish a relationship between the claim and your support. Decide whether your argument would be more powerful if the warrants were stated or left unstated.

4. **Anticipate your readers' opinions and values.** Decide whether your warrants will require backing. Anticipate rebuttals and answer them. Consider whether or not your claim would be more acceptable if it were qualified.

5. **Use the Toulmin model to evaluate your argument.** When you have finished writing your argument, use the Toulmin model to examine each element in it. Then test it with the question "Will the reader be convinced that this argument is probably true?"

EXERCISES AND ACTIVITIES

1. CLASS DISCUSSION: TRUTH VERSUS PROBABILITY

Write one of these titles on the board: *television, health, rewards in life,* or *the successful life.* Now draw a vertical line under the title to establish two columns. Label them as follows:

| **Absolute Facts** | **Probabilities** |
| (No argument) | (Possibility for argument) |

Brainstorm the topic you selected and put each item you think of in one of the two columns. Take a look at the items in both columns and circle some that would be good topics for argument.

2. GROUP WORK: APPLYING THE TOULMIN MODEL TO AN ADVERTISEMENT

Clip advertisements and bring them to class. Answer these questions:

What is the claim?
What is the support?
What are the warrants?
Do you accept them?
What types of rebuttal might you offer?
Is the claim acceptable, or should it be qualified?

3. INDIVIDUAL EXAMPLE OF THE TOULMIN MODEL

Clip an advertisement or a letter to the editor and identify the *claim,* some *support,* and one or more *warrants.* Write a one-page paper in which you identify the claim, support, and warrants and attach it to your clipping. Give a 2–3 minute oral report in which you describe these parts of the argument to the class. Submit the paper.

4. CLASS DISCUSSION: APPLYING THE TOULMIN MODEL TO AN ESSAY

Read the essay "The Great Alaska Wolf Kill" by Gordon C. Haber. Then answer the following questions:

a. What is the claim of the entire essay?
b. Now apply the Toulmin model to the subclaims. The first subclaim is "A wolf-kill policy will not significantly increase the caribou herds."
   (1) What is the support for this subclaim?
   (2) What is an unstated warrant?
   (3) Is there any backing for the warrant, or does the author assume the audience will accept it?

    (4) What is the rebuttal? (What do state officials want to do?)

    (5) Are any qualifiers used? What is qualified? Why?

  c. The second subclaim is "Wolves are intelligent, socially organized animals."

    (1) What is the support for this subclaim?

    (2) What is a stated warrant?

    (3) What is the stated backing?

    (4) If there were a rebuttal of this subclaim, what might it be?

    (5) Are there any qualifiers of this subclaim, or does the author expect the reader to accept it?

THE GREAT ALASKA WOLF KILL

Gordon C. Haber

Anchorage

Alaska's wolves face another hard winter, but not only because of the snow and cold. Under regulations that took effect yesterday, the state will begin killing up to 80 percent of the wolves in a 4,500-square-mile area south of Fairbanks and East of Denali National Park. State officials say that these wolves must be killed to provide better caribou- and moose-hunting opportunities.

My nearly 28 years of field research on wolves and their prey in Denali National Park and nearby areas indicates that the state is wrong. Acceptable caribou- and moose-hunting opportunities can be assured without this wolf-control plan.

The state is portraying the wolf kill as an emergency measure to boost the size of what is called the "Delta caribou herd," which ranges east of Denali. But the herd's population decrease since 1989—from 11,000 to 4,000—represents little more than a return to the numbers that prevailed for decades until the mid-80's. The short-lived increase to 11,000 probably resulted largely from a temporary shift of caribou from a neighboring herd.

The Delta herd didn't even exist until about 60 years ago; it is probably an offshoot of a much larger herd farther to the east. There is no major caribou-hunting tradition in this area, so the plan is not a matter of restoring something that hunters had enjoyed for generations. Over the past 12 months, most of the Delta herd has spent most of its time well outside the wolf-control area.

In fact, the state's view that this and other caribou herds should be managed at stable or minimum sizes is a mistake. Virtually all of Alaska's caribou belong to a single population within which, over the span of decades, there are shifting centers of abundance. Thousands of caribou may abandon a range they have inhabited for decades and move to an area where numbers have traditionally been low. Despite recent declines in the Delta herd and in several nearby areas, other herds have increased dramatically. Statewide, the number of caribou has more than tripled over the past 15 years to about a million animals and is continuing to increase rapidly.

Thus, it is biologically inappropriate, as well as a waste of time and money, to develop long-term management policies based on individual herds. Yet it is precisely this kind of thinking that underlies the latest wolf-kill plan.

Instead, hunters should travel to the areas where caribou are abundant, where they could harvest thousands more caribou per year than are being projected in the wolf-control plan. Occupants of what is now Alaska followed the shifting caribou herds for at least 8,000 years prior to the mid-20th century. Armed with superior technology—airplanes, all-terrain vehicles—today's hunters could do the same.

Sadly, the state has ignored this bit of common sense. As soon as there is a suitable snow cover for tracking, state biologists and contractors will begin to bait, shoot, trap and snare wolves in the control area with the aid of snowmobiles, airplanes and helicopters. Up to 150 wolves will be killed this winter, and probably at least as many over the next few years, in a speculative attempt to guarantee a harvest of several hundred caribou per year, mostly for the convenience of Fairbanks-area hunters.

The public can participate in the killing. So-called sportsmen can use an aerial hunting technique that was approved by the Alaska Board of Game in June for most of the state. By purchasing a $15 trapping license, hunters will be allowed to land ski-planes near wolves that are struggling through the snow. After moving only 300 feet from the airplane, the hunters can open fire with semi-automatic assault rifles. For the holder of a trapping license, there are no limits on the number of wolves that can be killed with this method. In the past, similar forms of "land and shoot" hunting resulted in statewide kills of 800 to 1,000 wolves per year.

It is already legal for anyone with a big-game license to kill up to five wolves per year using assault rifles, snowmobiles and other methods. Some hunting and trapping of wolves, even with snowmobiles, is allowed in Alaska's national parks, including Denali. Under current laws, hunters can shoot and trap wolves with fully dependent young. They can also kill the young wolves. For no other big-game species is such indiscriminate killing allowed.

Wolves are creatures of extraordinary intelligence and emotional depth—much more so than dogs. Their social systems, which are based primarily on extended families or packs, are of the most sophisticated form known in the animal kingdom. Society generally recognizes that it is wrong to kill creatures of such high intelligence and advanced social organization, such as whales, dolphins and gorillas.

I am not opposed to hunting in general. But to kill wolves in order to make caribou-hunting more convenient is unconscionable, especially when the plan could easily fail because of other natural variables. Alaska's Governor, Walter Hickel, should reconsider his support for the wolf-control plan and order his officials to halt it. He should then initiate a scientifically and ethically defensible overhaul of Alaska's backward wolf-management policies.[6]

---

[6]*New York Times*, October 2, 1993, Sec. A, Op-Ed.

5. CLASS DISCUSSION ON WARRANTS: GROUP WORK TO PLAN AND WRITE AN ARGUMENT STRUCTURED BY THE TOULMIN MODEL

Prepare for class discussion by reading the following article, "Not All Men Are Sly Foxes." Notice that the author identifies some of the warrants present in current children's literature. What are they? What is his claim in this argument? What are his own warrants? Now, in small groups, brainstorm a related issue using the Toulmin model to structure the argument. Complete the claim "Men (or women) seem to be more privileged than women (or men) in . . ."

a. Add at least two subclaims and support for each subclaim.
b. Identify the warrants and discuss whether they should be stated or left unstated. Do they need backing, or will the audience accept them?
c. Can you anticipate rebuttal arguments? What would they be? How can you refute them? Decide whether to acknowledge them and refute them in your paper.
d. Do you need to qualify anything? How?

Now, write the paper: make it 2–3 pages, double-spaced.

NOT ALL MEN ARE SLY FOXES

Armin A. Brott

If you thought your child's bookshelves were finally free of openly (and not so openly) discriminatory materials, you'd better check again. In recent years groups of concerned parents have persuaded textbook publishers to portray more accurately the roles that women and minorities play in shaping our country's history and culture. "Little Black Sambo" has all but disappeared from library and bookstore shelves; feminist fairy tales by such authors as Jack Zipes have, in many homes, replaced the more traditional (and obviously sexist) fairy tales. Richard Scarry, one of the most popular children's writers, has reissued new versions of some of his classics; now female animals are pictured doing the same jobs as male animals. Even the terminology has changed: males and females are referred to as mail "carriers" or "firefighters."

There is, however, one very large group whose portrayal continues to follow the same stereotypical lines as always: fathers. The evolution of children's literature didn't end with "Goodnight Moon" and "Charlotte's Web." My local public library, for example, previews 203 new children's picture books (for the under-5 set) each *month*. Many of these books make a very conscious effort to take women characters out of the kitchen and the nursery and give them professional jobs and responsibilities.

Despite this shift, mothers are by and large still shown as the primary caregivers and, more important, as the primary nurturers of their children. Men in these books—if they're shown at all—still come home late after work and participate in the child rearing by bouncing baby around for five minutes before putting the child to bed.

In one of my 2-year-old daughter's favorite books, "Mother Goose and the Sly Fox," "retold" by Chris Conover, a single mother (Mother Goose) of seven tiny goslings is pitted against (and naturally outwits) the sly Fox. Fox, a neglectful and presumably unemployed single father, lives with his filthy, hungry pups in a grimy hovel littered with the bones of their previous meals. Mother Goose, a successful entrepreneur with a thriving lace business, still finds time to serve her goslings homemade soup in pretty porcelain cups. The story is funny and the illustrations marvelous, but the unwritten message is that women take better care of their kids and men have nothing else to do but hunt down and kill innocent, law-abiding geese.

The majority of other children's classics perpetuate the same negative stereotypes of fathers. Once in a great while, people complain about "Babar's" colonialist slant (little jungle-dweller finds happiness in the big city and brings civilization—and fine clothes—to his backward village). But I've never heard anyone ask why, after his mother is killed by the evil hunter, Babar is automatically an "orphan." Why can he find comfort only in the arms of another female? Why do Arthur's and Celeste's mothers come alone to the city to fetch their children? Don't the fathers care? Do they even have fathers? I need my answers ready for when my daughter asks.

I recently spent an entire day on the children's floor of the local library trying to find out whether these same negative stereotypes are found in the more recent classics-to-be. The librarian gave me a list of the 20 most popular contemporary picture books and I read every one of them. Of the 20, seven don't mention a parent at all. Of the remaining 13, four portray fathers as much less loving and caring than mothers. In "Little Gorilla," we are told that the little gorilla's "mother loves him" and we see Mama gorilla giving her little one a warm hug. On the next page we're also told that his "father loves him," but in the illustration, father and son aren't even touching. Six of the remaining nine books mention or portray mothers as the only parent, and only three of the 20 have what could be considered "equal" treatment of mothers and fathers.

The same negative stereotypes also show up in literature aimed at the *parents* of small children. In "What to Expect the First Year," the authors answer almost every question the parents of a newborn or toddler could have in the first year of their child's life. They are meticulous in alternating between references to boys and girls. At the same time, they refer almost exclusively to "mother" or "mommy." Men, and their feelings about parenting, are relegated to a nine-page chapter just before the recipe section.

Unfortunately, it's still true that, in our society, women do the bulk of the child care, and that thanks to men abandoning their families, there are too many single mothers out there. Nevertheless, to say that portraying fathers as unnurturing or completely absent is simply "a reflection of reality" is unacceptable. If children's literature only reflected reality, it would be like prime-time TV and we'd have books filled with child abusers, wife beaters and criminals.

Young children believe what they hear—especially from a parent figure. And since, for the first few years of a child's life, adults select the reading material, children's literature should be held to a high standard. Ignoring men who share equally in raising their children, and continuing to show nothing but part-time or no-time fathers is only going to create yet another generation of men who have been told since boyhood—albeit subtly—that mothers are the truer parents and that fathers play, at best, a secondary role in the home. We've taken major steps to root out discrimination in what our children read. Let's finish the job.[7]

6. CLASS DISCUSSION AND WRITING ASSIGNMENT: A TOULMIN ANALYSIS

Do a Toulmin analysis of the following essay, "Learning by Intimidation?" In class discussion, identify the claim. Identify and discuss the effectiveness of the support. Describe the warrants, including the mother's warrants, the coach's warrants, and the young athletes' warrants, as well as any conflict regarding them.

Do not worry about finding the "right answers." There aren't any. Instead, use the model to help you read and analyze the essay, and then argue for your interpretation of it by writing about what it has helped you discover. Limit your paper to 2–3 pages.

7. INDIVIDUAL ONGOING ASSIGNMENT: CLAIMS AND SUBCLAIMS

Look back at the examples of issues, claims, and subclaims on page 152. Write a similar scheme to show how your issue relates to a broad issue area and to a specific related issue. Write a claim about your issue and develop it with some tentative subclaims as in the example. Later you will use this scheme to help you plan your research and your paper.

Now read two articles in "The Reader" that are related to your issue. Write brief summaries of them in either phrases or sentences. Then write an explanation of how they are related to your issue and how you might use them to help you think about and develop it.

8. UNDERSTANDING THE CHAPTER: GROUP OR INDIVIDUAL SUMMARIES. SUMMARIZE THE MAJOR IDEAS IN THIS CHAPTER BY COMPLETING THE FOLLOWING SENTENCES:

a. People do not argue about what is certainly true. Instead, they argue about . . . Examples are . . .
b. The three essential parts of the Toulmin model are . . . The three optional parts are . . .
c. Synonyms for each of the three essential parts of the Toulmin model are . . .
d. The Toulmin model works for all forms of argument, including those that aim at consensus, because of the warrants which . . .
e. Reading and writing strategies I can start using as a result of reading this chapter are . . .

---

[7]*Newsweek*, June 1, 1992, pp. 14–15.

LEARNING BY INTIMIDATION?

Rosemary Parker

His narrowed eyes burn like hot little coals, and he screams through clenched teeth, his face thrust into hers. She's young and scared and stands with head hung, eyebrows raised in an expression that, while failing to acknowledge his accusations, is careful not to challenge them. Even in her obvious distress she's practiced and automatically leans back a bit from time to time to avoid the spray of spit he spews as he spells it out for her: she's stupid, lazy and worthless, and if she doesn't shape up someone else will soon be doing her job.

The first time I witnessed it I was genuinely alarmed and thought of trying to intervene, or perhaps of calling in the authorities. But there were others there who knew these two better than I, and no one else batted an eye. He didn't hit her. I don't think he cursed. I tried to put myself in her mother's place—but her mother was there watching with me, and did nothing.

Then it was my daughter, and still I did nothing. Hey, if he were her boyfriend or her husband I like to think I'd be there in his face, or at least on the phone to social services trying to find counseling help. But this guy was my daughter's *coach*. And from what I hear from other parents, dads especially, this guy knows the game. He can teach her the skills she'll need, help her improve her game. And if he wants to, he can make her sit the bench. Which is why she beseeches me to mind my own business.

And I do. Other mothers, once bothered as I, tell me it is better for our children to be screamed at than ignored. It's a sure sign of that nebulous desirable called potential, they say. I'll get used to it and so will the kids. Though it does seem to me that submissiveness is considered a part of that potential. The few girls with faces marked by defiance are more likely found near the end of the bench.

Besides, this guy's not alone. Why is that a comfort, knowing someone else has it worse? There's the coach at a neighboring school who takes it right down to a foot-stamping, bleacher-kicking tirade. And the boys get it worse than the girls. The boys' varsity-team players are a bunch of "f——pussies" when they falter; a band instructor preparing for competition screams threats of what will happen unless more precision is achieved, using words that shock even those kids whose language is an adolescent shade of blue.

What's going on here? In any other scenario, wouldn't this behavior be stopped? Haven't we agreed that abuse and humiliation are not appropriate instructional aids? And isn't it especially chilling to allow—to encourage—our daughters to accept such treatment at the hands of a man, to shrug it off as "part of the game"? After all, it wasn't that long ago when the playing field was much broader, when it was all "the game" and women were all required to put up with it if they wanted to keep their jobs or their marriages.

But somehow even women seem to see school competitions in a context all their own. Their daughters are at last competing and they'll need to learn to do their best to win. And if that means coaches' using the traditional unkindnesses of pitting kids against their own teammates for playing time, yanking them out for a tongue-lashing in front of a gym full of their friends and relatives, or screaming out their mistakes as they try to play the game, well so be it.

In any case, isn't it necessary for kids to learn how to perform well under stress?

Actually not even the armed forces buys the old stress routine anymore, and drill instructors have been told to cool it a bit. Fraternity hazing is frowned upon and it's no longer tacitly acceptable to beat your wife or kids. I can't think of any other situation in which a collection of nice, middle-class parents would sit quietly by while an adult publicly reduced their children to tears. But short of corporal punishment or a technical foul (you can heap abuse on the children in your charge, but not on an adult referee), anything goes on the gym floor or the playing field.

I hate the way it works and I haven't gotten used to it. I still cringe along with the kids and sometimes can't bear to watch. I'm angry with myself for failing to challenge a wrong when my gut insists I should. I'm not sure I believe my children when they tell me they'd be the ones to pay for my speaking out, but I've not been willing to risk it, either. And when I witness the same thing in another sport or at another school, I tell myself it's none of my business, really. I recall the other arguments, too—that coaches are dedicated guys and that I am unable and unwilling to coach, so I should have no voice in how others do the job.

So while I wait for the answer to come to me I do silly little things, like yelling out "Good job!" to any player who exerts an effort, yelling it a little louder to the ones who screw up.

I tell myself it's not important anyway, that these are just children's games, after all, and that if their love of the game weren't enough to offset the guff, they'd quit. But I fume to think that those are the choices, and I wait for someone to take up the fight for our children's dignity.

Maybe one of the good coaches, one of the ones the kids adore, will step in. Maybe parents with more clout, whose kids are stars? But they have even more to lose. They may approve of these methods. It's gotten their kid further than the others, right? Maybe someone with kids who are not involved in sports, some outsider who could bring attention to the problem from a safer distance?

That's what I tell myself, but I'm not buying it. I know it's really my job, even though I am just an out-of-shape, over-40 mom with no credibility in this world of jocks. I know that with their eyes on the prize, their vision is different from mine. My children are the first to tell me that I just don't understand. But I thought I recognized harm when I saw it come a child's way—the least I can do is point to it.[8]

---

[8]*Newsweek*, November 8, 1993, p. 14. Rosemary Parker is a mother of five who lives in Michigan.

CHAPTER 6

Types of Proof

In the last chapter, the claim, the support, and the warrants were identified as the three essential parts of an argument. This chapter and the one that follows provide additional information about these three parts. This chapter focuses on the support and the warrants, which, when considered together, provide the proofs for the claim. Claims are the subject of the next chapter. The proofs are described before the claims because some of them are particularly appropriate for developing certain types of claims. An understanding of the proofs at this point will improve your understanding of claims when you encounter them in the next chapter.

The material in this chapter is organized to introduce you first to logical, ethical, and emotional proofs, next to the language and style associated with each of them, and finally to some of the logical, ethical, and emotional fallacies or pseudo-proofs that sometimes occur in argument.

As you understand and begin to work with the proofs, you will discover that they are not simply uniform patterns that are obvious and easy to recognize. Rather, slippery and imperfect as they are, they represent an attempt to describe what goes on in the real world of argument and in the minds of writers and readers of argument. Understanding them can put you closer to an author, so that you may better understand how that individual thought about, interpreted, and developed a particular subject. Then, when you switch roles and become the author yourself, your knowledge of what can happen in argument will help you develop your own thoughts and create your own effective arguments.

THE TRADITIONAL CATEGORIES OF PROOF

The traditional categories of proof, like much of our most fundamental and useful argument theory, were first articulated by classical theorists, and they are still useful for describing what goes on in real-world argument today. Recall from the last chapter that Aristotle, in the *Rhetoric*, said that an arguer must state a claim (or a proposition) and prove it. He also went into detail about the broad categories of proof that can be used to prove the probability of a claim. Aristotle's categories of proof are still useful either because they accurately describe what classical arguers did then and what modern arguers still do, or because Aristotle's ideas have become such an accepted part of our intellectual heritage that, like generations before us, we learn these methods and use them to observe, think about, and interpret reality. In either case, Aristotle's ideas and observations about argument still apply. They provide accurate descriptions of what goes on in argument.

Aristotle distinguishes between proofs that can be produced and laid on the table, so to speak, like a murder weapon, fingerprints, or a written contract, and proofs that are invented and represent the creative thinking and insights of clever and intelligent people.

Aristotle divides this second categories of proof into three subcategories: logical, ethical, and emotional. The Greek words used to refer to the proofs are *logos* (logical), *ethos* (ethical), and *pathos* (emotional). *Logical proof* appeals to people's reason, understanding, and common sense. It is consistent with what we know and believe, and it gives us fresh insight and ideas about issues. As proof, it relies mainly on such support as reasoned opinion and factual data and also on warrants that suggest the soundness and truth of such support. Aristotle declared that logical proof is the most important type of proof in argument, and most modern theorists agree with him. Richard M. Weaver, a well-known modern rhetorician, for example, says that argument has its primary basis in reasoning and that it appeals primarily to the rational part of man. Logical proof, he says, provides, "the plot" of argument.[1] The other two types of proof are also present and important, however.

Ethical proof appeals to the audience's impressions, opinions, and judgments about the individual stating the argument. Arguers who demonstrate competence, good character, fair-mindedness, and goodwill toward the audience are more convincing than people who lack these qualities. Individuals who project such favorable qualities to an audience have established good *ethos*. Audiences are more likely to trust and believe individuals with good ethos than those without it. At times, arguers also need to establish the ethos of the experts whom they quote in their arguments. They usually accomplish this purpose by providing information about them so that audiences will appreciate these individuals' degree of expertise and, consequently, be more willing to accept what they say.

Emotional proof is used to appeal to and arouse the feelings of the audience. Audience's feelings are aroused primarily through emotional language, examples, personal narratives, and vivid descriptions of events that contain emotional elements and that arouse strong feelings in other people. Emotional proof is appropriate in an argument when it is used to develop the claim and when it contributes to the sense of logical conviction or agreement that are argument's intended outcomes. A well-reasoned set of logical proofs contributes to such outcomes. But emotion can also contribute to a strong acceptance of a logical conclusion. Imagine, for example, an argument in favor of increasing taxes to build housing for homeless

---

[1] Richard M. Weaver, "Language Is Sermonic," in Richard L. Johannesen, ed., *Contemporary Theories of Rhetoric: Selected Readings*. (New York: Harper & Row, 1971), pp. 163–179.

people. The logical argument would describe reasons for these taxes, methods for levying them, and recommendations for spending them. The argument would be strengthened, however, by a few vivid and emotional examples of homeless people who lead miserable lives.

The next three sections will introduce you to seven types of logical proof, one type of ethical proof, and two types of emotional proof that are commonly used in argument. The number and variety of logical proofs is greater than the others because logical thinking dominates and provides "the plot" for most argument. Most arguments rely on a variety of proofs because several types of proof usually provide a stronger argument than reliance on only one.

Each type of proof will be explained as follows:[2]

Description and Example. The proof is described and an example is provided.
Claim and Support. You are then told what to look for, or what types of support you can expect to find on the printed page and how to find the claim.
Warrant. You are told what you are expected to assume to make logical connection between the support and the claim. The warrants associated with types of proof suggest specific ways of thinking about support and its function in an argument.
Tests of Validity. You are provided with questions to ask to help you test the reliability and validity of the proof. These questions will focus your attention on both support and warrant and how they do or do not function together as effective proof. They will also help you locate the weaknesses in an argument which can help you plan rebuttal and formulate argument of your own.

At the end of the chapter, in the exercise section, some of the proofs in a short essay are identified and analyzed so that you can also see how they operate in a written argument.

SOME TYPES OF LOGICAL PROOF: *LOGOS*

Logical proofs (also called substantive proofs) are based on reality and include substantial factual information, data, and accounts of actual events, both past and present. The support used in logical proof is real and drawn from experience. Logical (or substantive) warrants guarantee the reliability and relevance of this support. Logical proofs represent common ways of thinking about and perceiving relationships among the events and data of the real world and then using those ideas and relationships as support for a line of argument.

---

[2]In this chapter I have drawn on some of Wayne Brockriede and Douglas Ehninger's ideas in "Toulmin on Argument: An Interpretation and Application," *Quarterly Journal of Speech*, 46, no. 1 (February 1969): 44–53. Specifically, I have expanded and adapted these authors' analysis of proofs to make it apply to the reading and writing of argument as explained in this book.

Argument from Deduction

Description and Examples. Deductive argument is also called argument from principle because its warrant is a general principle. Remember that the warrant may or may not be stated explicitly in an argument. Etymology can help you remember the special features of deductive argument. The prefix *de-* means "from" and the root *duc* means "lead." *A deductive argument leads from a general principle,* which is the warrant, applies it to an example or specific case, which is described in the support, and draws *a conclusion,* which is the claim.

In the last chapter you learned that argument deals with matters that are probably rather than certainly true. People do not argue about matters that are certainly true because they already agree about them. Here is an example of a deductive argument based on a general principle that people would agree with and accept as true. Thus, they would not argue about it.

General warrant:	Every person has a unique set of fingerprints.
Support:	The accused is a person.
Claim:	The accused has a unique set of fingerprints.

This example might be used as a minor argument to support a claim that someone is guilty of a crime. It would never be the main issue in an argument, however, because it is not arguable.

Most of the deduction you will encounter in argument, on the other hand, is arguable because it deals with probabilities rather than with certainties. Sherlock Holmes used deduction to reach his sometimes astonishing conclusions. Holmes examined the supporting evidence—footprints, for example—and deduced that the man who left them walked with a limp. The general principle, that most uneven footprints are left by people with limps, is an assumption that is important in Holmes's deductive thinking even though it is not stated in the argument. It does not need to be spelled out for readers who are able to supply that warrant themselves as they accept Holmes's conclusion. The Holmes deduction can be summarized as follows. The purpose of this argument is to establish the type of person who left these footprints.

Unstated warrant:	Most uneven footprints are left by people with limps.
Support:	These footprints are uneven.
Claim:	Thus the person who left these footprints walks with a limp.

Is there any part of that argument that you might challenge as only possibly or probably rather than as certainly true? If so, you can argue about it.

Claim and Support. Locate the claim by answering this question: "On the basis of a general principle (warrant), implied or stated, what does the author expect me to conclude about this specific example or case?"

Deductive Warrants. You are expected to assume that a general principle about a whole category of phenomena (people, places, events, and so forth) has been stated or implied in the argument and that it is accurate and acceptable. You are expected to decide that, since the general principle, or warrant, and the support for the specific case are both accurate and acceptable, then the conclusion also is acceptable and probably true.

Tests of Validity. Ask, Is the warrant acceptable and believable? Does the warrant apply to the example or case? Is the support for the case accurate? How reliable, then, is the conclusion?

If the reader has a problem with either the warrant or the example in a deductive argument, the conclusion will not be acceptable. Consider Holmes's warrant that uneven footprints are left by people with limps. That may be convincing to some readers but not convincing to others. For instance, a reader who reflects that a person who pretends to limp or one who carries a heavy valise in one hand could also leave uneven footprints will also question the warrant and decide the proof is not even probably true.

Here is another example of a deductive argument that would not be equally successful with all audiences:

(*Unstated warrant*:	Families cannot be happy when the mother works outside the home.)
Support:	The mother in this family works outside the home
Claim:	This is an unhappy family.

For some readers who come from happy homes with working mothers the warrant in this example would seem faulty.

In the next example of a deductive argument, the support could be a problem for some readers who might have trouble accepting it because they think baby boomers are smart and responsible and would make excellent presidents. Thus they would reject the conclusion also.

Warrant:	People who are irresponsible and have materialistic lifestyles should not be president.
Support:	Baby boomers were irresponsible in the 1960s and are materialistic now.
Claim/conclusion:	A baby boomer should not be president.

All parts of a deductive argument need to be accurate and acceptable to the audience for it to be convincing.

Argument from Definition

Description and Examples. Definition is extremely important in argument. It is difficult to argue about any subject unless there is general agreement about the meanings of the key terms, especially when they are part of the claim. Sometimes an entire argument is based on the audience's acceptance of a certain meaning of a key term. If the audience accepts the definition, then the arguer says that the claim should be accepted "by definition." For example, if abortion is defined as willful taking of human life, then, by definition, it is murder. Here is this argument laid out as deduction:

(*Unstated warrant:* Willful taking of human life is murder.)
(*Unstated support:* Abortion is willful taking of human life.)
Claim: Abortion is murder.

Here is another example:

Warrant: Family values characterize the good citizen.
Support: Radical feminists lack family values.
Claim: Radical feminist are not good citizens.

We will accept the claim that radical feminists, by definition, are poor citizens only if we also accept the warrants that define the good citizen as one who possesses family values and radical feminists as people who lack these values. (See the article "Family Values" on page 218 to see how this argument appears in print.)

Even though argument by definition takes the form of deductive argument, it is listed separately here to emphasize the important function of definitions in arguments that depend on it as major proof.

Claim and Support. Look for all definitions or explanations of words or concepts. These may be a sentence, several paragraphs, or an entire essay in length. Notice if the definition is used simply to define a word or if it is used as part of the proof in the argument. Look for a claim that you are expected to accept as a result of the definition.

Definition Warrants. You are expected to assume that the definition describes the fundamental properties and qualities of the term accurately so that it can be used to prove the claim.

Tests of Validity. Is this an accurate and complete definition? Is it convincing in this context? Are there exceptions or other definitions for this term that would make the final claim less reliable?

Argument from Cause

Description and Example. Argument from cause places the subject in a cause-effect relationship to show that it is either the cause of an effect or the effect of a cause. It is very common in argument to explain or to justify a claim with cause-effect reasoning. Here is an example. Notice in this example that the claim is stated first. This is to remind you that in actual argument there is in no fixed order for the three parts of the argument.

Claim: Children read better in school when their parents read to them at home.
Support: Specific examples of parents reading to children who then read well at school.
Warrant: The parents' reading caused the children to do better.

Claim and Support.   Look for examples, events, trends, and people that have caused certain things to happen. Look for the effects. For example, "Television violence causes children to become violent." Or turn it around and look for the effects first and then the causes: "Many children are violent as a result of watching too much violence on television." Look, also, for clue words such as *cause, effect, resulted in, as a result, as a consequence,* or *because* to indicate that cause-effect reasoning is being used. Finally, the claim states what you are expected to conclude as a result of this cause-effect reasoning: "Parents should be trained to read to their children, " or, "Children should not watch violent television."

Causal Warrants.   You are expected to assume that the causes really do create the identified effects, or that the effects really are the results of the named causes.

Tests of Validity.   Are these causes alone sufficient to create these effects? Could these effects result from other causes? Can I think of exceptions to the cause-effect outcome that is claimed here?

Argument from Sign

Description and Example.   A specific visible sign is sometimes used to prove a claim. A sign can be used to prove with certainty: Someone breaks out in chicken pox, and the claim, based on that certain sign, is that the person has chicken pox. Or a sign can be used to prove the probability of a claim: A race riot, someone argues, is probably a sign of the claim that people think they are unfairly treated. Or the sign may turn out to be the pseudoproof of a false claim. A child asks, "Why should I believe in Santa Claus?" and the parent answers, "Look at all the toys under the tree that weren't there yesterday." That support is used as a sign for the claim that Santa Claus exists. Here is an example of a sign used to prove nationality. Would you say this is a certain or only probable sign?

Claim:	That person is Russian.
Support (sign):	She is speaking in Russian.
Warrant:	Speaking Russian is a sign of Russian nationality.

Claim and Support.   Look for visible clues, symptoms, and occurrences that are explained as obvious and clear signs of a certain belief or state of affairs. Look for the conclusion or claim that is made on the basis of these signs.

Sign Warrants.   You are expected to assume that the sign is actually a sign of what the author claims it to be.

Tests of Validity.   Is this really a sign of what the author claims it to be? Is there another explanation for the sign?

Argument from Induction

Description and Example.   Inductive argument provides a number of examples and draws a claim, in the form of a conclusion, from them. The audience is expected to accept the group of examples as adequate and accurate enough to make the inductive leap to the claim. Inductive argument is also called argument from generalization or argument from example because the claim is a generalization made on the basis of the examples. To help you remember the special features of inductive argument, learn its prefix *in-*, which means "in" or "into," and the root *duc*, which means "lead." *An inductive argument uses examples to lead into a claim or generalization about the examples.* Here is an example: Four different people take their cars to the same car repair shop and are overcharged. The claim is then made that anyone who takes a car to that repair shop will probably be overcharged.

Inductive reasoning is the basis of the scientific method. Most scientific conclusions are reached inductively. When a sufficient number of phenomena are observed repeatedly, then a generalization is made to explain them. Here is an example:

Claim: The sun always comes up.
Support: The sun has come up every day of recorded history.
Warrant: That is a sufficient number of days to make that claim.

Induction demonstrates only probability when there is the possibility of an exceptional example. Someone may get a good deal at the repair shop. On the other hand, an apple always falls from a tree and thus demonstrates gravity, or the sun always comes up. No one has been able to find exceptional examples to disprove these generalizations.

To be effective, inductive argument requires a sufficient number of examples. When a generalization is made on the basis of only one, or a few, examples, it is called a "hasty generalization." To claim, for instance, that an office worker should always be able to enter a certain amount of data because he did it once may not be accurate. To make a broad generalization, such as *all* office workers ought to be able to enter a certain amount of data because *one* employee was able to, is called a "sweeping" generalization. An inadequate sample of cases weakens or invalidates an inductive argument.

Claim and Support. Look for a group of examples followed by a generalization (claim) based on the examples; or the generalization (claim) may be stated first and then be followed by several examples.

Inductive Warrants. You are expected to assume that the list of examples is representative and that it shows a definite trend. You are also expected to assume that if you added more examples of the same general type the resulting conclusion would not change.

Test of Validity. Is the sample adequate? Would more examples continue to show the trend? Are there examples that show an opposite trend, that provide an exception? (Was someone charged a reasonable amount at the repair shop?) Can we make the inductive leap from the examples to the generalization to demonstrate that it is probably true?

Argument from Statistics

Description and Example. Like other forms of logical proof, statistics describe relationships among data, people, occurrences, and events in the real world, only they do so in quantitative terms. Modern readers have considerable faith in numbers and statistics. They seem more "true" than other types of support to many people. It is more convincing to some people, for example, to make the claim that we should end draft registration because it costs $27.5 million per year than to simply claim that we should end it because we no longer need it.

Read statistical proofs carefully to determine where they come from and how reliable, accurate, and relevant they are. Note also whether the original figures have been *changed* or *interpreted* in some way. Figures are often *rounded off* or *stated in different terms*, such as percentages or graphs. They are also sometimes *compared* to other material that is familiar to the audience to make them more interesting or memorable.[3] Various types of graphs or charts, such as those used on pages 46–51, also make data and statistics visual and even easier to grasp and remember.

Here is an example of a typical use of statistics in an article entitled "Child-Killing Increases in Rio"[4]

Claim: Child killing is increasing in Rio de Janeiro.
Support: Forty percent more children may be killed this year than last year.
Warrant: Forty percent represents an increase.

The source for these statistics is cited only as "preliminary statistics." On close reading, one realizes that 424 people under 18 were killed in one year in Rio compared with 348 who were killed in seven months of the next year. Thus the claim of a 40 percent increase is qualified to read "may be killed," since it is based on a projection of what might occur in the next five months. The figures are also converted to percentages. The author goes on to compare these figures with one that is more familiar to the reader, the number of child killings in the United States. It is claimed that 6,000 to 7,000 children, or 20 a day, died from gunshot wounds during the comparable period of time in the United States. Notice that these figures, also, are rounded off. The source for these last figures is cited as a news conference interview with the executive director of Unicef. You might have to read other sources on this subject to begin to test the validity of these figures.

Claim and Support.   Look for numbers and data, in both their original and their converted form, graphs and charts of figures, as well as interpretations of them, including comparisons. Look for a claim based on the data.

Statistical Warrants.   You are expected to assume that the data have been gathered and reported accurately by competent people, that they are representative and complete unless stated otherwise, and that they have been interpreted fairly and truthfully.

Tests of Validity.   Where did these statistics come from? To what dates do the statistics apply? How reliable is the source? How accurate are they? How are

---

[3]James Wood, *Speaking Effectively* (New York: Random House, 1988), pp. 121–127.
[4]James Brooke, "Child-Killing Increases in Rio," *Fort Worth Star-Telegram*, January 3, 1994, p. 7.

they presented? Have they been rounded off, changed, or converted? How has the change affected their accuracy? Do they prove what they are supposed to prove? Have they been interpreted fairly, or are they exaggerated or skewed? Has enough backing been provided to prove their reliability? What are they compared to, and how does this comparison contribute to their final significance?

Argument from Historical, Literal, or Figurative Analogy

Description and Examples. *Historical and literal analogies* explore similarities and differences between items in the same general category, and figurative analogies do the same, only with items in very different categories. In drawing analogies, we show how something we may not know much about is like something we know in greater detail. In other words, we interpret what we do not know in the light of what we do know. We then supply the warrant that what happened in one case will happen in the other, we draw conclusions, and we make a claim based on the comparisons in the analogy.

Historical analogies explain what is going on *now* in terms of what went on in similar cases in the *past*. Future outcomes are also often projected from past cases. The idea is that what happened in the past will probably repeat itself in the present. Also, the two events are so similar that the results of the former will surely be the end result of the latter. For example:

> *Claim*:   Many people will die of AIDS.
> *Support*:   Many people died of the black death.
> *Warrant*:   AIDS and the black death are similar.

Literal analogies compare two items in the same category: two school systems, two governments, two religions, two individuals. Outcomes are described as for historical analogies, that is, what happened in one case will happen in the other because of the similarities or the differences. For example:

> *Claim*:   The state should spend more money on education.
> *Support*:   Another state spent more money with good results.
> *Warrant*:   The two states are similar, and the results of one will be the results of the other.

Figurative analogies compare items from two different categories, as in metaphor, only the points of comparison in a figurative analogy are usually spelled out in more detail than they are in a metaphor. Many figurative analogies appeal to the emotions rather than to reason. Figurative analogies are only effective as logical proof when they are used to identify *real qualities* that are shared by both items and that can then be applied to help prove the claim logically. When the items in a figurative analogy are compared to add ornament or to stir up an emotional response, the analogy functions as emotional proof. It engages the emotions rather than the reason.

Here are some examples of figurative analogies used as logical proof. To prove that reading a difficult book should take time, Francis Bacon compares that activity with taking the time to chew and digest a large meal. The qualities of the two activities, rather than the activities themselves, are compared. Since these qualities are not spelled out, the audience must infer that both take time, and understanding, like digestion, benefits and becomes a permanent part of the individual. Here is this argument laid out so that you can see how it works:

Claim: Reading a difficult book should take time.
Support: Digesting a large meal takes time.
Warrant: Reading and eating are sufficiently alike that they can be compared.

Or, as another example of logical proof, the human fossil record is compared to an apple tree in early winter that has only a few apples on it. The quality that the fossil record and the tree have in common, which the reader must infer, is that both tree and fossil record have a complicated system of branches and limbs. Also, the few apples on the tree are like the few available fossils. At one time there were many of both. The qualities compared in these two instances improve a rational understanding of the fossil record.

Here is an example of a figurative analogy that is used as emotional proof and ornament rather than as logical proof: Warren Hinckle, in an article critical of political commentators, makes this statement about their writing: "Words such as 'Bonapartist,' even 'fascist,' run through their writing like beer through a fraternity boy."[5] The comparisons implied by that analogy do not result in logical proof. The analogy is, however, striking and memorable, and would encourage a reader to adopt a certain emotional attitude toward such writers.

Claim and Support.   Look for examples of items, events, people, and periods of times that are being compared. Whether these items are drawn from the past or present, as in the case of historical or literal analogies, they must be drawn from the same category: two types of disease, two types of school systems, two types of government, and so on. Look for the clue words *compare, contrast, like, similar to,* and *different from* to signal that comparisons are being made.

In the case of figurative analogies, look for two items being compared that are from totally different categories. Identify the qualities that they have in common. Look for the clue words *like, as, similar to,* or *compare.* Discover claims that are made as a result of comparing similarities or differences.

Comparison Warrants.   You are expected to assume that the items being compared are similar as described, and that what happens in one case probably will occur in the other. For figurative analogies you are expected to assume that the qualities of the two items are similar and significant enough so that reference to one will help to explain the other and will serve as convincing proof.

---

[5]Warren Hinckle, "Ross Perot: Hero of the Counterculture," *New York Times,* July 10, 1992, p. A29.

Sign
Induction
Cause
Deduction
Analogies (literal, historical, figurative)
Definition
Statistics

Sic dads refuted by logical proof.

Figure 6.1   The Logical Proofs

Tests of Validity.   Are the two items similar as claimed? Can I think of ways they are not similar or of other qualities they share that would change the claim? Are the outcomes really likely to be the same in both cases? Why? Or why not?

For figurative analogies, ask, Are the qualities of these two items similar, significant, and real enough to help prove a logical argument? Or are they so dissimilar, so far-fetched, or so trivial that the comparison does not prove anything? Does the analogy serve as an ornament, an emotional appeal, or a logical proof?

It is handy to be able to remember the logical proofs both when you are reading and when you are developing your paper so that you can use them more readily. Figure 6.1 provides a mnemonic device that will help you remember them. It shows the first letter of each proof rearranged to make a nonsense word, and a picture of that word to help you remember it. You can run through this mnemonic mentally when you are thinking about ways to develop the ideas in your paper.

A TYPE OF ETHICAL PROOF: *ETHOS*

All of the materials provided in argument that help the audience gain a favorable impression of the arguer, the group the arguer represents, or the authorities and experts the arguer cites or quotes are known as ethical proofs or arguments from authority.

Argument from Authority

Description and Example.   We are usually inclined to accept the opinions and factual evidence of people who are authorities and experts in their fields. In an article that claims California will have another earthquake, for example, the author describes and provides the professional credentials for several professors of geology from the major universities in southern California as well as scientists from the U.S. Geological Survey Office before quoting their opinions as support:

Claim: California will have an earthquake.
Support: Professors and scientists say so.
Warrant: These experts are reliable.

Authors themselves sometimes establish their own credentials by making references to various types of past experience that qualify them to write about their subject. They also sometimes establish the ethos of the group they represent, like "the great Republican Party."

Claim and Support. Look for all references to the author's credentials, whether made by the author or by an editor. Look for references to the author's training, education, professional position, background, and experience. Notice, also, references to the audience's concerns, beliefs, and values that demonstrate the author's effort to establish common ground and to show fairness and goodwill toward the audience. Look for references to groups the author may represent, and notice how they are described. Look for direct or paraphrased quotations from experts. Differentiate between facts and statements of opinion. Look for credential statements about these experts. Look for claims that are made more valid as a consequence of this expert opinion.

Authoritative Warrants. You are expected to assume that the information provided about the author, the group, or the expert is accurate, that these authorities are honorable, fair, reliable, knowledgeable, and experienced, and that they also exhibit goodwill toward the audience.

Tests of Validity. Is there enough information to establish the true character and experience of the author? Is this information complete and accurate? Is there enough information about the group to believe what the author says about it? Are the credentials of the experts good enough to make their contributions reliable? Also, are the credentials relevant to the issue? (A star athlete may not be the best judge of soft drinks or fast food.) If a source is quoted, is it reliable? Argument based on authority is as good as the authorities themselves.

SOME TYPES OF EMOTIONAL PROOF: *PATHOS*

Some argument theorists would say that there should be no appeals to emotion or attempts to arouse the emotions of the audience in argument. The idea is that an argument should appeal only to reason. Emotion, they claim, clouds reasoning and judgment and gets the argument off course. Richard M. Weaver, quoted earlier in this chapter, would disagree. Weaver points out that people are not just austerely unemotional logic machines who are interested only in deduction, induction, and cause-effect reasoning. People also use language to communicate feelings, values, and motives.[6]

Furthermore, when we consider that the source of much argument lies in the dramatic, emotionally laden occurrences of everyday life, we realize how impossible it is to eliminate all emotion from argument. As you read the many argumentative essays included in this book, study the emotional material that is used by professional writers. Try to develop a sense of when emotion contributes to ar-

---

[6]Weaver elaborates on some of the distinctions between logic and emotion in "Language Is Sermonic."

gument in effective and appropriate ways and when it does not. In general, emotional proofs are appropriate in argument when the subject itself is emotional and when it creates strong feelings in both the writer and the reader. For writers of argument, emotion leads to positions on issues, influences the tone of the writing, and informs some of the interpretations. For readers, emotion leads to a stronger engagement with the issue and influences the final outcomes. Emotional proof is appropriate when the occasion justifies it and when it strengthens logical conviction. It is inappropriate when it merely ventilates feelings, serves as an ornament, or distracts the audience from the logical conclusion of the argument. Types of emotional proof focus on *motivation*, or what all people want, and on *values*, or what we consider good or bad, favorable or unfavorable, acceptable or unacceptable.

Motivational Proofs

Description and Example.   Some proofs appeal explicitly to what all audiences are supposed to want, such as food, drink, warmth and shelter, sex, security, belongingness, self-esteem, creativity, or self-expression. (See Box 8.1, p. 271, for a more complete list of human needs.) The purpose of motivational proof is to urge the audience to take prescribed steps to meet an identified need. Advertisements and speeches by political candidates provide obvious examples of motivational proof. Drink a certain beer or buy a brand of blue jeans, and you will be irresistible to others. Or support a particular candidate and you will gain job security and safe neighborhoods:

Claim:	You should support this candidate.
Support:	This candidate can help you get job security and safe neighborhoods.
Warrant:	You want job security and safe neighborhoods.

Claim and Support.   To find the claim, look for what you are asked to believe or do to get what you want.

Motivational Warrants.   Look for references to items or qualities that you might need or want.

Tests of Validity.   What am I supposed to need? Do I really need it? What am I supposed to do? Will doing what is recommended satisfy the need in the ways described?

Value Proofs

Description and Example.   Some proofs appeal to what all audiences are expected to value, such as reliability, honesty, loyalty, industry, patriotism, courage, integrity, conviction, faithfulness, dependability, creativity, freedom, equality, devotion to duty, and so on. Here is an example that claims the curriculum can contribute to the values of equality and acceptance if it is multicultural:

Claim:	The curriculum should be multicultural.

> *Support:* A multicultural curriculum will contribute to equality and acceptance.
>
> *Warrant:* You value equality and acceptance.

Claim and Support. Look for value statements that are generally accepted by everyone because they have been proved elsewhere many times. Examples include "Freedom of speech is our constitutional right" or "There should be no freedom without responsibility" or "Individuals who have the courage of conviction are to be trusted." Look for slogans that display such values as "Honest Abe," "The home of the free and the brave," or "Honesty is the best policy." Or look for narratives and examples that display values, such as the story of an industrious, thrifty, and ambitious mother who is on welfare. When the values are not directly stated, ask, What value or belief is causing the author to say this? Look for a claim that shows what will result if the recommended values are accepted.

Value Warrants. You are expected to assume that you share the author's values and that they are as important as the author says they are.

Tests of Validity. What are the values expressed or implicit in this argument? Do I share these values with the author? If not, how do we differ? What effect do these differences have on my final acceptance of the claim?

The mnemonic VAM (value, authority, and motivation) may help you remember and use the ethical and emotional proofs.

HOW ARE *LOGOS, ETHOS,* AND *PATHOS* COMMUNICATED THROUGH LANGUAGE AND STYLE?

You can learn to recognize logical, ethical, and emotional argument not only by the use of proofs, but also by the language and style associated with them. Actually, you will not often encounter pure examples of one of these styles, but instead you will encounter a mix, with one of the styles predominating. The same is true of writing. You may plan to write in logical style, but emotion and *ethos* creep in and actually help you create a richer and more varied style for your argument.

The Language of Logical Argument

The language of logical argument, which is the language associated with reason, is sometimes called rational style. Words that carry mainly denotative meaning are favored in rational style over connotative and emotionally loaded language. The denotative meaning of a word is the commonly held meaning that most people would agree on and that is also found in the dictionary. Examples of words that have predominantly denotative meanings and that are emotionally neutral include *introduction, facts, information,* or *literal meaning.* Most people would agree on the meanings of those words and could produce synonyms. Words with strong connotative meaning may have many extra, unique, and personal meanings or associations attached to them that vary from person to person. Examples of words with connotative meaning, include *rock star, politician, mugger, family values,* or *human rights.* Several people, when asked to define such words, would usually provide a variety of personal meanings and examples that would not be exactly alike or match the denotative meanings of these words in a dictionary.

For support, rational style relies on opinion in the form of reasons, literal or historical analogies, explanations, and definitions, and also on factual data, quotations, and citations from experts and authorities. Furthermore, the reader is usually not required to make as many inferences as for other, more informal styles of writing. Most parts of the argument are spelled out explicitly for the sake of agreement and a better adherence of minds.

Slogans that elicit emotional response, such as "America is the greatest country," "The American people want change," or "Now is the time for healing," are also usually omitted in rational style. Slogans of this type substitute for logical thinking. Readers think better and draw better conclusions when provided with well-reasoned opinion, quotations from authorities, and facts.

For example, in the opening paragraph of an essay entitled "The Lost Art of Political Argument," Christopher Lasch argues in favor of argument and debate. (The entire essay appears in "The Reader" on pages 477–482.)

> Let us begin with a simple proposition: What democracy requires is public debate, not information. Of course it needs information too, but the kind of information it needs can be generated only by vigorous popular debate. We do not know what we need to know until we ask the right questions, and we can identify the right questions only by subjecting our own ideas about the world to the test of public controversy. Information, usually seen as the precondition of debate, is better understood as its by-product. When we get into arguments that focus and fully engage our attention, we become avid seekers of relevant information. Otherwise, we take in information passively—if we take it in at all.[7]

Rational style, you can see, evokes mainly a cognitive, rational response from its readers.

The Language of Ethical Argument

Authors who seek to establish their own credentials and thereby create positive ethos with an audience deliberately use language that is appropriate to that audience and its special characteristics and interests. The language used maintains an appropriate and consistent tone throughout. I. A. Richards, a modern rhetorical theorist, suggests that tone reflects an author's attitude toward the audience and establishes a relationship between author and reader.[8] For example, rap musicians write lyrics that use the language of rap to reflect a certain attitude toward the fans

---

[7]Christopher Lasch, "The Lost Art of Political Argument," *Harper's*, September 1990, p. 17.
[8]I. A. Richards, *Practical Criticism* (New York: Harcourt Brace, 1929), pp. 175-176.

of rap music, professors write articles that use academic language to reflect their attitude toward an academic audience, and newspaper writers use journalistic language to reflect their attitude toward the readers of newspaper articles. It would be inappropriate, unless there were an unusual context or purpose, for a rap musician to suddenly break out in academic language because doing so would destroy the tone of the lyrics. There is also a difference in tone between comparatively formal academic and comparatively informal journalistic writing. These differences result from the author's perceptions of the audience. An academic audience expects a certain vocabulary level that includes formal, abstract language, and a newspaper reader expects less formal, more concrete language or the language of everyday life.

A consistent tone reflected by a certain level and type of language that is appropriate for the audience helps an author establish *ethos*. Conversely, an author can destroy *ethos* and alter an audience's favorable impression by changing the tone. A student who uses colloquial, everyday expressions in a formal essay written for a professor, a commencement speaker who shouts obscenities at the student audience, or a father who uses formal, abstract language to talk to his five-year-old all reflect inappropriate attitudes toward their audiences, exhibit inappropriate tone, and damage their *ethos* with that audience. When you read argument, notice how an author uses language to build connections, establish reliability with the audience, and thereby establish effective *ethos*. When you write argument, use language that is appropriate for your audience and your subject. Appropriate language is particularly important when you write academic discourse. The use of slang, slogans, and colloquial expressions in otherwise formal writing changes the tone and damages your *ethos* and credibility with your readers. Writing errors, including mistakes in spelling, punctuation, and grammar, also damage *ethos* because they indicate a lack of concern and goodwill for your readers.

Here is an example of tone and style that builds connections and reassures the audience of the reliability and sincerity of the speaker. It is from a speech by President Boris N. Yeltsin of Russia delivered to the U.S. Congress shortly after the fall of communism in Russia:

> It is indeed a great honor for me to address the Congress of the great land of freedom as the first ever over 1,000 years of history as Russia's popularly elected president, as a citizen of the great country which has made its choice in favor of liberty and democracy.
>
> For many years, our two nations were the two poles, the two opposites. They wanted to make us implacable enemies. That affected the destinies of the world in a most tragic way.
>
> The world was shaken by the storms of confrontation. It was close to exploding, close to perishing beyond salvation.
>
> The evil scenario is becoming a thing of the past. Reason begins to triumph over madness. We have left behind the period when America and Russia looked at each other through gunsights, ready to pull the trigger at any time.
>
> Despite what we saw in the well-known American film "The Day After," it can be said today, tomorrow will be a day of peace, less of fear and more of hope for the happiness of our children. The world can sigh in relief. The idol of Communism, which spread everywhere social strife, animosity, and unparalleled brutality, which instilled

fear in humanity, has collapsed. It has collapsed never to rise again. I am here to assure you, we will not let it rise again in our land.[9]

Notice how Yeltsin's language establishes a complimentary, reassuring, and positive tone that reveals his attitude toward his American audience. He established excellent *ethos* in this speech, and the speech was enthusiastically received. Further excerpts from this speech appear in the exercise section of Chapter 8, pp. 277–279.

The Language of Emotional Argument

References to values and motives evoke feelings about what people regard as good and bad and about what they want, and authors use the language associated with emotional style in a variety of ways to express and evoke feelings about these matters. The following paragraphs describe a few special techniques that are characteristic of emotional style. Examples are drawn from the essay by Sara Rimer, "Jobs Illuminate What Riots Hid: Young Ideals," which appears in full in the exercise section of Chapter 3, pp. 95–98.

Emotionally loaded language evokes connotative meaning and causes the audience to experience feelings and associations at a personal level that are not described in dictionaries. Underline the emotional language in this passage:

> America has been bombarded with television images of the youth of South-Central Los Angeles: throwing bricks, looting stores, beating up innocent motorists. The Disneyland staff who interviewed the job applicants, ages 17 to 22, found a different neighborhood.
>
> "They were wonderful kids, outstanding kids," said Greg Albrecht, a spokesman for Disneyland. "We didn't know they were there." Nor, Mr. Albrecht added, had they known that the young people of South-Central Los Angeles would be so eager to work at Disneyland.[10]

There are several examples of emotional language here. Did you, for example, underline the words used to describe the two types of kids the author claims live in South-Central Los Angeles: *throwing, looting,* and *beating up* in contrast to *wonderful* and *outstanding*?

Emotional examples engage the emotions, as in this example: "One of the 600 who wanted to work at Disneyland was Olivia Miles, at 18 the youngest of seven children of a nurse's aide and a disabled roofer." Miss Miles has humble origins but achieves success. Success stories of this type usually result in positive emotional responses from the reader.

---

[9]Boris Yeltsin, "There Will Be No More Lies," *New York Times*, June 18, 1992, Sec. A, p. 8.

[10]Sara Rimer, "Jobs Illuminate What Riots Hid: Young Ideals," *New York Times*, June 18, 1992, Sec. A, pp. 1, 12.

Vivid description of an emotional scene creates an emotional reader response, as in this example:

> Aubrey Miles, who is 45, says he has taken pains to tell his daughter that there are good white people. They saved his life, he told her. He was putting a roof on an office building seven years ago when a vat of hot tar exploded. He was severely burned.
>
> "The guys on the job, who were white, helped me," he said. "I was on the ground, on fire. They put the fire out. One guy sat me up and put his back against my back. I could feel the connection. Then, afterward in the hospital, it was the same thing with the doctors."

Notice how this description brings you into the scene, causes you to share the physical sensations and emotions of the individuals described, and then to share in the conclusion about the people who helped.

Narratives of emotional events draw readers into a scene just as vivid description does. Here is a story about Olivia Miles and her reaction to the looting during the riots in Los Angeles:

> The riots presented Olivia Miles with the biggest ethical quandary of her life. "I saw people on television coming out with boxes of shoes and pretty furniture," she said. Her smile was embarrassed. "It was like Christmas. I wanted to get some. I was asking my sister if we could go. She said, 'No, you can't go out.' I thought: 'She's going to go to work. Should I get it, or shouldn't I get it? It's not fair that I can't. Everyone else is going to get stuff.' "
>
> This, too, her father had foreseen. "I told her, 'There are going to be a lot of opportunities for you to get things, so just stay in the house,' " Mr. Miles said. "She knew automatically that stealing was a no-no."
>
> That Sunday, Olivia was in her regular pew at the Mt. Sinai Baptist Church. "The pastor was saying, 'If you took something, shame on you. That's a sin,' " she said. She looked relieved all over again. "I was so happy."

By describing the emotions of the characters in a narrative, the author invites the reader to share them also.

Emotional tone, created by emotional language and examples, indicates that the author has a strong feeling about the subject and wants the audience to share that feeling. Also, irony and sarcasm should always be viewed as examples of emotional tone. They indicate strong feeling and a desire for change.

Figurative analogies contribute to emotion in an argument, particularly when two emotional subjects are compared and the resulting effect appeals more to emotion than to reason.

Emotional style is the easiest of all the styles to recognize because it is emotionally charged, and it is often close to our own experiences. Do not commit the common reading error of noticing only emotional style, ignoring logical and ethical style, and even missing the main point of the entire text because you become distracted by emotional material. Remember, in argument logic is the plot, and emotion and ethos add further support. Table 6.1 provides a summary of the characteristics of logical, ethical, and emotional style.

TABLE 6.1   A Summary of the Characteristics of Logical, Ethical, and Emotional Style

LOGICAL STYLE	ETHICAL STYLE	EMOTIONAL STYLE
Theoretical, abstract language	Language appropriate to audience and to subject	Vivid, concrete language
Denotative meanings	Consistent and appropriate tone	Emotionally loaded language
Reasons	Demonstrates author's reliability, competency, and respect for audience through reliable and appropriate use of support and general accuracy	Connotative meanings
Literal and historical analogies		Emotional examples
Explanations		Vivid descriptions
Definitions		Narratives of emotional events
Factual data		Emotional tone
Quotations		Figurative analogies
Citations from experts and authorities		Evokes an emotional response
Informed opinion		
Explicit, spelled out		
Evokes a cognitive, rational response		

THE FALLACIES OR PSEUDOPROOFS

In an advertisement for a health club, an attractive muscular man is embracing a beautiful slim woman. The caption reads, "Studies show diets don't work. This picture shows exercise does." No further evidence is provided. You do not have to be an expert in argument theory to sense that something is wrong with this proof.

Successful proof relies on skillful use of support and acceptable warrants to prove a claim. Since argument deals with probability instead of certainty, an argument may be perceived as very convincing, somewhat convincing, or not convincing at all. The success of the argument depends on the proofs, which include the quantity and quality of the support and the acceptability of the warrants. Weak support or a faulty or unacceptable warrant weakens an argument, but it is still an argument. The reader must ask the questions identified in this chapter to test the reliability and strength of the proofs and, ultimately, of the entire argument itself to decide whether it is well developed or underdeveloped, acceptable or unacceptable.

Sometimes, as in the case of the advertisement just described, a reader will encounter material that may appear at first to be a proof, but really isn't a proof at all. It is a pseudoproof, which is commonly called a fallacy. Fallacies lead an audience astray, they distort and distract, they represent inadequate reasoning or nonreasoning, and they oversimplify a claim instead of proving it.

You will encounter fallacies in advertisements, letters to the editor, and other argumentative writings. Avoid using them in your own writing because they weaken your argument and damage your *ethos*. Recognize fallacies by asking, Is this material even relevant? Is it adequate? Do I agree? Does it support the claim? Learning some of the common types of fallacies will also help you recognize them. Here are some of the most common ones categorized under the same categories we have used for genuine proofs: logical, ethical, and emotional.

Some Logical Fallacies

These fallacies pose as logical proof, but you will see that they are really pseudo-proofs that prove nothing at all. You may have trouble remembering all of their names; many people do. Concentrate, instead, on the fallacious thinking that is characteristic of each of them, such as introducing irrelevant material, providing wrong, unfair, inadequate, or even no support, drawing inappropriate conclusions, and oversimplifying the choices.

Begging the Question.   No support is provided by the arguer who begs the question, and the claim is simply restated, over and over again, in one form or another. For example, "Capital punishment deters crime because it keeps criminals from committing murder," simply restates the same idea, only in other words. Or here are other familiar examples: "Why is this true? It's true because I know it's true." Or "Everyone knows that the president of the United States has done his best for the environment because he said so." You can remember the name of this fallacy, begging the question, by recalling that the arguer, when asked for support, begs off and simply restates the claim in the same or different words.

Red Herring.   A red herring provides irrelevant and misleading support that pulls the audience away from the real argument. For example, "I don't believe we should hire this individual as chief executive officer of this company because his wife cannot cook, she does not stay home and care for her husband, and she does not meet the standards of a good American housewife." Authors of detective fiction sometimes use red herrings in their plots as false clues to divert the reader's attention from the real murderer. Remember the red herring fallacy by recalling that the fish, the red herring, was at one time used to train hunting dogs to follow a scent. It was not a true scent, however. The herring scent was irrelevant to the real smells of the real hunt, and the fallacy, the red herring, is irrelevant to an argument when it introduces such support as a wife's vocation as an influence on the husband's qualifications for a job.

Non Sequitur.   *Non sequitur* is Latin for "it does not follow." In this type of fallacy, the conclusion does not follow from the evidence and the warrant. In the example of the advertisement for the health club described at the beginning of this section, the statement "Studies show diets don't work. This picture shows exercise does" follows a picture of two slim, attractive people embracing. Most of us would agree that the picture, used as evidence, has little if anything to do with the claim that exercise works. The warrant, that exercise results in slimness, personal beauty, and romance, does not provide a convincing link between support and claim. Consequently, there is really no argument at all. Here is another example of a *non sequitur:* Women should not be placed in executive positions because they cannot drive cars as well as men.

   Straw Man.   A straw man is a proof that has nothing to do with the subject. The arguer sets up an irrelevant idea, refutes it, and appears to win, even though the idea may have little or nothing to do with the issue being discussed. For example, in an argument aimed at establishing the competence and experience of a political candidate, the arguer sets up a straw man that suggests the candidate's honesty in business dealings be examined and then gives evidence to prove that he has always been honest in business. This approach is irrelevant to the real issue of competency and experience in politics.

   Stacked Evidence.   Stacking evidence to represent only one side of an issue that clearly has two sides gives a distorted impression of the issue. For example, to prove that television is an inspiring and uplifting medium, the only evidence given is that "Sesame Street" is educational, "The Cosby Show" promotes family values, and news programs and documentaries keep audiences informed. The sex and violence programming is never mentioned.

   Either-Or.   Some arguments are oversimplified by the arguer and presented as black-or-white, either-or choices, when there are actually other alternatives. Some examples are "This country can either have a strong defense program or a strong social welfare program"; "We can either develop a strong space program or an urban development program"; "A woman can either be a mother or have a career"; and "A man can either go to graduate school or become a company man." No alternative, middle-ground, or compromise positions are acknowledged.

Some Ethical Fallacies

Ethical fallacies are aimed at attacking character or at using character instead of evidence as proof.

   Ad Hominem.   An *ad hominem* argument attacks a person's character rather than a person's ideas. The press is notorious for such attacks during political campaigns, and so are some of the candidates themselves. Negative information is provided about the candidates' personal lives rather than about their ideas and the issues. The purpose is to discredit them with the public. Or, here is another example: Christianity is said to have no validity because of the careless personal and financial habits of television evangelists. *Ad hominem* means "to the man" in Latin. An ad hominem argument directs attention away from the issues and to the man. Thus we become prejudiced and biased against an individual personally instead of evaluating that person's ideas.

Guilt by Association.   The fallacy of guilt by association suggests that people's character can be judged by examining the character of their associates. For example, an employee in a company that defrauds the government is declared dishonest because of his association with the company, even though he may have known nothing of the fraud. Or an observer is thrown into jail along with some political protestors simply because she was in the wrong place at the wrong time. It is assumed that she is a member of the group and guilty by association.

Using Authority instead of Evidence.   This is a variation of begging the question. The arguer relies on personal authority to prove a point rather than on evidence. For example, a salesman tells you to buy the used car because he is honest and trustworthy, and he knows your neighbor.

Some Emotional Fallacies

Irrelevant, unrelated, and distracting emotional materials are often introduced into argument to try to convince the audience. Here are some examples:

The Bandwagon Appeal.   The argument is that everyone is doing something, so you should also. For example, everyone is learning country-western dancing, so you should jump on the bandwagon and learn it also. Political and other public opinion polls are sometimes used to promote the bandwagon appeal. The suggestion is that since a majority of the people polled hold a certain opinion, you should adopt it also.

Slippery Slope.   The slippery-slope fallacy is a scare tactic that suggests that if we allow one thing to happen, we will immediately be sliding down the slippery slope to disaster. This fallacy is sometimes introduced into environment and abortion issues. Thus, if we allow loggers to cut a few trees, we will soon lose all the forests. Or, if a woman is required to wait 24 hours to reconsider her decision to have an abortion, soon no one will be permitted to have an abortion. This fallacy is similar to the saying about the camel that gets its nose into the tent. If we permit the nose today, we have the whole camel to deal with tomorrow. It is better not to start because disaster may result.

Creating False Needs.   Emotional proofs, as you have learned, appeal to what people value and think they need. Sometimes an arguer will create a false sense of need where none exists or will unrealistically heighten an existing need. The intent is to make the argument more convincing. Advertising provides excellent examples. The housewife is told she needs a shining kitchen floor with a high gloss that only a certain wax can provide. Parents are reminded that they want smart, successful children, so they should buy a set of encyclopedias.

These examples of fallacies will provide you with a good sense of what constitutes fallacious reasoning. Armed with this list and with the questions that test the validity of genuine proofs, you now have what you need to evaluate the strength and validity of the proofs in an argument. This information will help you make evaluations, form rebuttals in challenge of weak arguments, and create arguments of your own.

THE BOTTOM LINE QUESTIONS

You have now been provided with new information and questions to help you locate and evaluate the logical, ethical, and emotional proofs in an argument. Here are two bottom line questions you should ask when you have completed your reading and analysis of someone else's argument. They are also useful questions to ask of your own argument.

Bottom Line Question 1: *Am I convinced*? Ask, in other words, does this argument work for me? Why, or why not? Is the support fair, accurate, and convincing? Can I accept the warrants? Should the claim be qualified if it isn't already?

Bottom Line Question 2: *Is this argument moral or immoral according to your values and standards of behavior*? People were struck by some letters discovered in Germany a few years ago that were perfect examples of excellent technical writing, but whose subject matter was totally immoral. These letters were the written orders for exterminating the Jews during World War II. Though Hitler was a convincing arguer, his claims were immoral. Another example comes from the poem *Paradise Lost* by John Milton, where Satan, in the form of the serpent, makes an expert and extremely convincing argument to Eve to eat the apple, and she does. But Satan's argument is immoral by most people's standards. The classical argument theorists, Aristotle, Cicero, and Quintilian, all recognized that an arguer should be a good person with moral principles who is arguing for good causes. You will need to judge the final moral worth of an argument by testing it against your own system of values.

WHAT STRATEGIES CAN YOU NOW ADD TO IMPROVE YOUR PROCESS FOR READING AND WRITING ARGUMENT?

Reading Strategies

1. **Analyze the proofs**. Recognize logical, ethical, and emotional proofs and evaluate their validity.
2. **Recognize fallacies**. Be prepared to refute pseudoproofs that provide easy answers or distract you from the issue.

3. **Differentiate between rational, ethical, and emotional styles** and analyze their effects.
4. **Be sensitive to tone** and what it demonstrates about the author's attitude toward the audience and feeling for the subject.
5. **Ask the bottom line questions:** Am I convinced? Is this argument moral or immoral?

Writing Strategies

1. **Use the lists of proofs to help you create support** for your claim. Select those that are particularly appropriate for your topic.
2. **Avoid fallacies** in your writing.
3. **Decide which should be the predominant style** in your paper, logical or emotional.
4. **Create good *ethos*** by using language and tone that is appropriate to your audience and subject.
5. **Judge whether your argument is convincing and, also, whether it is moral or immoral** according to your own standards.

EXERCISES AND ACTIVITIES

1. CLASS DISCUSSION: ANALYZING AND TESTING PROOFS, ASKING THE BOTTOM LINE QUESTIONS, AND ANALYZING STYLE

a. Prepare for class discussion by reading the following essay, "The Two Nations," as well as the annotations in the margin that identify and describe the proofs in this essay.
b. Test the validity of these proofs by asking the *test of validity questions:*
Induction: Are the examples adequate? Would more examples continue to show the trend? Are there examples that show an opposite trend, that provide an exception? Can we make the inductive leap from the examples to the generalization to demonstrate that it is probably true?
Authority: Are the credentials of the person quoted good enough to make this contribution reliable? Are the credentials relevant to the issue?
Sign: Is this really a sign of what the author claims it to be? Is there another explanation for the sign?
Cause: Do these causes create these effects? Do these effects result from these causes? Can I think of exceptions that would change or alter the cause-effect outcome that is claimed here?
Historical analogy: Are the two items similar as claimed? Can I think of ways they are not similar or of other qualities they share that would change the claim? Will history repeat itself? Why? Why not?
Deduction: Is the warrant acceptable and believable? Is there enough support, and is it fair and accurate? Is it an example of the generalization expressed in the warrant? Is the conclusion also probably true?

c. Ask the bottom line questions:
    Are you convinced, or would you argue with one or more of the proofs?
    Do you accept the claim? Why? Why not?
    Is this argument moral or immoral by your standards?
d. What is the predominant language style in this essay—logical, ethical, or emotional? What other language and styles are also present? Explain your answer with examples.

THE TWO NATIONS

Anthony Lewis

Induction: Generalization that upper-income Americans live a better life than ordinary families, followed by examples in paragraphs 2 through 5.

1. Upper-income Americans generally, whether in public or private employment, live not just a better life but one quite removed from that of ordinary families. They hardly experience the problems that weigh so heavily today on American society. And that fact has dangerous political consequences.

Example: Health care

2. Health care, for example. The possibility of serious illness without insured care is now said to be the number one worry of Americans: not just the 40 million without any health insurance but the many millions more who have inadequate coverage or who are afraid to change jobs lest they lose protection.

3. The president does not have those concerns. He gets socialized medicine: care at public expense. Members of Congress and other top officials may also be treated in government hospitals. Nor is health insurance likely to be a concern for private Americans with incomes in the top 20 percent. Comprehensive coverage goes with the territory for them.

Example: Education

4. Or consider education. Public schools are among the most depressing features of contemporary life in this country, turning out young people unable to cope with the demands of a technological society—and culturally backward. Better-off families simply opt out of that problem. In large numbers, they send their children to private schools.

Example: Security

5. Crime is a menacing fact of daily life for millions of Americans; whole neighborhoods are unsafe. Of course the better-off may also be victims. But they increasingly protect themselves by living with alarm systems or in units with private security guards.

Induction: Generalization that top 20 percent is a varied group with examples of group members

6. All this refers not just to the super rich, the Lee Iacoccas whose inflated earnings have lately been so much discussed. The top-20-percent-income bracket includes business and financial people and professionals of all kinds: lawyers, doctors, journalists.

Authority: Establishes credentials of person quoted in next paragraph. Improves *ethos* of author because he is a friend of this writer and editor.

Sign: Food, hotels, etc. are signs of the sweet life.

Statistics: Summary and interpretation of who gets what.

Cause: Tax policies have caused the rich to become richer.

Historical analogy: The *ancien regime* in 1789 provided luxury for a few and was destroyed in the French Revolution.

Cause: The rich have the most political influence, which has caused or allowed them to create lower tax structures for themselves.

Deduction: *Warrant stated*: A democracy is not healthy when the top slice is isolated from the real problems.
Support: Twenty percent is isolated. (The rest of the essay proves this point.)
Conclusion (claim): We do not have a healthy democracy.

7. A friend of mine, a writer and editor, was at an economic conference in Switzerland recently. He is certainly not among the American rich. But he said he realized during that meeting how people of his professional class had come to have a qualitatively different life from most Americans.

8. "For the elite, life really is sweeter than it used to be," he said. "Food is so much better. Hotels are more sumptuous. The variety of amusements available, the sports, the travel—it's a cornucopia. For the few." And there's the rub: it *is* for the few. The top 20 percent of Americans now get 47 percent of the country's total income. The bottom fifth get 3.9 percent.

9. The gap between rich and poor in America is far and away the widest in the developed world. It has widened dramatically in the last 10 years, both because real incomes have grown at the top and shrunk at the bottom and because tax and other policies have exacerbated the differential.

10. America is more like the ancien regime in France than ever before. But luxury is not just for royalty and a handful of nobles. It is for the top 20 percent. That is a lot of people. And therein lie political consequences.

11. The professionals, the rich and the upper-middle-class families in the top 20 percent have the most political influence in this country. They care, they vote, they contribute to politicians. And quite naturally, not out of evil, they will tend to favor their own interest.

12. No one should really be surprised then, that tax rates on upper incomes are so much lower in the United States than in Japan or European countries. It is not hard to understand why a president talks about the need to improve public education but puts no money where his mouth is.

13. *In a democracy where a substantial top slice of the population is insulated from the country's most corrosive problems, it is politically very difficult to deal with those problems.* And the rest of the people, the majority who live with them, become increasingly cynical about government and politics.

14. *It is not a recipe for a healthy democratic society.*[11]

2. WRITING ASSIGNMENT: EMPLOYING PROOFS

Write a 2–3 page argument of your own in which you state one of the following claims and prove it. Limit yourself to one subclaim as in "The Two Nations."

a. The United States is a healthy democracy.

b. The United States is not a healthy democracy.

c. My college puts the interest and concerns of its students first.

d. My college does not put the interests and concerns of its students first.

---

[11]*New York Times*, February 13, 1992, Sec. A, p. 15.

Discuss with the class or your small group some proofs that you could use to support the claim you select. Remember SICDADS (sign, induction, cause, deduction, analogy, definition, statistics) and VAM (value, authority, motivation). Include at least two types of proof in your paper, and label them in the margin.

3. GROUP WORK AND DISCUSSION: EMOTIONAL PROOFS AND EMOTIONAL LANGUAGE AND STYLE

Prepare for group work and discussion by reading the following article, "The Whiny Generation." Focus on the emotional proofs and style in the essay. Answer the following questions, and have a member of your group report your findings to the class.

a. Identify *motivational proofs* in the essay. Look for references to items or qualities that the author claims the twentysomething generation wants, and also the items or qualities that the author claims they should want.
   Tests of validity: What are twentysomethings supposed to need, according to the author? Do they really need those things? What are they supposed to do to get them? Will doing what is recommended satisfy the need in the ways described?

b. Identify *value proofs* in the essay. Look for statements, stories, slogans, or examples that display the values that the author claims twentysomethings have. Look also for the values the author claims they should have. What does the author claim will result if twentysomethings accept the author's values?
   Tests of validity. Do you share the author's ideas about twentysomething values? Do you share the author's values? How do you differ? What effect do these differences have on your final acceptance of the claim?

THE WHINY GENERATION

David Martin

Ever since the publication of Douglas Coupland's book "Generation X," we've been subjected to a barrage of essays, op-ed pieces and feature articles blaming us baby boomers for the sad face of the twentysomething generation: the boomers took all the good jobs; the boomers are destroying the planet, the media is boomer-dominated and boomer-obsessed. The litany is never-ending. If you believe the Generation X essayists, all the troubles of the world can be traced to us fortysomethings.

Well, enough is enough. As a baby boomer, I'm fed up with the ceaseless carping of a handful of spoiled, self-indulgent, overgrown adolescents. Generation Xers may like to call themselves the "Why Me?" generation, but they should be called the "Whiny" generation. If these pusillanimous purveyors of pseudo-angst would put as much effort into getting a life as they do into writing about their horrible fate, we'd be spared the weekly diatribes that pass for reasoned argument in newspapers and magazines.

Let's examine for a moment the horrible fate visited on Generation X. This is a generation that was raised with the highest standard of living in the history of the world. By the time they arrived on the scene, their parents were comfortably established in the middle class and could afford to satisfy their offspring's every whim. And they did, in spades.

Growing up in the '70s and '80s, the twentysomethings were indulged with every toy, game and electronic device available. They didn't even have to learn how to amuse themselves since Mom and Dad were always there to ferry them from one organized activity to another. If we baby boomers were spoiled, the Whiny Generation was left out to rot. They had it all.

That's the essence of the Generation X problem. We have a generation (or at least part of a generation) whose every need has been catered to since birth. Now, when they finally face adulthood, they expect the gift-giving to continue. I'm 28 and I'll never own a house, whines the Generation Xer. I'm 25 and I don't have a high-paying job, says another.

Are these realistic expectations? Of course not. It's the rare individual in the last 40 years who had a high-paying job and owned a home prior to his or her 30th birthday. But the Whiners want everything now. A generation raised on the principle of instant satisfaction simply can't understand the concepts of long-term planning and deferred gratification. What's their reaction when they don't get what they want? That's right—they throw a tantrum.

The Whiners' most common complaint is that they've been relegated to what Mr. Coupland calls McJobs—low-paying, low-end positions in the service industry. I don't doubt that many Whiners are stuck in such jobs. But whose fault is that? Here's a generation that had enormous educational opportunities. But many Whiners squandered those chances figuring that a good job was a right not a privilege.

My parents' generation provided a better shot at post-secondary education for their boomer children than they themselves had enjoyed. And we took advantage of that situation in droves as the number of college and university graduates soared. The Whiners were afforded even greater scope for educational success but many of them failed to maximize their opportunities. They had the chance to reach higher but often chose not to or chose foolishly or unwisely.

Those who pursued a liberal-arts degree with a view to obtaining a job were either wealthy or naive. Those who thought that fine arts or film studies would yield more than a subsistence living were only fooling themselves. And those who entered law school will find sympathy hard to come by. More lawyers is one thing we definitely don't need.

The twentysomethings who planned their education wisely and spent the required years specializing in the technologies of the '90s now have the inside track in the job market. Those who chose to slide through high school to achieve semi-literacy are understandably unemployed or underemployed. Their cries of anguish do not now ring true. In fact, the youth unemployment rate is lower today than it was during the baby-boom recession of the early '80s. And despite the current recession, there are still plenty of positions available for highly skilled workers who exhibited the foresight and determination to achieve the necessary abilities.

The Whiners decry the lack of entry-level professional positions in the marketplace. Granted, during this current recession there are fewer such jobs. But that was also true in the early '80s. Instead of blaming everyone for this state of affairs, the Whiners should acquire more skills, education and specialized knowledge for the careers of the 21st century that will be awaiting those who have prepared themselves. Forget a career in law; start thinking about computers, telecomunications and health care.

POSITIONS OF POWER

As for the Whiners' complaint about the media being boomer-dominated and boomer-obsessed, that's nothing new. Once a generation has worked long and hard enough, it's only natural that some of its members become ensconced in positions of power. And once in power, it's not that surprising that they reflect the views, tastes and concerns of their contemporaries. Why should the media revolve around the lives of 25-year-olds? Remember, this is the generation whose biggest achievement to date is something called grunge rock. Once they've accomplished more, they'll get the media coverage.

So, I invite the Whiners to put aside their TV-generation values and accept cold, hard reality. Interesting, high-paying jobs and rich lifestyles are not automatic; they're not even commonplace. Most people live ordinary lives of quiet desperation stuck in uninteresting jobs that they're afraid to lose. If you want more than that, move out of your parents' houses, start working and, for heaven's sake, stop whining.[12]

   c. *Bottom line questions*:
     Are you convinced? Why, or why not?
     Is this argument moral or immoral by your standards? Why, or why not?
   d. *Language and style*.
     Identify examples of logical, ethical, and emotional argument.
     Which, would you say, predominates?

4. WRITING ASSIGNMENT: USING EMOTIONAL PROOFS

Write a two-page reaction to "The Whiny Generation" in which you either agree or disagree with the author's emotional proofs and provide original proofs of your own. Experiment with emotional language and style.

5. CLASS DISCUSSION AND WRITING ASSIGNMENT: PROOFS AND STYLE IN THE DECLARATION OF INDEPENDENCE

The Declaration of Independence, a classic argument, was written by Thomas Jefferson in 1776 and was used to separate the American colonies from Great Britain. It established America as independent states, and thus it is a revolutionary document with a revolutionary purpose.

---

[12]*Newsweek*, November 1, 1993, p. 10. David Martin, 43, is a lawyer and bureaucrat who lives in Ottawa.

a. Read the Declaration of Independence, and to understand it better, divide it into its three major component parts. Draw a line at the end of part 1, which explains the general principles behind the revolutionary action. Then draw a line at the end of part 2, which lists the reasons for the action. Finally, identify the purpose of the third and last brief part of the document.

b. The document presents a deductive argument with the warrants in part 1, the support in part 2, and the conclusion in part 3. Summarize this structure as a deductive argument. Follow the examples in the chapter.

c. Test the argument by questioning the warrants and the support. If you accept them, you accept the conclusion.

d. Identify other types of proof in the document.

e. Describe the predominant style in the document and give examples.

THE DECLARATION OF INDEPENDENCE

Thomas Jefferson

When in the course of human events, it becomes necessary for one people to dissolve the political bands which have connected them with another, and to assume among the Powers of the earth, the separate and equal station to which the Laws of Nature and of Nature's God entitle them, a decent respect to the opinions of mankind requires that they should declare the causes which impel them to the separation.

We hold these truths to be self-evident, that all men are created equal, that they are endowed by their Creator with certain unalienable Rights, that among these are Life, Liberty and the pursuit of Happiness.

That to secure these rights, Governments are instituted among Men, deriving their just powers from the consent of the governed.

That whenever any Form of Government becomes destructive of these ends, it is the Right of the People to alter or to abolish it, and to institute a new Government, laying its foundation on such principles and organizing its powers in such form, as to them shall seem most likely to effect their Safety and Happiness. Prudence, indeed, will dictate that Governments long established should not be changed for light and transient causes; and accordingly all experience hath shown that mankind are more disposed to suffer, while evils are sufferable, than to right themselves by abolishing the forms to which they are accustomed. But when a long train of abuses and usurpations pursuing invariably the same Object evinces a design to reduce them under absolute Despotism, it is their right, it is their duty, to throw off such government, and to provide new Guards for their future security.

Such has been the patient sufferance of these Colonies; and such is now the necessity which constrains them to alter their former Systems of Government. The history of the present King of Great Britain is a history of repeated injuries and usurpations, all having in direct object the establishment of an absolute Tyranny over these States. To prove this, let Facts be submitted to a candid world.

He has refused his Assent to Laws, the most wholesome and necessary for the public good.

He has forbidden his Governors to pass Laws of immediate and pressing importance, unless suspended in their operation till his Assent should be obtained; and when so suspended, he has utterly neglected to attend to them.

He has refused to pass other Laws for the accommodation of large districts of people, unless those people would relinquish the right of Representation in the Legislature, a right inestimable to them and formidable to tyrants only.

He has called together legislative bodies at places unusual, uncomfortable, and distant from the depository of their Public Records, for the sole purpose of fatiguing them into compliance with his measures.

He has dissolved Representative Houses repeatedly, for opposing with manly firmness his invasions on the rights of the people.

He has refused for a long time, after such dissolutions, to cause others to be elected; whereby the Legislative Powers, incapable of Annihilation, have returned to the People at large for their exercise; the State remaining in the mean time exposed to all the dangers of invasion from without, and convulsions within.

He has endeavored to prevent the population of these States; for that purpose obstructing the Laws for Naturalization of Foreigners; refusing to pass others to encourage their migration hither, and raising the conditions of new Appropriations of Lands.

He has obstructed the Administration of Justice, by refusing his Assent to Laws for establishing Judiciary Powers.

He has made Judges dependent on his Will alone, for the tenure of their offices, and the amount and payment of their salaries.

He has erected a multitude of New Offices, and sent hither swarms of Officers to harass our People, and eat out their substance.

He has kept among us, in time of peace, Standing Armies without the consent of our legislatures.

He has affected to render the Military independent of and superior to the Civil Power.

He has combined with others to subject us to jurisdictions foreign to our constitution, and unacknowledged by our laws; giving his Assent to their acts of pretended Legislation:

For quartering large bodies of armed troops among us:

For protecting them, by a mock Trial, from Punishment for any Murders which they should commit on the Inhabitants of these States:

For cutting off our Trade with all parts of the world:

For imposing Taxes on us without our Consent:

For depriving us in many cases of the benefits of Trial by Jury:

For transporting us beyond Seas to be tried for pretended offenses:

For abolishing the free System of English Laws in a neighbouring Province, establishing therein an Arbitrary government, and enlarging its Boundaries so as to render it at once an example and fit instrument for introducing the same absolute rule into these Colonies:

For taking away our Charters, abolishing our most valuable Laws, and altering fundamentally the Forms of our Governments.

For suspending our own Legislatures, and declaring themselves invested with Power to legislate for us in all cases whatsoever.

He has abdicated Government here, by declaring us out of his Protection and waging War against us.

He has plundered our seas, ravaged our Coasts, burnt our towns, and destroyed the Lives of our people.

He is at this time transporting large Armies of foreign Mercenaries to compleat the works of death, desolation and tyranny, already begun with circumstances of Cruelty & perfidy scarcely paralleled in the most barbarous ages, and totally unworthy the Head of a civilized nation.

He has constrained our fellow Citizens taken Captive on the high Seas to bear Arms against their Country, to become the executioners of their friends and Brethren, or to fall themselves by their Hands.

He has excited domestic insurrections amongst us, and has endeavored to bring on the inhabitants of our frontiers, the merciless Indian Savages, whose known rule of warfare, is an undistinguished destruction of all ages, sexes and conditions.

In every stage of these Oppressions We have Petitioned for Redress in the most humble terms: Our repeated Petitions have been answered only by repeated injury. A Prince, whose character is thus marked by every act which may define a Tyrant, is unfit to be the ruler of a free people.

Nor have We been wanting in attention to our British brethren. We have warned them from time to time of attempts by their legislature to extend an unwarrantable jurisdiction over us. We have reminded them of the circumstances of our emigration and settlement here. We have appealed to their native justice and magnanimity, and we have conjured them by the ties of our common kindred to disavow these usurpations, which would inevitably interrupt our connections and correspondence. They too have been deaf to the voice of justice and of consanguinity. We must, therefore, acquiesce in the necessity, which denounces our Separation, and hold them, as we hold the rest of mankind, Enemies in War, in Peace Friends.

We, therefore, the Representatives of the *United States of America*, in General Congress, Assembled, appealing to the Supreme Judge of the world for the rectitude of our intentions, do, in the Name, and by authority of the good People of these Colonies, solemnly publish and declare, That these United Colonies are, and of Right ought to be Free and Independent States; that they are Absolved from all Allegiance to the British Crown, and that all political connection between them and the State of Great Britain, is and ought to be totally dissolved; and that as Free and Independent States, they have full power to levy War, conclude Peace, contract Alliances, establish Commerce, and to do all other Acts and Things which Independent States may of right do. And for the support of this Declaration, with a firm reliance on the protection of Divine Providence, we mutually pledge to each other our Lives, our Fortunes and our sacred Honor.

f. Write a paper in which you explain the insights you now have about the structure, proofs, and style of the Declaration of Independence. Include an explanation of its parts, its deductive argument, its other types of proof, and its style.

6. GROUP WORK: FALLACIES

This exercise should help you understand, recognize, and remember some of the common fallacies. Read the following story and bring it up-to-date. Substitute a leather jacket or $200 athletic shoes for the raccoon coat. Each small group should take a fallacy. They are numbered in the margin. Change the slang and invent a modern example of each fallacy. (Note that there are some fallacies in this piece not mentioned in this chapter. You will be able to figure out why they are fallacies, however.) When you have finished your update, read or describe the changes you made to the class. Have fun with this exercise.

LOVE IS A FALLACY

Max Shulman

Cool was I and logical. Keen, calculating, perspicacious, acute, and astute—I was all of these. My brain was as powerful as a dynamo, as precise as a chemist's scales, as penetrating as a scalpel. And—think of it!—I was only eighteen.

It is not often that one so young has such a giant intellect. Take, for example, Petey Bellows, my roommate at the university. Same age, same background, but dumb as an ox. A nice enough fellow, you understand, but nothing upstairs. Emotional type. Unstable. Impressionable. Worst of all, a faddist. Fads, I submit, are the very negation of reason. To be swept up in every new craze that comes along, to surrender yourself to idiocy just because everybody else is doing it—this, to me, is the acme of mindlessness. Not, however, to Petey.

One afternoon I found Petey lying on his bed with an expression of such distress on his face that I immediately diagnosed appendicitis. "Don't move," I said. "Don't take a laxative. I'll get a doctor."

"Raccoon," he mumbled thickly.

"Raccoon?" I said, pausing in my flight.

"I want a raccoon coat," he wailed.

I perceived that his trouble was not physical, but mental. "Why do you want a raccoon coat?"

"I should have known it," he cried, pounding his temples. "I should have known they'd come back when the Charleston came back. Like a fool I spent all my money for textbooks, and now I can't get a raccoon coat."

"Can you mean," I said incredulously, "that people are actually wearing raccoon coats again?"

"All the Big Men on Campus are wearing them. Where've you been?"

"In the library," I said, naming a place not frequented by Big Men on Campus.

He leaped from the bed and paced the room. "I've got to have a raccoon coat," he said passionately. "I've got to!"

"Petey, why? Look at it rationally. Raccoon coats are unsanitary. They shed. They smell bad. They weigh too much. They're unsightly. They—"

"You don't understand," he interrupted impatiently. "It's the thing to do. Don't you want to be in the swim?"

"No," I said truthfully.

"Well, I do," he declared. "I'd give anything for a raccoon coat. Anything!"

My brain, that precision instrument, slipped into high gear. "Anything?" I asked, looking at him narrowly.

"Anything," he affirmed in ringing tones.

I stroked my chin thoughtfully. It so happened that I knew where to get my hands on a raccoon coat. My father had had one in his undergraduate days; it lay now in a trunk in the attic back home. It also happened that Petey had something I wanted. He didn't *have* it exactly, but at least he had first rights on it. I refer to his girl, Polly Espy.

I had long coveted Polly Espy. Let me emphasize that my desire for this young woman was not emotional in nature. She was, to be sure, a girl who excited the emotions, but I was not one to let my heart rule my head. I wanted Polly for a shrewdly calculated, entirely cerebral reason.

I was a freshman in law school. In a few years I would be out in practice. I was well aware of the importance of the right kind of wife in furthering a lawyer's career. The successful lawyers I had observed were, almost without exception, married to beautiful, gracious, intelligent women. With one omission, Polly fitted these specifications perfectly.

Beautiful she was. She was not yet of pin-up proportions, but I felt sure that time would supply the lack. She already had the makings.

Gracious she was. By gracious I mean full of graces. She had an erectness of carriage, an ease of bearing, a poise that clearly indicated the best of breeding. At table her manners were exquisite. I had seen her at the Kozy Kampus Korner eating the specialty of the house—a sandwich that contained scraps of pot roast, gravy, chopped nuts, and a dipper of sauerkraut—without even getting her fingers moist.

Intelligent she was not. In fact, she veered in the opposite direction. But I believed that under my guidance she would smarten up. At any rate, it was worth a try. It is, after all, easier to make a beautiful dumb girl smart than to make an ugly smart girl beautiful.

"Petey," I said, "are you in love with Polly Espy?"

"I think she's a keen kid," he replied, "but I don't know if you'd call it love. Why?"

"Do you," I asked, "have any kind of formal arrangement with her? I mean are you going steady or anything like that?"

"No. We see each other quite a bit, but we both have other dates. Why?"

"Is there," I asked, "any other man for whom she has a particular fondness?"

"Not that I know of. Why?"

I nodded with satisfaction. "In other words, if you were out of the picture, the field would be open. Is that right?"

"I guess so. What are you getting at?"

"Nothing, nothing," I said innocently, and took my suitcase out of the closet.

"Where you going?" asked Petey.

"Home for the week end." I threw a few things into the bag.

"Listen," he said, clutching my arm eagerly, "while you're home, you couldn't get some money from your old man, could you, and lend it to me so I can buy a raccoon coat?"

"I may do better than that," I said with a mysterious wink and closed my bag and left.

"Look," I said to Petey when I got back Monday morning. I threw open the suitcase and revealed the huge, hairy, gamy object that my father had worn in his Stutz Bearcat in 1925.

"Holy Toledo!" said Petey reverently. He plunged his hands into the raccoon coat and then his face. "Holy Toledo!" he repeated fifteen or twenty times.

"Would you like it?" I asked.

"Oh yes!" he cried, clutching the greasy pelt to him. Then a canny look came into his eyes. "What do you want for it?"

"Your girl," I said, mincing no words.

"Polly?" he said in a horrified whisper. "You want Polly?"

"That's right."

He flung the coat from him. "Never," he said stoutly.

I shrugged. "Okay. If you don't want to be in the swim, I guess it's your business."

I sat down in a chair and pretended to read a book, but out of the corner of my eye I kept watching Petey. He was a torn man. First he looked at the coat with the expression of a waif at a bakery window. Then he turned away and set his jaw resolutely. Then he looked back at the coat, with even more longing in his face. Then he turned away, but with not so much resolution this time. Back and forth his head swiveled, desire waxing, resolution waning. Finally he didn't turn away at all; he just stood and stared with mad lust at the coat.

"It isn't as though I was in love with Polly," he said thickly. "Or going steady or anything like that."

"That's right," I murmured.

"What's Polly to me, or me to Polly?"

"Not a thing," said I.

"It's just been a casual kick—just a few laughs, that's all."

"Try on the coat," said I.

He complied. The coat bunched high over his ears and dropped all the way down to his shoe tops. He looked like a mound of dead raccoons. "Fits fine," he said happily.

I rose from my chair. "Is it a deal?" I asked, extending my hand.

He swallowed. "It's a deal," he said and shook my hand.

I had my first date with Polly the following evening. This was in the nature of a survey; I wanted to find out just how much work I had to do to get her mind up to the standard I required. I took her first to dinner. "Gee, that was a delish dinner," she said as we left the restaurant. Then I took her to a movie. "Gee, that was a marvy movie," she said as we left the theater. And then I took her home. "Gee, I had a sensaysh time," she said as she bade me good night.

I went back to my room with a heavy heart. I had gravely underestimated the size of my task. This girl's lack of information was terrifying. Nor would it be enough merely to supply her with information. First she had to be taught to *think*. This loomed as a project of no small dimensions, and at first I was tempted to give her back to Petey. But then I got to thinking about her abundant physical charms and about the way she entered a room and the way she handled a knife and fork, and I decided to make an effort.

I went about it, as in all things, systematically. I gave her a course in logic. It happened that I, as a law student, was taking a course in logic myself, so I had all the facts at my fingertips. "Polly," I said to her when I picked her up on our next date, "tonight we are going over to the Knoll and talk."

"Oo, terrif," she replied. One thing I will say for this girl: you would go far to find another so agreeable.

We went to the Knoll, the campus trysting place, and we sat down under an old oak, and she looked at me expectantly. "What are we going to talk about?" she asked.

"Logic."

She thought this over for a minute and decided she liked it. "Magnif," she said.

"Logic," I said, clearing my throat, "is the science of thinking. Before we can think correctly, we must first learn to recognize the common fallacies of logic. These we will take up tonight."

"Wow-dow!" she cried, clapping her hands delightedly.

1   I winced, but went bravely on. "First let us examine the fallacy called Dicto Simpliciter."

"By all means," she urged, batting her lashes eagerly.

"Dicto Simpliciter means an argument based on an unqualified generalization. For example: Exercise is good. Therefore everybody should exercise."

"I agree," said Polly earnestly. "I mean exercise is wonderful. I mean it builds the body and everything."

"Polly," I said gently, "the argument is a fallacy. *Exercise is good* is an unqualified generalization. For instance, if you have heart disease, exercise is bad, not good. Many people are ordered by their doctors *not* to exercise. You must *qualify* the generalization. You must say exercise is *usually* good, or exercise is good *for most people*. Otherwise you have committed a Dicto Simpliciter. Do you see?"

"No," she confessed. "But this is marvy. Do more! Do more!"

"It will be better if you stop tugging at my sleeve," I told her, and when she 2   desisted, I continued. "Next we take up a fallacy called Hasty Generalization. Listen carefully: You can't speak French. I can't speak French. Petey Bellows can't speak French. I must therefore conclude that nobody at the University of Minnesota can speak French."

"Really?" said Polly, amazed. *"Nobody?"*

I hid my exasperation. "Polly, it's a fallacy. The generalization is reached too hastily. There are too few instances to support such a conclusion."

"Know any more fallacies?" she asked breathlessly. "This is more fun than dancing even."

3 I fought off a wave of despair. I was getting nowhere with this girl, absolutely nowhere. Still, I am nothing if not persistent. I continued. "Next comes Post Hoc. Listen to this: Let's not take Bill on our picnic. Every time we take him out with us, it rains."

"I know somebody just like that," she exclaimed. "A girl back home—Eula Becker, her name is. It never fails. Every single time we take her on a picnic—"

"Polly," I said sharply, "it's a fallacy. Eula Becker doesn't *cause* the rain. She has no connection with the rain. You are guilty of Post Hoc if you blame Eula Becker."

"I'll never do it again," she promised contritely. "Are you mad at me?"

I sighed. "No, Polly, I'm not mad."

"Then tell me some more fallacies."

4 "All right. Let's try Contradictory Premises."

"Yes, let's," she chirped, blinking her eyes happily.

I frowned, but plunged ahead. "Here's an example of Contradictory Premises: If God can do anything, can He make a stone so heavy that He won't be able to lift it?"

"Of course," she replied promptly.

"But if He can do anything, He can lift the stone," I pointed out.

"Yeah," she said thoughtfully. "Well, then I guess He can't make the stone."

"But He can do anything," I reminded her.

She scratched her pretty, empty head. "I'm all confused," she admitted.

"Of course you are. Because when the premises of an argument contradict each other, there can be no argument. If there is an irresistible force, there can be no immovable object. If there is an immovable object, there can be no irresistible force. Get it?"

"Tell me some more of this keen stuff," she said eagerly.

I consulted my watch. "I think we'd better call it a night. I'll take you home now, and you go over all the things you've learned. We'll have another session tomorrow night."

I deposited her at the girl's dormitory, where she assured me that she had had a perfectly terrif evening, and I went glumly home to my room. Petey lay snoring in his bed, the raccoon coat huddled like a great hairy beast at his feet. For a moment I considered waking him and telling him that he could have his girl back. It seemed clear that my project was doomed to failure. The girl simply had a logic-proof head.

But then I reconsidered. I had wasted one evening; I might as well waste another. Who knew? Maybe somewhere in the extinct crater of her mind a few embers still smoldered. Maybe somehow I could fan them into flame. Admittedly it was not a prospect fraught with hope, but I decided to give it one more try.

Seated under the oak the next evening I said, "Our first fallacy tonight is called Ad Misericordiam."

5

She quivered with delight.

"Listen closely," I said. "A man applies for a job. When the boss asks him what his qualifications are, he replies that he has a wife and six children at home, the wife is a helpless cripple, the children have nothing to eat, no clothes to wear, no shoes on their feet, there are no beds in the house, no coal in the cellar, and winter is coming."

A tear rolled down each of Polly's pink cheeks. "Oh, this is awful, awful," she sobbed.

"Yes, it's awful," I agreed, "but it's no argument. The man never answered the boss's question about his qualifications. Instead he appealed to the boss's sympathy. He committed the fallacy of Ad Misericordiam. Do you understand?"

"Have you got a handkerchief?" she blubbered.

6

I handed her a handkerchief and tried to keep from screaming while she wiped her eyes. "Next," I said in a carefully controlled tone, "we will discuss False Analogy. Here is an example: Students should be allowed to look at their textbooks during examinations. After all, surgeons have X rays to guide them during an operation, lawyers have briefs to guide them during a trial, carpenters have blueprints to guide them when they are building a house. Why, then, shouldn't students be allowed to look at their textbooks during an examination?"

"There now," she said enthusiastically, "is the most marvy idea I've heard in years."

"Polly," I said testily, "the argument is all wrong. Doctors, lawyers, and carpenters aren't taking a test to see how much they have learned, but students are. The situations are altogether different, and you can't make an analogy between them."

"I still think it's a good idea," said Polly.

7

"Nuts," I muttered. Doggedly I pressed on. "Next we'll try Hypothesis Contrary to Fact."

"Sounds yummy," was Polly's reaction.

"Listen: If Madame Curie had not happened to leave a photographic plate in a drawer with a chunk of pitchblende, the world today would not know about radium."

"True, true," said Polly, nodding her head. "Did you see the movie? Oh, it just knocked me out. That Walter Pidgeon is so dreamy. I mean he fractures me."

"If you can forget Mr. Pidgeon for a moment," I said coldly, "I would like to point out that the statement is a fallacy. Maybe Madame Curie would have discovered radium at some later date. Maybe somebody else would have discovered it. Maybe any number of things would have happened. You can't start with a hypothesis that is not true and then draw any supportable conclusions from it."

"They ought to put Walter Pidgeon in more pictures," said Polly. "I hardly ever see him any more."

8   One more chance, I decided. But just one more. There is a limit to what flesh and blood can bear. "The next fallacy is called Poisoning the Well."

"How cute!" she gurgled.

"Two men are having a debate. The first one gets up and says, 'My opponent is a notorious liar. You can't believe a word that he is going to say.' . . . Now, Polly, think. Think hard. What's wrong?"

I watched her closely as she knit her creamy brow in concentration. Suddenly a glimmer of intelligence—the first I had seen—came into her eyes. "It's not fair," she said with indignation. "It's not a bit fair. What chance has the second man got if the first man calls him a liar before he even begins talking?"

"Right!" I cried exultantly. "One hundred percent right. It's not fair. The first man has *poisoned the well* before anybody could drink from it. He has hamstrung his opponent before he could even start. . . . Polly, I'm proud of you."

"Pshaw," she murmured, blushing with pleasure.

"You see, my dear, these things aren't so hard. All you have to do is concentrate. Think—examine—evaluate. Come now, let's review everything we have learned."

"Fire away," she said with an airy wave of her hand.

Heartened by the knowledge that Polly was not altogether a cretin, I began a long, patient review of all I had told her. Over and over and over again I cited instances, pointed out flaws, kept hammering away without letup. It was like digging a tunnel. At first everything was work, sweat, and darkness. I had no idea when I would reach the light, or even *if* I would. But I persisted. I pounded and clawed and scraped, and finally I was rewarded. I saw a chink of light. And then the chink got bigger and the sun came pouring in and all was bright.

Five grueling nights this took, but it was worth it. I had made a logician out of Polly; I had taught her to think. My job was done. She was worthy of me at last. She was a fit wife for me, a proper hostess for my many mansions, a suitable mother for my well-heeled children.

It must not be thought that I was without love for this girl. Quite the contrary. Just as Pygmalion loved the perfect woman he had fashioned, so I loved mine. I decided to acquaint her with my feelings at our very next meeting. The time had come to change our relationship from academic to romantic.

"Polly," I said when next we sat beneath our oak, "tonight we will not discuss fallacies."

"Aw, gee," she said, disappointed.

"My dear," I said, favoring her with a smile, "we have now spent five evenings together. We have gotten along splendidly. It is clear that we are well matched."

2   "Hasty Generalization," said Polly brightly.

"I beg your pardon," said I.

"Hasty Generalization," she repeated. "How can you say that we are well matched on the basis of only five dates?"

I chuckled with amusement. The dear child had learned her lesson well. "My dear," I said, patting her hand in a tolerant manner, "five dates is plenty. After all, you don't have to eat a whole cake to know that it's good."

6   "False Analogy," said Polly promptly. "I'm not a cake. I'm a girl."

I chuckled with somewhat less amusement. The dear child had learned her lesson perhaps too well. I decided to change tactics. Obviously the best approach was a simple, strong, direct declaration of love. I paused for a moment while my massive brain chose the proper words. Then I began:

"Polly, I love you. You are the whole world to me, and the moon and the stars and the constellations of outer space. Please, my darling, say that you will go steady with me, for if you will not, life will be meaningless. I will languish. I will refuse my meals. I will wander the face of the earth, a shambling, hollow-eyed hulk."

There, I thought, folding my arms, that ought to do it.

5   "Ad Misericordiam," said Polly.

I ground my teeth. I was not Pygmalion; I was Frankenstein, and my monster had me by the throat. Frantically I fought back the tide of panic surging through me. At all costs I had to keep cool.

"Well, Polly," I said, forcing a smile, "you certainly have learned your fallacies."

"You're darn right," she said with a vigorous nod.

"And who taught them to you, Polly?"

"You did."

"That's right. So you do owe me something, don't you, my dear? If I hadn't come along you never would have learned about fallacies."

7   "Hypothesis Contrary to Fact," she said instantly.

I dashed perspiration from my brow. "Polly," I croaked, "you mustn't take all these things so literally. I mean this is just classroom stuff. You know that the things you learn in school don't have anything to do with life."

1   "Dicto Simpliciter," she said, wagging her finger at me playfully.

That did it. I leaped to my feet, bellowing like a bull. "Will you or will you not go steady with me?"

"I will not," she replied.

"Why not?" I demanded.

"Because this afternoon I promised Petey Bellows that I would go steady with him."

I reeled back, overcome with the infamy of it. After he promised, after he made a deal, after he shook my hand! "That rat!" I shrieked, kicking up great chunks of turf. "You can't go with him, Polly. He's a liar. He's a cheat. He's a rat."

8   "Poisoning the Well," said Polly, "and stop shouting. I think shouting must be a fallacy too."

With an immense effort of will, I modulated my voice. "All right," I said. "You're a logician. Let's look at this thing logically. How could you choose Petey Bellows over me? Look at me—a brilliant student, a tremendous intellectual, a man with an assured future. Look at Petey—a knothead, a jitterbug, a guy who'll never know where his next meal is coming from. Can you give me one logical reason why you should go steady with Petey Bellows?"

"I certainly can," declared Polly. "He's got a raccoon coat."[13]

---

[13]Harold Matson Company, Inc., 1951. Renewed 1979 by Max Shulman.

7. INDIVIDUAL ONGOING PROJECT: SUPPORT YOUR CLAIM WITH PROOFS

You may want to prepare for this writing assignment by discussing possible proofs for your claim with your writing group.

a. Write your claim.
b. Review the proofs and select at least one but probably no more than three to use to prove the claim.
c. Write a two-page paper in which you state your claim and prove it.
d. In a two-minute oral report, summarize your claim and proofs for the class. This report will provide many brief examples of how proofs are used to support claims.

8. UNDERSTANDING THE CHAPTER: WHOLE CLASS, GROUPS, OR INDIVIDUALS

Summarize the major ideas in this chapter by completing the following sentences briefly and in your own words:

a. Logical proof appeals to . . . Examples are . . .
b. Ethical proof appeals to . . . An example is . . .
c. Emotional proof appeals to . . . Examples are . . .
d. The types of language and style identified were . . . Special characteristics of each are . . .
e. Fallacies are . . . Examples of the faulty thinking found in fallacies include . . .
f. The bottom line questions are . . .
g. Strategies to add to your reading process include . . .

CHAPTER 7

Types of Claims

Argument theorists categorize claims according to types, and these types suggest the fundamental purposes of given arguments. Knowing possible categories for claims and the special characteristics associated with each of them will help you better understand the purposes and special features of the arguments you read, and will also improve your writing of them. When reading, as soon as you identify the type of claim in an argument, you can predict and anticipate certain features of that type of argument. This technique helps you follow the author's line of thought more easily. When writing, knowing the types of claims can provide you with frameworks for developing your purpose and strategy.

When you begin to read argument with the idea of locating the claim and identifying it by type, your ability to identify and understand all the parts of an argument will increase. The next section presents a strategy for analyzing an argument to get a sense of its purpose and to identify its parts.

GET A SENSE OF THE PURPOSE AND PARTS OF AN ARGUMENT

Survey. Follow the procedure for surveying a book on page 84 or for surveying an article on page 85. Your objective is to find the claim and some of the main subclaims or parts.

Divide the Argument into Its Parts. Draw a line across the page (or make a light dot in the margin) each time the subject changes. This physical division of a written argument into its parts is called *chunking*. For example, in a policy paper that proposes a solution to a problem, the explanation of the problem would be a major chunk, as would be the explanation of the solution.

Ask Why the Parts Have Been Placed in the Particular Order. Try to determine if the parts have been placed in a logical order to facilitate understanding, for instance, or whether they have been placed in a psychological order, leading up to the conclusion or action step at the end. There are other possibilities as well. Try to get a sense of how the author thought about and organized the parts.

Analyze the Relationships among the Parts.   When you have speculated about why the author put the parts in a particular order, go a step further and think about the relationships among these parts. Do they all contribute to a central idea, such as a specialized definition? Or are other relationships apparent, such as causes for effects or solutions for problems?

When you begin to write argument, write a claim, list a few supporting reasons that represent the tentative parts, and then think about the best sequence for these parts. The relationships among them will become clearer to you as you rearrange them in an order that is logical to you.

Once you have a sense of the overall purpose and shape of an argument, you can then identify the type of claim that predominates in it.

FIVE CATEGORIES OF CLAIMS

Virtually all arguments can be categorized according to one of five types of claims. You can identify each argument type by identifying the questions the argument answers. In general, certain types of organization and proof are associated with certain types of claims, as you will see in the following discussion. There are no hard-and-fast rules about using specific organizational strategies or types of proof to develop specific types of claims. Knowing common patterns and tendencies, however, helps readers make predictions about the course of an argument and helps writers plan and write their own arguments.

Here are the five categories of claims, along with the main questions that they answer:

1. *Claims of fact*. Did it happen? Is it true?
2. *Claims of definition*. What is it? How should we interpret it?
3. *Claims of cause*. What caused it? Or, what are the effects?
4. *Claims of value*. Is it good or bad? What criteria do we use to decide?
5. *Claims of policy*. What should we do about it? What should be our future course of action?

The sections that follow provide additional explanations of the five types of claims, along with the general questions they answer, some examples of actual claims, a list of the types of proof most typically associated with each type, the organizational strategies that one might expect for each type, and a short written argument that illustrates each type as it appears in practice.

Claims of Fact

Questions Answered by Claims of Fact.   Did it happen? Is it true? Does it exist? Is it a fact?

Examples of Claims of Fact.   (Note that all of the "facts" in these claims need to be proved as either absolutely or probably true in order to be acceptable to an audience. All of these claims, also, are controversial.) The ozone layer is becoming depleted. Increasing population threatens the environment. American drivers are becoming more responsible. America's military is prepared for any likely crisis. The abominable snowman exists in certain remote areas. Women are not as effective as men in combat. A mass murderer is evil and not insane. The American judicial system operates successfully.

Types of Proof Associated with Claims of Fact.

Types of Proof Associated with Claims of Fact. Factual proof, as you might guess, is especially appropriate for claims of fact. Such proof includes both past and present *facts, statistics, real examples,* and *quotations from reliable authorities. Inductive reasoning,* which cites several examples and then draws a probable conclusion from them, is also a common type of proof for claims of fact. *Analogies* that establish comparisons and similarities between the subject and something else that is commonly accepted as true are useful. *Signs* that present evidence of a past or present state of affairs are also useful to establish claims of fact. *Opinions* are used to support claims of fact and are usually also supported by factual data.

Possible Organizational Strategies. Chronological order, which traces what has occurred over a period of time, usually in the order in which it occurred, can be used to develop claims of fact. For example, the history of the increase in population might be provided to show how it has happened over a period of time. Or topical order may be used. In topical order a group of reasons to support a fact may be identified and developed topic by topic. Thus reasons might be given for the existence of the abominable snowman, with each of them developed at length. This chapter is organized according to topics: the five types of claims.

The claim of fact itself is often stated at or near the beginning of the argument unless there is a psychological advantage for stating it at the end. Most authors make claims of fact clear from the outset, revealing early what they seek to establish.

An Example of an Argument That Contains a Claim of Fact. The fact being established in the article from which the following excerpt was taken is that Americans have grown pessimistic about the current state of the country. This is controversial. A rebuttal might use different evidence to establish a different fact, that Americans are optimistic.

Real example of someone who is pessimistic about the country

Brian Williams is part of the great American dream.

Born one of eight children in a poor black family whose father worked in the meat-packing houses here, he has scratched and struggled his way up to the point here now, at the age of 25, he holds a degree from Princeton University and runs his own printing company.

But Brian Williams is worried.

"Given all the trouble we're having governing this country and keeping the economy going," he says, "I'm not sure the great American dream will come true for my children the way it did for me. It seems to me that for the first time in American history, *there is a real possibility that the next generation may have less opportunity than the current generation.*"

Claim of fact

Sign to support
the claim
    Mr. Williams is far from alone in his concern.... *In dozens of interviews* conducted during a 1,500-mile journey across the country to this heartland city, *pessimism emerged* again and again as the dominant mood.[1]

Claims of Definition

Questions Answered by Claims of Definition. What is it? What is it like? How should it be classified? How should it be interpreted? How does its usual meaning change in a particular context?

Examples of Claims of Definition. (Note that here we are looking at definition claims that dominate the argument in the essay as a whole. Definition also serves at the level of a proof for other types of claims.) We need to define what constitutes a family before we talk about family values. In order to determine whether a publication is pornography or a work of art, we need to define what we mean by pornography in this context. To determine whether the police were doing their job or were engaging in brutality, we need to establish what we mean by police brutality. In order to determine whether a person is mentally competent, we need to define what we mean by that term. Should we describe what occurred during the 1992 Los Angeles riots as civil disobedience or vandalism? If we have established the fact that young men killed their parents, shall we define this killing as self-defense or premeditated murder?

Types of Proof Associated with Claims of Definition. The main types of proof used to prove claims of definition are *references to reliable authorities and accepted sources* that can be used to establish clear definitions and meanings, such as the dictionary or a well-known work. Also useful are *analogies* and other comparisons, especially to other words or situations that are clearly understood and that can consequently be used to shed some light on what is being defined. *Examples*, both real and hypothetical, and *signs* can also be used to clarify or develop definitions.

Possible Organizational Strategies. Comparison-and-contrast organization can dominate the development of a claim of definition and serve as the main structure. In this structure two or more objects are compared and contrasted throughout. For example, in an essay that expands the notion of crime to include white-collar crime, conventional crime would be compared with white-collar crime to prove that they are similar. In the previous chapter, we showed how some people compare abortion to murder to prove how they are similar.

    Topical organization may also be used. Several special qualities, characteristics, or features of the word or concept are identified and explained as discrete

---

[1]Drummond Ayres, Jr., "Shadow of Pessimism Eclipses a Dream," *New York Times,* February 9, 1992, Sec. 1, pp. 1, 12.

topics. Thus, in an essay defining a criminal as mentally competent, the characteristics of mental competence would be explained as separate topics and applied to the criminal. Another strategy is to explain the controversy over the term and give reasons for accepting one view over another.

An Example of an Argument That Contains a Claim of Definition.   The following excerpt suggests the confusion that can be created if people do not agree on a definition for a term. William Safire writes a regular column on language for the *New York Times Magazine*, and his analysis in a column entitled "Family Values" identifies some of the definition arguments of the 1992 political campaign when family values were a political issue.

FAMILY VALUES

William Safire

Quote from reliable authority and first definition

"Integrity, courage, strength"—those were the *family values* as defined by Barbara Bush at the Republican convention in Houston. She added "sharing, love of God and pride in being an American." Not much controversy in that definition.

Another authority and a second definition

But on "family values night," as Marilyn Quayle described the session dominated by Republican women, the values took on an accusatory edge: after recalling that many in the baby boom had not "joined the counterculture" or "dodged the draft," the Vice President's wife made clear to cheering conservatives what she felt was at the center of family values: "Commitment, marriage and fidelity are not just arbitrary arrangements."

Another authority and a third definition

Pat Robertson, the religious broadcaster who sought the Presidential nomination four years ago, eschewed such innuendo and slammed home the political point: "When Bill and Hillary Clinton talk about family values, they are not talking about either families or values. They are talking about a radical plan to destroy the traditional family."

Another authority and a fourth definition

Claim of definition: the meaning that emerges this year

We have here the G.O.P.'s political attack phrase of the 1992 campaign. When Mario Cuomo stressed the words *family* and *values* in his speech to the 1984 Democratic convention, he used them in a warmly positive sense. But *this year*, packaged in a single phrase, *the terms are an assertion of moral traditionalism* that carries an implicit charge: the other side seeks to undermine the institution of the family by taking a permissive line on (a) abortion rights, (b) homosexual rights and (c) the "character issue," code words for marital infidelity.

Signs of a lack of family values according to new definition

Sometimes pot smoking is included, but sex is most often the common denominator, and the pointing finger includes women who do not center their lives inside the home: the defeated candidate Pat Buchanan includes "radical feminist" in his angry denunciation of those who lack what he considers to be family values.[2]

Claims of Cause

Questions Answered by Claims of Cause. What caused it? Where did it come from? Why did it happen? What are the effects? What probably will be the results both on a short-term and a long-term basis?

Examples of Claims of Cause. The United States champions human rights in foreign countries to further its own economic self-interests. Clear-cutting is the main cause of the destruction of ancient forests. Legalizing marijuana could have beneficial effects for medicine. The American people's current mood has been caused by a lack of faith in political leaders. The long-term effects of inadequate funding for AIDS research will be a disastrous worldwide epidemic. The Los Angeles riots were caused by social service programs that failed. Censorship can have good results by protecting children.

Types of Proof Associated with Claims of Cause. The argument must establish the probability of a cause-effect relationship. The best type of proof for this purpose is *factual data*, including *statistics* that are used to prove a cause or an effect. You can also expect *analogies*, including both *literal* and *historical analogies* that parallel cases in past history to show that the cause of one event could also be the cause of another similar event. You can, furthermore, expect *signs* of certain causes or effects, and you can also expect *induction*. Several examples cited as a cause will invite the inductive leap to a possible effect as the end result. *Deduction* is also used to develop claims of cause. Premises about effects are proposed, as in the Sherlock Holmes example in Chapter 6, and a conclusion about the possible cause is drawn.

Possible Organizational Strategies. One strategy is to describe causes and then effects. Thus clear-cutting would be described as a cause that would lead to the ultimate destruction of the forests, which would be the effect. Or effects may be described and then the cause or causes. The effects of censorship may be described before the public efforts that caused that censorship. You may also encounter refutation of other actual or possible causes or effects.

An Example of an Argument That Contains a Claim of Cause. The causes of heart disease have been an issue and the subject of scientific inquiry for some time. Also controversial has been the question of the similarities and differences between men and women in regard to this issue. The next article claims that the causes of heart disease in women may be different from those in men. Note the inductive proof that is used in this article, that is, a scientific hypothesis is derived from a number of examples or cases.

---

[2]*New York Times Magazine*, September 6, 1992, p. 14.

WOMEN TAKE UN–TYPE A BEHAVIOR TO HEART

B. Bower

Claim of cause

In affairs of the heart, women often differ from men. *A new study indicates that personality traits linked to an early death from heart disease may also vary between the sexes.*

Induction: Generalizations about the cause of male and female heart disease derived from examples

Research conducted over the past 30 years finds that male heart-attack survivors stand a greater chance of dying from a heart ailment if they display a Type A personality, one bursting with hostility, cynicism, and impatience. The converse appears true for women. Female heart-attack survivors who keep a lid on their anger and react slowly to external events prove most likely to suffer fatal heart problems, report Lynda H. Powell, a psychologist at Rush-Presbyterian-St. Luke's Medical Center in Chicago, and her colleagues.

Their investigation, a rare effort to identify psychological and social factors that put women at risk for suffering recurrences of physical disease, appears in the September/October *Psychosomatic Medicine*.

Authority

"[This study] challenges our current models of psychosocial factors of heart disease that focus on hostility," writes Margaret A. Chesney, a psychologist at the University of California, San Francisco, in an accompanying comment.

Faulty analogy

Many researchers assume that findings derived from studies of emotions and heart disease among men apply to women as well, Chesney asserts.

Powell and her colleagues studied 83 women enrolled in clinical trials to determine whether altering Type A behavior diminishes heart problems among heart-attack survivors. Participants entered the project in 1978 and ranged in age from 30 to 63. None smoked cigarettes or suffered from diabetes. At least six months had passed since their first heart attack.

Induction

In the following eight to 10 years, six women died of heart attacks or coronary complications.

Induction

Women with heart disease and un–Type A traits whose aspirations to a traditional, stable family life go unfulfilled appear to face the bleakest survival prospects, according to Powell's group. Participants in their study married and had children in the 1940s and 1950s and apparently did not expect to need extensive education for paid employment. When forced to work outside the home following divorce, death of a husband, or reduction in a spouse's income, they could obtain only low-paying jobs. In the study, women who died of heart disease were more often divorced, worked full-time, lacked a college education, and earned no more than $20,000 per year.

Signs

Deduction

Overall, financial and emotional stress appeared to surge in the absence of an intimate relationship. In these cases, women often tried to suppress their anger, resentment, loneliness, and dissatisfaction, the researchers say.

Authority

"For women with coronary disease, this combination of factors may be lethal," Powell and her co-workers contend.

Caution against hasty generalization

The findings require confirmation in a larger sample, the investigators caution. But a strong link between specific psychosocial measures and the risk of death in a group this size suggests that the same pattern will emerge in further studies, they argue.

Signs

Most strikingly, women who died of heart disease displayed an absence of any urgency to finish tasks and expressed no anger or agitation during a stress-

Cause and effect

ful interview, Powell's group notes. This antithesis of Type A responses may indicate a tendency to suppress unpleasant emotions, they suggest.[3]

Claims of Value

Questions Answered by Claims of Value.   It is good or bad? How bad? How good? Of what worth is it? Is it moral or immoral? Who thinks so? What do those people value? What values or criteria should I use to determine its goodness or badness? Are my values different from other people's values or from the author's values?

Examples of Claims of Value.   Computers are a valuable addition to modern society. School prayer has a moral function in the public schools. Viewing television is a wasteful activity. Mercy killing is immoral. The contributions of homemakers are as valuable as those of professional women. Animal rights are as important as human rights.

Types of Proof Associated with Claims of Value.   *Value proofs* are important in developing claims of value. Recall that value proofs appeal to what the audience is expected to value. Thus a sense of a common, shared system of values between the arguer and the audience is important for the argument to be convincing. These shared values must be established either explicitly or implicitly in the argument. *Motivational proofs* that appeal to what the audience wants are also important in establishing claims of value. People place value on the things that they work to achieve. Other types of proof used to establish claims of value include *analogies*, both *literal* and *figurative*, that establish links with other good or bad objects or qualities. Also, quotations from *authorities* who are admired help establish both expert criteria and judgments of good or bad, right or wrong. *Induction* is also used through the use of good examples to demonstrate that something is good, or through bad examples to show that something is bad. *Signs* that something is good or bad are sometimes cited. *Definitions* are used to clarify criteria for evaluation.

Possible Organizational Strategies.   *Applied criteria* is one way to develop a claim of value. Criteria for evaluation are established and then applied to the subject that is at issue. For example, in arguing that a particular television series is the best on

---

[3]*Science News,* October 16, 1993, p. 244.

television, criteria for what makes a superior series would be identified and then applied to the series to defend it as best. The audience would have to agree with the criteria to make the argument effective. Or suppose the claim is made that toxic waste is the worst threat to the environment. A list of criteria for evaluating threats to the environment would be established and applied to toxic waste to show that it is the worst of all. Another possibility is to use *topical* organization by developing a list of reasons about why something is good or bad and then to develop each of the reasons as a separate topic. You may also expect that *narrative* structure will sometimes be used to develop a claim of value. Narratives are real or made-up stories that can illustrate values in action, with morals or generalizations being noted either explicitly or implicitly along the way. An example of a narrative used to support a claim of value is the parable of the good Samaritan who helped a fellow traveler. The claim is that helping one another in such circumstances is valued and desirable behavior.

An Example of an Argument That Contains a Claim of Value. The following article examines the value of the men's movement from the author's point of view. Notice the author's refutation of some of the opposing evidence. Also notice the author's conclusion and his major reasons for reaching this conclusion.

THE MEN'S MOVEMENT

Christopher Evans

Value proofs that are ironic. He believes the opposite.

The term pops up almost daily now, in print or on the air. The "men's movement." The "Men's Movement."

Either way, I wince. And it's not that we American men are OK. We're not.

Depending on the source, enough male-critical data are around these days to justify shooting us all, or at least emasculating all but the highest forms of us and sending us somewhere far away.

We don't support our families, either when we're with them or after we leave them. We do most of the killing, the chemical abuse, the power abuse, and on and on. We can't feel or "emote" or do any number of other things women can. So, the thinking goes, we deserve being passed over in favor of women in the job market, in the promotion derby.

Does this make me mad? Absolutely. Does it make me feel like a victim? To be honest, yes, at times.

Yet when I think of a men's movement, I start to squirm. And that's because the thought conjures the picture of a bunch of gun-waving, jock-torching loonies hitting the streets to protest, and then to litigate, on my behalf.

It's not that I'm against men, privately or in groups, working to remedy their inadequacies. I have no qualms with Wildman Gatherings

... [where] problemed males retreat to the wild to work, play, grunt, spit, croon and hug in order to nurture such qualities as compassion, sensitivity and all the rest.

Literal analogy; then compares the men's movement with other groups taken over by lunatic fringes

My problem with a men's movement is that I fear the various male-driven hate groups—whose underlying premise is always "Poor little me" and whose figurative finger is always pointed at other groups who have seized the American dream and done something with it—will latch onto it. And pretend to be speaking for me.

Then there is certain trivialization of the subgroup-advocacy phenomenon, something at the very heart of democracy and every human rights struggle worth its bloodshed. Subgroup-advocacy movements spring up when people with a common trait—in this case men, but it could be the one-legged transvestite plumbers of North America—band together to battle wrongs done them by somebody else.

If we have learned anything from subgroup-advocacies past, it is that the honorable and just causes behind most of them often are lost when sometimes self-serving folk join the movement to perpetuate their piece of the cause. What happens is that "the movement," be it civil rights, women's or anything else, becomes known by its most oddball and radical fringes, not by the masses within its mainstream.

Why bring this up now? Because there is growing evidence that suggests American men—heretofore known as the gender of power in the world's most opulent nation—are being preyed upon. And some of the evidence seems compelling. At first.

Farrell, the opposition, argues from signs and statistics that men lack power and need help

"If any other group—blacks, Jews, women or gays—were singled out to register for the draft based merely on characteristics at birth, we would immediately recognize it as genocide," writes Warren Farrell in the book *The Myth of Male Power*. "But when men are singled out based on their sex at birth, it is called power.

"What any other group would call powerlessness, men have been taught to call power. We don't call male-killing sexism, we call it glory. We don't call it a slaughter when 1 million men are killed or maimed in the battles of the Somme in World War I, we call it serving the country. We don't call those who selected only men to die murderers, we call them voters."

Farrell portrays American males as whipping boys—i.e. women commit one-third of domestic homicides, only 4 percent of custodial fathers in this country get child support, 94 percent of workplace fatalities are men, and so forth. Then he leads us to believe that American males suddenly are hapless, helpless wimps with no control over our own destiny.

Horse ... feathers!

Refutation of Farrell

The problems most able-bodied American men face that are peculiar to males are by and large created by men. If child-support or child-custody laws or policies by which we draft people into the military are unfair, it's because men until recently not only made the laws and policies, but were responsible for carrying them out.

Cause: Men caused these problems and can solve them

So, men, let's be concerned with our rights as a gender, sure. But first, let's shore up what we can without the hue and cry of a "movement," which surely sooner or later will become a refuge for the losers amongst us, namely the hate groups and their ilk, whose real forte is self-pity.

Motivational proofs: Men can be better people

The rhetoric of the so-called "men's movement" can seem enticing. At first. We can blame testosterone for our woes. Or we can get on about the business of rectifying our part of the problem with the race—the human one.

Value claim: Negative reaction to men's movement

If it means seeing a psychotherapist to find out who we are and how we can be better, so be it. If it means dropping our macho defense mechanisms and paying child support—or heading to the woods with a group of males to learn to communicate—let's get at it.

But a "men's movement?" Nah. Not for me.[4]

Claims of Policy

Questions Answered by Claims of Policy.   What should we do? How should we act? What should future policy be? How can we solve this problem? What course of action should we pursue? Notice that policy claims focus on the future more than the other types of claims, which tend to deal with the past or present.

Examples of Claims of Policy.   The criminal should be sent to prison rather than to a mental institution. Everyone should be taught to recognize and report sexual harassment in the workplace. Every person in the United States should have access to health care regardless of cost. Small business loans must be made available to help people reestablish their businesses after a natural disaster. Both filmmakers and recording groups should make objectionable language and subject matter known to prospective consumers. Battered women who take revenge should not be placed in jail. Genetic engineering should be discouraged. Parents should have the right to choose the schools their children attend.

Types of Proof Associated with Claims of Policy.   *Data* and *statistics* are used to support a policy claim, but so are moral and commonsense appeals to what people value and want. *Motivational appeals* are especially important for policy claims. The audience needs to become sufficiently motivated to think or even act in a different way. In order to accomplish this degree of motivation, the arguer must convince the audience that it wants to change. *Value* proofs are also used for motivation. The audience becomes convinced it should follow a policy to achieve important values. Also typical of policy claims is proof from *literal analogy*. The arguer establishes what other similar people or groups have done and suggests the same thing can work in this case also. Or a successful effort is described, and the claim is made that it could work even better on a broader scale. This is another type of literal

---

[4]*Fort Worth Star-Telegram,* September 21, 1993, Sec. D, p. 1.

analogy, because it compares a small-scale effort to a large-scale, expanded effort. *Argument from authority* is also often used to establish claims of policy. The authorities quoted, however, must be trusted and must have good ethos. Effort is usually made to establish their credentials. *Cause* can be used to establish the origin of the problem, and *definition* can be used to clarify it. Finally, *deduction* can be used to reach a conclusion based on a general principle.

Possible Organizational Strategies. The problem-solution structure is typical of policy claims. The problem is first described in sufficient detail so that the audience will want a solution. Then the solution is spelled out. Furthermore, the solution suggested is usually shown to be superior to other solutions by anticipating and showing what is wrong with each of the others. Sometimes the problem and solution sections are followed by a visualization of how matters will be improved if the proposed solution is accepted and followed. Sometimes problem-solution arguments end with an action step that directs the audience to take a particular course of action (vote, buy, and so forth).

An Example of an Argument That Contains a Claim of Policy. The following argument identifies a problem, discusses its origins, explains why it is a problem now, and recommends a solution.

DRAFT REGISTRATION IS DUMB. END IT.

Murray Polner

Problem

Does anyone remember why draft registration resumed in 1980? A failing Jimmy Carter used millions of men as pawns to try to recapture his diminishing political base by sending the Soviets a "signal" after their invasion of Afghanistan. Even his Selective Service director considered the step unnecessary.

Cause of problem

Quote from authority followed by refutation

But this vestige of past wars became a part of the permanent bureaucracy. It was praised in 1991 by Gen. Samuel K. Lessey Jr., then the Selective Service director, as "a rite of passage, an American thing to do."

Statistics: Cost of problem

Draft registration has served no purpose except to provide a costly budget, most recently $27.5 million, for jobs and fringe benefits for several hundred Selective Service data processors and record-keepers.

Value-proofs: No one values or needs it

Since 1980, about 15.5 million 18-year-olds have been forced to register for a draft nobody wants or expects to see again, and that was aimed at the Soviet Union, which no longer exists.

Effects of problem

Lists are regularly combed in the hunt for prey who may have failed to register. While this failure may no longer bring prosecution, the law weighs heavily on young men (but not women): no registration, no Federal education aid, no Pell grants, no Federal civil service jobs. Thirteen states deny nonregistrants financial assistance, and states such as South Dakota and Tennessee require registration before acceptance into state schools and as a prerequisite for state jobs.

Induction: A generalization drawn from a single example

The lightning victory in the gulf war relied exclusively on volunteers. In addition, Defense Secretary Dick Cheney made it clear the gulf war would never lead to a draft. So why maintain the fiction that registration is vital to national security?

Quote from authority followed by refutation

"Threats to national security and world peace can occur at any time," Robert W. Gambino, the Selective Service director, said in his recent report to Congress. Another spokesman called it "mobilization insurance." But for what? Against whom?

Solution

The $27.5 million saved could finance 135 medical research grants of $200,000 each for AIDS, cardiovascular disease or cancer. Or 1,200 postdoctoral fellowships for training in biochemistry, molecular biology or epidemiology. Or 220 fully furnished homes for homeless families in the greater New York area. Or 1,000 rookie police officers in New York City. Or 1,000 more New York City teachers.

Statistics

Quote from authority

Representative Peter A. DeFazio, Democrat of Oregon, has introduced a bill to terminate registration and put Selective Service in "deep standby" status, maintaining its computer lists but putting everything else on hold. "Draft registration has nothing to do with military readiness," he said. "If there were a true national emergency, draft registration would not put a single soldier on the front line one hour earlier." He's right. *It's time to end the charade.*[5]

Policy claim

CLAIMS AND ARGUMENT IN REAL LIFE

In argument, one type of claim may predominate, but other types may be present as subclaims. It is not always easy to establish the predominant claim in an argument or to establish its type. You may find some disagreement in your class discussions when you try to categorize a claim according to type. The reason for this disagreement is that often two or more types of claim will be present in an argument. But close reading will usually reveal a predominant type with the other types serving as subclaims. For example, a value claim that the popular press creates harm by prying into the private lives of public figures may establish the fact that this is a pervasive practice, may define what should be public and what should not be public information, may examine the causes or, more likely, the effects of this type of reporting, and may suggest future policy for dealing with this problem. All may occur in the same article. Still, the dominant claim is one of value, that this practice of news writers is bad.

It is useful when reading argument to identify the predominant claim because doing so helps you identify (1) the predominant purpose of the argument, (2) the

---

[5]*New York Times*, February 13, 1992, Sec. A, p. 15. Polner has also written a book about Vietnam veterans.

types of proofs that may be used, and (3) the possible organizational strategies. It is also useful, however, to identify other types of subclaims, and to analyze why they are used and how they contribute to the argumentative purpose. When planning and writing argument, you can, in turn, identify a predominant claim as well as other types of subclaims, proofs, and organization (see Table 9.1 on p. 291 and Table 10.1 on p. 318) to help you develop your main claim and purpose.

As you read and write argument, you will also notice that claims follow a predictable sequence when they originate in real-life situations. In fact, argument appears most vigorous in dramatic, life-and-death situations, or when a person's character is called into question. We see claims and rebuttals, many kinds of proofs, and every conceivable organizational strategy in these instances. For example, in the 1992 Los Angeles riots, the issues that emerged included these: Is the justice system adequate? Do all people possess adequate civil rights? Was police brutality involved? What is the present status of racial discrimination? How can we make inner cities more livable? How can we improve social programs?

Such real-life situations, particularly when they are life-threatening, not only generate issues; they also usually generate many arguments. Interestingly, the types of argument usually appear in a fairly predictable order. The first arguments made in response to a new issue-generating situation usually involves claims of fact and definition. People first have to come to terms with the fact that something significant has happened. Then they need to define what happened so that they can better understand it.

The next group of arguments that appear after fact and definition often inquire into cause. People need to figure out why the event happened. Multiple causes are often considered and debated. Next, people begin to evaluate the goodness or badness of what has happened. It is usually after all of these other matters have been dealt with that people turn their attention to future policy and how to solve the problems. Often the proofs associated with these claims are logical, but emotional proofs are frequently invoked as well because of the nature of the event.

We can use the Los Angeles riots as an example of this typical sequence of claims. The riots started quite suddenly in the spring of 1992 just hours after the court decision that allowed the police officers who had beaten Rodney King to go free. People around the country were caught off guard by the sudden rioting and looting in Los Angeles. The first newspaper article and even speeches by President Bush sought to establish and clarify what exactly was going on in that city. People asked, Is this a class riot? A race riot? War? Civil disobedience? Looting and law-breaking? Civil demonstrations? Or what?

These initial fact and definition articles were followed by many others that speculated and argued about the causes of the riots. Were they caused by racial discrimination? Economic problems? Desire for power? A lack of home and community values? Anger at the court decision? One African-American civil rights leader argued that the cause was slavery, that people were still angry that their ancestors had been brought from Africa as slaves, and that the riots were an expression of their anger. Another African-American leader of an organization that fostered productive family life argued that civil rights leaders themselves incited the riots in order to keep their power base and government relief programs strong.

After much speculation about cause, people began to turn their attention to value and to argue about whether any good could be found in these riots. The president pointed out that not all people rioted and looted, and that some actually gave others a helping hand. But many bad or mixed good and bad results were identified as well. Racial tensions between African-Americans and Koreans had surfaced during the riots and were regarded as bad. Considerable property was destroyed, and many people lost their homes or jobs.

It was not until most of these initial matters were analyzed and debated that discussion of future policy began to surface. Finally, headlines like "What Los Angeles Needs" began to appear. One individual recommended that the citizens of South-Central Los Angeles organize themselves as a Third World country and declare war on the United States. Other individuals outside of the area thought troops should be sent in to beat the rioters into submission. Other suggestions for dealing with the problems caused by the riots included new training and job programs, a retrial of the police officers, government loans to rebuild small businesses, a reconception of inner-city neighborhoods, and so on.

The same pattern of argument can be found in the sexual correctness issue that has been gathering speed since the Anita Hill–Clarence Thomas hearings, where Ms. Hill accused Mr. Thomas of sexual harassment, and the U.S. Navy Tailhook scandal, where male naval personnel harassed and abused women at an annual party. Many of the first articles written in response to these events and others like them focus on fact, or what happened. Were these actual incidents of sexual harassment, the authors ask, or were they just incidents of flirting, the type of thing that goes on all the time between men and women? Definitions of sexual harassment usually follow with attempts to define it in terms of actions, comments, or looks, and to distinguish it from generally cloddish, insensitive behavior. Once people establish that an incident of harassment has occurred and that it can be defined, cause next becomes an issue. Did the woman cause it by leading on the man? Was liquor at fault? Were hormones to blame, or perhaps the age-old war between the sexes? Value arguments surface next that focus on who has been harmed and whether that person has been badly or only mildly harmed. Policy issues, or what to do about it, come later. Should Clarence Thomas be denied a seat on the U.S. Supreme Court? Should the annual navy parties be discontinued? In 1993 policy to govern sexual correctness was established at Antioch College that required each person to obtain permission from the member of the opposite sex before making any advances of a sexual nature.

You may be able to think of other issues that have inspired a variety of arguments and claims in this same roughly predictable order. It is useful to pay attention to the issues that come out of dramatic events, to the types of claims that are generated by them, and to the order in which these claims appear. Such analysis will help you anticipate the course an issue will take. It will also help you determine at what point in the ongoing conversation about an issue you happen to be at the present time. You can then speculate about the aspects of the issue that have already been argued and what are likely to be argued in the future.

WHAT STRATEGIES CAN YOU NOW ADD TO IMPROVE YOUR PROCESS FOR READING AND WRITING ARGUMENT?

Reading Strategies

1. **Survey** to identify the organizational strategy of an argument, and **then break it into meaningful chunks,** speculate why the chunks are in this order, and analyze the relationships among them.
2. **Identify the predominant type of claim**.
3. **Read to determine which other types of claims are also present** as subclaims.
4. **Analyze the types of proofs** used to support a particular type of claim and speculate about the effects of these proofs on the audience.
5. **Determine how the present claim contributes to the ongoing conversation** about an issue. What has probably gone before? What will probably come next?

Writing Strategies

1. **Decide which type of claim** will predominate in your paper.
2. **Decide on appropriate types of subclaims** as well.
3. **Write a claim** followed by a few subclaims, and place them in a logical order.
4. **Decide on some types of proofs** and organizational strategies you might use.
5. **Consider where you are in the ongoing conversation** about your issue. What has gone before? What will come next?

EXERCISES AND ACTIVITIES

1. **CLASS DISCUSSION: PREDICTING TYPES OF CLAIMS**
   Bring in the front page of a current newspaper. Discuss headlines that suggest controversial topics. Anticipate from each headline the type of claim that you predict will be made.

2. **GROUP WORK: READING AND ANALYSIS OF TYPES OF CLAIMS**
   The class is divided into five groups, and each group is assigned one of the five articles that follow. Prepare for group work by reading the article assigned to your group. Then get in your groups and apply the new reading strategies described in this chapter by answering the following questions. Assign a person to report your answers to the class.

   a. How can you describe the organization of this argument? How might you chunk it into parts? Why are the parts in the order in which you find them? What are some of the relationships among the parts?
   b. What is the predominant type of claim?
   c. What other types of claims are present in the argument as subclaims?
   d. What are the major types of proofs? What are their effects on the audience?

e. Where might you position this argument in an ongoing conversation about the issue? At the beginning, the middle, or the end? Why?

The articles:

"How to Save Science in the Classroom"
"We're Too Busy for Ideas"
"And a Purple Dinosaur Shall Lead Them"
"Rap's Embrace of 'Nigger' Fires Bitter Debate"
"Malling of America Puts Planet in Peril"

HOW TO SAVE SCIENCE IN THE CLASSROOM

Leon M. Lederman

As an ever-grateful graduate of New York public schools—kindergarten through City College—it was gratifying to learn of plans for a drastic overhaul of science instruction in the city's schools. As New York considers its changes, which are supposed to be aimed at invigorating science education for all, not just the most talented, I have some advice.

A debate used to rage over whether to invest in gifted students or the other 99 percent. It should be obvious that we need to do both: there is no real conflict for resources. We must take care of the super-bright: New York has a glorious tradition with Bronx High School, Stuyvesant High School, Brooklyn Tech. The returns have been extraordinary. In my state, the Illinois Math and Science Academy, a three-year public high school in Aurora, spends four times as much on its students as other schools do—and it is a wise investment.

But we are also rightly concerned with the rest of kids. Science and math could be tremendously attractive to inner-city children—if teachers let the children talk and work in groups rather than passively listen, if the teacher is the facilitator rather than the font of all knowledge, striving not for correct answers but for clues as to how the child thinks. But the sad fact is that the average teacher's science and mathematics preparation is about zero.

In Chicago, an effort begun by the city's universities is aimed at changing that. A group of us designed a massive retraining of the 17,000 public-school teachers who must teach math and science, most of whom were never trained to do so. We hastily concocted a 16-week intensive training program, realizing it would evolve in time. We supplemented this with evening, weekend and summer follow-up and enrichment work, technology workshops, parent programs—every possible form of outreach.

Support for this fairly expensive program came from the U.S. Department of Energy and the National Science Foundation. To train the 17,000 teachers, we planned to take 100 the first year, 1,000 the second year and 2,500 from then on.

Now, beginning our third year, we are way behind schedule, but wiser and more determined than ever. We know that about 80 percent of teachers really care about their children, and most of the 700 teachers we have retrained take to our programs. But constant follow-up is essential. This takes time, money, manpower.

These programs work with the simplest of kits: dry ice, beads, soap bubbles, graph paper. Everyone glows when the computers are brought in. The results of the new approach have been tremendous. Children love it, the teacher loves it, the principal can't believe it. Science is actually being taught in the Chicago elementary schools!

In addition, children do better in reading, writing and speaking because the new methodology in math and science has inspired change in teachers and the joy of learning in them and their kids. Here is a key to true reform of American education. If this type of early schooling can help break the cycle of poverty, crime, dropping out and pregnancy that traps so many minority students, then we will have shown a way to genuine change.

To extend programs similar to ours to 25 other cities would require something less than $1 billion annually. Washington officials plead gridlock and deficits. But is this too much to invest in an escape ladder out of poverty and joblessness and in the rejuvenation of the waning science-literate work force?

Education takes patience and commitment. The current rhetoric—choice, national exams, you-can't-throw-money-at-the-problem, privatization—does not seem relevant to the problems of the 400,000 children of Chicago's public schools.

The lesson is that a city can mobilize the resources to create a flexible private entity to work with public schools—not to whittle them away but to make them work.[6]

WE'RE TOO BUSY FOR IDEAS

Michele McCormick

I recently became one of the last people in America to acquire a portable radio/headphone set. This delay was out of character—normally I ride the crest of every trend. But in this case I sensed a certain dangerous potential. So I put off the purchase for ages, feeling wary of such an inviting distraction. Too much headphone time, I worried, could easily impair my business performance, if not ruin my way of life completely.

As it turns out, my concerns were right on target.

The problem isn't the expense, or the constant exposure to musical drivel, or even the endangerment of my hearing—and I do like to keep the volume set on "blast." No, the problem is more subtle and insidious. It's simply that, once I was fully plugged in, things stopped occurring to me.

---

[6]*New York Times,* September 5, 1992, Sec. A, p. 13. Leon M. Lederman is professor of science at Illinois Institute of Technology and is a Nobel laureate in physics.

I get excited about good ideas. Especially my own. I used to have lists of them in all my regular haunts. My office desk, kitchen, car and even my gym bag were littered with bits of paper. Ideas ranging from a terrific brochure headline or a pitch to a new client for my public-relations agency to finding a new route to avoid the morning rush—each notion began as an unsummoned thought, mulled over and jotted down.

I'm convinced that such musings are the key to business and social vitality. They are the initial source of the innovative problem solving, creative solutions and even radical departures, without which success and progress are elusive. I've found that a lot of my better ideas originate in those times when I allow my mind to range freely.

The old story has it that Isaac Newton identified the concept and presence of gravity while sitting under an apple tree. One fruit fell and science gained a new dimension. While there may be some historic license in that tale, it's easy to see that if Newton had been wearing his Walkman, he probably would have overlooked the real impact of the apple's fall.

This is the problematic side of technological evolution. As tools become more compact, portable and inescapable, they begin to take away something they cannot replace. The car phone, battery-powered TV, portable fax and notepad-size computer do everything for accessibility. They make it easy to be in touch, to be productive, to avoid the tragedy of a wasted second. But there are worse things than empty time. A calendar packed to the max makes it easy to overlook what's missing. A dearth of good ideas isn't something that strikes like a lightning bolt. It's a far more gradual dawning, like the slow unwelcome recognition that one's memory has become less sharp.

If that dawning is slow, it's because our minds are fully occupied. It now takes an unprecedented depth of knowledge to stay on top of basic matters, from choosing sensible investments to keeping up on job skills to purchasing the healthiest food. There is literally no end to the information that has become essential.

When there is a chance to relax, we don't stop the input; we change channels. With earphones on our heads or televisions in our faces, we lock in to a steady barrage of news, views and videos that eliminate the likelihood of any spontaneous thought.

THWARTED INSIGHT

Still, we are not totally oblivious. We work hard to counter the mind-numbing impact of the river of information and factoidal jetsam we are forced to absorb. There is a deliberate emphasis on the importance of creative thought as a daily factor. Many businesses try to ensure that the workplace is conducive to clear thinking. They can provide employees with a comfortable environment and stimulating challenges, and summon them to brainstorming sessions. From seminars to smart drinks, from computer programs to yoga postures, there's no end to the strategies and products that claim to enhance creativity. It would be unfair to say that all of these methods are without value. But beyond a certain point they are, at best, superfluous. Trying too hard to reach for high-quality insight can thwart the process in the worst way.

The best ideas occur to me when my mind is otherwise unchallenged and there is no pressure to create. I have mentally composed whole articles while jogging, flashed upon the solution to a software dilemma while sitting in the steam room, come up with just the right opening line for a client's speech while pushing a vacuum. These were not problems I had set out to address at those particular times. Inventiveness came to my uncluttered mind in a random, unfocused moment.

Certainly not every idea that pops up during a quiet time is a winner. But a surprising number do set me on the path to fresh solutions. And I have found that a free flow of ideas builds its own momentum, leapfrogging me along to answers that work.

The bonus is that creative thought is joyful. It doesn't matter if the idea is for a clever party decoration, a better way to rearrange the living-room furniture or the definitive antigravity machine. When a fine idea emerges there is a moment of "Eureka!" that simply beats all.

The simple fact is that time spent lost in thought isn't really lost at all. That's why "unplugged time" is vital. It's when new directions, different approaches and exciting solutions emerge from a place that can't be tapped at will.

It is unwise to take this resource for granted. Better to recognize it, understand something about where it resides and thereby ensure it is not lost.

Clearly, this is far easier said than done. Technology is seductive. It chases us down, grabs hold and will not let us go. Nor do we want it to. The challenge is to keep it in its place and to remember that time spent unplugged brings unique rewards. This doesn't mean I will abandon my new radio headset toy. But I will take the precaution of leaving it in my dresser drawer on a regular basis.

Otherwise, unlike wise old Newton, I may see the fall but never grasp its meaning.[7]

AND A PURPLE DINOSAUR SHALL LEAD THEM

Adam Cadre

When I was very little, I had a reason to get up in the morning. The world was a scary place—stagflation, Three Mile Island, and scariest of all, disco—but I didn't care, because I knew that at four o'clock sharp I could sweep the clouds away and spend an hour where the air was sweet. That's right: Sesame Street. I was a "Sesame Street" freak. I watched it every single day. In fact, the one time I accidentally slept through it I was so distraught that I spent the next several days in a sort of existential despair (and if you think confronting the ultimate absurdity of existence is hard now, try it when you're four years old). Seriously, though, for a couple of

---

[7]*Newsweek*, March 29, 1993, p 10. Michele McCormick is the owner of a small public relations firm in California.

years there my life really did revolve around "Sesame Street," and even after I grew out of it, it was always sort of heartwarming to know that Big Bird and friends were continuing to bring joy and enlightenment into the lives of generation after generation of little kids.

Now, suddenly, Big Bird is passe.

That's right—the powers that be seem to have decided that "Sesame Street" is not the ideal children's show it was once thought to be. Among the complaints that have been leveled against it by child psychologists and media watchdogs are: it's too fast; the world it presents is too unsettling for young children; most of the humor goes over the kids' heads; and so on. In the end, they conclude "Sesame Street" may be an effective educational tool, but it can also be quite harmful. After all, the first generation to grow up on "Sesame Street" has now come of age—and look how *they* turned out: alienated, cynical, completely devoid of any kind of attention span. And I suppose the critics have a point. "Sesame Street" *is* fast. It'll cut from the live-action storyline to an unrelated vignette between Bert and Ernie to a cartoon about the letter V to a quick documentary about dolphins to a news flash with Kermit the Frog to a cartoon about the number 7 and then back to the storyline, all in the space of a couple of minutes. You might even say that "Sesame Street" is a perfect primer for—no! not that! anything but that!—MTV. (Insert dramatic "DUM-DUM-dum" sound here.) So, yeah, it's fast. And true, while it may seem kind of hard to believe at first, the world of "Sesame Street" might well be a little unsettling. After all, Bert and Ernie are constantly squabbling, various muppets are collapsing from exhaustion or extreme pain every five minutes, and there's a nasty green guy lurking in the trash can. So it's not all bliss and harmony. And while I didn't realize this when I was four, a lot of the humor on "Sesame Street" *is* aimed at adults. A surprising amount of "Sesame Street" is satirical in nature. While the kids are learning about different kinds of animals, their parents are laughing at the Springsteen parody in "Barn in the USA"; while the kids are giggling at the sight of pigs with tennis rackets, it's for their parents' benefit that Old MacDonald mentions that the withdrawal of government subsidies has forced him to convert his farm into a condominium complex complete with health spa; and while the kids happily watch Oscar the Grouch groan in distress while some strange woman praises his candor, their parents (and college students doing research for "Bad Subjects" articles) are getting a kick out of the fact that the woman in question is Jodie Foster slumming on PBS between films. So it's true that "Sesame Street" isn't completely accessible to the kids. But people have been making these kinds of complaints for years now. Why are they suddenly gaining so much attention? Because now there's an alternative, one that's earned the praise of child psychologists and the undying love of little children everywhere: Barney. (Insert another dramatic "DUM-DUM-dum" sound here.)

Those of you who have spent the last year or so in a deep coma are probably wondering who or what Barney is. Well, Barney is a dinosaur from our imagination, and when he's tall he's what you'd call a dinosaur sensation. At least that's what the opening jingle says. It's a good thing they tell us, too, because otherwise it's kind of hard to tell. I suppose he does look vaguely reptilian, but then he's also purple, cuddly, and five feet tall, qualities not normally associated with your typical T. rex or velociraptor. But it's not his appearance that separates Barney from the "Sesame Street" crew—after all, if you can accept an eight-foot yellow talking bird, you can accept a five-foot purple talking dinosaur thing. No, what sets him apart from "Sesame Street" (and related programs like the dearly departed "Electric Company") is his disposition and the world he inhabits. In the world of "Barney & Friends," there is no conflict whatsoever. None. No one fights or disagrees, nothing bad ever happens. They just hang around and sing songs and learn how to count to ten over and over and over and play games and sing some more songs and then the credits roll. The songs themselves are also very different from those in "Sesame Street." The songs in "Sesame Street" are quite sophisticated, with complex melodies and often borrowing from rock, rap, music from other cultures, and in my day, disco. The songs in "Barney & Friends" are very, very simple, usually featuring tunes borrowed from other children's songs like "Yankee Doodle" and "This Old Man." And there is absolutely nothing in "Barney & Friends" that is not completely comprehensible to any three-year-old. So the child psychologists love Barney. And most little kids would gladly fall on a grenade for him. Why, then, does everybody else seem to hate him?

Barney, you see, has become the victim of one of the most vicious backlashes in recent memory. This backlash comes in two flavors. First, there are the parents of all the little Barneyphiles. Forced to buy every single scrap of Barney merchandise, forced to play the Barney videotapes over and over and over, and worst of all, forced to listen to the "I love you, you love me, we're a happy family" song roughly eighty thousand times a day, theirs is a classic case of backlash due to overexposure. (Others who have fallen prey to this phenomenon include Nirvana, the Energizer Bunny, and Ross Perot.) But then there's the curious case of all the people who hate Barney with a passion despite having never seen the show. Among these are the kids who quite literally beat the stuffing out of Barney in a Texas shopping mall. They haven't been forced to listen to the saccharine songs, they haven't had to suffer through the wretched acting, they haven't had to deal with Barney's grating voice clawing at their eardrums. So why does their hatred match, if not surpass, that of the parents who've had to deal with Barney firsthand?...

This, I think, is why [people] who have never ever seen the show hate Barney so much: he goes against all their values. The most important thing for a member of [the Sesame Street] generation to be is "cool"—and Barney is pretty much the definition of "uncool." Let's take a quick look at the kind of education Barney's legions are getting. First of all, it's much more structured. Every show is built around one theme, and sticks to it fairly faithfully—if the show's about how to count to ten, ninety percent of the show is going to be about how to count to ten. Over and over and over. Secondly, unlike "Sesame Street," there is only one authority figure in "Barney & Friends": Barney himself. Barney has all the answers and the kids follow him without question. And what does Barney preach? Universal love, community, sincerity, friendship, team spirit; but also conformity, unquestioning adherence to authority, and enforced happiness. (One recent episode revolved around the attempts of Barney and some other kids to pester a little girl into cheering up—they simply *would not let* her be sad for a while.) These are the kind of values, both positive and negative, associated with [Barney]. ...[8]

RAP'S EMBRACE OF "NIGGER" FIRES BITTER DEBATE

Michel Marriott

One of America's oldest and most searing epithets—"nigger"—is flooding into the nation's popular culture, giving rise to a bitter debate among blacks about its historically ugly power and its increasingly open use in an integrated society.

Whether thoughtlessly or by design, large numbers of a post–civil rights generation of blacks have turned to a conspicuous use of "nigger" just as they have gained considerable cultural influence through rap music and related genres.

Some blacks, mostly young people, argue that their open use of the word will eventually demystify it, strip it of its racist meaning. They liken it to the way some homosexuals have started referring to themselves as "queers" in a defiant slap at an old slur.

But other blacks—most of them older—say that "nigger," no matter who uses it, is such a hideous pejorative that it should be stricken from the national vocabulary. At a time when they perceive a deepening racial estrangement, they say its popular use can only make bigotry more socially acceptable.

"Nigger," of course, has long been an element of black vernacular, almost an honorific of the streets, strictly, and still, off limits to whites. But as the word has found voice in black music, dance and film, the role of black culture in popular culture has driven it into the mainstream.

For the last several years, rap artists have increasingly used "nigger" in their lyrics, repackaging it and selling it not just to their own inner-city neighborhoods but to the largely white suburbs. In his song "Straight Up Nigga," Ice-T raps, "I'm a nigga in America, and that much I flaunt," and indeed, a large portion of his record sales are in white America.

In movies and on television, too, "nigger" is heard with unprecedented regularity these days. In "Trespass," a newly released major-studio film about an inner-city treasure hunt, black rappers portraying gang members call one another "nigger" almost as often as they call one another by their names.

And every Friday at midnight, Home Box Office televises "Russell Simmons' Def Comedy Jam," a half-hour featuring many black, cutting-edge comedians who frequently use "nigger" in their acts.

---

[8]*Bad Subjects: Political Education for Everyday Life*, 12, 1994 (Electronic journal, Internet address: bad subjects-request@uclink.berkeley.edu). Adam Cadre, who was born in 1974, wrote this while he was a senior English major at the University of California at Berkeley. This essay first appeared in a journal which is published monthly on the Internet. Its purpose is "to promote radical thinking and public education about the political implications of everyday life."

Sometimes, the use of the word is simply a flat-out repetition of the street vernacular. In rap and hip-hop music, a genre in which millions of its listeners adopt the artists' style and language, "nigger" is virtually interchangeable with words like "guy," "man" or "brother."

But often it is a discussion of the word's various uses and meanings in society, black or white. Not only is black popular culture the focus of the debate, it is often the medium for it.

"MAKES MY TEETH WHITE"

Paul Mooney, a veteran black stand-up comic and writer, recently released a comedy tape titled "Race." On the tape, which includes routines called "Nigger Vampire," "1-900-Blame-a-Nigger," "Niggerstein," "Nigger Raisins" and "Nigger History," Mr. Mooney explains why he uses the word so often.

"I say nigger all the time," he said. "I say nigger 100 times every morning. It makes my teeth white. Nigger-nigger-nigger-nigger-nigger-nigger-nigger-nigger-nigger. I say it. You think, 'What a small white world.'"

Blacks who say they should use the word more openly maintain that its casual use, especially in the company of whites, will shift the word's context and strip "nigger" of its ability to hurt. That is precisely what blacks have been doing for years, say linguists who study black vernacular. By using the word strictly among themselves, the linguists say, they change its context and in doing so dull its edge whenever whites use it.

Kris Parker, a leading rap artist known as KRS-One, predicts that through black culture's ability to affect popular American culture through the electronic media, "nigger" will be deracialized by its broader use and become just another word.

"In another 5 to 10 years, you're going to see youth in elementary school spelling it out in their vocabulary tests," he said. "It's going to be that accepted by the society."

But other blacks, especially members of the generation for whom Malcolm X and the Rev. Dr. Martin Luther King Jr. were living heroes, say no one should ever be permitted to forget what "nigger" has meant, and still means, in America.

"That term encapsulates so much of the indignities forced on our people," said the Rev. Benjamin F. Chavis Jr., a longtime civil-rights leader who is executive director of the United Church of Christ Commission for Racial Justice. "That term made us less than human, and that is why we must reject the usage of that term.

"We cannot let that term be trivialized," he said. "We cannot let that term be taken out of its historical context."

Some blacks say they are so traumatized by the oppressive legacy of "nigger," that they cannot even bring themselves to say the word. Instead, they choose linguistic dodges like "the N-word" or simply spelling the word out. Other blacks say they are "ambivalent" about the growing public use of "nigger."

"Does it signal a new progressive step forward toward a new level of understanding or a regressive step back into self-hate?" asked Christopher Cathcart, a black 29-year-old public relations specialist in New York. "I fear it is the latter."

Throughout history, nearly all minority groups have found themselves branded by hateful terms. Early in the century, such seemingly innocent words as "Irish" and "Jew" were considered pejoratives, said Edward Bendix, a professor of linguistic anthropology at the Graduate Center of the City University of New York.

In time the groups have used some of the same terms as passwords to their particular groups, which is what happened with "nigger" in the black vernacular. Indeed, Bob Guccione Jr., editor and publisher of the popular music magazine *Spin*—which reports extensively on the rap music scene—said that while whites are very reluctant to use "nigger" because it has "such an incredible weight of ugliness to it," blacks often use it in the presence of whites as a verbal demarcation point.

"In a sense, it empowers the black community in the white mainstream," said Mr. Guccione, who is white. "They can use a very powerful word like a passkey, and whites dare not, or should not, use it."

But seldom has a word like "nigger" been pushed into the mainstream while its negative connotations exist, said Dr. Robin Lakoff, a social linguist and author of the book *Talking Power* (Basic Books, 1990). "That's harder with 'nigger,' especially with so many people around who still use it in its racist meaning," said Dr. Lakoff, a professor of linguistics at the University of California at Berkeley.

Many of the blacks who defend their open use of the word acknowledge that whites still cannot publicly say "nigger" without stirring up old black-white antagonisms.

"Race in America is like herpes because you can never get rid of it," said James Bernard, who is black and senior editor of *The Source*, a magazine that covers the rap and hip-hop scene. "There is still a line."

"A HORRENDOUS WORD"

The magazine's multiracial staff recently published a story about Spike Lee and the basketball star Charles Barkley under a headline "NINETIES NIGGERS." Kris Parker, the rapper, said such uses represent progress. But to the white Chicago writer Studs Terkel, whose latest book, *Race* (The New Press, 1992), is a series of interviews with blacks and whites about race in America, the increased use of "nigger" represents anything but progress.

"It is a horrendous word," he said, adding that the new permissiveness may have more to do with the "wink and nod" of the Reagan-Bush years of dismantling civil rights gains than with rap artists naming themselves N.W.A., for Niggas With an Attitude.

Examples abound that "nigger" has not lost its wounding power when used by whites. Whether scratched into a restroom stall or scrawled on the house of a black family in a white neighborhood, "nigger" remains a graffito of hate—the most commonly heard epithet used during anti-black crimes, the authorities say.

When a black man from New Jersey was abducted and set ablaze by three white men in Florida on New Year's Day, one of the first things they said to him, according to the victim's mother, was "nigger."

BLURRING A LINE

The changing uses of the word have made for some curious situations on the white side of an increasingly blurred line.

Alex T. Noble, a white public relations intern in New York, said he has white friends who use "nigger" with one another as a term of endearment. Mr. Noble, who works with rappers, said when a black friend calls him a "nigger," "I feel flattered, like I'm part of something."

But, he adds, he is extremely reluctant to return the salutation.

"As a white person I would never go up to a black person and say, 'Yo, nigger,'" Mr. Noble said. "I think it's hard to outrun the legacy of oppression that word signifies. Anytime a white person says that word it is troublesome."

The attempts to demystify "nigger" are by no means new. One of the more publicized cases came in the early 1970's, when Richard Pryor used "nigger" in his stand-up comedy act with the express purpose of defanging its racist bite. He titled his seminal comedy album in 1974 "That Nigger's Crazy." Some years later, however, after a trip to Africa, Mr. Pryor told audiences he would never use the word again as a performer. While abroad, he said, he saw black people running governments and businesses. And in a moment of epiphany, he said he realized that he did not see any "niggers."[9]

MALLING OF AMERICA PUTS PLANET IN PERIL

Alan Thein Durning

In Minnesota last month, developers opened the doors to one of the world's largest shopping centers, a dazzling circuit of boutiques a mile in circumference and four stories tall surrounding a seven-acre indoor amusement park. Its designers call it the Mall of America, and if their projections pan out, it will attract more visitors each year than Mecca or the Vatican.

History rarely encapsulates itself as perfectly as in the Mall of America. It's a monument to higher consumption—the unifying ambition of our globalizing consumer culture. Unfortunately, that consumer society is hazardous to our planet's health.

Thousands of U.S. shopping malls are the centerpieces of the most environmentally destructive way of life yet devised. In combination, the suburbs that surround them, the cars that stream into them, the packaged throwaways that stream out of them, and the fast-food outlets and convenience franchises that mimic them

---

[9]*New York Times*, January 24, 1993, pp. 1, 11. Michel Marriott wrote this in response to the increasingly frequent use of the word "nigger" in new and different contexts.

cause more harm to the biosphere than anything else except perhaps rapid population growth.

Yet more than ever before, the United States is organizing itself around its malls. We visit them more often than we go to church, and our teen-agers spend more time there than anywhere but home or school. (Ninety-three percent of teen-age girls rank shopping their favorite activity.) Malls have become the town squares of our public life, and the brand names and chain stores they host have become the icons of our popular culture.

This trend isn't uniquely American, of course. Europeans and Japanese are following our lead, abandoning community as the focus of their lives in favor of private consumption and building malls to rival our own. And the richer citizens of poor nations emulate consumer ways as best they can, constructing walled-in shopping palaces amid the squalor of their cities.

Still, in the perception of most of the world's people, the consumer lifestyle is made in America. To them, the Mall of America is all of America. Those who can't afford to consume on our level know all about our lifestyle: They watch us on television. *Dynasty* is the most popular show in Poland, and, as *Fortune* reports, the whole world watches *Dallas*.

But the American Dream is unattainable for all of humanity. The mall-centered consumer lifestyle requires enormous and continuous inputs of the very commodities that are most damaging to the earth to produce: energy, chemicals, metals and paper. Americans consume close to their own weight in basic raw materials each day.

Since mid-century, we mall shoppers of the world—the billion-strong global consumer class—have spewed out virtually all the ozone-depleting chlorofluoro-carbons, two-thirds of greenhouse gases and acid rain and similar shares of everything from pesticide runoff to radioactive waste. In the tropics, meanwhile, our demand for mahogany and teak, rare birds and fish, coral paperweights and other exotica (including drugs such as cocaine) wreaks havoc on habitats.

If our planet is ill-equipped to support 1 billion people living the Mall of America way, how would it withstand all the world's 5 billion inhabitants doing so? Consumerism, no matter how tastefully trimmed with green, is a recipe for ecological decline.

On the other hand, the opposite of overconsumption—poverty—is worse for the human spirit and harms the environment, too, as when desperate Third World peasants put forests to the torch and steep slopes to the plow. If the Earth suffers when people have either too little or too much, the question arises, how much is enough?

What level of consumption can the planet support for all? An environmentally sound lifestyle might combine traditional techniques of living in lesser-developed societies with advanced technologies. It could employ American laptop computers, Japanese high-speed trains with a Chinese-style low-meat diet emphasizing local produce, an Indian-style transportation system of bicycles and buses, a Latin American-style urban design of moderate dwellings nearby one another and a Korean-style system of materials use that puts a premium on durability and repair. Shifting from the consumer society to a sustainable society would generate a steady stream of challenges and opportunities for individuals, communities and nations.[10]

3. GROUPS AND INDIVIDUALS, WRITING ASSIGNMENT: TYPES OF CLAIMS

Write a one-page paper organized around a single type of claim. Use the following claims as starter sentences for your paper. Use the information about types of proofs and organizational strategies for each type of claim in this chapter to help you plan and write. Work in groups to generate the ideas and support for these papers.

a. Fact: Too many people own guns.
b. Definition: A definition of family values requires first a definition of a family.
c. Cause: Closing the college library on the weekends could have disastrous results.
d. Value: Computers are indispensable in modern education.
e. Policy: Parents should have the right to choose the schools their children attend.

4. INDIVIDUAL ONGOING PROJECT: WRITE YOUR ISSUE; USE THE TYPES OF CLAIMS TO GENERATE IDEAS

Ask questions about your issue that are associated with each of the five types of claims, and write at least a paragraph in response to each question. These questions are listed in part b. This exercise will help you begin to generate ideas for the argument paper on your issue that is assigned in Part Three.

a. Write your issue in the form of a question. Example: Have the Great Lakes become too polluted? Your issue: _____
b. Answer these questions:
Did it happen? Does it exist?
What is it?
What caused it?
Is it good or bad?
What should we do about it?

5. GROUP OR INDIVIDUAL SUMMARIES

Summarize the major ideas in the chapter by completing the following sentences:

a. The five types of claims are ...
b. The questions associated with each type are ...
c. A predictable sequence that claims follow when they originate in a dramatic, real-life situation is ...

---

[10]*Fort Worth Star-Telegram*, September 13, 1992, Sec. A, p. 34. Alan Thein Durning, a past senior researcher at Worldwatch Institute, is now the director of Northwest Environment Watch in Seattle. He writes about consumerism and the environment. He wrote this piece originally for the *Washington Post*.

d. Even though an argument may confine itself to proving only one type of claim, a more typical pattern is ...

SYNTHESIS OF READING AND WRITING

ASSIGNMENT: CRITICAL READING AND THE CRITICAL ANALYSIS PAPER. This final assignment will help you synthesize the information you have learned in these first seven chapters and apply it to a well-known argument, "Letter from Birmingham Jail" by Martin Luther King, Jr. It will also teach you to write the type of critical analysis paper sometimes required in other classes.

1. **Read the twenty questions** entitled "A Synthesis of Strategies for Reading Argument." These questions can be employed to help you read and analyze any argument. You will practice answering them as you read the two letters printed here, the clergymen's letter and King's answer.

2. **Read the background information** that places these letters in their historical context. This information will help you analyze the rhetorical situation in which these letters were produced.

3. **Read the letters and answer the brief versions of the twenty questions** as they appear at the beginning, in the margins, and at the end of the letters.

4. **Write a critical analysis paper.** Write a four-page double-spaced critical-analysis paper of the two letters by the clergymen and King. Explain the issue from both points of view, and summarize the positions taken in both letters. State the claims in both letters, and describe and evaluate the support and warrants in both. Finally, state your final evaluation and reaction to these letters. Which letter is more effective? Why? Have your own views been modified or changed?

A SYNTHESIS OF STRATEGIES FOR READING ARGUMENT

1. What is the issue area?
2. What specific issues are associated with it?
3. What do you already know about it?
4. What is at issue here, and what position does the author take?
5. How would you describe the rhetorical situation?
6. What is the claim?
7. What type of claim is it?
8. Divide the material into its parts, and analyze the organization. What are the parts? Why are they in this order? How do they relate to each other?
9. Study the specific support. What predominates? Facts, opinions, examples? Is there enough? Is it carefully selected or stacked to reveal bias? What effect does it have on the audience?
10. What are the warrants? Do you share them? Or do they need backing? Is there common ground between you and the author?
11. Are rebuttal arguments included? If not, can you think of possible rebuttals?

12. Should the claim be qualified to make it more convincing, or is it acceptable as it is?

13. Does the author use logical proofs and logical style? Describe them. What is the effect on the audience?

14. Does the author use ethical proofs and style? Describe them. What is the effect on the audience?

15. Does the author use emotional proofs and style? Describe them. What is the effect on the audience?

16. Are there any fallacies? What are they?

17. Is the argumentative intention clear, admitted, and straightforward, or is it concealed and presented under the guise of objective reporting?

18. Is this part of an ongoing conversation on this issue? What has gone before? What will come later?

19. Is the argument moral or immoral according to your standards? Why do you think so? Where are you coming from?

20. Are you convinced? Do you think others will be convinced? What do you perceive as the outcomes of this argument?

Background Information for Martin Luther King, Jr.'s "Letter from Birmingham Jail"

The two letters printed here were written in response to a dramatic situation that took place in Birmingham, Alabama, in 1963. Birmingham was a very strange place at that time. Black people were allowed to sit only in certain parts of buses and restaurants, they were required to drink out of separate water fountains, and they were not allowed in white churches, schools, or various other public places.

Martin Luther King, Jr., was a black Baptist minister who was a leader in the civil rights movement at that time. The purpose of the movement was to end segregation and discrimination and to create equal rights and access for black people.

King and others carefully prepared for demonstrations that would take place in Birmingham in the spring of 1963. The demonstrators began by sitting-in at lunch counters that had never served blacks before and by picketing stores. Twenty people were arrested the first day on charges of trespassing. Next, the civil rights leaders applied for permits to picket and hold parades against the injustices of discrimination and segregation. They were refused permission, but they demonstrated and picketed anyway. King was served an injunction by a circuit judge that said civil rights leaders could not protest, demonstrate, boycott, or sit-in. King and others decided that this was an unfair and unjust application of the law, and they decided to break it.

King, himself, decided to march on Good Friday, and he expected to go to jail. He was, in fact, arrested and jailed along with 50 other people before he had walked half a mile. King was in jail for eight days. During that time he wrote the "Letter from Birmingham Jail." It was written in response to the letter from eight white clergymen that had been published in the newspaper.

After King left jail, there were further demonstrations and some violence. Thousands of people demonstrated, and thousands were jailed. Finally, black and white leaders began to negotiate, and some final terms were announced May 10, 1963.

All lunch counters, restrooms, fitting rooms, and drinking fountains in downtown stores were to be desegregated within 90 days; blacks were to be placed in clerical and sales jobs in stores within 60 days; the many people arrested during the demonstrations were to be released on low bail; and permanent lines of communication were to be established between black and white leaders. The demonstrations ended then, and the city settled down and began to implement the agreements.[11]

Read the letters and answer these questions about the rhetorical situation:

1. What is the *exigence* for these two letters? What caused the authors to write them? What was the problem? Was it a new or recurring problem?
2. Who is the *audience* for the clergymen's letter? For King's letter? What is the nature of these audiences? Can they be convinced? What are the expected outcomes?
3. What are the *constraints*? Speculate about the beliefs, attitudes, habits, and traditions that were in place that limited or constrained both the clergymen and King. How did these constraining circumstances influence the audience at that time?
4. Think about the *authors* of both letters. Who are they? Speculate about their background, experience, affiliations, and values. What motivates them to write?
5. What kind of *text* is this? What effect do its special qualities and features have on the audience?
6. Think about *yourself as the reader*. What is your position on the issue? Do you experience constraints as you read? Do you perceive common ground with either the clergymen or King or both? Describe it. Are you influenced by these letters? How?

LETTER FROM EIGHT WHITE CLERGYMEN

A CALL FOR UNITY

April 12, 1963

What is the issue area?

What is the issue?

What is the clergymen's position?

We the undersigned clergymen are among those who, in January, issued "An Appeal for Law and Order and Common Sense," in dealing with racial problems in Alabama. We expressed understanding that honest convictions in racial matters could properly be pursued in the courts, but urged that decisions of those courts should in the meantime be peacefully obeyed.

---

[11]This account is drawn from Lee E. Bains, Jr., "Birmingham, 1963: Confrontation over Civil Rights," in *Birmingham, Alabama, 1956–1963: The Black Struggle for Civil Rights*, ed. David J. Garrow (Brooklyn: Carlson, 1989), pp. 175–183.

<table>
<tr><td>

What is the
claim?

What type of
claim is it?

</td><td>

Since that time there had been some evidence of increased forebearance and a willingness to face facts. Responsible citizens have undertaken to work on various problems which cause racial friction and unrest. In Birmingham, recent public events have given indication that we all have opportunity for a new constructive and realistic approach to racial problems.

However, we are now confronted by a series of demonstrations by some of our Negro citizens, directed and led in part by outsiders. We recognize the natural impatience of people who feel that their hopes are slow in being realized. But we are convinced that these demonstrations are unwise and untimely.

We agree rather with certain local Negro leadership which has called for honest and open negotiation of racial issues in our area. And we believe this kind of facing of issues can best be accomplished by citizens of our own metropolitan area, white and Negro, meeting with their knowledge and experience of the local situation. All of us need to face

</td></tr>
</table>

What is the
support?

that responsibility and find proper channels for its accomplishment.

Just as we formerly pointed out that "hatred and violence have no sanction in our religious and political traditions," we also point out that such actions as incite to hatred and violence, however technically peaceful those actions may be, have not contributed to the resolution of our local problems. We do not believe that these days of new hope are days when extreme measures are justified in Birmingham.

What are the
warrants?

We commend the community as a whole, and the local news media and law enforcement officials in particular, on the calm manner in which these demonstrations have been handled. We urge the public to continue to show restraint should the demonstrations continue, and the law enforcement officials to remain calm and continue to protect our city from violence.

Do you have
common
ground?

Can you
anticipate
rebuttals?

We further strongly urge our own Negro community to withdraw support from these demonstrations, and to unite locally in working peacefully for a better Birmingham. When rights are consistently denied, a cause should be pressed in the courts and in negotiations among local leaders, and not in the streets. We appeal to both our white and Negro citizenry to observe the principles of law and order and common sense.

Describe the style.

C. C. J. Carpenter, D.D., L.L.D., Bishop of Alabama; Joseph A. Durick, D.D., Auxiliary Bishop, Diocese of Mobile-Birmingham; Rabbi Milton L. Grafman, Temple Emanu-El, Birmingham, Alabama; Bishop Paul Hardin, Bishop of the Alabama–West Florida Conference of the Methodist Church; Bishop Nolan B. Harmon, Bishop of the North Alabama Conference of the Methodist Church; George M. Murray, D.D., L.L.D., Bishop Coadjutor, Episcopal Diocese of Alabama; Edward V. Ramage, Moderator, Synod of the Alabama Presbyterian Church in the United States; Earl Stallings, Pastor, First Baptist Church, Birmingham.

LETTER FROM BIRMINGHAM JAIL*

Martin Luther King, Jr.

April 16, 1963

My Dear Fellow Clergymen:

What is the
issue?

What is King's
position?

Make three
predictions.

Ask one big
question.

Underline
selectively and
jot key ideas
in the margin.

Survey.

Draw a line at
the end of the
introduction.

While confined here in the Birmingham city jail, I came across your recent statement calling my present activities "unwise and untimely." Seldom do I pause to answer criticism of my work and ideas. If I sought to answer all the criticisms that cross my desk, my secretaries would have little time for anything other than such correspondence in the course of the day, and I would have no time for constructive work. But since I feel that you are men of genuine good will and that your criticisms are sincerely set forth, I want to try to answer your statement in what I hope will be patient and reasonable terms.

I think I should indicate why I am here in Birmingham, since you have been influenced by the view which argues against "outsiders coming in." I have the honor of serving as president of the Southern Christian Leadership Conference, an organization operating in every southern state, with headquarters in Atlanta, Georgia. We have some eighty-five affiliated organizations across the South, and one of them is the Alabama Christian Movement for Human Rights. Frequently we share staff, educational and financial resources with our affiliates. Several months ago the affiliate here in Birmingham asked us to be on call to engage in a nonviolent direct-action program if such were deemed necessary. We readily consented, and when the hour came we lived up to our promise. So I, along with several members of my staff, am here because I was invited here. I am here because I have organizational ties here.

But more basically, I am in Birmingham because injustice is here. Just as the prophets of the eighth century B.C. left their villages and carried their "thus saith the Lord" far beyond the boundaries of their home towns, and just as the Apostle Paul left his village of Tarsus and carried the gospel of Jesus Christ to the far corners of the Greco-Roman world, so am I compelled to carry the gospel of freedom beyond my own home town. Like Paul, I must constantly respond to the Macedonian call for aid.

Moreover, I am cognizant of the interrelatedness of all communities and states. I cannot sit idly by in Atlanta and not be concerned about

---

*Author's Note: This response to a published statement by eight fellow clergymen from Alabama (Bishop C. C. J. Carpenter, Bishop Joseph A. Durick, Rabbi Milton L. Grafman, Bishop Paul Hardin, Bishop Nolan B. Harmon, the Reverend George M. Murray, the Reverend Edward V. Ramage, and the Reverend Earl Stallings) was composed under somewhat constricting circumstances. Begun on the margins of the newspaper in which the statement appeared while I was in jail, the letter was continued on scraps of writing paper supplied by a friendly Negro trusty, and concluded on a pad my attorneys were eventually permitted to leave me. Although the text remains in substance unaltered, I have indulged in the author's prerogative of polishing it for publication.

Draw other lines at the end of each of the other major sections of material. Identify the subject of each section.

Described the organization.

What is the claim?

What type of claim is it?

Is it qualified?

What other types of claims can you identify in the letter?

What are they?

Identify and analyze the logical proof.

what happens in Birmingham. Injustice anywhere is a threat to justice everywhere. We are caught in an inescapable network of mutuality, tied in a single garment of destiny. Whatever affects one directly, affects all indirectly. Never again can we afford to live with the narrow, provincial "outside agitator" idea. Anyone who lives inside the United States can never be considered an outsider anywhere within its bounds.

You deplore the demonstrations taking place in Birmingham. But your statement, I am sorry to say, fails to express a similar concern for the conditions that brought about the demonstrations. I am sure that none of you would want to rest content with the superficial kind of social analysis that deals merely with effects and does not grapple with underlying causes. It is unfortunate that demonstrations are taking place in Birmingham, but it is even more unfortunate that the city's white power structure left the Negro community with no alternative.

In any nonviolent campaign there are four basic steps: collection of the facts to determine whether injustices exist; negotiation; self-purification; and direct action. We have gone through all these steps in Birmingham. There can be no gain-saying the fact that racial injustice engulfs this community. Birmingham is probably the most thoroughly segregated city in the United States. Its ugly record of brutality is widely known. Negroes have experienced grossly unjust treatment in the courts. There have been more unsolved bombings of Negro homes and churches in Birmingham than in any other city in the nation. These are the hard, brutal facts of the case. On the basis of these conditions, Negro leaders sought to negotiate with the city fathers. But the latter consistently refused to engage in good-faith negotiation.

Then, last September, came the opportunity to talk with leaders of Birmingham's economic community. In the course of the negotiations, certain promises were made by the merchants—for example, to remove the stores' humiliating racial signs. On the basis of these promises, the Reverend Fred Shuttlesworth and the leaders of the Alabama Christian Movement for Human Rights agreed to a moratorium on all demonstrations. As the weeks and months went by, we realized that we were the victims of a broken promise. A few signs, briefly removed, returned; the others remained.

As in so many past experiences, our hopes had been blasted, and the shadow of deep disappointment settled upon us. We had no alternative except to prepare for direct action, whereby we would present our very bodies as a means of laying our case before the conscience of the local and the national community. Mindful of the difficulties involved, we decided to undertake a process of self-purification. We began a series of workshops on nonviolence, and we repeatedly asked ourselves: "Are you able to accept blows without retaliating?" "Are you able to endure the ordeal of jail?" We decided to schedule our direct-action program for the Easter season, realizing that except for Christmas, this is the main shopping period of the year. Knowing that a strong economic-withdrawal program would be the by-product of direct action, we felt that this would be the best time to bring pressure to bear on the merchants for the needed change.

Then it occurred to us that Birmingham's mayoral election was coming up in march, and we speedily decided to postpone action until after election day. When we discovered that the Commissioner of Public Safety, Eugene "Bull" Connor, had piled up enough votes to be in the runoff, we decided again to postpone action until the day after the runoff so that the demonstrations could not be used to cloud the issues. Like many others, we waited to see Mr. Connor defeated, and to this end we endured postponement after postponement. Having aided in this community need, we felt that our direct-action program could be delayed no longer.

You may well ask: "Why direct action? Why sit-ins, marches and so forth? Isn't negotiation a better path?" You are quite right in calling for negotiation. Indeed, this is the very purpose of direct action. Nonviolent direct action seeks to create such a crisis and foster such a tension that a community which has constantly refused to negotiate is forced to confront the issue. It seeks so to dramatize the issue that it can no longer be ignored. My citing the creation of tension as part of the work of the nonviolent-resister may sound rather shocking. But I must confess that I am not afraid of the word "tension." I have earnestly opposed violent tension, but there is a type of constructive, nonviolent tension which is necessary for growth. Just as Socrates felt that it was necessary to create a tension in the mind so that individuals could rise from the bondage of myths and half-truths to the unfettered realm of creative analysis and objective appraisal, so must we see the need for nonviolent gadflies to create the kind of tension in society that will help men rise from the dark depths of prejudice and racism to the majestic heights of understanding and brotherhood.

The purpose of our direct-action program is to create a situation so crisis-packed that it will inevitably open the door to negotiation. I therefore concur with you in your call for negotiation. Too long has our beloved Southland been bogged down in a tragic effort to live in monologue rather than dialogue.

One of the basic points in your statement is that the action that I and my associates have taken in Birmingham is untimely. Some have asked: "Why didn't you give the new city administration time to act?" The only answer that I can give to this query is that the new Birmingham administration must be prodded about as much as the outgoing one, before it will act. We are sadly mistaken if we feel that the election of Albert Boutwell as mayor will bring the millennium to Birmingham. While Mr. Boutwell is a much more gentle person than Mr. Connor, they are both segregationists, dedicated to the maintenance of the status quo. I have hope that Mr. Boutwell will be reasonable enough to see the futility of massive resistance to desegregation. But he will not see this without pressure from devotees of civil rights. My friends, I must say to you that we have not made a single gain in civil rights without determined legal and nonvio-

Identify and describe the rebuttals.

Identify and analyze the ethical proof.

lent pressure. Lamentably, it is an historical fact that privileged groups seldom give up their privileges voluntarily. Individuals may see the moral light and voluntarily give up their unjust posture; but, as Reinhold Niebuhr has reminded us, groups tend to be more immoral than individuals.

Identify and analyze the emotional proof.

We know through painful experience that freedom is never voluntarily given by the oppressor; it must be demanded by the oppressed. Frankly, I have yet to engage in a direct-action campaign that was "well-timed" in the view of those who have not suffered unduly from the disease of segregation. For years now I have heard the word "Wait!" It rings in the ear of every Negro with piercing familiarity. This "Wait" has almost always meant "Never." We must come to see, with one of our distinguished jurists, that "justice too long delayed is justice denied."

We have waited for more than 340 years for our constitutional and God-given rights. The nations of Asia and Africa are moving with jetlike speed toward gaining political independence, but we still creep at horse-and-buggy pace toward gaining a cup of coffee at a lunch counter. Perhaps it is easy for those who have never felt the stinging darts of segregation to say, "Wait." But when you have seen vicious mobs lynch your mothers and fathers at will and drown your sisters and brothers at whim; when you have seen hate-filled policemen curse, kick and even kill your black brothers and sisters; when you see the vast majority of your twenty million Negro brothers smothering in an airtight cage of poverty in the midst of an affluent society; when you suddenly find your tongue twisted and your speech stammering as you seek to explain to your six-year-old daughter why she can't go to the public amusement park that has just been advertised on television, and see tears welling up in her eyes when she is told that Fun-town is closed to colored children, and see ominous clouds of inferiority beginning to form in her little mental sky, and see her beginning to distort her personality by developing an unconscious bitterness toward white people; when you have to concoct an answer for a five-year-old son who is asking: "Daddy, why do white people treat colored people so mean?"; when you take a cross-country drive and find it necessary to sleep night after night in the uncomfortable corners of your automobile because no motel will accept you; when you are humiliated day in and day out by nagging signs reading "white" and "colored"; when your first name becomes "nigger," your middle name becomes "boy" (however old you are) and your last name becomes "John," and your wife and mother are never given the respected title "Mrs."; when you are harried by day and haunted by night by the fact that you are a Negro, living constantly at tiptoe stance, never quite knowing what to expect next, and are plagued with inner fears and outer resentments; when you are forever fighting a degenerating sense of "nobodiness"—then you will understand why we find it difficult to wait. There comes a time when the cup of endurance runs over, and men are no longer willing to be plunged into the abyss of despair. I hope, sirs, you can understand our legitimate and unavoidable impatience.

Draw a line where the subject changes and identify the subject of the next section.

You express a great deal of anxiety over our willingness to break laws. This is certainly a legitimate concern. Since we so diligently urge people to obey the Supreme Court's decision of 1954 outlawing segregation in the public schools, at first glance it may seem rather paradoxical for us consciously to break laws. One may well ask: "How can you advocate breaking some laws and obeying others?" The answer lies in the fact that there are two types of laws: just and unjust. I would be the first to advocate obeying just laws. Conversely, one has a moral responsibility to disobey unjust laws. I would agree with St. Augustine that "an unjust law is no law at all."

What are some types of support?

Does one type predominate?

Now, what is the difference between the two? How does one determine whether a law is just or unjust? A just law is a man-made code that squares with the moral law or the law of God. An unjust law is a code that is out of harmony with the moral law. To put it in the terms of St. Thomas Aquinas: An unjust law is a human law that is not rooted in eternal law and natural law. Any law that uplifts human personality is just. Any law that degrades human personality is unjust. All segregation statutes are unjust because segregation distorts the soul and damages the personality. It gives the segregator a false sense of superiority and the segregated a false sense of inferiority. Segregation, to use the terminology of the Jewish philosopher Martin Buber, substitutes an "I-it" relationship for an "I-thou" relationship and ends up relegating persons to the status of things. Hence segregation is not only politically, economically, and sociologically unsound, it is morally wrong and sinful. Paul Tillich has said that sin is separation. Is not segregation an existential expression of man's tragic separation, his awful estrangement, his terrible sinfulness? Thus it is that I can urge men to obey the 1954 decision of the Supreme Court, for it is morally right; and I can urge them to disobey segregation ordinances, for they are morally wrong.

Let us consider a more concrete example of just and unjust laws. An unjust law is a code that a numerical or power majority group compels a minority group to obey but does not make binding on itself. This is *difference* made legal. By the same token, a just law is a code that a majority compels a minority to follow and that it is willing to follow itself. This is *sameness* made legal.

Let me give another explanation. A law is unjust if it is inflicted on a minority that, as a result of being denied the right to vote, had no part in enacting or devising the law. Who can say that the legislature of Alabama which set up that state's segregation laws was democratically elected? Throughout Alabama all sorts of devious methods are used to prevent Negroes from becoming registered voters, and there are some counties in which, even though Negroes constitute a majority of the population, not a single Negro is registered. Can any law enacted under such circumstances be considered democratically structured?

Sometimes a law is just on its face and unjust in its application. For instance, I have been arrested on a charge of parading without a permit. Now, there is nothing wrong in having an ordinance which requires a permit for a parade. But such an ordinance becomes unjust when it is used to maintain segregation and to deny citizens the First-Amendment privilege of peaceful assembly and protest.

I hope you are able to see the distinction I am trying to point out. In no sense do I advocate evading or defying the law, as would the rabid segregationist. That would lead to anarchy. One who breaks an unjust law must do so openly, lovingly, and with a willingness to accept the penalty. I submit that an individual who breaks a law that conscience tells him is unjust, and who willingly accepts the penalty of imprisonment in order to arouse the conscience of the community over its injustice, is in reality expressing the highest respect for law.

Of course, there is nothing new about this kind of civil disobedience. It was evidenced sublimely in the refusal of Shadrach, Meshach and Abednego to obey the laws of Nebuchadnezzar, on the ground that a higher moral law was at stake. It was practiced superbly by the early Christians, who were willing to face hungry lions and the excruciating pain of chopping blocks rather than submit to certain unjust laws of the roman empire. To a degree, academic freedom is a reality today because Socrates practiced civil disobedience. In our own nation, the Boston Tea Party represented a massive act of civil disobedience.

We should never forget that everything Adolf Hitler did in Germany was "legal" and everything the Hungarian freedom fighters did in Hungary was "illegal." It was "illegal" to aid and comfort a Jew in Hitler's Germany. Even so, I am sure that, had I lived in Germany at the time, I would have aided and comforted my Jewish brothers. If today I lived in a Communist country where certain principles dear to the Christian faith are suppressed, I would openly advocate disobeying that country's antireligious laws.

I must make two honest confessions to you, my Christian and Jewish brothers. First, I must confess that over the past few years I have been gravely disappointed with the white moderate. I have almost reached the regrettable conclusion that the Negro's great stumbling block in his stride toward freedom is not the White Citizen's Counciler or the Ku Klux Klanner, but the white moderate, who is more devoted to "order" than to justice; who prefers a negative peace which is the absence of tension to a positive peace which is the presence of justice; who constantly says: "I agree with you in the goal you seek, but I cannot agree with your methods of direct action"; who paternalistically believes he can set the timetable for another man's freedom; who lives by a mythical concept of time and who constantly advises the Negro to wait for a "more convenient season." Shallow understanding from people of good will is more frustrating than absolute misunderstanding from people of ill will. Lukewarm acceptance is much more bewildering than outright rejection.

I had hoped that the white moderate would understand that law and order exist for the purpose of establishing justice and that when they fail in this purpose they become the dangerously structured dams that block the flow of social progress. I had hoped that the white moderate would

Draw a line where the subject changes and identify the next subject.

What are King's warrants?

How do they differ from the clergymen's?

What does King do to establish common ground?

understand that the present tension in the South is a necessary phase of the transition from an obnoxious negative peace, in which the negro passively accepted his unjust plight, to a substantive and positive peace, in which all men will respect the dignity and worth of human personality. Actually, we who engage in nonviolent direct action are not the creators of tension. We merely bring to the surface the hidden tension that is already alive. We bring it out in the open, where it can be seen and dealt with. Like a boil that can never be cured so long as it is covered up but must be opened with all its ugliness to the natural medicines of air and light, injustice must be exposed, with all the tension its exposure creates, to the light of human conscience and the air of national opinion before it can be cured.

In your statements you assert that our actions, even though peaceful, must be condemned because they precipitate violence. But is this a logical assertion? Isn't this like condemning a robbed man because his possession of money precipitated the evil act of robbery? Isn't this like condemning Socrates because his unswerving commitment to truth and his philosophical inquiries precipitated the act by the misguided populace in which they made him drink hemlock? Isn't this like condemning Jesus because his unique God-consciousness and never-ceasing devotion to God's will precipitated the evil act of crucifixion? We must come to see that, as the federal courts have consistently affirmed, it is wrong to urge an individual to cease his efforts to gain his basic constitutional rights because the quest may precipitate violence. Society must protect the robbed and punish the robber.

Are there any fallacies? Describe them.

I had also hoped that the white moderate would reject the myth concerning time in relation to the struggle for freedom. I have just received a letter from a white brother in Texas. He writes: "All Christians know that the colored people will receive equal rights eventually, but it is possible that you are in too great a religious hurry. It has taken Christianity almost two thousand years to accomplish what it has. The teachings of Christ take time to come to earth." Such an attitude stems from a tragic misconception of time, from the strangely irrational notion that there is something in the very flow of time that will inevitably cure all ills. Actually, time itself is neutral; it can be used either destructively or constructively. More and more I feel that the people of ill will have used time much more effectively than have the people of good will. We will have to repent in this generation not merely for the hateful words and actions of the bad people but for the appalling silence of the good people. Human progress never rolls in on wheels of inevitability; it comes through the tireless efforts of men willing to be coworkers with God, and without this hard work, time itself becomes an ally of the forces of social stagnation. We must use time creatively, in the knowledge that the time is always ripe to do right. Now is the time to make real the promise of democracy and transform our pending national elegy into a creative psalm of brotherhood. Now is the time to lift our national policy from the quicksand of racial injustice to the solid rock of human dignity.

Is King's intention clear?

You speak of our activity in Birmingham as extreme. At first I was rather disappointed that fellow clergymen would see my nonviolent efforts as those of an extremist. I began thinking about the fact that I stand in the middle of two opposing forces in the Negro community. One is a force of complacency, made up in part of Negroes who, as a result of long years of oppression, are so drained of self-respect and a sense of "somebodiness" that they have adjusted to segregation; and in part of a few middle-class Negroes who, because of a degree of academic and economic security and because in some ways they profit by segregation, have become insensitive to the problems of the masses. The other force is one of bitterness and hatred, and it comes perilously close to advocating violence. It is expressed in the various black nationalist groups that are springing up across the nation, the largest and best-known being Elijah Muhammad's Muslim movement. Nourished by the Negro's frustration over the continued existence of racial discrimination, this movement is made up of people who have lost faith in America, who have absolutely repudiated Christianity, and who have concluded that the white man is an incorrigible "devil."

I have tried to stand between these two forces, saying that we need emulate neither the "do-nothingism" of the complacent nor the hatred and despair of the black nationalist. For there is the more excellent way of love and nonviolent protest. I am grateful to God that, through the influence of the Negro church, the way of nonviolence became an integral part of our struggle.

If this philosophy had not emerged, by now many streets of the South would, I am convinced, be flowing with blood. And I am further convinced that if our white brothers dismiss as "rabble-rousers" and "outside agitators" those of us who employ nonviolent direct action, and if they refuse to support our nonviolent efforts, millions of Negroes will, out of frustration and despair, seek solace and security in black-nationalist ideologies—a development that would inevitably lead to a frightening racial nightmare.

Oppressed people cannot remain oppressed forever. The yearning for freedom eventually manifests itself, and that is what has happened to the American negro. Something within has reminded him of his birthright of freedom, and something without has reminded him that it can be gained. Consciously or unconsciously, he has been caught up by the *Zeitgeist*, and with his black brothers of Africa and his brown and yellow brothers of Asia, South America and the Caribbean, the United States Negro is moving with a sense of great urgency toward the promised land of racial justice. If one recognizes this vital urge that has engulfed the Negro community, one should readily understand why public demonstrations are taking place. The Negro has many pent-up resentments and latent frustrations, and he must release them. So let him march; let him make prayer pilgrimages to the city hall; let him go on freedom rides—and try to understand why he must do so. If his repressed emotions are not released in nonviolent ways, they will seek expression through violence; this is not a threat but a fact of history. So I have not said to my people: "Get rid of your discontent." Rather, I have tried to say that this normal and healthy discontent can be channeled into the creative outlet of nonviolent direct action. And now this approach is being termed extremist.

But though I was initially disappointed at being categorized as an extremist, as I continued to think about the matter I gradually gained a measure of satisfaction from the label. Was not Jesus an extremist for love: "Love your enemies, bless them that curse you, do good to them that hate you, and pray for them which despitefully use you, and persecute you." Was not Amos an extremist for justice: "Let justice roll down like waters and righteousness like an ever-flowing stream." Was not Paul an extremist for the Christian gospel: "I bear in my body the marks of the Lord Jesus." Was not Martin Luther an extremist: "Here I stand; I cannot do otherwise, so help me God." And John Bunyan: "I will stay in jail to the end of my days before I make a butchery of my conscience." And Abraham Lincoln: "This nation cannot survive half slave and half free." And Thomas Jefferson: "We hold these truths to be self-evident, that all men are created equal...." So the question is not whether we will be extremists, but what kind of extremists we will be. Will we be extremists for hate or for love? Will we be extremists for the preservation of injustice or for the extension of justice? In that dramatic scene on Calvary's hill three men were crucified. We must never forget that all three were crucified for the same crime—the crime of extremism. Two were extremists for immorality, and thus fell below their environment. The other, Jesus Christ, was an extremist for love, truth, and goodness, and thereby rose above his environment. Perhaps the South, the nation and the world are in dire need of creative extremists.

I had hoped that the white moderate would see this need. Perhaps I was too optimistic; perhaps I expected too much. I suppose I should have realized that few members of the oppressor race can understand the deep groans and passionate yearnings of the oppressed race, and still fewer have the vision to see that injustice must be rooted out by strong, persistent and determined action. I am thankful, however, that some of our white brothers in the South have grasped the meaning of this social revolution and committed themselves to it. They are still all too few in quantity, but they are big in quality. Some—such as Ralph McGill, Lillian Smith, Harry Golden, James McBride Dabbs, Ann Braden and Sarah Patton Boyle—have written about our struggle in eloquent and prophetic terms. Others have marched with us down nameless streets of the South. They have languished in filthy, roach-infested jails, suffering the abuse and brutality of policemen who view them as "dirty nigger-lovers." Unlike so many of their moderate brothers and sisters, they have recognized the urgency of the moment and sensed the need for powerful "action" antidotes to combat the disease of segregation.

Draw a line where the subject changes and identify the next subject.

Let me take note of my other major disappointment. I have been so greatly disappointed with the white church and its leadership. Of course, there are some notable exceptions. I am not unmindful of the fact that each of you has taken some significant stands on this issue. I commend you, Reverend Stallings, for your Christian stand on this past

Reconsider the rhetorical situation: What went before? What will come later?

Sunday, in welcoming Negroes to your worship service on a non-segregated basis. I commend the Catholic leaders of this state for integrating Spring Hill College several years ago.

But despite these notable exceptions, I must honestly reiterate that I have been disappointed with the church. I do not say this as one of those negative critics who can always find something wrong with the church. I say this as a minister of the gospel, who loves the church; who was nurtured in its bosom; who has been sustained by its spiritual blessings and who will remain true to it as long as the cord of life shall lengthen.

When I was suddenly catapulted into the leadership of the bus protest in Montgomery, Alabama, a few years ago, I felt we would be supported by the white church. I felt that the white ministers, priests and rabbis of the South would be among our strongest allies. Instead, some have been outright opponents, refusing to understand the freedom movement and misrepresenting its leaders; all too many others have been more cautious than courageous and have remained silent behind the anesthetizing security of stained-glass windows.

In spite of my shattered dreams, I came to Birmingham with the hope that the white religious leadership of this community would see the justice of our cause and, with deep moral concern, would serve as the channel through which our just grievances could reach the power structure. I had hoped that each of you would understand. But again I have been disappointed.

I have heard numerous southern religious leaders admonish their worshipers to comply with a desegregation decision because it is the law, but I have longed to hear white ministers declare: "Follow this decree because integration is morally right and because the Negro is your brother." In the midst of blatant injustices inflicted upon the Negro, I have watched white churchmen stand on the sideline and mouth pious irrelevancies and sanctimonious trivialities. In the midst of a mighty struggle to rid our nation of racial and economic injustice, I have heard many ministers say: "Those are social issues, with which the gospel has no real concern." And I have watched many churches commit themselves to a completely otherwordly religion which makes a strange, un-Biblical distinction between body and soul, between the sacred and the secular.

Are these letters part of an ongoing conversation? Describe it.

I have traveled the length and breadth of Alabama, Mississippi and all the other southern states. On sweltering summer days and crisp autumn mornings I have looked at the South's beautiful churches with their lofty spires pointing heavenward. I have beheld the impressive outlines of her massive religious-education buildings. Over and over I have found myself asking: "What kind of people worship here? Who is their God? Where were their voices when the lips of Governor Barnett dripped with words of interposition and nullification? Where were they when Governor Wallace gave a clarion call for defiance and hatred? Where were their voices of support when bruised and weary Negro men and women decided to rise from the dark dungeons of complacency to the bright hills of creative protest?"

Yes, these questions are still in my mind. In deep disappointment I have wept over the laxity of the church. But be assured that my tears have been tears of love. There can be no deep disappointment where there is not deep love. Yes, I love the church. How could I do otherwise? I am in the rather unique position of being the son, the grandson and the great-grandson of preachers. Yes, I see the church as the body of Christ. But, oh! How we have blemished and scarred that body through social neglect and through fear of being nonconformists.

There was a time when the church was very powerful—in the time when the early Christians rejoiced at being deemed worthy to suffer for what they believed. In those days the church was not merely a thermometer that recorded the ideas and principles of popular opinion; it was a thermostat that transformed the mores of society. Whenever the early Christians entered a town, the people in power became disturbed and immediately sought to convict the Christians for being "disturbers of the peace" and "outside agitators." But the Christians pressed on, in the conviction that they were a colony of heaven," called to obey God rather than man. Small in number, they were big in commitment. They were too God-intoxicated to be "astronomically intimidated." By their effort and example they brought an end to such ancient evils as infanticide and gladiatorial contests.

Things are different now. So often the contemporary church is a weak, ineffectual voice with an uncertain sound. So often it is an arch-defender of the status quo. Far from being disturbed by the presence of the church, the power structure of the average community is consoled by the church's silent—and often even vocal—sanction of things as they are.

But the judgment of God is upon the church as never before. If today's church does not recapture the sacrificial spirit of the early church, it will lose its authenticity, forfeit the loyalty of millions, and be dismissed as an irrelevant social club with no meaning for the twentieth century. Every day I meet young people whose disappointment with the Church has turned into outright disgust.

Perhaps I have once again been too optimistic. Is organized religion too inextricably bound to the status quo to save our nation and the world? Perhaps I must turn my faith to the inner spiritual church, the church within the church, as the true *ekklesia* and the hope of the world. But again I am thankful to God that some noble souls from the ranks of organized religion have broken loose from the paralyzing chains of conformity and joined us as active partners in the struggle for freedom. They have left their secure congregations and walked the streets of Albany, Georgia, with us. They have gone down the highways of the South on tortuous rides for freedom. Yes, they have gone to jail with us. Some have been dismissed from their churches, have lost the support of their bishops and fellow ministers. But they have acted in the faith that right defeated is stronger than evil triumphant. Their witness has been the spiritual salt that has preserved the true meaning of the gospel in these troubled times. They have carved a tunnel of hope through the dark mountain of disappointment.

I hope the church as a whole will meet the challenge of this decisive hour. But even if the church does not come to the aid of justice, I have no despair about the future. I have no fear about the outcome of our struggle in Birmingham, even if our motives are at present misunderstood. We will reach the goal of freedom in Birmingham and all over the nation, because the goal of America is freedom. Abused and scorned though we may be, our destiny is tied up with America's destiny. Before the pilgrims landed at Plymouth, we were here. Before the pen of Jefferson etched the majestic words of the Declaration of Independence across the pages of history, we were here. For more than two centuries our forebears labored in this country without wages; they made cotton king; they built the homes of their masters while suffering gross injustice and shameful humiliation—and yet out of a bottomless vitality they continued to thrive and develop. If the inexpressible cruelties of slavery could not stop us, the opposition we now face will surely fail. We will win our freedom because the sacred heritage of our nation and the eternal will of God are embodied in our echoing demands.

Before closing I feel impelled to mention one other point in your statement that has troubled me profoundly. You warmly commended the Birmingham police force for keeping "order" and "preventing violence." I doubt that you would have so warmly commended the police force if you had seen its dogs sinking their teeth into unarmed, nonviolent Negroes. I doubt that you would so quickly commend the policemen if you were to observe their ugly and inhumane treatment of Negroes here in the city jail; if you were to watch them push and curse old Negro women and young Negro girls; if you were to see them slap and kick old Negro men and young boys; if you were to observe them, as they did on two occasions, refuse to give us food because we wanted to sing our grace together. I cannot join you in your praise of the Birmingham police department.

It is true that the police have exercised a degree of discipline in handling the demonstrators. In this sense they have conducted themselves rather "nonviolently" in public. But for what purpose? To preserve the evil system of segregation. Over the past few years I have consistently preached that nonviolence demands that the means we use must be as pure as the ends we seek. I have tried to make clear that it is wrong to use immoral means to attain moral ends. But now I must affirm that it is just as wrong, or perhaps even more so, to use moral means to preserve immoral ends. Perhaps Mr. Connor and his policemen have been rather nonviolent in public, as was Chief Pritchett in Albany, Georgia, but they have used the moral means of nonviolence to maintain the immoral end of racial injustice. As T. S. Eliot has said: "The last temptation is the greatest treason: To do the right deed for the wrong reason."

I wish you had commended the Negro sit-inners and the demonstrators of Birmingham for their sublime courage, their willingness to suffer and their amazing discipline in the midst of great provocation. One day the South will recognize its real heroes. They will be the James Merediths, with the noble sense of purpose that enables them to face jeering and

Draw a line where the subject changes and identify the next subject.

hostile mobs, and with the agonizing loneliness that characterizes the life of the pioneer. They will be old, oppressed, battered Negro women, symbolized in a seventy-two-year-old woman in Montgomery, Alabama, who rose up with a sense of dignity and with her people decided not to ride segregated buses, and who responded with ungrammatical profundity to one who inquired about her weariness: "My feets is tired, but my soul is at rest." They will be the young high school and college students, the young ministers of the gospel and a host of their elders, courageously and nonviolently sitting in at lunch counters and willingly going to jail for conscience' sake. One day the South will know that when these disinherited children of God sat down at lunch counters, they were in reality standing up for what is best in the American dream and for the most sacred values in our Judaeo-Christian heritage, thereby bringing our nation back to those great wells of democracy which were dug deep by the founding fathers in their formulation of the Constitution and the Declaration of Independence.

Draw a line to set off the conclusion. What is the concluding idea?

Never before have I written so long a letter. I'm afraid it is much too long to take your precious time. I can assure you that it would have been much shorter if I had been writing from a comfortable desk, but what else can one do when he is alone in a narrow jail cell, other than write long letters, think long thoughts and pray long prayers?

What is the predominant style? Defend your answer.

If I have said anything in this letter that overstates the truth and indicates an unreasonable impatience, I beg you to forgive me. If I have said anything that understates the truth and indicates my having a patience that allows me to settle for anything less than brotherhood, I beg God to forgive me.

Are you convinced by either letter? Describe.

I hope this letter finds you strong in the faith. I also hope that circumstances will soon make it possible for me to meet each of you, not as an integrationist or a civil-rights leader but as a fellow clergyman and a Christian brother. Let us all hope that the dark clouds of racial prejudice will soon pass away and the deep fog of misunderstanding will be lifted from our fear-drenched communities, and in some not too distant tomorrow the radiant stars of love and brotherhood will shine over our great nation with all their scintillating beauty.

Are the clergymen's and King's arguments moral or immoral according to your standards?

Yours for the cause of Peace and Brotherhood,
MARTIN LUTHER KING, JR.

Write a Summary of the Core of the Argument

Claim: King wants to convince me to think that . . .
Support: Because . . .
Warrants: Where is King coming from?
Backing: Do you need backing for these warrants? Does King supply it?
What is probably the best position that you can take on this issue yourself with your present information?
What are your current reflections and ideas that are generated by this text?
Answer your big question.
Check your predictions. Were they correct? Do you need to change them?

PART THREE

Writing a Research Paper That Presents an Argument

The purpose of these last three chapters is to teach you to write an argument paper from your own perspective that incorporates research materials from outside sources. Since other professors or even employers may also ask you to produce such papers, this instruction should be useful to you not only now but in the future as well. Chapter 8 teaches you to write a claim, clarify the purpose for your paper, and analyze your audience. Chapter 9 teaches you various creative strategies for inventing and gathering research material for your paper. Chapter 10 teaches ways to organize this material, write and revise the paper, and prepare the final copy. Methods for locating and using resource materials from the library are also included in Chapters 9 and 10. When you finish reading Part Three:

- You will know how to write your claim and determine the main argumentative purpose of your paper.
- You will know how to analyze your audience and predict how it might change.
- You will know how to think about your claim and gather material from your own background and experience to support it.
- You will know how to organize and conduct library research to support your claim further.
- You will know a variety of possible ways to organize the ideas for your paper.
- You will know how to incorporate research materials into your paper and prepare the final copy.

CHAPTER 8

Clarifying Purpose and Understanding the Audience

This chapter and the two that follow will help you plan, research, and write an argument paper in which you state your claim and prove it. Chaim Perelman's definition of argument quoted in Chapter 1 will help you focus on your final objective in writing this paper: you will seek "to create or increase the adherence of minds to the theses presented for their [the audience's] assent."[1] In other words, you will try to get your reading audience to agree, at least to some extent, with your claim and the ideas you use to support it.

WRITE A CLAIM AND CLARIFY YOUR PURPOSE

Write your claim as early in the process as possible. To help you with the process of writing your claim, refer to the information in Chapter 1, which will help you find and test an issue that will be of compelling interest to you. (See pp. 16–20, 33). Then, either map your issue (see pp. 94 and 102) or freewrite about it (see p. 113) to help you narrow and focus it so that you can finally write a claim about it. You may have to do some background reading at this point as well. A number of examples of claims are provided in Chapter 7 (starting on p. 215), which you can look at again when you write your own claim. This chapter will also provide additional information to help you write a claim.

Your claim is important because it provides purpose, control, and direction for everything else that you include in your paper. The claim questions from Chapter 7 will help you identify the type of claim you are writing and establish the fundamental argumentative purpose for your paper. Your main purpose will be either to establish fact (What happened?), to define (What is it?), to show cause (What caused it?), to establish value (Is it good or bad?), or to propose policy (What

---

[1]Chaim Perelman and L. Olbrechts-Tyteca, *The New Rhetoric: A Treatise on Argumentation* (Notre Dame, IN: Notre Dame Press, 1969), p. 45.

should we do?). The examples in the following list demonstrate how the claim questions can be used to establish purpose for your claim and your paper. But first, here is a detailed explanation of a rhetorical situation for an issue of crime and the treatment of criminals that will be used as an example in this chapter and that could serve as motivation for a written argument: A teenage white supremacist murdered a black middle-class family man. This crime was committed in Texas, where juries are impaneled both to decide guilt and to sentence the criminal. The jury decided the white supremacist was guilty and, in ignorance, sentenced him both to probation and a jail term. The law does not permit both sentences, and so the murderer ended up with probation. As you can imagine, there was public concern, and issues began to surface. Here is how the claim questions can be used in this situation to decide on a purpose and a claim.

Using Claim Questions to Plan Purpose and Claim

1. To establish a claim of fact, ask: What happened? Does it exist? Is it a fact? Is it true?

> *Example*: You and the audience know about the murder and have just learned about the probationary sentence. Something seems very wrong. Your purpose is to analyze what is wrong, especially since some people are satisfied and others are dissatisfied with the sentence. Your claim is a claim of fact, *The murderer escaped an appropriate sentence.* Your strategy will be to organize the paper chronologically, giving a history of what has happened, and quoting both facts and expert opinion to prove your claim.

2. To establish a claim of definition, ask: What is it? What is it like? How should we interpret it? How does its usual meaning change in this context?

> *Example*: You think there was a definition problem in the sentencing procedure. The jury was supposed to assign an appropriate sentence for a murder. You decide your audience needs a definition of an appropriate sentence for a murder. Your claim is, *Probation is not an appropriate sentence for murder.* Your argument relies on expert opinion and the citation of similar cases to illustrate what an appropriate sentence for murder should be.

3. To establish a claim of cause, ask: What caused it? Where did it come from? Why did it happen? What are the effects? What will the short-term and long-term results be?

> *Example*: Personal conversations and media reports indicate considerable confusion over the cause of the sentence. Some people think the jury was racially prejudiced, others think the murderer was assigned probation because he is young, and others are baffled. You decide the cause was the jury's lack of information, and your claim is, *The jury did not know and did not receive information about how to sentence murderers, and as a result it recommended an inappropriate sentence.* To prove this claim, you examine the training provided jurors. You interview people who have served on juries. You try to learn what training was available for this particular jury.

4. To establish a claim of value, ask: Is it good or bad? How bad? How good? Of what worth is it? Is it moral or immoral? Who thinks so? What criteria should I use to decide goodness or badness? Are these the same criteria the audience would apply?

Example: There seems to be some disagreement about whether this sentence was good or bad, and you decide to declare it a bad sentence. Your claim is, *It was wrong of the jury to assign the murderer probation and no jail sentence.* To prove this, you appeal to the standard needs and values you assume your audience holds, including a desire for physical safety, a sense of fairness and justness, and a respect for the jury system which, you argue, has failed in this case.

5. To establish a claim of policy, ask: What should we do about it? What should be our future course of action? How can we solve the problem?

Example: By the time you write your paper, everyone has decided that the jury has made a mistake. In fact, the criminal is back in jail on another charge waiting for a new trial. You decide to write a policy paper in which you recommend jury training so that this same problem will not recur. Your claim is, *Juries need pretrial training in order to make competent judgments.* An example of a policy paper organized around this claim and written in response to this actual rhetorical situation appears at the end of Chapter 10 in the Exercise section.

When you have decided on your main purpose and written your claim, you can now begin to think about ways to develop your claim.

SOME PRELIMINARY QUESTIONS TO HELP YOU DEVELOP YOUR CLAIM

Ask the following questions to further clarify and develop your claim. Some tentative answers to these questions now can help you stay on track and avoid problems with the development of your paper later.

Is the Claim Narrow and Focused? You may have started with a broad issue area, such as technology or education, that suggests many specific related issues. You may have participated in mapping sessions in class to discover some of the specific issues related to an issue area, and this work may have helped you narrow your issue. You may now need to narrow your issue even further by focusing on one prong or aspect of it. Here is an example:

Issue area: The environment
 Specific related issue:
 What problems are associated with nuclear energy?
  Aspects of that issue:
  What should be done with nuclear waste?
  How hazardous is it, and how can we control the hazards?
  What are the alternatives to nuclear energy?

In selecting a narrowed issue to write about, you may want to focus on only one of the three aspects of the nuclear energy problem. You might, for instance, decide to make this claim: Solar power is better than nuclear energy. Later, as you write, you may need to narrow this topic even further and revise your claim: Solar power is best for certain specified purposes. Any topic can turn out to be too broad or complicated when you begin to write about it.

You may also need to change your focus or perspective to narrow your claim. You may, for example, begin to research the claim you have made in response to your issue, but while doing research, discover that the real issue is something else. As a result, you decide to change your claim. For example, suppose you decide to write a policy paper about freedom of speech. Your claim is, Freedom of speech should be protected in all situations. As you read and research, however, you discover that an issue for many people is a narrower one related to freedom of speech specifically as it relates to violence on television and children's behavior. In fact, you encounter an article that claims, Television violence should be censored even if doing so violates free-speech rights. You decide to refocus your paper and write a value paper that claims, Television violence is harmful and not subject to the protection of free-speech rights.

Which Controversial Words in Your Claim Will You Need to Define? Identify the words in your claim that may need defining. In the example just used, you would need to be clear about what you mean by *television violence, censorship,* and *free-speech rights.*

Can You Learn Enough to Cover the Claim Fully? If the information for an effective paper is unavailable or too complicated, write another claim, one that you know more about and can research more successfully. Or narrow the claim further to an aspect that you can understand and develop.

What Are the Different Perspectives on Your Issue? Make certain that your issue invites two or more perspectives. If you have written an exploratory paper on your issue, you already know what several views are. If you have not written such a paper, explore your issue by writing several claims that represent several points of view, and then select the one you want to prove. For example:

- Solar power is better than nuclear power.
- Solar power is worse than nuclear power.
- Solar power has some advantages and some disadvantages when compared to nuclear power.
- Solar power is better than nuclear power for certain specified purposes.

As you identify the different perspectives on your issue, you can also begin to plan some refutation that will not alienate your audience. An angry or insulted audience is not likely to change.

How Can You Make Your Claim Both Interesting and Compelling to Yourself and Your Audience? Develop a fresh perspective or "take" on your issue when writing your claim. Suppose, for example, you are writing a policy paper that claims public education should be changed. You get bored with it. You keep running into old reasons that everyone already knows. Then you discover a couple of new aspects of the issue that you could cover with more original ideas and material. You learn that some people think parents should be able to choose their children's school, and you learn that competition among schools might lead to improvement. You refocus your issue and your perspective. Your new fact claim is, Competition among schools, like competition in business, leads to improvement. The issue and your claim now have new interest for you and your audience because you are looking at them in a whole new way.

At What Point Are You and the Audience Entering the Conversation on the Issue? Consider your audience's background and initial views on the issue to decide how to write a claim about it. If both you and your audience are new to the issue, you may decide to stick with claims of fact and definition. If they partially understand it, but need more analysis, you may decide on claims of cause or value. If both you and your audience have adequate background on the issue, you may want to write a policy claim and try to solve the problems associated with it. Keep in mind, also, that issues and audiences are dynamic. As soon as audiences engage with issues, both begin to change. So you need to be constantly aware of the current status of the issue and the audience's current stand on it.

What Secondary Purpose Do I Want to Address in My Paper? Even though you establish your predominant purpose as policy or cause, you may still want to answer the other claim questions, particularly if you think your audience needs that information. You may need to explain what happened or speculate on causes as part of the background information you provide. You may need to provide definitions for the key words in your claim. You may want to address value questions in order to engage your audience's motives and values. Finally, you may want to suggest policy briefly even though your paper has another predominant purpose.

MAKE A PRELIMINARY OUTLINE

Make a preliminary outline to guide your future thinking and research and to help you maintain the focus and direction you have already established. Even though you may not know very much about your issue and your claim at this point, it can be valuable, nevertheless, to write what you want to learn. Attach to your outline a preliminary research plan and some ideas to help you get started on a first draft. Here is an example:

A Preliminary Outline

VALUE CLAIM.
 Television violence is harmful and should not be subject to the protection of free speech rights, because

1. Violence on television and in life seem to be related.
2. Children do not always differentiate between television and reality.
3. Parents do not supervise their children's television viewing.
4. Even though free speech is a constitutional right, it should not be invoked to project what is harmful to society.

continued

RESEARCH NEEDS.

I need to find out how free speech is usually defined. Does it include all freedom of expression, including violence on television? Also, I will need to find the latest studies on television violence and violent behavior, particularly in children. Will there be a cause-effect relationship? Even though I want to focus mainly on value and show that violent television is bad, I will also need to include definition and cause in this paper.

DRAFT PLAN.

I will define television violence and free speech. I need to do some background reading on censorship and freedom of speech, and summarize some of this information for my readers. My strongest material will probably be on the relationship between violence on television and in real life. I think now I'll begin with that and end with the idea that the Constitution should not be invoked to protect harmful elements like television violence. I'm going to imagine an audience that either has children or that values children. I will use examples from an article I clipped about how children imitate what they see on television.

You now have the beginning of an argument paper: a claim, some reasons, and some ideas to explore further. Your claim may change, and your reasons will probably change as you think, read, and do research. Before you go further, however, you need to think more about the audience. The nature of your audience can have a major influence on how you will finally write your argument paper.

UNDERSTAND THE AUDIENCE TO HELP YOU ACHIEVE SUCCESSFUL ARGUMENT OUTCOMES

Why is it important to understand your audience? Why not just argue for what you think is important? Some definitions and descriptions of effective argument emphasize the techniques of argument rather than the outcomes. They encourage the arguer to focus on what he or she thinks is important. For example, an argument with a clear claim, clear logic and reasoning, and good evidence will be described by some theorists as a good argument. The position in this book, however, has been different. If the argument does not reach the audience and create some common ground in order to convince or change it in some way, then the argument, no matter how skillfully crafted, is not productive. Productive argument, according to the definitions we used in Chapter 1, must create common ground and achieve some definable audience outcomes.

In order for the writer of argument to reach the audience, create common ground, and bring about change, two essential requirements need to be met. First, the audience must be willing to listen and perhaps also be willing to change. Second, the author must be willing to study, understand, and appeal to the audience. Such analysis will enable the author to appeal to the audience's present opinions, values, and motives, and to show as often as possible that the author shares them to achieve the common ground essential for effective argument. Thus both audience and author need to cooperate to a certain degree for argument to achieve any outcomes at all.

Here are four strategies to help you begin the process of understanding and appealing to your audience:

1. Assess the audience's size and familiarity to you.
2. Determine how much you have in common with your audience.
3. Determine the audience's initial position and what changes in views or actions might occur as a result of your argument.
4. Identify the audience's discourse community.

Assess the Audience's Size and Familiarity.   Audiences come in all sizes and may or may not include people you know. The smallest and most familiar audience is always yourself; you must convince yourself in internal argument. The next smallest audience is one other person. Larger audiences may include specific, known groups such as family members, classmates, work associates, or members of an organization you belong to. You may also at times write for a large unfamiliar audience composed of either local, national, or international members. And, of course, some audiences are mixed, including both people you do and do not know. Your techniques will vary for building common ground with both large and small, familiar and unfamiliar audiences, but your argumentative aim will not change.

Determine What You and the Audience Have in Common.   You may or may not consider yourself a member of your audience, depending on how closely you identify with it and share its views. For example, if you are a member of a union, you will probably identify and agree with its official position, particularly on work-related issues. If you work with management, you will hold other views about work-related issues. Your methods of achieving common ground with either of these audiences will be somewhat different, depending on whether you consider yourself a member of the group or not.

Determine the Audience's Initial Position and How It Might Change.   As part of your planning, project what you would regard as acceptable audience outcomes for your argument. Think about the degree of common ground you initially share with your audience, because it is then easier to imagine audience change. There are several possibilities of initial audience positions and possible changes or outcomes.

You may be writing for a *friendly* audience that is in near or total agreement with you from the outset. The planned outcome is to *confirm this audience's beliefs and strengthen its commitment*. You can be straightforward with this audience, addressing it directly and openly with the claim at the beginning, supported with evidence and warrants that it can accept. Political rallies, religious sermons, and public demonstrations by special interest groups, such as civil rights or prolife groups, all serve to make members more strongly committed to their original beliefs. When you write for a friendly audience, you will achieve the same effect.

Another type of audience either *mildly agrees* with you or *mildly opposes* you. This audience may possess no clear reasons for its tendencies or beliefs. Possible outcomes in this case usually include (1) *final agreement* with you, (2) *a new interest* in the issue and a commitment to work out a position on it, or (3) *a tentative decision* to accept what seems to be true for now. To establish common ground with this type of audience, get to the point quickly and use support and warrants that will establish connections.

Other audiences may be *neutral* on your issue, uncommitted and uninterested in how an issue is resolved one way or another. Your aim will be to *change the level of their indifference* and encourage them to take a position. You may only be able to get their attention or raise their level of consciousness. As with other audiences, you will establish common ground with a neutral audience by analyzing its needs and by appealing to those needs.

A *hostile* audience that disagrees with you may be closed to the idea of change, at least at first. Anticipated outcomes for such audiences might include *avoiding more hostility* and *getting them to listen* and *consider possible alternative views*. Rogerian argument or a delayed claim may be necessary to get such an audience to listen at all. It is always possible that a hostile audience might *change its mind*, or at least *compromise*. If all else fails, sometimes you can get a hostile audience to *agree to disagree*, which is much better than increasing the hostility.

Think of your relationship with your audience as if it were plotted on a sliding scale. At one end are those who agree with you, and at the other end are those who disagree. In the middle is the neutral audience. Other mildly hostile or mildly favorable audiences are positioned at various points in between. Your knowledge of human nature and argument theory will help you plan strategies of argument that will address all these audience types.

Identify the Audience's Discourse Community.   An audience's affiliations can help define its nature. Specialized groups that share subject matter, background, experience, values, and a common language (including specialized and technical vocabulary, jargon, or slang) are known as *discourse communities*. Common ground automatically exists among members of a discourse community because they understand one another easily.

Consider discourse communities composed of all scientists, all engineers, or all mathematicians. Their common background, training, language, and knowledge make it easier for them to connect, achieve common ground, and work toward conclusions. The discourse community itself, in fact, creates some of the common ground necessary for successful academic inquiry or for other types of argument.

You are a member of the university or college discourse community where you attend classes. This community is characterized by reasonable and educated people who share common background and interests that enable them to inquire into matters that are still at issue. You are also a member of the discourse community in your argument class, which has a common vocabulary and common tasks and assignments. Outsiders visiting your class would not be members of this community in the same way that you and your classmates are.

What other discourse communities do you belong to? How do the discourse communities in your home, among your friends, and at work differ from your university and argument class discourse communities? For some students, the differences are considerable. The strategies for connecting with others, building common ground, and arguing within the context of each of your discourse communities can vary considerably. With some reflection, you will be able to think of examples of the ways you have analyzed and adapted to each of them already. You can improve your natural ability to analyze and adapt to audiences by learning some conscious strategies for analyzing and adapting to both familiar and unfamiliar audiences.

SOME WAYS TO ANALYZE A FAMILIAR AUDIENCE

At an early stage in the writing process, you need to answer certain key questions about your audience. To get this information you may simply ask members of your audience some questions. Asking questions isn't always possible or advisable, however. More often, you will have to answer for your audience by studying them and even doing research.

The following list presents a set of 13 questions to ask about a familiar audience. You do not have to answer every question about every audience. You may need to add a question or two, depending on your audience. Answer questions that are suggested by the particular rhetorical situation for your argument. For example, the age range of the audience might be a factor to consider if you are writing about how to live a successful life; the diversity of the class might be important if you are writing about racial issues; or class interests, particularly outdoor interests, might be useful to know if you are writing about the environment.

As you read through the audience analysis questions, imagine that you are continuing to work on the argument paper on the topic of jury trials. Recall that your claim is, Juries need pretrial training in order to make competent judgments. The information that you uncover about your audience follows each question.

1. Describe the audience in general. Who are they? What do you have in common with them?

Example: My audience is my argument class. We have common educational goals, language, assignments, campus interests, and experiences.

2. What are some of the demographics of the group? Consider size, age, gender, nationality, education, and professional status.

Example: Two-thirds of the 25 students are 18–20 years old, and one-third are over 30. Fifty-six percent are female, and 44 percent are male. Slightly less than half are white; about a third are black, Hispanic, and Asian; and the rest are international students. About three-fourths are freshmen and sophomores, and the rest are upperclassmen. More than half of the class works at part-time outside jobs. Two have full-time professions in insurance and sales.

3. What are some of their organizational affiliations? Consider political parties, religion, social and living groups, and economic status.

Example: Roughly half say they are Democrat, and half Republican. Three say they are Libertarians. Fifty percent say they attend Christian churches, 20 percent are Jewish, and the rest either are Islamic or Hindu or say they are not religious. Four belong to fraternities or sororities, a few live in the dorms, and the rest live at home or in apartments. Most are in the middle or lower-middle class with aspirations to graduate, get better jobs, and move up.

4. What are their interests? Include outside interests, reading material, and perhaps majors.

Example: The group lists the following interests and activities: sports, movies, television, exercise and fitness, camping and hiking, attending lectures, repairing and driving cars, listening to music, reading local newspapers, and reading news magazines. They are all college students. Five are in engineering, six are in business, one is in nursing, and the rest are in humanities and social sciences.

5. What is their present position on your issue? What audience outcomes can you anticipate?

Example: My issue is jury trials, and my claim is, Juries need pretrial training in order to make competent judgments. Most of the class have not thought about this issue and either are neutral or mildly agree. A show of hands reveals that five think juries need more training, fifteen don't know, and five favor the status quo. I can expect the neutral and status quo members to become interested and perhaps even agree. I can expect the others to agree more strongly than they do now.

6. Will they interpret the issue in the same way you have?

Example: This issue comes from a local event, and some class members may see a double-jeopardy issue or some other issue emerging from it. I will have to focus their attention on my issue and make it important to them.

7. How significant is your issue to the audience? Will it touch their lives or remain theoretical for them?

Example: This is a personally significant issue for the people planning to be lawyers. It has some personal significance for most of the others, also, because everyone who votes is a potential jury member. The international students will have interest in it, depending upon their background and experience. I need to find out what their experiences have been.

8. Are there any obstacles that will prevent your audience from accepting your claim as soon as you state it?

Example: Part of this audience believes that juries are always effective and need no improvement. I will have to challenge that idea.

9. At what point are they in the ongoing conversation about the issue? Will they require background and definitions? Are they knowledgeable enough to contemplate policy change?

Example: Ninety percent know about the recent local case in which the jury made a poor judgment because of ignorance of procedures. Half of the class have been called for jury duty, and two have served. Three intend to go to law school and have considerable background and interest in juries. This audience knows enough to think about policy changes.

10. What is the attitude of your audience toward you?

Example: I think I have a friendly audience, and I am an insider, a part of it. We have established an open atmosphere in this class, and there are no personal hostilities that I can see. We share the same discourse community.

11. What beliefs and values do you and your audience share?

Example: In regard to my issue, they value trial by jury, they value a job well done, and they value education.

12. What motivates your audience? What are their goals and aims?

Example: My audience would be personally motivated to do a good job if they were on a jury.

13. What argument style will work best with your audience?

Example: I don't want to debate this issue. I would like to get consensus and a sense of cooperation instead. In fact, I picked this issue because it is one that people will probably not fight about. I want to use examples that will appeal to my audience's experiences. I am willing to negotiate or qualify my conclusion if the class members who critique my paper have trouble with it.

Go through these questions and try to answer them for a potential audience, as has been done here, at an early stage of the writing process. To help you answer questions 11 and 12 about values and motives, refer to Box 8.1.

1. Survival needs: food, warmth, and shelter; physical safety.
2. Health: physical well-being, strength, endurance, energy; mental stability, optimism.
3. Financial well-being: accumulation of wealth; increased earning capacity; lower costs and expenses; financial security.
4. Affection and friendship: identification in a group; being accepted, liked, loved; being attractive to others; having others as friends or objects of affection.
5. Respect and esteem of others: having the approval of others, having status in a group, being admired, fame.
6. Self-esteem: meeting one's own standards in such virtues as courage, fairness, honesty, generosity, good judgment, and compassion; meeting self-accepted obligations of one's role as employee, child or parent, citizen, member of an organization.
7. New experience: travel; change in employment or location; new hobbies or leisure activities; new food or consumer products; variety in friends and acquaintances.
8. Self-actualization: developing one's potential in skills and abilities; achieving ambitions; being creative; gaining the power to influence events and other people.
9. Convenience: conserving time or energy; the ease with which the other motives can be satisfied.

BOX 8.1 Needs and Values That Motivate Most Audiences[2]

---

[2]This list is based on Abraham Maslow's hierarchy of needs and motives from his book *Motion and Personality*, expanded by James A. Wood in *Speaking Effectively* (New York: Random House, 1988), pp. 203–204. Reproduced with permission.

CONSTRUCT AN UNFAMILIAR AUDIENCE

Sometimes you will not be able to gather direct information about your audience because it will be unfamiliar to you and unavailable for study. In this case, you will need to draw on your past experience for audience analysis. To do so you will have to imagine a particular kind of audience, a *universal audience*, and write for it when you cannot get direct audience information.

Chaim Perelman, who has written extensively about the difficulty of identifying the qualities of audiences with certainty, has developed the concept of the universal audience.[3] He suggests planning an argument for a composite audience that has individual differences but also important common qualities. This universal audience is educated, reasonable, normal, adult, and willing to listen. Every arguer constructs the universal audience from his or her own past experience, and, consequently, the concept of the universal audience varies somewhat from individual to individual and culture to culture.

The construct of the universal audience can be useful when you write argument and other papers for your other college classes. It is especially useful when the audience is largely unknown and you cannot obtain much information about it. Imagine writing for a universal audience on those occasions. Your professors and classmates as a group possess the general qualities of this audience.

It is also useful to try to construct an unfamiliar audience's possible initial position on your issue. When you do not know your audience's position, it is best to imagine it as neutral to mildly opposed to your views and direct your argument with that in mind. Imagining an unfamiliar audience as either hostile or friendly can lead to extreme positions that may cause the argument to fail. Imagining the audience as neutral or mildly opposed ensures an even tone to the argument that promotes audience interest and receptivity. The following excerpt from a speech report illustrates some of the problems that were created when the speaker assumed total agreement from the audience. Notice that the author, who describes himself as an audience member, is obviously different from the audience members imagined by the speaker. How is he different? What is the effect? What changes could this speaker make to create better common ground with all of her audience members? Consider what this speaker might have done differently if she had imagined a neutral or mildly opposed audience, instead of a strongly friendly audience.

> I am listening to a lecture by Helen Caldicott, the environmental activist. Dr. Caldicott is in top form, holding forth with her usual bracing mixture of caustic wit and prophetical urgency. All around me, an audience of the faithful is responding with camp-meeting fervor, cheering her on as she itemizes a familiar checklist of impending calamities: acid rain, global warming, endangered species.
>
> She has even come up with a fresh wrinkle on one of the standard environmental horrors: nuclear energy. Did we know, she asks, that nuclear energy is producing scores of anencephalic births in the industrial shanty-towns along the Mexican border? "Every time you turn on an electric light," she admonishes us, "you are making another brainless baby."

---

[3]See Perelman and Olbrechts-Tyteca, *The New Rhetoric*, for additional details on the universal audience.

Dr. Caldicott's presentation is meant to instill unease. In my case, she is succeeding, though not in the way she intends. She is making me worry, as so many of my fellow environmentalists have begun to make me worry—not simply for the fate of the Earth, but for the fate of this movement on which so much depends. As much as I want to endorse what I hear, Dr. Caldicott's effort to shock and shame just isn't taking. I am as sympathetic a listener as she can expect to find, yet rather than collapsing into self-castigation, as I once might have, I find myself going numb.

Is it possible that green guilt, the mainstay of the movement has lost its ethical sting?

Despite my reservations, I do my best to go along with what Dr. Caldicott has to say—even though I suspect (as I think most of her audience does) that there is no connection between light bulbs and brainless babies.[4]

USING INFORMATION ABOUT YOUR AUDIENCE

When you complete your analysis of your audience, you need to go back through the information you have gathered and consciously decide which audience characteristics to appeal to in your paper. As an example, look back through the audience analysis of the argument class that was done for you. Suppose that you are the student who is planning to write the paper about jury training. You decide that the general questions about the makeup of the group suggest that you have a fairly typical college audience. They are varied enough in their background and experience so that you know they will not all share common opinions on all matters. They do have in common, however, their status as college students. Furthermore, all of you belong to the same group, so you can assume some common values and goals. All of them, you assume, want to be successful, to graduate, and to improve themselves and society; you can appeal to these common motives. All or most of them read local newspapers or watch local news programs, so they will have common background on the rhetorical situation for your issue. You have asked about their present views on jury training, and you know that many are neutral. Your strategy will be to break through this neutrality and get commitment for change.

You decide, furthermore, that you may have to focus the issue for them because they are not likely to see it your way without help. They should also, you decide, know enough to contemplate policy change. You can appeal to their potential common experience as jurors and their need for physical safety, fairness, and good judgment in dealing with criminals. You can further assume that your audience values competence, expertise, and reasonableness, all important outcomes of the training system you intend to advocate. Your argument style will work with the group because you have already analyzed styles, and yours is familiar to them. They either share your style or are flexible enough to adapt to it. You are now in a position to gather materials for your paper that will be convincing to this particular audience. You will develop reasoning, including support and warrants, that they can link to their personal values, motives, beliefs, knowledge, and experience.

You need to show the same care in adapting to the needs of a universal audience. Since this audience is reasonable, educated, and adult, support and war-

---

[4]Theodore Roszak, "Green Guilt and Ecological Overload," *New York Times*, June 9, 1992, Sec. A, p. 13.

rants must be on its level and should also have broad applicability and acceptance. Odd or extreme perspectives or support will usually not be acceptable. An example is the electric light causing brainless babies in "Green Guilt and Ecological Overload." This example does not have universal appeal. Notice, also, that the universal audience, as a reasonable and educated audience, should inspire a high level of argumentative writing. Careful research, intelligent reasoning, and clear style will be requirements for this audience.

WHAT STRATEGIES CAN YOU NOW ADD TO IMPROVE YOUR PROCESS FOR WRITING ARGUMENT?

1. **Write a claim**, and decide on a purpose.
2. **Use the claim questions** to develop primary and secondary purposes for your paper.
3. **Narrow your claim, get an original perspective**, and begin to think about refutation and research needs.
4. **Write a preliminary outline** with a research plan and draft plan to guide future reading, thinking, and writing activities.
5. **Analyze a familiar audience**.
6. **Construct an unfamiliar audience**.
7. **Adapt to your audience** by discovering ways to build common ground.

EXERCISES AND ACTIVITIES

1. INDIVIDUAL ONGOING PROJECT, THE ARGUMENT PAPER: WRITE A CLAIM AND CLARIFY YOUR PURPOSE

Complete the following worksheet by writing answers to the questions. They will help you focus on your claim and ways to develop it. Discuss your answers with the other members in your writing group, or discuss some of your answers with the whole class.

Claim Development Worksheet

1. Write your claim in a complete sentence (refer to page 263 for help).
2. What is your original slant on the issue, and is it evident in the claim?
3. Is the claim too broad, too narrow, or okay for now?
4. Which will be your predominant argumentative purpose in developing the claim? Fact? Definition? Cause? Value? Policy?
5. What additional minor purposes will you include in your paper? Fact? Definition? Cause? Value? Policy?

continued

6. Can you learn enough to develop the claim? How?
7. What are the other perspectives on this issue?
8. What strategies will you use to develop common ground with your audience?
9. At what point are you entering the conversation about your issue? What has gone before? What may come later?
10. How will you define the controversial words in your claim?
11. Do you predict at this point that you may have to qualify your claim to make it acceptable to the audience? How?

2. INDIVIDUAL ONGOING PROJECT, THE ARGUMENT PAPER: MAKE A PRELIMINARY OUTLINE

Use the following worksheet to help you construct a preliminary outline and a guide for thinking and research:

Preliminary Outline Worksheet

1. Write your claim. Write the word *because*. List three to five possible reasons or subclaims that you might develop in your paper.
2. Anticipate your research needs. Which reasons can you develop with your present knowledge and information? Which will you need to think about and research further? What types of research materials will you seek?
3. How much additional background reading do you need to do, and where should you do it? Is an encyclopedia sufficient, or should you ask your professor or a librarian for a better source? What other readings and research will you need to do?
4. How much background will you need to provide your readers?
5. What are your strongest opinions? Your best reasons?
6. What is a tentative way to begin your paper? What is a tentative way to end it?
7. What original examples, descriptions, or comparisons occur to you now?

3. CLASS DISCUSSION: THE CLASS AS AUDIENCE

Conduct an audience analysis of your class. Answer questions 1 through 4 (pages 269–270) to get a general idea of the nature of your group. These questions have to do with the audience in general, its demographic makeup, its organizational affiliations, and its interests. Follow the model provided by the examples. Make a list of additional audience factors that class members might keep in mind when they narrow their issues, define their purposes, and state their claims. (Note that audience-analysis questions 5 through 13, pages 270–271, are related to how the audience regards specific issues. These questions can be used when class members have their issues in mind and want to get some initial reaction to them.)

4. INDIVIDUAL ONGOING PROJECT, THE ARGUMENT PAPER: AUDIENCE ANALYSIS OF YOUR WRITING GROUP

Do an analysis of the small group of four or five individuals in your class who will serve as readers and critics of your paper from now until you hand it in. Prepare for this discussion by going through the following list and checking the questions that you want answered. For example, you may want to skip questions 1 to 4, particularly if you have already discussed them as a class. Focus on the questions that will help you develop your issue so that your audience members will be interested in reading your paper and perhaps even in changing their minds. Do this as a group project, with each group member, in turn, interviewing the others and jotting down answers to the following questions:

Audience Analysis Worksheet

1. Describe the audience in general. Who are they? What do you have in common with them?
2. What are some of the demographics of the group? Consider size, age, gender, nationality, education, and professional status.
3. What are some of their organizational affiliations?
4. What are their interests? Include outside interests and reading material.
5. What is their present position on your issue? What audience outcomes can you anticipate? If you wrote an exploratory paper (Exercise section, Chapter 4), describe the different perspectives on your issue, and ask for a show of hands to see how audience members view your issue at present. How might they change?
6. Will they interpret the issue in the same way you have?
7. How significant is your issue to the audience?
8. Are there any obstacles that will prevent them from accepting your claim as soon as you state it?
9. At what point are they in the ongoing conversation about the issue? What do they already know about your issue?
10. What is the attitude of your audience toward you?
11. What beliefs and values do you and your audience share?
12. What motivates your audience?
13. What argument style will work best with them?
14. List the special characteristics from this analysis that you plan to appeal to with your paper. Include values and motives in your list.

---

5. ORAL REPORTS: WRITING FOR AN AUDIENCE

Clip and bring to class either an advertisement or a letter to the editor from any magazine or newspaper. In a 2–3-minute oral report, describe it, read it, or show it to the class; describe in as much detail as possible the audience to whom it is addressed; and point out some ways the author has worked to establish common ground with the audience.

6. SMALL GROUP WORK AND WRITING ASSIGNMENTS: ADAPTING TO AN AUDIENCE AND ACHIEVING OUTCOMES

Prepare for group work by reading the following written transcripts of public speeches. Each is accompanied by a description of the rhetorical situation for the speech and an account of the immediate audience outcomes.

a. *Small group work.* In groups, analyze and describe what each speaker did to achieve particular audience outcomes.

b. *Writing assignments.* Write a two-page paper on one of the speeches.

Follow the instructions below for each speech:

Speech 1: Describe Boris Yeltsin's strategies for reducing threat and bringing his hostile audience into enthusiastic agreement with him.

Speech 2: Analyze Bill Clinton's efforts to adapt to and change the attitudes of a hostile audience.

A. RUSSIAN PRESIDENT BORIS YELTSIN'S SPEECH TO THE U.S. CONGRESS ON JUNE 18, 1992

Rhetorical situation: The February 1992 speeches that signaled the end of the cold war between Russia and the United States are in the exercise section of Chapter 2. At that time Yeltsin indicated he would welcome financial aid for Russia, but it was not forthcoming, and he was frustrated. Four months later, he returned to the United States and gave the following speech. The outcomes were described in an article in the *New York Times* entitled "Yeltsin Speaks, and Congressional Wall Tumbles." The lead sentence was "With oratory that thrilled even Congressional critics of aid, President Boris N. Yeltsin of Russia appeared today to have virtually eliminated an important obstacle to passage of an aid program for the former Soviet republics."[5] Yeltsin managed to bring an audience that was at least slightly hostile into enthusiastic agreement with him. Here are some of the most important excerpts from his speech. Analyze what he did to achieve such extremely positive audience outcomes.

THERE WILL BE NO MORE LIES

Boris Yeltsin

It is indeed a great honor for me to address the Congress of the great land of freedom as the first ever over 1,000 years of history as Russia's popularly elected president, as a citizen of the great country which has made its choice in favor of liberty and democracy.

[5]*New York Times*, June 18, 1992, Sec. 9, p. 9.

For many years, our two nations were the two poles, the two opposites. They wanted to make us implacable enemies. That affected the destinies of the world in a most tragic way.

The world was shaken by the storms of confrontation. It was close to exploding, close to perishing beyond salvation.

That evil scenario is becoming a thing of the past. Reason begins to triumph over madness. We have left behind the period when America and Russia looked at each other through gunsights, ready to pull the trigger at any time.

Despite what we saw in the well-known American film "The Day After," it can be said today, tomorrow will be a day of peace, less of fear and more of hope for the happiness of our children. The world can sigh in relief. The idol of Communism, which spread everywhere social strife, animosity, and unparalleled brutality, which instilled fear in humanity, has collapsed. It has collapsed never to rise again. I am here to assure you, we will not let it rise again in our land. . . .

You will recall August 1991, when for three days Russia was under the dark cloud of dictatorship. I addressed the Muscovites who were defending the White House of Russia. I addressed all the people of Russia. I addressed them standing on top of the tank whose crew had disobeyed criminal orders.

"I WILL NOT SAY UNCLE"

I will be candid with you. At that moment, I feared. But I had no fear for myself. I feared for the future of democracy in Russia and throughout the world, because I was aware what could happen if we failed to win.

Citizens of Russia upheld their freedom and did not allow the continuation of the 75 years of nightmare. From this high rostrum, I want to express our sincere thanks and gratitude to President Bush and to the American people for their invaluable moral support for the just cause of the people of Russia. . . .

We must carry through unprecedented reforms in the economy, that over the seven decades, has been stripped of all market infrastructure, lay the foundations for democracy, and restore the rule of law in the country that for scores of years was poisoned with political strife and political oppression. We must guarantee domestic social and political stability, as well as the maintenance of civil peace.

We have no right to fail in this most difficult endeavor, for there will be no second try, as in sports. Our predecessors have used them all up. The reforms must succeed. . . .

Today I am telling you what I tell my fellow countrymen. I will not go back on the reforms. And it is practically impossible to topple Yeltsin in Russia. I am in good health, and I will not say "uncle" before I make the reforms irreversible. We realize our great responsibility for the success of our changes, not only toward the people of Russia, but also toward the citizens of America, and of the entire world. Today the freedom of America is being upheld in Russia. Should the reforms fail, it will cost hundreds of billions to upset that failure. . . .

Russia has brought its policies toward a number of countries in line with its solemn declarations of the recent years. We have stopped arms deliveries to

Afghanistan, where the senseless military adventure has taken thousands of Russians and hundreds of thousands of Afghan lives.

"NO MORE LIES"

With external props removed, the puppet regime collapsed.

We have corrected the well-known imbalances in relations with Cuba. At present that country is one of our Latin American partners. Our commerce with Cuba is based on universally accepted principles and world prices.

It is Russia that once and for all has done away with double standards in foreign policy. We are firmly resolved not to lie any more, either to our negotiating partners, or to the Russians or Americans or any other people.

There will be no more lies—ever. The same applies to biological weapons experiments, and the facts that have been revealed about American prisoners of war, the KAL 007 flight, and many other things. That list could be continued.

The archives of the K.G.B. and the Communist Party Central Committee are being opened. Moreover, we are inviting the cooperation of the United States and other nations to investigate these dark pages.

I promise you that each and every document in each and every archive will be examined in order to investigate the fate of every American unaccounted for. As President of Russia, I assure you that even if one American has been detained in my country, and can still be found, I will find him. I will get him back to his family. . . .

History is giving us a chance to fulfill President Wilson's dream, namely, to make the world safe for democracy.

More than 30 years ago, President Kennedy addressed these words to humanity: My fellow citizens of the world, ask not what America can do for you, but what together we can do for the freedom of man.

I believe that his inspired call for working together toward a democratic world is addressed above all to our two peoples, to the people of America, and to the people of Russia. Partnership and friendship of our two largest democracies, in strengthening democracy, is indeed a great goal. Joining the world community, we wish to preserve our identity, our own image and history, promote culture, and strengthen the moral standards of our people. . . .

I would like now to conclude my statement with the words from a song by Irving Berlin, an American of Russian descent—God bless America, to which I add, and Russia.[6]

B. PRESIDENT BILL CLINTON'S MEMORIAL DAY SPEECH AT THE VIETNAM VETERANS MEMORIAL, MAY 31, 1993

> *Rhetorical situation:* President Clinton has been perceived as a draft dodger by some people, and when he spoke at the Vietnam Memorial on Memorial Day in 1993, he faced a mixed audience of overtly hostile to mildly hostile people. Here is the account in the *New York Times* that describes the audience: "As Mr. Clinton rose to speak on this balmy

---

[6]*New York Times*, June 18, 1992, Sec. A, p. 8.

Washington afternoon on Memorial Day, he was greeted with a cacophony of enthusiastic applause, peppered by catcalls of 'Draft dodger!' 'Liar!' and 'Shut up, coward!' Many veterans in the audience, some wearing their green war fatigues and crumpled jungle hats, turned their backs when Mr. Clinton began his remarks."[7] Clinton made some special efforts to adapt to this hostile audience, and there was a mixed response at the end. Some people praised him, and others remained angry. Read the speech and analyze what Clinton did to make his audience more friendly and accepting of him and his views.

TEXT OF CLINTON SPEECH AT VIETNAM MEMORIAL

Bill Clinton

Thank you, thank you very much. General Powell, General McCaffrey and my good friend Lou Puller, whom I did not know was coming here today, I thank you so much.

To all of you who are shouting, I have heard you. I ask you now to hear me. I have heard you.

Some have suggested that it is wrong for me to be here with you today because I did not agree a quarter of a century ago with the decision made to send the young men and women to battle in Vietnam. Well, so much the better. Here we are celebrating America today. Just as war is freedom's cost, disagreement is freedom's privilege. And we honor it here today.

But I ask all of you to remember the words that have been said here today, and I ask you at this monument, Can any American be out of place? And can any Commander in Chief be in any other place but here on this day? I think not.

Many volumes have been written about this war and those complicated times, but the message of this memorial is quite simple: These men and women fought for freedom, brought honor to their communities, loved their country and died for it.

They were known to all of us. There's not a person in this crowd today who did not know someone on this wall. Four of my high school classmates are there, four who shared with me the joys and trials of childhood and did not live to see the three score and 10 years the Scripture says we are entitled to.

Let us continue to disagree if we must about the war, but let us not let it divide us as a people any longer.

No one has come here today to disagree about the heroism of those whom we honor. But the only way we can really honor their memory is to resolve to live and serve today and tomorrow as best we can and to make America the best that she can be. Surely that is what we owe to all those whose names are etched in this beautiful memorial.

As we all resolve to keep the finest military in the world, let us remember some of the lessons that all agree on. If the day should come when our service men

---

[7] *New York Times*, June 1, 1993, Sec. A, p. 1.

and women must again go into combat, let us all resolve they will go with the training, the equipment, the support necessary to win, and, most important of all, with a clear mission to win.

Let us do what is necessary to regain control over our destiny as a people here at home, to strengthen our economy and to develop the capacities of all of our people, to rebuild our communities and our families where children are raised and character is developed. Let us keep the American dream alive.

Today let us also renew a pledge to the families whose names are not on this wall because their sons and daughters did not come home. We will do all we can to give you not only the attention you have asked for but the answers you deserve.

Today I have ordered that by Veterans Day we will have declassified all United States Government records related to P.O.W.'s and M.I.A.'s from the Vietnam War—all those records except for a tiny fraction which could still affect our national security or invade the privacy of their families.

As we allow the American public to have access to what our Government knows, we will press harder to find out what other governments know. We are pressing the Vietnamese to provide this accounting not only because it is the central outstanding issue in our relationship with Vietnam, but because it is a central commitment made by the American Government to our people. And I intend to keep it.

You heard General Powell quoting President Lincoln: "With malice toward none and charity for all, let us bind up the nation's wounds."

Lincoln speaks to us today across the years. Let us resolve to take from this haunting and beautiful memorial a renewed sense of our national unity and purpose, a deepened gratitude for the sacrifice of those whose names we touched and whose memories we revere and a finer dedication to making America a better place for their children and for our children, too.

Thank you all for coming here today. God bless you, and God bless America.[8]

7. UNDERSTANDING THE CHAPTER: WHOLE CLASS, GROUP, OR INDIVIDUALS

Summarize the major ideas in this chapter by completing the following sentences briefly and in your own words:

a. Using claim questions can help you decide . . .
b. Asking additional questions about your claim can help you . . .
c. A preliminary outline is useful for . . .
d. It is easier to build common ground with an audience that is . . . It is more difficult with an audience that is . . .
e. Discourse communities have in common . . .
f. In analyzing the audience for your paper, you may want to ask about . . .
g. A universal audience has special qualities that include . . .
h. As you adapt to your audience, you should keep in mind their background, their values, . . .

---

[8]*New York Times*, June 1, 1993, Sec. A, p. 10.

CHAPTER 9

Invention and Research

The writing process is both creative and critical. For example, invention and research are creative, and rewriting and revision are critical. This chapter is about creativity. It encourages you to think about what you already know and believe before you seek the opinions of others. As a result, your voice will become the major voice in your paper, and your ideas will predominate over those of others. Information and ideas from other sources will be brought in later to back up what you finally think.

The invention strategies presented here are appropriate for helping you think about and develop your ideas for a single-perspective argument paper. Use them along with the prewriting invention strategies that appear in Chapter 4. All of the invention strategies from both chapters are summarized on the invention worksheet on page 308.

The first two strategies described here are logical thinking methods to help you expand on your topic. These are followed by some strategies for using argument theory from earlier chapters to help you invent ideas and identify the parts of your paper. The last sections of the chapter will help you do library research, another creative source of information and opinion for your paper.

USE BURKE'S PENTAD TO ESTABLISH CAUSE

Asking the question *why* will help you establish cause for controversial incidents and human motives. So will a systematic application of Kenneth Burke's pentad as he describes it in his book *A Grammar of Motives*.[1] In his first sentence, Burke poses the question "What is involved when we say what people are doing and why they are doing it?" Burke identified five terms and associated questions that can be used to examine possible causes for human action and events. Since establishing cause is an important part of many arguments, and especially of fact, cause, and policy arguments, the pentad is potentially very useful to the writer of argument. Here

---

[1] Kenneth Burke, *A Grammar of Motives* (New York: Prentice Hall, 1945), p. xv. James Wood pointed out to me the value of Burke's pentad in attributing cause in argument.

are Burke's terms and questions along with some examples to demonstrate application. These examples, by the way, are intended to be controversial. As you read the examples drawn from the Los Angeles riots of 1992 and the U.S. budget deficit, go a step further and apply these questions to your own issue to help you think about cause. Burke's pentad, by the way, is similar to the journalist's questions *who, what, where, when,* and *why* except that it yields even more information than they do.

1. **Act.** *What was done?* What took place in thought or deed?

Example: The rioting in L.A. got out of control, and, like many big riots, it could not be controlled by the police.
Example: Lowered taxes and undisciplined spending occurred over a period of time and contributed to the national debt.

2. **Scene.** *When or where was it done?* What is the background or scene in which it occurred?

Example: The L.A. ghettos were the scene for the riots in 1992. Racial tension, anger at the police over the Rodney King beating, and gangs are all part of the scene.
Example: The entire U.S. economy, including government and private spending, is the scene. The 1980s are usually cited as the time when spending was particularly uncontrolled.

3. **Agent.** *Who did it?* What person or kind of person performed the act?

Example: The people who rioted, stole, broke into buildings, burned them, and fought are agents. So are the police. Peer pressure, or the predisposition to riot because others are doing it, is a characteristic of the agent in this case.
Example: Politicians, particularly the Republicans in the 1980s, are agents. So are greedy, wealthy American citizens.

4. **Agency.** *How did he (she) do it?* What means or instruments were used?

Example: Guns were available that provided the means. Television news coverage was also part of the agency because it allowed rioters to know what was going on and communicate with one another.
Example: Lower taxes for the wealthy were used to increase private spending but also to increase government debt.

5. **Purpose.** *Why did it happen?* What was the main motivation?

Example: The purpose was to protest the King verdict and the racism behind it.
Example: The purpose was to reduce the income tax and protect wealthy people.

Notice that you can focus on the answer to any one of the five questions and argue that it is the main cause of what happened. Also, each of the five questions provides a different perspective on the cause of the problem. Furthermore, the answers to these questions stir controversy. You may, in fact, have found yourself disagreeing with the answers in the examples. As Burke puts it, "Men may violently disagree about the purposes behind a given act, or about the character of the person who did it, or how he did it, or in what kind of situation he acted; or they may even insist upon totally different words to name the act itself."[2] Still, he goes on to say, one can begin with some kind of answers to these questions, which then provide a starting point for inquiry and argument. Apply Burke's pentad to every issue you write about to provide you with a deeper perspective on the causes or motives behind it.

USE CHAINS OF REASONS TO DEVELOP GREATER DEPTH OF ANALYSIS AND DETAIL

Another method of developing a claim or subclaim in your paper is to use chains of reasons to help you get a line of thinking going. You use this method quite naturally in verbal argument when you make a claim, someone asks you questions like "Why?" or "What for?" and you give additional reasons and evidence as support. For example:

You claim: The university should be more student-friendly.
Someone asks: Why do you think so? I think it's okay.
You answer: Because students are its customers, and without us it would not exist.
Someone asks: Why wouldn't it?
You answer: Because we pay the money to keep it going.
Someone asks: Why do students keep it going? There are other sources of income.
You answer: Because our tuition is much more than all of the other sources combined.

You get the idea. Imagining that you are in a dialogue with another person who keeps asking why enables you to create quantities of additional support and detailed development for your claim. Also, by laying out your argument in this way you can see where you need more support. In the preceding example, you need to provide support to show what portion of the operating budget is funded by student tuition. You might also give examples of insensitive treatment of students. You should also explain what students have in common with customers.

Here is another example of how a chain of reasons creates the structure for Anna Quindlen's essay "A Political Correction." First, read the chain as abstracted, and then read the essay for an example of how this chain of reasoning creates the structure for the essay.

Claim (end of paragraph 3): "The right to free speech must include the right to objectionable speech." Why?

Because of the way things are in the real world (examples of the sailor, the Louisiana man, the Secret Service agents, and Jesse Helms).

---

[2]Ibid.

Why should we be concerned with the real world?

Because we learn to distinguish good from bad in the real world. (Open exchange is better than censorship and makes Helms look bad.)

Why is this important?

Because understanding good and bad creates tolerance for people. Tolerance must be learned through tolerance for words.

Here is the entire essay:

A POLITICAL CORRECTION

Anna Quindlen

Discussions of political correctness on campus always puzzle me a bit, because they usually have as their starting point a view of the academy, in fact the world, that is contrary to established reality. That is, that into this calm pool of egalitarian rational discourse comes the bigfoot of racial and gender politics, ready to stomp down anyone who offends, diverges, challenges liberal orthodoxy.

The stomping part I understand. But that calm egalitarian pool? Oh, phooey, boys and girls.

Claim: Free speech should include objectionable speech. Why?

During the last few months there has been gnashing of teeth about pilfered student newspapers at various institutions of [higher] education, spirited away in the night by students who found certain free speech objectionable and so imprisoned it. This is no good. The right to free speech must include the right to objectionable speech.

That is the overarching argument, and I buy it. But the uproar implies that these students are being insulated from counterorthodoxy, thought-policed in liberal bastions.

Because of the nature of the real world.

Let's let real life intrude for a minute among ivory tower discussions of hate speech, free speech and the now ritual complaint that variations from some P.C. party line are put down.

During the final weeks of school, graduating college seniors could get a quick current events education about how the world works:

Example: Sailor

• A sailor was sentenced to life in prison for punching and kicking one of his fellows to death in a bathroom. The dead man was gay and had requested a discharge because of frequent harassment; his assailant admitted that he had lied to investigators when he said the beating had been prompted by the gay sailor's sexual advances.

Example: Louisiana man

• A Louisiana man was acquitted of shooting and killing an unarmed 16-year-old Japanese exchange student who came to the wrong house looking for a Halloween party.

Example: Secret
Service agents

• Twenty-one Secret Service agents in Annapolis preparing for a visit by the President stopped for breakfast at a Denny's restaurant. All but six were served in short order. The six were black. The restaurant chain faces a lawsuit in California based on similar complaints from 32 black customers.

Example: Jesse Helms

And finally, Senator Jesse Helms said he would not support Roberta Achtenberg for Assistant Secretary of Housing and Urban Development because she was a "damn lesbian."

Why should we be concerned with the real world? *Because* we learn from it how to distinguish good from bad and how to respond to bad, and open exchange also makes the opposition look bad.

Ideas should be freely exchanged not only because one woman's obscenity is another's Bovary, but because you can learn a lot of good stuff from bad stuff. At Penn, a group of black students seized and destroyed thousands of copies of the campus paper because they found offensive the writings of a conservative columnist.

During the course of their Ivy education, someone should have taught those students that a pointed exchange of letters, columns and countercolumns always does more to further human understanding—and usually the just cause—than censorship. Look at Senator Helms's comments. They do not reflect badly on Ms. Achtenberg, who was confirmed, as she deserved to be. They prove that the Senator speaks his mind, and that he is not working with much when he does so. Ignorant free speech often works against the speaker. That is one of several reasons why it must be given rein instead of suppressed.

Why is this important?

There are complaints that because of incidents like the one at Penn, students feel inhibited about airing their opinions on campuses that have become oversensitive to minority groups. But let's remember that for every highly publicized incident of overreaction or suppression, there is plenty of small-scale incivility and bigotry. Let's remember that there are good inhibitions, and there are bad inhibitions. If people can no longer discuss their differences, that is bad. If people make fewer racist jokes, that is just fine.

Because understanding good and bad creates tolerance for people, which can be learned through a tolerance for words.

The class of '93 has gone out to meet the world. And no matter how loud the hue and cry about political correctness, this is the fact behind the fracas: After four short years these students enter a world in which intolerance for discourse is overwhelmed by intolerance for people—for people waiting to be served breakfast or for people being beaten to death in a bathroom. Liberal orthodoxy? Phooey, boys and girls. Most of what you learn in life is something altogether different.[3]

In summary, to chain an argument, repeat the *why . . . because* sequence three or four times, both for your main claim and also for each of your subclaims. Add evidence in all the places where your argument is sketchy. You will end up with a detailed analysis and support for your claim that will make it much less vulnerable to attack.

[3]*New York Times*, June 13, 1993, Sec. 1, p. 19.

USE ARGUMENT THEORY TO THINK SYSTEMATICALLY ABOUT YOUR ISSUE

Use what you have learned about argument in earlier chapters to help you think about your claim and some ways to develop it.

Analyze the Rhetorical Situation. Focus your attention on the total context for your argument, including the motivation for the issue, how you will write about it, and how your reader-audience will react to it. Use the rhetorical situation questions, and apply them to your paper:

1. What is the *exigence* (context, dramatic real-life situation) that makes me and others perceive this issue as controversial?
2. Who is the *audience*; that is, who besides me thinks the issue is a problem? How do they view it?
3. What are the *constraints* (other people, events, affiliations, organizations, values, beliefs, or traditions) that influence the audience's perceptions of this issue, and will they bring us together or drive us apart?
4. What is motivating *me*, the *author*, to write about this issue; what makes me qualified?
5. What will be the purpose and strategies of the text I produce?

Use the Toulmin Model. The following paragraphs present a brief review of the six parts of the Toulmin model with suggestions to help you use them as guides for thinking and planning the parts of your argument paper. They are written as questions, and by the time you have answered them, you will have the essential parts of your paper.

What Is My Claim? What type of claim is it? What are my subclaims, or reasons? If you used the claim development worksheet on page 274, your claim will be well developed. Your claim is the thesis statement of your paper. It tells your readers what you are trying to prove. Decide whether it will be stronger to place it at the beginning, in the middle, or at the end. Classify your claim as fact, definition, cause, value, or policy to establish your fundamental purpose and help you plan support and organization. You will also need to invent subclaims or reasons that will develop your claim. Take another look at the brief outlines of claims and subclaims on page 152 for some examples. Your reasons should be "good" reasons, or ones that are acceptable to your audience.

What Support Should I Use? You will need to develop the subclaims in your paper with support. Research is a necessity for many argument papers because support (facts, opinions, reasoning, examples) creates convincing argument. When you think about *facts*, consider using descriptions of events you or others you know have observed, or specific examples or accounts of other real happenings. You may also use narratives of both historical and recent events and statistical reports. Facts should be vivid, real, and verifiable to be convincing. Plan also to include *opinion*. Opinions and reasoning are your interpretations, explanations, and ideas about factual information. While facts, by themselves, are comparatively lifeless and boring, they become interesting and convincing when they are presented along with explanations about their significance and relevance. Besides your own opinions, you may also want to include expert opinion that can be summarized, paraphrased, or quoted directly in your paper. You must also tell your reader in the text who these experts are and where you found their ideas. The next chapter provides you with details on these techniques. When you quote opinions, select those that seem to you to be "informed," that is, based on knowledge, experience, and good judgment. Think also of some *examples*. They clarify points, make them interesting and easier to remember and, in argument, help prove the claim. Remember that examples can be real or made up, long or short; and real examples are more convincing than hypothetical examples.

What Are My Warrants? Remember that support and warrants, taken together, constitute the proofs or lines of argument for your paper. Every time you use a particular piece of support, a warrant, usually implicit, will cause your audience either to accept or reject it as appropriate support for the claim. Write down the warrants that are working in your paper, and answer three questions about them: (1) Do they link the evidence and the claim? You want the audience to think, "Ah, yes, I see how that evidence supports that claim and makes it convincing." (2) Do you believe your own warrants? If you do not, make some changes. Argument from personal conviction is the most convincing argument. (3) Will your audience share your warrants or reject them? If you think they will reject them, consider the possibility of stating them and providing some backing for them.

What Backing Might I Provide to Make My Warrants More Acceptable and Convincing? You may use additional support, including facts, expert opinion, reports, studies, and polls, to back up your warrants. You can do the same to back up evidence when necessary. Add material, in other words, to make your paper more convincing whenever you think your audience requires it.

How Should I Handle Rebuttal? Not all argument papers include rebuttal. You will usually strengthen your own position, however, if you decide to include rebuttal. It is particularly important to identify the arguments on the other side and point out what is wrong with them when the issue is familiar and obviously controversial. Your audience will be familiar with the other views and will expect your opinion on them in your paper.

When you plan rebuttal, here are some specific strategies to consider: Use your exploratory paper or do some background research to get a sense of the different perspectives on your issue. Then write your own claim and state reasons in favor of it; next, write an opposing claim and state reasons to support it; and finally, write a claim that represents a middle or neutral view and write reasons for it. Now, study the claims and reasons that are different from your own and attack their weakest features. Is it the support, the warrants, or the claims themselves that are the most vulnerable? Name some of the weakest features of these other perspectives, and point out the problems associated with them in your paper.

Another strategy for rebuttal is to build a strong case of your own that undercuts an opposing position but does not specifically acknowledge it. State and demonstrate that yours is the strongest position available. Or you can always examine the opposition's major proofs and apply the tests of validity explained in Chapter 6. In your paper, point out all problems with these proofs. Finally, for a hostile audience, use Rogerian argument to restate one or more opposing positions and show the special circumstances in which they might be valid. Then present your own position as better than all of the others. Remember that rebuttal should not offend the audience. Angry people won't pay serious attention or change their minds. Watch members of the U.S. Congress on C-SPAN television for examples of cordial rebuttal. They constantly engage in rebuttal, but they are polite and usually compliment the opposition while they disagree with them. This courtesy reduces hostility both in the opposition and the audience.

Will You Need to Qualify Your Claim? If you believe strongly in your claim, you may want to state it as absolutely true. You must realize, however, that absolute positions will only be acceptable to people who already agreed with you. To gain the adherence of more members of your audience, you may need to qualify your claim by using such words as *usually, often, probably, sometimes,* or *almost always.*

Plan Your Proofs.   Here is a review of the types of proof. A variety of types in your paper will make it more interesting and convincing. Refer to Chapter 6 or the summary chart (p. 191) for explanations as needed.

Logical Proofs. Logical proofs are convincing because they are real and drawn from experience. Here they are for quick reference:

1. *Deduction*, or applying a general principle or premise to a specific case or example and reaching a conclusion.
2. *Definitions*, which can be very short, a word or phrase only, or very long, from several sentences to several paragraphs to the entire essay.
3. *Cause*, or attributing cause or effect to your claim.
4. *Sign*, or pointing out the symptoms or signs that something is so.
5. *Induction*, or drawing a conclusion based on representative cases or examples.
6. *Statistics*, or numbers, data, graphs, and charts along with your interpretations of them.
7. *Analogies* (figurative, historical, and literal), or explaining what we do not understand in terms of what we do understand.

Ethical Proofs. Ethical proofs provide opinion and establish the ethos or authority of the quoted individuals. Mention the professions and affiliations of the people you quote along with their background, education, or experience to show that they are particularly qualified to provide information and opinions about your issue. Recall that ethical proofs include *your own opinions* as well as *the opinions of experts and authorities.*

Emotional Proofs. When the subject itself is emotional, when the audience will accept it, and when the occasion justifies it, emotional proofs are appropriate. As a general rule, use emotion to strengthen logical conviction rather than for its own sake. You can introduce feeling into your argument by using emotionally loaded language, emotional examples, personal narratives with an emotional impact, and vivid descriptions of emotional scenes. Two specific types of emotional proof are *motivational proofs*, or appealing to what your audience needs or wants and showing them how to get it; and *value proofs*, or establishing what your audience values and showing them how to achieve it. Keep in mind that the audience will be convinced only by appeals to specific needs or values that they can accept or agree with.

Use Proofs Appropriate for the Purpose or Type of Claim Some proofs work better than others to establish different types of claims.[4] The following are not rules, just suggestions for you to consider.

Fact and Cause. Fact and cause papers call for substantive, factual support, including data and statistics. In developing either a fact or a cause paper, consider naming specific *causes* and *effects*, naming and describing *symptoms* and *signs*, using *induction* to suggest that if one exists others do also, using *analogies* to suggest that items coexist and share qualities and outcomes, and using *definitions* that place items in classes or categories. Also, consider quoting an *authority* to demonstrate that a reputable person says something is a fact or can identify what caused it. Emotional proofs are less valuable than *logical* and *ethical* proofs in establishing fact or cause.

Definition. Definition papers can be developed with *literal analogies* that invite comparisons of similar items, with *historical analogies* that suggest that if one thing happens, another thing will also, and with *classification*, or putting the item in a category with known characteristics. *Authorities* can be used to define it or support a particular view or interpretation of it. *Emotional proofs* are only relevant if the subject is emotional and you want the audience to accept an emotional definition—for example, abortion is a bloodbath.

Value Argument. Value arguments require *motivational proofs* and *value proofs*, and they must be connected to the needs and values of the audience. *Authorities* may also be used to establish the value of something. *Definition* can be used to put an item in a good or bad category or class. *Analogies* that compare good or bad items or outcomes may also be used. Value arguments also require criteria for making value judgments. You will need to establish these criteria and describe where they came from. They may be your own, society's, a particular group's, or those of the universal audience.

---

[4]I am indebted to Wayne E. Brockriede and Douglas Ehninger for some of the suggestions in this section. They identify some types of proof as appropriate for different sorts of claims in their article "Toulmin on Argument: An Interpretation and Application," *Quarterly Journal of Speech*, 46 (February 1960): 44–53.

TABLE 9.1 Proofs That Are Particularly Appropriate for Developing Specific Types of Claims

CLAIMS OF FACT	CLAIMS OF DEFINITION	CLAIMS OF CAUSE	CLAIMS OF VALUE	CLAIMS OF POLICY
Facts	Reliable	Facts	Value proofs	Data
Statistics	authorities	Statistics	Motivational	Motivational
Real	Accepted	Historical	proofs	proofs
examples	sources	analogies	Literal	Value proofs
Quotes from	Analogies	Literal	analogies	Literal
reliable	with the	analogies	Figurative	analogies
authorities	familiar	Signs	analogies	Reliable
Inductions	Examples	Induction	Quotes from	authorities
Literal and	Real	Deduction	reliable	Deduction
historical	Made up	Quotes from	authorities	Definition
analogies	Signs	reliable	Induction	Statistics
Signs		authorities	Signs	Cause
Informed			Definitions	
opinion			Cause	

Policy. Policy papers can be developed with *literal analogies* showing that what worked in one case will also work in another. *Authorities* can be used to establish either the severity of the problem or the efficacy of the solution. *Motivational proofs* may be used to demonstrate how certain solutions or policies meet the needs of the audience. Table 9.1 summarizes the proofs that are appropriate for developing specific types of claims.

When you have worked through a few of the invention strategies described so far, you will be ready to do some research and get additional information from outside sources for your paper. Continue to interweave inventional strategies with library research as you go along. All of the strategies in this chapter, although described separately, should be integrated to maintain a high level of creativity through the information-gathering phase.

SOME SUGGESTIONS TO HELP YOU WITH LIBRARY RESEARCH

Library research is a creative process that allows you to expand your ideas. Here are some suggestions to streamline your research:

Get Organized for Research. First, get acquainted with the library itself. Locate the card or computer catalogs and indexes to books and articles, the books and articles themselves (including those on microfilm), and the government documents and reference books. Also, find out where the copy center or copy machines are located in your library. Finally, find the reference desk and the reference librarians who will answer your questions when you get stuck. Now get prepared to write. Bring pens, sheets of paper, 3 x 5 cards, and something to keep them in. Think about buying three different colors of cards to color code the three types of information you will write on them: white for bibliography, yellow for all material you will cite in your paper, and blue for your own ideas. Also, bring money for the copy machine.

Use Your Preliminary Outline and Tentative Research Plan. Be specific about the material you seek in the library so that you do not get off course and waste time reading aimlessly. Once you begin research, you quite possibly will change some of your ideas about your topic. When you have new ideas, change your outline so that it continues to focus and guide your research. Every piece of research material that you examine should be related to an item on your outline unless you are reading creatively to get ideas.

Start with the Bibliography. The bibliography is the list of sources you will locate and read to add information to your paper. Search for books and for articles in magazines, journals, and newspapers. Locate books by consulting the card catalog or the computer index. If your library still maintains a card catalog, you will find that each book is represented in it with three different cards: the first, with the author's name printed at the top, is filed in the *author section* of the catalog; the second, with the title of the book printed at the top, is filed in the *title section*; and the third, with the subject of the book printed at the top, is filed in the *subject section* of the catalog. The subject section will be particularly useful to you in the early stages of research because all of the library's books on your subject will be cataloged there in one place. You can often read the titles and decide which books might be useful.

Your library may have closed down the card catalog and now store the same information in a computer index. You will use a computer terminal to call up the same information you would find in the card catalog. That is, you may search for a book by looking for its author, title, or subject. Computer indexes also permit you to search by "key word." Enter a key word that represents your topic, such as "clear-cutting," and the computer will print all titles of books and articles that contain that word. Key-word searches are the quickest way to build a bibliography. Read the titles of the books and articles as they appear on the screen to locate those that might be useful. When you have found a book title that looks promising, move to the screen that gives complete information about that book. There you will find all of the other subject headings under which that book is listed in the index. Use those subject headings, or key words extracted from them, to expand your search. Computer indexes are "user-friendly" and will tell you on the screen how to use them. Follow the directions exactly and ask for help when you get frustrated.

To find articles in the library you will need to consult indexes to periodical literature, such as *The Reader's Guide to Periodical Literature, The Social Sciences Index, The Humanities Index, The Education Index,* and *The Engineering Index.* There are quite a few of these indexes, representing a variety of subject areas. They are usually shelved together in one area of the library. Take some time to read their titles and browse in them. Browsing will help you discover the ones that will be most useful for directing you to articles on your issue.

Check to see if you can access some of these indexes on the computer. Many libraries now have periodical indexes for the last four or five years available on the computer screen. You will then only need to consult bound volumes for highly specialized topics or for articles more than five years old.

Newspapers, such as the *New York Times,* the *Wall Street Journal,* the *Christian Science Monitor,* or the *London Times,* along with news magazines like *Time* and *Newsweek,* are kept on microfilm in a special section of the library. Some books and many other journals are kept in this form also. When you encounter the abbreviations *mic, mf, mc,* or *mfc* as part of the catalog information for a book or magazine, you will need to locate it in the microfilm section. Machines are available there that enlarge the tiny images so that you can read them. Other machines enable you to print copies of microfilm material.

Indexes to newspapers and some magazines are available in the microfilm section as well. *Newsbank* is a particularly useful index for authors of argument papers. Check if your library has it. It collects newspaper articles from 150 urban newspapers starting from 1970 on almost any contemporary issue you can think of. Look up your issue in the *Newsbank* index, and it will lead you to a microfiche card that may contain 15 to 20 articles on your issue. Indexes to large daily newspapers and news magazines are also available in the microfilm section. Look up your subject in one of them, and then locate the articles they identify in the microfilm files.

You may also want to do research in other areas of the library, such as the reference room or the government documents. Or you may decide to do a computer search. The reference room contains a variety of volumes that provide biographical information. If you need to establish the credibility of one of your authorities, you can get biographical information from the *Biography Index, Current Biography,* or the various editions of *Who's Who.*

Government documents contain considerable data and other factual information useful for argument. Indexes to consult to help you locate material in government documents include the *Public Affairs Information Bulletin,* the *Monthly Catalog,* and the *Index to U.S. Government Periodicals.* Look up your issue in each of them. Your librarian will help you locate the actual materials among the government documents.

Most libraries also provide a computer search service that allows you to access huge data bases that index the world's literature on your issue. You usually have to pay a fee for this service. It may be worth it, however, to get a quick bibliography. You will need to provide the librarian who does the search with your preliminary research outline. Key words will be extracted from your claim and list of subclaims and used to search for relevant information. You will end up with a printed bibliography on your issue. Sometimes it will also be annotated. Some of the sources will be immediately available in your library. Others you will have to order from other libraries through interlibrary loan.

Make a separate bibliography card for every book, article, or pamphlet that looks useful and that you want to locate. A bibliography card for a book must include the author, title, place of publication, publisher, date of publication, and call number so that you can find it later in the library. Add an annotation or explanation of how you will use the source in your paper. Figure 9.1 provides an example.

Wishman, Seymour. <u>Anatomy of a Jury</u>: <u>The System on Trial</u>.

New York: Times Books, 1986.

Annotation | Use to demonstrate problems with present system. Author has been trial lawyer for 20 years and has tried hundreds of cases. Objective, but with some lawyer's bias. Wide audience appeal. | KF 8972 .W57 Stacks | Call number

Figure 9.1 A Bibliography Card for a Book with Annotation and Call Number[5]

A bibliography card for an article must include the author's name (if there is one), the title of the article, name of the publication, volume (if there is one), the date of publication, the page numbers, and the call number or other description of location in the library. Add an annotation to each card about how you will use the source in your paper. Figure 9.2 provides an example.

The call numbers for periodicals will be easy to find if they are listed in the computer. If they are not, ask the librarian. Often, a library's list of periodicals and corresponding call numbers are printed in books that are located throughout the library. Be forewarned. Some of the older issues of a periodical may be in bound

Robinson, Archie S. "We the Jury: Who Serves, Who Doesn't." <u>U.S.A. Today</u>: <u>The Magazine of the American Scene</u>. 120 (January 1992): 62–63.

Annotation | Use for background information on characteristics of juries. Author has examined current surveys of data. Very objective source. Wide appeal. | L11 S36 | Call number and location

Figure 9.2 A Bibliography Card for an Article in a Magazine with Annotation and Location in Library

---

[5]I am indebted to Peggy Kulesz for the idea of adding annotations.

volumes in the book stacks, some of the newer ones may be on microfilm, and the newest issues may be stacked on shelves in the current-periodicals section of the library. You may have to look for a while to find what you want.

When you complete your bibliography search, you will have a card for each item you want to find along with its location in the library. You will also have written on the card how you now think you will use each source in your paper. You can add author information and a general evaluation to this annotation later when you get your hands on the source itself.

Now you are ready to go find the books and articles. Be prepared for a certain amount of frustration. If your book is checked out, for example, look at the other books shelved in the same area. They will also be on your subject and may be as useful as the one you can't find. Also, make enough bibliography cards for articles so that if you cannot find some of them, you will be able to find others.

Survey and Skim. When you have located your research material, do not try to read all the way through all of it. You will never finish. It is important, however, to understand the context of the material you quote and to learn something about the author. Survey rather than read books and articles (see Chapter 3). Use this technique to locate information quickly. It is especially important to read the preface to a book to learn the author's position on the issue. Then use the table of contents and index to find specific information. After you have surveyed, you can then skim relevant parts to find the specific information you need. To skim, read quickly every fourth or fifth line, or sweep your eyes across the page in large diagonal movements. If you know what you are looking for and you are concentrating on finding it, you will be able to use these means to locate information quickly and successfully.

Read Creatively to Generate Ideas. Surveying and skimming may not always yield the understanding that you require, particularly if the material is difficult or dense or if you do not know what information you are looking for. In these situations, switch from surveying or skimming to creative reading to help you think and get additional ideas for your paper.

Creative reading is different from some of the other types of reading that you do. For example, *leisure reading* is done for relaxation and pleasure. *Study reading* requires you to read, understand, learn, and remember material so that you can pass a test. *Critical reading*, which you learned to do in Parts One and Two of this book, has you identify and analyze the parts of an argument within an overall context. *Creative reading* enables you to get ideas and think critically. Here are some questions that you can keep in mind to guide creative reading.

1. What strikes me in this text? What interests me? Why?
2. What new ideas and answers are occurring to me as I read?
3. How can I relate (compare, elaborate, apply, associate) this new material with what I already know?
4. Do these new ideas challenge any of my existing ideas? How? Can I reconcile the differences?
5. What are the implications of these new ideas?
6. How can I use these new ideas in my paper?

Remember to use the Toulmin model to read all argument. It will help you focus on the important parts: the claim, the support, and the warrants. It will also call your attention to the different ways that other authors handle rebuttal. You may want to follow someone's example when you write your own.

Take Some Notes and Fill In Your Outline.   Keep your preliminary outline handy as you read and take notes, and then take notes to fill in your outline. Revise your outline as needed.

Either write notes on cards or copy the material you intend to use on one of the copy machines. Whichever system you use, you must differentiate among the material you quote, the material you write in your own words (paraphrase), the material you summarize, and your own ideas. Code the different types of information by using different colors of cards, by writing with different colors of pens, or by labeling the type of information on each card. Place all of your own ideas in square brackets [ ], and always indicate directly quoted material by placing it in quotation marks.

If you decide to use the copy machine instead of writing note cards, make sure to copy the entire article or entire section of a book and write source information on it: the name of the publication, the volume, and the date for an article, and the author, title, city of publication, publisher, and date for a book. Get all of the information you need the first time so that you will not have to go back to find this material again.

Indicate at the top of the card or in the margin of copied material where you intend to use it in your paper. Use a brief version of a heading on your preliminary outline for this cross-referencing.

Write only brief source information on your note cards because complete information is available on your bibliography cards. The author's name is usually enough, unless you are using two books by the same author. Then write the author's name and a short title at the top of each note card. Copy quoted material ex-

---

Problems—current system

Wishman.

"Jury instructions are often incomprehensible because they are drafted by lawyers and judges who do not realize how much of their 'legalese' vocabulary and syntax was acquired in law school… little effort is made to write clear and simple language for those not legally trained." p. 224

Figure 9.3   A Note Card with Quoted Material

actly, and place it in quotes so that it will go into your paper that way. Add the page number at the end. See Figure 9.3 for an example of a note card with a direct quote.

Paraphrased material should also be recorded carefully and accurately with the page number at the end. Since you are condensing or changing the wording of this material, do not place it in quotation marks. You will still have to let your reader know where you got it when you write your paper, so include on the card the author's name and page number. Also indicate where you will use it in your paper. Figure 9.4 provides an example. Figure 9.5 provides an example of a note card with the student essayist's original idea on it.

Arrange these cards as you go along according to the categories that are written at the top. Then place the categories in the sequence you think you will follow in your paper. The cards are now ready to work into your paper when you write the first draft.

> Introduction—statistics
>
> Robinson.
>
> He quotes survey done by defense trial lawyers assoc.
> 45% adult Americans have been called for jury duty.
> 17% have served through a trial.
>
> p. 62

Figure 9.4   A Paraphrased Note Card

> need for change
>
> mine.
>
> If the judge gives instructions to the jury only once and in unfamiliar legal language, the jury will forget or confuse them. The current system needs to be improved.

Figure 9.5   A Note Card with an Original Idea or Reaction on It

EVALUATE YOUR RESEARCH MATERIALS

Your main concern in evaluating research materials is to determine that it is relevant to the particular points you are making in your paper. Research materials, when worked into a paper, can clarify, prove, justify, elaborate on, illustrate, and add interest to the major ideas. But before they can function in any of those ways, they must first be relevant and related to the topics they support.

You will also discover that each book or article you locate for research will fit into categories similar to those described at the beginning of Chapter 3. Identifying this material by category will make you more aware of what you are using and will also help you interpret it for your audience.

Extremist, Biased, True-Believer Writing.   Recognize biased material by the emotional language, extreme examples, and implicit value systems that are associated with extremist rather than mainstream groups. One student doing research on changing the two-party system in the United States encountered so much odd, extreme material that she almost had to change to a new issue. She knew that if she used only the extremist material in her paper, she would be appealing to a very small audience.

Deliberate Argumentative Writing with Wider Audience Appeal.   Recognize argumentative material by its obvious position on a controversial issue and, specifically, by its claim, support, and warrants. Learn what you can about the author's credentials and about the sources consulted to provide support. The purpose will be clear, and the reasons and support will have appeal for a specific audience. Discover which audience, and decide whether the material has sufficiently wide appeal so that it might even be acceptable to a universal audience.

Exploratory Writing.   Recognize exploratory material by its objective explanation of several different views or perspectives on any issue. Use this material to help you define your own position and plan ways to refute others.

Objective Writing with a Hidden or Unconscious Argumentative Purpose. An unusual amount of emotional language, carefully selected or stacked evidence, and quotes from biased sources and authorities characterize this material. Use such material to support your own position if the audience will accept it. Or attack the obvious bias in this material if you want to refute it.

Objective, Factual Writing.   Genuinely objective writing contains facts and information that do not change from one source to another. It may include surveys, almanacs, data lists, polls, reports (including scientific reports), and some news articles. It will be acceptable as proof to your audience if you convince them also that the data were compiled, interpreted, and reported by objective, unbiased, responsible, and experienced researchers.

You can further evaluate each research source by comparing it with other sources on the same subject, by analyzing the warrants, by applying the tests for the validity of the proofs, by determining whether or not the source in which you found it is biased, by looking up reviews, and by asking your professor for an opinion about it.

WHAT STRATEGIES CAN YOU NOW ADD TO IMPROVE YOUR PROCESS FOR WRITING ARGUMENT?

1. **Use Burke's pentad** to discover the cause of the human actions and events associated with your issue.
2. **Use chains of reasons** to develop depth of analysis and detail in your argument.
3. **Use argument theory** to think systematically about your issue by considering the rhetorical situation, applying the Toulmin model, deciding which proofs to use, and selecting proofs appropriate for the claim.
4. **Let your preliminary outline guide your research** and your bibliography work.
5. **Read creatively** for ideas or survey and skim for information.
6. **Take research notes**.
7. **Evaluate your resource sources**.

EXERCISES AND ACTIVITIES

1. SMALL GROUPS: PRACTICE DEVELOPING PROOFS FOR DIFFERENT TYPES OF CLAIMS

Each group works on one of the five tasks in the following lettered list. Use a claim that a group member has already written, or make a claim about a familiar campus issue such as parking, registration, overloaded classes, or opportunities for social life. Write this claim in five different ways, for example:

Fact: Social life on this campus is nonexistent.
Definition: To determine whether social life exists on this campus, we need to define and describe an acceptable social life for college students.
Cause: The lack of social life on campus is caused by programming plans that have failed.
Value: Social life on this campus is worse than it was in high school.
Policy: Social life needs to be improved through direct action by students, faculty, and administration.

Note that all of these claims are controversial. See other examples of claims in Chapter 7, pp. 215–226.

   a. *Write a claim of fact.* Develop it with one-sentence proofs of the following types:
   - (1) Causes and/or effects
   - (2) Symptoms and signs
   - (3) Induction
   - (4) Analogies or comparisons
   - (5) Definition

   b. *Write a claim of definition.* Develop it with one-sentence proofs of the following types:
   - (1) Comparison to a similar case
   - (2) Literal or historical analogy
   - (3) Figurative analogy
   - (4) Classifying or placing it in a category with known characteristics

   c. *Write a claim of cause.* Develop it with one-sentence proofs of the same types used above for claim of fact.

   d. *Write a value claim.* Develop it with one-sentence proofs of the following types:
   - (1) A value proof
   - (2) A motivational proof
   - (3) A quotation from an authority
   - (4) A definition
   - (5) A comparison

   e. *Write a policy claim.* Develop it with one-sentence proofs of the following types:
   - (1) Literal analogies
   - (2) A quotation from an authority
   - (3) A motivational proof

Number or arrange your proofs in the best logical order and read your brief arguments aloud to the class.

2. SMALL GROUPS: USING AUDIENCE VALUES AND CONSTRAINTS TO HELP PLAN MOTIVATIONAL AND VALUE PROOFS

Read the descriptions of the six value systems in the article "American Value Systems." Each group should then be assigned one value system and be directed to write the claims and the needs and value statements described in the following list so that they are acceptable to the particular audiences.

   a. Use a claim that a group member has already written, and rewrite it so that it would be immediately acceptable to people holding the values your group has been assigned.

   b. Write your claim so that they would immediately find it unacceptable.

   c. Write a value statement they would accept.

   d. Write a value statement they would not accept.

   e. Write a needs statement they would accept.

   f. Write a needs statement they would not accept.

Read what you have written to the class.

AMERICAN VALUE SYSTEMS

Richard Rieke and Malcolm Sillars

As we have noted, by careful analysis individual values can be discovered in the arguments of ourselves and others. There is a difficulty, however, in attempting to define a whole system of values for a person or a group. And as difficult as that is, each of us, as a participant in argumentation, should have some concept of the broad systems that most frequently bring together certain values. For this purpose, it is useful for you to have an idea of some of the most commonly acknowledged value systems.

You must approach this study with a great deal of care, however, because even though the six basic value systems we are about to define provide a fair view of the standard American value systems, they do not provide convenient pigeon-holes into which individuals can be placed. They represent broad social categories. Some individuals (even groups) will be found outside these systems. Many individuals and groups will cross over value systems, picking and choosing from several. Note how certain words appear as value terms in more than one value system. The purpose of this survey is to provide a beginning understanding of standard American values, not a complete catalog.[1]

THE PURITAN-PIONEER-PEASANT VALUE SYSTEM

This value system has been identified frequently as the *puritan morality* or the *Protestant ethic*. It also has been miscast frequently because of the excessive emphasis placed, by some of its adherents, on restrictions of personal acts such as smoking and consuming alcohol.[2] Consequently, over the years, this value system has come to stand for a narrow-minded attempt to interfere in other people's business, particularly if those people are having fun. However, large numbers of people who do not share such beliefs follow this value system.

We have taken the liberty of expanding beyond the strong and perhaps too obvious religious implications of the terms *puritan* and *Protestant*. This value system is what most Americans refer to when they speak of the "pioneer spirit," which was not necessarily religious. It also extends, we are convinced, to a strain of values brought to this country by Southern and Eastern European Catholics, Greek Orthodox, and Jews who could hardly be held responsible for John Calvin's theology or even the term *Protestant ethic*. Thus, we have the added word *peasant*, which may not be particularly accurate. Despite the great friction that existed between these foreign-speaking immigrants from other religions and their native Protestant counterparts, they had a great deal in common as do their ideological descendants today. On many occasions after describing the puritan morality we have heard a Jewish student say, "That's the way my father thinks," or had a student of Italian or Polish descent say, "My grandmother talks that way all the time."

The Puritan-Pioneer-Peasant value system is rooted in the idea that persons have an obligation to themselves and those around them, and in some cases to their God, to work hard at whatever they do. In this system, people are limited in their abilities and must be prepared to fail. The great benefit is in the striving against an unknowable and frequently hostile universe. They have an obligation to others, must be selfless, and must not waste. Some believe this is the only way to gain happiness and success. Others see it as a means to salvation. In all cases it takes on a moral orientation. Obviously, one might work hard for a summer in order to buy a new car and not be labeled a "puritan." Frequently, in this value system, the instrumental values of selflessness, thrift, and hard work become terminal values where the work has value beyond the other benefits it can bring one. People who come from this value system often have difficulty with retirement, because their meaning in life, indeed their pleasure, came from work.

Likewise, because work, selflessness, and thrift are positive value terms in this value system, laziness, selfishness, and waste are negative value terms. One can see how some adherents to this value system object to smoking, drinking, dancing, or cardplaying. These activities are frivolous; they take one's mind off more serious matters and waste time.

Some of the words that are associated with the Puritan-Pioneer-Peasant value system are:

Positive: *activity, work, thrift, morality, dedication, selflessness, virtue, right-eousness, duty, dependability, temperance, sobriety, savings, dignity*

Negative: *waste, immorality, dereliction, dissipation, infidelity, theft, vandalism, hunger, poverty, disgrace, vanity*

THE ENLIGHTENMENT VALUE SYSTEM

America became a nation in the period of the Enlightenment. It happened when a new intellectual era based on the scientific finding of men like Sir Isaac Newton and the philosophical systems of men like John Locke were dominant. The founders of our nation were particularly influenced by such men. The Declaration of Independence is the epitome of an enlightenment document. In many ways America is an enlightenment nation, and if enlightenment is not the predominant value system, it is surely first among equals.

The enlightenment position stems from the belief that we live in an ordered world in which all activity is governed by laws similar to the laws of physics. These "natural laws" may or may not come from God, depending on the particular orientation of the person examining them; but unlike many adherents to the Puritan value system just discussed, enlightenment persons theorized that people could discover these laws by themselves. Thus, they may worship God for God's greatness, even acknowledge that God created the universe and natural laws, but they find out about the universe because they have the power of reason. The laws of nature are harmonious, and one can use reason to discover them all. They can also be used to provide for a better life.

Because humans are basically good and capable of finding answers, restraints on them must be limited. Occasionally, people do foolish things and must be restrained by society. However, a person should never be restrained in matters of the mind. Reason must be free. Thus, government is an agreement among individuals to assist the society to protect rights. That government is a democracy. Certain rights are inalienable, and they may not be abridged; "among these are life, liberty and the pursuit of happiness." Arguments for academic freedom, against wiretaps, and for scientific inquiry come from this value system.

Some of the words that are associated with the Enlightenment value system are:

Positive: *freedom, science, nature, rationality, democracy, fact, liberty, individualism, knowledge, intelligence, reason, natural rights, natural laws, progress*

Negative: *ignorance, inattention, thoughtlessness, error, indecision, irrationality, dictatorship, fascism, bookburning, falsehood, regression*

THE PROGRESSIVE VALUE SYSTEM

Progress was a natural handmaiden of the Enlightenment. If these laws were available and if humans had the tool, reason, to discover them and use them to advantage, then progress would result. Things would continually get better. But although progress is probably an historical spin-off of the Enlightenment, it has become so important on its own that it deserves at times to be seen quite separate from the Enlightenment.

Richard Weaver, in 1953, found that "one would not go far wrong in naming progress" the "god term" of that age. It is, he said, the "expression about which all other expressions are ranked as subordinate. . . . Its force imparts to the others their lesser degrees of force, and fixes the scale by which degrees of comparison are understood."

Today, the unmediated use of the progress value system is questioned, but progress is still a fundamental value in America. Most arguments against progress are usually arguments about the definition of progress. They are about what "true progress is."

Some of the key words of the Progressive value system are:

Positive: *practicality, efficiency, change, improvement, science, future, modern, progress, evolution*

Negative: *old-fashioned, regressive, impossible, backward*

THE TRANSCENDENTAL VALUE SYSTEM

Another historical spin-off of the Enlightenment system was the development of the Transcendental movement of the early nineteenth century. It took from the Enlightenment all its optimism about people, freedom, and democracy, but rejected the emphasis on reason. It argued idealistically that there was a faculty higher than reason; let us call it, as many transcendentalists did, intuition. Thus, for the transcendentalist, there is a way of knowing that is better than reason, a way which *transcends* reason. Consequently, what might seem like the obvious solution to problems is not necessarily so. One must look, on important matters at least, to the intuition, to the feelings. Like the enlightenment thinker, the transcendentalist believes in a unified universe governed by natural laws. Thus all persons, by following their intuition will discover these laws, and universal harmony will take place. And, of course, little or no government will be necessary. The original American transcendentalists of the early nineteenth century drew their inspiration from Platonism, German idealism, and Oriental mysticism. The idea was also fairly well limited to the intellectuals. By and large, transcendentalism has been the view of a rather small group of people throughout our history, but at times it has been very important. It has always been somewhat more influential among younger people. James Truslow Adams once wrote that everyone should read Ralph Waldo Emerson at sixteen because his writings were a marvel for the buoyantly optimistic person of that age but that his transcendental writings did not have the same luster at twenty-one.[5] In the late 1960s and early 1970s, Henry David Thoreau's *Walden* was the popular reading of campus rebels. The emphasis of anti-establishment youth on Oriental mysticism, like Zen, should not be ignored either. The rejection of contemporary society and mores symbolized by what others considered "outlandish dress" and "hippie behavior" with its emphasis on emotional response and "do your own thing" indicated the adoption of a transcendental value system. Communal living is reminiscent of the transcendental "Brook Farm" experiments that were attempted in the early nineteenth century and described by Nathaniel Hawthorne in his novel *The Blithedale Romance.*

In all of these movements the emphasis on humanitarian values, the centrality of love for others, and the preference for quiet contemplation over activity has been important. Transcendentalism, however, rejects the common idea of progress. Inner light and knowledge of one's self is more important than material well-being. There is also some tendency to reject physical well-being because it takes one away from intuitive truth.

It should be noted that not everyone who argues for change is a transcendentalist. The transcendental white campus agitators of the late 1960s discovered that, despite all their concern for replacing racism and war with love and peace, their black counterparts were highly pragmatic and rationalistic about objectives and means. Black agitators and demonstrators were never "doing their thing" in the intuitive way of many whites.

It should also be noted that while a full adherence to transcendentalism has been limited to small groups, particularly among intellectuals and youth, many of the ideas are not limited to such persons. One can surely find strains of what we have labeled, for convenience, transcendentalism in the mysticism of some very devout older Roman Catholics, for instance. And perhaps many Americans become transcendental on particular issues, about the value to be derived from hiking in the mountains, for example.

Here are some of the terms that are characteristic of the Transcendental value system:

Positive: *humanitarian, individualism, respect, intuition, truth, equality, sympathetic, affection, feeling, love, sensitivity, emotion, personal kindness, compassion, brotherhood, friendship, mysticism*

Negative: *science,[6] reason, mechanical, hate, war, anger, insensitive, coldness, un-emotional*

THE PERSONAL SUCCESS VALUE SYSTEM

The least social of the major American value systems is the one that moves people toward personal achievement and success. It can be related as a part of the Enlightenment value system, but it is more than that because it involves a highly pragmatic concern for the material happiness of the individual. To call it selfish would be to load the terms against it, although there would be some who accept this value system who would say "Yes, I'm selfish." "The Lord helps those who help themselves" has always been an acceptable adage by some of the most devout in our nation.

You might note that the Gallup poll, cited earlier in this chapter, is very heavily weighted toward personal values. Even "good family life" rated as the top value can be seen as an item of personal success. This survey includes only a few social values like "helping needy people" and "helping better America" and even those are phrased in personal terms. That is, the respondents were asked "how important you feel each of these is to you." The personal orientation of the survey may represent a bias of the Gallup poll, but we suspect it reflects much of American society. We are personal success-oriented in an individual way which would not be found in some other cultures (e.g., in the Japanese culture).

Here are some of the terms that tend to be characteristic of the Personal Success value system:

Positive: *career, family, friends, recreation, economic security, identity, health, individualism, affection, respect, enjoyment, dignity, consideration, fair play, personal*

Negative: *dullness, routine, hunger, poverty, disgrace, coercion, disease*

THE COLLECTIVIST VALUE SYSTEM

Although there are few actual members of various socialist and communist groups in the United States, one cannot ignore the strong attachment among some people for collective action. This is, in part, a product of the influx of social theories from Europe in the nineteenth century. It is also a natural outgrowth of a perceived need to control the excesses of freedom in a mass society. Its legitimacy is not limited to current history, however. There has always been a value placed on cooperative action. The same people today who would condemn welfare payments to unwed mothers would undoubtedly praise their ancestors for barnraising and taking care of the widow in a frontier community. Much rhetoric about our "pioneer ancestors" has to do with their cooperative action. And anticollectivist presidents and evangelists talk about "the team." At the same time many fervent advocates of collective action in the society argue vehemently for their freedom and independence. Certainly the civil rights movement constituted a collective action for freedom. Remember the link in Martin Luther King, Jr.'s speech between "freedom" and "brotherhood"?

But whether the Collectivist value system is used to defend socialist proposals or promote "law and order" there is no doubt that collectivism is a strong value system in this nation. Like transcendentalism, however, it is probably a value system that, at least in this day cannot work alone.

Here are some of the terms that tend to characterize the Collectivist value system:

Positive: *cooperation, joint action, unity, brotherhood, together, social good, order, humanitarian aid and comfort, equality*

Negative: *disorganization, selfishness, personal greed, inequality*

Clearly, these six do not constitute a complete catalog of all American value systems. Combinations and reorderings produce different systems. Two values deserve special attention because they are common in these systems and sometimes operate alone: *nature* and *patriotism*. Since the beginning of our nation the idea has prevailed that the natural is good and there for our use and preservation. Also, since John Winthrop first proclaimed that the New England Puritans would build "a city on the hill" for all the world to see and emulate, the idea has endured that America is a fundamentally great nation, perhaps God-chosen, to lead the world to a better life. This idea may be somewhat tarnished in some quarters today, but there is no doubt that it will revive as it has in the past. Linked to other value systems we have discussed, it will once more be a theme that will draw the adherence of others to arguments.[6]

NOTES

1. The following material draws from a wide variety of sources. The following is an illustrative cross section of sources from a variety of disciplines: Virgil I. Baker and Ralph T. Eubanks, *Speech in Personal and Public Affairs* (New York: David McKay, 1965), pp. 95–102; Clyde Kluckhohn, "An Anthropologist Looks at the United States," *Mirror for Man* (New York: McGraw-Hill, 1949), pp. 228–261; Stow Persons, *American Minds* (New York: Holt, Rinehart and Winston, 1958); Jurgen Ruesch, "Communication and American Values; A Psychological Approach," *Communication: The Social Matrix of Psychiatry*, Jurgen Ruesch and Gregory Bateson (New York: W. W. Norton, 1951), pp. 94–134; Edward D. Steele and W. Charles Redding, "The American Value System: Premises for Persuasion," *Western Speech*, 26 (Spring 1962), pp. 83–91; Richard Weaver, "Ultimate Terms in Contemporary Rhetoric," *The Ethics of Rhetoric* (Chicago: Henry Regnery, 1953), pp. 211–232; Robin M. Williams, Jr., *American Society*, 3rd ed. (New York: Alfred A. Knopf, 1970), pp. 438–504.
2. It is ironic that the original American Puritans did not have clear injunctions against such activity.
3. Weaver, p. 212.
4. Note that "old-fashioned" is frequently positive when we speak of morality and charm but not when we speak of our taste in music.
5. James Truslow Adams, "Emerson Re-read," *The Transcendental Revolt*, George F. Whicher, Ed. (Boston: D. C. Heath, 1949), pp. 31–39.

[6]From Richard D. Rieke and Malcolm O. Sillars, *Argumentation and the Decision Making Process*, 2nd ed. (Glenview, IL: Scott, Foresman, 1984).

6. It is interesting to note, however, that one of the major organizations in the United States with transcendental origins, the Christian Science Church, combines transcendentalism with science.

3. PAIRS OF STUDENTS: PRACTICE BURKE'S PENTAD AND WRITE A PAPER

Use Burke's pentad to analyze the whole context and particularly the cause either of the claim you have written for your paper or a claim generated in response to a recent event that is stirring controversy on the national or local scene: a change in policy, a crime, a riot or demonstration, a diplomatic visit, a political appointment, job layoffs, and so on. Check the newspaper. Then answer the following questions:

a. *Act:* What was done?
b. *Scene:* When or where was it done?
c. *Agent:* Who did it?
d. *Agency:* How did he (she, they) do it?
e. *Purpose:* Why did it happen?

Decide which of the five perspectives provides the strongest and most easily defensible cause. Express it in the form of a causal claim. Read your claims to the class, and write a one-page paper in which you explain the cause you selected.

4. PAIRS OF STUDENTS: CREATE A CHAIN OF REASONS AND WRITE A PAPER

Get in a dialogue with a fellow student either about the claim you have written for your paper or the following claim: "Students today will have better (or worse) opportunities than their parents had at the same age." Imagine a questioner who asks, "Why? Why not? Why do you think so? What for?" after each reason that you give. Repeat the *claim, question, answer* sequence five times, and write out the results. Go back and identify the places in this chain that could be strengthened with evidence. Indicate what kinds of evidence.

Read the results of your group work to the class. Write a two-page paper in which you express the line of thinking you have developed.

5. INDIVIDUAL ONGOING PROJECT, THE ARGUMENT PAPER: INVENTION OF IDEAS

Read through the list of invention strategies in the following worksheet. They represent a composite of those described in this chapter and in Chapter 4. Some of them will be "hot spots" for you. That is, they will immediately suggest profitable activity for developing your paper. Check those that you want to use at this point and complete them. There may be only two or three. Include the Toulmin model, however. It is one of the best invention strategies for argument.

6. PAIRS OF STUDENTS: BECOMING FAMILIAR WITH THE LIBRARY

Visit your library with a partner and begin to do research. This exercise will take roughly one class period if you and your partner work quickly.

You and your partner should explore the issues you have selected to write about in your papers. Or select an issue from the following list. Use the library

Invention Worksheet

Write your claim _____ .

    Begin to develop your claim by using some of the following invention strategies. If you cannot generate information and ideas, do some background reading and then come back to these.

1. Freewrite for five minutes.
2. Brainstorm additional ideas and details in brief phrases for another five minutes.
3. Make a list or map that shows the parts of your paper.
4. Explain to someone in your class or group about what you expect to accomplish in your paper, or talk into a tape recorder about it.
5. Write your insights in a journal or on sheets of paper filed in a folder.
6. Mentally visualize and write a description of a scene related to your claim.
7. Make a preliminary outline. Add research and draft plans.
   a. Write a claim and some subclaims.
   b. Plan definitions for all controversial terms in your claim.
   c. Plan background reading and research.
   d. Plan background information for the reader.
   e. Identify your strongest opinions and best reasons.
   f. Think of tentative ways to begin and end your paper.
   g. Think of original examples, descriptions, or comparisons.
8. Think through the rhetorical situation. Remember TRACE: text, reader, author, constraints, exigence.
9. Use the Toulmin model to come up with the key parts of your paper.
   a. Classify your claim according to its type.
   b. Describe the support you will need.
   c. Describe one or more of your warrants.
   d. Decide on backing for your warrants.
   e. Plan your rebuttal strategy.
   f. Plan qualifiers if necessary.
10. Decide on some proofs that are appropriate for your type of claim. Remember SICDADS and VAM: sign, induction, cause, deduction, analogies (literal, figurative, historical), definition, and sign; and also value, authoritative, and motivational proofs.
11. Apply critical thinking prompts. Start with your claim, but then make these recursive; that is, apply them at any point and more than once during the process.

Associate it.	Think about it as it is now.	Evaluate it.
Describe it.	Think about it over time.	Elaborate on it.
Compare it.	Decide what it is a part of.	Project and predict.
Apply it.	Analyze its parts.	Ask why.
Divide it.	Synthesize it.	

12. Use Burke's pentad to establish cause: act, scene, agent, agency, purpose.
13. Use chains of reasons to develop your claim through five repetitions of *claim, why, because*: Describe where you need to add evidence.

to practice finding sources. To find your sources, work through the six library stations until you have completed the assignment. If you need help locating a source, ask a librarian for assistance.

Gun control
Violence on television
Death penalty
Sex education
Pollution
Censorship
Gang violence
The ozone layer

Library Stations

Station 1—On-line catalog or card catalog and periodical indexes.
At this station, locate books and articles about your subject by using the computer to do a key-word or subject search; or use the card catalog to find books about your subject, and one of the periodical indexes to find articles. Determine also how to find the call numbers for the periodicals if they are not listed in the computer. You will need to find a variety of sources that focus on your topic. Write down the call numbers of a book about your subject, a current periodical (one that has not yet been bound), a bound periodical, and an article that has been preserved on microfilm or microfiche, such as a weekly news magazine.

Station 2—The stacks.
Next, go to the stacks and use the call number to locate the book about your subject. When you find it, locate a copy machine, and make a copy of the title page or of the title page and the pages you will quote, paraphrase, or summarize in your paper. Bring the copy to your next class meeting.

Station 3—Bound periodicals.
Locate the bound periodicals in your library, and find the magazine article you selected. Make a copy of the first page of the article or of the entire article if you intend to draw information from it for your paper. (If for some reason the volume you need is not on the shelf, find another article in a bound volume and make a copy of the first page of it to demonstrate that you located these volumes.)

Station 4—Current periodicals.
Locate the current periodicals and find the article you selected. Make a copy of the first page of the article or of the entire article if you intend to use it. (Again, if you can't find the particular issue of the periodical you need, make a copy from another current periodical. Remember, the main goal of this orientation exercise is to familiarize you with the library. It is desirable to locate specific articles you can use.)

Station 5—Microfilm/microfiche.
Next, go to the part of your library that houses the microforms. Using the viewer, find your article and write down one interesting quote from the article. Bring the quote to class with you along with the name of the source, the date, and the page number where you found your quote.

Station 6—Reference desk.

Find the reference desk at your library. Ask the assistant working there to sign your assignment sheet. Now you will know where to go to receive assistance from reference librarians.[7]

7. INDIVIDUAL ONGOING PROJECT, THE ARGUMENT PAPER: RESEARCH FOR PAPER

Research Worksheet

1. Get organized for research: gather cards, pencils, money for the copy machine, paper, and a big envelope or folder. Review your preliminary outline and research plan.
2. Create a bibliography of ten to 12 sources. Plan to locate and use at least four to six for your paper. Include both books and articles, and write pertinent information on cards. Add annotations to the cards about possible use, author, and evaluation of evidence.
3. Survey and skim for specific information. Take notes.
4. Read creatively for original ideas. Take notes.
5. Make evaluative judgments about each source.

---

8. UNDERSTANDING THE CHAPTER: WHOLE CLASS, GROUPS, OR INDIVIDUALS

Summarize the major ideas in this chapter by completing the following sentences briefly and in your own words:

a. The inventional strategies to access what you already know that you are most likely to use include . . .
b. The five elements of Burke's pentad are . . . The pentad is useful in argument to establish . . .
c. Create chains of reasons by . . .
d. Argument theories and models that you can use to review ideas and think about the parts of your paper include . . .
e. Bibliography cards provide information about . . .
f. Three types of information you will write on note cards are . . .
g. Evaluate your research sources by . . .

---

[7]This exercise was prepared by Leslie Snow.

CHAPTER 10

Organizing, Writing, and Revising

T his chapter will provide you with the information you will need to create some order in the material you have gathered so that you can now write your argument paper. Specifically, you will be taught some ways to organize and outline, to incorporate research into your first draft, and to revise and prepare the final copy. Organization, or deciding on a framework of ideas for your paper, will be dealt with first.

HOW DOES ORGANIZATION HELP YOU AND YOUR READER?

Everyone has a natural tendency to associate or group ideas and to place them in an order so that they make sense and are easier to remember. You have probably already begun to do this with the materials for your paper. You may have made a preliminary outline, labeled note cards, and written some lists. Eventually, these activities will help your reader, who will understand organized ideas far more easily than disorganized ones. To illustrate this fact, here are two examples. The ideas and information in Example 1 are a collection of ideas for a value paper that have not yet been organized.

Example 1.   *Claim: Women have more opportunities for variety in their lives now than they had 50 years ago.*

Women's movement.
Several causes for changes in women's opportunities.
Comparison between women at mid-twentieth and at end of twentieth century.
Some women are dysfunctional.
Examples of three contemporary women.
Not all changes are good—signs of stress in women, men, children.

Women are now self-actualized.

Statistical data suggesting the variety of positions occupied by women in 1990s and in 1950s.

Labor-saving devices, education, economy, and women's ambitions contribute to change.

A review of human needs and motivation and how they relate to women.

Improved opportunities for women.

The effects of the changes on men and children.

Analysis of the causes for the changes in opportunities for women.

Donna Reed and Murphy Brown.

How can this jumble of ideas and information be organized for an effective argument paper? Thinking about organization requires that you identify the *parts*, place them in an *order*, and establish some *relationships* among them. In other words, one must establish reasons for discussing one idea before another.

In Example 2 the parts have been rearranged. The same items appear in both examples, but they have been organized in Example 2 according to the following rationale:

1. The issue is introduced as a fact, that women have more opportunity now. This fact is illustrated with examples and statistics to focus the issue and get attention and interest.
2. Burke's pentad is used to explore causes for the changes: agency (labor-saving devices), scene (education and economy), agent (women and women's movement), and purpose (to satisfy personal needs) are cited as causes.
3. The effects of the changes are explained and illustrated with examples.
4. The opposition is refuted and negative perceptions are changed to positive values.
5. The value claim, that the changes are good, is stated and made more convincing with a quote.

Example 2. *Title: Improved Opportunities for Women*

Introduction: Women now have a wide range of opportunities.

A comparison between women at mid-twentieth and end of twentieth century. Example, two television characters who reflect social mores: Donna Reed (1950s) and Murphy Brown (1990s).

Statistical data suggesting the variety of roles occupied by women in the 1990s and in the 1950s.

I. Analysis of the causes for the changes in women's roles.

Labor-saving devices—freed-up time.

Education—improved competencies.

Economy—requires two incomes.

Women's movement—made women more aware of human needs and motivation and how they relate to women.

II. Effects of the changes.

Women now able to meet needs for self-actualization in a variety of ways, some of which were formerly reserved for men.
Examples of three contemporary women who are satisfied with their lives: professional, military, homemaker.

III. Rebuttal: Some people argue that not all changes have been good and that there are signs of stress in women, men, and children. Actually, the effects they perceive as bad are good.

The stress for women is good stress because they now choose what they want to do.
Men are closer to their children because they share responsibility.
Children learn to take more initiative and shoulder more responsibility.
People made dysfunctional by the changes would probably have problems in any setting.

IV. Conclusion: *Claim: Women have more opportunities for variety in their lives now than they had 50 years ago.*

The benefits outweigh the problems.
Quote from an authority about women's current satisfaction.
No one would want to go back.

This is not the only organizational strategy that could have been used for this paper. The rebuttal, for example, could have been placed first. The effects could have been described before the causes. The value claim could have been placed at the beginning instead of at the end. Any one of these alternatives might have worked as well as another provided they made sense to the author and were convincing to the audience.

Read the materials you have gathered for your own paper and think about (1) how they can be divided into *parts*, (2) how these parts can be placed in an *order*, and (3) what the logical *relationships* are among them. List the parts, tentatively number them to reflect order, and explain the rationale for your decisions.

To help you plan the *parts*, keep the Toulmin model in mind. Your parts should include a claim, support, and warrants, and possibly also backing for the warrants, a rebuttal, and a qualifier for the claim. Think also about the subclaims that represent the major sections of the paper and the facts, examples, and opinions that support them. Tentatively plan the introduction and conclusion and what to include in them. The usual functions of the introduction are to focus and introduce the topic, provide some background, and get the attention of the audience. The conclusion usually refocuses the claim through restatement and final, compelling reasons.

To help you think about *order*, keep in mind that the beginning of your paper is a strong position for arguments, but that the end is even stronger. Put your strongest material at or near the end, other strong material at the beginning, and the less impressive material in the middle. Also, think about your audience when determining order. For instance, for a hostile audience you might argue about women's roles by admitting that the 1950s were a good time for women, but adding that times have changed, and finally showing how the 1950s way of life is now impractical. For a neutral audience, you might want to present strong and interesting examples at the beginning to get attention and create interest. For a friendly audience, you can show how things are better right away and thus confirm an already favorable opinion.

To focus on *relationships*, use words that name the relationships you have worked out. As in Example 2, write the words *causes, effects*, and *rebuttals* into your plan to clarify the main sections and suggest the relationships among them.

HOW CAN ORGANIZATIONAL PATTERNS HELP YOU THINK AND ORGANIZE?

For centuries, authors have used certain established patterns of thought to help them think about, develop, and organize ideas. This practice benefits both authors and readers who, as a result, are able to follow and understand the material more easily. Some of these patterns of thought are particularly helpful for organizing the ideas in argument. The following list describes those most commonly used. These patterns, by the way, can dominate your paper as the dominant pattern or can combine as minor patterns within the dominant pattern to organize some of the sections.

1. **Claim-with-reasons (or reasons-followed-by-claim) pattern.** This pattern takes the following form:

> Statement of claim
> > Reason 1
> > Reason 2
> > Reason 3, and so forth

Set this pattern up by writing the claim, following it with the word *because*, and listing some reasons. Or list some reasons, follow them with the word *therefore*, and write the claim. For example, you may present the claim that we need a national health care program, which is followed by reasons: the unemployed have no insurance, the elderly cannot afford medicine, many children do not receive adequate health care. The reasons may be distinct and different from one another and set up like separate topics in your paper. Or you may have created a chain of related reasons by asking *why* and answering *because* five or six times. Also, some of your reasons may be used to refute, others to prove, and still others to show how your claim will meet the needs and values of the audience. Support all reasons with facts, examples, and opinions. You may use transitional phrases such as *one reason, another reason*, a *related reason*, or a *final reason* to emphasize your reasons and make them stand out in your paper.

2. **Cause-effect (or effect-cause) pattern.** The cause-effect pattern may be used to identify one or more causes followed by one or more effects or results. Or you may reverse this sequence and describe effects first and then the cause(s). For example, the causes of water pollution might be followed by its effects on both humans and

animals. You may use obvious transitions to clarify cause-effect, such as "Those are the causes; now, let us look at the effects," or simply the words *cause, effect*, or *result*.

3. **Applied criteria pattern.** This pattern establishes criteria or standards for evaluation and judgment and then shows how the claim meets them. For example, in an argument about children in day care, the criteria of physical safety, psychological security, sociability, and creativity are established as successful criteria for day-care centers. Then the claim is made that day care meets those criteria as well as or even better than home care, and support is provided. Or criteria for great poems are established, and the claim and evidence demonstrate how a particular poem meets those criteria. The applied criteria pattern is obviously useful for value arguments. It is also useful in policy arguments to establish a way of evaluating a proposed solution. You may want to use the words and phrases *criteria, standards, needs*, and *meets those criteria or needs* to clarify the parts of your paper.

4. **Problem-solution pattern.** The problem-solution pattern is commonly used in policy papers. There are at least three ways to organize these papers. The problem is described followed by the solution. In this case, the claim is the solution, and it may be stated at the beginning of the solution section or at the end of the paper. An alternative is to propose the solution first and describe the problems that motivated it last. Or a problem may be followed by several solutions, one of which is selected as the best. When the solution/claim is stated at the end of the paper, the pattern is sometimes called the delayed proposal. For a hostile audience, it may be effective to describe the problem, show why other solutions do not work, and finally suggest the favored solution. For example, you may want to claim that labor unions are the best solution for reducing unemployment. First, you describe the unemployment problem in vivid detail so that the audience really wants a solution. Then you show how government mandates and individual company initiatives have not worked. Finally, you show how labor unions guarantee employment for workers. You may use the words *problem* and *solution* to signal the main sections of your paper for your reader.

5. **Chronological/narrative pattern.** Material arranged chronologically is explained as it occurs in time. This pattern may be used to establish what happened for an argument of fact. For example, you may want to give a history of childhood traumas to account for an individual's current criminal behavior. Or you may want to tell a story to develop one or more points in your argument. Use transitional words like *then, next*, or *finally* to make the parts of the chronology clear.

6. **Deductive pattern.** Recall that deductive reasoning involves reasoning from a generalization, applying it to cases or examples, and drawing a conclusion. For example, you may generalize that the open land in the west is becoming overgrazed; follow this assertion with examples of erosion, threatened wildlife, and other environmental harms; and conclude that the government must restrict grazing to designated areas. The conclusion is the claim. You may use such transitional phrases as *for instance, for example*, or *to clarify* to set your examples off from the rest of the argument, and *therefore, thus, consequently*, or *in conclusion* to lead into your claim.

7. **Inductive pattern.** The inductive pattern involves citing one or more examples and then making the "inductive leap" to the conclusion. For instance, five

or six examples of boatloads of illegal immigrants landing in the United States who require expensive social services lead some people to conclude that they should be sent home. Others may conclude that they should be allowed to stay. No matter which claim/conclusion is chosen, it can be stated at the beginning or at the end of the paper. The only requirement is that it be based on the examples. The same transitional words used for the deductive pattern are also useful for the inductive: *for instance, for example,* or *some examples* to emphasize the examples, and *therefore, thus,* or *consequently* to lead into the claim.

8. **Comparison-contrast pattern.** This pattern is particularly useful in definition arguments and in other arguments that show how a subject is like or unlike other similar subjects. It is also often used to demonstrate a variety of similarities or differences. For example, the claim is made that drug abuse is a medical problem instead of a criminal justice problem. The proof consists of literal analogies that compare drug abuse to AIDS, cancer, and heart disease in a number of areas to redefine it as a medical problem. The transitional words *by contrast, in comparison, while, some,* and *others* are sometimes used to clarify the ideas in this pattern.

9. **Rogerian pattern.** You were introduced to Rogerian argument in Chapter 2. Here is a review of the recommended strategy for this pattern of argument: You first introduce the issue and state the opponent's position on it. Then you show that it is understood, valued, and viable in certain contexts or conditions. Next, you state your own position and show the contexts in which it is valid. Finally, you show how the opponent's position would be improved by adopting all or at least some elements of your position. In other words, you finally show how the positions complement one another.

For example, the issue of gays in the military, each time it surfaces, results in particularly adamant positions on either side. Military leaders oppose openly gay behavior in the military, and gay service personnel want the same rights and opportunities as other people, including the right to be open about their sexual preferences. Rogerian strategy aimed at convincing military leaders to change their minds requires an opening statement that explains their position and gives reasons and evidence to show that it is understood and considered valid in certain circumstances. Next, the counterposition that gays should be allowed to be openly gay is offered along with reminders that gay military personnel have served well in the past and that their gay behavior has not been harmful. Finally, the claim is made that the military is improved by allowing gays and lesbians to serve as openly gay personnel because they are happier and better-adjusted employees.

10. **Motivated sequence pattern.** A common distinction between argument and persuasion is that argument results in agreement or conviction and persuasion results in action or changed behavior. The motivated sequence is a persuasive pattern that is used to motivate an audience to do something. You may find it useful when you want to persuade your audience to act. There are five steps. We will use, as an example, the campus issue that is a problem at some schools: insufficient numbers of classes for all the students who want to enroll.

a. *Attention.* First, create some interest and desire.
   Example: How often have you tried to register for a class only to be told that it is closed and you must try again next semester?
b. *Need.* Now, heighten the audience's need to do something about this situation.
   Example: A problem arises because you, like many other students, had planned to graduate at the end of this semester. If you cannot get into the classes you need to graduate, once again you put your life on hold for another half year. And what guarantee exists that the needed classes will be available to you next semester? The frustration may continue.
c. *Satisfaction.* Next, show that your proposed plan of action will solve the problem and satisfy the audience's needs.
   Example: There is a way of dealing with this problem. Enroll in the nearby college, take the course there, and transfer it back here to be counted as credit toward your graduation. You will complete your course work on schedule, learn just as much, and be ready to take that job you lined up at the time you agreed to start. You may have to drive more and complete some extra paperwork, but it will finally be worth it.
d. *Visualization.* Describe how things will be if the plan is put into action. Be positive.
   Example: Imagine yourself six months from now with your diploma in hand, ready to tackle the real world, take on an interesting job, and make some money for a change. You'll be able to make car payments, get into a nice apartment, and put aside the pressures of school, including trying to get into closed classes.
e. *Action.* Finally, tell the audience what it needs to do to satisfy its needs and create the desired outcomes.
   Example: It's easy to enroll at the other college. Call the registrar and start the necessary paperwork today.

Note that the motivated sequence includes the introduction and conclusion in its total structure. The other organizational patterns do not.[1]

11. **Exploratory pattern.** The pattern you used to write your exploratory paper can be expanded for a single-perspective argument paper. Recall that you explained the positions of those in favor of the issue, those against it, and those with various views in between. Your objective was to explain the range of different perspectives on the issue. Having stated these positions, you can now expand your exploratory paper by refuting some of them, and by stating and supporting your own. You may want to use another pattern, such as the claim with reasons, to organize your own position on the issue.

Some of these organizational patterns are particularly appropriate for specific types of claims. Table 10.1 suggests patterns you might want to consider as promising for particular argumentative purposes. You may, of course, combine more than one pattern to develop a paper. For example, you may begin with a narrative of what happened, then describe its causes and effects, and finally propose a solution for dealing with the problems created by the effects.

---

[1]The motivated sequence pattern is popularized by Alan Monroe in his public speaking textbooks.

TABLE 10.1 Appropriate Patterns for Developing Types of Claims (The first in each list is the one most commonly used.)

CLAIM OF FACT	CLAIM OF DEFINITION	CLAIM OF CAUSE	CLAIM OF VALUE	CLAIM OF POLICY
Claim + reasons	Deductive	Cause-effect	Applied criteria	Problem-solution
Inductive	Claim + reasons	Claim + reasons	Cause-effect	Applied criteria
Chronological/ narrative	Comparison	Rogerian	Claim + reasons	Motivated sequence
	Rogerian	Deductive	Chronological/ narrative	Cause-effect
Cause-effect	Exploratory	Exploratory	Rogerian	Claim + reasons
Rogerian	Inductive		Inductive	Rogerian
Exploratory			Deductive	Exploratory
			Comparison	
			Exploratory	

Use organizational patterns to help you think and organize your ideas. The patterns may be too constraining if you start with one and try to fill it in with your own material. You may prefer to work with your ideas first, without the conscious constraints of a pattern to guide you. At some point, however, when you are finished or nearly finished organizing your ideas, move out of the creative mode and into the critical mode to analyze what you have done. You may find that you have arranged your ideas according to one or more of the patterns without being consciously aware of it. This is a common discovery. Now use what you know about the patterns to improve and sharpen the divisions among your ideas and to clarify these ideas with transitions. You will ultimately improve the readability of your paper by making it conform more closely to one or more specific patterns of organization.

OUTLINE THE PAPER AND CROSS REFERENCE NOTE CARDS

You have already been provided with a rationale and some ideas for outlining in Chapter 4. Most people need some sort of outline to guide their writing when they are working not only with their own ideas but also with outside sources. Make the kind of outline that works best for you. Think of it as a guide that will help you write later. At the very least, indicate on your outline the major ideas or headings, and list under them the ideas and research you will use for support and development. Read through your invention and research notes, and check to make certain that all are cross-referenced in some way to the outline. Identify the places where you need more information and research. If you have gathered research material on cards, paperclip the cards to the places on the outline where they will be used later. Or if you have copied material, use numbers to cross-reference the passages you intend to quote to your outline. Work with your outline until it flows logically and makes sense.

If you have the opportunity, discuss your outline with your instructor, a peer editing group, or a friend. Someone else can often tell you if the organization is clear and logical, point out places where you will need more support and evidence, and also tell you whether or not the warrants will be generally acceptable.

Here is an example. The following outline is more complete than a preliminary outline to guide research. It would be complete enough to guide writing for some

---

Outline: Working title for paper: Is Technology Good or Bad? The Technophobic Perspective

Introduction: Value claim: Even though most people claim to be technophiles, many are really closet technophobes, and that may represent a desirable state of affairs.

(Define technophobia as a fundamental distrust of modern technology, and give some examples, like getting the answering machine when you need to talk with a human, the old typewriter that was updated to a computer on "Murder, She Wrote," and automated teller machines and credit cards that cause some people to lose control over their financial resources.)

Reasons:

I. Technology is advancing too rapidly, which causes some people to lag behind and resent it.
   - It's hard to learn the new ways and give up the old ones.
   - It's hard to adjust to constant change.

II. Technology is perceived as dehumanizing by many people.
   - Technology reduces human initiative.
   - New machines sometimes have a higher profile than individual people.

III. Technology changes the way many of us use our time, and we resent it.
   - We spend less time thinking and reflecting and more time engaged with machines (Example: People who spend hours a day on the Internet).
   - We spend less time outdoors communing with nature and more time inside watching movies and television.
   - We are losing our sense of what is "real."

IV. Many people become nostalgic for the way things were.

Conclusion: It is time for technophobes to declare themselves, and they should not be ashamed of their technophobia. It may lead to a healthy skepticism about technology that will help humans maintain their humanity while they objectively evaluate what technology can and cannot contribute to their lives.

people. Other people might want to add more detail to it before attempting the first draft. It is the sort of outline one might take to a peer editing group to discuss and get suggestions for the actual writing of the paper.

Note that this outline is worked out in detail in some areas but not in others. The ideas in it so far, however, belong to the author. The peer group that critiques it at this stage would be able to identify the areas in which this paper is likely to need more development and would suggest areas for research. The author goes to the library and finds three relevant articles about: (1) students who spend too much time on the Internet, (2) a professor who will not give up his old typewriter for a computer, and (3) a teacher who likes her old bicycle.

The following are some examples of notes that this author has taken to use in the rough draft of the paper (see Figures 10.1–10.5). They have been taken from the essay about the old bicycle that appears on pp. 322–323.

Mednick, Johanne, "The Highs of Low Technology." <u>Toronto Globe and Mail</u>. 23 July 1993:

Use as an example of 4, nostalgia.

Figure 10.1 The Bibliography Card for the Article by Mednick with Annotation

<u>4. Nostalgia</u>

Mednick

"Perhaps my bike is representative of a world gone by, . . . My bike is certainly not built for speed, . . . It's built for taking time. It makes people feel relaxed." p. 16

Figure 10.2 A Direct Quote. The ellipsis (. . .) indicate that material has been omitted from the material quoted in paragraph 6 of Mednick's article.

> 2. Dehumanizing
>
> Mednick
>
> She says that her microwave and her computer make her feel that life is getting too complicated and out of control. p. 16

Figure 10.3 A Paraphrase of the Ideas in Paragraph 7 of Mednick's Article

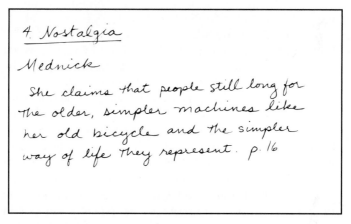

> 4. Nostalgia
>
> Mednick
>
> She claims that people still long for the older, simpler machines like her old bicycle and the simpler way of life they represent. p. 16

Figure 10.4 A Summary of the Article by Mednick

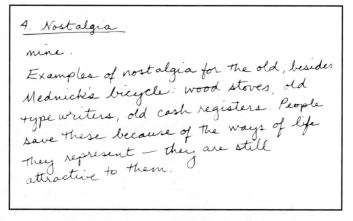

> 4. Nostalgia
>
> mine.
> Examples of nostalgia for the old, besides Mednick's bicycle: wood stoves, old typewriters, old cash registers. People save these because of the ways of life they represent — they are still attractive to them.

Figure 10.5 A Card with the Author's Original Insight Written on It

THE HIGHS OF LOW TECHNOLOGY

Johanne Mednick

1. I have a wonderful bicycle. Most people refer to it as "the old clunker," an ancient piece of metal the likes of which can be found in the dump or, if you're lucky, at garage sales.

2. In other words, people trashed these things a long time ago. Mine is a souped-up version of the basic "no-speeder," vintage 1930 or '40—two large wheels, seat, handle bars, basket, bell and the simple mechanism that allows me to pedal my way to wherever I'm going. I go uphill and downhill, easily gliding past all the riders on racers and mountain bikes intent on engaging the right gear for the occasion.

3. It's not that I'm an Amazon bike rider or anything. In fact, I won't make it up those hills if I don't get the necessary run at the start. But I have confidence in my bike. It gives me power, and I cherish its simplicity.

4. What intrigues me, in this age of technological innovation (which is nowhere more apparent than in the bicycle world), is the number of people who stop me and comment on my bike. It's a regular conversation piece. "Where did you get that thing?" "I haven't seen one of those in ages." "What a great bike." I get all kinds of comments—the best one being from a motorcycle gang who cornered me while I was locking it up. They politely suggested to me that I wear gloves while riding to protect my hands. Maybe I should also don a leather jacket.

5. But really, what is it that people are admiring? Are they admiring me for re-sisting the lure toward mass bicycle consumerism? I must look like an eyesore ped-alling behind my family, who all ride the latest model of designer-coloured mountain bike. (To them, I'm some sort of anomaly, an embarrassment not fit to be on the road.) On the other hand, maybe people are just genuinely curious, as they would be if confronted with a dinosaur bone. I never get the feeling that they think I'm crazy for riding something archaic when I could be fiddling with gears and having a presumably easier time of things. I believe that this curiosity runs deeper. My bike seems to touch a sensitive chord in people, and I'm not quite sure what or why that is.

6. Perhaps my bike is representative of a world gone by, the world before gim-micks and gadgets, accessories and attachments. A time when people thought in terms of settling into a cushioned seat, stopping the movement with their heel and travelling a bit slower than we are travelling now. My bike is certainly not built for speed, but who needs speed when I can coast along the streets, hold my head high and deliciously feel the wind on my face? It's built for taking time. It makes people feel relaxed.

7. When I'm riding my bike, I feel as though I have control. And I don't feel that way about most things these days. I don't deny that my computer or my microwave make my life a lot easier. I use these things, but they also make me feel rather small and, in a strange way, inadequate. What if I press the wrong button? What if some-thing goes wrong? Maybe if I learned to understand these appliances I'd feel bet-ter, more secure about my relationship with technology. But frankly, I'm not

comforted by manuals and how-to courses. Of course there are always "experts" I could go to who seem to know everything about anything. Relative, friend or salesperson, these people seem to breathe the latest invention and revel in ingenuity.

8.   I just don't get excited over yet another thing I could do if I pulled the right lever or set the right program. Nervous and unsure in the beginning, I eventually adapt to these so-called conveniences and accept them as a part of life, but I'm not entirely convinced of their merit. I crave simplicity and I have a sneaking suspicion that many people feel the same way. That's why they admire my bike. It comforts them and gives them a sense of something manageable, not too complicated.

9.   I'm not suggesting that we go back to a pioneer-village mentality. But I do think it's important to respect that which is simple and manageable—no doubt difficult in a time when more is better and new is best. I'm proud that my clunker makes me and others feel good. It allows me the opportunity to relax and, at best when I'm heading down the road, escape what I don't understand.[2]

Now look back at the note cards on pp. 320–321 and the outline on p. 319. Note that at the top of each card the number and a short title of the relevant subidea on the outline are recorded. Thus "4. Nostalgia" refers to *point IV* on the outline. Note also that the quoted material is placed in quotation marks to remind the author that these are the essayist's exact words. The paraphrase, or rephrasing of the ideas in paragraph 7, is written in the author's words and thus is without quotes. The summary, also in the author's words and without quotes, states the main point of the article. When all of the notes have been taken on all of the articles, they can be stacked in the order in which they will be used in the paper and placed next to the outline. The author is now ready to begin the draft. Most of the material in the paper will be the insights, observations, ideas, and examples of the author. Some other material from the cards, however, will be incorporated into the paper to add interest and improve the clarity and credibility of the final paper.

HOW TO INCORPORATE RESEARCH INTO THE FIRST DRAFT

Use your common sense in working your research materials into your draft. Your objective is to create a smooth document that can be easily read while at the same time demonstrating to your readers exactly which materials are yours and which are drawn from outside sources. Introduce each quote as you write it into the draft, so that it is clear where your words and ideas leave off and where someone else's begin. Then write all quoted and paraphrased material into the context of the draft so that your entire paper will be in place for smooth reading. The following are

---

[2]*Toronto Globe and Mail*, July 23, 1993, p. A16. Johanne Mednick is a teacher who lives in Canada. She wrote this article in 1993.

three paragraphs that show the quoted, paraphrased, and summarized material from the Mednick article worked into the first draft so that it is absolutely clear what is the author's and what is Mednick's.

An Example of Incorporating Research Material

> Many people become nostalgic for the ways things were. Some people keep old cash registers at their businesses to remind customers of days gone by. Other people fire up wood stoves to help them remember earlier times. Johanna Mednick, a teacher in Canada, claims that many people still long for older, simpler machines and also for the way of life they represent (16).
>
> Mednick uses her old bicycle as an example. "Perhaps my bike is representative of a world gone by . . . ," she says. "My bike is certainly not built for speed . . . It's built for taking time. It makes people feel relaxed" (16).
>
> New computers and microwave ovens, by contrast, make people feel that life is getting too complicated and out of control (Mednick, 16).

Notice that in the first two paragraphs Mednick's name is used in the text to introduce the material that is attributed to her. Since it is clear from the context where her material begins and where it leaves off, it is only necessary to insert the page number of her article at the end of the borrowed material. In the third paragraph, Mednick's name is not included in the text and it is less clear whose idea this is. To make it absolutely clear to the reader that this is another idea of Mednick's, her last name along with the page number is placed at the end of the borrowed idea. The full information about this source and where it was first located will be placed on final bibliography pages at the end of the paper. The reader who wants to know when and where Mednick published her article can refer to those pages.

A Common Student Error

Avoid mixing your words with those of another author while neglecting to put the quoted words in quotation marks. Sometimes it is obvious to the reader where your words leave off and those of another author's begin since individual authors commonly differ in their style and voice. However, this creates a problem for the reader who cannot sort out your ideas from those of others. Example 1 shows what students often do without realizing they are mismanaging quoted material. Example 2 shows how to correct the problem. Read the first two paragraphs of the Mednick article first and then read Examples 1 and 2 below.

Example 1: The wrong way to incorporate research.

```
Low technology can be a high for many people. A wonderful bicycle that
most people would refer to as an old clunker might bring its owner con-
siderable pleasure. Its two large wheels, seats, handle bars, basket,
bell, and pedals help its owner glide past all of the riders on racers
and mountain bikes who are intent on engaging the right gear for the
occasion (Mednick, 16).
```

The problem with that paragraph is that the author has simply copied much of Mednick's original language without putting it in quotation marks to indicate which of it is her own and which has been supplied by the author. Example 2 shows the acceptable way of writing this same material. Notice how in this second example it is absolutely clear which of this paragraph belongs to Mednick and which belongs to the author.

Example 2: The right way to incorporate research.

```
"Low technology," according to Johanna Mednick, can be a "high" for
many people. She owns a "wonderful" bicycle that most people would call
an "old clunker." Still, it brings its owner considerable pleasure.
What she likes best about it are its "two large wheels, seat, handle
bars, basket, bell, and pedals," which help its owner pass up other
riders who are on more modern bikes (16).
```

Avoid Plagiarism

As you add quoted, paraphrased, and summarized material from other sources to your paper, you must indicate where your words leave off and someone else's begin, and you must also indicate the original source for all borrowed material. The next sections of this chapter will teach you how.

To simply use other people's ideas or words in your paper without acknowledging where they came from or to whom they belong is a form of academic theft called *plagiarism*. Although some students might think that they had not committed plagiarism in Example 1, above, because they quoted the source at the end of the paragraph, they actually have because they have used a considerable amount of Mednick's language verbatim without indicating that it is hers. Penalties for plagiarism can be severe and range from a failing grade to probation or suspension from college. Avoid plagiarism by differentiating between your ideas and those of others at all stages of the paper-writing process. In fact, you were advised to color code your note cards to keep your ideas separate from the direct quotes, paraphrases, and summaries that you draw from other people's works. If you use the color-coding method, you will be less likely to confuse your work with that of others.

Cite Your Sources

Some of the main features of source acknowledgment appear at the end of the Exercise section in this chapter. Use this material as a handy reference guide when you are working borrowed material into your paper and also when you are preparing the final list of the works you have used. These methods will inform your reader exactly what material in your paper is yours, what belongs to other people, and where you found the material in the first place. You will first be shown a number of examples of ways to incorporate borrowed material into the text of your paper and to use in-text citations (page numbers in parentheses) to show in brief form where it originally appeared. You will then be shown how to prepare entries for the list of sources that you have used. This list will appear at the end of your paper. Read through the types of sources that might appear on your list, beginning on page 332. They may suggest examples of resources for your paper that you have not thought of.

As you incorporate borrowed material from other sources, you will need to follow a system and a set of conventions that has been prescribed for this purpose. There are several such systems. The two that are taught at the end of this chapter are MLA style, which is recommended by the Modern Language Association for papers written in the humanities, and APA style, recommended by the American Psychological Association for papers written in the social sciences. Both give advice on how to acknowledge the work of other individuals in your paper and also how to give full information about these sources in a list of "Works Cited" (MLA) or "References" (APA) at the end of the paper. The Council of Biology Editors publishes the *CBE Manual*, now in a fifth edition, which shows how to document sources in scientific papers in such areas as the natural sciences, chemistry, geography, and geology. No matter which system you use, be consistent throughout your paper.

Additional examples of incorporating quoted, paraphrased, and summarized material along with lists of works cited and references appear in the two student argument papers that begin on page 338. Study the annotations in the margins of these papers. They demonstrate how quoted and summarized material can be incorporated into papers and acknowledged according to MLA style in the first paper and APA style in the second.

MAKE FINAL REVISIONS AND PREPARE THE FINAL COPY

There is considerable additional information in Chapter 4 that you can review to help you write and rewrite your paper. It may take several tries, but you will eventually get a version of your paper that you are content to show to other readers. Seek the help of your peer editing group, a tutor, your instructor, or other readers once again, when you have improved your paper as much as possible on your own. When you get to this point, you will think your paper is pretty good. Now is the time, however, to put aside your pride and let others take a final look at it. During this final revision process, you and your readers can use the Toulmin model to help you identify and revise the major elements in your paper.

1. Find your claim. Is it clear? Is it well positioned?
2. Check the quantity and quality of your support.
3. Check to see if your warrants are acceptable to your audience.
4. Decide if backing for your warrants would make them stronger.
5. Focus on your rebuttal, if you have one. Does it address all of the opposing arguments, and does it do so effectively?
6. Would it make your argument stronger to qualify your claim?

As you go through your paper these final times, make all the remaining changes, large and small. Write a title, if you haven't already. Rewrite parts by using better, different words; cut out anything that doesn't contribute to the meaning; add where necessary; rearrange if you have a good reason to do so; and make all final corrections. You will finally reach a point where you are satisfied and ready to quit. Now it is time to prepare the final copy.

Type your paper on $8\frac{1}{2} \times 11$ inch paper, and double space it. Leave one-inch margins all around. One inch from the top of the first page, by the left margin, type and double space your name, your instructor's name, the course number, and the date. Double space again and type the title. Skip four spaces and begin typing your paper. You do not need to number the first page. Number all other pages, however, at the top right-hand corner with your last name before the page number. Attach the "Works Cited" or "References" page(s). Your paper is now ready for submission.

WHAT STRATEGIES CAN YOU NOW ADD TO IMPROVE YOUR PROCESS FOR WRITING ARGUMENT?

1. **Think in terms of parts, order, and relationships** to help you organize ideas.
2. **Use the Toulmin model** to help you organize your paper and also to review and revise it.
3. **Use organizational patterns** to help you think about the ideas in your paper and also to organize them.
4. **Write some kind of an outline** to guide your writing and cross reference your research to it.
5. **Write the first draft quickly** to catch the flow of ideas. Include quoted and paraphrased material and in-text citations.
6. **Use transitions** to make your organization clear.
7. **Rewrite and revise** the first draft so that someone else can read it and make suggestions for improvement.
8. **Seek some outside opinion,** such as that provided in peer editing groups in class.
9. **Prepare the final copy** using MLA, APA, or another style with consistency throughout.

EXERCISES AND ACTIVITIES

1. SMALL GROUPS, INDIVIDUAL ONGOING PROJECT, ARGUMENT PAPER: PEER CRITIQUE OF OUTLINE

Make some sort of an outline or write a partial manuscript that will serve as a plan for your paper and bring it to class. Organize peer editing groups of three or four students. Explain to the group what your paper is about and how you plan to develop it. Get ideas from the others to help with drafting and possibly also with adding research.

2. WHOLE CLASS, INDIVIDUAL ONGOING PROJECT, ARGUMENT PAPER: CREATE A PEER CRITIQUE SHEET

The peer critique sheet is a worksheet that provides a guide for revision. Make a list on the board of all of the special requirements for a good argument paper: clear claim, acceptable warrants, etc. Select five to ten items from this list that you believe are essential elements to consider during revision. Organize them on a peer critique sheet. The peer editing groups can now use these sheets to critique individual student papers and make recommendations for revision.

3. SMALL GROUPS, INDIVIDUAL ONGOING PROJECT, ARGUMENT PAPER: PEER CRITIQUE OF DRAFT

Draft and revise your paper and bring it to class. In your group, read all of the papers either silently or aloud, and make observations and recommendations about each of them on the peer critique sheets you created in Exercise 2. Discuss each paper in turn, giving strengths, weaknesses, and recommendations for improvement. Give the filled-in peer critique sheets to the student authors for further guidance.

4. INDIVIDUAL ONGOING PROJECT, ARGUMENT PAPER: FINAL COPY

Make final revisions and prepare the final copy. Your paper should be five or six pages long, be double-spaced, and use approximately four or five outside sources. Use MLA format throughout unless advised to use APA or some other format. The two student papers on pp. 338–347 can be used as examples. The first demonstrates general format, in-text citations, and the "Works Cited" page required for MLA style. The second demonstrates similar requirements for APA style. Notice, also, that in both papers the ideas that control the papers are the authors' original ideas and opinions and that the quoted and paraphrased material provides support for their ideas.

5. INDIVIDUAL ONGOING PROJECT: ARGUMENT PAPER

Write a one-page Toulmin analysis of your paper and submit it with your paper.

6. INDIVIDUAL ONGOING PROJECT: ARGUMENT PAPER

Write a letter to your instructor and submit it with your final paper. Describe what you like about your paper and what still dissatisfies you. Identify problems or passages where you would like some opinion.

7. GROUP OR INDIVIDUAL SUMMARIES

Summarize the major ideas in this chapter by completing the following sentences:

a. Organization is important because it helps the reader . . .

b. To organize material, you need to divide it into parts, place these parts in an order, and . . .

c. Some examples of organizational patterns that you might use in a paper are . . .

d. The value of an outline to you is . . .

e. The value of peer editing sessions to you is . . .

f. Your first draft should be . . .

g. Some things to keep in mind when you revise are . . .

h. In-text citations and the final list of sources inform the reader . . .

HOW TO DOCUMENT SOURCES USING THE MLA AND APA STYLES

The following material will demonstrate how to use in-text citations and lists of works cited (MLA) or references (APA) to indicate where borrowed source material first appeared. For additional detail on how to use MLA style, consult *The MLA Handbook for Writers of Research Papers* (3rd ed., 1988), published by the Modern Language Association, and the *Publication Manual of the American Psychological Association* (3rd ed., 1983), published by the American Psychological Association.

How to Write In-Text Parenthetical Citations

Both the MLA and APA systems of documentation ask that you show where you originally found a direct quote, a paraphrase, or a summary by inserting a brief parenthetical citation at the end of the borrowed material in your written text. The MLA system requires that you provide the author and the page number: (Jones 13), and APA requires that you provide the author, the date of publication, and the page numbers, which are introduced by "p." or "pp.": (Jones, 1983, p. 5). If, however, you mention the name of the author in the text, you do not need to include the author's name in the parenthetical material. The following are examples.

1. **Direct quote with the author mentioned in the text.**

MLA: As Howard Rheingold describes his first trip into virtual reality, "My body wasn't in the computer world" (15–16).

APA: As Howard Rheingold (1991) describes his first trip into virtual reality, "My body wasn't in the computer world" (pp. 15–16).

2. **Direct quote with the author not mentioned in the text.**

MLA: Virtual reality changes perceptions radically. As one participant explains it, "My body wasn't in the computer world. I could see around me, but one of my hands had accompanied my point of view onto the vast electronic plain that seemed to surround me" (Rheingold 15–16).

APA: As one participant explains it, "My body wasn't in the computer world. I could see around me" (Rheingold, 1991, pp. 15–16).

3. **Paraphrase or summary with the author mentioned in the text.**

MLA: Howard Rheingold describes his first trip into virtual reality as one that involved his hand and arm but not his whole body (15–16).

APA: Howard Rheingold (1991) describes his first trip into virtual reality as one that involved his hand and arm but not his whole body (pp. 15–16).

4. **Paraphrase or summary with the author not mentioned the text.**

MLA: One's whole body is not always a part of the virtual reality experience. Sometimes only a hand and arm enter that reality (Rheingold 15–16).

APA: One's whole body is not always a part of the virtual reality experience. Sometimes only a hand and arm enter that reality (Rheingold, 1991, pp. 15–16).

5. **Two or more authors.** If two or three authors have written the material you have borrowed, include all of their names either in the introductory material or the citation.

MLA: "Virtual reality is all about illusion" (Pimentel and Teixeira 7).

APA: Pimentel and Teixeira (1993) remind us, "Virtual reality is all about illusion" (p. 7).

For more than three authors, use only the first author's name and add "et al." to the citation for MLA. For APA, list all of the authors' names for the first reference, but use the first name and et al. for subsequent references.

6. **Corporate author.** Sometimes written materials are attributed to a corporate rather than to an individual author. In this case, use the name of the corporation or group, preferably in the material that precedes the quote.

MLA: According to the <u>Notebook</u> published by the Network Project, "The quote" (7).

Or you can mention the corporate author at the end:

APA: "The quote" (Network Project, 1992, p. 7).

7. **Title only.** When no author is listed for either a book or an article, use the title or the first words of an abbreviated title in your citation.

MLA: Article: ("Creativity and Television" 14).
   Book: (<u>Nielsen Television</u> 17).

APA: Article: ("Creativity and Television," 1973, p. 14).
   Book: (<u>Nielsen television</u>, 1975, p. 17).

8. **Article in a book.** If you quote an article that appears in a book such as this one, use the name of the author of the article in your citation, not the author or editor of the book.

The following is one additional tip to help you work borrowed material into your paper:

Typing short and long quotations. Type short quotes (4 lines or less for MLA or 40 words or less for APA) right into your paper. Make them visually part of it by double spacing, running them out to the margins, and putting them in quotation marks. Longer quotes should be indented ten spaces (five for APA) from the left-hand margin and printed as a block. The parenthetical citations for long quotes appear right after the final period and are positioned in the same way for both the MLA and APA systems.

How to Write the List of "Works Cited" (MLA) or "References" (APA)

Attach to your draft a list of all of the works you have quoted or paraphrased in your paper. This list is entitled either "Works Cited" (MLA) or "References" (APA). Look also at the examples of the student papers beginning on page 338. The first of them follows MLA format, and the second follows APA. Include on your list only the works you have actually used in your paper. The easiest way to prepare this list is to alphabetize your bibliography cards according to the authors' last names or, if no author is listed, by the title of the work. Omit *a, an,* and *the* in alphabetizing. Type the bibliography by double spacing it throughout and by indenting the second line of each citation five spaces for MLA, or three spaces for APA.

Basic Format for Books and Articles

	MLA	*APA*
For a book:	Author, <u>Title of Book.</u> City: Publisher, date.	Author. (Date). <u>Title of book.</u> City: Publisher.
For an article:	Author. "Title of Article." <u>Name of Periodical</u> volume number (year of publication): page numbers.	Author. (Date). Title of article. <u>Name of Periodical,</u> p. or pp.

Note that MLA capitalizes all important nouns in a title, headline style, and that APA capitalizes only the first word in a title, sentence style. Also, for articles, MLA uses quotation marks and APA does not. The titles of magazines and journals, however, are written in headline style for both MLA and APA.

Here are some examples of the types of sources that are most commonly cited for argument papers. Examples of both MLA and APA styles are provided.

How to List Books

1. *Book by One Author*

MLA: Rheingold, Howard. Virtual Reality. New York: Simon & Schuster, 1991.

APA: Rheingold, H. (1991). Virtual reality. New York: Simon & Schuster.

2. *Book by Two or Three Authors*

MLA: Pimentel, Ken and Kevin Teixeira. Virtual Reality: Through the New Looking Glass. New York: McGraw Hill, 1993.

APA: Pimentel, K., & Teixeira, K. (1993). Virtual reality: Through the new looking glass. New York: McGraw Hill.

Use the same format to add a third author.

3. *Book by More Than Three Authors*

MLA: Comstock, George, et al. Television and Human Behavior. New York: Columbia UP, 1978.

APA: Comstock, G., Chaffee, S., Katzman N., McCombs, M., & Roberts, D. (1978). Television and human behavior. New York: Columbia University Press.

4. *How to List Two or More Books by the Same Author*

MLA: Rheingold, Howard. Tools for Thought. New York: Simon & Schuster, 1985.
    ---. Virtual Reality. New York: Simon & Schuster, 1991.

APA: Rheingold, H. (1985). Tools for thought. New York: Simon & Schuster.
    Rheingold, H. (1991). Virtual reality. New York: Simon & Schuster.

5. *Books by a Corporate Author*

MLA: VPL Research, Inc., Virtual Reality at Texpo '89. Redwood City, CA: VPL Research, Inc., 1989.

APA: VPL Research, Inc. (1989). Virtual reality at Texpo '89. Redwood City, CA: VPL Research, Inc.

6. *Book with No Author Named*

MLA: Virtual Reality Marketplace. Westport: Meckler, 1992.

APA: Virtual reality marketplace (1992). Westport: Meckler.

7. *Book Reprinted in a Later Edition*

MLA: Malthus, Thomas R. An Essay on the Principle of Population. 1798. London: William Pickering, 1986.

APA: Malthus, T. R. (1986). An essay on the principle of population. London: William Pickering. (Original work published in 1798).

8. *Translation*

MLA: Rousseau, Jean-Jacques. La Nouvelle Héloïse. 1761. Trans. Judith H. McDowell. University Park: Pennsylvania State UP, 1968.

APA: Rousseau, J.-J. (1968). La Nouvelle Héloïse. (J. H. McDowell, Trans.) University Park: Pennsylvania State University Press. (Original work published in 1761).

9. *Subsequent Editions*

MLA: Thompson, Warren S. Population problems. 4th ed. New York: McGraw Hill, 1953.

APA: Thompson, W. S. (1953). Population problems. (4th ed.). New York: McGraw Hill.

10. *Proceedings from Conference or Symposium*

MLA: McKerrow, Raymie E., ed. Argument and the Postmodern Challenge: Proceedings of the Eighth SCA/AFA Conference on Argumentation. 5–8 Aug 1993. Annandale, VA: Speech Communication Assn., 1993.

APA: McKerrow, R. E. (Ed.). (1993). Argument and the postmodern challenge: Proceedings of the eighth SCA/AFA conference on argumentation. Annandale, VA: Speech Communication Association.

11. *Introduction, Preface, Foreword, or Afterword*

MLA: Schneiderman, Ben. Foreword. Interacting with Virtual Environments, eds. Lindsay MacDonald and John Vince. Chichester, NY: J. Wiley, 1994.

APA: Schneiderman, B. (1994). Foreword. In L. MacDonald and J. Vince (Eds.), Interacting with virtual environments. Chichester, NY: Wiley.

12. *Government Documents*

MLA: United States. F.B.I. U.S. Dept. of Justice. Uniform Crime Reports for the United States. Washington: GPO, 1990.

APA: Federal Bureau of Investigation, U.S. Department of Justice (1990). Uniform crime reports for the United States. Washington, DC: U.S. Government Printing Office.

How to List Articles

13. *Article from a Periodical*

MLA: Monastersky, Richard. "The Deforestation Debate." Science News 10 July 1993:26–27.

APA: Monastersky, R. (1993, July 10). The deforestation debate. Science News, pp. 26–27.

14. Article from a Newspaper

MLA: Weinstein, Jack B., "The War on Drugs Is Self-Defeating." <u>New York Times</u> 8 July 1993: A11.

APA: Weinstein, J. B. (1993, July 8). The war on drugs is self-defeating. <u>New York Times</u>, p. A11.

15. Article with No Author Listed

MLA: "A Democratic Army." <u>The New Yorker</u> 28 June 1993: 4+.

For MLA, use a plus sign when the pages are interrupted with ads and other material in the magazine. For APA, list all pages on which the article is printed.

APA: A democratic army. (1993, June 28). <u>The New Yorker</u>, pp. 4, 6.

16. Article in a Journal with Continuous Pagination from January to December

MLA: Jasinski, James. "Rhetoric and Judgment in the Constitutional Ratification Debate of 1787–1788: An Exploration of the Relationship between Theory and Critical Practice." <u>Quarterly Journal of Speech</u> 78 (1992): 197–218.

APA: Jasinski, J. (1992). Rhetoric and judgment in the constitutional ratification debate of 1787–1788: An exploration of the relationship between theory and critical practice. <u>Quarterly Journal of Speech</u>, 78, 197–218.

17. Article in a Journal That Pages Each Issue Separately

MLA: Rosenbloom, Nancy J. "In Defense of the Moving Pictures: The People's Institute, The National Board of Censorship and the Problem of Leisure in Urban America." <u>American Studies</u> 33.2 (1992): 41–60.

APA: Rosenbloom, N. J. (1992). In defense of the moving pictures: The people's institute, the National Board of Censorship and the problem of leisure in urban America. <u>American Studies</u>, 33(2), 41–60.

18. Edited Collection of Articles or an Anthology

MLA: Forester, Tom, ed. <u>The Information Technology Revolution</u>. Cambridge, MA: MIT Press, 1985.

APA: Forester, T. (Ed.). (1985). <u>The information technology revolution</u>. Cambridge, MA: MIT Press.

19. Article in an Edited Collection or an Anthology

MLA: Boden, Margaret A. "The Social Impact of Thinking Machines." <u>The Information Technology Revolution</u>, ed. Tom Foster. Cambridge, MA: MIT Press, 1985. 95–103.

APA: Boden, M. A. (1985). The social impact of thinking machines. In T. Foster (Ed.), <u>The information technology revolution</u> (pp. 95–103). Cambridge, MA: MIT Press.

20. *Reprinted Article in an Edited Volume or Collection (like "The Reader" in this book)*

MLA: Brott, Armin A. "Not All Men Are Sly Foxes." *Newsweek* 1 June 1992: 14–15. Rpt. in Perspectives on Argument, ed. Nancy V. Wood. Englewood Cliffs, NJ: Prentice Hall.

APA: Brott, A. A. (1995). Not all men are sly foxes. In N. Wood (Ed.), Perspectives on argument (pp. 293–295). Englewood Cliffs, NJ: Prentice Hall.

21. *Signed Article in a Reference Work*

MLA: Davidson II, W. S. "Crime." Encyclopedia of Psychology, ed. Raymond J. Corsini. 4 vols. New York: Wiley, 1984.

APA: Davidson II, W. S. (1984). Crime. In R. J. Corsini (Ed.), Encyclopedia of psychology (pp. 310–312). New York: Wiley.

22. *Unsigned Article in a Reference Work*

MLA: "Anna Quindlen." Current Biography. Apr. 1993.

APA: Anna Quindlen (1993, April). In Current Biography.

23. *Review*

MLA: Watts, Steven. "Sinners in the Hands of an Angry Critic: Christopher Lasch's Struggle with Progressive America." Rev. of The Tru and Only Heaven: Progress and Its Critics, by Christopher Lasch. American Studies 33.2 (1992): 113–120.

APA: Watts, S. (1992). Sinners in the hands of an angry critic: Christopher Lasch's struggle with progressive America. [Review of The true and only heaven: progress and its critics]. American Studies, 33 (2), 113–120.

24. *Letter to the Editor*

MLA: McCaffrey, Mark. Letter. Utne Reader July/Aug. 1993: 10.

APA: McCaffrey, M. (1993, July/August). Letter to the editor. Utne Reader, p. 10.

25. *Editorial*

MLA: "A Touch of Class for the Court." Editorial. New York Times 25 July 1993: E16.

APA: A touch of class for the court. (1993, July 25). [Editorial.] New York Times, p. E16.

How to List Media: Film, Video, Computers, Television

26. *Article in an Electronic Journal*

MLA: Cadre, Adam. "And a Purple Dinosaur Shall Lead Them." Bad
Subjects: Political Education for Everyday Life. 12 (1994).
Electronic journal. Electronic mail address (Internet):
badsubjects-request@uclink.berkeley.edu.

APA: Cadre, A. (1994). And a purple dinosaur shall lead them. Bad subjects:
Political education for everyday life, 12. [Electronic journal].
Electronic mail address (Internet): badsubjects-request@uclink.berke-
ley.edu.

27. *ERIC Information Service*

MLA: Land, Warren A. and Elizabeth R. Land The Effect of Changing a
Professional Educational Program on National Teacher
Education Test Scores. ERIC ED 365 729.

APA: Land, W. A., & Land, E. R. The effect of changing a professional
educational program on national teacher education test scores.
(ERIC Document Reproduction Service No. ED 365 729).

28. *Videotapes*

MLA: Composition Videotape. Prod. ABC/Prentice Hall Video Library.
Prentice Hall, 1993.

APA: ABC/Prentice Hall Video Library (Producer). (1993). Composition
[Video]. Englewood Cliffs, NJ: Prentice Hall.

29. *Radio and Television Programs*

MLA: Resolved: Political Correctness Is a Menace and a Bore. Prod. and dir.
Warren Steibel. With William F. Buckley, Jr., Firing Line. PBS.
KDTN, Dallas. 2 December 1993.

APA: Steibel, W. (Producer and Director), Buckley, Jr., W. F. (Moderator).
(1993, December 2). Resolved: Political correctness is a menace and
a bore. [Television program]. Dallas: KDTN, PBS Firing Line.

30. *Computer Software*

MLA: The Home Reference Library. Computer Software. Ellis Enterprises
Inc., 1989. CD-ROM.

APA: The home reference library. [Computer software]. (1989). Ellis
Enterprises Inc. CD-ROM.

How to List Interviews and Speeches

31. *Published Interviews*

MLA: Hardin, Garrett. Interview. With Cathy Spencer. Omni June, 1992:
55–63.

APA: Hardin, G. (1992, June). [Personal interview with C. Spencer]. <u>Omni</u>, pp. 55–63.

32. *Personal Interview*

MLA: Wick, Audrey. Personal Interview. 27 May 1994.
APA: Wick, A. (1994, May 27). [Personal interview].

33. *Lectures, Speeches, Addresses*

MLA: Yeltsin, Boris. Address to the U.S. Congress. Washington, DC, June 18, 1992.
APA: Yeltsin, B. (1992, June 18). Address. Speech presented to the U.S. Congress. Washington, DC.

MLA STYLE

Tanya Pierce

Professor Snow

English 3102

February 1995

The Importance of Jury Instructions

The right to a trial by jury is a fundamental right guaranteed
by our United States Constitution. The Supreme Court has consistently protected this right and has extended it to all but the
most trivial of cases. However, our jury system is not without
flaws. On the contrary, many critics of the jury system argue
that juries are simply uneducated in the basic concepts of law
necessary to intelligently decide cases. Others claim that juries are too biased, and this taints the judicial process. These
criticisms are not totally unfounded in many cases. In spite of
its problems, however, the jury system is a valuable institution. It provides a buffer between our often harsh and inflexible legal system and the average citizen on trial. It is
critical to our democratic society. In fact, one conclusion of a
recent survey on jury service conducted by an association of defense trial lawyers is that "the more involvement people have in
the jury process, the more they seem to take to heart their responsibilities as citizens in our democratic society" (Robinson
62). Still because of recent mistakes made by juries and the
growing scrutiny of the decisions made by juries, it is necessary to improve our jury system.

Serving on a jury takes a great deal of time. Because jury
service does require one to spend a lot of time, many Americans
will do just about anything to get out of jury duty. In addition
many segments of the population are exempt from jury duty either

Margin annotations:

Author speaking: Summaries of different perspectives on issue drawn from exploratory paper.

Direct quote cited: Author of quote not mentioned in text.

Author speaking: Introduction to policy claim.

Problems: Time, exemptions.

by permissible judicial rule, by law, or by custom. Among the
occupational groups generally exempt in the vast majority of jurisdictions are professionals such as lawyers, licensed physi-

Summary cited.

cians and dentists, members of the armed forces, officers of all
three branches of government, police officers, fire fighters,
clergy, and teachers (Abraham 117). The average jury in America

Summary cited.

consists of housewives or househusbands, retirees, blue-collar
workers, and the unemployed. According to the survey quoted
above, only forty-five percent of all adult Americans have been
called for jury duty, and only seventeen percent have served
through an actual trial (Robinson 62). These people often are
not indispensable in their jobs and are not as limited by time
constraints as are the exempt groups. Critics of the jury system
argue that these juries are often not educated enough to handle

**Author speaking:
More problems:
Unprepared jurors.**

the responsibility of deciding important cases.

It is sad to say but in many cases the jurists are ignorant
of the legal issues surrounding a given case. In many instances
they do not understand the facts in the case, and they often do

**Supported by
specific example.**

not understand the consequences of their decisions. For example,
the jury in the recent Brosky hate crime case thought that it
was sentencing Brosky to five years in jail plus ten years probation. It is an either-or situation. Because of this lack of
understanding by the jury and the ineffective instructions given
by the judge and attorneys involved in the case, a grave and irreversible injustice was done. Brosky was only given ten years
probation for the murder of another human being. This is just
one of numerous cases where the jury's lack of knowledge has led
to disastrous decisions.

Something clearly needs to be done to educate these jurors.

**Transition: Current
solutions and their
problems.**

Current practice requires the judge to give instructions, called
a charge, to the jury before it begins deliberations. According
to Henry Abraham, who has written extensively on the judicial
process, "Much thought goes--or should go--into this charge,

Direct quote cited. Author in text.

which is intended as an exposition of the law and is delivered orally in most, although not all, cases" (131).

One of the problems with the judge's charge, however, is that most states do not permit the jury to take either a copy or a tape recording of it with them when they leave the courtroom

Summary cited. Author in text.

to make their deliberations. Seymour Wishman, a criminal lawyer who has tried hundreds of cases before juries, quotes one judge who supports the idea of allowing jurors to take written or audiotaped instructions with them. According to this judge, we expect people to listen to instructions once and remember them well enough to make "monumental decisions" (224).

Transition.

The judge's instructions are not only difficult to remember; they are also sometimes difficult for the jury to understand. Wishman goes on to claim, "Jury instructions are often incompre

Direct quotes cited. Authors in text.

hensible because they are drafted by lawyers and judges who do not realize how much of their 'legalese' vocabulary and syntax was acquired in law school. . . . little effort is made to write clear and simple language for those not legally trained" (224). Abraham, agreeing that there can be significant problems with the judge's charge, says, "Many a charge has, ultimately, been instrumental in causing a mistrial; many another has been found to be defective on points of law by appellate courts" (131).

Transition.

Obviously the educational process for jurors needs to be improved, and judges and lawyers need to become active participants in this educational process. They need to take the respon

Author speaking.

sibility for informing jurors about the relevant legal issues in each case. They must educate jurors on the rules of law applica

Solution: Establish new policy.

ble to the cases at hand and in language they can understand. Some may argue that this system may be abused by lawyers who want to bias a jury in their favor. This is, of course, possible. But one must realize that juries are inherently biased.

Refutation of those who may disagree.

Each jurist walks in with his or her own distinct set of values and beliefs. The lawyers are always trying to influence them to

Author speaking.

see their side. I would argue, however, that it is better to risk the possibility of some additional bias in order for the juries to be better informed. It is more desirable to have a knowledgeable jury, even at the risk of some bias, rather than to have a jury that is totally in the dark about the legal issues surrounding a particular case.

Support for solution.

Some research suggests that juries should be given lessons in the law before the trial begins and also at various points during the trial. Psychological studies have consistently shown that early exposure and frequent exposure to legal principles correlate with juries that are more likely to presume innocence in a case until sufficient evidence is provided to decide otherwise.

Summary cited.

Experimental mock juries questioned midway through testimony showed a significantly higher indecision rate when they had been informed about the legal issues involved before the start of testimony than those who had not been instructed earlier (Heuer and Penrod 429). This suggests that juries instructed prior to the presentation of evidence are more likely to consider all of the evidence of a case before arriving at a decision of guilt or innocence.

Although some may interpret this psychological data as suggesting that informing juries early and frequently would delay the judicial process, I believe the opposite is true.

Author speaking: More refutation and benefits of solution.

Instructing juries on the basic legal concepts will help them be more open-minded. They will have more intelligent discussions during deliberations because they will know what issues to concentrate on. Psychological tests have also demonstrated that juries who are informed on legal concepts frequently are less

Summary cited.

likely to result in a hung jury (Goldberg 456). This latter finding is especially valuable since so much government money in the form of our tax dollars is wasted when juries are unable to arrive at a unanimous decision.

**Author speaking:
Summary of
perspective in
paper.**

**Policy claim in
last sentence.**

The right to be judged by a group of one's peers is a right most Americans value highly. It helps insure that all citizens will be given a fair chance in our legal system. It is valuable because it allows the American public to play an active role in our judicial process. However, like all institutions our jury system is not without its flaws. It is important for us to recognize the shortcomings in this process and try to improve it. A positive start towards improving the jury system would be for judges and lawyers to take a more active role in educating jurors at several crucial points during the course of a trial.[3]

Works Cited

Abraham, Henry J. The Judicial Process: An Introductory Analysis of the Courts of the United States, England, and France, 5th ed. New York: Oxford University Press, 1986.

Goldberg, Janice C. "Memory, Magic, and Myth: The Timing of Jury Instructions." Oregon Law Review 59 (1981): 451-475.

Heuer, Larry and Steven Penrod. "A Field Experiment with Written and Preliminary Instructions." Law and Human Behavior 13 (1989): 409-430.

Robinson, Archie S. "We the Jury: Who Serves, Who Doesn't." USA Today: The Magazine of the American Scene 120 (Jan. 1992): 62-63.

Wishman, Seymour. Anatomy of a Jury: The System on Trial. New York: Times Book, 1986.

---

[3]Used by permission.

APA STYLE

Darrell D. Greer

Professor Snow

English 1302

February 1995

Alaskan Wolf Management

Introduction and background of problem. Quotes from authorities and statistics to establish extent of problem.

In the past few years Alaska has been witnessing a decline in the populations of caribou and moose in the Fortymile, Delta, and Nelchina Basin areas. This decline in the caribou and moose populations is due mainly to the uprising of the wolf populations in these three areas. Robert Stephenson of the Alaska Department of Fish and Game claims, "Wolf packs will kill one caribou every two days or so, and one moose every three to ten days" (Keszler, 1993, p. 65). The Delta caribou herd alone declined from about eleven thousand in 1989 to less than four thousand this spring ("Alaska Wolf," 1993, p. 6). With statistics like these the caribou and moose population in Alaska is clearly a problem that needs immediate attention.

Quotations worked into text that suggest the unique character of the problem in Alaska.

This rapid decline in caribou and moose populations is devastating to the state. Not only are they a valuable resource for Alaska in terms of nonresident hunting and tourist sight-seeing, but for many remote residents, caribou and moose are their main source of food. The way of life for many Alaskans is one that the average American cannot vaguely understand. Max Peterson, the executive director of the International Association of Wildlife Agencies, says that in Alaska, "People interact as another predator in the ecosystem," and, as a result, "the interest in Alaska by people outside Alaska certainly is greater than their knowledge of Alaska" (Keszler, 1993, p. 67). Ted Williams

(1993) clarifies the lifestyle that many rural Alaskans lead:

A long quotation of more than 40 words is indented and written in block form. No quotation marks are necessary for indented quotes. The source is indicated at the end. Note that the author is mentioned in the text.

> Genuine subsistence is the most environmentally benign of all possible lifestyles. Subsisters do not--indeed cannot--deplete fish and wildlife because if they do, they will subsist no more. But even in the remotest native villages, Alaska as trackless wilderness where people blend with nature is just an old dream. Many villagers are now on social welfare programs and are therefore cash dependent. (p. 49)

Failing to protect existing caribou and moose populations could lower the subsistence level for some Alaskans, even more than it is at present.

The biologists of the state of Alaska believe that wolf populations are nowhere close to being endangered. They estimate the total wolf population in Alaska to be between 5,900 and 7,200. In the three areas up for wildlife management (about 3.5 percent of the state), Rodney Boertje, an Alaskan Department of Fish and Game wildlife biologist, says, "Wolf populations can sustain harvest rates of twenty-five to forty percent. So sixty to eighty-five percent of wolves must be removed for control efforts to be effective" (Keszler, 1993, p. 66). This amount totals between three hundred and four hundred wolves in these three areas. Wildlife management experts believe the most humane and efficient way of accomplishing this task is through aerial shootings of wolves.

Statistics and quotations from authorities to strengthen the solution preferred by this author.

Refutation of the animal rights groups and their solutions to the problem.

With the announcement of the wolf management plan proposed by Alaska Governor Walter Hickel and the Alaska Department of Fish and Game involving aerial shootings of wolves, the animal rights groups started an all-out war with the state. They organized widespread mailings to the governor and threatened massive boycotts of tourism in Alaska if the plan was not repealed (Keszler, 1993, p. 65). The animal rights groups believe that other methods of management could increase caribou and moose populations. One such method is reducing bag limits, shortening hunting seasons, or totally eliminating hunting in these three areas. This type of management will not be effective in this situation, however, since hunters are not the real cause of the problem. Pete Buist, a Fairbanks, Alaska, resident, says, "In control areas, hunters are taking less than five percent of the annual production of meat animals. Predators are taking more than seventy-five percent" (1993, p. 12). Animal rights groups commonly point to hunters as the culprits in animal conservation efforts. According to Arms (1994), however, "Nowadays in developed countries, groups representing hunting and fishing interests are the most active conservationists. They understand that their sport and, sometimes, their livelihood depend on sustained or increasing populations of the organisms they hunt or fish" (p. 347). As mentioned earlier, rural Alaskans who depend on caribou and moose for subsistence are some of these hunters who continue to take these animals but not in dangerously large numbers.

Another alternative management method that has been brought up by the animal rights groups is tranquilizing and capturing the wolves and chemically sterilizing them or using some other sort of contraception. This method has not been scientifically proven to work. Even if it did work, this method would take entirely too long to be effective for this situation. Contraception only deals with the wolf numbers down the road, and not with existing numbers, which would remain the same for now. Existing wolves in the immediate future may devastate the caribou and moose populations so drastically that they will not be able to recover.

In the United States Constitution the management of fish and wildlife is left up to the individual states. When Alaska made the professional decision that the best way to control their wolf population was by aerial shootings, the animal rights

Evaluation and refutation of other solutions.

groups picked only that part of a larger plan to attack. In media reports activists "portrayed the plan simply as a mass extermination of wolves designed to increase game numbers for out-of-state hunters and wildlife watchers" (Keszler, 1993, p. 39). They showed through commercials "visions of helicopter gunships slaughtering wolves by the hundreds" (Keszler, 1993, p. 39) when, in fact, the aerial shooting of wolves is just one small part of the plan. The animal rights groups did not focus on the parts of the plan that dealt with the restrictions to help the wolves in other areas. In Denali National Park and Preserve, Alaskan conservationists plan to do away with all hunting and trapping to give the wolves a sanctuary with no outside pressure (Keszler, 1993, p. 65). Other laws and bans on hunting and trapping to protect wolves would take place in areas around Anchorage and Fairbanks. The practice of land-and-shoot hunting (a practice used by many trappers to locate game by helicopter, land the helicopter, and start hunting) would be banned statewide (Keszler, 1993, p. 65). But none of these efforts to protect the wolf population were even discussed by the animal rights activists.

Establishment of ethos of conservationists in Alaska to make their plan acceptable.

The professional wildlife biologists at the Alaska Department of Fish and Game have taken a lot of heat from the animal rights media reports on their decision to go ahead with the original plan to manage wolf populations through aerial shooting and other methods not mentioned by the media. The biologists of the state of Alaska have devoted their lives to the preservation of wildlife. They know Alaska and Alaska's wildlife

Claim in last sentence. Author has identified a problem, evaluated several solutions, and arrived at this solution as the best possible. This is a value argument because it claims one of several considered solutions is the best.

better than anyone else. After researching and trying other methods, they believe the best solution to their problem is through aerial shooting. Their main concern is to protect the wildlife population as a whole, and not just to wage a "war on wolves." While the animal rightists are sitting around in their offices wondering which animals to save, the biologists at

Problem solution and policy are also strong features in this argument.

Alaska's Department of Fish and Game are in the field research-ing the range conditions and overall population conditions to better manage the wildlife community as a whole. As inhumane and immoral as it might seem, the aerial shooting of wolves is still the best solution for game management in this situation.[4]

References

Alaska wolf update. (1993, August). <u>American Hunter</u>, p. 6.

Arms, K. (1994). <u>Environmental science</u> (2nd ed.). Fort Worth, TX: Harcourt Brace.

Buist, P. (1993, September). Letter to the editor. <u>American Hunter</u>, p. 12.

Keszler, E. (1993, May). Wolves and big game: Searching for balance in Alaska. <u>American Hunter</u>, pp. 38-39, 65-67.

Williams, T. (1993, May/June). Alaska's war on the wolves. <u>Audubon</u>, pp. 44-47, 49-50.

---

[4]Used by permission.

SYNTHESIS OF CHAPTERS 1–10: SUMMARY CHARTS

TRACE

The Rhetorical Situation

For You as the Reader

Text. What kind of text is it? What are its qualities and features?

Reader. Are you one of the readers the writer anticipated? Do you share common ground with the author and other audience members? Are you open to change?

Author. Who is the author? How is the author influenced by background, experience, education, affiliations, values? What is the author's motivation to write?

Constraints. What beliefs, attitudes, habits, affiliations, or traditions will influence the way you and the author view the argument?

Exigence. What caused the argument, and do you perceive it as a defect or problem?

For the Targeted Reader at the Time It Was Written

Text. What kind of text is it? Is it unique to its time?

Reader. What was the nature of the targeted readers? Were they convinced? How are they different from other or modern readers?

Author. Who is the author? What influenced the author? Why was the author motivated to write?

Constraints. What beliefs, attitudes, habits, affiliations, or traditions influenced the author's and the readers' views in this argument?

Exigence. What happened to cause the argument? Why was it a problem? Has it recurred?

For You as the Writer

Text. What is your argumentative strategy? What is your purpose and perspective? How will you make your paper convincing?

Reader. Who are your readers? Where do they stand on the issue? How can you establish common ground? Can they change?

Constraints. How are your training, background, affiliations, and values either in harmony or conflict with your audience? Will they drive you apart or help build common ground?

Exigence. What happened? What is motivating you to write on this issue? Why is it compelling to you?

THE PROCESS

(Be selective and flexible in using the strategies, and remember there is no best order. You will backtrack and repeat.)

When You Are the Reader

Prereading Strategies
- Read the title and first paragraph. Ask, "What is at issue?"
- Background the issue. Free-associate and write words and phrases that the issue brings to mind.
- Evaluate your background. Do you know enough? If not, read or discuss to get background. Look up a key word or two.
- Jot down your present position.
- Survey the material. Locate the claim and some of the subclaims; notice how they are organized.
- Analyze and make some guesses about the rhetorical situation.
- Predict and jot down two or three ideas you think the author may discuss.
- Write one big question you would like answered.

Reading Strategies
- Anticipate and read the information in the introduction, body, and conclusion.
- Identify claim, subclaims, and support, and underline selectively. Box the transitions to highlight relationships between ideas and changes of subject.
- Annotate the ideas that seem important.
- Abstract the organizational scheme in your mind. Continue to analyze the rhetorical situation.
- Circle key words that represent major concepts and jot down meanings if necessary.
- Monitor your comprehension with brief summaries and notes.
- Check the accuracy of your predictions and change any that are wrong.

Postreading Strategies
- Write a summary or make a map of the ideas.

When You Are the Writer

Prewriting Strategies
- Get organized to write: gather materials, create motivation to write.
- Break the assignment into parts and find time.
- Identify an issue, read to get basic information, and apply the 12 tests.
- Analyze the rhetorical situation.
- Write what you already know and think about the issue.
- Read for the different perspectives on the issue.
- Think of a new perspective or approach.
- Take a position, write a claim, and begin to list reasons. Decide which words to define.
- Decide on your argumentative purpose.
- Write a guide to research: a list of ideas and what you need to find and read.
- Read and take notes.
- Use the Toulmin model, rhetorical situation, list of proofs to invent ideas and support.
- Use reading strategies to help you plan structure, read, and revise.
- Use critical thinking strategies: associate, apply, elaborate, think of examples.
- Make an expanded list or outline to guide your writing.

Writing Strategies
- Write a first draft.
- Read more and take more notes if necessary.
- Rearrange or cut down the outline if necessary.
- Freewrite if you get blocked; or read more and then freewrite.
- Do not aim for perfection on the first draft.

Postwriting Strategies
- Read your draft critically.

continued

THE PROCESS *(continued)*

When You Are the Reader

- Reflect and write an answer to your big questions.
- Write out all original ideas inspired by your reading.
- Write a comparison of the author's position with your own.
- Compare your present position with your initial position.
- Evaluate the argument to decide whether it is convincing.
- Decide what value this material has for you and how you will use it.
- Judge whether the argument is moral or immoral by your standards.

When You Are the Writer

- Evaluate your paper to see if it meets the criteria of a good argument paper.
- Apply the Toulmin model.
- Reorganize, cross out, rewrite, and make additions.
- Read it aloud and make further changes.
- Write a title.
- Check it for final mechanical and spelling errors; type or print it on a word processor.

THE TOULMIN MODEL

When You Are the Reader

1. *What is the claim?* What is this author trying to prove? Look for the claim at the beginning or at the end, or infer it.
2. *What is the support?* What information does the author use to convince you of the claim? Look for reasons, explanations, facts, opinions, personal narratives, and examples.
3. *What are the warrants?* What assumptions, general principles, values, beliefs, and appeals to human motives are implicit in the argument? Where is the author coming from? Does the support develop the claim? Are the warrants stated, or must they be inferred?
4. *Is backing supplied for the warrants?* See if additional support is provided to make the warrants more acceptable to the reader.
5. *Is there a rebuttal?* Are other perspectives on the issue stated in the argument? Are they refuted? Are counterarguments given?
6. *Has the claim been qualified?* Look for qualifying words like *sometimes, most, probably, possibly*. Decide what is probably the best position to take on the issue, for now.

When You Are the Writer

1. *What is my claim?* Decide on the type of claim and the subclaims. Decide where to put the claim in your paper.
2. *What support will I use?* Invent reasons, opinions, and examples. Research and quote authorities and facts.
3. *What are my warrants?* Write out the warrants. Do they strengthen the argument by linking the support to the claim? Do you believe them yourself? Will the audience share them or reject them?
4. *What backing for the warrants should I provide?* Add polls, studies, reports, expert opinion, or facts to make your warrants convincing.
5. *How should I handle rebuttal?* Include other perspectives and point out what is wrong with them. Make counterarguments.
6. *Will I need to qualify my claim?* Decide if you can strengthen your claim by adding qualifying words like *usually, often, probably*.

TYPES OF PROOF AND TESTS OF VALIDITY

Logical Proofs (7)

(Rearrange the logical proofs to form the mnemonic SICDADS: sign, induction, cause, deduction, analogies, definition, statistics.)

When You Are the Reader		When You Are the Writer
Locate or infer the general principle (warrant).	I. **Deduction.** Applying a general principle (warrant) to an example or a case and drawing a conclusion.	Make a general statement.
Apply it to the example or case.	*Example:*	Apply it to an example or a case.
Draw a conclusion/claim.		Draw a conclusion.
	Warrant: Most uneven footprints are left by people with limps.	Decide whether to make the general statement (warrant) explicit or implicit.
	Support: These footprints are uneven.	
	Claim: The person who left these footprints walks with a limp.	
	Test of Validity. Ask if the general principle (warrant) and the support are probably true, because then the claim is also probably true.	
Look for definitions of key words or concepts.	II. **Definition.** Describing the fundamental properties and qualities of a term or placing an item in a category and proving it "by definition."	Isolate the key terms and concepts, especially those in your claim.
They can be short, a word or sentence, or long, several paragraphs or an entire essay.	*Example:*	Define all terms that you and your reader must agree on for the argument to work.
Notice if the reader is supposed to accept the claim "by definition" because it has been placed in an established category.	Warrant: Family values characterize the good citizen.	Place some ideas or items in established categories and argue that they are so "by definition."
	Support: Radical feminists lack family values.	
	Claim: Radical feminists are not good citizens.	

continued

353

TYPES OF PROOF AND TESTS OF VALIDITY (*continued*)

When You Are the Reader	When You Are the Writer
	Tests of Validity. Ask if the definition is accurate and reliable, or if there are exceptions or other definitions that would make it less reliable. Ask if the item belongs in the category in which it has been placed.	
Look for examples, trends, people, events that are cited as causes for the claim.	III. ***Cause.*** Placing the claim in a cause-effect relationship to show that it is either the cause of an effect or an effect of a cause.	Make a claim and ask what caused it. Apply Burke's pentad to focus the main cause:
Look for effects of the claim.	*Example:*	What was done?
	Claim: Children read better in school when their parents read to them at home.	Where was it done? Who did it? How did he/she do it?
	Support: There are specific examples of parents reading to children who then read well at school.	Why did it happen?
	Warrant: The parents' reading caused the children to do better.	
	Tests of Validity. Ask if these causes alone are sufficient to create these effects or could these effects result from other causes. Try to think of exceptions to the cause-effect outcome.	
Look for clues, symptoms, occurrences that are explained as signs or symptoms that something is so.	IV. ***Sign.*** Pointing out the symptoms or signs that something is so.	Think of symptoms or signs that you can use to demonstrate that something is so.
	Example:	
	Claim: The child has chicken pox.	
	Support: The child had spots.	
	Warrant: Those spots are a sign of chicken pox.	
	Test of Validity. Ask if this is really a sign of what the author claims, or if there is another explanation.	

continued

TYPES OF PROOF AND TESTS OF VALIDITY (continued)

When You Are the Reader		When You Are the Writer
Look for a conclusion/claim based on examples or cases.	**V. *Induction*.** Drawing a conclusion (claim) from a number of representative cases or examples. *Example:* Claim: Everyone liked that movie. Support: I know three people who liked it. Warrant: Three examples are enough. **Tests of Validity.** Ask if there are enough examples, or if this is a "hasty" conclusion/claim? Try to think of an exception that would change the conclusion/claim. See if you can make the "inductive leap" from the examples to the conclusion/claim and accept it as probably true.	Give some examples and draw a conclusion/claim based on them; *or* make the claim and back it up with a series of examples.
Look for numbers, data, tables of figures along with interpretations of them.	**VI. *Statistics*.** Using figures or data to prove a claim. *Example:* Claim: We should end draft registration. Support: It costs 27.5 million dollars per year. Warrant: This is too much; it proves we should end it. **Tests of Validity.** Ask where the statistics came from, to what dates they apply, and if they are fair and accurate. Ask if they have been exaggerated or skewed. Ask if they prove what they are supposed to prove.	Find data, statistics, and tables of figures to use as evidence to back up your claim. Make clear where you get the statistics, and add interpretations of experts.

355

TYPES OF PROOF AND TESTS OF VALIDITY *(continued)*

When You Are the Reader

Literal and historical analogy:
Look for items, events, people, or periods of time that are being compared.

VII. **Analogies: *literal, historical, and figurative.*** Interpreting what we do not understand by comparing it with something we do. Literal and historical analogies compare similar items, and figurative analogies compare items from radically different categories.

Example of historical analogy:

Claim: Many people will die of AIDS.

Support: Many people died of the black death.

Warrant: AIDS and the black death are similar.

Example of literal analogy:

Claim: The state should spend more money on education.

Support: Another state spent more money with good results.

Warrant: The two states are similar, and the results of one will be the results of the other.

Example of figurative analogy:

Claim: Reading a difficult book should take time.

Support: Digesting a large meal takes time.

Warrant: Reading and eating are sufficiently alike that they can be compared.

When You Are the Writer

Literal and historical analogy:
Think of items in the same category that can be compared. Show that what happened in one case will also happen in the other. Or demonstrate that history repeats itself.

continued

TYPES OF PROOF AND TESTS OF VALIDITY (continued)

When You Are the Reader		When You Are the Writer
Figurative analogy: Look for extended metaphors or items compared that are from totally different categories.	*Figurative analogy:* Look for extended metaphors or items compared that are from totally different categories. **Tests of Validity.** For literal analogies, ask if the cases are so similar that the results of one will be the results of the other. For historical analogies, ask if history will repeat itself. For figurative analogies, ask if the qualities of the items being compared are real enough to provide logical support, or if they are so dissimilar that they do not prove anything.	*Figurative analogy:* Think of comparisons with items from other categories. Try to compare items that have similar qualities, characteristics, or outcomes.

Ethical Proof (1)

When You Are the Reader		When You Are the Writer
Look for references to the author's credentials, background, and training. Look for credential statements about quoted authorities.	I. *Authority.* Quoting established authorities or experts or establishing one's own authority and credibility. *Example:* Claim: California will have an earthquake. Support: Professors and scientists say so. Warrant: These experts are reliable. **Test of Validity.** Ask if the experts, including both outside authorities and the author, are really experts. Remember that argument from authority is only as good as the authorities themselves.	Refer to your own experience and background to establish expertise. Quote the best and most reliable authorities. Establish common ground and respect by using appropriate language and tone.

Emotional Proofs (2)

When You Are the Reader		When You Are the Writer
Look for references to items or qualities you might need or want and advice on how to get them. Look for emotional language, description, and tone.	I. *Motives.* Appealing to what all audiences are supposed to need, such as food, drink, warmth and shelter, sex, security, belongingness, self-esteem, creativity, and self-expression. Urging audiences to take steps to meet their needs.	Think about what your audience needs, and show how your ideas will help them. Use emotional language and tone where appropriate.

continued

357

TYPES OF PROOF AND TESTS OF VALIDITY (continued)

When You Are the Reader	When You Are the Writer
	Example:
	Claim: You should support this candidate.
	Support: The candidate can help you get job security and safe neighborhoods.
	Warrant: You want job security and safe neighborhoods.
	Tests of Validity. Ask if you really need what the author assumes you need. Ask if doing what is recommended will satisfy the need as described.
Look for value statements generally accepted by most people. Look for examples or narratives that display values. Infer values (warrants) that are not explicitly stated. Look for emotional language and tone.	II. *Values.* Appealing to what all audiences are supposed to value, such as reliability, honesty, loyalty, industry, patriotism, courage, integrity, conviction, faithfulness, dependability, creativity, freedom, equality, devotion to duty, and acceptance by others.
	Example:
	Claim: The curriculum should be multicultural.
	Support: A multicultural curriculum will contribute to equality and acceptance.
	Warrant: You value equality and acceptance.
	Tests of Validity. Ask if you share the author's values. Ask about the effect that differences in values will have on the argument.
	Appeal to your audience's values through warrants, explicit value statements, and narratives or illustrate values. Use emotional language and tone where appropriate.

TYPES OF CLAIMS (5)

I. *Claims of fact.* What happened? Is it true? Does it exist? Is it a fact?
Examples:

> Increasing population threatens the environment.
> Television content promotes violence.
> Women are not as effective as men in combat.

Readers	Writers
• Look for claims that state facts. • Look for facts, statistics, real examples, quotes from reliable authorities. • Anticipate induction, analogies, and signs. • Look for chronological or topical organization or a claim plus reasons.	• State the claim as a fact even though it is controversial. • Use factual evidence and expert opinion. • Use induction, historical and literal analogies, and signs. • Consider arranging your material as a claim with reasons.

II. *Claims of definition.* What is it? What is it like? How should it be classified? How should it be interpreted? How does its usual meaning change in a particular context?
Examples:

> We need to define what constitutes a family before we discuss family values.
> A definition will demonstrate that the riots were an instance of civil disobedience.

Readers	Writers
• Look for a claim that contains or is followed by a definition. • Look for reliable authorities and sources for definitions. • Look for comparisons and examples. • Look for comparison-and-contrast, topical, or deductive organization.	• State your claim and define the key term/terms. • Quote authorities, or go to dictionaries, encyclopedias, or other reliable sources for definitions. • If you are comparing to help define, use comparison-contrast and organization. • Use deductive organization.

III. *Claims of cause.* What caused it? Where did it come from? Why did it happen? What are the effects? What probably will be the results on a short-term and long-term basis?
Examples:

> Clear-cutting is the main cause of the destruction of ancient forests.
> Censorship can result in limits on freedom of speech.
> The American people's current mood has been caused by a faltering economy.

Readers	Writers
• Look for a claim that states or implies cause or effect.	• Make a claim that states or implies cause or effect.

continued

TYPES OF CLAIMS (5)   *(continued)*

Readers	Writers
• Look for facts and statistics, comparisons, such as historical analogies, signs, induction, deduction, and causal arguments. • Look for cause-effect or effect-cause organization.	• Use facts and statistics. • Apply Burke's pentad to focus the main cause. • Use historical analogies, signs, induction, deduction. • Consider using cause-effect or effect-cause organization.

IV. *Claims of value.* Is it good or bad? How good? How bad? Of what worth is it? Is it moral or immoral? Who thinks so? What do those people value? What values or criteria should I use to determine its goodness or badness? Are my values different from other people's or the author's?

Examples:

Computers are a valuable addition to modern education.

School prayer has a moral function in the public schools.

Mercy killing is immoral.

Readers	Writers
• Look for claims that make a value statement. • Look for value proofs, motivational proofs, analogies, both literal and figurative, quotes from authorities, signs, and definitions. • Expect emotional language. • Look for applied-criteria, topical, or narrative patterns of organization.	• State your claim as a judgment or value statement. • Analyze your audience's needs and values, and appeal to them. • Use literal and figurative analogies, quotes from authorities, signs, and definitions. • Use emotional language appropriately. • Consider the applied-criteria, claim-and-reasons, or narrative organizational patterns.

V. *Claims of policy.* What should we do? How should we act? What should future policy be? How can we solve this problem? What course of action should we pursue?

Examples:

The criminal should be sent to prison rather than to a mental hospital.

Sex education should be part of the public school curriculum.

Battered women who take revenge should not be placed in jail.

Readers	Writers
• Look for claims that state that something should be done. • Look for data, motivational appeals, literal analogies, and argument from authority. • Anticipate the problem-solution pattern of organization.	• State the claim as something that should be done. • Use data, motivational appeals, analogies, and authorities as proof. • Use emotional language appropriately. • Consider the problem-solution pattern of organization.

PART FOUR
The Reader

Introduction to "The Reader": Reading and Writing About Issue Areas

"T he Reader" contains eight sections. The first seven introduce you to the broad issue areas of men's and women's roles, education, crime and the treatment of criminals, freedom of speech, the environment, racism in America, and modern technology. Articles are then organized under specific related issues in each broad category. Section VIII provides you with the opportunity to organize class debates and attempt to establish common ground on an inflammatory issue about the value of life. It also invites you to organize a class symposium and practice academic inquiry on an issue of your choice. "The Reader" contains both classical and contemporary essays. These explore some of the individual perspectives and positions people have taken in regard to issues both now and in the past. You may quickly bring them up to date by reading what is being written about them now as you read this book.

THE PURPOSE OF "THE READER"

"The Reader" serves three main purposes:

1. It introduces you to big issue areas and a few of their specific related issues. It also helps you build background and provides you with information to quote in your papers.
2. It provides you with models of different types of arguments and thus gives you a better idea of how argument works in general. It provides you with examples and strategies for improving your own written arguments.
3. It helps you think and invent arguments and ideas of your own by providing you with essays that function as springboards for your own thoughts and reactions.

HOW TO USE "THE READER"

See chapters for details or review.

1. Select an issue area that is compelling for you. Background it. Anticipate ways to build common ground with those who oppose you. (Chapters 1 and 2)
2. Survey it: Read the titles and summaries of the articles in the table of contents; read the introductory material and "The Rhetorical Situation" at the beginning of the issue area; read the introductions to the articles. (Chapter 3)
3. Select the related issue area that interests you the most. (Chapters 1 and 3)
4. Read the articles in the related issue area and jot down the claim and some of the major support and warrants for each. (Chapter 3)
5. Make a map or write a list of all of the smaller related issues that you can think of that are related to the issue you have read about. (Chapter 3)
6. Select an issue to write about. Narrow and focus it. (Chapter 8)
7. Write an exploratory paper in which you explain the perspectives presented by the articles in "The Reader." You may also want to do outside research. Explain at least three perspectives on your issue. (Chapter 4)
8. Take a position on the issue, and phrase it as a question. Apply the 12 tests on page 33 to make certain you have an arguable issue. (Chapter 1)
9. State your claim, clarify your purpose, plan, and write a single-perspective argument paper. (Chapters 8, 9, and 10)

QUESTIONS TO HELP YOU READ CRITICALLY AND ANALYTICALLY

1. What is at issue?
2. What is the claim? What type of claim is it?
3. What is the support?
4. What are the warrants?
5. What are the weaknesses in the argument, and how can I refute them?
6. What are some other perspectives on the issue?
7. Where do I stand now?

QUESTIONS TO HELP YOU READ CREATIVELY AND MOVE FROM READING TO WRITING

1. What is my exigence for writing about this topic?
2. What is my general position compared to the author's?
3. Which specific ideas do I agree or disagree with?
4. Do the essays confirm what I think, or do they cause me to change my mind?
5. What original or related ideas are occurring to me as I read?
6. What original perspective can I take?
7. What type of claim do I want to make?
8. What can I quote, paraphrase, or summarize?

SECTION I
Issues Concerning Men's and Women's Roles

WHAT ARE THE ISSUES?

1. Are Men and Women Fundamentally Different or Basically the Same?

Of course, men and women are different. But people argue about how great these differences are as they occur in the workplace, in the public sphere, at home, and even in the classroom. A related issue is whether men and women should expect different or special treatment from employers, editors, teachers, and others. See also "Love Is a Fallacy," pp. 205–212, and "Women Take Un–Type A Behavior to Heart," pp. 220–221.

2. How Do Women Define Their Roles?

Two modern feminists give their views on women's roles. Friedan is often credited with starting the most recent women's movement that began in the 1960s. Faludi examines recent opinions regarding the outcomes and value of this movement. Another article explores the problems of the mother who works outside the home.

3. How Do Men Define Their Roles?

Rotundo explores contemporary roles for men and contrasts modern men's roles with those of men in the nineteenth century. Kipnis explains some of the benefits of belonging to men's groups. Finally, Theroux complains about the traditional male roles. See also "Not All Men Are Sly Foxes," pp. 167–169, and "The Men's Movement," pp. 222–224.

THE RHETORICAL SITUATION

The roles that men and women should assume in the home, at work, and in society have been debated since humans first organized themselves into societies. Every age has produced writings on this subject, and the issues associated with it are some of the most enduring. The world's religions, along with societal customs and traditions, provide both the constraints and many of the warrants. In this section, current authors give their perspectives on men's and women's roles, beginning with Betty Friedan, whose book *The Feminine Mystique*, published in 1963, provided much of the energy for the women's movement in the second half of the twentieth century.

A basic question is raised in these writings again and again: Are men and women really different, or are they fundamentally the same? If they are basically the same, they should have equal opportunity and treatment at home, at school, in the public sphere, and in the workplace. They should also be free to assume a variety of types of roles. If they are different, they should expect different treatment and traditional roles.

Men's and women's issues touch everyone's lives eventually, so there is a constant exigency. Look at the best-seller list. Browse in the magazine section of a bookstore. What are the related issues on this subject now? Which of them affect you? Men's and women's issues are intensely personal, and you will probably want to consult your own experience as you read and write about them.

1. Are Men and Women Fundamentally Different or Basically the Same?

TEACHERS' CLASSROOM STRATEGIES SHOULD RECOGNIZE THAT MEN AND WOMEN USE LANGUAGE DIFFERENTLY

Deborah Tannen

The author of You Just Don't Understand: Men and Women in Conversation *describes how her research for that book has made her sensitive to the differences in men and women students' class discussion patterns in her classrooms. Tannen is a professor of linguistics at Georgetown University.*

When I researched and wrote my latest book, *You Just Don't Understand: Women and Men in Conversation*, the furthest thing from my mind was reevaluating my teaching strategies. But that has been one of the direct benefits of having written the book.

The primary focus of my linguistic research always has been the language of everyday conversation. One facet of this is conversational style: how different regional, ethnic, and class backgrounds, as well as age and gender, result in different ways of using language to communicate. *You Just Don't Understand* is about the conversational styles of women and men. As I gained more insight into typically male and female ways of using language, I began to suspect some of the causes of the troubling facts that women who go to single-sex schools do better in later life, and that when young women sit next to young men in classrooms, the males talk more. This is not to say that all men

Chronicle of Higher Education, June 19, 1991, pp. B1, B3.

talk in class, nor that no women do. It is simply that a greater percentage of discussion time is taken by men's voices.

The research of sociologists and anthropologists such as Janet Lever, Marjorie Harness Goodwin, and Donna Eder has shown that girls and boys learn to use language differently in their sex-separate peer groups. Typically, a girl has a best friend with whom she sits and talks, frequently telling secrets. It's the telling of secrets, the fact and the way that they talk to each other, that makes them best friends. For boys, activities are central: Their best friends are the ones they do things with. Boys also tend to play in larger groups that are hierarchical. High-status boys give orders and push low-status boys around. So boys are expected to use language to seize center stage: by exhibiting their skill, displaying their knowledge, and challenging and resisting challenges.

These patterns have stunning implications for classroom interaction. Most faculty members assume that participating in class discussion is a necessary part of successful performance. Yet speaking in a classroom is more congenial to boys' language experience than to girls', since it entails putting oneself forward in front of a large group of people, many of whom are strangers and at least one of whom is sure to judge speakers' knowledge and intelligence by their verbal display.

Another aspect of many classrooms that makes them more hospitable to most men than to most women is the use of debate-like formats as a learning tool. Our educational system, as Walter Ong argues persuasively in his book *Fighting for Life* (Cornell University Press, 1981), is fundamentally male in that the pursuit of knowledge is believed to be achieved by ritual opposition: public display followed by argument and challenge. Father Ong demonstrates that ritual opposition—what he calls "adversativeness" or "agonism"—is fundamental to the way most males approach almost any activity. (Consider, for example, the little boy who shows he likes a little girl by pulling her braids and shoving her.) But ritual opposition is antithetical to the way most females learn and like to interact. It is not that females don't fight, but that they don't fight for fun. They don't *ritualize* opposition.

Anthropologists working in widely disparate parts of the world have found contrasting verbal rituals for women and men. Women in completely unrelated cultures (for example, Greece and Bali) engage in ritual laments: spontaneously produced rhyming couplets that express their pain, for example, over the loss of loved ones. Men do not take part in laments. They have their own, very different verbal ritual: a contest, a war of words in which they vie with each other to devise clever insults.

When discussing these phenomena with a colleague, I commented that I see these two styles in American conversation: Many women bond by talking about troubles, and many men bond by exchanging playful insults and put-downs, and other sorts of verbal sparring. He exclaimed: "I never thought of this, but that's the way I teach: I have students read an article, and then I invite them to tear it apart. After we've torn it to shreds, we talk about how to build a better model."

This contrasts sharply with the way I teach: I open the discussion of readings by asking, "What did you find useful in this? What can we use in our own theory building and our own methods?" I note what I see as weaknesses in the author's approach, but I also point out that the writer's discipline and purposes might be different from ours. Finally, I offer personal anecdotes illustrating the phenomena under discussion and praise students' anecdotes as well as their critical acumen.

These different teaching styles must make our classrooms wildly different places and hospitable to different students. Male students are more likely to be comfortable attacking the readings and might find the inclusion of personal anecdotes irrelevant and "soft." Women are more likely to resist discussion they perceive as hostile, and, indeed, it is women in my classes who are most likely to offer personal anecdotes.

A colleague who read my book commented that he had always taken for granted that the best way to deal with students' comments is to challenge them; this, he felt it was self-evident, sharpens their minds and helps them develop debating skills. But he had noticed that women were relatively silent in his classes, so he decided to try beginning discussion with relatively open-ended questions and letting comments go unchallenged. He found, to his amazement and satisfaction, that more women began to speak up.

Though some of the women in his class clearly liked this better, perhaps some of the men liked it less. One young man in my class wrote in a questionnaire about a history professor who gave students questions to think about and called on people to answer them: "He would then play devil's advocate . . . *i.e.,* he debated us. . . . That class *really* sharpened me intellectually. . . . We as students do need to know how to defend ourselves." This young man valued the experience of being attacked and challenged publicly. Many, if not most, women would shrink from such "challenge," experiencing it as public humiliation.

A professor at Hamilton College told me of a young man who was upset because he felt his class presentation had been a failure. The professor was puzzled because he had observed that class members had listened attentively and agreed with the student's observations. It turned out that it was this very agreement that the student interpreted as failure: Since no one had engaged his ideas by arguing with him, he felt they had found them unworthy of attention.

So one reason men speak in class more than women is that many of them find the "public" classroom setting more conducive to speaking, whereas most women are more comfortable speaking in private to a small group of people they know well. A second reason is that men are more likely to be comfortable with the debate-like form that discussion may take. Yet another reason is the different attitudes toward speaking in class that typify women and men.

Students who speak frequently in class, many of whom are men, assume that it is their job to think of contributions and try to get the floor to express them. But many women monitor their participation not only to get the floor but to avoid getting it. Women students in my class tell me that if they have spoken up once or twice, they hold back for the rest of the class because they don't want to dominate. If they have spoken a lot one week, they will remain silent the next. These different ethics of participation are, of course, unstated, so those who speak freely assume that those who remain silent have nothing to say, and those who are reining themselves in assume that the big talkers are selfish and hoggish.

When I looked around my classes, I could see these differing ethics and habits at work. For example, my graduate class in analyzing conversation had 20 students, 11 women and 9 men. Of the men, four were foreign students: two Japanese, one Chinese, and one Syrian. With the exception of the three Asian men, all the men spoke in class at least occasionally. The biggest talker in the class was a woman, but there were also five women who never spoke at all, only one of whom was Japanese. I decided to try something different.

I broke the class into small groups to discuss the issues raised in the readings and to analyze their own conversational transcripts. I devised three ways of dividing the students into groups: one by the degree program they were in, one by gender, and one by conversational style, as closely as I could guess it. This meant that when the class was grouped according to conversational style, I put Asian students together, fast talkers together, and quiet students together. The class split into groups six times during the semester, so they met in each grouping twice. I told students to regard the groups as examples of interactional data and to note the different ways they participated in the different groups. Toward the end of the term, I gave them a questionnaire asking about their class and group participation.

I could see plainly from my observation of the groups at work that women who never opened their mouths in class were talking away in the small groups. In fact, the Japanese woman commented that she found it particularly hard to contribute to the all-woman group she was in because "I was overwhelmed by how talkative the female students were in the female-only group." This is particularly revealing because it highlights that the same person who can be "oppressed" into silence in one context can become the talkative "oppressor" in another. No one's conversational style is absolute; everyone's style changes in response to the context and others' styles.

Some of the students (seven) said they preferred the same-gender groups; others preferred the same-style groups. In answer to the question "Would you have liked to speak in class more than you did?" six of the seven who said Yes were women; the one man was Japanese. Most startlingly, this response did not come only from quiet women; it came from women who had indicated they had spoken in class never, rarely, sometimes, and often. Of the 11 students who said the amount they had spoken was fine, 7 were men. Of the four women who checked "fine," two added qualifications indicating it wasn't completely fine: One wrote in "maybe more," and one wrote, "I have an urge to participate but often feel I should have something more interesting/relevant/wonderful/intelligent to say!!"

I counted my experiment a success. Everyone in the class found the small groups interesting, and no one indicated he or she would have preferred that the class not break into groups. Perhaps most instructive, however, was the fact that the experience of breaking into groups, and of talking about participation in class, raised everyone's awareness about classroom participation. After we had talked about it, some of the quietest women in the class made a few voluntary contributions, though sometimes I had to insure their participation by interrupting the students who were exuberantly speaking out.

Americans are often proud that they discount the significance of cultural differences: "We are all individuals," many people boast. Ignoring such issues as gender and ethnicity becomes a source of pride: "I treat everyone the same." But treating people the same is not equal treatment if they are not the same.

The classroom is a different environment for those who feel comfortable putting themselves forward in a group than it is for those who find the prospect of doing so chastening, or even terrifying. When a professor asks, "Are there any questions?," students who can formulate statements the fastest have the greatest opportunity to respond. Those who need significant time to do so have not really been given a chance at all, since by the time they are ready to speak, someone else has the floor.

In a class where some students speak out without raising hands, those who feel they must raise their hands and wait to be recognized do not have equal opportunity to speak. Telling them to feel free to jump in will not make them feel free; one's sense of timing, of one's rights and obligations in a classroom, are automatic, learned over years of interaction. They may be changed over time, with motivation and effort, but they cannot be changed on the spot. And everyone assumes his or her own way is best. When I asked my students how the class could be changed to make it easier for them to speak more, the most talkative woman said she would prefer it if no one had to raise hands, and a foreign student said he wished people would raise their hands and wait to be recognized.

My experience in this class has convinced me that small-group interaction should be part of any class that is not a small seminar. I also am convinced that having the students become observers of their own interaction is a crucial part of their education. Talking about ways of talking in class makes students aware that their ways of talking affect other students, that the motivations they impute to others may not truly reflect others' motives, and that the behaviors they assume to be self-evidently right are not universal norms.

The goal of complete equal opportunity in class may not be attainable, but realizing that one monolithic classroom-participation structure is not equal opportunity is itself a powerful motivation to find more-diverse methods to serve diverse students—and every classroom is diverse.

ARE OPINIONS MALE?

Naomi Wolf

Feminist author Naomi Wolf wrote this article about "the barriers that shut women up" for The New Republic *in 1993. She is also the author of* Fire with Fire: The New Female Power and How It Will Change the Twenty-First Century *and* The Beauty Myth.

What is that vast silent wavelength out on the opinion superhighway? It is the sound of women not talking.

Despite women's recent strides into public life, the national forums of debate—op-ed pages, political magazines, public affairs talk shows, newspaper columns—remain strikingly immune to the general agitation for female access. The agora of opinion is largely a men's club.

A simple count of the elite media bears out the charge. In 1992, the putative Year of the Woman, "Crossfire" presented fifty-five female guests, compared with 440 male guests. Of the print media, the most elite forums are the worst offenders: according to a survey conducted by Women, Men and Media, during a one-month period in 1992, 13 percent of the op-ed pieces published in *The Washington Post* were written by women; 16 percent of the articles on the *The New York Times* op-ed page were by women. Over the course of the year, *The New Republic* averaged 14 percent female contributors; *Harper's*, less than 20 percent; *The Nation*, 23 percent; *The Atlantic Monthly*, 33 percent. *The National Interest* ran the remarkable ratio of eighty male bylines to one female. *The Washington Monthly* ran thirty-three women to 108 men; *National Review*, fifty-one female bylines to 505 male (and twelve of those female bylines belonged to one columnist, Florence King). Talk radio, an influential forum for airing populist grievances, counts fifty female hosts in its national association's roster that totals 900. Eric Alterman's book about opinion-makers, *Sound and Fury*, chronicles female pundits only in passing.

What is going on here? Is there an unconscious—or conscious—editorial bias against women's opinions? Or are opinions themselves somehow gendered male—does female socialization conspire against many women's ability or desire to generate a strong public voice?

The answer to the first question is an unhesitant yes: on the nuts-and-bolts level of feminist analysis, women are being left out of the opinion mix because of passive but institutionalized discrimination on the part of editors and producers. General-interest magazines, newspapers and electronic forums tend to view public affairs as if they can be clothed exclusively in gray flannel suits, and rely on an insular Rolodex of white men.

The New Republic, November 29, 1993, pp. 20, 22, 24–26.

In self-defense some male (and female) public opinion editors point to the allegedly "personal" way in which women tend to write about politics and express their public opinions. Women are accused of writing too much about their "feelings" and their "bodies"—as if such subjects were by nature ill-suited to respectable public discussion. And yes, this charge has some merit. But a double standard is at work here. Men, too, write about their feelings and bodies, but that discussion is perceived as being central and public. Though masculinists lay claim to passionless "objectivity," "logic" and "universality" as being the hallmarks of male debate, a glance shows how spurious is their position. What, after all, was the gays-in-the-military debate except a touchy-feely all-night boys-only slumber party, in which Dad—in the form of Sam Nunn—came downstairs to have a bull session with earnest youths lying on bunk beds? What were the snuggled-up military boys asked about but their feelings—feelings about being ogled, objectified, harassed; fears of seduction and even rape? Had it been young women interviewed in their dorm rooms about their fears of men, the whole exercise, cloaked in the sententious language of "national preparedness," would have been dismissed as a radical-feminist fiesta of victim-consciousness, encouraging oversensitive flowers to see sexual predators under every bed.

Indeed, the nationalism of German skinheads, the high melodrama of the World Cup and the recent convulsion of Japan-bashing—all of these are, on one level, complex sociopolitical developments; on another, they are a continuing global C.R. session on vulnerability and self-esteem conducted primarily by men about men. One could read the Western canon itself as a record of men's deep feelings of alternating hope and self-doubt—whether it recounts Dick Diver destroying himself because his wife is wealthier than he, or King Lear raging on a heath at the humiliation of being stripped of his world.

So women and men often actually theorize about parallel experiences, but the author's maleness will elevate the language as being importantly public, while the author's femaleness stigmatizes it as being worthlessly private. Women writing about the stresses and failures of maternity, for instance, are deviating onto the literary mommy track, but when men write about the stresses and failures of paternity, they are analyzing "the plight of inner-city youths," "cultural breakdown" or "child abuse hysteria." A woman recounting her own experience of systematic oppression is writing a "confessional"; but when a man writes intensely personal, confessional prose—whether it is Rousseau in his *Confessions* or Bob Packwood in his diaries—he is engaged in pioneering enlightenment, or, even in William Safire's terms, acting as "a Pepysian diarist . . . [who] has kept voluminous notes on life as a lightning rod."

Of course, many women write about issues unmarked by gender, from city council elections to computer chips. But when women talk about politics, culture, science and the law in relation to female experience—i.e., rape statutes, fertility drugs, misogyny in film or abortion rights—they are perceived as talking about their feelings and bodies. Whereas when men talk about their feelings and bodies—i.e., free speech in relation to their interest in pornography, gun ownership in relation to their fear of criminal assault, the drive for prostate cancer research in relation to their fears of impotence, new sexual harassment guidelines in relation to their irritation at having their desire intercepted in the workplace—they are read as if they are talking about politics, culture, science and the law.

Thus, much of what passes for rational public debate is an exchange of subjective *male* impressions about *masculine* sensibilities and the *male* body—an exchange that appears "lucid" and "public" because men arrogate the qualities of transparency and generalization when discussing male emotions and the experiences of male flesh, but assign to women the qualities of opacity and particularity when they discuss their own.

The lack of media oxygen for women writers of opinion can strangle voice, putting them into an impossible double bind. Many women also write from a personal vantage point alone because they feel it is one realm over which they can claim authority. As Jodie Allen, an editor at *The Washington Post*, puts it, "When they sit down to write, they think, why should anyone listen to me? At least if I take it from the 'women's' point of view, they can't deny I'm a woman. It becomes a self-fulfilling prophecy." With the "public/male, private/female" split so schematized, many other women writers of opinion must assume "the female perspective," as if shouldering a heroic but cumbersome burden. They are forced, by the relative paucity of female pundits at the highest levels, to speak "for women" rather than simply hashing out the issues in a solitary way.

This extreme is represented sometimes by an Anna Quindlen, whose "maternal punditry" beats a lonely drum on the guy terrain of the *Times* op-ed page. The meager allocation of space for female pundits at the highest levels, what Quindlen calls "a quota of one," does indeed force the few visible women writers of opinion who take a feminist stance into becoming stoic producers of that viewpoint, counted upon to generate a splash of sass and color, a provocative readerly-writerly tussle, in the gray expanses of male perspectives and prose. Editors seem to treat these few female pundits as cans in six-packs marked, for instance, "Lyrical African American Women Novelists"; "Spunky White Female Columnists with Kids"; or, perhaps, the reliable category, "Feminists (Knee-Jerk to Loony)." As Quindlen once remarked, a newspaper editor explained that he could not syndicate her column because "we already run Ellen Goodman." Popular discourse treats such writers as sound bite producers when it needs someone to say "multiculturalism is good" or "rape is bad."

So the few "pundits of identity" achieve, in the minds of those who decide what ideas inhabit the op-ed pages and who should argue with whom about what, a hard-won commerce in the perspectives inflected by gender, or by gender and race. But few can hope to take for granted the sweet oxygen that any writer needs in order to flourish: space to speak for no one but oneself.

The other extreme of the female public voice is perhaps represented by a Jeane Kirkpatrick: a voice so Olympian, so neck-up and uninflected by the experiences of the female body, that the subtle message received by young female writers is: to enter public voice, one must abide by the no-uterus rule. This voice gives a publication the benefit of a woman's name on the title page, without the mess and disruption of women's issues entering that precious space. This is the message absorbed by the legions of young women I meet. Though many writers are avidly trying to seek it out, we still lack the space and encouragement to range from the personal to the political, from identity to universality, with the ease and un-self-consciousness assumed by men.

So women are left out, or included under conditions of constraint. But do we leave ourselves out of the public forum as well? When I have asked editors at *The New Republic, The Washington Post, Harper's* and *The New York Times* op-ed page about the gender imbalance in their forums, this is the overwhelming message. Women simply do not submit articles in the same numbers that men do. And this is accurate: during one randomly selected month at *TNR* (February 1992), eight women submitted unsolicited manuscripts, versus fifteen men; during another month (October 1993), the ratio was eight women to fifty-five men. According to Toby Harshaw, staff member of *The New York Times* op-ed page, in the morning mail of November 8, of about 150 unsolicited manuscripts, the ratio of men to women was 10-to-1.

Why is this? Some editors argue that one reason for the imbalance is that women have not yet reached the highest echelons of public life: "Our biggest groups that submit are think tanks, lawyers, universities and government officials," says Harshaw. And the overwhelming majority of pieces from these groups, he notes, are by men. Yet while that argument has some validity, it cannot account for the extent of the imbalance: at the middle ranks of the law and the academy, women are reaching parity with men. What makes many women reluctant to write and submit opinion journalism, compared with men?

There is, I think, a set of deeply conditioned, internal inhibitions that work in concert with the manifest external discrimination to keep fewer women willing to submit opinion pieces, and to slug it out in public arenas. The problem is not, of course, that women can't write. They write, one can argue, with more facility than men do: women have dominated the novel—at least in its popular form—since its birth; and, if anything, social enculturation encourages girls to be more literary than most boys. No, the problem is that the traits required by writing opinion journalism or appearing on adversarial public affairs shows are often in conflict with what are deemed "appropriate" female speech patterns and behavior.

Dr. Deborah Tannen, the Georgetown University linguist, asserted that women and men often speak in different ways—women seek intimacy and consensus, she claims, while men seek status and independence. She notes that boys are raised to see boy-to-boy conflict as a way to express bonding, while girls are raised to avoid conflict in their play and enforce consensus. Psychologists Jean Baker Miller and Carol Gilligan suggest that women are more "relational" and men more "autonomous."

I don't agree with Miller or Gilligan that these tendencies are due to any primal psychic development; but women are surely encouraged to show such traits by virtue of social conditioning. And the act of writing an opinion piece—or appearing on "Crossfire"—calls for skills that are autonomous, contrarian and independent (not to say bloody-minded). Writing opinion journalism is a cranky, self-satisfied and, in traditionally feminine terms, extremely rude way to behave in public. The momentum to thrash out an opinion piece often begins with the conviction that others are wrong and that oneself is right, or that others are not saying the one thing that must be said. One is not *listening*; one is not set on enhancing others' well-being; one is certainly not demonstrating a "fusion of identity and intimacy," which pursuit Gilligan claims motivates women.

Unfortunately, you can't write strong, assertive prose if you are too anxious about preserving consensus; you can't have a vigorous debate if you are paralyzed with concern about wounding the sensitivities of your opposite number. Writing a bold declarative sentence that claims that the world is this way and not that, or that President Clinton should do X and is a fool to do Y, demands the assumption of a solitary, even arrogant, stance. In Gilliganesque "different voice" terms, it is lonely and emotionally unrewarding; it is, according to such theories, almost by definition an engagement in "masculine" values and patterns of speech.

Without a countervailing encouragement into speech, the social pressure on women to exhibit "connection" and suppress "autonomy" can inhibit many women's public assertiveness. Tannen describes English Professor Thomas Fox's observations of male and female freshman students' different approaches to writing analytical papers. He looked at a Ms. M. and a Mr. H. "In her speaking as well as her writing [to be read by the class]," Tannen reports, "Ms. M. held back what she knew, appearing uninformed and uninterested, because she feared offending her classmates. Mr. H. spoke with authority and apparent confidence because he was eager to persuade his peers. She did not worry about persuading; he did not worry about offending." But in Ms. M.'s papers that were to be read only by the professor—her "private" writing—Ms. M. was clear, forceful and direct. In this anecdote we see, essentially, that of the two, Mr. H., at 17, is being socialized to write opinion journalism and shout down interruptions on "The McLaughlin Group"; whereas Ms. M. is being socialized to write celebrity puff pieces in *Entertainment Weekly*.

Many women are raised to care—or to feel guilty if they don't care—about wounding the feelings of others. And yet, to write most purely out of herself, a writer must somehow kill off the inhibiting influence of the need for "connection." The woman writer of opinion must delve into what early feminists called "the solitude of self." When Camille Paglia claims that women have not produced great artists for the same reasons that they have not produced a Jack the Ripper, she touches, perhaps inadvertently, upon a real creative problem for women: fidelity to nothing but one's own voice can in fact depend upon a kind of radical solipsism, an ecstatic, highly unfeminine disregard for the importance of others if their well-being obtrudes upon the emergence of that transcendent vision.

Virginia Woolf returned often in her diaries to this theme, to the need to be impervious both to criticism and approval: "I look upon disregard or abuse as part of my bargain," Woolf wrote. "I'm to write what I like and they're to say what they like." Woolf's opinion of unsuccessful women's novels says volumes about the social disincentives many women face in writing damn-the-torpedoes opinion pieces: "It was the flaw in the center that had rotted them. [The novelist] had altered her values in deference to the opinions of others." And yet the world conspires against us, and within us, to have us do just that.

This internal dilemma is compounded by an external convention: even for the many women who are willing and eager to express strong opinions, conventions about how women are permitted to speak in print or on T.V. hem them in. The authoritative female voice asserting judgments about the real world is an unseemly voice. The globalizing tone that the conventions of opinion journalism or T.V. debate require involves an assumption of authority that women are actively dissuaded from claiming. A female writer of opinion at the *Post* concurs: "Op-ed language is the language of a certain level of abstraction; this is a language more often used by more men because more men are expert at it—you have to learn that language." As Professor Rhonda Garelick, who teaches French literary theory at the University of Colorado, put it to me, "It is just now becoming true for me that I can make 'sweeping' statements. But even as I make them, I am aware that it is an unusual verbal structure for me because I'm a woman. And I am always pleasurably surprised when they are accepted. The effect is good, but it is certainly something I am trained not to do by a lifetime of being a woman. I always opted for carefulness, precision, detail in what I said or wrote—but to take that leap [and write]: I must mean this large thing—that is disconcerting. And that's what opinion journalism is."

Since the authoritative voice can be so disconcerting for many women to use, women writers often have turned to fiction to give safe cover to their longing to express their political points of view: *Jane Eyre* conceals a passionate outburst about feminism; *Uncle Tom's Cabin* sugar-coats an anti-slavery polemic. As Emily Dickinson warned, "Tell all the truth but tell it slant." A prominent feminist muckraker keeps on her refrigerator the motto, "Tell the truth and run."

We know as women that the act of "taking a position" in a sweeping way—"standing one's ground" above one's own byline, asserting one's view about the world of fact rather than fantasy—is a dangerous one, an act that will be met with punishment. When I have interviewed college women about their fears of leadership and public voice, they often use metaphors of punitive violence when describing their anxiety about expressing opinions in public: "having it blow up in my face"; "I'll be torn apart"; "ripped to shreds"; "they'll shoot me down."

Punishment—is that not too strong a word? This is the end of the twentieth century, after all; women no longer need to write under pseudonyms to conceal the force of their opinions. Yet when we look at what happens when women "take a stand," the common female fear of punishment for expressing an opinion suggests no phantom anxiety. A woman who enters public debate is indeed likely to be punished. A complex set of rules ensures it. Some involve ad feminam attacks: the absurd attacks on Chelsea Clinton's appearance that flitted across the public stage in the last year or so were in fact attacks on her mother, a message to all women contemplating entering public life that their children can be held hostage in retribution.

Others involve chivalry: when a woman tries to argue with men—as Rodham Clinton did in presenting her views on health care—the debate can be neatly sidestepped by labeling her "charming" and "disarming." These terms ensure that she cannot be seen to fight and win by virtue of her wits, for her potential adversaries preemptively "disarm" themselves—yield their weapons—and let themselves be "charmed"—go into a trance of delight that, presumably, mere reason cannot penetrate. Rodham Clinton's experience eerily re-evokes the debate-evasive reaction that Virginia Woolf anticipated after she finished the immensely (if elegantly) confrontational essay that became *A Room of One's Own*: "I forecast, then, that I shall get no criticism, except of the evasive, jocular kind . . . that the press will be kind and talk of its charm and sprightliness; Also I shall be attacked for a feminist and hinted at for a Sapphist. . . . I am afraid it will not be taken seriously."

Still others involve stigmatizing the woman's anger: if the female antagonist is less than universally admired (or doesn't happen to be married to the president), she is called "shrill," as Geraldine Ferraro was when she debated George Bush ("rhymes with rich"). Female radio personalities have told me that when they ask male guests tough questions, their listeners call in and tell them to stop being rude to the men. It was front-page news when, in a speech, President Clinton lost his temper at the press—something that a cool-headed leader is rightly expected not to do; but it was front-page news when his wife directed anger at the insurance industry—something that a leader in her position should do, if she is to serve her constituency well.

I do not believe that the "different voice" concerns lie deep in women; granted permission to do so without punishment, as many women as men would write blustery, cantankerous prose and flock to the delights of public argument. Women do not lack the desire or ability to fight hard or write fiercely; we lack a behavioral paradigm that makes doing so acceptable.

When a woman does engage in public debate, she is often torn in two. She may be anguished by her own sense that her strong voice is in a state of conflict with her longing for approval and her discomfort with conflict. I feel this role conflict often myself: in a recent book, I argued hard with a certain writer's ideas; when I subsequently met her and liked her, I wanted to beg forgiveness—even though my views of her work had not changed. I feel a kind of terror when I am critical in public and experience a kind of nausea when I am attacked. The knowledge that another person and I publicly disagree makes me feel that I have left something unresolved, raw in the world; even if I "win"—expecially if I win—I also lose, because I am guilty, in traditionally feminine terms, of a failure to create harmony and consensus; this bruise to identity manifests at the level of my sense of femininity.

Now I know that this anxiety is unhelpful, even retrograde; and it is directly at odds with my even stronger wish to enjoy the fray without this grief. But there it is. And if I, with my strong feminist upbringing, feel this sense of two drives in a state of absolute conflict when I enter public debate, I doubt that I can be alone. If a woman thinks of herself as someone who is warm and kind in private life, how can she also be a critic in public life, an agonist? This sense of role conflict can feel to many as if it is built in to women's participation in public life.

Women also lack any paradigm for expressing dissent with other women in a way that is perceived as a sign of respect. Men have rituals for expressing conflict as a form of honor, even of friendship; British male parliamentarians are famous for braying at one another and then joking over the urinal. But women lack any such social patterns. If a woman engages in hard debate with another woman, she is a "spoiler" or a "mudslinger," as Liz Holtzman was accused of being when she attacked Ferraro in the 1992 Senate race; the fact that Senator Nancy Kassebaum *disagreed* with Senator Patty Murray about what to do with the Packwood investigation made news. Woman-to-woman argument is seen, even by women, as a breakdown of precious consensus, or a catfight, or a "betrayal of sisterhood"—a situation that can force women in public to suppress their legitimate differences of opinion; whereas man-to-man argument is understood as being the stuff of democracy.

Why is all this "subjective," "emotional" stuff a fit subject for the pages of a policy journal? Because the psychic disincentives for women to argue in public, or to write strong opinionated journalism, have profound implications for the health of democracy. Woolf wrote, "The effect of discouragement upon the mind of the artist should be measured." These psychological and social barriers to women's opinionated public speech make it literally not worth it, in many women's minds, to run for office, contradict an adversary or take a controversial public stance. If many women feel ridicule and hostility more acutely than men do, if they are uncomfortable with isolation, then ridicule, hostility and the threat of isolation can be—and are—standard weapons in the arsenal used to scare women away from public life.

In essence, certain kinds of forceful speech and interchange are defined as male and prohibited to women, as a subtle but immensely effective means to maintain the world of opinion and policy-making as an all-male preserve. And then, in a vicious circle, many women pre-emptively internalize the barriers, which keeps them wary of storming their way into the marketplace of opinions.

The response to this state of affairs has to be a complex one. To begin with, editors and producers must root out their own often unwitting bias. They are welching on their commitment to inform citizens of a real range of views, leaving half the population ill-prepared to pursue their interests within the democratic process. They are also shortchanging us as a nation, for their unacknowledged warp in perspective leaves "women's issues" and female talking heads, no matter how pressing the topic nor how perspicacious the voices, to languish in the journalistic harem of women's magazines, crowded in among celebrity pets and the latest news on the French manicure. Because of this omission of "women's perspectives" and hard facts about women, we endure wildly off-the-mark debate and create faulty policy in a vacuum of information.

Further gender polarization is not the answer. Just as we are learning to integrate "male" and "female" perspectives about sexual harassment as we seek a newer, fairer social contract in the workplace, we must integrate "male" and "female" views and patterns of expression as we renegotiate the contract about what it is appropriate to say, and how it is appropriate to say it, in the forums of opinion.

The last solution to this dilemma, for all of us who are women still ambivalent about waging opinion, is internal: the only way forward is through. We must realize that public debate may starve the receptors for love and approval, but that it stimulates the synapses of self-respect. Let us shed the lingering sense that authority is something that others—male others—bestow upon us; whenever we are inclined to mumble invective into our coffee, let us flood the airwaves instead. Let's steal a right that has heretofore been defined as masculine: the right to be in love with the sound of one's own voice.

ENDING THE BATTLE BETWEEN THE SEXES

Aaron R. Kipnis and Elizabeth Herron

This article is written by authors who are active members of the men's and women's movements and who are also leaders for men's and women's groups. Aaron R. Kipnis is the author of Knights Without Armor. *He and Elizabeth Herron, a seasoned women's group leader, codirect the Santa Barbara Institute for Gender Studies in Santa Barbara, California. They are authors of the book* Gender War, Gender Peace.

Have you noticed that American men and women seem angrier at one another than ever? Belligerent superpowers have buried the hatchet, but the war between the sexes continues unabated. On every television talk show, women and men trade increasingly bitter accusations. We feel the tension in our homes, in our workplaces, and in our universities.[. . .]

Often, however, these changes are seen to benefit one sex at the expense of the other, and the mistrust that results creates resentment. Most men and

Utne Reader, January/February 1993, pp. 69–76.

women seem unable to entertain the idea that the two sexes' differing perspectives on many issues can be equally valid. So polarization grows instead of reconciliation, as many women and men fire ever bigger and better-aimed missiles across the gender gap. On both sides there's a dearth of compassion about the predicaments of the other sex.

For example:

• Women feel sexually harassed; men feel their courting behavior is often misunderstood.

• Women fear men's power to wound them physically; men fear women's power to wound them emotionally.

• Women say men aren't sensitive enough; men say women are too emotional.

• Women feel men don't do their fair share of housework and child care; men feel that women don't feel as much pressure to provide the family's income and do home maintenance.

• Many women feel morally superior to men; many men feel that they are more logical and just than women.

• Women say men have destroyed the environment; men say the women's movement has destroyed the traditional family.

• Men are often afraid to speak about the times that they feel victimized and powerless; women frequently deny their real power.

• Women feel that men don't listen; men feel that women talk too much.

• Women resent being paid less than men; men are concerned about the occupational hazards and stress that lead to their significantly shorter life spans.

• Men are concerned about unfairness in custody and visitation rights; women are concerned about fathers who shirk their child support payments.

It is very difficult to accept the idea that so many conflicting perspectives could all have intrinsic value. Many of us fear that listening to the story of another will somehow weaken our own voice, our own initiative, even our own identity. The fear keeps us locked in adversarial thinking and patterns of blame and alienation. In this frightened absence of empathy, devaluation of the other sex grows. . . .

In an attempt to address some of the discord between the sexes, we have been conducting gender workshops around the country. We invite men and women to spend some time in all-male and all-female groups, talking about the opposite sex. Then we bring the two groups into an encounter with one another. In one of our mixed groups this spring, Susan, a 35-year-old advertising executive, told the men, "Most men these days are insensitive jerks. When are men going to get it that we are coming to work to make a living, not to get laid? Anita Hill was obviously telling the truth. Most of the women I work with have been harassed as well."

Michael, her co-worker, replied, "Then why didn't she tell him ten years ago that what he was doing was offensive? How are we supposed to know where your boundaries are if you laugh at our jokes, smile when you're angry, and never confront us in the direct way a man would? How am I supposed to learn what's not OK with you, if the first time I hear about it is at a grievance hearing?"

We've heard many permutations of this same conversation:

Gina, a 32-year-old school teacher in Washington, D.C., asks, "Why don't men ever take *no* for an answer?"

Arthur, a 40-year-old construction foreman, replies that in his experience, "some women *do* in fact say no when they mean yes. Women seem to believe that men should do all the pursuing in the mating dance. But then if we don't read her silent signals right, we're the bad guys. If we get it right, though, then we're heroes."

Many men agree that they are in a double bind. They are labeled aggressive jerks if they come on strong, but are rejected as wimps if they don't. Women feel a similar double bind. They are accused of being teases if they make themselves attractive but reject the advances of men. Paradoxically, however, as Donna, a fortyish divorcée, reports, "When I am up front about my desires, men often head for the hills."

As Deborah Tannen, author of the best-seller about male-female language styles *You Just Don't Understand,* has observed, men and women often have entirely different styles of communication. How many of us have jokingly speculated that men and women actually come from different planets? But miscommunication alone is not the source of all our sorrow.

Men have an ancient history of enmity toward women. For centuries, many believed women to be the cause of our legendary fall from God's grace. "How can he be clean that is born of woman?" asks the Bible. Martin Luther wrote that "God created Adam Lord of all living things, but Eve spoiled it all." The "enlightened" '60s brought us Abbie Hoffman, who said: "The only alliance I would make with the women's liberation movement is in bed." And from the religious right, Jerry Falwell still characterizes feminism as a "satanic attack" on the American family.

In turn, many feel the women's movement devalues the role of men. Marilyn French, author of *The Women's Room,* said, "All men are rapists and that's all they are." In response to the emerging men's movement, Betty Friedan commented, "Oh God, sick . . . I'd hoped by now men were strong enough to accept their vulnerability and to be authentic without aping Neanderthal cavemen."

This hostility to the men's movement is somewhat paradoxical. Those who are intimately involved with the movement say that it is primarily dedicated to ending war and racism, increasing environmental awareness, healing men's lives and reducing violence, promoting responsible fatherhood, and creating equal partnerships with women—all things with which feminism is ideologically aligned. Yet leaders of the men's movement often evoke indignant responses from women. A prominent woman attorney tells us, "I've been waiting 20 years for men to hear our message. Now instead of joining us at last, they're starting their *own* movement. And now they want us to hear that they're wounded too. It makes me sick."

On the other hand, a leader of the men's movement says, "I was a feminist for 15 years. Recently, I realized that all the men I know are struggling just as much as women. Also, I'm tired of all the male-bashing. I just can't listen to women's issues anymore while passively watching so many men go down the tubes."

Some of our gender conflict is an inevitable by-product of the positive growth that has occurred in our society over the last generation. The traditional gender roles of previous generations imprisoned many women and men in soul-killing routines. Women felt dependent and disenfranchised; men felt distanced from feelings, family, and their capacity for self-care.

With almost 70 percent of women now in the work force, calls ... for women to return to the home full time seem ludicrous, not to mention financially impossible. In addition, these calls for the traditional nuclear family ignore the fact that increasing numbers of men now want to downshift from full-time work in order to spend more time at home. So if we can't go back to the old heroic model of masculinity and the old domestic ideal of femininity, how then do we weave a new social fabric out of the broken strands of worn-out sexual stereotypes?

Numerous participants in the well-established women's movement, as well as numbers of men in the smaller but growing men's movement, have been discovering the strength, healing, power, and sense of security that come from being involved with a same-sex group. Women and men have different social, psychological, and biological realities and receive different behavioral training from infancy through adulthood.

In most pre-technological societies, women and men both participate in same-sex social and ceremonial groups. The process of becoming a woman or a man usually begins with some form of ritual initiation. At the onset of puberty, young men and women are brought into the men's and women's lodges, where they gain a deep sense of gender identity.

Even in our own culture, women and men have traditionally had places to meet apart from members of the other sex. For generations, women have gathered over coffee or quilts; men have bonded at work and in taverns. But in our modern society, most heterosexuals believe that a member of the opposite sex is supposed to fulfill all their emotional and social needs. Most young people today are not taught to respect and honor the differences of the other gender, and they arrive at adulthood both mystified and distrustful, worried about the other sex's power to affect them. In fact, most cross-gender conflict is essentially *conflict between different cultures*. Looking at the gender war from this perspective may help us develop solutions to our dilemmas.

In recent decades, cultural anthropologists have come to believe that people are more productive members of society when they can retain their own cultural identity within the framework of the larger culture. As a consequence, the old American "melting pot" theory of cultural assimilation has evolved into a new theory of diversity, whose model might be the "tossed salad." In this ideal, each subculture retains its essential identity, while coexisting within the same social container.

Applying this idea to men and women, we can see the problems with the trend of the past several decades toward a sex-role melting pot. In our quest for gender equality through sameness, we are losing both the beauty of our diversity and our tolerance for differences. Just as a monoculture is not as environmentally stable or rich as a diverse natural ecosystem, androgyny denies the fact that sexual differences are healthy.

In the past, perceived differences between men and women have been used to promote discrimination, devaluation, and subjugation. As a result, many "we're all the same" proponents—New Agers and humanistic social theorists, for example—are justifiably suspicious of discussions that seek to restore awareness of our differences. But pretending that differences do not exist is not the way to end discrimination toward either sex.

Our present challenge is to acknowledge the value of our differing experiences as men and women, and to find ways to reap this harvest in the spirit of true equality. Carol Tavris, in her book *The Mismeasure of Women*, suggests that instead of "regarding cultural and reproductive differences as problems to be eliminated, we should aim to eliminate *the unequal consequences that follow from them*."

Some habits are hard to change, even with an egalitarian awareness. Who can draw the line between what is socially conditioned and what is natural? It may not be possible, or even desirable, to do so. What seems more important is that women and men start understanding each other's different cultures and granting one another greater freedom to experiment with whatever roles or lifestyles attract them.

Lisa, a 29-year-old social worker from New York participating in one of our gender workshops, told us, "Both Joel [her husband] and I work full time. But it always seems to be me who ends up having to change my schedule when Gabe, our son, has a doctor's appointment or a teacher conference, is sick at home or has to be picked up after school. It's simply taken for granted that in most cases my time is less important than his. I know Joel tries really hard to be an engaged father. But the truth is that I feel I'm always on the front line when it comes to the responsibilities of parenting and keeping the home together. It's just not fair."

Joel responds by acknowledging that Lisa's complaint is justified; but he says, "I handle all the home maintenance, fix the cars, do all the banking and bookkeeping and all the yard work as well. These things aren't hobbies. I also work more overtime than Lisa. Where am I supposed to find the time to equally co-parent too? Is Lisa going to start mowing the lawn or help me build the new bathroom? Not likely."

In many cases of male-female conflict, as with Lisa and Joel, there are two differing but *equally valid* points of view. Yet in books, the media, and in women's and men's groups, we only hear about most issues from a woman's point of view or from a man's. This is at the root of the escalating war between the sexes.

For us, the starting point in the quest for gender peace is for men and women to spend more time with members of the same sex. We have found that many men form intimate friendships in same-sex groups. In addition to supporting their well-being, these connections can take some of the pressure off their relationships with women. Men in close friendships no longer expect women to satisfy *all* their emotional needs. And when women meet in groups they support one another's need for connection and also for empowerment in the world. Women then no longer expect men to provide their sense of self-worth. So these same-sex groups can enhance not only the participants' individual lives, but their relationships with members of the other sex as well.

If men and women *remain* separated, however, we risk losing perspective and continuing the domination or scapegoating of the other sex. In women's groups, male-bashing has been running rampant for years. At a recent lecture we gave at a major university, a young male psychology student said, "This is the first time in three years on campus that I have heard anyone say a single positive thing about men or masculinity."

Many women voice the same complaint about their experiences in male-dominated workplaces. Gail, a middle management executive, says, "When I make proposals to the all-male board of directors, I catch the little condescending smirks and glances the men give one another. They don't pull that shit when my male colleagues speak. If they're that rude in front of me, I can only imagine how degrading their comments are when they meet in private."

There are few arenas today in which women and men can safely come together on common ground to frankly discuss our rapidly changing ideas about gender justice. Instead of more sniping from the sidelines, what is needed is for groups of women and men to communicate directly with one another. When we take this *next step* and make a commitment to spend time apart and then meet with each other, then we can begin to build a true social, political, and spiritual equality. This process also instills a greater appreciation for the unique gifts each sex has to contribute.

Husband-and-wife team James Sniechowski and Judith Sherven conduct gender reconciliation meetings—similar to the meetings we've been holding around the country—each month in Southern California. In a recent group of 25 people (11 women, 14 men), participants were invited to explore questions like: What did you learn about being a man/woman from your mother? From your father? Sniechowski reports that, "even though, for the most part, the men and women revealed their confusions, mistrust, heartbreaks, and bewilderments, the room quickly filled with a poignant beauty." As one woman said of the meeting, "When I listen to the burdens we suffer, it helps me soften my heart toward them." On another occasion a man said, "My image of women shifts as I realize they've been through some of the same stuff I have."

Discussions such as these give us an opportunity to really hear one another and, perhaps, discover that many of our disagreements come from equally valid, if different, points of view. What many women regard as intimacy feels suffocating and invasive to men. What many men regard as masculine strength feels isolating and distant to women. Through blame and condemnation, women and men shame one another. Through compassionate communication, however, we can help one another. This mutual empowerment is in the best interests of both sexes, because when one sex suffers, the other does too.

Toward the end of our meetings, men and women inevitably become more accountable for the ways in which they contribute to the problem. Gina said, "I've never really heard the men's point of view on all this before. I must admit that I rarely give men clear signals when they say or do something that offends me."

Arthur then said, "All my life I've been trained that my job as a man is to keep pursuing until 'no' is changed to 'yes, yes, yes.' But I hear it that when a woman says no, they want me to respect it. I get it now that what I thought was just a normal part of the dance is experienced as harassment by some women. But you know, it seems that if we're ever going to get together now, more women are going to have to start making the first moves."

After getting support from their same-sex groups and then listening to feedback from the whole group, Joel and Lisa realize that if they are both going to work full time they need to get outside help with family tasks, rather than continuing to blame and shame one another for not doing more.

Gender partnership based on strong, interactive, separate but equal gender identities can support the needs of both sexes. Becoming more affirming or supportive of our same sex doesn't have to lead to hostility toward the other sex. In fact, the acknowledgment that gender diversity is healthy may help all of us to become more tolerant toward other kinds of differences in our society.

Through gender reconciliation—both formal workshops and informal discussions—the sexes can support each other, instead of blaming one sex for not meeting the other's expectations. Men and women clearly have the capacity to move away from the sex-war rhetoric that is dividing us as well as the courage necessary to create forums for communication that can unite and heal us.

Boys and girls need regular opportunities in school to openly discuss their differing views on dating, sex, and gender roles. In universities, established women's studies courses could be complemented with men's studies, and classes in the two fields could be brought together from time to time to deepen students' understanding of both sexes. The informal discussion group is another useful format in which men and women everywhere can directly communicate with each other. [. . .] In the workplace the struggle for gender understanding needs to go beyond the simple setting up of guidelines about harassment; it is essential that women and men regularly discuss their differing views on gender issues. Outside help is often needed in structuring such discussions and getting them under way. Our organization, the Santa Barbara Institute for Gender Studies, trains and provides "reconciliation facilitators" for that purpose.

These forums must be fair. Discussions of women's wage equity must also include men's job safety. Discussions about reproductive rights, custody rights, or parental leave must consider the rights of both mothers and fathers—and the needs of the children. Affirmative action to balance the male-dominated political and economic leadership must also bring balance to the female-dominated primary-education and social-welfare systems.

We call for both sexes to come to the negotiating table from a new position of increased strength and self-esteem. Men and women do not need to become more like one another, merely more deeply themselves. But gender understanding is only a step on the long road that must ultimately lead to fundamental institutional change. We would hope, for example, that in the near future men and women will stop arguing about whether women should go into combat and concentrate instead on how to end war. The skills and basic attitudes that will lead to gender peace are the very ones we need in order to meet the other needs of our time—social, political, and environmental—with committed action.

2. How Do Women Define Their Roles?

THE PROBLEM THAT HAS NO NAME

Betty Friedan

> *This is an excerpt from* The Feminine Mystique, *published in 1963, a book that explains the reasons for the current women's movement.*

The problem lay buried, unspoken, for many years in the minds of American women. It was a strange stirring, a sense of dissatisfaction, a yearning that women suffered in the middle of the twentieth century in the United States. Each suburban wife struggled with it alone. As she made the beds, shopped for groceries, matched slipcover material, ate peanut butter sandwiches with her children, chauffeured Cub Scouts and Brownies, lay beside her husband at night—she was afraid to ask even of herself the silent question—"Is this all?"

For over fifteen years there was no word of this yearning in the millions of words written about women, for women, in all the columns, books and articles by experts telling women their role was to seek fulfillment as wives and mothers. Over and over women heard in voices of tradition and of Freudian sophistication that they could desire no greater destiny than to glory in their own femininity. Experts told them how to catch a man and keep him, how to breastfeed children and handle their toilet training, how to cope with sibling rivalry and adolescent rebellion; how to buy a dishwasher, bake bread, cook gourmet snails, and build a swimming pool with their own hands; how to dress, look, and act more feminine and make marriage more exciting; how to keep

From Betty Friedan, *The Feminine Mystique* (New York: W. W. Norton, 1963), pp. 15–16, 22, 23–24, 30–31, 32.

their husbands from dying young and their sons from growing into delinquents. They were taught to pity the neurotic, unfeminine, unhappy women who wanted to be poets or physicists or presidents. They learned that truly feminine women do not want careers, higher education, political rights—the independence and the opportunities that the old-fashioned feminists fought for. Some women, in their forties and fifties, still remembered painfully giving up those dreams, but most of the younger women no longer even thought about them. A thousand expert voices applauded their femininity, their adjustment, their new maturity. All they had to do was devote their lives from earliest girlhood to finding a husband and bearing children.

By the end of the nineteen-fifties, the average marriage age of women in America dropped to 20, and was still dropping, into the teens. Fourteen million girls were engaged by 17. The proportion of women attending college in comparison with men dropped from 47 per cent in 1920 to 35 per cent in 1958. A century earlier, women had fought for higher education; now girls went to college to get a husband. By the mid-fifties, 60 per cent dropped out of college to marry, or because they were afraid too much education would be a marriage bar. Colleges built dormitories for "married students," but the students were almost always the husbands. A new degree was instituted for the wives—"Ph.T." (Putting Husband Through).

In 1960, the problem that has no name burst like a boil through the image of the happy American housewife. In the television commercials the pretty housewives still beamed over their foaming dishpans and *Time*'s cover story on "The Suburban Wife, an American Phenomenon" protested: "Having too good a time . . . to believe that they should be unhappy." But the actual unhappiness of the American housewife was suddenly being reported—from the *New York Times* and *Newsweek* to *Good Housekeeping* and CBS Television ("The Trapped Housewife"), although almost everybody who talked about it found some superficial reason to dismiss it. It was attributed to incompetent appliance repairmen (*New York Times*), or the distances children must be chauffeured in the suburbs (*Time*), or too much PTA (*Redbook*). Some said it was the old problem—education: more and more women had education, which naturally made them unhappy in their role as housewives. "The road from Freud to Frigidaire, from Sophocles to Spock, has turned out to be a bumpy one," reported the *New York Times* (June 28, 1960). "Many young women—certainly not all—whose education plunged them into a world of ideas feel stifled in their homes. They find their routine lives out of joint with their training. Like shut-ins, they feel left out. In the last year, the problem of the educated housewife has provided the meat of dozens of speeches made by troubled presidents of women's colleges who maintain, in the face of complaints, that sixteen years of academic training is realistic preparation for wifehood and motherhood." [. . .]

A number of educators suggested seriously that women no longer be admitted to the four-year colleges and universities: in the growing college crisis, the education which girls could not use as housewives was more urgently needed than ever by boys to do the work of the atomic age.

The problem was also dismissed with drastic solutions no one could take seriously. (A woman writer proposed in *Harper's* that women be drafted for compulsory service as nurses' aides and baby-sitters.) And it was smoothed over with the age-old panaceas: "love is their answer," "the only answer is inner help," "the secret of completeness—children," "a private means of intellectual fulfillment," "to cure this toothache of the spirit—the simple formula of handing one's self and one's will over to God."[1]

The problem was dismissed by telling the housewife she doesn't realize how lucky she is—her own boss, no time clock, no junior executive gunning for her job. What if she isn't happy—does she think men are happy in this world? Does she really, secretly, still want to be a man? Doesn't she know yet how lucky she is to be a woman? [. . .]

Can the problem that has no name be somehow related to the domestic routine of the housewife? When a woman tries to put the problem into words, she often merely describes the daily life she leads. What is there in this recital of comfortable domestic detail that could possibly cause such a feeling of desperation? Is she trapped simply by the enormous demands of her role as modern housewife: wife, mistress, mother, nurse, consumer, cook, chauffeur; expert on interior decoration, child care, appliance repair, furniture refinishing, nutrition, and education? Her day is fragmented as she rushes from dishwasher to washing machine to telephone to dryer to station wagon to supermarket, and delivers Johnny to the Little League field, takes Janey to dancing class, gets the lawnmower fixed and meets the 6:45. She can never spend more than 15 minutes on any one thing; she has no time to read books, only magazines; even if she had time, she has lost the power to concentrate. At the end of the day, she is so terribly tired that sometimes her husband has to take over and put the children to bed.

This terrible tiredness took so many women to doctors in the 1950's that one decided to investigate it. He found, surprisingly, that his patients suffering from "housewife's fatigue" slept more than an adult needed to sleep—as much as ten hours a day—and that the actual energy they expended on housework did not tax their capacity. The real problem must be something else, he decided—perhaps boredom. Some doctors told their women patients they must get out of the house for a day, treat themselves to a movie in town. Others prescribed tranquilizers. Many suburban housewives were taking tranquilizers like cough drops. "You wake up in the morning, and you feel as if there's no point in going on another day like this. So you take a tranquilizer because it makes you not care so much that it's pointless."

It is easy to see the concrete details that trap the suburban housewife, the continual demands on her time. But the chains that bind her in her trap are chains in her own mind and spirit. They are chains made up of mistaken ideas and misinterpreted facts, of incomplete truths and unreal choices. They are not easily seen and not easily shaken off.[. . .]

---

[1]See the seventy-fifth anniversary issue of *Good Housekeeping*, May, 1960, "The Gift of Self," a symposium by Margaret Mead, Jessamyn West, *et al.*

If I am right, the problem that has no name stirring in the minds of so many American women today is not a matter of loss of femininity or too much education, or the demands of domesticity. It is far more important than anyone recognizes. It is the key to these other new and old problems which have been torturing women and their husbands and children, and puzzling their doctors and educators for years. It may well be the key to our future as a nation and a culture. We can no longer ignore that voice within women that says: "I want something more than my husband and my children and my home."

BACKLASH: BLAME IT ON FEMINISM

Susan Faludi

This is an excerpt from Backlash: The Undeclared War against American Women, *published in 1991, which provides a defense for the women's movement.*

To be a woman in America at the close of the 20th century—what good fortune. That's what we keep hearing, anyway. The barricades have fallen, politicians assure us. Women have "made it," Madison Avenue cheers. Women's fight for equality has "largely been won," *Time* magazine announces. Enroll at any university, join any law firm, apply for credit at any bank. Women have so many opportunities now, corporate leaders say, that we don't really need equal opportunity policies. Women are so equal now, lawmakers say, that we no longer need an Equal Rights Amendment. Women have "so much," former President Ronald Reagan says, that the White House no longer needs to appoint them to higher office. Even American Express ads are saluting a woman's freedom to charge it. At last, women have received their full citizenship papers.

And yet . . .

Behind this celebration of the American woman's victory, behind the news, cheerfully and endlessly repeated, that the struggle for women's rights is won, another message flashes. You may be free and equal now, it says to women, but you have never been more miserable.

This bulletin of despair is posted everywhere—at the newsstand, on the TV set, at the movies, in advertisements and doctors' offices and academic journals. Professional women are suffering "burnout" and succumbing to an "infertility epidemic." Single women are grieving from a "man shortage." The *New York Times* reports: Childless women are "depressed and confused" and

From Susan Faludi, *Backlash: The Undeclared War against American Women* (New York: Doubleday, 1991), pp. ix–xv, xxiii.

their ranks are swelling. *Newsweek* says: Unwed women are "hysterical" and crumbling under a "profound crisis of confidence." The health advice manuals inform: High-powered career women are stricken with unprecedented outbreaks of "stress-induced disorders," hair loss, bad nerves, alcoholism, and even heart attacks. The psychology books advise: Independent women's loneliness represents "a major mental health problem today." Even founding feminist Betty Friedan has been spreading the word: she warns that women now suffer from a new identity crisis and "new 'problems that have no name.' "

How can American women be in so much trouble at the same time that they are supposed to be so blessed? If the status of women has never been higher, why is their emotional state so low? If women got what they asked for, what could possibly be the matter now?

The prevailing wisdom of the past decade has supported one, and only one, answer to this riddle: it must be all that equality that's causing all that pain. Women are unhappy precisely *because* they are free. Women are enslaved by their own liberation. They have grabbed at the gold ring of independence, only to miss the one ring that really matters. They have gained control of their fertility, only to destroy it. They have pursued their own professional dreams—and lost out on the greatest female adventure. The women's movement, as we are told time and again, has proved women's own worst enemy.

"In dispensing its spoils, women's liberation has given my generation high incomes, our own cigarette, the option of single parenthood, rape crisis centers, personal lines of credit, free love, and female gynecologists," Mona Charen, a young law student, writes in the *National Review*, in an article titled "The Feminist Mistake." "In return it has effectively robbed us of one thing upon which the happiness of most women rests—men." The *National Review* is a conservative publication, but such charges against the women's movement are not confined to its pages. "Our generation was the human sacrifice" to the women's movement, *Los Angeles Times* feature writer Elizabeth Mehren contends in a *Time* cover story. Baby-boom women like her, she says, have been duped by feminism: "We believed the rhetoric." In *Newsweek*, writer Kay Ebeling dubs feminism "the Great Experiment That Failed" and asserts "women in my generation, its perpetrators, are the casualties." Even the beauty magazines are saying it: *Harper's Bazaar* accuses the women's movement of having "lost us [women] ground instead of gaining it."

In the last decade, publications from the *New York Times* to *Vanity Fair* to the *Nation* have issued a steady stream of indictments against the women's movement, with such headlines as WHEN FEMINISM FAILED or THE AWFUL TRUTH ABOUT WOMEN'S LIB. They hold the campaign for women's equality responsible for nearly every woe besetting women, from mental depression to meager savings accounts, from teenage suicides to eating disorders to bad complexions. The "Today" show says women's liberation is to blame for bag ladies. A guest columnist in the *Baltimore Sun* even proposes that feminists produced the rise in slasher movies. By making the "violence" of abortion more acceptable, the author reasons, women's rights activists made it all right to show graphic murders on screen.[. . .]

Some "liberated" women themselves have joined the lamentations. In confessional accounts, works that invariably receive a hearty greeting from the publishing industry, "recovering Superwomen" tell all. In *The Cost of Loving: Women and the New Fear of Intimacy*, Megan Marshall, a Harvard-pedigreed writer, asserts that the feminist "Myth of Independence" has turned her generation into unloved and unhappy fast-trackers, "dehumanized" by careers and "uncertain of their gender identity." Other diaries of mad Superwomen charge that "the hard-core feminist viewpoint," as one of them puts it, has relegated educated executive achievers to solitary nights of frozen dinners and closet drinking. The triumph of equality, they report, has merely given women hives, stomach cramps, eye-twitching disorders, even comas.

But what "equality" are all these authorities talking about?

If American women are so equal, why do they represent two-thirds of all poor adults? Why are nearly 75 percent of full-time working women making less than $20,000 a year, nearly double the male rate? Why are they still far more likely than men to live in poor housing and receive no health insurance, and twice as likely to draw no pension? Why does the average working woman's salary still lag as far behind the average man's as it did twenty years ago? Why does the average female college graduate today earn less than a man with no more than a high school diploma (just as she did in the '50s)—and why does the average female high school graduate today earn less than a male high school dropout? Why do American women, in fact, face one of the worst gender-based pay gaps in the developed world?

If women have "made it," then why are nearly 80 percent of working women still stuck in traditional "female" jobs—as secretaries, administrative "support" workers and salesclerks? And, conversely, why are they less than 8 percent of all federal and state judges, less than 6 percent of all law partners, and less than one half of 1 percent of top corporate managers? Why are there only three female state governors, two female U.S. senators, and two Fortune 500 chief executives? Why are only nineteen of the four thousand corporate officers and directors women—and why do more than half the boards of Fortune companies still lack even one female member?

If women "have it all," then why don't they have the most basic requirements to achieve equality in the work force? Unlike virtually all other industrialized nations, the U.S. government still has no family-leave and child care programs—and more than 99 percent of American private employers don't offer child care either. Though business leaders say they are aware of and deplore sex discrimination, corporate America has yet to make an honest effort toward eradicating it. In a 1990 national poll of chief executives at Fortune 1000 companies, more than 80 percent acknowledged that discrimination impedes female employees' progress—yet, less than 1 percent of these same companies regarded *remedying* sex discrimination as a goal that their personnel departments should pursue. In fact, when the companies' human resource officers were asked to rate their department's priorities, women's advancement ranked last.

If women are so "free," why are their reproductive freedoms in greater jeopardy today than a decade earlier? Why do women who want to postpone childbearing now have fewer options than ten years ago? The availability of different forms of contraception has declined, research for new birth control has virtually halted, new laws restricting abortion—or even *information* about abortion—for young and poor women have been passed, and the U.S. Supreme Court has shown little ardor in defending the right it granted in 1973.

Nor is women's struggle for equal education over; as a 1989 study found, three-fourths of all high schools still violate the federal law banning sex discrimination in education. In colleges, undergraduate women receive only 70 percent of the aid undergraduate men get in grants and work-study jobs—and women's sports programs receive a pittance compared with men's. A review of state equal-education laws in the late '80s found that only thirteen states had adopted the minimum provisions required by the federal Title IX law—and only seven states had anti-discrimination regulations that covered all education levels.

Nor do women enjoy equality in their own homes, where they still shoulder 70 percent of the household duties—and the only major change in the last fifteen years is that now middle-class men *think* they do more around the house. (In fact, a national poll finds the ranks of women saying their husbands share equally in child care shrunk to 31 percent in 1987 from 40 percent three years earlier.) Furthermore, in thirty states, it is still generally legal for husbands to rape their wives; and only ten states have laws mandating arrest for domestic violence—even though battering was the leading cause of injury of women in the late '80s. Women who have no other option but to flee find that isn't much of an alternative either. Federal funding for battered women's shelters has been withheld and one third of the 1 million battered women who seek emergency shelter each year can find none. Blows from men contributed far more to the rising numbers of "bag ladies" than the ill effects of feminism. In the '80s, almost half of all homeless women (the fastest growing segment of the homeless) were refugees of domestic violence.

The word may be that women have been "liberated," but women themselves seem to feel otherwise. Repeatedly in national surveys, majorities of women say they are still far from equality. Nearly 70 percent of women polled by the *New York Times* in 1989 said the movement for women's rights had only just begun. Most women in the 1990 Virginia Slims opinion poll agreed with the statement that conditions for their sex in American society had improved "a little, not a lot." In poll after poll in the decade, overwhelming majorities of women said they needed equal pay and equal job opportunities, they needed an Equal Rights Amendment, they needed the right to an abortion without government interference, they needed a federal law guaranteeing maternity leave, they needed decent child care services. They have none of these. So how exactly have we "won" the war for women's rights?

Seen against this background, the much ballyhooed claim that feminism is responsible for making women miserable becomes absurd—and irrelevant.

[. . .] The afflictions ascribed to feminism are all myths. From "the man shortage" to "the infertility epidemic" to "female burnout" to "toxic day care," these so-called female crises have had their origins not in the actual conditions of women's lives but rather in a closed system that starts and ends in the media, popular culture, and advertising—an endless feedback loop that perpetuates and exaggerates its own false images of womanhood.

Women themselves don't single out the women's movement as the source of their misery. To the contrary, in national surveys 75 to 95 percent of women credit the feminist campaign with *improving* their lives, and a similar proportion say that the women's movement should keep pushing for change. Less than 8 percent think the women's movement might have actually made their lot worse.[. . .]

To blame feminism for women's "lesser life" is to miss entirely the point of feminism, which is to win women a wider range of experience. Feminism remains a pretty simple concept, despite repeated—and enormously effective—efforts to dress it up in greasepaint and turn its proponents into gargoyles. As Rebecca West wrote sardonically in 1913, "I myself have never been able to find out precisely what feminism is: I only know that people call me a feminist whenever I express sentiments that differentiate me from a doormat."

The meaning of the word "feminist" has not really changed since it first appeared in a book review in the *Athenaeum* of April 27, 1895, describing a woman who "has in her the capacity of fighting her way back to independence." It is the basic proposition that, as Nora put it in Ibsen's *A Doll's House* a century ago, "Before everything else I'm a human being." It is the simply worded sign hoisted by a little girl in the 1970 Women's Strike for Equality: I AM NOT A BARBIE DOLL. Feminism asks the world to recognize at long last that women aren't decorative ornaments, worthy vessels, members of a "special-interest group." They are half (in fact, now more than half) of the national population, and just as deserving of rights and opportunities, just as capable of participating in the world's events, as the other half. Feminism's agenda is basic: It asks that women not be forced to "choose" between public justice and private happiness. It asks that women be free to define themselves—instead of having their identity defined for them, time and again, by their culture and their men.

The fact that these are still such incendiary notions should tell us that American women have a way to go before they enter the promised land of equality.

DEFINING THE GOOD MOTHER

Susan Chira

This article was written in 1992, when the family values issue was being debated.

FREMONT, Mich.—The American mother—that self-sacrificing, self-effacing, cookie-baking icon—has been shoved into the center of a political morality play, one where stick-figure mothers battle in a debate that does not begin to suggest the complexity, diversity and confusion of being a mother in 1992.

Instead of Marilyn Quayle and Hillary Clinton, those emblems of stay-at-home and working mothers, talk to Toni Rumsey, who cried when her first child was born and realized she would have to keep her factory job at Gerber Baby Foods here in Fremont or face living in a trailer.

Or Stacy Murdock, who watches every penny on her farm in Murray, Ky., because her family's income dropped by more than half when she quit teaching, unable to bear leaving her children.

Or Nancy Cassidy, a garment worker in Easton, Pa., who loves to work and believes her children are the better for it.

These mothers are haunted by the ghost of the mythical 1950's television mother—one that most women today cannot be, even if they want to. Caught between a fictional ideal, changing expectations of women's roles and the re-ality that many mothers now work because they must, women around the country are groping for a new definition of the good mother.

RESHAPING MOTHERHOOD

The old images linger, but they fit fewer people's lives. Motherhood in America has undergone a breathtaking transformation in little more than 30 years, pro-pelled by shrinking wages of husbands and changing social attitudes.

In 1960, 20 percent of mothers with children under 6 years old were in the labor force; by last year the figure had swelled to 58 percent, with most of them working full time. Twenty-nine percent of all American families are now headed by one parent.

Some more affluent women choose to work for self-fulfillment, and some who started out that way found that they could not afford to leave their jobs as the economy soured. Whether or not a conservative backlash movement is trying to shame women into staying at home, more and more mothers see work as a financial and personal necessity.[. . .]

"I never feel like I'm a full mom," said Mrs. Rumsey, a 34-year-old mother of two who checks Gerber's baby food for shards of glass and signs of spoilage from 7 A.M. to 3 P.M. "I make the cookies, the homemade costumes for

Halloween. I volunteer for everything to make up to them for not being here. When I do all that, I make myself so tired that they lose a happy cheerful mom, and then I'm cheating them again. It's hard when you were raised with Donna Reed and the Beav's mom."

In another factory in Easton, Pa., Mrs. Cassidy inspects sportswear, and her life as a working mother, for flaws. "I think you can work and be a good mother," said the 42-year-old mother of two. "We're doing it. When people compliment you that they're nice children, then I think you've been a terrific mother." [. . .]

Instead of family breakfasts and school volunteer work, Jan Flint works nights and her husband works days in a Welch's juice and jam plant in Lawton, Mich., so that one of them can always be home with the children.

"That's what God meant for me—to stay at home, cook and sew, and I can't do that," said Mrs. Flint, who had to return to work seven years ago when money got tight. "I used to have a clean house all the time. I always enjoyed being involved in my older two's education. Last night was open house and my children wanted me to go. I bribed them—'I'll let you bring friends over if I don't go.' That's what's happening to the American family. Nobody's there, and children don't have full-time guidance."

Measuring themselves against such an exacting, idealized standard, where good mothering equals how much time is spent with the children rather than how secure or happy the children are, many working women feel they fall short. For the most part, these women struggle without help from society or their employers, who seldom give them long maternity leaves or flexible hours.

And because motherhood itself has been transformed in less than a generation, these mothers have no guides. "What is happening now is that parents are relying on child care who themselves were often raised by their mothers," said Deborah Phillips, a psychologist and expert in child development at the University of Virginia. "So there is incredible anxiety and uncertainty, especially in a society that holds firmly to the belief that mother care is superior."

Sheila Lencki, a mother of four who works as a school secretary in Murray, Ky., says she fears she is failing to meet the standard her own mother set.

"My own mother stayed at home, and that's what I wanted to do," she said. "I respect my mother so much. I think that everything she does is right."

Even more troubling, many women fear they have somehow relinquished their children. "When I put them in day care, I did feel a pull; I'm not the one raising my children," said Mrs. Moorefield, who raised her two children alone for seven years until her remarriage several years ago. "Who's teaching them values?"

That anxiety deepens if mothers suspect their child care is not very good, a suspicion that experts in the field say is often correct. Working-class women usually cannot afford to buy one-on-one attention for their children; most of the women interviewed either left their children with relatives or took them to the home of another mother who was looking after several children for pay.

The quality of such care, in both the physical settings and the attention the children receive, varies considerably. The best care is also often the most expensive, and many women said government could help them most by giving them some financial help with child care.

Many women said they felt lucky to have found help from their families or loving baby sitters. But some said they were making compromises that disturbed them, either leaving children as young as 9 at home alone until they returned from work or having to switch baby sitters frequently.

Although she loves her work, Mrs. Moorefield is torn because she believes her recent change to a 12-hour shift may be hurting her children, who are not doing well in school. She is considering sharing a job, but she must first wait to see whether her husband, who works in an airline stockroom, goes on strike.

Generally, though, most women say, with an air of surprise, that they believe their children are actually turning out all right, even if working interferes with their ideal of a good mother.

"For me, looking at my kids tells me I'm doing O.K.," Mrs. Rumsey said. "My kids are excellent students. They are outgoing. They have minds of their own. No matter how much I've never wanted to work, there's never been any drastic indication from my kids that I shouldn't."

With little chance of living out their ideal of the good mother, many mothers are searching for a new way to think about motherhood.

Elesha Lindsay works days checking references at Forsyth Memorial Hospital in Winston-Salem, N.C., and two nights a week studying for a higher-paying job as a medical stenographer while her husband juggles four jobs as a cook. She leaves her 16-month-old daughter at the hospital's day-care center, where she believes her daughter is happy and well-cared for. Yet she cried all week when she first had to return to work, when her daughter was 9 weeks old. She and a friend filled in for each other so she could add three weeks onto the hospital's normal six-week maternity leave.

Although she would rather work part time when her daughter is small, Mrs. Lindsay sees herself as a good mother, and work as a welcome part of her life.

"Being a good mother depends on what type of person you are and what you instill," she said. "My mother wasn't there the majority of the time, but I was watching her, knowing the type of person she was. We knew what our mother expected from us. That child is spending more time with that day-care giver than you, but I still feel like I'm a better person for her, out working, financially helping the family."

Mrs. Cassidy, the garment worker, also believes that too many mothers become obsessed with motherhood's gestures rather than its substance. "It doesn't matter if you bake cookies for them, and don't take them to Cub Scouts every time," she said. "You're not going to be there for their first step. But I never heard mine say, 'You were never there when I needed you.'"

Still, many mothers worry that they may be deluding themselves. "It looks fine to me," Mrs. Lencki said, "but maybe I'm not looking."

While there is debate about the effects of extensive nonmaternal care early in life, experts agree that with conscientious, loving parents and high-quality care the vast majority of children do just fine, by any measurement of intellectual and emotional development. Some studies suggest that mothers' attitudes are crucial; if they are happy, whether staying at home or working, that will have an enormous impact on their relationship with their children.

Employer flexibility clearly makes a difference, said Arlie Hochschild, a sociologist and author of *The Second Shift: Working Parents and the Revolution at Home* (Viking, 1989), who is now studying the workplace and its effects on family life. "We have to acknowledge that the majority of American women will work for the majority of their lives through their childbearing years and we have to adapt the workplace," she said. "Don't pretend they're men who have wives at home to do this."

One reason Mrs. Cassidy feels little guilt is that she was able to take off work to watch her children in school plays, or tend them when they were sick. But other companies, particularly factories where workers' absences may slow assembly lines, are not so lenient. Several women said their employers required 24-hour notice for sick days—an impossibility with children—or docked their pay if they wanted to go to an event at their children's schools.

But even if they did not choose to work, some mothers have found that working has brought unexpected benefits: a new sense of identity, a role in a broader community, pride in their independence, a temporary escape from children that may allow them to be better mothers in the time they share.

And while women may yearn for the safe world of mythic families, they have seen enough of the sobering reality of divorce and widowhood to cherish the financial independence that working confers. "My mother stayed home, and when my father divorced her she had nothing to fall back on," said Donna King, a hospital laboratory supervisor who is a mother of four.

In fact, most of the women interviewed said they would prefer working to staying at home—but most wanted to work part time.

These days, some more affluent and educated women say they would feel embarrassed to tell their friends that they did not work. Yet many working-class mothers who have found that they are happy working treat it like a guilty secret. Mrs. Lencki dropped her voice almost to a whisper when she talked about enjoying her job, despite her guilt that her youngest son had not had her full-time presence.

Pride, embarrassment and defiance competed as Mrs. Moorefield talked about work. "For me, the ideal mother is one who is able to choose," Mrs. Moorefield said. "Even if we could financially afford that I could not work, I still think I would need at least some other contact, part time. You want to be there for your children, and on the other hand you want to be able to provide for them well. This sounds like I'm anti-family values . . ."

3. How Do Men Define Their Roles?

MANHOOD IN THE TWENTIETH CENTURY

E. Anthony Rotundo

These excerpts about some of the possible role models for modern males are taken from Rotundo's book American Manhood: Transformations in Masculinity from the Revolution to the Modern Era. *It was published in 1993.*

From the late eighteenth century to the late twentieth, "manhood" has changed along with its environment. Two centuries ago, the town and the extended family formed the matrix of life in the Northern states. For some, the church congregation also provided a society in which a man (or woman) might develop an identity. Now, at the end of the 1900s, those institutions have faded in importance for most middle-class folk. Our primary community is the nuclear family, which is an isolated unit under the best of circumstances—and current circumstances are not the best, for a large proportion of nuclear families are riven by divorce. The large bureaucratic institutions where so many middle-class men work resemble eighteenth-century communities in certain ways: they are hierarchical, and they make elaborate demands on the individual. Unlike the more genuine communities of the colonial and revolutionary eras, however, the great corporate bodies of our time do not provide the individual with security, nor with any sense of organized connection to other people or to the flow of human history.

In the twentieth century, some of our most engaging experiences of community come from our participation in communities of consumption.[1] To be moved as part of a concert audience or to discover someone who shares one's tastes can be exciting experiences, but neither of them guarantees the sense of personal connection or support that a human community can provide.

As many social critics have recently noted, we lack even the rudiments of a language to discuss community and connection.[2] This point is starkly illustrated when a president of the United States, trying to praise the voluntary help that some people give to others, resorts again and again to the image of "a thousand points of light" to describe what he praises. Surely, a society that valued connectedness would be able to produce a more accurate image of human help and kindness than this vision of separation in a vast, cold darkness.

Of course, in losing a strong sense of community, we have gained something else vitally important. Once, men had their positions in society ascribed to them largely by birth; now, those positions are a matter of individual achievement. The weight of the community and the dead hand of the past rest more

From E. Anthony Rotundo, *American Manhood: Transformations in Masculinity from the Revolution to the Modern Era* (New York: Basic Books, 1993), pp. 284–287, 289, 362–363.

lightly upon the individual—especially the male individual—than they once did. Individual initiative, as a principle, has been applied far beyond matters of social status. Middle-class men of the last two centuries have had profoundly individualistic experiences; each one must earn approval, win love, attain power, make friendship, mold an identity.[3] Since the early 1800s, these have all become individual quests. They are (as we like to think of it) detached from social necessity in a way that was not possible two hundred or more years ago. Even where we have genuine communities in our own time (be it in the nuclear family, in friendship groups, or in small, informal organizations), they are created by individual effort. We cherish our belief in individual initiative, our sense that the fate of each person lies in that person's hands.

We also cherish our modern notion that the core of each individual is an inner essence, a unique combination of temperament, passion, and personal experience untouched by society. This idea of a deep, true passionate self has been with us for at least two centuries, but not until the turn of the twentieth century did middle-class men and women begin to rethink the relationship between the self and the molding efforts of the individual. For the American bourgeoisie, the nineteenth century was a time of self-making, both in the economic sense and in the sense of shaping the desires and talents of the inner self to fit the proper moral and social forms. The twentieth century, by contrast, has been increasingly a time of self-realization, when individuals have worked to let their impulses and personal potentials flourish. In little more than a hundred years, the balance of bourgeois values has tipped from self-discipline to self-expression, from self-denial to self-enjoyment.

The true male nature is thought to deserve the same thing that any other portion of the deepest self deserves—an outlet in the real world. Men are still perceived as more aggressive, more primitive, more lustful, more dominating, and more independent than women—but how can these manly passions fit into the organized civilization of the twentieth century? This is nearly the same question that men and women asked at the start of the nineteenth century, when men's aggressive ambitions were set loose from the restraints of hierarchy and communal opinion; but the context for asking the question is very different today.

Middle-class observers at the dawn of the nineteenth century treated "male" passions—assertive and competitive drives—with fearful condemnation. The cultural structure of separate spheres was erected to allow expression of those drives for the greater economic and political good in a way that would also isolate them from sanctuaries of civilization and provide their male carriers with a source of constant purification. In the twentieth century, the competitive, aggressive drives—though still defined as male—are seen with less fear and more reverence. We think of them as vital contents of a man's true self in an era when the true self is regarded as sacrosanct. Although impulses to dominance and assertion are still viewed with some suspicion, there is general agreement that they can be productive and that they deserve a social outlet without stigma. This, in turn, raises an important question for twentieth-century men: What are the best outlets for the "male" passions in the twentieth century?

Men have developed several ideals of manhood that have offered answers to this question. One ideal is the "team player." Based on an ethic of sublimation, this ideal takes competitive athletics as a model for fitting aggression and rivalry into the new bureaucratic work settings of the twentieth century.[4] While a man struggles to reach the top within his own organization through fierce competition with his teammates, he also cooperates with them in the contest between his organization and others. In this way, the old investment of aggressive, selfish passions in economic competition has gained new life in the modern world.

Another strategy for establishing a relationship between male passion and modern life is represented by the "existential hero." This ideal grows out of a belief that there is, in fact, no proper place for true masculine impulse within modern society. The hero who lives by this belief is suspicious of authority, wary of women, and disgusted with corrupt civilization. If he would be true to the purity of his male passions and principles, he must—and can only—live at the margins of society. This romantic ideal has been embodied in such popular figures as Humphrey Bogart, Ernest Hemingway, and John Wayne.[5] It has an economic counterpart in the cult of the entrepreneur who pursues his vision outside the contaminating influence of corporate institutions.

A third approach is signified by the ideal of the "pleasure seeker." This is a man who works hard at his job so that he can afford as much satisfaction of his passions after work as possible. Some men might find such outlets in exciting, dangerous sports like skydiving or rock climbing. They may seek adventure through risky drugs, risky driving, and risky games with money (speculation and other forms of high-stakes gambling). A pleasure-seeking middle-class man can become a consumer connoisseur, pursuing the finest clothes, the finest cars, the finest art and entertainment, or the finest women. One form of this ideal has found expression in *Playboy* magazine. Its pages make explicit what is only implied in other commercial media—that sex and beautiful women are consumer products, accoutrements to the good life. They are one outlet for the masculine passions of the pleasure seeker.[6]

In the late twentieth century, one more symbolic ideal of manhood has emerged, the "spiritual warrior." Conjured up in the teaching of Robert Bly and other leaders of the mythopoeic men's movement, this ideal was born of dissatisfaction with the other ideals and images of men that have recently dominated American culture. It grows from a direct, conscious focus on the passions that its advocates assume are naturally male.[7] The spiritual warrior believes he has lost touch with those passions and lost his ability to connect directly with other men. In the process, he has been prevented from fulfilling his deepest spiritual needs as well.[8]

This understanding of manhood appeals intensely to many men because of its focus on fatherhood. Bly and others lament the growing distance between fathers and sons in the modern world. The teachers of the spiritual warrior ideal see the disconnection of sons from their fathers repeating itself in the disconnection of men from passion, from the spirit, from their fellow men. Here begins a striking series of parallels with the movement toward primitive masculinity at the turn of the twentieth century. For the spokesmen of that movement voiced the same concerns about the absence of fathers that men are voicing today. They also expressed the same anxiety about the dangers of a boy learning his vision of manhood through the eyes of mothers and other women.[9][. . .]

There is one important trait that all four ideals share. [. . .] Each of them signifies a turning away from women. The ideal of the spiritual warrior represents a ritual quest for manhood in an all-male setting. The ideal of the pleasure seeker may treat women as objects of pleasure or as accessory companions in his pursuit of enjoyment, but considers them largely irrelevant to the fulfillment of his yearnings. The ideal of the existential hero endorses separation from the confinement of civilization and the halter of permanent, personal commitment—and, given our cultural associations between women and the bonds of civilization, it is no surprise that adherents of this ideal view women's world with suspicion.

The world of the team player is less intrinsically exclusive of women than that of the other ideals. Pristine in its blindness to personal history, the great contest for success is technically open to anyone who can play and win according to its competitive rules. As we have seen historically, however, the middle-class male workplace was constructed by men according to shared male values and customs that are culturally alien to women. In recent years, women have made statistical inroads in the world of the team player, but as yet there is little change—culturally or statistically—at the level where most power is wielded.[13] In reality, the ideal of the team player posits a world where women have difficulty surviving even though they are not explicitly forbidden to enter.

NOTES

1. The term "communities of consumption" is Daniel Boorstin's. See Boorstin, *The Americans: The Democratic Experience* (New York, 1973), 89–164.
2. The central text here is Robert N. Bellah et al., *Habits of the Heart: Individualism and Commitment in American Life* (New York, 1985). For an earlier statement of this theme, see Philip Slater, *The Pursuit of Loneliness: American Culture at the Breaking Point* (Boston, 1970).
3. Alexis de Tocqueville in *Democracy in America* (trans. Henry Reeve [New York, 1945]) described much of this and anticipated its consequences. Most poignantly, see vol. 2, 144–47.
4. In his study of male heroes in magazines, Theodore P. Greene (*America's Heroes: The Changing Models of Success in American Magazines* [New York, 1970]) notes the rise of "Idols of Organization" in the mid-1910s. Greene describes these men as hard-working, efficient organizers who brought nineteenth-century persistence and industry into a bureaucratic work setting. The new hero was a team player who believed deeply in efficient organization and cooperation. As Greene depicts him, "the new 'Idol of Organization' was neither the creator nor the owner of the enterprise which he ran. The new demand was for men who could take over existing organizations and run them with a minimum of human friction and a maximum of practical results" (Greene, *America's Heroes*, 333–34).

5. On Hemingway as a model of manhood, see Leonard Kriegel, *On Men and Masculinity* (New York, 1979), 89–112. The existential hero—and variations on the ideal—in American movies are treated in Donald Spoto, *Camerado: Hollywood and the American Man* (New York, 1978). See also an essay on Clint Eastwood as a late twentieth-century hero: Robert Mazzocco, "The Supply-Side Star," *New York Review of Books*, Apr. 1, 1982.

6. The very term *playboy* shows how old standards of manhood have been turned on their heads. The idea that a man should aspire to be a boy would have been sufficiently shocking to an eighteenth-century Yankee. The idea that this boy-man's goal in life was to play would have seemed downright effeminate. For an analysis of *Playboy* that stresses rebellion against domesticity rather than regression, see Barbara Ehrenreich, *The Hearts of Men: The American Dream and the Flight from Commitment* (New York, 1984), 42–51. See also her analysis of the Beat movement of the 1950s as another reaction to twentieth-century middle-class concepts of home and family (52–67). Harvey Cox, looking at the surface of the magazine more than its underlying philosophy, has described *Playboy* as a guide to a style of manhood (based largely on consumption) that emphasizes the pursuit of pleasure. See Harvey Cox, *The Secular City: Secularization and Urbanization in Theological Perspective* (New York, 1966), 172–78.

7. The mythopoeic men's movement differs with this book in its basic assumptions about gender. Its stance is "essentialism": manhood begins with a timeless, unchanging core of qualities that all men ultimately possess. The stance of this book is one of "cultural construction": manhood is a mental category created and recreated by cultures as they, and their social and physical environments, change.

8. For a useful summary of what the men's movement is about, see Jack Thomas, "The New Man: Finding Another Way to Be Male," *Boston Globe*, Aug. 21, 1991, 43, 46–47; "Following the Beat of a Different Drum," Aug. 21, 1991, 43, 46; and "The Bible of the Men's Movement," Aug. 21, 1991, 43, 47.

9. These concerns are summarized in Edward S. Martin, "The Use of Fathers," *Harper's New Monthly Magazine*, 117 (1908); G. Stanley Hall, "Feminization in Schools and Home: The Undue Influence of Women Teachers—The Need of Different Training for the Sexes," *World's Work*, 16 (1908); and C. P. Seldon, "Rule of Mother," *North American Review* (1895). Joe L. Dubbert explores the turn-of-the-century literature on absent fathers in *A Man's Place: Masculinity in Transition* (Englewood Cliffs, N.J., 1979), 140–44.

. . .

13. Some of the changes and the roadblocks are summarized in Lisa Belkin, "Bars to Equality of Sexes Seen as Eroding, Slowly," *New York Times*, Aug. 20, 1989, 1, 26; Alison Leigh Cowan, "Women's Gains on the Job: Not without a Heavy Toll," *New York Times*, Aug. 21, 1989, 1, 14.

BREAKING THE SPELL: MEN AND MEN'S GROUPS

Aaron Kipnis

These are excerpts from an article written by a leader of the men's movement and author of the book Knights Without Armor.

In the years since the new knights, the men's group I belong to, began meeting, we've frequently been asked by other men, "How do you start a men's group?" or "What do you do in your men's group?" A number of men expressed interest in joining our group. But we wanted to keep the core group small and intimate, so we would invite them to visit our group just for an evening or two. As a result of their experience, quite a few went on to start groups of their own. Several of us visited those groups in the early stages. We would offer what we could in the way of support and direction, and then withdraw.

Through my work as a psychologist concerned with gender issues, moreover, I've initiated numerous men's and mixed-gender groups, visited many existing groups, and attended dozens of men's conferences. Most of the new knights also have attended workshops, visited other groups and been mentors as well. Along the way we've compared our notes from these experiences and integrated them with our personal work in the new knights. It has become increasingly important to us as an element of our recovery to reach out and be available to other men.

In our experience, groups can form around many diverse issues. A few examples are:

1. Men's-rights groups, which address inequities in the social and legal system. Much of this work involves fathers' rights and advocacy for male victims of abuse and discrimination.
2. Mythopoetic groups that focus on ritual, men's spirituality and building male community. These groups reclaim sacred images of masculinity.
3. Groups that focus on gay rights and other gay issues, such as the three levels of coming out—personal, private and public—overcoming internalized homophobia (building gay-affirming self-esteem); fighting discrimination; increasing intimacy (moving beyond sex addiction); understanding the complexities of same-sex couples; and building gay-affirming community.
4. Male codependency groups, which focus on the issues of men who give too much. These groups focus on different issues from the oft-repeated women's issues depicted in the popular literature. Men benefit from looking at their relationship problems through a lens that affirms masculine ethics and examines the ways in which women equally contribute to relationship problems.

Man!, Winter, 1991, pp. 10–14.

5. Groups like our new knights, which focus on recovery in a broad sense. This work also led us to men's-rights issues, healing the wounds of childhood abuse and concerns with recovering soul—the mythopoetic query.

6. Other 12-step-inspired groups work with issues of specific addictions. The principles taught in these programs and the guidelines offered for meetings also offer valuable directions for men's work.

From our point of view, recovery issues underlie the work of all men's groups. It's doubtful you'll get much out of a mythopoetic quest or adequately claim your rights to be a parent if you haven't faced the tyranny of your own addictive behaviors. However, focusing only on pathologies may keep you identifying yourself as a victim, an adult child—not really a man. So it's important to take what you can from this 12-step work and leave the rest.

Once men gather for the first time, they often ask: Now that we're all here, what do we say? What should we do?

Many of us are habitually rational, goal-directed and focused on the content and outcome of things. When men come together, there's often a tendency to talk around issues, instead of about them. We may tend to fill the space swapping old tales and discussing current events. Our early meetings of the knights focused more on the poker game in front of us, news of the day and business concerns than on our sobriety. This traditional men's-club sort of activity is enjoyable and natural. It's also what comes easiest for us all.

The easiest route, however, isn't always the most direct road toward healing and transformation. For example, Carl Jung points out that the individuation process is an operation *contra naturum*—opposite to our nature. The same may be true about the process of claiming a new vision of masculinity.

Talking about our personal issues—our hopes, fears, frustrations and weaknesses—is more difficult. Expressing our uncensored feelings to one another is even more challenging. But it's more healing, valuable and a better use of the limited time we have available for men's work. Through revealing our wounds, we also engender support for whatever crisis or difficult challenge we're facing at the moment. At any time we may be slipping in our sobriety; experiencing conflict in our relationships, problems with our children, or stress at work; confronting health or financial problems; or having some other form of distress. Through including the men of the lodge in our struggles, our load is lightened. We receive new perspectives and commiseration. We no longer feel we must face everything alone. Our relationships with women no longer have to carry the entire burden of our emotional needs. This alone can improve our relationships significantly.

Sharing our hope, strength and experience with one another will undoubtedly affect our relations with one another, our families and the community at large. For that and for many other reasons, it's important to hold confidentiality as a basic tenet of our work. We don't want to risk muddying the group's waters with gossip. So we don't share the details of our meetings, even with our mates. This isn't easy, but it's a measure of respect for the other men in our group. On that note, all of the new knights have read this manuscript. Nothing has been included that they have not wanted to divulge for the benefit of the reader.

In addition to talking openly about our personal issues, we also try to incorporate some non-verbal work. Drumming, making music, movement, working with art forms to express our feelings, hiking, cooking for each other, and even dancing have found their way into our meetings. This gets us out of our heads and breaks the rigid hold of tensions or problems we may be carrying.

The major benefit we've all reaped, however, has been from our regular conversations about issues that are central to our lives and our recovery. In our shadowy, neglected and funky places are often found the keys to personal transformation. Outside of private therapy, our group is one of the few places we've ever felt supported for discussing our addictions, depressions, failures, inferiorities, dark fantasies, fears, and wild, hopeful dreams.

Many men feel wounded by failures to live up to the heroic ideal and by the lack of support for radical change that we often encounter in our environment. Through sharing our failures with one another, we've healed much of this shame. We now believe that our failures are badges of honor earned for trying to succeed at all. Our lodge is also a place to celebrate our successes and transformations. We acknowledge one another for our triumphs, both small and large. It gives our lives greater meaning when our accomplishments are heralded by others.

BEING A MAN

Paul Theroux

This author was born in 1941 and writes travel literature. He first published this essay in Sunrise with Seamonsters *in 1985.*

There is a pathetic sentence in the chapter "Fetishism" in Dr. Norman Cameron's book *Personality Development and Psychopathology*. It goes, "Fetishists are nearly always men; and the commonest fetish is a woman's shoe." I cannot read that sentence without thinking that it is just one more awful thing about being a man—and perhaps it is an important thing to know about us.

Excerpts from Paul Theroux, "Being a Man," *Sunrise with Seamonsters: Travels and Discoveries* (Boston: Houghton Mifflin, 1985).

I have always disliked being a man. The whole idea of manhood in America is pitiful, in my opinion. This version of masculinity is a little like having to wear an ill-fitting coat for one's entire life (by contrast, I imagine femininity to be an oppressive sense of nakedness). Even the expression "Be a man!" strikes me as insulting and abusive. It means: Be stupid, be unfeeling, obedient, soldierly and stop thinking. Man means "manly"—how can one think about men without considering the terrible ambition of manliness? And yet it is part of every man's life. It is a hideous and crippling lie; it not only insists on difference and connives at superiority, it is also by its very nature destructive—emotionally damaging and socially harmful.

The youth who is subverted, as most are, into believing in the masculine ideal is effectively separated from women and he spends the rest of his life finding women a riddle and a nuisance. Of course, there is a female version of this male affliction. It begins with mothers encouraging little girls to say (to other adults) "Do you like my new dress?" In a sense, little girls are traditionally urged to please adults with a kind of coquettishness, while boys are enjoined to behave like monkeys towards each other. The nine-year-old coquette proceeds to become womanish in a subtle power game in which she learns to be sexually indispensable, socially decorative and always alert to a man's sense of inadequacy.

Femininity—being lady-like—implies needing a man as witness and seducer; but masculinity celebrates the exclusive company of men. That is why it is so grotesque; and that is also why there is no manliness without inadequacy—because it denies men the natural friendship of women.

It is very hard to imagine any concept of manliness that does not belittle women, and it begins very early. At an age when I wanted to meet girls—let's say the treacherous years of thirteen to sixteen—I was told to take up a sport, get more fresh air, join the Boy Scouts, and I was urged not to read so much. It was the 1950s and if you asked too many questions about sex you were sent to camp—boy's camp, of course: the nightmare. Nothing is more unnatural or prisonlike than a boy's camp, but if it were not for them we would have no Elk's Lodges, no pool rooms, no boxing matches, no Marines.

And perhaps no sports as we know them. Everyone is aware of how few in number are the athletes who behave like gentlemen. Just as high school basketball teaches you how to be a poor loser, the manly attitude towards sports seems to be little more than a recipe for creating bad marriages, social misfits, moral degenerates, sadists, latent rapists and just plain louts. I regard high school sports as a drug far worse than marijuana, and it is the reason that the average tennis champion, say, is a pathetic oaf.

Any objective study would find the quest for manliness essentially right-wing, puritanical, cowardly, neurotic and fueled largely by a fear of women. It is also certainly philistine. There is no book-hater like a Little League coach. But indeed all the creative arts are obnoxious to the manly ideal, because at their best the arts are pursued by uncompetitive and essentially solitary people. It makes it very hard for a creative youngster, for any boy who expresses the desire to be alone seems to be saying that there is something wrong with him.

It ought to be clear by now that I have something of an objection to the way we turn boys into men. It does not surprise me that when the President of the United States has his customary weekend off he dresses like a cowboy—it is both a measure of his insecurity and his willingness to please. In many ways, American culture does little more for a man than prepare him for modeling clothes in the L. L. Bean catalogue. I take this as a personal insult because for many years I found it impossible to admit to myself that I wanted to be a writer. It was my guilty secret, because being a writer was incompatible with being a man.

There are people who might deny this, but that is because the American writer, typically, has been so at pains to prove his manliness that we have come to see literariness and manliness as mingled qualities. But first there was a fear that writing was not a manly profession—indeed, not a profession at all. (The paradox in American letters is that it has always been easier for a woman to write and for a man to be published.) Growing up, I had thought of sports as wasteful and humiliating, and the idea of manliness was a bore. My wanting to become a writer was not a flight from that oppressive role-playing, but I quickly saw that it was at odds with it. Everything in stereotyped manliness goes against the life of the mind. The Hemingway personality is too tedious to go into here, and in any case his exertions are well-known, but certainly it was not until this aberrant behavior was examined by feminists in the 1960s that any male writer dared question the pugnacity in Hemingway's fiction. All the bullfighting and arm wrestling and elephant shooting diminished Hemingway as a writer, but it is consistent with a prevailing attitude in American writing: one cannot be a male writer without first proving that one is a man.

It is normal in America for a man to be dismissive or even somewhat apologetic about being a writer. Various factors make it easier. There is a heartiness about journalism that makes it acceptable—journalism is the manliest form of American writing and, therefore, the profession the most independent-minded women seek (yes, it is an illusion, but that is my point). Fiction-writing is equated with a kind of dispirited failure and is only manly when it produces wealth—money is masculinity. So is drinking. Being a drunkard is another assertion, if misplaced, of manliness. The American male writer is traditionally proud of his heavy drinking. But we are also a very literal-minded people. A man proves his manhood in America in old-fashioned ways. He kills lions, like Hemingway; or he hunts ducks, like Nathanael West; or he makes pronouncements like, "A man should carry enough knife to defend himself with," as James Jones once said to a *Life* interviewer. Or he says he can drink you under the table. But even tiny drunken William Faulkner loved to mount a horse and go fox hunting, and Jack Kerouac roistered up and down Manhattan in a lumberjack shirt (and spent every night of *The Subterraneans* with his mother in Queens). And we are familiar with the lengths to which Norman Mailer is prepared, in his endearing way, to prove that he is just as much a monster as the next man.

When the novelist John Irving was revealed as a wrestler, people took him to be a very serious writer; and even a bubble reputation like Eric (*Love Story*)

Segal's was enhanced by the news that he ran the marathon in a respectable time. How surprised we would be if Joyce Carol Oates were revealed as a sumo wrestler or Joan Didion active in pumping iron. "Lives in New York City with her three children" is the typical woman writer's biographical note, for just as the male writer must prove he has achieved a sort of muscular manhood, the woman writer—or rather her publicists—must prove her motherhood.

There would be no point in saying any of this if it were not generally accepted that to be a man is somehow—even now in feminist-influenced America—a privilege. It is on the contrary an unmerciful and punishing burden. Being a man is bad enough; being manly is appalling (in this sense, women's lib has done much more for men than for women). It is the sinister silliness of men's fashions, and a clubby attitude in the arts. It is the subversion of good students. It is the so-called "Dress Code" of the Ritz-Carlton Hotel in Boston, and it is the institutionalized cheating in college sports. It is the most primitive insecurity.

And this is also why men often object to feminism but are afraid to explain why: of course women have a justified grievance, but most men believe—and with reason—that their lives are just as bad.

QUESTIONS TO HELP YOU THINK AND WRITE ABOUT MEN'S AND WOMEN'S ROLES

1. Do you agree or disagree with Tannen about the differences in conversation and discussion styles of men and women? Have some of your instructors in the past been better teachers of one gender than the other? Why? Support your answer with evidence from Tannen's article as well as with examples and narratives from your own experience. What would improve the environment in your argument class and make it easier for you to contribute to class discussion?

2. Respond to Wolf's claim that women do not contribute to public argument as much as men, not because they can't, but because they are not expected to. Do you agree or disagree? Give reasons. Should women, in your opinion, participate more? What would be required to create better participation from women? It may be useful to consider this issue from a variety of points of view: Is it a fact? What has caused it? Would it be valuable if more women participated? What can be done to create more female participation in public argument?

3. Read "Ending the Battle between the Sexes" and mark a passage that you either strongly agree with or strongly disagree with. Take five minutes to freewrite the reasons for your opinions. Discuss your ideas with your writing group or with a group composed only of members of your gender. Then report the conclusions of your group to the class. Now make a claim and write an argument that has been inspired by this discussion.

4. Read Friedan's essay and answer the question, What is the problem that has no

name? Seek the perspective of students in class who remember the 1950s. Was it a problem then for all women? For a few? Bring it up to date. Is it a problem now? How severe a problem? How do those who perceive it as a problem try to solve it? Are the solutions good or bad? Evaluate them from a personal and a societal perspective.

5. What does Faludi mean by a "backlash" in feminism? What is your position on feminism as it is described in this article? Think of some reasons to support Faludi's position. Think of other reasons why she might be wrong. Describe some personal examples to support both of the following claims: women are more equal now than they were before; women are less equal now than they were before. Which do you agree with? Why?

6. Imagine Friedan, Faludi, and Chira in conversation about women's roles. On which points about women's roles as wife, mother, and worker outside of the home would they agree and on which would they disagree? Now join this conversation yourself. Which of these authors best represents your views about contemporary women's roles at home, at work, and in society?

7. Consider the four roles described for modern men in Rotundo's article. Are they sufficient? Or would you add to the list? What? Why? Evaluate these roles. Why are they good? Why are they bad? Is a mix possible? What would be a good mix? Why?

8. Compare the article on men's groups by Kipnis with the article on the same subject on page 222. What are the two views expressed in these articles? Which author presents the more convincing argument? Why? Which author do you agree with? Why?

9. Theroux challenges some of the male stereotypes. What do you think his exigence was for writing on this subject? Do you share this exigence? Why or why not?

10. Imagine Rotundo and Chira married with children and trying to work out the problem of child care. How do you think they would solve this problem? Would you agree or disagree with their solutions? Consider what your own policy for child care might be if you had children.

SECTION II

Issues in Education

WHAT ARE THE ISSUES?

1. What Should Schools Teach?

Three authors continue the enduring argument about what students should learn. Specifically, they focus on some areas that are not traditionally associated with the traditional curriculum. They examine the controversies associated with teaching students to value the diversity associated with modern culture, to develop self-esteem, and to develop a stronger sense of spirituality. See also "How to Save Science in the Classroom," pp. 230–231, "A Cultural Diversity Course Requirement," pp. 554–556, and "Special Education's Best Intentions," pp. 74–77.

2. How Should Learning Be Graded/Evaluated?

The articles in this section explore the problems associated with grading, grade inflation, and national testing. See also "Learning by Intimidation," pp. 170–171

3. How Far Should Schools Go to Eliminate Bias in Education?

Four articles give evidence for bias against women and minorities in education and describe efforts to eliminate it.

4. What Can Be Done about Educational Costs?

See the article on pages 21–22, "Some College Costs Should Be Tax Deductible" to help you think about this issue.

THE RHETORICAL SITUATION

In classical times, Plato argued that students should not be allowed to read poetry because it appealed to emotion and warped the perception of truth. In the seventeenth century, Milton made a strong case for introducing writing instruction late in students' careers, after they had read widely and deeply on many subjects. What students should learn, when they should learn it, and who should teach it are enduring issues that continue to receive lively attention.

     For example, some people argue that the traditional curriculum that focuses mainly on the European cultural heritage should be broadened to include the study of minority and third world cultural heritages. Another issue, what schools should and should not teach in addition to the traditional subjects, is familiar to all of you. For some people, athletics, art, and music are unnecessary additions that threaten the essential core of instruction. For others, a variety of skills and even personal values are considered essential additions to the traditional core. What students should know and be able to do when they leave school and take their places as workers and citizens is at the heart of this issue. Successful education, in most people's minds, leads to successful lives and a successful society. What constitutes a successful life and a successful society provide some of the warrants for this issue.

Because everyone in the United States is expected to attend school, there is a constant exigency for a wide variety of education issues. Only a few of them are represented here. They include what schools should teach, grading and other forms of evaluation, the problems of bias and unequal opportunity in school, and the high costs of education. As a student yourself, you will undoubtedly be able to add your own related issues to this list.

1. What Should Schools Teach?

THE VALUE OF MULTICULTURALISM

Ronald Takaki

Ronald Takaki is professor of ethnic studies at the University of California at Berkeley and the author of From Different Shores: Perspective on Race and Ethnicity in America. *This article first appeared in the* Chronicle of Higher Education *in 1989 and was reprinted in* Liberal Education *in 1991.*

In Palolo Valley, Hawaii, where I lived as a child, my neighbors were Japanese, Chinese, Portuguese, Filipino, and Hawaiian. I heard voices with different accents and I heard different languages. I played with children of different colors. Why, I wondered, were families representing such an array of nationalities living together in one little valley? My teachers and textbooks did not explain our diversity.

After graduation from high school, I attended a college on the mainland where students and even professors would ask me how long I had been in America and where I had learned to speak English. "In this country," I would reply. "I was born in America, and my family has been here for three generations."

Today, some twenty years later, Asian American as well as African American, Chicano/Latino, and Native American students continue to find themselves perceived as strangers on college campuses. Moreover, they are encountering a new campus racism. The targets of ugly racial slurs and violence, they have begun to ask critical questions about why knowledge of their histories and communities is excluded from the curriculum. White students also are realizing the need to understand the cultural diversity of American society.

Liberal Education, 77, no. 3 (1991): 9–10.

In response, colleges and universities across the country have been discussing the institution of required courses designed to help students understand diverse cultures. The debate is taking place within a general context framed by academic pundits like Allan Bloom and E. D. Hirsch. Both ask: What is an educated, culturally literate person? I think Bloom is right when he says: "There are some things one must know about if one is to be educated. . . . The university should try to have a vision of what an educated person is." I also agree with Hirsch when he insists that there is a body of cultural information that "every American needs to know."

But the question is: What should be the content of education and what does cultural literacy mean? The traditional curriculum reflects what Howard Swearer, former president of Brown University, has described as a "certain provincialism," an overly Eurocentric perspective. Concerned about this problem, a Brown University visiting committee recommended that the faculty consider requiring students to take an ethnic studies course before they graduate. "The contemporary definition of an educated person," the committee said, "must include at least minimal awareness of multicultural reality. . . ."

What would be the focus and content of such multicultural courses? There is a wide range of possibilities. For many years I have been teaching "Racial Inequality in America: A Comparative Historical Perspective." Who we are in this society and how we are perceived and treated have been conditioned by America's racial and ethnic diversity. My approach is captured in the phrase "from different shores." By "shores," I intend a double meaning. One is the shores that immigrants left to go to America. . . . The second is the different and often conflicting shores or perspectives from which scholars have viewed the experiences of racial and ethnic groups.

My students read Thomas Sowell's *Ethnic America: A History* and my *Iron Cages: Race and Culture in 19th-Century America*. Readings also include Winthrop Jordan on racism, John Higham on nativism, Clara Rodríguez on Puerto Ricans, and William J. Wilson as well as Charles Murray on the black underclass. By critically examining different "shores," students are able to address complex comparative questions: How have the experiences of racial minorities such as blacks and Asians been similar to, and different from, one another? Is "race" the same as "ethnicity"? How have race relations been shaped by economic developments, as well as by culture? What impact have these forces had on moral values about how people should think and behave, beliefs about human nature and society, and images of the past as well as the future? . . .

The need to open the American mind to greater cultural diversity will not go away. We can resist it by ignoring the changing ethnic composition of our student bodies and the larger society, or we can realize how it offers colleges and universities a timely and exciting opportunity to revitalize the social sciences and humanities, giving both a new sense of purpose and a more inclusive definition of knowledge.

The University of California–Berkeley has responded by establishing an American cultures requirement: to fulfill a general-education requirement, students must take a course (from a list offered by fifteen to twenty-six departments) which examines comparatively African Americans, Asian Americans, Chicanos/Latinos, Native Americans, and European Americans.

We seem to be in the throes of racial tensions on campuses across the country, but we are also on the threshold of understanding how America's *unum* has sprung from our *pluribus* and how places like Palolo Valley fit into American society.

READING, WRITING, NARCISSISM

Lilian G. Katz

Lilian Katz is a professor of early childhood education at the University of Illinois. This article first appeared in the American Educator, *and it was later adapted for the* New York Times *Op-Ed page in 1993.*

Developing and strengthening children's self-esteem has become a major goal of our schools. Although it is true that many children, especially the youngest students, have low self-esteem, our practice of lavishing praise for the mildest accomplishments is not likely to have much success. Feelings cannot be learned from direct instruction, and constant reminders about how wonderful one is may raise doubts about the credibility of the message and the messenger.

A project by a first grade class in an affluent Middle Western suburb that I recently observed showed how self-esteem and narcissism can be confused. Working from copied pages prepared by the teacher, each student produced a booklet called "All About Me." The first page asked for basic information about the child's home and family. The second page was titled "what I like to eat," the third was "what I like to watch on TV," the next was "what I want for a present" and another was "where I want to go on vacation."

The booklet, like thousands of others I have encountered around the country, had no page headings such as "what I want to know more about," "what I am curious about," "what I want to solve" or even "to make."

Each page was directed toward the child's basest inner gratifications. Each topic put the child in the role of consumer—of food, entertainment, gifts and recreation. Not once was the child asked to play the role of producer, investigator, initiator, explorer, experimenter or problem-solver.

It is perhaps this kind of literature that accounts for a poster I saw in a school entrance hall. Pictures of clapping hands surround the title "We Applaud Ourselves." While the sign's probable purpose was to help children feel good about themselves, it did so by directing their attention inward. The poster urged self-congratulation; it made no reference to possible ways of earning applause—by considering the feelings or needs of others.

Another common type of exercise was a display of kindergartners' work I saw recently that consisted of large paper-doll figures, each having a balloon containing a sentence stem that began "I am special because. . ." The children completed the sentence with the phrases such as, "I can color," "I can ride a bike," and "I like to play with my friends." But these children are not likely to believe for very long that they are special because they can color or ride a bike. What are they going to think when they discover just how trivial these criteria for being special are?

This overemphasizing self-esteem and self-congratulation stems from a legitimate desire to correct previous generations' traditions of avoiding compliments for fear of making children conceited. But the current practices are vast over-corrections. The idea of specialness they express is contradictory: If everybody is special, nobody is special.

Adults can show their approval for children in more significant ways than awarding gold stars and happy faces. Esteem is conveyed to students when adults and peers treat them with respect, ask for their views and preferences and provide opportunities for decisions and choices about things that matter to them. Children are born natural and social scientists. They devote much time and energy to investigating and making sense of their environments. During the pre-school and early school years, teachers can capitalize on this disposition by engaging children in investigations and projects.

Several years ago, I saw this kind of project at a rural British school for 5- to 7-year-olds. A large display on the bulletin board read: "We Are a Class Full of Bodies. Here Are the Details." The display space was filled with bar graphs showing birth dates, weights and heights, eye colors, number of lost teeth, shoe sizes and other data of the entire class. As the children worked in small groups to take measurements, prepare graphs and help one another post displays of their analyses, the teacher was able to create an atmosphere of a community of researchers looking for averages, trends and ranges.

Compare this to the American kindergarten I visited recently in which the comments made by the children about a visit to a dairy farm were displayed on the bulletin board. Each sentence began with the words "I liked." For example, "I liked the cows" and "I liked the milking machine." No sentences began "What surprised me was . . ." and "What I want to know more about is . . ."

Of course children benefit from positive feedback. But praise and rewards are not the only methods of reinforcement. More emphasis should be placed on appreciation—reinforcement related explicitly and directly to the *content* of the child's interest and effort. For example, if a child poses a thoughtful question, the teacher might come to class the next day with a new reference book on the same subject. It is important that the teacher shows appreciation for pupils' concerns without taking their minds off the subjects at hand or directing their attention inward.

When children see that their concerns and interests are taken seriously, they are more likely to raise them in discussion and to take their own ideas seriously. Teachers can strengthen children's disposition to wonder, reflect, raise questions and generate alternative solutions to practical and intellectual problems. Of course, when children are engaged in challenging and significant activities, they are bound to experience failures and rebuffs. But as long as the teacher accepts the child's feelings and responds respectfully—"I know you're disappointed, but you can try again tomorrow"—the child is more likely to learn from the incident than be harmed by it.

Learning to deal with setbacks, and maintaining the persistence and optimism necessary for childhood's long road to mastery are the real foundations of lasting self-esteem. Children who are helped to develop these qualities will surely respect themselves—though they probably will have better things to think about.

THE HOLLOW CURRICULUM

Robert N. Sollod

Robert Sollod teaches psychology at Cleveland State University. This argument first appeared in The Chronicle of Higher Education *in 1992.*

The past decade in academe has seen widespread controversy over curricular reform. We have explored many of the deeply rooted, core assumptions that have guided past decisions about which subjects should be emphasized in the curriculum and how they should be approached. Yet I have found myself repeatedly disappointed by the lack of significant discussion concerning the place of religion and spirituality in colleges' curricula and in the lives of educated persons.

I do not mean to suggest that universities should indoctrinate students with specific viewpoints or approaches to life; that is not their proper function. But American universities now largely ignore religion and spirituality, rather than considering what aspects of religious and spiritual teachings should enter the curriculum and how those subjects should be taught. The curricula that most undergraduates study do little to rectify the fact that many Americans are ignorant of religious and spiritual teachings, of their significance in the history of this and other civilizations, and of their significance in contemporary

The Chronicle of Higher Education, March 18, 1992, p. A60.

society. Omitting this major facet of human experience and thought contributes to a continuing shallowness and imbalance in much of university life today.

Let us take the current discussions of multiculturalism as one example. It is hardly arguable that an educated person should approach life with knowledge of several cultures or patterns of experience. Appreciation and understanding of human diversity are worthy educational ideals. Should such an appreciation exclude the religious and spiritually based concepts of reality that are the backbone upon which entire cultures have been based?

Multiculturalism that does not include appreciation of the deepest visions of reality reminds me of the travelogues that I saw in the cinema as a child—full of details of quaint and somewhat mysterious behavior that evoked some superficial empathy but no real, in-depth understanding. Implicit in a multicultural approach that ignores spiritual factors is a kind of critical and patronizing attitude. It assumes that we can understand and evaluate the experiences of other cultures without comprehension of their deepest beliefs.

Incomprehensibly, traditionalists who oppose adding multicultural content to the curriculum also ignore the religious and theological bases of the Western civilization that they seek to defend. Today's advocates of Western traditionalism focus, for the most part, on conveying a type of rationalism that is only a single strain in Western thought. Their approach does not demonstrate sufficient awareness of the contributions of Western religions and spirituality to philosophy and literature, to moral and legal codes, to the development of governmental and political institutions, and to the mores of our society.

Nor is the lack of attention to religion and spirituality new. I recall taking undergraduate philosophy classes in the 1960's in which Plato and Socrates were taught without reference to the fact that they were contemplative mystics who believed in immortality and reincarnation. Everything that I learned in my formal undergraduate education about Christianity came through studying a little Thomas Aquinas in a philosophy course, and even there we focused more on the logical sequence of his arguments than on the fundamentals of the Christian doctrine that he espoused.

I recall that Dostoyevsky was presented as an existentialist, with hardly a nod given to the fervent Christian beliefs so clearly apparent in his writings. I even recall my professors referring to their Christian colleagues, somewhat disparagingly, as "Christers." I learned about mystical and spiritual interpretations of Shakespeare's sonnets and plays many years after taking college English courses.

We can see the significance of omitting teaching about religion and spirituality in the discipline of psychology and, in particular, in my own field of clinical psychology. I am a member of the Task Force on Religious Issues in Graduate Education and Training in Division 36 of the American Psychological Association, a panel chaired by Edward Shafranske of Pepperdine University. In this work, I have discovered that graduate programs generally do not require students to learn anything about the role of religion in people's lives.

Almost no courses are available to teach psychologists how to deal with the religious values or concerns expressed by their clients. Nor are such courses required or generally available at the undergraduate level for psychology majors. Allusions to religion and spirituality often are completely missing in textbooks on introductory psychology, personality theory, concepts of psychotherapy, and developmental psychology.

Recent attempts to add a multicultural perspective to clinical training almost completely ignore the role of religion and spirituality as core elements of many racial, ethnic, and national identities. Prayer is widely practiced, yet poorly understood and rarely studied by psychologists. When presented, religious ideas are usually found in case histories of patients manifesting severe psychopathology.

Yet spiritual and mystical experiences are not unusual in our culture. And research has shown that religion is an important factor in the lives of many Americans; some studies have suggested that a client's religious identification may affect the psychotherapeutic relationship, as well as the course and outcome of therapy. Some patterns of religious commitment have been found to be associated with high levels of mental health and ego strength. A small number of psychologists are beginning to actively challenge the field's inertia and indifference by researching and writing on topics related to religion and spirituality. Their efforts have not as yet, however, markedly affected the climate or curricula in most psychology departments.

Is it any wonder that religion for the typical psychotherapist is a mysterious and taboo topic? It should not be surprising that therapists are not equipped even to ask the appropriate questions regarding a person's religious or spiritual life—much less deal with psychological aspects of spiritual crises.

Or consider the field of political science. Our scholars and policy makers have been unable to predict or understand the major social and political movements that produced upheavals around the world during the last decade. That is at least partly because many significant events—the remarkable rise of Islamic fundamentalism, the victory of Afghanistan over the Soviet Union, the unanticipated velvet revolutions in Eastern Europe and in the Soviet Union, and the continuing conflicts in Cyprus, Israel, Lebanon, Northern Ireland, Pakistan, Sri Lanka, Tibet, and Yugoslavia—can hardly be appreciated without a deep understanding of the religious views of those involved. The tender wisdom of our contemporary political scientists cannot seem to comprehend the deep spirituality inherent in many of today's important social movements.

Far from being an anachronism, religious conviction has proved to be a more potent contemporary force than most, if not all, secular ideologies. Too often, however, people with strong religious sentiments are simply dismissed as "zealots" or "fanatics"—whether they be Jewish settlers on the West Bank, Iranian demonstrators, Russian Baptists, Shiite leaders, anti-abortion activists, or evangelical Christians.

Most sadly, the continuing neglect of spirituality and religion by colleges and universities also results in a kind of segregation of the life of the spirit from the life of the mind in American culture. This situation is far from the ideals of Thoreau, Emerson, or William James. Spirituality in our society too often represents a retreat from the world of intellectual discourse, and spiritual pursuits are often cloaked in a reflexive anti-intellectualism, which mirrors the view in academe of spirituality as an irrational cultural residue. Students with spiritual interests and concerns learn that the university will not validate or feed their interests. They learn either to suppress their spiritual life or to split their spiritual life apart from their formal education.

Much has been written about the loss of ethics, a sense of decency, moderation, and fair play in American society. I would submit that much of this loss is a result of the increasing ignorance, in circles of presumably educated people, of religious and spiritual world views. It is difficult to imagine, for example, how ethical issues can be intelligently approached and discussed or how wise ethical decisions can be reached without either knowledge or reference to those religious and spiritual principles that underlie our legal system and moral codes.

Our colleges and universities should reclaim one of their earliest purposes—to educate and inform students concerning the spiritual and religious underpinnings of thought and society. To the extent that such education is lacking, our colleges and universities are presenting a narrow and fragmented view of human experience.

Both core curricula and more advanced courses in the humanities and social sciences should be evaluated for their coverage of religious topics. Active leadership at the university, college, and departmental levels is needed to encourage and carry out needed additions and changes in course content. Campus organizations should develop forums and committees to examine the issue, exchange information, and develop specific proposals.

National debate and discussion about the best way to educate students concerning religion and spirituality are long overdue.

2. How Should Learning Be Graded/Evaluated?

DESPERATELY SEEKING SUMMA

Craig Lambert

This article about grade inflation at Harvard, which appeared in Harvard Magazine *in 1993, was written by one of its associate editors. How big a problem is grade inflation in your experience?*

In some respects, grades in most Harvard courses now resemble the progeny of Garrison Keillor's Lake Wobegon, "where all the women are strong, all the

Harvard Magazine, May–June 1993, pp. 36–40.

men are good looking, and all the children are above average." The grade of C, which nominally signifies an "average" performance, has virtually disappeared from Harvard transcripts: last year about 91 percent of undergraduate grades were B– or higher. D's and E's are virtually extinct. "The five-letter system has gone to three letters," says Katherine Tulenko '93, a biochemistry concentrator and a marshal of the Radcliffe chapter of Phi Beta Kappa. Her fellow PBK marshal, Elaine Goldenberg '93, notes that "a lot of people today would consider a C as equivalent to what a D or even an E used to mean—a very poor grade." Tulenko amplifies: "Ask any student how they would feel about getting a B–. They'll make an ugly face."

At the high end, the marks A and A–, which are said to denote an "excellent" performance, together accounted for about 22 percent of all grades in 1966–67. Twenty-five years later, excellence had apparently exploded; A and A– made up 43 percent of all grades last year. "In some departments A stands for 'Average,' " says Dianne Reeder '93, a student participant in a recent panel on grade inflation at the Kennedy School. "It's impossible to earn an above-average grade. Since so many of us have A– averages, our grades are meaningless." [. . .]

Inflation is not confined to Harvard. At Princeton during the last four years, the proportion of A's has zoomed up from 33 to 40 percent of all grades, according to a report in the *Princeton Alumni Weekly*. Stanford saw the A's on its transcripts grow from 29 percent of all grades in 1968–69 to 35 percent by 1986–87; over the same period, C's shrank from 16 to 6 percent.

The contraction of letter grades to the three choices of A, B, and C has been official policy at Brown University since the early 1970s. Brown students also have an option to elect satisfactory/no-credit grading, and last year they chose it in 22 percent of their courses. Between 1981 and 1992, the percentage of A's at Brown rose from 31 to 37 percent (exceeding B's, at 29 percent), while C's fell from 10 to 8 percent.

At Harvard College, the average grade has ascended from a point between B and B– in 1966–67 to about B+ today. But inflation has not been uniform across the scale. "I went over to the archives and looked at Harvard grades across a period of a hundred years, going back to the 1800s," says Dean Whitla, director of the Office of Instructional Research and Evaluation. "Considering the change in talent over the past century, there hasn't been a lot of grade inflation. We've been very constant over that period in the A's given out, until very recently. The big difference is in the A– and B+ grades."

Students concur that the A– is far more accessible than the A. "For me to go from a B+ to an A– in a course might require one or two more hours of work a week," says Tulenko. "But to go from an A– to an A could mean *ten* extra hours per week." Goldenberg agrees that "an A has to some extent retained its meaning, even if an A– has not."

The B range, which accounts for nearly half of all undergraduate grades, is a battlefield of controversy. "B is a very fat grade at Harvard," says Parimal Patil, a resident tutor in Currier House. "It includes students who are fighting for A's and don't quite make it, who get B+'s, and others who treat the course with no respect, miss lots of classes, turn in papers late, and still get B–'s." Alan Ackerman, a tutor in English in Kirkland House, notes that "in our department people rarely receive a grade lower than a B–. Even B– is kind of beneath mediocre."

The convergence of grades at the top of the spectrum narrows the range of distinctions available to instructors. Medieval literature specialist William Cole, Ph.D. '91, a teaching assistant in the Core program, says that "in a lot of fields, especially in the humanities, I can't figure out the purpose of grades, because they're so close together. Everyone gets an A or an A–." In a recent article in *The Chronicle of Higher Education* (see *Harvard Magazine*, "The Vanishing C," March–April, page 59), Cole asserted that "by rewarding mediocrity we discourage excellence. Many students who work hard at the outset of their college careers, in pursuit of good grades and honors degrees, throw up their hands upon seeing their peers do equally well despite putting in far less effort."

Ackerman says that "the ability to give a range of grades is pedagogically valuable. Students would benefit from a grading system that was more equitable—one in which the range of grades represents the range of work that is turned in. Narrowly limiting the number of grades that we can give also limits what students can learn from their mistakes."

Whitla explains another consequence of grade convergence: "If grade inflation continues, admissions to graduate and professional schools will not be made on the basis of grades but of test scores. Recommendations are already generous: if grades can't be used to distinguish between scholars, nothing would be left but test scores. While scores have merit, they could become too important in this process." [. . .]

Theodore Sizer, who is professor of education at Brown University and was dean of Harvard's Graduate School of Education from 1964 to 1972, says that the issue of grade inflation "masks more fundamental problems. One is our absolutely myopic concern about assessment, grading, and evaluation. We have this mania for rating people. It's a plague at the school level. It has gone too far; it washes over everybody in the system. The grade is an end in itself. It's really kind of sick."

The grasping focus on the grade, rather than learning, is illustrated by a student who once took a history course from James Wilkinson, director of the Derek Bok Center for Teaching and Learning. "He told me that he needed a better grade in my course because he needed to get into medical school," Wilkinson recalls. " 'I may not be very good at history,' he said, 'but I'm going to be a very good doctor, and I really reject the idea that you have the right to keep me out of medical school.' " [. . .]

One way for a teacher to help students, Sizer says, is to publish explicit criteria for achieving A, B, or C rankings: "I hand published criteria out at the start of the course, and it scares them half to death because they've never seen such a thing. They argue with you, but it's a good argument."

Lurking beneath every academic controversy regarding grade inflation is another, less genteel issue that invariably turns out to be driven by economics. Courses that grade generously may attract large enrollments and thus create teaching jobs for section leaders and so bring money into a department to support its graduate students. If they are respected institutions, colleges whose transcripts abound with A's will succeed in placing their students in top graduate and professional schools; these alumni will later prosper and reward their alma maters. "A Harvard diploma is almost like a stock certificate whose value is driven by prestige," says Cole. "Alumni and parents are concerned that it maintain and increase its value. By donating money to hire prestigious faculty, they're protecting their investment."

"Universities have lost sight of their goal, which should be education," Cole continues. "Learning has become marginal to the business of higher education. Teaching ability has nothing to do with becoming a professor. The highest rank in academia is that of University Professor, and the great privilege of that rank is that *you don't have to teach!* You are relieved of your teaching 'load.' Scholarship, not teaching, is what brings prestige; it is the coin of the realm. If you want to minimize your teaching time, give an A on a paper and write no comments. If you give a C, you have to write comments to justify that grade.

"The trouble now is that everyone is happy," Cole continues. "Students get their degrees with minimal effort. Professors discharge their teaching duties with minimal effort. The administration collects millions of dollars in tuition and fees. And everyone associated with this gets Harvard's prestige. The question is, How long will this last? How long will it be before corporations ask, Why should we pay a Harvard graduate, or any college graduate, extra money to come and work here? If these people aren't really learning a lot in college, why shouldn't we just hire people straight out of high school and train them specifically to do what our company does?

"Colleges are becoming no more than holding tanks to prevent massive unemployment in this country, keeping lots of 17-to-22 year-olds out of the job market," Cole concludes. "If Harvard focused on education, the prestige would inevitably accompany that educational excellence. But if Harvard continues to traffic in prestige, the education will disappear, and eventually the prestige will disappear as well."

A LIBERATING CURRICULUM

Roberta F. Borkat

Roberta Borkat is a professor of English and comparative literature at San Diego State University. Use what you learned about claims on pages 149–153 to help you establish the claim of this essay.

A blessed change has come over me. Events of recent months have revealed to me that I have been laboring as a university professor for more than 20 years under a misguided theory of teaching. I humbly regret that during all those years I have caused distress and inconvenience to thousands of students while providing some amusement to my more practical colleagues. Enlightenment came to me in a sublime moment of clarity while I was being verbally attacked by a student whose paper I had just proved to have been plagiarized from "The Norton Anthology of English Literature." Suddenly, I understood the true purpose of my profession, and I devised a plan to embody that revelation. Every moment since then has been filled with delight about the advantages to students, professors and universities from my Plan to Increase Student Happiness.

The plan is simplicity itself: at the end of the second week of the semester, all students enrolled in each course will receive a final grade of A. Then their minds will be relieved of anxiety, and they will be free to do whatever they want for the rest of the term.

The benefits are immediately evident. Students will be assured of high grade-point averages and an absence of obstacles in their march toward graduation. Professors will be relieved of useless burdens and will have time to pursue their real interests. Universities will have achieved the long-desired goal of molding individual professors into interchangeable parts of a smoothly operating machine. Even the environment will be improved because education will no longer consume vast quantities of paper for books, compositions and examinations.

Although this scheme will instantly solve countless problems that have plagued education, a few people may raise trivial objections and even urge universities not to adopt it. Some of my colleagues may protest that we have an obligation to uphold the integrity of our profession. Poor fools, I understand their delusion, for I formerly shared it. To them, I say: "Hey, lighten up! Why make life difficult?"

Those who believe that we have a duty to increase the knowledge of our students may also object. I, too, used to think that knowledge was important and that we should encourage hard work and perseverance. Now I realize that the concept of rewards for merit is elitist and, therefore, wrong in a society that aims for equality in all things. We are a democracy. What could be more democratic than to give exactly the same grade to every single student?

One or two forlorn colleagues may even protest that we have a responsibility to significant works of the past because the writings of such authors as Chaucer, Shakespeare, Milton and Swift are intrinsically valuable. I can empathize with these misguided souls, for I once labored under the illusion that I was giving my students a precious gift by introducing them to works by great poets, playwrights and satirists. Now I recognize the error of my ways. The writings of such authors may have seemed meaningful to our ancestors, who had nothing better to do, but we are living in a time of wonderful improvements. The writers of bygone eras have been made irrelevant, replaced by MTV and *People* magazine. After all, their bodies are dead. Why shouldn't their ideas be dead, too?

JOYOUS SMILES

If any colleagues persist in protesting that we should try to convey knowledge to students and preserve our cultural heritage, I offer this suggestion: honestly consider what students really want. As one young man graciously explained to me, he had no desire to take my course but had enrolled in it merely to fulfill a requirement that he resented. His job schedule made it impossible for him to attend at least 30 percent of my class sessions, and he wouldn't have time to do much of the reading. Nevertheless, he wanted a good grade. Another student consulted me after the first exam, upset because she had not studied and had earned only 14 points out of a possible 100. I told her that, if she studied hard and attended class more regularly, she could do well enough on the remaining tests to pass the course. This encouragement did not satisfy her. What she wanted was an assurance that she would receive at least a B. Under my plan both students would be guaranteed an A. Why not? They have good looks and self-esteem. What more could anyone ever need in life?

I do not ask for thanks from the many people who will benefit. I'm grateful to my colleagues who for decades have tried to help me realize that seriousness about teaching is not the path to professorial prestige, rapid promotion and frequent sabbaticals. Alas, I was stubborn. Not until I heard the illuminating explanation of the student who had plagiarized from the anthology's introduction to Jonathan Swift did I fully grasp the wisdom that others had been generously offering to me for years—learning is just too hard. Now, with a light heart, I await the plan's adoption. In my mind's eye, I can see the happy faces of university administrators and professors, released at last from the irksome chore of dealing with students. I can imagine the joyous smiles of thousands of students, all with straight-A averages and plenty of free time.

My only regret is that I wasted so much time. For nearly 30 years, I threw away numerous hours annually on trivia: writing, grading and explaining examinations; grading hundreds of papers a semester; holding private conferences with students; reading countless books; buying extra materials to give students a feeling for the music, art and clothing of past centuries; endlessly worrying about how to improve my teaching. At last I see the folly of grubbing away in meaningless efforts. I wish that I had faced facts earlier and had not lost years because of old-fashioned notions. But such are the penalties for those who do not understand the true purpose of education.

A TEST OF DEMOCRACY

Theodore R. Sizer

Theodore Sizer is chairman of the Coalition of Essential Schools at Brown University. This article first appeared in 1992. The exigence for national testing is similar to that of much standardized testing.

In the name of raising the standards of public schools, calls have gone out for a national examination—American Achievement Tests, the Bush Administration

New York Times, January 30, 1991, p. A15.

calls them—or at least for some regionally based but universally calibrated assessment system. The rhetoric suggests a voluntary approach, but the intent of the effort belies this. The Administration would like to make these exams America's educational scorecard.

The argument for this venture is seductively simple. The "nation" will set the standards, children will be tested and schools that yield successful students will be honored while those that falter will be chastised. In this way, the "nation" expects to shape the schools and thus drive educational reform. Supporters of this approach point to the apparent success of national examinations in other countries to persuade those of us who harbor doubts about American-wide tests.

Yet before we jump to such a solution, we must ask several questions:
• Who sets the standards and by what right? Who in this democracy, elected or appointed, shall be qualified to speak for all parents, students and school people? How can we insure that all constituencies in our rich tapestry of cultures are accommodated by a unitary group of "expert" examiners?

Education poses complex questions of rights. My children are compelled to attend school. This is not a voluntary act. Therefore, shouldn't I as the parent have rights over the ideas to which my child is exposed? To cede most curricular matters—in particular, content beyond the three R's—to authorities far from my local school board strips me of democratic rights that should be respected.

• Must our search for higher standards inevitably lead to the national level? Is the Federal Government smarter and more statesmanlike than local communities? Less prone to special-interest pressures?

• Can examinations be designed to test what we value most in a student? Will they test the informed and imaginative use of knowledge, not just a grasp of the facts? Can the habits of thoughtful behavior and the ability to address new situations be tested in a standardized way? For example, can results from a test not only prove that one understands the nature of law, but that one acts civilly when not supervised? Such "scores" tell us little about developing the qualities Americans seem to care about most.

Experts in testing insist that we must have more "authentic" assessment, like expecting students to prepare essays rather than simply criticizing other people's writing in multiple-choice questions. While this direction seems promising, what is the evidence that it can be done well and fairly? And if, as some experts say, this approach costs five to 10 times that of existing testing, will the public buy it? If not, what then?

• How will a national exam insure fairness and equity? There is sweeping evidence that many existing tests discriminate by race, gender, ethnicity and class. A universal test will only worsen severe inequities in American education.

The drift of educational authority from localities to state capitals and Washington represents a fundamental shift. Merely asserting that U.S. schools are "failing" and that we must move decisively is no argument that a more centralized direction is wiser. That this decisiveness comes at the expense of democratic rights and our nation's rich cultural diversity is chilling and astonishingly wasteful.

There are less dangerous paths for raising standards. We can use the best testing methods (however limited) combined with creative "auditing" of the schools by the states. We can insist on rigorous, open progress reports from each school every year. We should consider these ideas carefully before settling on a national examination. The stakes are enormous.

3. How Far Should Schools Go to Eliminate Bias in Education?

MINORITY STUDENTS TELL OF BIAS IN QUEST FOR HIGHER EDUCATION

Susan Chira

Susan Chira writes about education. This article appeared in 1992.

ANDOVER, Mass.—When Denise Galarza Sepúlveda told her high school guidance counselor that she dreamed of one day teaching at a university, the counselor looked at her and rolled her eyes.

Ms. Galarza Sepúlveda had good grades, but she was the only Puerto Rican in her class. Her guidance counselor had approached other, nonminority, students and suggested they apply to college. With deadlines looming, Ms. Galarza Sepúlveda asked for an appointment and offered up her dreams.

"That's all she did, then just silence," Ms. Galarza Sepúlveda said, recalling her counselor rolling her eyes. "I don't even know how I managed to leave the room. I felt like crying. Actually, I did go to the bathroom and just started crying, because I felt completely worthless."

AN OFT-TOLD TALE

Her tale of a put-down of academic ambitions is one told by black, Hispanic and American Indian students around the country. All too often, they say, they are discouraged from believing they can succeed in intellectually demanding professions. For example, Guy Bluford, the first black astronaut, was told by a high school adviser that he was only smart enough for trade school.

Minorities are particularly scarce among teachers and Ph.D.'s. Of the 24,721 Ph.D. degrees awarded to Americans last year, blacks received 993, Hispanic Americans 708 and American Indians 128. Eight percent of public school teachers are black and 3 percent Hispanic American in the country at large, although in large cities the percentages are higher. In New York City, 19.2 percent of the public school teachers are black and 10.2 percent are Hispanic.

New York Times, August 14, 1992, pp. A1, A7.

Ms. Galarza Sepúlveda eventually found a sympathetic teacher who guided her through the maze of college applications, and now attends the University of Connecticut.

But experiences like hers suggest that the scarcity of black and Hispanic teachers and professors is not only a matter of finding enough money for advanced degrees, or of navigating a complex application process to graduate school. Minority students' confidence has also been undermined by years of assumptions that because they are not white they are not smart enough to make it.

What college students like Lisette Nieves say they hear is, "You don't have that 'thought gene.' "

Ms. Nieves did not let such discouraging words deter her from becoming the first Rhodes Scholar from Brooklyn College. This July, she joined more than 40 other minority college students, graduate students and professors in a program that aims to send a different message—that they have the brains for graduate school and that they are not alone.

FOUR WEEKS OF STUDY

The program, the Institute for the Recruitment of Teachers, brings promising college students to the campus of Phillips Academy here for four weeks of study, guides them through graduate school applications and continues to monitor them once they enter graduate school.

The program is one of several designed to swell the ranks of minority teachers and Ph.D.'s. There are many reasons for the shortages. Talented students often choose better-paying jobs in law or business, partly because many minority students are saddled with huge loan repayments for their college education. Many students do not even consider graduate school and have no one in their families or neighborhoods who can guide them.

But students also talk of being pushed aside, discouraged from intellectual pursuits by people blinded by the color of their skin.

Jeffrey L. Pegram recalls a guidance counselor who told him he was only good enough to get into a two-year college—this to a student whose high grades put him on the dean's list three years in a row.

"Out of 2,000 students, I was one of five Native Americans, and we found out that this guidance counselor had told a lot of people of color that they should go into the Army or a two-year school," said Mr. Pegram, who graduated this year from the University of Massachusetts and wants to study American Indian history.

A FAMILIAR MESSAGE

This sometimes unspoken, sometimes brazen message is one familiar to experts who work with minority college students.

"I hear examples from students coming from high schools all the time," said Freeman Hrabowski 3d, interim president of the University of Maryland Baltimore County. "Sometimes we say so much without ever using words. We can discourage a student in so many ways."

Mr. Hrabowski directs the university's Meyerhoff Scholars program, which seeks to encourage black students to pursue advanced degrees in science and engineering. The program was founded by Robert Meyerhoff, a Baltimore philanthropist.

For all the slights and barriers, students are also quick to praise those who believed in them and helped them believe in themselves.

"My guidance counselor spoon-fed me through the application process," said Ray Blakeney, a senior at the University of Dayton in Ohio whose father is black and mother is Korean. "People are out there who really want to help. A lot of time people tend to focus on the negative and don't realize the positive."

THE QUOTA QUESTION

But the wounds linger for many students. Gonzalo Zeballos still stiffens when he tells what happened after he was admitted to the honors program at the College of the Holy Cross: "One of my closest friends said, 'You're just the token minority.' "

Comments like these made Mr. Zeballos wonder if, after all, his friends could be right. "At one point you start to believe that you got into school because of a quota," he said. "Once I got in, I wasn't sure I deserved to be there. It makes it difficult to function because you're afraid to fail, and you tell yourself not to perform."

His first year in college, away from his close, traditional Chilean family, was difficult. His grades were low, but one of his professors noticed how articulate he was in class and recommended him for the honors program. He graduated with a very high grade-point average.

"By my senior year, I learned to accept that I could do the work as well as anybody else," Mr. Zeballos said. "People who want to belittle you or your accomplishments are always going to find a way, and you have to find a way to get beyond that."

A SENSE OF COMMUNITY

Painful as such encounters were, they also fired some students with a determination not only to excel, but also to smooth the path for others. At first, Noel Anderson was ready to give up when an English professor in his freshman year told him he was not good enough to be at Brooklyn College.

"I was close to dropping out," he said. "Of course, my mother wouldn't allow me to. Not until my junior year did I meet a couple of professors who helped me out. As a black male, I want representation on that campus. Hopefully, when I become a professor I can encourage someone else."

Experiences like Mr. Anderson's explain why the teachers at the Andover program—themselves all minorities—work to rebuild confidence and create a sense of community that students can draw on once they enter the isolating and mostly white world of graduate study.

"It's really staggering how many students say, 'I don't think I can do this,' " said Nicholas Rowe, a graduate student in 18th-century English and

French history at Boston College who is one of eight teachers in the summer program. "Even after they start graduate school, the message to them is, 'When are you going to drop out?' We tell them, 'You can do this.' We show them how we were able to succeed and overcome."

Hearing stories like these inspired Kelly Wise, a former dean of the faculty at Phillips Academy, to create the Institute for the Recruitment of Teachers in 1990. As dean, Mr. Wise had recruited many minority faculty members as teachers, and as he stepped down he realized that he had built a network of contacts that he could draw upon to find talented minority students and encourage them to choose teaching at the high school or college level.

"It has become my passion in the last 10 years to recruit people of color," he said.

So he raised money, at first from former students and later from a number of foundations, to pay for a four-week summer session and an intensive follow-through program. The cost this year is close to $300,000.

Over the summer, the teachers at Andover work intensively with these students to sharpen their writing and analytical skills, offering far more personal attention than most students get even in college.

A PROVOCATIVE CURRICULUM

Ms. Nieves, who attended the program's first session two years ago, said her writing improved dramatically. The curriculum is provocative, challenging students to defend deeply held convictions about such inflammatory topics as race with the cool logic expected in graduate school.

"We get into fights here," said Luis Cosme, a graduate student at the University of Wisconsin who is an alumnus of the program. "But they have to bring their analytical skills."

The program also concentrates on practical barriers to graduate school. Teachers tell what graduate school is like and offer guidance on such crucial decisions as how to select a dissertation adviser. Students go over difficult questions on the Graduate Record Examination, which is required to enter graduate school.

Mr. Wise has followed each student's graduate school application, making sure all paperwork is complete, calling admissions officers and even raising money to pay for the standardized tests.

AN UNBLEMISHED RECORD

He organized a consortium of 19 universities, including the University of Chicago and the University of Michigan, that relies on him to recruit minority graduate students and pledge in return to provide them with mentors and financial support.

So far, all students in the program who have applied to graduate school have been admitted; by this fall, the program will have placed 110 students in graduate programs.

Directors of graduate affairs at the universities, and officers at foundations, including the Ford Foundation, that help pay for the program, say it stands out in two ways: it focuses on humanities and social sciences rather than math and science, and it offers an intensive summer session.

The most fervent endorsements, though, come from students like Désirée Y. Blackman, a senior at the State University of New York College at Purchase. "This is the only time in my entire life I've had six people who are determined to get me into graduate school," she said, fighting back tears. "Just getting into the program was something I didn't think I could do."

BOYS GET CALLED ON

Jillian Mincer

This author claims that gender bias is still found in America's classrooms. This essay was first published in 1994.

Susie Van Scoyk was stunned by the findings in a report on gender bias in schools. Mrs. Van Scoyk, a sixth-grade teacher in Arvada, Colo., a Denver suburb, couldn't imagine why teachers would discriminate against girls in the classroom. "I thought, truly, I don't do this," she said.

But a videotape taken several weeks later showed that she clearly gave more attention to the boys in her class and encouraged them more through words and gestures. "I was appalled," she said. "I saw that I really focused on the boys. The sexism was so subtle, that's what's so striking."

FREQUENT OCCURRENCE

Mrs. Van Scoyk's discovery was not unusual. Numerous studies now confirm what many educators have long suspected: gender bias still occurs frequently in America's classrooms two decades after the passage of Title IX, which prohibits discrimination on the basis of sex in federally funded school programs.

Girls receive significantly less attention from classroom teachers than boys do, according to "How Schools Short-change Girls," a report commissioned by the American Association of University Women Educational Foundation. Gender bias undermines girls' self-esteem and often discourages them from taking math and science courses. The study also found that although black girls initiate teacher contact more than white girls, the black youngsters are more likely to be rebuffed by teachers.

The report, conducted by the Wellesley College Center for Research on Women, added that the curriculum frequently ignores or stereotypes females and that many standardized tests contain elements of sex bias. "I think in gen-

New York Times, Education Life Special Section, January 9, 1994, p. 27.

eral the lesson girls learn from this is that they're not encouraged to speak up or speak out," said Susan McGee Bailey, director of the Wellesley Center and the principal author of the A.A.U.W. report.

In their new book, "Failing at Fairness: How America's Schools Cheat Girls," published by Scribners, two American University professors, Myra and David Sadker, explain that because "gender bias is not a noisy problem, most people are unaware of secret sexist lessons and the quiet losses they engender."

Girls enter school ahead of boys in almost every subject except science, where boys have a slight edge, said Myra Sadker, dean of the School of Education. But girls graduate from high school behind in almost every subject. "The impact on girls is that they lose self-esteem as they go through school," she said. "They come in with so much promise, and there's a systematic robbery."

In their research, the Sadkers found that boys in elementary and middle school spoke out in class eight times more often than girls. Teachers generally listened to the boys who spoke out but told girls who did so to raise their hands if they wanted to speak.

Girls are being shortchanged in several areas, said Anne L. Bryant, executive director of the A.A.U.W. She said the lack of role models in education affected girls. Although 70 percent of teachers from kindergarten through 12th grade are women, only 27 to 30 percent are principals and only 5 to 6 percent are superintendents, she said.

The survey found that while boys and girls both experience a loss of self-esteem as they grow older, the loss is most dramatic among girls. A key finding of the 1992 report was that a relationship exists between self-esteem and enjoyment of math and science. Girls and boys who like those subjects have higher self-esteem and greater career aspirations, it concluded.

In response to the A.A.U.W. studies, a package of nine bills on gender equity and education was introduced in the House of Representatives last year. The omnibus package, H.R. 1793, addresses gender bias in the schools, calling for the establishment of an office of women's equity in the Department of Education, equity training for teachers, efforts to improve girls' achievement and participation in math and science. It also includes provisions to eliminate sexual harassment in schools. Another bill would require schools to disclose their expenditures on men's and women's athletics.

Diane Ravitch, an assistant secretary of education in the Bush Administration and now a visiting fellow at the Brookings Institution, opposes the bills. "You can't say schools are biased against girls when boys are having a harder time in schools," she said. "The data show that women have made remarkable success in education."

But David Sadker, noting that statistics and studies can be interpreted many ways, said, "The key numbers suggest slow progress but a substantial problem remaining."

TO HELP GIRLS KEEP UP, GIRLS-ONLY MATH CLASSES

Jane Gross

The exigence for the educational experiments described here, which involve segregating girls in their own math classrooms, was provided by girls achieving lower math scores on the SATs than boys.

In Laura Gamb's high school mathematics and science classes last year, the boys would make fun of her if she said million when she meant billion, and she learned to deflect their ridicule by saying, "Just kidding," or "Never mind."

In Amber West's middle school math class, she was so afraid of sounding stupid when she didn't understand something that she swallowed her questions, whispered them to a teacher between periods or waited until she got home and asked her mother.

And in Cara Raysinger's high school math class, she often couldn't concentrate or get the teacher's attention because there were so many rowdy boys jumping out of their seats and throwing pencils across the room and making noises like airplanes.

But Laura, Amber and Cara don't feel embarrassed, intimidated, distracted or ignored anymore because now they are learning math and science in all-girl classrooms in three California schools. The schools have adopted segregation as a way of solving the widely acknowledged problem of girls lagging behind boys in math and science from middle school onward.

A wealth of research shows that girls are largely shortchanged in traditional classrooms, particularly in math and science, where boys tend to dominate discussion, receive more of their teachers' time and wring the self-confidence from girls who enter school equal in achievement and attitude but leave with lower test scores and diminished dreams.

In response to that research, which shows girls scoring generally lower on standardized tests—there is a 50-point gap on the math S.A.T.—and avoiding advanced math and science classes, three California schools are segregating girls in some classes: Ventura High School and Anacapa Middle School, both public schools in this oceanside city north of Los Angeles, and Marin Academy, a private high school north of San Francisco.

"It may not be the solution to the world's problems, but it seems to be serving our young women," said Evelyn A. Flory, the assistant principal at Marin Academy, which was first to experiment with an all-girl algebra class for first-year students last year. The pilot was so popular that the program was expanded this year to include two math and two science classes for both freshman and sophomore girls.

It is the public schools, however, that could face legal challenges and the loss of state or Federal money by offering segregated instruction: in this case, two algebra classes for junior and senior girls at Ventura High School and a pair of seventh-grade math classes just for girls and another pair just for boys at Anacapa Middle School here.

California education officials said the all-girl classes are permissible under state law because they are technically open to boys, even though none have enrolled. But Federal officials said they doubted that the classes would survive a more rigorous constitutional challenge because there were alternative ways to improve the educational environment for girls.

"There are less segregatory means to reach the same end," said Norma Cantu, the Assistant Secretary for civil rights in the Federal Department of Education. "Have they really exhausted the possibilities of training teachers to handle the different learning styles of boys and girls?"

While several all-boy public schools with an Afrocentric curriculum in Detroit were forced to accept girls after a court challenge, there has not been a legal challenge to single-sex classes within schools.

Even researchers who led the way in documenting sexual bias in education seem wary of the single-sex approach. Many prefer better teacher training and restructured classrooms that include cooperative learning and other techniques known to help girls.

Susan Baily, director of the Wellesley College Center for Research on Women and the main author of a recent report on the subject for the American Association of University Women, said she was concerned about "sending a message that girls are so special, so in need of extra help, that they must be taught separately."

But, she added, the all-girl classes will illuminate "what works for girls" and thus could eventually enhance coeducational teaching.

While it is too soon to say whether the single-sex classes in California are effective, the girls enrolled in them uniformly say they are delighted. When a reporter visited all three schools last week, scores of girls clamored to talk about how happy they were to be in classrooms with no boys to badger them into silence or to consume the teacher's attention, often with their misbehavior.

Many of the girls also said it was a relief to be able to learn at their own pace and help each other rather than be rushed along by the boys. "The boys want to hurry up and get it done so they can say, 'I beat you,' " said Misty West, a seventh-grader at Anacapa.

In fact, the boys in one single-sex middle school class flew through their problems, egging each other on to move faster, to do better. "I did it!" one boy shouted. Another countered, "I did it before him!"

By contrast, the all-girl classes ground to a halt if someone did not understand triangulation or matrix logic. Round and round the conversation went while those who got it tried to explain it to those who did not.

"If I know a problem and somebody else doesn't, I go slowly," said Bernice Motter, a senior at Ventura High, where the teacher, Chris Mikles, gives out her home telephone number for after-hours help and pairs her students with female mentors in various careers.

The girls added that they were more comfortable taking leadership roles in single-sex classes and acknowledging that they were smart—the same outcomes noted by proponents of all-female colleges. "You don't have to hide a part of your personality and pretend you're confused when you know what's happening," said Miya Drucker, a freshman at Marin Academy.

Many of the boys made fun of the experimental classes when left to their own devices. But when asked about it by an adult, they gave relatively thoughtful answers.

Typical was Dawud Lankford, a Marin freshman who barged up to a group of girls talking about how much they liked the classes and imitated them in a falsetto voice. The girls blushed and fell silent.

Later, Dawud said that he was "just playing, messing with them." He added that if the new classes "will help the girls, you know, with their study habits or whatever, I guess it's good."

A few boys, like Jeff Taish, a Marin Academy sophomore, said that if the girls did better academically, it would put the boys at a competitive disadvantage. And some, like Ian Borchert, a seventh-grader at Anacapa, complained that he missed having girls to look at.

The boys assigned to the all-boys classes, which were instituted at Anacapa Middle School because it made scheduling the all-girls classes easier, seemed at worst indifferent and at best mildly pleased. "Girls are, like, hard to talk to," said Jeff Kearney. "You want to impress them and stuff."

At both Marin Academy and Anacapa Middle School, administrators said they were now considering separate classes for boys in art or language arts, where they tend to trail the girls in performance. But limited research on the subject shows that boys do not benefit from such segregation, and several teachers and students here wondered if it did not hurt them.

"One of my beefs about this is that girls are a calming influence," said Adrian Sears, whose coed class, "Foundations of Natural Science," at Marin Academy this year has only two girls, in part because there is also an all-girl section. "They are not so testosterone-driven, not so me, me, me."

Steven Kahn, a Marin freshman, agreed, saying: "Girls in the class neutralize things and keep you in check. Without them, it's more edgy."

One tentative concern about the all-girl classes, voiced by a few teachers but not by any female students, is that the girls move too slowly, ask too many questions and discuss things endlessly.

Anita Mattison, a math teacher at Marin Academy who is in her second year with all-girl classes, said her girls "kept on with something that we'd pretty much exhausted, like each of them had to explain it their way." The repetitious comments, she said, seemed a sign that the girls "needed reinforcement."

Cinda Beem, a teacher at Anacapa, said her boys were five lessons ahead of her girls, boosted to greater accomplishment by their competitive natures. She said she worried that the meeker girls would not complete the year's work.

But another Anacapa teacher, Pam Belitski, said her girls had kept pace with the boys by working fewer problems for each lesson once they understand the concept. And the boys, she said, often barrel forward regardless of whether they all understand.

Even if the girls lagged behind, Mrs. Belitski added, she would encourage their inquiries. "How many years have they not been able to ask questions?" she said.

In most of the single-sex classes, everybody raised a hand and had a say. But occasionally, one girl dominated, as a boy might. In Jim Morris's geometry class at Marin Academy, for instance, Laura Gamb, her fingers flying across a Texas Instruments T1-81 calculator, was first with the answer to every question, yelling each out while others struggled.

The three experiments are too new to have yielded hard and fast results. At Marin Academy, which is furthest along, the girls have yet to take any standardized tests, and Mrs. Flory said grades were a poor measure because four teachers were involved. Last year, the school interviewed students in all-girl and coed algebra classes and found that far more girls from the all-girl class would take math if it was not required.

At Ventura High, the students in the all-girl classes recently took preliminary college boards but have yet to receive their scores. Asked if they were getting better grades, virtually every girl said yes. How much better, they were asked? D's to A's was the common shouted reply.

At Anacapa the children have written essays about their experience. In a typical one, Amber West said, "Math was my worst subject, and now it's turned out to be pretty fun."

Irene Gonzalez offered this verbal testimonial: "Before, my teacher wrote notes to my mom saying, 'Irene is embarrassed to ask questions and she needs to ask them.' I don't get those notes no more."

BABAR THE RACIST

Kay Sunstein Hymowitz

This article appeared in The New Republic *in 1991. The author is a freelance writer in New York.*

Perhaps it was inevitable, but the latest minority to join the plethora of ethnic, sexual, and cultural groups now seeking the status of victimhood are, yes, witches. According to the *Anti-Bias Curriculum*, a publication of the National Association for the Education of Young Children that is gaining prestige in teachers' colleges, they have suffered too long from disparaging prejudice. The book advises teachers to explain that Halloween witches are not evil hags who like to eat children, like the one in *Hansel and Gretel*, but actually good women who use herbal remedies to "really help people." Deborah Goldsbury, a preschool teacher at the Happy Medium School in Seattle, sings a song about witches with her four- and five-year-old preschoolers, which includes the line: "Maybe your great, great grandmother was one." "I also tell the children about women I know who consider themselves witches," says Goldsbury. "And I bring in some interesting herbs so we can make potions together."

Higher education came first, then the high schools, but the latest educational area for extrasensitive pedagogy is kindergarten. In classrooms across the country, experiments—some sensible, some plain crazy—are proliferating to put the pc into abc. The practice begins with the essentials. Many kindergarten teachers find in Columbus Day and Thanksgiving an excellent opportunity for object lessons in ethnocentrism. Take Lawrence Zilke, a teacher at the Center for Early Education in West Hollywood. He shows his first-graders old educational films about the founding of America in order to demonstrate the bias on which their parents were raised. In Monica Marsh's kindergarten class in University Heights, Ohio, children celebrate an "international Thanksgiving" during which everyone contributes food and flags from his own country. In a Brooklyn classroom, when one boy began to cry in confusion because his ancestry was English, Scottish, Irish, German, and Jewish, the teacher relented from an earlier prohibition and allowed the child to bring in an American flag.

A number of teachers have some interesting ideas about the spring holidays as well—like Passover, Easter, International Women's Day, Japanese Boy's Day, Japanese Girl's Day (of little importance in Japan, evidently), Cinco de Mayo, and Family Day. The last is the brainchild of Patricia Ramsey, director of the Gorse Child Studies Center in Mount Holyoke, Massachusetts. It is designed to replace Mother's Day, which Ramsey says is a regressive symbol of a sexist organization of labor. Family Day allows "all the members of the family [to] be honored." To play it safe, other school districts like Shaker Heights and Cleveland Heights in Ohio discourage the teaching of all holidays. A similar measure was adopted in Madison, Wisconsin.

In Iowa (the first state to mandate "multicultural, nonsexist education"), the Area Education Agency in Cedar Falls recognizes that story time presents a special moral challenge for enlightened early childhood teachers. It has put out the "Multicultural Nonsexist Teaching Strategies" to help. Among its kindergarten reading recommendations: *Hi Mrs. Mallory*, about "an intergenerational relationship," and *Leo the Lop*, "to make students aware of how diversity is not always accepted in a positive way." Students should also be acquainted with *William's Doll*, about a boy who wants to play with a doll, and *Max*, about a boy who learns to warm up for his baseball game at his sister's ballet class.

Further suggestions for story-telling include giving a sensitive twist to children's classics—for example, reading *'Twas the Night Before Christmas* and "pretending there is no 'Papa' in the story. Why not have Mama run to the window?"

But sadly many of the great children's books are beyond help. *Babar*, for instance, "extols the virtues of a European middle-class lifestyle and disparages the animals and people who have remained in the jungle," to quote Ramsey once more.

A helpful resource for the teacher wishing to eschew subversive stories of this sort is the Council on Interracial Books for Children, whose bulletin circulates to educators in all fifty states. It "analyzes the content of new children's books and educational materials for racism, sexism, ageism, handicapism, and other anti-human values." Some of the older books critiqued by the council bulletin include *Rumpelstiltskin* ("sexist"), *Snow White, Peter Pan, Mary Poppins* (all "racist" and "sexist"), and Shel Silverstein's *The Giving Tree* ("a male supremacist fantasy": the generous, nurturing tree is referred to with a feminine pronoun). The council bulletin also reminds teachers to be leery of books in which "law enforcers are depicted as the people's best friend" or in which "teachers are portrayed as loving, kind, bilingual, and as having answers to all problems."

Should a retro book somehow find its way into the classroom, however, it can always be grasped as an opportunity to teach the young children to "think critically," in the parlance of the au courant educator. At the Longfellow School in Teaneck, New Jersey, children are indulged in their reading of *Cinderella*, but they will then be asked, according to the principal, incisive questions like: "Will Cinderella be happy after she and the prince are married?" "Wouldn't it be better if Cinderella had wanted other things to make her happy?" Goldsbury uses a more direct approach. She suggests confronting any tot who may have enjoyed the fairy tale with the observation: "You seem to think this story is fun, but it's not fun for me. This person isn't making decisions for herself or taking charge of her own life." Other educators recommend considering the point of view of the giant in *Jack and the Beanstalk* and the wolf in *Little Red Riding Hood*.

Playtime in general is full of incorrect temptations. But remedies are at hand. In the dress-up corner a teacher can ensure that there are more briefcases than pocketbooks and that there are plenty of scarves to wrap the head and body like people in other countries so that, as Ramsey points out, the girls won't be tempted to "clomp around in high heels with pocketbooks like middle-class Americans." She would also make sure that toys like earthmovers and dump trucks are banned from the playroom, as they reflect the American desire to "conquer nature." Marsh noticed that many times a crowd of boys surrounded the workbench or "inventor's table," so she made a rule: there must always be two boys and two girls in those areas, evidently to ensure that girls and boys will conquer nature in equal numbers. Heaven knows what regulations apply in the sandbox.

QUESTIONS TO HELP YOU THINK AND WRITE ABOUT EDUCATION ISSUES

1. Read the three articles by Takaki, Katz, and Sollod. Draw a line down the middle of three sheets of paper, and make lists of the advantages and disadvantages

of the multicultural curriculum in the columns on the first sheet, the advantages and disadvantages of teaching self-esteem on the second, and the advantages and disadvantages of teaching spirituality on the third. What do you value? Why? What is consistent with your current educational experiences? Explain in detail.

2. Identify the claim, support, and warrants in the article by Katz. Do you share her opinions about teaching self-esteem in the public schools? Have you noticed any differences in the efforts of your primary and secondary school teachers and your college professors in their efforts to teach self-esteem? Is a student's self-esteem a legitimate concern of college professors? Why or why not? Try to think in terms of human motivation and values as you work with this issue.

3. Sollod offers yet another possible subject for the schools to teach. What do you think the public schools should be responsible for teaching? What do you think the colleges and universities should be responsible for teaching? Think in terms of what constitutes a successful life and a successful society by your standards. Discuss how schools can contribute to success in some areas and how they should not be expected to contribute in others.

4. The articles by Lambert and Borkat deal with the problem of grade inflation in different ways. What is your response to these authors' ideas? Do you think this is a problem? What is its cause? Is it harmful? Why or how? What should be done about it?

5. What is Borkat's claim in her essay? Why do you think so? What technique is she using to state her claim?

6. Read Sizer's essay. Now draw a line down the middle of a piece of paper and list the reasons in favor of a national exam in one column and the reasons against it in the other. What conclusions does Sizer draw? What are your conclusions on this issue? Give reasons.

7. How far do you think schools should go to eliminate bias in education? Think in terms of your own experience. Have you ever experienced bias in an educational setting, or have you witnessed bias? Provide a narrative with details as support. What could the school have done differently to eliminate bias in this situation? Read the articles by Chira, Mincer, and Gross to help you think about solutions to this problem.

8. Think of both advantages and disadvantages of the practice used to eliminate bias in the article "Babar the Racist." What is your final conclusion about this practice?

SECTION III

Issues Concerning Crime and the Treatment of Criminals

WHAT ARE THE ISSUES?

1. How Tough Should Drug Sentencing Be?

A senator and a federal judge provide perspectives on minimum sentences for drug cases. The third article provides an account of prison life for an individual who received a life sentence for a drug offense.

2. What Can Be Done to Reduce Crime?

Several authors propose policies for reducing crime and dealing with criminals. See also "Reading, Writing, Rehabilitation," pp. 100–101.

3. How Should We Punish the Worst Crimes?

Arguments about capital punishment question its effectiveness, give reasons for retaining it, provide a firsthand account of an execution, explain the psychology behind it, and suggest how some positive social good could come from it.

THE RHETORICAL SITUATION

Everyone seems to have opinions about the issues associated with crime and criminals. All of the recent presidents of the United States have made it a major issue in their campaigns and presidencies, yet the problems persist. According to the perceptions of many, the country is becoming increasingly lawless. Motivational warrants linked to the need for safety are implicit in many of the arguments about crime issues.

A poll of more than 2,500 Americans representative of the population as a whole was conducted by *Parade* magazine in 1993. It highlighted some of the major crime issues, as well as popular opinion about them. Here are some of the questions that were asked, along with the responses:

Are the police doing a good job? 82% yes 18% no
Do juries convict the guilty and free the innocent? 23% yes 77% no
Does the criminal justice system treat all people equally? 13% yes 87% no
Should repeat offenders be eligible for parole? 8% yes 92% no
Should 13–16-year-olds be tried in adult courts? 71% yes 29% no
Should people who commit nonviolent crimes such as tax evasion, petty theft,

prostitution, or forgery be sentenced to community service instead of prison? 83% yes   17% no[1]

The issues related to crime that are included in this section deal with the degree of severity that should be required in sentencing drug cases, with policies for reducing crime and dealing with criminals, and with the punishment of murderers and others who commit particularly horrible crimes. Drug sentencing causes severe overcrowding in jails and prisons, so some people question whether first offenders should receive mandatory jail sentences. Finding creative ways to reduce crime by protecting neighborhoods, reducing or increasing the use of handguns, rehabilitating criminals, or preventing them from becoming criminals in the first place seems important to some people and impossible to others. And finally, even though 87 percent of the people in the *Parade* survey favor the death penalty, it is still debatable, as you will see. It was banned in 1972 and ruled constitutional again in 1976.

1. How Tough Should Drug Sentencing Be?

DON'T LET JUDGES SET CROOKS FREE

Phil Gramm

Phil Gramm is a Republican U.S. senator from Texas. He wrote this article for the New York Times *in 1993. It was printed along with the following article by Judge Weinstein.*

Two Federal judges recently announced that they would refuse to take drug cases because they oppose mandatory minimum sentences. One judge, Jack Weinstein of Brooklyn, confessed to a "sense of depression about much of the cruelty I have been party to in connection with the war on drugs." The other, Whitman Knapp of Manhattan, heartened that President Clinton "has not committed himself to the war on drugs in such a way as the Republican Administration had," hoped his action would influence the President to abandon tough mandatory sentencing.

If the Clinton Administration listens to these voices, and their echoes, and tries to roll back minimum mandatory sentences, it will certainly win applause from some criminal defense lawyers, judges and the media—and no doubt many criminals—but it will betray millions of Americans who took the President at his word when he promised to be tough on crime.

Contrary to conventional wisdom, most criminals are perfectly rational men and women. They don't commit crimes because they're in the grip of some irresistible impulse. They commit crimes because they think it pays.

---

[1] *Parade*, April 18, 1993, pp. 4, 7.
New York Times, July 8, 1993, p. A11.

Unfortunately, in most cases they are right: In America today, crime *does* pay.

Morgan Reynolds, an economist at Texas A&M University, has calculated the amount of time that a person committing a serious crime in 1990—the last year for which we have complete statistics—could reasonably expect to spend in prison. By analyzing the probability of arrest, prosecution, conviction, imprisonment and the average actual sentence served by convicts for particular crimes, Professor Reynolds has reached some shocking conclusions.

On average, a person committing murder in the United States today can expect to spend only 1.8 years in prison. For rape, the expected punishment is 60 days. Expected time in prison is 23 days for robbery, 6.7 days for arson and 6.4 days for aggravated assault. And for stealing a car, a person can reasonably expect to spend just a day and a half in prison.

Given this extremely low rate of expected punishment, is it any wonder that our nation is deluged by a tidal wave of crime? In trying to account for the six million violent crimes committed annually, analysts point to the breakdown of the family, the effects of television violence and the failure to teach moral values in our schools. While these factors have an impact, they overlook the main culprit: a criminal justice system in which the cost of committing crimes is so shamelessly cheap that it fails to deter potential criminals.

Mandatory minimum sentences deal with this problem directly. When a potential criminal knows that if he is convicted he is *certain* to be sentenced, and his sentence is *certain* to be stiff, his cost-benefit calculus changes dramatically and his willingness to engage in criminal activity takes a nose dive.

Again, Professor Reynolds's statistics are revealing. He found that since 1950, the expected punishment for a serious criminal has declined by two-thirds, while the annual number of crimes has risen seven-fold. In 1950, each perpetrator of a serious crime risked, on average, 24 days in prison. By 1988, the amount of risked time was 8.5 days. Over 38 years, soft sentencing—treating criminals as victims of dysfunctional families, of predatory capitalism, of society at large—has brought a dramatic decline in the cost of committing a crime and a dramatic increase in crime.

Critics of mandatory minimum sentences point out, often with considerable indignation, that mandatory sentencing denies judges discretion in imposing sentences. And they are perfectly right. That's what we want.

Americans have lost faith in our criminal justice systems. Too many violent criminals have walked away with light or even no prison sentences. Mandatory minimum sentencing is a massive no-confidence vote by the American people in the discretionary powers of our judges. If judges and parole boards were legally liable for the actions of convicted felons who walk the streets due to their decisions, I would have more confidence in their judgment. But they are not.

"But what about fairness?" critics of mandatory minimum sentencing ask. "Is it fair that someone who has never committed a crime in his life should go to prison for 10 years because one day he sold drugs to some kid? Shouldn't we distinguish between a major drug dealer and a minor drug offense?"

Once again, the critics are right: There is a distinction between major and minor drug offenses. A minor drug offense takes place when a pusher sells drugs to somebody else's child; a major drug offense takes place when he pushes drugs on yours. Only when our nation's elites are as outraged about what happens to someone else's child as they would be were it happening to their own will we deal with crime effectively.

Of course, there is the cost issue to be considered. At a time when we are desperately trying to reduce the Federal deficit, can we really afford to sentence more criminals to jail for lengthier periods of time?

Of course we can. In 1990, the Department of Justice's bureau of statistics found that it costs from $15,000 to $30,000 to keep a felon in prison for a year. A Rand Corporation study calculated that the active street criminal imposes a financial cost of $430,000 a year on the general public—not to mention such immeasurable but very real costs as grief, fear and anger. By Washington standards (or anybody's, for that matter), spending $30,000 a year to save $430,000 a year is a brilliant allocation of resources.

In dealing with our nation's crime problem, cost is not the fundamental issue. Indifference is. I am appalled by the shoulder-shrugging approach some Americans take to the issue of crime in this country. Americans saw the pictures of starving children in Somalia and were outraged; we saw "ethnic cleansing" in Bosnia and were furious. But our outrage and fury evaporate when American children are the victims of criminals.

Like Judge Weinstein, all too many are ready to agonize over the "cruelty" that mandatory sentencing inflicts on drug pushers, and to overlook the cruelty that mandatory sentencing avoids by keeping these criminals off the streets and preventing them from brutalizing your children, mine or even Judge Weinstein's.

With the end of the cold war, domestic crime is now the greatest threat to the safety and well being of Americans. And just as the U.S. developed a military strategy—"containment"—to deter Soviet aggression by raising its costs, so today we need a legal strategy to contain, and reverse, the growth of violent crime.

That is why, along with many other Americans, I am a strong supporter of mandatory minimum sentences. In fact, I will go so far as to say that as long as I am in the Senate, we will be imposing more minimum sentences, not repealing them.

THE WAR ON DRUGS IS SELF-DEFEATING

Jack B. Weinstein

Jack Weinstein is a judge in the Federal District Court in Brooklyn. This article
was published with Gramm's article in the New York Times *in 1993 to provide*
another perspective on mandatory drug sentencing.

In the debate over national drug policy, too many policy makers, unsure of
what might work or why, appear to rely upon what seems politically safe:
harsher law enforcement based on more prison time.

A nonpartisan Federal Commission on Drugs needs to be formed. Its object should be to report candidly on the costs, benefits, risks and advantages of
present and potential national drug policies. Such a commission could provide
the fact-finding and serious analysis lacking in the political climate surrounding drugs.

The nation can look for guidance to the Wickersham Commission, appointed by President Hoover in 1929, whose report led to a full debate on
Prohibition laws and a constitutional amendment returning responsibility to
the states for control of alcohol. Also instructive is the National Commission
on Marijuana and Drug Abuse, appointed by President Nixon in 1971, which
recommended ending prosecution for possession of marijuana for private
use.

So urgent is the issue that Chief Justice William H. Rehnquist in a speech
in June said, "The law by itself is not going to solve the problems of drugs and
violence," raising "questions of public policy which must be decided, not by
lawyers, judges or other experts, but by the popularly elected branches of government"—and ultimately, I think, by a well-informed electorate.

Attorney General Janet Reno, confronting the problem of drug crime immediately upon assuming office, emphasized the importance of reconsidering
the existing policy.

America has had three national drug policies. Before 1914, a freedom
model reigned. Opiates were sold as over-the-counter household remedies and
marijuana was a legal crop. In 1914, we began to tax narcotics to control them,
but we, like Britain, relied primarily on a medical model of treatment and pre-
scriptions.

In the 1930's, we embarked upon a strict punitive model, and the medical profession was largely pushed out of the field. The drug supplier—law enforcement complex was enormously expanded by the war on drugs in the 1980's
at an annual cost of tens of billions of dollars.

Meanwhile, in my judicial district, the Federal probation service has had
to radically cut its drug-testing and medical treatment program; many parents

have no place to send their children for help; educational and other nonpenal controls are ineffective, and, too frequently, ghetto youths seek to emulate sellers and thugs who brazenly walk city streets.

Largely because of drug prosecutions, our justice system is in crisis. Nationally, over one-third of all new inmates are drug offenders. Over 60 percent of those in Federal prisons have been convicted of drug offenses.

In the Eastern District of New York, we sentence about 400 drug "mules" each year. These are usually poor people who smuggle drugs, primarily heroin from Nigeria and cocaine and heroin from Colombia. They are cheaply hired for one trip. Before the adoption of guideline sentencing, they were sentenced to 30 months and paroled in about one year.

Now they must serve an average of two additional years, and sometimes a 10-year minimum, leading to at least 800 more penal years, at millions of dollars of added expense for incarceration in our district alone.

Largely because of mandated and unnecessarily harsh sentences for minor drug offenders, which fail to deter, I have exercised my option as a senior Federal judge not to try minor drug cases.

When I wrote a report on drug laws for the City Bar Association in the early 1950's and then served as chairman of the lay board of the North Brothers Island Hospital—the first for teen-age narcotics users—I believed a modified medical model was desirable. In the 60's, as a father I supported some form of criminal model because I thought that it might discourage drug use by young people. As a judge, in the 80's and 90's, I have become increasingly despondent over the cruelties and self-defeating character of our war on drugs.

A national commission could address the difficult questions. How should marijuana be treated? Has it become such a large and widely available cash crop that prohibition is neither attainable nor affordable? (In some districts Federal prosecutors decline cases involving less than a ton, while in other places people are sent to prison for years when they possess a few plants for their own use.)

How dangerous is marijuana? Does it have useful therapeutic values? How much money could be saved in law enforcement by decriminalizing its use? Would savings be offset by an increase in health and other costs attributable to a rise in consumption? Or would we find that noncriminal social controls—ranging from taxation and bans on smoking in public places to peer pressure—would reduce use, as they have for cigarette smoking?

For hard drugs, a national commission should consider the tradeoffs between medical controls and education, and our current punitive approach. Our investments in increased law enforcement are no longer providing adequate returns. If we reduce our criminal-penal efforts, how much of the savings could be better utilized for education and medical efforts to decrease demand? What is the optimal balance?

We must also consider moral and religious issues. Would decriminalization imply society's approval? Is there an overlooked moral dilemma in our penal approach that results, for example, in one in four black males in their 20's being under the control of the criminal justice system?

Different strategies might be required in dealing with different sectors of society. An airplane mechanic testified before me that he stopped using cocaine and marijuana when random drug testing was imposed, for fear of losing his job. Should we take greater advantage of alternative forms of control? Would such forms of control help those who may have lost hope for better lives?

Many such questions require analysis by economists, scientists, law enforcement specialists, sociologists, ethicists, religious leaders and others.

In considering loosening legal controls on narcotics, we must weigh the claim that our inner cities would be devastated against the price we now pay in daily body counts from gunfire. Unthinking acceptance of the current policy is unreasonable. It is time to compile the likely results of different drug policies. Only a national commission can do this. If we are fortunate, a national debate would follow. Perhaps then we could reduce the violence, moral degradation and waste associated with drugs in a more humane, effective and cost-efficient way.

A TRAGIC MISCARRIAGE OF JUSTICE CONTINUES

Mike Sager

These are excerpts from an article in Rolling Stone *magazine published in 1993. Gary Fannon has been interviewed on television and has had other stories written about him. Those who support his release from prison note that the present Michigan law does not discriminate between the actual delivery and the conspiracy to deliver drugs. Some seek to change the law.*

Gary Fannon was just 18 when he stood before the court to hear his sentence, a skinny blue-eyed kid with long hair and an earring who liked cars and heavy metal and hanging out at the mall. He'd made a mistake, the first time in his life. The jury found him guilty. The judge had no choice. Gary's knees buckled. His mother fainted. They both knew what the sentence would be: Life without possibility of parole.

Seven years ago, Gary Fannon became another victim of Michigan's mandatory-minimum laws for sentencing in drug cases. Lured into the drug trade by a detective who later left the force after he tested positive for cocaine, the teenager was tried and convicted of delivery of cocaine. He was sentenced to die in jail.

Today, you'd hardly recognize him. He's put on 50 pounds, thick muscle swaddled in a glutinous wrapper of farina and macaroni, fried fish, polish sausage, mashed potatoes and peanut butter, the stuff that passes in here for chow. And the face, how hard it has become, no more the handsome teenager with his date before the high-school prom, smiling broadly, a pink boutonniere to match her dress, the photo his mother likes to show. After six and a half years of nightmares on the top bunk in an 8-by-10-foot cell, the kid who used to turn heads goes by a new name. To his fellow inmates, he is Bulldog. [. . .]

"I guess I have some pent-up aggression," says Gary.

He is met this morning wearing a Hard Rock Cafe Orlando T-shirt, turquoise sweat pants, in the visiting room at Ryan Regional Correctional Facility, a red brick monolith surrounded with fences and razor wire in the middle of bombed-out Detroit. It's a fairly new prison, though there are newer ones in the state, some of which haven't even opened yet for lack of operating funds. The Michigan legislature passed recently the highest prison budget in state history, $1.12 billion, jumping the corrections line item from 12th largest to third, right behind social services and education. With the notion of rehabilitation long ago given up for impossible, the latest words in penal technology have become *deterrent* and *warehouse*. More than 60 percent of federal prisoners in the nation are in for drug crimes. Violent felons are being paroled early to make space. Lock them up, throw away the key: the marching orders in the war on drugs. [. . .]

Gary was a regular kid who was turned on to cocaine for the first time by an undercover cop. The cop duped him into setting up a large drug deal. First grass, then coke, then more coke. And though Gary got scared and fled—he wasn't even in the state of Michigan when the delivery went down—he was found guilty of delivering more than 650 grams of cocaine. It was his first offense. His mandatory sentence was life, as legislated by state officials in an obscure amendment to an 800-page public-health act passed in 1978.

The cop, by the way, a man named Kurt Johnston, was later dismissed from the force for using drugs. He went back to school, got a psychology degree. He is currently in private practice, counseling drug abusers. His office is just a few miles from Gary's mom's house.

There are about 150 other such drug lifers in Michigan, the state with the oldest and toughest mandatory-minimum drug penalties in the nation. Roughly 40 percent of Michigan's drug lifers are first-time offenders like Gary. Most of them were lookouts, drivers, unfortunate accessories, little fish caught accidentally in a net designed for kingpins. Some of them had nothing at all to do with drugs. One grandmother was given life for picking up a friend of her sister-in-law's at the airport. Unbeknownst to her, he had a bagful of coke.

Six and a half years down at Ryan Regional, every day the same. Wake around 4:30, usually from a nightmare, in a cold sweat. You don't want to hear Gary's dreams, man. Dreams of guys chasing him, trying to kill him. Dreams of guys capturing his friends, taking a razor blade and cutting them from the forehead down to the nose because they won't tell where Gary is, and when they still don't tell, they cut them all the way down to their chins and start peeling their faces away. Every once in a while, he has a dream of being home. It's so real. Just before he wakes up and looks around and real-izes where he is, he has this feeling, like, I don't want to wake up, because I know I'm going to be in prison. You wake up and you're like, *damn, I thought I was home.* Sometimes he dreams of going to a movie. Or walking down the street. Sitting on a couch with his girlfriend. Going to McDonald's. Playing with his brother. Just having a phone, being able to pick it up when it rings and say hello. Not having to call collect. Those kinds of dreams are worse than night-mares.

Anyway, he wakes up, dozes off again, gets up around 6:15 to brush his teeth and go to chow hall. They serve slop. A lot of oatmeal and grits and fa-rina, whatever the hell that is, Gary doesn't know, but he eats it. Eating is like a focus. Something to count on three times a day. Since he's been here so long, his system is set to eat at certain times. Like if he doesn't eat, he starts to feel famished and weak. They call you state raised if you never miss a meal. "I'm pretty much state raised by now," says Gary.

After chow, he comes back to the house, flosses, brushes, watches a few minutes of the *Today* show to catch up on Katie Couric. He'd like to meet Katie. Drew Barrymore is another. Drew. He wishes she would write. The news befuddles him. He sees 13-year-olds getting busted for murder, schools and community centers shutting down for lack of funds, new prisons being built constantly, more and more people arrested for drugs. He doesn't un-derstand the politicians. Don't they see that they're breeding another gener-ation of trouble?

He watches all this on a 12-inch black-and-white on a shelf above his bunk, ordered from the prison catalog. His mother, Linda, had a 12-inch black-and-white at home, but she couldn't give it to him. Instead, she had to deposit $65 into his account so he could buy a new one. She wonders where Gary would be today if she had been able to bring that man the $1,500 he'd asked for. Before Gary's trial, Linda claims, a man approached her and said that for $1,500 he'd make sure the testimony against Gary wouldn't be so bad. If only she'd had it. Divorced mother, two boys to raise, long hours as a waitress—she couldn't come up with the cash. Like she told her state senator, William Faust: She grew up in a Donna Reed household. Her mom and dad always taught her that if you work hard, you're honest, you don't steal, you don't cheat, then you have a good life. But the truth is, you got to be rich to get justice. That's just the way it is. Linda wishes she was rich. She has seen Gary change.

To order something from the catalog, you have to fill out a disbursement form, give it to a counselor. The counselor has to turn it into the business of-fice, then it goes to the front desk. The front desk has to process. It goes on and on. It doesn't matter, really. Where do you have to go? And you can't have too much stuff anyway. Each man is allowed one duffel bag-ful. You're supposed to be ready to ride out to another prison at short notice. Whatever won't fit gets left behind. Gary also has a radio Walkman from the catalog. The guitar and amp in his footlocker he had before he went to jail.

"I brought those with me from the world," says Gary.

The reception on his 12-inch isn't so great. He gets the basics, 2, 4 and 7. They're supposed to be getting cable soon. Recently, in a poll, the inmates decided on four sports stations, BET and FLIX. Presumably, cable is a more manageable investment than college coursework, which has been discontinued at Ryan due to budget cuts. Gary collected 46 credits before the cuts—psychology, sociology, business math, the basics. He has a 3.5 GPA.

Just before 7:30, Gary leaves his house and goes to work as a tutor in the prison school. You tell the guard where you're going. If you're late, they'll give you a ticket. It's all recorded in the log, on the detail sheets. Where you're supposed to be when. The guys he tutors are trying to get their GEDs. Mostly, they don't ask for help, so he just sits there. It's about pride. Begging makes them feel weak. Weak in here will get you killed.

Back to the house at 10:15, count at 10:25. The whole prison population is locked in their houses so the guards can make sure everyone's still there. If you're excused from your house for some reason, at count time, wherever you are, you have to show your ID and give your numbers. Gary's are 4A-16-upper. Cellblock 4A, cell number 16, upper bunk. Gary takes a nap during count, wakes at 11:30, brushes his teeth again. He has a thing for brushing his teeth. He thinks it has something to do with dignity, with keeping his humanity. He's read how people in gulags and POW camps hold on to some obscure detail of their former lives with a fervor approaching mania. So be it, if that's what it takes. Brushing his teeth is his.

The news comes on again at noon, so he goes to the day room to watch. By Gary's estimate, 90 percent of the inmates are black, and the majority of the rest are Hispanic. Though most people kind of hang with one group or the other, Gary hangs to himself. That's how you get by doing time. You do your own time. If something happens, you look the other way, whatever; you don't get involved.

He does have a few pals. One of them is a beefy, 6-foot-2 white guy from the suburbs who looks like he spent his earlier life heaving bales of hay onto a truck. The guy committed a murder and didn't get caught, only he felt so guilty he turned himself in. It felt like everywhere he went, everyone was looking at him. He got 20 to 40, something like that. The rest of the guys Gary hangs with are Mexicans. White guys in here are looked upon as weak. Or as people who might be stepped on. And if you can't protect yourself, Gary's not going to be hanging around with you just to protect you. Like why should he stand by your side if you can't even stand alone? The Mexicans can stand alone. Only problem is, they smoke a lot of pot. Gary will have nothing to do with all the drugs in prison; it takes some effort, there are a lot of drugs. Though he's lost two appeals, his attorney plans to fight all the way to the U.S. Supreme Court. [. . .] What if he did get a chance for parole? He stays clear [of drugs].

Lunch is polish sausage, chop suey, turkey fried stew, a hamburger the size of a silver dollar. After that, it's out to the yard, Bulldog. Besides the lifting, he's also started studying Kendo, the martial art made popular by Steven Seagal. Another inmate is teaching him. Gary says he's learning it just for the peace of mind. The yard closes at 3:45. Then comes lock-down. Another count at 4.

More news, some collect calls, more chow, the yard again. Weights or softball, maybe just a walk around the track. Then back to his house to write letters. Gary tries to answer all the letters he gets. He's kind of renting a guy's typewriter for the purpose. His description of the conditions of rent are somewhat vague. You learn how to get things done. The letters have made a big difference so far. [. . .]

Nightly, Gary types letters to legislators, to supporters, to anyone who cares. He'd write letters all night long if they didn't turn the power off at 12. But Bulldog Gary Fannon is a ward of the state, and when they say lights out, it's lights out. Gary climbs up to his rack, the end of another day. That's when the thoughts kick in.

You try to keep pretty busy all day long, but when you're just lying there, nothing going on, no lights to read or nothing, your mind just starts going into thoughts like "Man, I've been here six and a half years now," or "This girl is doing this to me," or you know, "My little brother had a baby, and I can't be there for him." And his mom. He thinks all the time about his mom. How she can't rest with him in there. How she's probably lying awake, too, thinking the same things this very moment, her first-born son in jail, nothing she can do.

To get himself to sleep, Gary pulls from his childhood, the Catholic Church. He recites the Our Father: Our Father, who art in Heaven, hallowed be thy name. . . . Over and over and over and over. Just to make his mind blank. Just to make him drowsy. Over and over and over. Our Father, who art in Heaven . . . Kind of like a mantra.

Yes, yes, Gary says, people always get religion in the big house. But over these last six and a half years, Gary has seen the hand of God in many ways. "I mean, who ever thought I'd be in *Rolling Stone*?" he says. "Or on national TV. Or have so many people writing and coming to my aid. Or having a mom like I do. Or having remained safe all this time in prison." You can see the little miracles happening.

"Now all we need is a big miracle," he continues. "I gotta get out of here. I can't die in here. That's got to be the loneliest death in the world. Just to die in here. Alone. That's what scares me the most."

"I know you won't remember this, Senator, but 20 years ago, you helped my boys and me get an apartment. . . ."

"Well, er, um, glad to have helped. What can we do for you today? I bet you're here about the bill, right?"

Gary's mother, Linda, is in visiting State Sen. Faust. [. . .]

Faust . . . has recently requested the drafting of a four-point bill to modify Michigan's drug-lifer laws. In short, the legislation would allow people convicted of delivery, conspiracy or possession of more than 650 grams of cocaine to come up for parole after ten years; create a one-year deadline for reviewing the cases of all drug lifers currently serving; eliminate mandatory-minimum sentences for first-time offenders; allow judges some discretion in sentencing, so that penalties can be meted out based on the particulars of a case rather than on legislated mandatory minimums. [. . .]

"First, Senator, I would like to say how appreciative my son and I are of the bill," says Linda. "How is it going, anyway?"

Says the senator: "I know it is going to be an uphill battle. One of my colleagues, when I approached him on the bill, said: 'Don't talk to me about logic on this, because people at home don't understand it. A drug dealer is a drug dealer.'

"But I'm convinced that at least half the drug lifers just shouldn't be in there," continues Faust, looking out the window in his corner office at the great dome of the state capitol. "Yes, some of them, like Gary, made stupid mistakes. But I've made mistakes. And there probably wouldn't be any legislators in the country if everyone was put in jail for stupid mistakes.

"To take away their whole life for a nonviolent crime, a first offense. That seems to me an injustice. It's just terribly wrong."

"When do you think the bill will be ready?" asks Linda.

2. What Can Be Done to Reduce Crime?

IF TEXAS SPENDS WISELY, FEWER PRISON CELLS WILL BE NEEDED

Molly Ivins

Molly Ivins is a Texas columnist who wrote this article in 1988.

In politics, fear is at the root of more evil than money. And people are terribly afraid of crime and of drugs these days.

No bloody wonder, you may say, crack is epidemic in our cities, there are drug murders daily, bizarre mass murderers keep showing up, vicious and brutal crimes regularly lead the television news. But does the perception fit the reality?

Not according to the numbers. The U.S. Bureau of Justice Statistics reports that the overall rate of violent crime dropped 13.9 percent between 1973 and 1987. That's especially interesting since an article in Monday's *New York Times* reports that during the same time, the percentage of Americans in prison more than doubled.

From the 1920s to the early 1970s, the national imprisonment rate remained at about 110 prisoners for every 100,000 Americans. It's now up to 228 prisoners and still shooting up. Prison population increased 6.7 percent nationally last year and the National Conference on Crime and Delinquency projects a 21 percent increase by 1992.

There are three reasons why our fears do not match the reality.

Dallas Times Herald, April 26, 1988, p. A9.

One is that certain kinds of crime are astonishingly visible. If you live in a neighborhood taken over by crack dealers, nothing's going to convince you that crime is not rampant in the streets—you can see it every day.

The second fear factor is television—not only the kind of sleazy television news that plays up blood and gore because it keeps people from switching to another channel, but fantasy television as well. People on TV shows are shot with such regularity that no child in the country winces to watch it anymore. Women on television are constantly cowering in fear as some faceless intruder threatens them. Sure it happens in life, but not nearly as often as it happens on television: studies have shown that the more television people watch, the more fearful they become—all the while sitting safely at home on their sofas.

The third player in encouraging our fears is politics. Law and order were a wonderful topic for right-wing demagogues long before Adolf Hitler turned them into notorious code words. Pols promising to clean up the streets, to lock 'em up and throw away the key and to put 'em under the jailhouse are a constant feature of our landscape. The more fearful people are, the better this stuff sells and the better it sells, the more pols use it.

Any pol fool enough to raise a question is written off as an ally of murderers, rapists and robbers. Ed Meese 3rd, that distinguished apostle of law and order, once referred to the American Civil Liberties Union as "the criminals' lobby," a sobriquet now a favorite with right-wing mailers.

The upshot of such uproar is that here in Texas we have a governor now calling for the Legislature to approve an *additional* 10,000 beds for the state prison system, on top of the 10,000 additional beds the Lege approved last session. This [. . .] will take care of our prison needs for 10 years into the future.

In construction costs alone, we're talking at least $160 million, with operating costs on top of that. William Bennett Turner, the lawyer in the Ruiz case, estimates that it will cost the state $2 billion to run and operate the additional prison space over 10 years, not counting interest on bonds, increased welfare, lost wages, divorce, etc.

Think about 10 years from now, when the state will be prepared like a Boy Scout to welcome the inmate class of 1998. Most of those future inmates are today, right now, boys of 7 and 8. Suppose, just suppose, instead of spending the $2 billion on them 10 years from now, we were to take a fraction of that money and use it to keep them from ever going to prison in the first place. Just the teeniest sliver of that money. Not for pie-in-the-sky programs, but for stuff we KNOW works.

We know pre-school works. An 18-year follow-up study on pre-school done in Michigan shows significantly lower rates of teen pregnancy, unemployment and incarceration. In Texas, we now have pre-K for some disadvantaged kids. In New York, Gov. Mario Cuomo is not calling for more prisons, he is asking for pre-K programs for *all* 4-year-olds. The Legislature in New York just put an additional $6 million into the existing program for low-income kids and a $12 million increase to augment the wages of day-care workers. Training funds for day care were provided, along with funds to encourage employers to set up pilot day-care programs. According to the *New York Times*, "a promising child-care resource and referral network will get an additional $1 million."

The New York Lege also voted for a $9 million increase in nutrition assistance for women, infants and children, but turned down Cuomo's proposal to extend Medicaid to 55,000 children without health insurance and to create a new category of health care coverage for 65,000 children of the working poor.

The centerpiece of Cuomo's program to help children was an ambitious anti-dropout effort called Liberty Scholarships that would guarantee poor high school graduates four years of higher education at a state university or college. The idea would eventually cost $60 million a year. This is the program that was so successful when it was tried by a Florida philanthropist a few years ago, it has been imitated all over the country with private money, but, of course, on nothing like the scale a state can offer.

Over at the Texas bonding authority, they issued $155 million for prison construction in March, the state wants another $85 million in June and $25 million to $30 million in September. This is just to build the cells where we put people away to rot at a cost of $14,000 each per year.

Where in hell are the fiscal conservatives this state used to be so famous for?

WHAT TO DO WITH OUR ADDICTION PROBLEM: WAGING PEACE ON DRUGS

Tom Dworetzky

Tom Dworetzky originally published this article in Omni *magazine in 1993. It appeared along with the question "Would you trade freedom for free drugs?" and a 900 number to call.*

People from the entire political spectrum are calling for the legalization of drugs. Others argue that it's both immoral and absurd to legalize substances that are destroying not only individuals, but communities—and that we should "crack down" harder.

No question that drug addiction is the immediate social problem today. The plight of junkies' ruined lives and 'hoods creates its own cancerous underground economy—and nourishes a thriving overground economy we can hardly afford: beefed-up police forces, overcrowded prisons, and understaffed health-care facilities.

Omni, September 1993, p. 22.

The stalemated debate on legalization focuses on the wrong thing: whether by legalizing drugs, we thus condone them. This is a false issue. Drugs are bad; no argument. But in truth, the war on drugs is a losing proposition. Trying to keep junkies and drugs separate (or any of us from our bad habits) can't be done. So perhaps it's time to consider a modest middle way, based on two seemingly contradictory propositions:

1. *Drugs should remain illegal.* Who could possibly advise easy drug access for anyone? The accidents and evils perpetrated while *under the influence* indirectly hold us all captive and infringe on our rights to safety.

2. *Drugs should be legal.* Why punish those weak-willed or tormented enough to fall into the monkey's grip? Drug addiction is a medical and psychological—not criminal—issue. Junkies have enough problems already.

At first glance, these two propositions seem totally at odds. How, then, to please all? What plan can satisfy the pragmatists trying to cut costs, the individual-freedom advocates, the moralists who argue that society must set standards for everyone, and, of course, the junkies?

But looking beneath the rhetoric, you'll observe a couple of things: first, that when you're rich, society looks the other way if you have a drug problem. There are many low-profile alternatives; just ask visitors to the Betty Ford Clinic. When the rich get in a jam, they go to a sanitarium or, if it's the kids, to a boarding school or academy. We don't need a bunch of law-enforcement agencies to shove the rich into rehab programs, either. All it takes is cash, check, or charge.

Then, acknowledge that whether a junkie has money or is broke, we can't keep him or her from the drugs. Several decades and billions of dollars after we declared war on drugs, we've won only minor battles. The conflict itself is lost. Drugs are easier to get than ever before.

We can end the war and at the same time keep junkies off the streets by making drugs freely available—in pharmacies located in minimum-security prisons. I've never known a junkie who'd waste time hassling people when he or she had drugs. With drugs available in prisons, we could at the same time and place offer cost-effective treatment services, high-school courses, and health care. So, instead of spending all of our money to catch junkies, we could encourage addicts to check into jail.

The deal would be, "If you do drugs, all right; but you can't leave high, and you won't find drugs on the outside. Do drugs, but pay with your freedom until you can leave clean." Make prisons the malls for the addicted, and cut out the middlemen who prey on their disease.

Think of the prisons as Betty Ford Clinics for the poor. Addicts do crimes to get drugs; they don't do drugs to commit crimes. Let the junkies live in peace and get on with their lives, confront their inner demons, work through their journeys. And let our neighborhoods experience a little peace and quiet, too.

Perhaps we should examine why we won't give drugs to people. There's a world of difference between condemnation and control. We can condemn addicts by making them check into secure drug-use and treatment facilities to pursue their chemical nightmares, to remain separated from civilized society until the time they're clean and ready to return. Or we can try to control them and fight over the long, strange trip they're on.

A PISTOL-WHIPPED NATION

William Greider

This article was written for Rolling Stone *magazine just before the Brady bill, which required a five-day waiting period to purchase a handgun, was passed in 1993. A common reaction at the time by people who opposed handgun ownership was that the bill would not accomplish enough. Greider's article presents some arguments for a bill that would ban handguns altogether.*

[. . .] Circumstances call for a brave new politics, a bold and honest campaign that takes aim at the real problem: the guns themselves. Now is the time to ban handguns.

Sen. John H. Chafee of Rhode Island is a middle-of-the-road Republican with liberal views on social issues, which puts him in a minority within the minority. That lonely position requires stamina and patience, since it means losing often. But it also provides a certain kind of freedom—the freedom to think independently. Chafee came to the gun issue by way of health-care reform. His study of the complexities of that topic led him to a radical conclusion on guns: The only genuine way to end the public-health threat of handguns is to ban their private ownership.

"A radical proposal? Hardly," the senator wrote in a *Washington Post* Op-Ed. "What I would call radical is allowing the terrible status quo to continue."

After Chafee introduced his handgun prohibition bill last year, the NRA [the National Rifle Association, which favors handgun ownership] naturally added him to its hit list, as did right-wing radio and TV talk shows. "Send Chafee back to Cuba," among other cries, was soon heard. "We're getting the crap beat out of us," a Chafee aide observed.

For a senator up for re-election next year, this is most impolitic behavior. "They will probably target me, but they should be careful about doing that because I fully intend to win that election," Chafee says. "The NRA likes to scare the daylights out of people, but if they target me and they lose, that will hurt them, not me."

Rolling Stone, September 30, 1993, pp. 31–32, 120.

Rhode Island, after all, is not exactly the Wild West. "I have to acknowl-edge my state isn't Montana or Wyoming," the senator says. "That might be another matter. I talk to my people, and while this thing isn't a political plus, it's not hurting me like it might in, say, Colorado."

Chafee's purpose is to push the gun-control debate past the NRA's scare tactics to confront the fundamentals. "This may not happen in my lifetime," he's told his staff, "but I'm going to keep putting it on the table and try to force a real debate on the issue."

Many of his Senate colleagues have expressed admiration for his coura-geous position—in private conversations. But Chafee's bill, reintroduced in May, attracted only one co-sponsor. "Many important voyages start with only a few travelers," Chafee says.

Politicians are wary because the senator does not hedge on the implica-tions of what he is proposing: a flat prohibition on the manufacturing, sale and possession of handguns and handgun ammunition. His bill allows common-sense exceptions. The military, law-enforcement officers, licensed security guards, antique-gun collectors and target-shooting clubs would be exempt.

Everyone else would be required to turn in their handguns. Chafee pro-poses a six-month grace period, in which gun owners would be compensated at fair-market value for their weapons. After that, owners who voluntarily sur-rendered their handguns would escape criminal prosecution but might be sub-ject to a civil fine. Anyone caught with a handgun could face hard time.

A one-time buyout of 60 million to 70 million handguns would be very expensive, Chafee concedes, but still cheap compared with the full costs of the warfare now under way. In any case, even with strong public cooperation, it would probably take years, perhaps a generation or more, to eradicate the guns in circulation.

In the meantime, the NRA would continue to inflame the public with raw appeals. That is the core of what makes Chafee's prohibition bill so provoca-tive—it challenges the conventional presumptions that have surrounded the gun-control debate for decades. The gun problem, Chafee argues, is not just about criminals. It is about everyone who owns guns. Guns are not primarily an issue of criminal justice. Guns constitute a large and expensive threat to pub-lic health as well as to public education.

The facts support him, of course, though that does not necessarily con-vince scared citizens. "The downside of the pressure for gun control is that many people say the answer to guns is that they want one, too," the senator acknowledges. "If we were starting out fresh and there were none available, no one would say let's have handguns. But if we try to put a ban on them now, that makes some people nervous, and I understand that."

"But you've got to turn off this spigot sometime," Chafee says. "I just feel very strongly that we can get handguns under control if we start now. We'll get all those handguns from the bad guys. We may not get them all right away, but by God, we'll get them. And we will save lots of lives by doing so."

In terms of society's most dangerous objects, guns rank second only to cars and trucks—and are closing fast. If present trends continue, it's conceivable that in a few years guns will surpass motor vehicles as the leading cause of fatalities. In 1990, Louisiana and Texas both had a death rate from firearms higher than the death rate from auto accidents. In 1991, accidental deaths dropped in most categories, including autos; firearms, however, increased by 8 percent.

Criminals do their share. For instance, 70 percent of the police officers killed in the line of duty in 1991 were shot with handguns. In the inner cities, the proliferation of drug commerce and enhanced firepower has changed the mortality statistics of black teenage boys. "For an entire generation of black males, guns are the leading cause of death," Chafee says. "These young men are being wiped out—obliterated—by guns."

But here is the unpleasant truth that many people (especially scared white suburbanites) find difficult to accept: The mere presence of guns in abundant numbers is by itself the leading killer, not just crime and habitual criminals. The NRA likes to say that guns don't kill people, people kill people. Right. But guns make the killing a lot easier.

According to Justice Department statistics, nearly half of all handgun murders are committed during an argument among friends or family. As Chafee points out: "Handguns are far, far more likely to kill a loved one than an intruder."

Likewise, suicides are made easier—especially for young people—by the easy availability of guns in homes. Handguns are the weapon of choice in 12,600 suicides every year. "Teens are particularly susceptible to impulse suicide," the senator notes, "and the odds that a suicidal teen will kill him- or herself more than double if a gun is available in the home."

Finally, children are among the major victims of handguns—usually killed by other children. A study of 266 accidental handgun shootings of children found that nearly 90 percent took place in the child's own home or a friend's home. In a little over half the cases, the shooters were other children.

Beyond these facts, there is the extraordinary cost. The annual health-care bill for treating gunshot wounds has been estimated at $4 billion—most of it borne by taxpayers. A study by University of California at Davis researchers calculated the average cost of hospital treatment for gunshot victims at $13,200, with individual cases ranging as high as $495,000. Spinal-cord injuries and paralysis, often associated with gun violence, are especially expensive. Three months of therapy at a rehab center typically costs $135,000.

"The type and severity of the trauma now seen in our hospitals is so similar to that seen on the battlefield," says Chafee, "that Navy and Army physicians are doing rotations at urban trauma centers as training for military combat."

The country, in other words, is at war with itself, and the guns are winning. [. . .]

Chafee's careful legal research has demolished a favorite red herring of the NRA's—the claim that the Second Amendment would prohibit his legislation. On the contrary, as a half-century of Supreme Court precedents makes clear, the Second Amendment does not proscribe a prohibition of handguns.

"One thing we've accomplished," Chafee says, "is that we've blown away the Second Amendment argument. They've backed away from peddling that scam anymore."

Other gun measures are now being put forward in Congress that fall somewhere between the Brady bill's waiting period and Chafee's flat-out prohibition. Having carried the banner for moderate reform measures for so many years, Handgun Control Inc. cannot quite deal with Chafee's provocative departure. "Prohibition has not been shown to work," says Cheryl Brolin, a spokesperson for HCL. "There are certain valid reasons people have to own guns. We don't believe Sen. Chafee's bill is realistically addressing the situation. We're trying to pursue more middle-ground proposals—one where gun owners and antigun people can find some common ground."

But the violent reality of American life has moved beyond such sweet compromises. Right now, it's time for a healthy, fundamental argument among the reformers themselves. This will be hastened, I think, as other groups representing public-health concerns, children and law enforcement come forward to redefine gun control in broader terms, just as Chafee is doing.

In the meantime, timid politicians still reluctant to take on the NRA, still afraid to pursue genuine solutions, should take note of public opinion. This summer, a Harris Poll found that for the first time ever, a majority of Americans—52 percent—actually favor the radical step of banning the private ownership of handguns. Once again, it seems, the folks are a step or two ahead of Washington.

GO AHEAD, CROOKS, MAKE MY DAY

Pamela James

Pamela James was a senior majoring in journalism when she wrote this article for her college newspaper in 1993. She had a strong exigence for writing, as you will discover when you read it.

I vividly recall the first time I ever pulled the trigger of a gun. My boyfriend had been attempting to instill in me the importance of women (or anyone) knowing how to properly fire a handgun. In his opinion, the police departments have become helpless and frustrated and [. . .] each and every one of us must learn the invaluable method of self defense.

The Shorthorn, October 1, 1993, p. 6. *The Shorthorn* is the official student newspaper of the University of Texas at Arlington.

Today, this memory is deeply shadowed by the travesty that has befallen us. I no longer kid my radical boyfriend about his "overreaction" to society's ills. The constant, senseless murder we see every day in this community has placed itself firmly in the consciousness of my existence. It's gotten too close to home.

A Mesquite newly-wed couple were [. . .] jogging on Eastfield Community College's track recently when a young man approached and demanded money. After explaining they had none, they were forced both to lie face-down in the grass. The gunman then matter-of-factly shot the young man once in the head and twice in the chest. The dying man's wife of merely 11 days was immediately assaulted by this same individual, who somehow decided to spare her life. She lives as the only witness to this unthinkable, senseless taking of a life. And the guy walked away without a dime.

The person responsible for this heinous act is still out there, somewhere, free to do it again.

A [. . .] letter to the editor by a . . . family therapist took the words right out of my wide-open mouth—we've become a bunch of "sheep."

A community should not have to blame a wife or daughter for "not being more careful." Our children should not have to be reminded not to talk with strangers.

By being sensitive to the criminals who perform these crimes, we've created a horrid problem that we must now learn to live with. I don't care just when or how a murderer became a murderer. We must stop them. If it means brandishing a weapon of our own—so be it.

The Brady Bill, designed primarily as a way to "slow down" the availability of weapons to potential criminals, is a nice gesture. We've all heard about how drug dealers get their "toys"—they simply steal them.

Solving society's ills is an extremely complex problem. This country continues to spend millions to rehabilitate these conscienceless individuals. But I think it's too late. We're letting "predators" out on "good time" to roam the wild—and devour us like defenseless sheep. And we continue to sit frightened like any helpless prey—waiting to die.

I'm not going to sit around and wait to die. I will learn how to properly fire a handgun. Classes are taught [. . .] for any citizen who makes the effort to find out about them. You must apply legally to own a gun, and must be willing to abide by the law.

But you can't defend yourself from these other "experts in firepower" if you don't know how to properly defend yourself with one. The last thing we want to do (and police departments rightfully fear this) is to allow a well-meaning, tax-abiding, gun-toting citizen to give these criminals another weapon to use.

I respect what our law enforcement and crime prevention teams are attempting to do. But they remain frustratingly limited. A police officer can't help me if I decide to jog at 10 P.M. on a college campus track. And he or she cannot help me if someone decides to jump in the back seat of my car at a red light.

The ultimate responsibility to protect our families and our property is ours. It always has been and always will be.

Heed the warning, criminals. You're wrong. Some of us are not sheep.

A NOT SO MODEST PROPOSAL FOR SAFER STREETS

Judy MacLean

This author has an original solution for the crime problem. Do you think she is serious in making her "not so modest proposal"? What do you think she expects you to infer?

I'm tired of not being able to go out at certain times and in certain neighborhoods just because it's too dangerous for a woman alone. There's such an obvious solution.

We can take a tip here from the Saudi Arabians. After all, they decree that one sex can only go out accompanied by the opposite sex. So why can't we? Only it makes a lot more sense for the sex that causes all the trouble to stay home.

What this country needs is a federal law forbidding men to go out on the streets unless they are accompanied by a woman. It would lead to an immediate drop in rape, street harassment, and gang activity. Men are much less likely to engage in these practices when they have to bring their mothers or girlfriends along.

There would be other benefits. Women who are now sitting home, waiting for the phone, would suddenly have more dates. When no man can go out without a woman, women's social calendars are bound to fill up.

And more housework would get done by men. If men can't find anyone to accompany them on that trip to the football game or bar, they'll just have to stay home. Leave them there long enough, they might discover the satisfactions of vacuuming and changing diapers.

Imagine the streets at night, full of women, children, and occasional male-female couples, strolling along safely. Teams of police officers (always at least 50% women) are on patrol. If they find a stray man, they simply take him home.

Now, some people will raise objections to this. How will men get to work, for instance? Very simple. If they don't have a wife, girlfriend, mother, sister, daughter or female friend to accompany them, they'll have to hire a woman.

It will give new respectability to the term "paid escort." And if women can pick up a few extra dollars riding to and from offices and construction sites

Funny Times, March 1992, pp. 1, 5.

with working men, it will help narrow the income gap between men and women, decreasing the feminization of poverty.

Another objection will come from gay men, who will say this is terribly unfair to them. So, to be fair, any man accompanied by a drag queen should also be allowed out on the street. After all, when was the last time you heard of a woman being assaulted by a man in a fuchsia evening gown, bouffant hairdo and 4-inch heels? Or even a man escorting such a man?

There's no need to worry that this will lead to muggers disguising themselves in female attire. Putting on false eyelashes and a bra tends to tame that old testosterone fast.

Some will also object to this proposal because it will bring a massive loss of civil rights for men. It traps *all* men at home just because *some* of them are responsible for violent crimes. Almost all violent crimes, to be exact.

Shouldn't men who really mean women no harm be glad to have one with them at all times?

Besides, women are already trapped in our homes, by something even more powerful than a law. If we dare to go out by ourselves to a neighborhood, or at a time, where it's "not safe" (meaning, where there might be hostile men), then we face a far worse threat than being taken home. Which is harsher, what I propose for men, or what women put up with now?

3. How Should We Punish the Worst Crimes?

WHY CAPITAL PUNISHMENT?

Clarence Darrow

> *These excerpts come from Clarence Darrow's autobiography,* The Story of My Life, *published in 1932. Darrow was a criminal lawyer who opposed the death penalty and was able to avoid it even for some of his most horrendous criminal cases. It was legal in his time.*

So long as men discuss crime and penalties they will discuss capital punishment. It is not easy to select the valid reasons for and against any sort of punishment. One who really seeks to know and understand goes over and over the question, and winds up at last by denying the validity of all punishment. Which means, of course, that society should not deliberately cause any one to suffer for any act that he commits. The difference between the one penalty and another depends entirely upon the reactions of the individual who fixes the penalties or discusses the subject.

It is almost universally believed that the death penalty is the most serious infliction that can be visited upon any individual. This is the reason peo-

Clarence Darrow, *The Story of My Life* (New York: Scribner and Sons, 1932), pp. 359–365.

ple range on the opposite sides of the much-mooted topic. Those who are for it believe in this penalty because it is the worst fate that man can visit upon his fellow man. Those who are against are influenced by the same reason. No one is either for or against it on account of the effect on society, for it is out of the question to tell whether it increases the number of murders or lessens it. Even if this could be told, it would not settle the question. If so, more men would believe in some obvious form of physical torture like regular beatings or maimings, or starving or branding, or burning or boiling, or continuous torment of the victim up to the time of death.

There are various reasons why this cannot be settled. First, no one knows the effect of the different sorts of punishment toward preventing others from killing. Nor do they know which gives the most pain to the sufferer, or just how the pain administered upon one human being will affect others who know it, or whether men, women and children in general should be allowed to see the sufferings of the guilty or be compelled to see these victims while in agony, so that the spectacle of agony shall be expected to keep others from committing the same crime. Neither do they know whether visualizing and hearing of the effects of punishment of one deters others, or induces others. Or whether, even if it served to deter in this particular way, it might not render men, women and children callous to human distress.

A Chicago sheriff once had an unusual brainstorm: Instead of hiding the condemned, the execution, and the excutioner, he took the other course. He had the scaffold erected in the jail corridor so that the prisoners would be obliged to see and hear all that occurred at the righteous killing. Of course, the brainstorm sheriff assumed that the jail contained the future murderers of Chicago, and assumed that if they saw and heard all the grim act, they would never kill, if, indeed, they ever got out. But this noble experiment does not seem to have produced the intended effect.

The hanging or electrocuting of a human sacrifice can be witnessed by only a few, although nothing else would draw such audiences as this everyday viciousness. Nor are the pictures allowed to be shown in the movies, although this would bring the matter most vividly before the people. And if capital punishment deters, nothing else than witnessing the hangings and other executions could produce the result. No one has yet settled whether the event of execution should be exploited or advertised. If not made public, how can it deter others? If made public, what effect will it have on the born and unborn? Before one starts on a journey, he should know where he wants to go, else he may take the wrong road. Only one thing is certain about capital punishment or its effect, that it is administered for no reason but deep and fixed hatred of the individual and an abiding thirst for revenge.

Whether one is for or against capital punishment depends, in the last analysis, on what sort of person he is; whether he is sensitive and imaginative and emotional, or whether he is cold and stolid and self-centred. And what he is depends on his inherited structure and his environment. So far as I can remember, I got my first impression of capital punishment from my father when I was very young, probably not over seven or eight years old. He told me about a murder that was committed when he was a young man, which happened in the town adjoining the one where he lived. In those days the murderer was hanged outdoors in broad daylight, and every one was invited to see the act and all the grewsome [sic] details that went with it. It was an eager, boisterous and anxious assembly, each pushing and crowding to be in at the moment of the death. My father managed to get well in front where he could watch the spectacle; but, he told me, when he saw the rope adjusted around the man's neck and the black cap pulled over his head, he could stand no more. My father turned away his head and felt humiliated and ashamed for the rest of his life to think that he could have had that much of a hand in killing a fellow man.

In most of the countries of the world the death penalty has been reserved for murder, on the theory, I suppose, that it is the most terrible crime ever committed. How is it so terrible? Is it because a human being has been put to death? If so, execution is just as bad, and much more deliberate. Is it, then, that it is more evil to take life than to commit any other act? If it is because to kill is evil, it means that he has what the law terms a wicked and malignant heart; although, as a matter of fact, the heart is not involved. Should the culprit be hanged because he has a wicked heart? Then all people merit death upon the same logic, for when one hates or despises another he usually wishes the other were dead, and has a feeling of pleasure if he learns of the death. Probably very few people have lived long in this world without wishing that some person or persons would die.

The killer's psychology is not different from that of any other man. Indeed, in a large proportion of the cases the murderer had no malice toward the dead. Is it, then, a worse crime if there is no malice? What then becomes of the wicked and malicious heart, said to be the reason for the crime and for the punishment? Something else must be found as a reason for putting the offender to death. Is he to suffer death because he has so grossly violated some other person's right? There are many other ways of destroying peoples' lives, and it is done day by day, by the slanderer, the libeller, and the one who takes away another's means of livelihood, whether in or out of the protection of the law.

But capital punishment is not administered for murder alone. Even in the State of Illinois there are two offenses punishable by death: murder and kidnapping. The latter is a recent statute passed, like all other new penal laws, when such reason as man has was lost through hatred and fear. Really, this law was passed so that in case a kidnapper takes a child and holds it for ransom, and for some reason the distracted parents cannot or do not pay the ransom, the kidnapper will kill the child to prevent its giving evidence in court. In some States rape is also subject to the death penalty; this, too, is a direct inducement for a ravisher to kill as well as rape; if caught, he must die anyhow, so he is persuaded by the law to kill the evidence of his guilt.

Up to a hundred and twenty-five years ago England punished some two hundred offenses by death. Amongst these were: picking pockets, gypsies remaining in the kingdom one month, the unlawful hunting or killing of deer, stealing fish out of a pond, injuring Westminster Bridge or any other bridge. The early American colonists made twelve offenses punishable by death, among which were blaspheming, the hitting or striking of a parent by a child over sixteen years old, and witchcraft, a favorite crime for which our Puritan fathers provided the death penalty; all the preachers and most of the judges abhorred this offense. To quote Warden Lewis Lawes, of Sing Sing prison, "When they stopped killing witches, witches ceased to exist."

Why does a portion of the world still insist upon the death penalty for murder? Different people would give different reasons for this, but the real reason is that human beings enjoy the sufferings of others. The issue is always clouded by false statements, foolish inferences, and a wild appeal to the mob. Are there any facts to justify the belief that the death penalty lessens murder? Most of Europe has either abolished it by law or has practically ceased to use it. Italy abolished it for more than fifty years. When Mussolini came into power it was revived for political offenses. But Italy is in the hands of one man who no doubt thinks that his rule rests on arbitrary power. England has kept the death penalty on its books for many years but seldom uses it. England and Wales together, with some fifty million population, do not execute more than from fifteen to twenty people a year. Perhaps thirty or thirty-five are convicted and given the death penalty, but nearly half of these are reprieved in the Home Office; and in England a life term means not more than twenty years.

It has for years been the stock-in-trade of the haters to tell how much better the law is enforced in England than in the United States, and that this is the reason that there is less crime in Great Britain. But the statement is absurd and untrue. In proportion to the population, the United States executes four times as many as England and Wales, and this takes no account of the quasi-judicial killing by lynching of negroes in the South, and even in the North. So long as the hangers here could get by with the statements of the stern enforcement of the law in England they seemed to rest content; but when every one learned the truth they took up a new refrain: It was not that England punished individuals, but that their punishments were surer and quicker. The deterrent is not many punishments, but sure and quick ones, they now say.

No one knows much about why men violate the law, or why they do not. It is probable that the criminal statutes and the convictions have little to do with the conduct that we call crime. Human conduct is not controlled by statutes. It is true that of the people arrested a much larger proportion are convicted in England than here, but what does this prove? Scotland Yard seldom takes any one into custody except on thorough investigation and convincing proof. This is not brought about by the third degree. No officer could remain on the police force in that country if he resorted to the shameless beating and brutality that everywhere prevails in America. When the English police take one into custody he is pretty sure to be guilty. In America it is not uncommon to arrest five or ten, or even fifty, and subject them all to all sorts of indignities in order to find the one man. In the meantime, if the matter is at all sensational, the police are spurred on by continuous startling stories broadcast by the press, and the whole populace gleefully and righteously joins in the man hunt. I do not know how swift and sure is justice in the United States, or in any other land. In truth, I know little about the meaning of the word, and in this all men are alike. But I know this, that there is no country in the world, so far as I have investigated, where in any case that attracts attention a defendant is placed on trial so soon after the alleged offense as in our country. Professionals who criticise the courts in the interest of cruelty are given to pointing to cases that have been long waiting for trial. These delays sometimes happen before trial, sometimes after conviction and retrial. In almost every instance these delays are caused by the prosecution, when they do not dare dismiss the case for fear of criticism and know that they cannot convict.

Here in America it often happens that one is indicted one day and on the way to doom the next; and sometimes on the very same day. In the last few months we have been regaled with the quick responses of judges to public opinion. Really there is no reason for judges to intervene between the mob and the prisoner. They do not, in fact, intervene, but obey orders, and frequently are a part of the mob. These judges have been giving sentences running all the way from one year to one hundred and fifty years. It is only fair to note that in England the public press cannot comment on the facts, or alleged facts, of a criminal case until it is on trial, and then give only the barest report of the testimony. In this country, every detail, clue, surmise, and theory is given out every day until the public is as certain of the guilt of the defendant as the prohibitionist is of the sanctity of the Volstead Act.

When men recover from the obsession that it is only punishment and its dread that keep others from crime, they will be able to undertake the question of social order sanely and scientifically. They will accomplish real results without violating the safeguards of freedom, destroying liberty, and making a nightmare of life. There are more violations of law in America than in any European country; probably many more. What is the cause and what is the remedy? Is it bigger and better laws, or more and harder laws, or bigger and better prisons, or bigger and hotter frying-pans on which to sizzle the victims of luck and chance? Or, is it nothing of the sort?

STATEMENTS IN FAVOR OF THE DEATH PENALTY

J. Edgar Hoover

J. Edgar Hoover directed the Federal Bureau of Investigation from 1924 until his death in 1972. The statements reprinted here about his opinions on the death penalty were made in 1959, 1960, and 1961.

I

The question of capital punishment has sent a storm of controversy thundering across our Nation—millions of spoken and written words seek to ex-

Reprinted from the *F.B.I. Law Enforcement Bulletin*, Vol. 29 (June 1960), Vol. 30 (June 1961), and *Uniform Crime Reports, 1959*, p. 14, respectively.

amine the question so that decisions may be reached which befit our civilization.

The struggle for answers concerning the taking of men's lives is one to which every American should lend his voice, for the problem in a democracy such as ours is not one for a handful of men to solve alone.

As a representative of law enforcement, it is my belief that a great many of the most vociferous cries for abolition of capital punishment emanate from those areas of our society which have been insulated against the horrors man can and does perpetrate against his fellow beings. Certainly, penetrative and searching thought must be given before considering any blanket cessation of capital punishment in a time when unspeakable crimes are being committed. The savagely mutilated bodies and mentally ravaged victims of murderers, rapists and other criminal beasts beg consideration when the evidence is weighed on both sides of the scales of Justice.

At the same time, nothing is so precious in our country as the life of a human being, whether he is a criminal or not, and on the other side of the scales must be placed all of the legal safeguards which our society demands.

Experience has clearly demonstrated, however, that the time-proven deterrents to crime are sure detection, swift apprehension, and proper punishments. Each is a necessary ingredient. Law-abiding citizens have a right to expect that the efforts of law enforcement officers in detecting and apprehending criminals will be followed by realistic punishment.

It is my opinion that when no shadow of a doubt remains relative to the guilt of a defendant, the public interest demands capital punishment be invoked where the law so provides.

Who, in all good conscience, can say that Julius and Ethel Rosenberg, the spies who delivered the secret of the atomic bomb into the hands of the Soviets, should have been spared when their treachery caused the shadow of annihilation to fall upon all of the world's peoples? What place would there have been in civilization for these two who went to their deaths unrepentant, unwilling to the last to help their own country and their own fellow men? What would have been the chances of rehabilitating Jack Gilbert Graham, who placed a bomb in his own mother's luggage and blasted her and forty-three other innocent victims into oblivion as they rode an airliner across a peaceful sky?

A judge once said, "The death penalty is a warning, just like a lighthouse throwing its beams out to sea. We hear about shipwrecks, but we do not hear about the ships the lighthouse guides safely on their way. We do not have proof of the number of ships it saves, but we do not tear the lighthouse down."

Despicable crimes must be dealt with realistically. To abolish the death penalty would absolve other Rosenbergs and Grahams from fear of the consequences for committing atrocious crimes. Where the death penalty is provided, a criminal's punishment may be meted out commensurate with his deeds. While a Power transcending man is the final Judge, this same Power gave man reason so that he might protect himself. Capital punishment is an instrument with which he may guard the righteous against the predators among men.

We must never allow misguided compassion to erase our concern for the hundreds of unfortunate, innocent victims of bestial criminals.

II

The capital punishment question, in which law enforcement officers have a basic interest, has been confused recently by self-styled agitators "against the evil of capital punishment." A brochure released not long ago, pleading for "rehabilitation" of murderers while passing lightly over the plight of the killers' innocent victims and families, charges that law enforcement officers "become so insensitized by their dealings with vicious criminals that they go to the extreme of feeling that the death penalty is absolutely necessary."

To add to the burden of conscience borne by peace officers, prosecutors, and jurists and to brand law enforcement officers as callous, unfeeling men "insensitized" to the sanctity of human life are gross acts of injustice to these servants of the public. This ridiculous allegation is mutely refuted by the compassion which wells up in quiet tears flowing down the cheeks of hardened, veteran officers who too often see the ravaged bodies of victims of child molesters.

There can be no doubt of the sincerity of many of those who deplore capital punishment. A realistic approach to the problem, however, demands that they weigh the right of innocent persons to live their lives free from fear of bestial killers against statistical arguments which boast of how few murderers kill again after "rehabilitation" and release. No one, unless he can probe the mind of every potential killer, can say with any authority whatsoever that capital punishment is not a deterrent. As one police officer has asked, how can these "authorities" possibly know how many people are not on death row because of the deterrent effect of executions?

Maudlin viewers of the death penalty call the most wanton slaver a "child of God" who should not be executed regardless of how heinous his crime may be because "God created man in his own image, in the image of God created he him." (Genesis 1:27) Was not this small, blonde six-year-old girl a child of God? She was choked, beaten, and raped by a sex fiend whose pregnant wife reportedly helped him lure the innocent child into his car and who sat and watched the assault on the screaming youngster. And when he completed his inhuman deed, the wife, herself bringing a life into the world, allegedly killed the child with several savage blows with a tire iron. The husband has been sentenced to death. Words and words and words may be written, but no plea in favor of the death penalty can be more horribly eloquent than the sight of the battered, sexually assaulted body of this child, truly a "child of God."

The proponents of "rehabilitation" for all murderers quote those portions of the Bible which they believe support their lavender-and-old-lace world where evil is neither recognized nor allowed. But the Bible clearly reveals that enforcement of moral justice is nothing new to our age. In fact, in referring to man as the "image of God," the Old Testament, so freely quoted by opponents of the death penalty, also states, "Whoso sheddeth man's blood, by man shall his blood be shed: for in the image of God made he man." (Genesis 9:6) There are many passages in the Old Testament which refer to capital punishment being necessary to enforce the laws of society. Since the Old Testament was written about and to a nation while the New Testament was written to individuals and to a nonpolitical body known as the Church, there is a difference in emphasis and approach. Certainly, however, the moral laws of the Old Testament remain with us today.

Misguided do-gooders frequently quote the Sixth Commandment, "Thou shalt not kill," to prove that capital punishment is wrong. This Commandment in the twentieth chapter, verse 13, of Exodus has also been interpreted to mean: "Thou shalt do no murder." Then the twenty-first chapter, verse 12, says, "He that smiteth a man, so that he die, shall be surely put to death." We can no more change the application to our society of this basic moral law in the Old Testament than we can change the meaning of Leviticus 19:18: "thou shalt love thy neighbor as thyself," which Jesus quoted in the New Testament.

To "love thy neighbor" is to protect him; capital punishment acts as at least one wall to afford "God's children" protection.

III

Most states have capital punishment; a few do not. For the most part, capital punishment is associated with the crime of murder. Some states have high murder rates; some do not. Of those states with low murder rates, some have capital punishment; some do not. The number of murders that occur within a state as indicated by rates is due to a wide range of social, human and material factors.

It would be convenient for a study of the effects of capital punishment as a deterrent if states fell neatly into two groups: (1) those with low murder rates and capital punishment; and (2) those with high murder rates and no capital punishment. Or, if the user of these statistics is making a case against capital punishment, he would prefer to demonstrate that the states with low murder rates are those that do not have capital punishment. But to expect such an oversimplification of a highly complex subject is to engage in wishful thinking or a futile groping for proof that is not there.

Some who propose the abolishment of capital punishment select statistics that "prove" their point and ignore those that point the other way. Comparisons of murder rates between the nine states which abolished the death penalty or qualified its use and the forty-one states which have retained it either individually, before or after abolition, or by group are completely inconclusive.

The professional law enforcement officer is convinced from experience that the hardened criminal has been and is deterred from killing based on the prospect of the death penalty. It is possible that the deterrent effect of capital punishment is greater in states with a high murder rate if the conditions which contribute to the act of murder develop more frequently in those states. For the law enforcement officer the time-proven deterrents to crime are sure detection, swift apprehension, and proper punishment. Each is a necessary ingredient.

WITNESS TO AN EXECUTION

Terry FitzPatrick

Terry FitzPatrick wrote this firsthand account of an execution in Texas for the Texas Observer *in 1992. You will need to infer his claim.*

I must confess that I *wanted* to see the execution of Johnny Frank Garrett. It took a bit of journalistic hustle to secure a place on the five-member press pool. My friends told me that I should examine my motives before I went. I didn't. I marched toward the Death House at midnight to satisfy insatiable journalistic curiosity. I just wanted to get *inside*.

The Death House is a brick bunker tucked inside The Walls prison unit in downtown Huntsville. Inside it's painted milky blue. It must be the most brightly lighted place in the entire Texas prison system. The room is small; only a few feet and silver, metal prison bars separated Garrett from his family. I stood directly behind Garrett's mother. The executioner stood in a separate room behind a pane of mirrored glass. Thin intravenous tubes ran through a small opening in the wall, into both arms of the prisoner.

Garrett was strapped to a gurney, with white leather belts across his chest, belly, thighs, knees, and ankles. His hands were concealed by tape. His arms were strapped outward at right angles. From above, it must have looked like he was on a crucifix.

Garrett was in a defiant mood and was clearly agitated. He was already on the gurney when the press contingent entered a few minutes past midnight. I'd seen Garrett many times before, in courtrooms, in jails, in those undignified hallway shuffles past the packs of reporters and cameras. He had always seemed calm, a bit detached. Back then, his prison haircuts, long sideburns, and thick eyebrows made him look like a Neanderthal. But here in the Death House, Garrett was clean shaven with his hair neatly combed back. He was very thin, clothed in pressed prison blues and new, white canvas shoes. His last meal had been chocolate ice cream. He had the look of panic: wide eyes, short breaths, tense movements of the head. Despite the psychiatrist's assessment that Garrett didn't believe a lethal injection would kill him, it seemed to me that Johnny Frank Garrett knew he was about to die.

His family was tightly huddled when I entered. His mother, two sisters, stepfather, and brother-in-law clutched the prison bars as Garrett strained to turn his head to the right to speak his final words.

"I'd like to thank my friends who tried to pull me through all this. My guru for helping me go through this. I'd like to thank my family for loving me. And the rest of the world can kiss my ass."

Garrett looked at the warden as he spoke that last part. Then he jerked his head toward the white ceiling to show he was ready. Garrett began to recite some kind of prayer or mantra to himself and the warden made a barely perceptible signal to the anonymous executioner behind the mirrored glass.

It was over in an instant: Garrett's mouth caught open in mid-speech, his eyes open—frozen with a small squint of recognition that poison was racing through his veins.

His mother kept saying "I love you son, it's okay. Go to sleep," as if it were a lullaby. Garrett's sisters were angry. "They're gonna' pay," one sister said.

With that, Garrett's mother tried to console her daughters. "God forgives those who forgive his brothers," she said. "He's at peace. He paid his debt. We all have to do that."

"He's in a better place than we are," the sister replied. "There aren't any assholes to tell him what to do."

The family sang Amazing Grace in broken tearful voices.

Texas uses three drugs in executions: sodium thiopental to relax the prisoner and induce sleep, pancuronium bromide to paralyze the muscles and prevent breathing, and potassium chloride to stop the heart. The dose is large enough to kill 10 people. The injection lasted four minutes, though life had slipped from Garrett's body just seconds after it began.

The executioner placed a roll of white adhesive tape in the small opening in the wall, beside the clear intravenous tubes, to indicate the injection was over. A prison doctor ambled in and searched perfunctorily for a pulse on Garrett's neck and arm, and then listened to Garrett's chest through a stethoscope for just an instant. He turned to the warden and compared the time on their watches. "I figure 12:18."

With that the heavy metal doors swung open with a startling thud. We filed out of the Death House behind the family. Nobody said a word. Officials looked at the floor as they walked. And Garrett lay there still. There were no gestures of respect for his corpse. Nobody covered him with a sheet, or closed his lifeless eyes. There was no dignity in this death.

We stepped outside the prison into the glare of television lights. A crowd of students from the nearby university broke out in cheers and applause, singing "na-na-na-na, hey-hey-hey, good bye." I felt ashamed as I walked with Garrett's family to the prison administration building across the street. The students weren't jeering at just the family, they were jeering at me. I felt my privileged press-pool access made me a participant in the execution as well as an observer. As a citizen of Texas, I realized that Johnny Frank Garrett had been executed in my name.

ON CRIMES AND THEIR PUNISHMENTS: THE PSYCHOLOGY OF RETRIBUTION

Graeme Newman

These are excerpts from Newman's book Just and Painful: A Case for the Corporal Punishment of Criminals, *published in 1983. Compare the ideas in this selection with the ideas in "Turning Bad into Good" on p. 471, which is a more recent article by Newman on the subject of how to treat criminals.*

From ancient myths to modern myths, retribution has played a central role in the resolution and definition of evil deeds. For example, Aeschylus borrowed the ideas for his Orestian tragedy from the dim beginnings of Greek history—an unending cycle of killings in which: King Agamemnon sacrifices his daughter Iphegenia for a propitious opening to his military campaign; his Queen Clytemnestra revenges their daughter by murdering the King; in turn, the Queen is murdered by their son Orestes. And the gods are hesitant to condemn any of the killings as totally unjustified.

Modern myths view retribution in a similar way. Take, for example, a modern play, the movie *Superman II*—not a tragedy, but a romance which is more typical of today's popular culture:

> Superman, having lost his super powers, accompanies Lois Lane as Clark Kent into that great belly of American culture, the diner. He leaves to make a telephone call, she sits up at the counter. A rough character takes Clark's seat and starts to bother Lois. Clark returns, asks the fellow to move, and a brawl ensues. The former Superman gets pummelled, and tastes his own blood for the first time.
>
> The audience sits on edge. Superman goes on to regain his super powers and perform the impossible: he defeats in mighty combat not one, but three evil persons who had equivalent super powers to his own.
>
> The audience lets out a sigh of relief. But the movie is not yet over.
>
> Clark Kent returns to the diner. The same ugly character is there insulting the diner's food. Clark picks a fight with him and—you guessed it—pummells the ruffian into the floor.
>
> The audience cheers loudly. Justice was done! And how the bully *deserved* what he got!

From Graeme Newman, *Just and Painful: A Case for the Corporal Punishment of Criminals* (New York: Macmillan, 1983), pp. 19–21, 22.

Why should a superman, one who had won a huge battle with three evil supermen, find it necessary to even up the score with a pathetic earthling? Surely a man so big and powerful could have shrugged it off?

The writers of this movie shrewdly saw that there would have been no end to this story had they not provided this last scene of redress. The need to settle a score, to even up old wrongs is deeply embedded into the meaning of justice in almost all cultures of the world.

This is the "psychological reality" of punishment—as Sigmund Freud called it—and it is well over two thousand years old. Philosophers and legal theorists call it "retribution" or "just deserts."

Here, justice is equated with the logic of the history and psychology of punishment.

Historically, punishment has always been linked to the crime: it has been made to fit the crime.

Psychologically we *feel* that the link between the crime and its punishment is right. We recognize that to reward crimes would make us feel extremely frustrated. (Indeed, this may be why so many people feel dissatisfied with our criminal justice system because it does seem to reward many criminals.) And at the very least, to sit by and do nothing about criminal behavior makes us jittery, even though we personally would rather not be those who actually meted out the punishment. Nevertheless, we insist that something be done to criminals who have committed offenses.

In the past, those who vociferously demanded retribution were considered to be conservatives. Today it has become a favorite banner of reformers such as Professor Von Hirsch in his book *Doing Justice*. In 1976 the Committee on Incarceration with Professor Von Hirsch as its Director, argued for a return to a just deserts model of punishment, claiming, among other things, that it would limit the overall length of time offenders spent in prison. It would replace the "treatment model" of criminal punishment which was blamed for the excesses of the "indeterminate sentence" (that is, the offender was incarcerated until such time that it was thought he was "cured"). The Committee argued that punishment according to just deserts would ensure that there were fixed limits to the punishment that could be applied to a particular crime, because the theory of just deserts requires that a person can only be punished:

1. For the particular crime, and only that crime, which he has committed and
2. By a punishment that fits the crime.

The oldest idea of making the punishment fit the crime was to reflect both the quality and gravity of the crime in the punishment. Thus, the hand of the thief was cut off—the old principle of an eye for an eye (often associated with the law of Moses, but the principle can be found to underlie the punishment systems of most cultures). There are many other variations of this theme. In colonial America, garrulous women who nagged at their husbands too much were, appropriately, gagged by the punishment of a metal bridle (called the "scold's bridle") that was placed over their heads and clamped on their mouths—a painful contraption which responded directly to the offense. Another reflection of the quality of the crime in the punishment was to punish a criminal on the very spot where he had committed the offense, a practice in English criminal law up until the 18th century. Or certain parts of the body were identified as the seat of the crime: to cut out the heart of a traitor, remove the kidneys of a thief.

The great Italian poet Dante Alighieri was a master at concocting reflecting punishments. In Dante's Hell, suicides, because they did not respect their own bodies, were turned into trees which were periodically snapped at and chewed by dogs. Thieves who had not respected the distinction between "mine" and "thine" were turned into reptiles, then transformed again into each other, destined never to retain their own true form. How apt, we say. There seems to be something inherently right about the choice of punishment. By "inherently" we mean that we have a "gut feeling" that it is right. This is why the audience cheers so loudly when Superman evens up the score.

MAKING THE PUNISHMENT FIT THE CRIME

This is a brief example of creative sentencing in an effort to make the punishment fit the crime. It was reported in The New Republic *in 1993. No author was listed.*

An Indiana judge recently sentenced fourteen abortion protesters to sit silently in an abortion clinic's waiting room for eight hours, without handing out anti-abortion literature. "I didn't want to send them to jail," said Judge Bernard Carter of the Lake County Superior Court, "but I did want them to do something that would make them uncomfortable, make them think about what they're doing." Carter's creative sentencing wins the prize for proportionate justice: a thought punishment for a thought crime.

TURNING BAD INTO GOOD

Graeme Newman

Graeme Newman, a professor at the School of Criminal Justice of the State University of New York at Albany, writes arguments about the treatment of criminals that have original slants. These are excerpts from an article that first appeared in the magazine Chronicles *in 1992.*

In 1983 I noted in *Just and Painful: A Case for the Corporal Punishment of Criminals* that there were approximately 315,000 individuals incarcerated in federal and state prisons, plus some 158,000 persons in jails of various kinds. The annual

The New Republic, December 13, 1993, p. 10.
Chronicles, May 1992, pp. 19–22.

cost of this incarceration was estimated then to be $20,000 per inmate, amounting to an annual expenditure of some $10 billion.

The solution I advocated at that time was to replace much of the punishment of prison with corporal punishment of a specific type: one that applied acute pain (that is, intense sharp pain of very brief duration). [. . .]

But I am humbled by the fact that hardly anyone takes my solution to the punishment problem seriously, especially since things have become much worse since 1983. Today there are over 600,000 persons in prison plus some 405,000 in jails. The annual cost is somewhere in the vicinity of $40,000 per inmate, and to build a new cell costs approximately $100,000. Why has the situation become so much worse? Why has no credible alternative to prison arisen? [. . .]

There have, of course, been alternatives to prison, but these attempts themselves demonstrate the very failure to understand the profound centrality of punishment to social life. The most well-known "alternative" was, of course, probation, introduced on a large scale in the United States early this century. It turned out to be largely an add-on "punishment" simply finding additional offenders. Worse, probation failed to convince the general public that it was in fact punitive enough. The great solution of the 1980's was supposed to be "community service," but unless its punitive element is sharpened, it will go the way of probation: people will see it, justifiably, as yet another attempt to subvert the punishment process. It turns "punishment" into "service" and "service" into "punishment" by taking away the intrinsic merit of service from those who would normally volunteer for it.

Yet the idea embedded in community service is morally attractive: it tries to draw out of the punishment process something "good"—service to the community. This is an important idea that, unfortunately in the way it is currently implemented, will go the way of other "alternatives" to punishment, because it does not address the fact that punishment must be punishment. The public, in my view, understands and demands this. Legislators understand this to a point, by enacting severe prison terms, but they ignore the fiscal implications of their legislation. These alternatives to prison have simply subverted the central idea of punishment: the intentional and deliberate infliction of pain and suffering on the offender. [. . .]

I propose, therefore, to turn to the other end of the criminal justice system, and ask what we might do to those few who have been condemned to death for the most hideous of crimes. Theirs is behavior that is not so difficult to pronounce as evil, and whose behavior we might try to avoid in our punishment. At the same time, though, in an effort to raise ourselves above the level of the murderer, we must try to extract something good out of the evil that we do to the murderer (such as the application of the death penalty) even though he may well deserve to suffer terribly for his crimes.

What "good" did the execution of the serial killer Ted Bundy do? We know that such penalties do not deter, so this was not the "good." Did it "satisfy" justice? But what kind of justice is it that feeds on the killing of individuals? Is it good to feel satisfied after killing someone, even though the person deserved it? I do not argue that the motives for killing are identical, but I do insist that there are psychological elements of both acts that are similar. The most obvious similarity is that both killings are intentional. I contend that there is no positive aspect in the infliction of pain or suffering on an individual, even when it is justified. We need to work hard, therefore, to turn this act of violence into something that *is* positive. The mere taking away of the murderer's life does not fulfill this need.

The answer lies in the very common complaint of murderers on death row. They announce that they are "sorry" for what they did (though it's often hard to believe them), but add, what can they do? Their victims are dead, they say, and they can't bring them back to life. True enough. But if we pause for a moment, we see the answer: while they cannot bring their victims back to life, they can save the life (and perhaps lives) of others. They could donate their body parts. In this way, one executed criminal's body could possibly save several lives. I would go so far as to say that the condemned murderer should be *made* to give up his body organs. The social and moral good could be enhanced tremendously by this practice.

There is a critical shortage of donor organs. As of 1987, for example, there were over 13,000 individuals waiting for organs of one kind or another, and the number is closer to 20,000 today. The U.S. government spent $300,000 in 1990 on Medicare assistance for each of the 60,000 Americans who require kidney dialysis. Thus, each executed murderer is "worth" at least $600,000 just for the two kidneys alone. In 1987 there were more than 12,000 individuals waiting for kidney transplants, and only some 2,500 donors. A liver transplant costs about $150,000. The need, therefore, is critical.

The fantastic service that executed murderers could provide by saving lives is tremendous. While their suffering may not make up for the specific suffering and loss of the particular victim, the victim's family and society as well can at least take comfort in the fact that two terrible deeds—the murder and the execution—have been turned at least to a truly positive outcome: saving lives and improving the quality of life of many others. This is true community service, while at the same time preserving the punitive element of the punishment.

There are, of course, many obvious objections to this idea. I anticipate, for example, complaints that the government will execute more murderers in order to obtain more body parts. This is indeed a cynical view of government. It should be possible to introduce legislative safeguards to fend off this pitfall, if it is a pitfall. There may also be some concern about an individual living with a serial murderer's heart or other body part. Patients receiving such organs would need to be counseled carefully. Whether it should even be known from whom the organs came is a question that would need to be addressed. Others might complain of a slippery slope, since some organs, such as kidneys, could be extracted from prisoners without killing them. Why not trade off years in prison for donating a kidney? And could an inmate "freely volunteer" parts of his body in order to get out of prison? For the moment, we should begin only with executed prisoners, and if this works, then look to its extension in other settings.

When I advocated corporal punishment for most offenders some nine years ago, I thought that the enormous cost of using prisons for punishment would sooner or later bring the system down. The massive increase in the use of prisons since that time has so far proven me wrong. The problem of punishment is not motivated or limited by fiscal concerns. Rather, it is a problem of moral psychology, as I have argued in this essay. We must try hard to solve this distinctly late-20th-century problem of punishment by beginning to acknowledge the deep-seated shame we have about punishing. We should not be ashamed to use punishment in order to save lives. In doing so, we may turn not only the bad of the offender into good, but also the bad of the punishment process itself into something good.

QUESTIONS TO HELP YOU THINK AND WRITE ABOUT THE ISSUES CONCERNING CRIME AND THE TREATMENT OF CRIMINALS

1. Read the first two selections about drug sentencing by Gramm and Weinstein. What is at issue in these selections? What is the position of each author? Which author provides the best logical appeal? Emotional appeal? Ethical appeal? Which author provides the most convincing argument for you? Why? (Consider the warrants that you share or do not share with each of them.)

2. What do you think Sager's purpose was in writing the article about Gary Fannon? Why do you think so? Provide some evidence for your answer. Do you agree with the author? Why or why not?

3. Read Sager's and Ivins's articles together and form some opinions about prison as a form of punishment. Consider imprisonment as a value issue. Is prison a good or bad form of punishment? Establish some criteria for effective punishment as you consider this issue. What are Ivins's alternatives to imprisonment? Can you think of others?

4. The articles by Sager and Dworetzky propose two different solutions to the issue of how to deal with drug criminals. Are either of these good solutions, or can you think of better ones?

5. Compare the articles by Greider and James as policies for dealing with crime. What are the strengths and weaknesses of each of their arguments? Which solutions do you favor? Why?

6. What do you think is the exigence for MacLean's article? What, in your opinion, was her purpose for writing it? Can you think of other "modest proposals" that would provide imaginative solutions to the crime problem?

7. Compare the articles about capital punishment written by lawyer Clarence Darrow, FBI director J. Edgar Hoover, and journalist Terry FitzPatrick. Do they rely on logical, emotional, or ethical proof? What are the strengths of each argument? What are the weaknesses? How would you refute each of these arguments? What is your own opinion on the issue of capital punishment? Were you influenced in your thinking by any of these authors?

8. Read Newman's essay about the psychology of retribution. Explain what he means by retribution. What are your opinions about Newman's claims concerning the "psychological reality" of punishment?

9. Read both of Newman's essays and the short piece "Making the Punishment Fit the Crime." What are some of the specific examples of the concept of making the punishment fit the crime? Evaluate this concept. Is it good or bad? Can you think of some other creative ways for making the punishment fit the crime?

SECTION IV
Freedom of Speech Issues

WHAT ARE THE ISSUES?

1. What Is the Responsibility of the Media in a Country That Values Free Speech?

Lasch and Katz provide two views on the special responsibilities of the media in a free-speech society. See also "And a Purple Dinosaur Shall Lead Them," pp. 233–236, and "Rap's Embrace of 'Nigger' Fires Bitter Debate," pp. 236–239.

2. Should Reading Material Be Screened to Protect Students?

Five authors provide different perspectives on the enduring issue of books that students should be allowed or forbidden to read in school. Value warrants are important in these arguments. See if you can discover the values involved and how they come into conflict with each other. See also "A Political Correction," pp. 285–286.

THE RHETORICAL SITUATION

No argument textbook would be complete without a section on freedom of speech. This is a right provided by the First Amendment to the U.S. Constitution, and one purpose of this book is to teach responsible and productive ways to exercise that right. Since freedom of speech is a constitutional issue, many legal controversies are referred to the U.S. Supreme Court for debate and final resolution. Consequently, much of what is written about free speech includes references to court decisions as one type of evidence. You will find examples in this collection of articles.

One way to develop a perspective on free-speech issues is to place the essays you read somewhere on a continuum that begins with genuinely objective writing like almanacs or weather reports at one end and proceeds to extremist writing that may use emotionally loaded language in a hateful or discriminatory manner at the other end. Objective writing does not usually spark controversy. Writing at the other end of this continuum does, however, because it arouses strong emotions that some people fear may result in antisocial behavior. Language that may influence people's value systems is also controversial, particularly for those who hold opposing values. Socrates was put to death for distorting the values of Athens's youth. The modern writer Salman Rushdie has had to remain in hiding to protect his life from those who have threatened to assassinate him because of his views and values. You may be able to think of other examples of conflict resulting from books or essays that are inflammatory to certain audiences.

In the 19th century, John Stuart Mill, in his famous essay "On Liberty," made the statement, "If all mankind minus one were of one opinion, and only one person were of the contrary opinion, mankind would be no more justified in silencing that one person, than he, if he had the power, would be justified in silencing mankind." The U.S. Constitution was written in this spirit. The First Amendment states,

> Congress shall make no law respecting an establishment of religion, or prohibiting the free exercise thereof; or abridging the freedom of speech, or of the press; or the right of the people peaceably to assemble, and to petition the Government for a redress of grievances.

In spite of the free-speech guarantee, however, the suspicions and fear of powerful language persists; every age debates what language should be permitted, and what, if any, should be suppressed. The issue surfaces when something happens: Someone says he shot a policeman because of a song he heard on the radio; someone leaves a note at a murder scene that contains hate language; a professor gives a biased, racially discriminatory lecture and claims he is exercising freedom of speech. Fear, the values associated with free speech, and the perceived responsibility to report and interpret free-speech infractions provide both exigence and constraints for authors who write about freedom of speech issues.

One of the issues examined in the articles collected here is the responsibility of the media in a free-speech society. Lasch and Katz view the media from different perspectives. Cadre's essay on pages 233–236 suggests the influence the media has on children. These articles will help you think about how the media should function in society. The question of screening or banning some of the books that students are assigned to read is addressed in the next set of articles. The issue for many people is whether students should develop their major value systems by reading books and, at the same time, be protected from reading certain books that may undermine certain value systems.

1. What Is the Role of the Media in a Country That Values Free Speech?

THE LOST ART OF POLITICAL ARGUMENT

Christopher Lasch

Christopher Lasch teaches history at the University of Rochester. This essay was first published in 1990 in the Gannett Center Journal *and reprinted later that same year in* Harper's *magazine.*

Let us begin with a simple proposition: What democracy requires is public debate, not information. Of course it needs information too, but the kind of information it needs can be generated only by vigorous popular debate. We do not know what we need to know until we ask the right questions, and we can identify the right questions only by subjecting our own ideas about the world

Harper's, September 1990, pp. 17–22.

to the test of public controversy. Information, usually seen as the precondition of debate, is better understood as its by-product. When we get into arguments that focus and fully engage our attention, we become avid seekers of relevant information. Otherwise, we take in information passively—if we take it in at all.

From these considerations it follows that the job of the press is to encourage debate, not to supply the public with information. But as things now stand the press generates information in abundance, and nobody pays any attention. It is no secret that the public knows less about public affairs than it used to know. Millions of Americans cannot begin to tell you what is in the Bill of Rights, what Congress does, what the Constitution says about the powers of the presidency, how the party system emerged or how it operates. Ignorance of public affairs is commonly attributed to the failure of the public schools, and only secondarily to the failure of the press to inform. But since the public no longer participates in debates on national issues, it has no reason to be better informed. When debate becomes a lost art, information makes no impression.

Let us ask why debate has become a lost art. The answer may surprise: Debate began to decline around the turn of the century, when the press became more "responsible," more professional, more conscious of its civic obligations. In the early nineteenth century the press was fiercely partisan. Until the middle of the century papers were often financed by political parties. Even when they became more independent of parties they did not embrace the ideal of objectivity or neutrality. In 1841 Horace Greeley launched his *New York Tribune* with the announcement that it would be a "journal removed alike from servile partisanship on the one hand and from gagged, mincing neutrality on the other." Strong-minded editors like Greeley, James Gordon Bennett, E. L. Godkin, and Samuel Bowles did not attempt to conceal their own views or to impose a strict separation of news and editorial content. Their papers were journals of opinion in which the reader expected to find a definite point of view, together with unrelenting criticism of opposing points of view.

It is no accident that journalism of this kind flourished during the period from 1830 to 1900, when popular participation in politics was at its height. Eighty percent of the eligible voters typically went to the polls in presidential elections. (After 1900 the percentage began to decline sharply.) Torchlight parades, mass rallies, and gladiatorial contests of oratory made nineteenth-century politics an object of consuming popular interest.

In the midst of such politics, nineteenth-century journalism served as an extension of the town meeting. It created a public forum in which the issues of the day were hotly debated. Newspapers not only reported political controversies but participated in them, drawing in their readers as well. And print culture rested on the remnants of an oral tradition: Printed language was still shaped by the rhythms and requirements of the spoken word, in particular by the conventions of verbal argumentation. Print served to create a larger forum for the spoken word, not yet to displace or reshape it.

The "best men," as they liked to think of themselves, were never altogether happy with this state of affairs, and by the 1870s and 1880s their low opinion of politics had come to be widely shared by the educated classes. The scandals of the Gilded Age gave party politics a bad name. Genteel reformers—"mugwumps," to their enemies—demanded a professionalization of politics, designed to free the civil service from party control and to replace political appointees with trained experts.

The drive to clean up politics gained momentum in the Progressive era. Under the leadership of Theodore Roosevelt, Woodrow Wilson, Robert La Follette, and William Jennings Bryan, the Progressives preached "efficiency," "good government," "bipartisanship," and the "scientific management" of public affairs, and declared war on "bossism." These reformers had little use for public debate. Most political questions were too complex, in their view, to be submitted to popular judgment. They liked to contrast the scientific expert with the orator—the latter a useless windbag whose rantings only confused the public mind.

Professionalism in politics meant professionalism in journalism. The connection between the two was spelled out by Walter Lippmann in the Twenties, in a series of books that provided a founding charter for modern journalism—an elaborate rationale for a journalism guided by the new idea of professional objectivity. Lippmann held up standards by which the press is still judged.

In Lippmann's view, democracy did not require that people literally govern themselves. Questions of substance should be decided by knowledgeable administrators whose access to reliable information immunized them against the emotional "symbols" and "stereotypes" that dominated public debate. The public, according to Lippmann, was incompetent to govern itself and did not even care to do so.

At one time this may not have been the case, but now, in the "wide and unpredictable environment" of the modern world, the old ideal of citizenship was obsolete. A complex industrial society required a government carried on by officials who would necessarily be guided—since any form of direct democracy was now impossible—by either public opinion or expert knowledge. Public opinion was unreliable because it could be united only by an appeal to slogans and "symbolic pictures." Lippmann's distrust of public opinion rested on the epistemological distinction between truth and mere opinion. Truth, as he conceived it, grew out of disinterested scientific inquiry; everything else was ideology. Public debate was at best a disagreeable necessity. Ideally, it would not take place at all; decisions would be based on scientific "standards of measurement" alone.

The role of the press, as Lippmann saw it, was to circulate information, not to encourage argument. The relationship between information and argument was antagonistic, not complementary. He did not take the position that argumentation was a necessary outcome of reliable information; on the contrary, his point was that information precluded argument, made argument unnecessary. Arguments were what took place in the absence of reliable information.

Lippmann had forgotten what he learned (or should have learned) from

William James and John Dewey: that our search for reliable information is it-self guided by the questions that arise during arguments about a given course of action. It is only by subjecting our preferences and projects to the test of de-bate that we come to understand what we know and what we still need to learn. Until we have to defend our opinions in public, they remain opinions in Lippmann's pejorative sense—half-formed convictions based on random im-pressions and unexamined assumptions. It is the act of articulating and de-fending our views that lifts them out of the category of "opinions," gives them shape and definition, and makes it possible for others to recognize them as a description of their own experience as well. In short, we come to know our own minds only by explaining ourselves to others.

The attempt to bring others around to our own point of view carries the risk, of course, that we may adopt their point of view instead. We have to enter imaginatively into our opponents' arguments, if only for the purpose of refut-ing them, and we may end up being persuaded by those we sought to persuade. Argument is risky and unpredictable—and therefore educational. Most of us tend to think of it (as Lippmann thought of it) as a clash of rival dogmas, a shout-ing match in which neither side gives any ground. But arguments are not won by shouting down opponents. They are won by changing opponents' minds.

If we insist on argument as the essence of education, we will defend democracy not as the most efficient but as the most educational form of gov-ernment—one that extends the circle of debate as widely as possible and thus forces all citizens to articulate their views, to put their views at risk, and to cul-tivate the virtues of eloquence, clarity of thought and expression, and sound judgment. From this point of view, the press has the potential to serve as the equivalent of the town meeting.

This is what Dewey argued, in effect—though not, unfortunately, very clearly—in *The Public and Its Problems* (1927), a book written in reply to Lippmann's disparaging studies of public opinion. Lippmann's distinction be-tween truth and information rested on a "spectator theory of knowledge," as James W. Carey explains in his recently published book, *Communication as Culture*. As Lippmann understood these matters, knowledge is what we get when an observer, preferably a scientifically trained observer, provides us with a copy of reality that we can all recognize. Dewey, on the other hand, knew that even scientists argue among themselves. He held that the knowl-edge needed by any community—whether it is a community of scientific in-quirers or a political community—emerges only from "dialogue" and "direct give and take."

It is significant, as Carey points out, that Dewey's analysis of communi-cation stressed the ear rather than the eye. "Conversation," Dewey wrote, "has a vital import lacking in the fixed and frozen words of written speech. . . . The connections of the ear with vital and outgoing thought and emotion are im-mensely closer and more varied than those of the eye. Vision is a spectator; hearing is a participator."

The proper role of the press is to extend the scope of debate by supplementing the spoken word with the written word. The written word is indeed a poor substitute for the spoken word; nevertheless, it can serve as an acceptable substitute as long as written speech takes spoken speech (and not, say, mathematics) as its model. According to Lippmann, the press was unreliable because it could never give us accurate representations of reality, only "symbolic pictures" and stereotypes. Dewey's analysis implied a more penetrating line of criticism. As Carey puts it, "The press, by seeing its role as that of informing the public, abandons its role as an agency for carrying on the conversation of our culture." Having embraced Lippmann's ideal of objectivity, the press no longer serves to cultivate "certain vital habits" in the community— "the ability to follow an argument, grasp the point of view of another, expand the boundaries of understanding, debate the alternative purposes that might be pursued."

The rise of the advertising and public-relations industries, side by side, helps to explain why the press abdicated its most important function—enlarging the public forum—at the same time that it became more "responsible." A responsible press, as opposed to a partisan or opinionated one, attracted the kind of readers advertisers were eager to reach: well-heeled readers, most of whom probably thought of themselves as independent voters. These readers wanted to be assured that they were reading all the news that was fit to print, not an editor's idiosyncratic and no doubt biased view of things. Responsibility came to be equated with the avoidance of controversy because advertisers were willing to pay for it. Some advertisers were also willing to pay for sensationalism, though on the whole they preferred a respectable readership to sheer numbers. What they clearly did not prefer was "opinion"—not because they were impressed with Lippmann's philosophical arguments but because opinionated reporting did not guarantee the right audience. No doubt they also hoped that an aura of objectivity, the hallmark of responsible journalism, would rub off on the advertisements that surrounded increasingly slender columns of print.

In a curious historical twist, advertising, publicity, and other forms of commercial persuasion themselves came to be disguised as information and, eventually, to substitute for open debate. "Hidden persuaders" (as Vance Packard called them) replaced the old-time editors, essayists, and orators who made no secret of their partisanship. And information and publicity became increasingly indistinguishable. Today, most of the "news" in our newspapers consists of items churned out by press agencies and public-relations offices and then regurgitated intact by the "objective" organs of journalism.

The decline of the partisan press and the rise of a new type of journalism professing rigorous standards of objectivity do not assure a steady supply of usable information. Unless information is generated by sustained public debate, most of it will be irrelevant at best, misleading and manipulative at worst. Increasingly, information is generated by those who wish to promote something or someone—a product, a cause, a political candidate or officeholder— without either arguing their case on its merits or explicitly advertising it as self-interested material. Much of the press, in its eagerness to inform the public, has become a conduit for the equivalent of junk mail. When words are used merely as instruments of publicity or propaganda, they lose their power to persuade. Soon they cease to mean anything at all. People lose the capacity to use language precisely and expressively, or even to distinguish one word from another. The spoken word models itself on the written word instead of the other way around, and ordinary speech begins to sound like the clotted jargon we see in print. Ordinary speech begins to sound like "information"—a disaster from which the English language may never recover.

THE MEDIA'S WAR ON KIDS: FROM THE BEATLES TO BEAVIS AND BUTT-HEAD

Jon Katz

> *This author claims that a new media is emerging that is for the young. He wrote this article for* Rolling Stone *magazine in 1993.*

The kids are gone. The we-need-to-reach-young-people features on dating and dressing "cool" and rock music were far too little and way too late. The young are abandoning conventional journalism in stunning and accelerating numbers. Step by step, from rock to rap, TV to computers—and now especially cable—the young are fighting for and building their own powerful media.

And the grown-ups—and their media—hate it.

No group of young people has ever had more choices to make regarding—or more control over—its own information, amusement and politics. Rock spawned one culture; TV, another; movies, hip-hop, computers, video games, still more. Now they're all converging toward the one medium that can accommodate them all with room to spare—cable.

On cable, the music never stops playing, movies never leave the screen, news never ends, politicians never stop talking. On cable, comedy, trials, the weather and sci-fi each get a whole channel. On cable, computers will soon join digital shopping. Most importantly, cable is where the boys and girls are. According to a survey by Peter Hart Research Associates, three-fifths of people under 45 would now choose cable if forced to choose between it and broadcast TV, a numbing statistic, given that the medium barely existed 20 years ago.

"Young people prefer choices," the Hart survey found. "A majority of those under age 45 believe more channels is a step in the right direction. The

Rolling Stone, November 25, 1993, pp. 46–49, 130.

majority of those age 60 and older disagree."

Journalism has presented this massive shift as an educational problem—look what's keeping the little blockheads from reading now—as well as a menace to society. But the giant communications companies spending billions to get into cable know better.

The percentage of people under 35 who said they "read a newspaper yesterday" plunged from 67 percent in 1965 to 30 percent in 1990. The number of adults 18 to 24 reading *Time, Newsweek* or *U.S. News and World Report* has declined by 55 percent in the past 14 years, according to media consultant David Lehmkuhl. A confidential study commissioned by one network news division last year found that the percentage of viewers between 18 and 34 watching commercial network newscasts has dropped more than 45 percent since 1980.

According to a Yankelovich study, only 20 percent of people 21 to 24 watch ABC's *World News Tonight*, although 35 percent of that age group watches *The Simpsons*, and 29 percent watches CNN.

"It's no longer possible for us to reach the young," says the marketing director of one of the country's biggest newspaper chains. "They're watching cable, playing videos, using and communicating on computers. We don't have any younger readers to speak of, surely not under 30, and there's no way anybody can see that we're going to get any. We are now a medium for the middle-aged and up, emphasis on *up*."

For the traditional media, this is grim news, but it should hardly be surprising. It's hard to think of anything the industry could have done to ignore or alienate younger consumers that it didn't do—or isn't doing still. It has resisted innovative design, clung to its deadly monolithic voice, refused to broaden or alter its definitions of news and—most importantly—trashed the culture of the young at every opportunity.

The attacks on kid culture are at least as old as rock itself. In 1956, the *New York Times* reported a psychologist's assertion that dancing outside an Alan Freed concert was "very much like the medieval type of spontaneous lunacy where one person goes off and lots of other persons go off with him." The *Times* found a Columbia University psychiatrist to join the fretting. He linked the "craze" to the "contagious epidemic of dance fury" that "swept Germany and spread to all of Europe" in the 14th century. This kind of dancing in medieval Italy, he said, was "popularly related to a toxic bite by the hairy spider called tarantula."

The psychologist and the psychiatrist were pioneers in one of journalism's laziest and most useless practices—the summoning of experts, therapists and spokespeople to advance their abiding conviction that kids are going to hell, and it's kid culture that's driving them there.

Today the academic, corporate and editorial factions that dominate journalism continue to see kid culture as repulsive and dangerous. Thus computers are a medium for invasion of privacy, not a new way to communicate. TV isn't a medium that has transformed the politics of the world as well as the lives of the young but a transmitter of crude, stupid, violence-inducing programs. Rap is not a powerful and influential form of racial and political expression but a trigger for bigotry, sexism and violence. Video games are dangerous and addictive, unhealthy breeders of illiteracy.

"The Age of Indifference," a 1990 study by the Times Mirror Center for the People and the Press, embodies such a rationale: "Younger Americans are 40 percent less likely to correctly identify frequent newsmakers, and 20 percent less likely to know such things as who won the recent presidential election in Nicaragua, what happened to Rumanian dictator Nicolae Ceausescu and what the Soviet Union's role was in the political changes in eastern Europe."

Like most producers and editors, the Times Mirror researchers presumed that these events were critically important to the young, that public awareness is measurable primarily in terms of news-media consumption and that youthful disinterest in absorbing whatever journalism offers reflects ignorance or indifference.

Or more bluntly: Whatever we publish and broadcast, kids should read and watch. If they don't, they're dumb. "Today's young Americans, aged 18 to 30, know less and care less about news and public affairs than any other generation of Americans in the past 50 years," the study clucked. "Only in sports coverage—and the abortion issue—do young people match their elders in news interest." The core audience for TV news, concluded the study, "is increasingly drawn from the ranks of older people."

The study did not, of course, explore whether it's the media's approach, rather than kids' responses, that has to change. Or whether young Americans have different—but still valid—editorial agendas. How much information about Ceausescu do people need in order to qualify as civic minded? How much do they need to know, in general? The Times-Mirror study pointed to the youthful popularity of "quasi-news" media like *People* or *A Current Affair* as part of the reason for the young's disinterest in "serious news."

In the '50s, journalists seemed genuinely shocked by rock. The media were too white, male and straight to comprehend it or make sense of the almost overnight transition from ballroom dancing to crooning so loud, sexual and uninhibited. But the news media are vastly more sophisticated now, their ranks stuffed with people who themselves once danced like medieval lunatics. Yet journalists still seem threatened. And if anything, the attacks have grown more frantic and nonsensical as pop culture has been transformed from medieval lunacy into something really dangerous: competition.

In their worst nightmares, '50s reporters and editors had no inkling that, say, music-video channels and talk shows would someday play a significant role in a presidential election. Journalists are losing control; their economic well-being and stature as guardians of the country's political life are being threatened. In this context, their assaults on pop culture, conscious or not, are more explicable.

There is a lot at stake. Aside from the $90 billion youth market, there are these issues: Who gets to decide what the big stories are, and who gets to tell about them? Who gets to control kids? Who gets to shape the media of the future? Perhaps the new culture is far more menacing than its worst critics even know. The dumber it is made to look, the less threatening it seems.

"Stupidity," said *Newsweek* in October, "served with knowing intelligence, is now TV's answer to real smarts." Calling television the "idiot box," *Newsweek* lumped together Ren and Stimpy, Ernie Kovacs, Beavis and Butthead, Bart Simpson, the Three Stooges, Wayne and Garth, Letterman's Stupid Pet Tricks and Howard Stern as examples of the pervasive stupidity driving programming. That tucked among them are the best, funniest, most innovative and popular programs says lots about the relative value systems of journalism and the culture that's displacing it. [. . .]

Coming from the traditional media, these warnings of stupidity and violence are transparently hypocritical. TV is dumb and bad for kids, but read our new Sunday TV section and expanded cable listings. Movies are vulgar and violent, but look at our full-page movie ads and Friday entertainment sections and profiles of Schwarzenegger and Snipes. Music is tasteless and dangerous, but read our expanded rock coverage, lists of Top 10 albums and syndicated profile of Pearl Jam.

What earthly reason would kids have to consume a medium that thinks the most interesting things in their lives are dumb and dangerous, yet continually tries to exploit and market them? If TV and music made kids as dumb as journalism says they do, lots more of those kids would be buying newspapers and watching the evening news.

Detailed studies by organizations like Yankelovich, Peter Hart Associates and Simmons Market Research have exhaustively documented the growing differences in the way the old and young gather information. Unlike journalists, the young like cable, appreciate its breadth and variety of information and view its growth as liberating and entertaining. They don't take TV, music or movies as literally as journalists seem to, understanding that cultural messages can be hyperbolic, shocking and exaggerated.

They like magazines that cater to their specific interests and tastes rather than their parents' newsmagazines, which attempt to portray a broad range of political, breaking and cultural news in one monotonously reassuring voice. They are more informal and prefer their information from informal people with informal voices.

They take themselves far less seriously than journalism takes itself, define news more broadly than a J-school dean and are attracted to satire and self-mockery, nonexistent in journalism. They like vivid writing, real opinion and point of view, all considered unethical or inappropriate by most journalists. "I've always maintained that what's bad for children is not violence but bad storytelling," says Matt Groening, Bart Simpson's creator.

The young are less focused on fixed-time programs and publications; they absorb information on the fly while they eat, drive, talk to friends, move about the house. This reflects not so much an age of indifference but busier, more frantic lives and new and diverting media. They move in and out of cable, TV, music and radio as their work and social schedules permit or when stories attract them. They learn of big stories—the Israeli-PLO treaty, the turmoil in Russia—not by reading through a paper or sitting and watching a newscast but in bits and pieces, some from radio, some from CNN, some from one another.

If they have a universal common denominator, it is probably the one thing journalism hates and fears the most—popular culture. They are instinctively drawn to the choice and diversity of cable, follow evolving forms of music closely, debate films, play or have played video games without visibly harming themselves. For the young, culture is politics, personal expression and entertainment all fused together, often the biggest and most important story in their lives.

This is precisely the big idea that journalism won't get, foolishly casting itself as the mean, old schoolmarm, handkerchief tucked into sleeve, whacking kids on the wrist when they spell a word wrong, warning about falling in with a bad crowd.

In 1966, John Lennon set off a firestorm by predicting that "Christianity will go." "It will vanish and shrink," he said. "We're more popular than Jesus Christ right now." To the established order—religion, politics, journalism—popular culture has become one enormous audiovisual Antichrist. In his book *Blasphemy*, Leonard Levy writes that "blasphemy is a litmus test of the standards a society believes it must enforce to preserve its unity, its peace, its morality, its feelings and road to salvation." These are the very values pop culture has been portrayed as destroying.

It's no accident that some of the most savage battles in modern revolutions are fought for TV stations or that the first kids over the Berlin Wall had risked their lives to get to record stores. Asked by an interviewer two years ago what happened to communism, Poland's Lech Walesa pointed to a TV set in a corner of the room. "It all came from there," he said.

Even as it transmitted the pictures, journalism couldn't grasp their meaning. The medium that has dominated national politics has never understood how political youth culture is. It seems that the stilted rhetoric of '60s rockers was true. Rock & roll was as much about politics and liberation as music. So, it turns out, are Beavis and Butt-head. And the popular culture that electronically spawned them.

This all adds up to a new world for information, one journalism appears to have willfully shut itself out of. While the Baby Bells merge with cable companies and communications companies like Viacom and QVC fight for control of cable's future, the institutions of journalism that brought down presidents and stopped wars just a few years ago have fallen too far behind. None of them are players in the new information world. They blew what turned out to be their biggest story and arrogantly insulted a whole generation.

According to *American Demographics* magazine, young adults are more liberal than their elders—including the baby boomers, who now make up most of the nation's journalists. Young adults are less likely to support the banning of books from public libraries or the firing of teachers because they are gay. They are more likely to feel that the women's movement has been a "good influence on the country." They also, according to the magazine, accept interracial dating more readily than older people. "And 49 percent of people aged 18 to 24 approve of giving preferential treatment to minorities to improve their situation, compared with only about one in three boomers."

The kids may be stupid. But the kids are all right.

2. Should Reading Material Be Screened to Protect Students?

WHAT IS CENSORSHIP?

Henry Reichman

This is an excerpt from the book Censorship and Selection: Issues and Answers for Schools, *published in 1988. It gives a brief definition of censorship and an account of some of the legislation in response to it. There is also a value claim. See if you can locate it.*

Put briefly, censorship is the removal, suppression, or restricted circulation of literary, artistic, or educational materials—of images, ideas, and information—on the grounds that these are morally or otherwise objectionable in light of standards applied by the censor. Frequently, the single occurrence of an offending word will arouse protest. In other cases, objection will be made to the underlying values and basic message conveyed—or said to be conveyed—by a given work. In the final analysis, censorship is simply a matter of someone saying: "No, you cannot read that magazine or book or see that film or videotape—because I don't like it." According to some, only agents of government may censor. Yet in reality, pressures exerted by private citizens or citizen groups can also result in removal or suppression of "objectionable" items. In such situations these private individuals and groups function as true and effective censors.

Pressures to remove allegedly "offensive" classroom or school library materials have attracted considerable media attention. Typically, individual parents or parent/citizen groups bring some kind of pressure upon school boards or administrators, who in turn might tell librarians not to circulate, or teachers not to assign, a challenged work. More often than not, school systems resist such pressure. In some cases, however, professional educators or school boards have initiated removal or restriction. In other instances, teachers, librarians, and school principals acceded to pressure, only to be reversed when counter-pressures were exerted on higher-level administrators or school boards. In March 1987, for the first time in U.S. history, a federal court took on the role of school book censor when a Mobile, Alabama, judge ordered public school

From Henry Reichman, *Censorship and Selection: Issues and Answers for Schools* (joint publication of the American Library Association, Chicago, and the American Association of School Administrators, Arlington, VA, 1988), pp. 2–3.

districts in that state to remove from classrooms 44 state-approved social studies, history, and home economics textbooks because they allegedly promoted "secular humanism," a violation, the judge ruled, of the constitutional separation of church and state. Fortunately, the U.S. Court of Appeals reversed that decision in August 1987.

That instance notwithstanding, the courts have tended to give local school districts wide discretion in determining what they will teach and with which materials. In the 1968 case of *Epperson* v. *Arkansas*, the U.S. Supreme Court declared: "Public education in our Nation is committed to the control of state and local authorities. Courts do not and cannot intervene in the resolution of conflicts which arise in the daily operation of school systems and which do not directly and sharply implicate basic constitutional values."[1]

Still, in *Epperson*, the Supreme Court struck down a state law that prohibited the teaching of evolution. Court decisions give school authorities broad discretion in making educational decisions, but not judgments that smack of ideological, political or religious motivations. The Supreme Court has frequently upheld the overriding importance of free expression. The First Amendment, the Court declared in 1976, "does not tolerate laws which cast a pall of orthodoxy over the classroom . . . students must always remain free to inquire, to study and to evaluate, to gain new maturity and understanding." In 1982, the Supreme Court ruled, in a plurality opinion written by Justice William J. Brennan, Jr., that "local school boards may not remove books from school library shelves simply because they dislike the ideas contained in those books and seek by their removal to prescribe what shall be orthodox in politics, nationalism, religion, or other matters of opinion."[2]

Although censors almost invariably claim to be defending American values, educational censorship is harmful precisely because it undermines those very democratic values of tolerance and intellectual freedom that our educational system must seek to instill. In the process of acquiring knowledge and searching for truth, students learn to discriminate and choose—to make decisions rationally and logically in light of evidence. Removing a book from a classroom or school library because it offends some members of the community increases the likelihood that students will see suppression as an acceptable way of responding to controversial ideas and images.

By suppressing materials containing ideas or themes with which they do not agree, censors produce a sterile conformity and a lack of intellectual and emotional growth in students. Freedom in the public schools is central to the quality of what and how students learn.

NOTES

1. *Epperson* v. *Arkansas*, 393 U.S. 97 (1968).
2. *Board of Education, Island Trees Union Free School District* v. *Pico*, 102 U.S. 2799 (1982).

WHAT SHOULD BE DONE ABOUT BIAS IN OUR CHILDREN'S TEXTBOOKS?

Paul C. Vitz

This excerpt is from the book Censorship: Evidence of Bias in Our Children's Textbooks, *published in 1986. Identify the value warrants in this selection.*

[. . .] Studies make it abundantly clear that public school textbooks commonly exclude the history, heritage, beliefs, and values of millions of Americans. Those who believe in the traditional family are not represented. Those who believe in free enterprise are not represented. Those whose politics are conservative are almost unrepresented. Above all, those who are committed to their religious tradition—at the very least as an important part of the historical record—are not represented.

Even those who uphold the classic or republican virtues of discipline, public duty, hard work, patriotism, and concern for others are scarcely represented. Indeed, the world of these virtues long advocated by believers, as well as by deists and skeptics such as Thomas Paine, Benjamin Franklin, and Thomas Jefferson, is not found here. Even what one might call the "noble pagan" has ample reason to reject these inadequate and sentimentalized books which seem to be about an equal mixture of pap and propaganda.

Over and over, we have seen that liberal and secular bias is primarily accomplished by exclusion, by leaving out the opposing position. Such a bias is much harder to observe than a positive vilification or direct criticism, but it is the essence of censorship. It is effective not only because it is hard to observe—it isn't *there*—and therefore hard to counteract, but also because it makes only the liberal, secular positions familiar and plausible. As a result, the millions of Americans who hold conservative, traditional, and religious positions are made to appear irrelevant, strange, on the fringe, old-fashioned, reactionary. For these countless Americans it is now surely clear that the textbooks used in the public schools threaten the continued existence of their positions.

A natural question to raise is: how could this textbook bias have happened? What brought it about? Some have suggested that religion is downplayed because of concern over maintaining the separation of church and state. This concern seems either unlikely or a rationalization of an underlying distaste for religion. After all, to identify the historical or contemporary importance of religion is to respect the facts; it is not to advocate religion. To teach *about* religion is not to teach religion.

Furthermore, the rejection of religion in these books is part of a very general rejection of the entire conservative spectrum of American life. Recall that

From Paul C. Vitz, *Censorship: Evidence of Bias in Our Children's Textbooks* (Ann Arbor, MI: Servant Books, 1986), pp. 77–81.

these books omit marriage and the traditional family, along with traditional sex roles, patriotism, and free enterprise. In short, the bias in these books is not accidental; much of it is certainly not the result of some misunderstanding about separating church and state.

Another possible answer is that the publishers of these books have attempted to avoid controversial subjects. According to this theory, the books have been written in a style which will avoid offending anyone. In fact, some publishers do give guidelines to authors on what kinds of people and issues to avoid. But the evidence of this study makes clear that a desire to avoid offense and controversy *cannot* explain much of the bias observed here. [. . .] Consider the profeminist position found in several social studies texts and throughout the basal readers for grades 3 and 6. That feminism is controversial cannot be seriously denied, even by feminists. And consider that positive representations of traditional feminine role models are obviously absent from these books. The regular procoverage of environmental issues also makes clear that the only people and topics which are avoided in these books are those on the political right, those that are "controversial" to a liberal frame of mind.

One explanation of the antireligious bias in these books is that religion is so especially controversial that publishers want to avoid the subject. Curiously, the religions that do get some mention, e.g., Catholicism, Judaism, and Islam, are hardly uncontroversial. (In any case, why religion is supposedly more controversial than race, ethnic identity, feminism, or politics remains to be explained.)

The real issue is how a book handles religion. For example, magazines like the *Reader's Digest* and others often have articles about the positive accomplishments of people of different religious denominations. Such articles celebrating the different religions and their contributions to this country are uncontroversial, well received, and appear to help sales. Yet, such a positive treatment of America's religious life is without any example in the ninety books evaluated in this entire study.

Religious concepts and vocabulary are certainly censored in these textbooks. A most revealing example of this censorship was recently published in the article "Censoring the Sources" by Barbara Cohen.[1] The issue centered on a children's story of hers called "Molly's Pilgrim." The story has an important Jewish religious theme; it focuses on the Jewish harvest holiday of Sukkos, a holiday that influenced the Pilgrims in initiating Thanksgiving. A major textbook publisher (Harcourt Brace Jovanovich) wanted to reprint part of the story for their third grade reader. But like most such stories, the publishers wanted to shorten it greatly and to rewrite parts to make it more acceptable. They phoned Ms. Cohen and asked her for permission to reprint their modified version. But her story wasn't just modified, it was maimed. "All mention of Jews, Sukkos, God, and the Bible"[2] had been removed. So Barbara Cohen refused to give them permission. They called back dismayed and tried to convince her to let them go ahead with the heavily censored version. They argued, "Try to understand. We have a lot of problems. If we mention God, some atheist will object. If we mention the Bible, someone will want to know why we don't give equal time to the Koran. Every time that happens, we lose sales."[3] "But the Pilgrims did read the Bible," Barbara Cohen answered.[4] Yes, you know that and we know that, but we can't have anything in it that people object to, was the reply!

After more debate and give and take, a compromise was reached. The publisher allowed a reference to worship and the Jewish harvest holiday of Sukkos to stay in. But God and the Bible were "eternally unacceptable"[5] and they had to go. The publisher claimed, "We'd get into terrible trouble if we mentioned the Bible."[6]

This true but incredible story ends with Barbara Cohen stating: "Censorship in this country is widespread, subtle, and surprising. It is not inflicted on us by the government. It doesn't need to be. We inflict it on ourselves."[7] At the very least, the publishers should hear from the millions of Christians and Jews that if God and the Bible are left out, the publishers will also lose sales. And, God willing, lots more sales will be lost than when publishers leave God and the Bible in. The schools and the publishers must learn that what is left out of a textbook can be just as offensive as what is let in.

Of course, the central issue hinges on the *facts* of America's past and present. And the facts are clear: religion, especially Christianity, has played and continues to play a central role in American life. To neglect to report this is simply to fail to carry out the major duty of any textbook writer—the duty to tell the truth.

To explain the liberal and secular prejudice of the texts, some have proposed that a deliberate, large-scale conspiracy is involved. I doubt very much, however, that this is the case. The number of people writing, editing, publishing, selecting, and using these books is far too large and varied for this explanation to be plausible. Instead, the bias is, I believe, the consequence of the widespread, dominant, secular worldview found throughout the upper levels of the field of education,[8] especially among those who control the schools of education, the publishers, the federal and state education bureaucracies, and the National Education Association. But, whatever the source of the bias, it certainly exists. Thus, the question is "What should be done?" Let us consider the major possibilities.

One possibility that I will call *Scenario One* is as follows. In this possible future the public school leadership acknowledges that the majority of America's parents are religious in their sympathies and generally conservative in their moral and social life. Recognizing this, educators move clearly and positively back into the mainstream of American life. Religion is given a positive and realistic portrayal in textbooks and other curriculum. The traditional family and moral values are recognized and integrated into the school programs. Finally, the new emphasis on character education continues to grow and become widely influential.

The result of making these changes is a revival of confidence in the public schools and increased community support. As a result, many religious Americans return their children to the public schools. Meanwhile more secular Yuppy parents note the increased morale of teachers and students and they also return to active public school support. After all, the private schools favored by many of the young upwardly mobile professionals are quite expensive. Revitalized public schools would be welcomed by many of them. In short, in this scenario the public schools are positively transformed and gain a new long lease on life.

NOTES

1. Barbara Cohen, "Censoring the Sources," *School Library Journal*, March 1986.
2. Cohen, 97.
3. Cohen, 98.
4. Cohen.
5. Cohen, 99.
6. Cohen.
7. Cohen.
8. This is also the opinion of Mel and Norma Gabler in *What Are They Teaching Our Children?* (Wheaton, IL: SP Publications, 1985).

WHY TEACH US TO READ AND THEN SAY WE CAN'T?

Nat Hentoff

Nat Hentoff has written many books about freedom of speech. This is an excerpt from Free Speech for Me—But Not for Thee: How the American Left and Right Relentlessly Censor Each Other, *published in 1992.*

Children in many American schools are instructed early in thought control. This is not the term use by their school boards and principals. They call it the removal of "inappropriate" books.

For a long time, a book near the top of the hit list has been J. D. Salinger's *Catcher in the Rye*. In Boron, California, in 1990, a parent noted in alarm that the book "uses the Lord's name in vain two hundred times. That's enough reason to ban it right there," she explained. "They said it describes reality. I say let's back up from reality. Let's go backwards. Let's go back to when we didn't have an immoral society."

That parent is more candid than most of those on the political and religious right who object to certain books on their children's required or optional reading lists. They genuinely fear that forces—some say satanic forces—beyond their control have taken over the majority culture. And their responsibility, as parents and as Christians, is to protect their children—and all other children—from the infectious permissiveness of the larger society.

From Nat Hentoff, *Free Speech for Me—But Not for Thee: How the American Left and Right Relentlessly Censor Each Other* (New York: HarperCollins, 1992), pp. 374–379.

Strategically, it is a mistake to underestimate the seriousness of purpose and strength of will of these book police. I've spoken to many of them. They are not "kooks."

The resolution of the *Catcher in the Rye* furor in Boron, North Carolina, was the removal of the book from the high school language arts supplemental reading list.

In Clay County, in north Florida, school officials banished *My Friend Flicka* from the optional reading lists of fifth- and sixth-grade kids. The book has become an outlaw because in it, a female dog is described as a "bitch."

The harm that can be found in writing that has previously been considered free of malignities has also been exposed by school officials in Citrus County, Florida. As reported by Howard Kleinberg in the Los Angeles legal newspaper, the *Daily Journal*, a school cultural contest in Citrus County was canceled in 1990 "on the grounds that Joyce Kilmer, whose poem was part of the project, used the words 'breast and bosom' in it."

Attempts to control what children read, and thereby think, have been increasing across the country, according to annual accounts by the American Library Association and People for the American Way. There is a great deal of underreporting, however, as I've discovered in interviews with teachers and librarians through the years.

Many principals, for instance, yield immediately to complaints rather than have to deal with the controversy that comes with review committees and public hearings. And once there has been trouble in a school, some librarians do their own self-censoring of books they decide not to order.

Judy Blume's books, for example, are widely popular, especially among girls, but because they deal with real problems familiar to real youngsters, they are often attacked. At a meeting of librarians a few years ago, two of them from Minnesota told me how much they admired Judy Blume's ability to understand what's troubling kids. Then one of them added: "But we're not going to buy another book of hers. Too much damn trouble."

An increasing preoccupation of many fundamentalist Christians—to whom the Devil is no abstraction—has to do with satanism in books for children. Since the Devil can take on many forms, one has to sniff very carefully for the scent of brimstone. In Yorba Linda, California, parents insisting that satanism be removed root and branch filed objections to the presence of Old Nick in, among other books in the school, *Romeo and Juliet*, Maurice Sendak's *Where the Wild Things Are*, and a story by Nathaniel Hawthorne.

In response to the complaints, most of the children of the Satan-detectors were moved to safe classrooms in which those works were not taught.

Not all the putative censors win. By and large, those schools with a clearly worded and structured review procedure can often withstand these attacks. The parent or other complainer has to fill out a form specifying his or her objections. Faced with the form, some parents let the issue drop. But others go on. The review committee—consisting of librarians, teachers, and sometimes members of the community—usually provide some due-process protections for both the objecting parents and the accused books. And then there is the school board for final review. That being a political body, it can be more concerned with the next election than the First Amendment. But not always.

Here's how this review procedure worked in Watanga County, North Carolina. A philosophy professor and father of a child in kindergarten challenged a 1901 edition of Rudyard Kipling's *Just So Stories*. In one of the stories, "How the Leopard Got His Spots," the word "nigger" appears. A five-member review committee decided to remove the book.

Two librarians, however, appealed to the school board to reverse the sentence. The chairman of the school board—as reported in the American Library Association's *Newsletter on Intellectual Freedom*—said: "Freedom of speech is the vehicle through which can come the defense against those who would use words to harm human beings."

But the philosophy professor disagreed: "There are two things I very much want my daughter not to become. I don't want her to be a drug addict, and I don't want her to be a racist."

One of the librarians, however carried the day: "In the end the only way we learn there are such issues as racism is by discussing them with our children. We ask that you vote to leave this book on the shelf."

The vote was unanimous. Rudyard Kipling's stories still have a home in the Watanga County elementary school library.

Another victory for free expression took place in Colonie, New York. At issue was the future in the Shaker High School Library of *The Progressive* magazine, a national liberal political journal. A sophomore—complaints do come from students as well as from all manner of school employees—wanted the magazine banned because it has contained ads for *The Anarchist Cookbook*, *Women Loving Women*, and *Prove Christ Fictional*. Also offensive to the student was a full-page ad by the Jewish Committee on the Middle East.

The student saw no reason that his family's tax dollars should be spent to enrich this offensive magazine. And 123 of his fellow students signed a petition agreeing with him. On the other hand, the library director brandished a petition signed by 395(!) students supporting the magazine: "Libraries should provide information on all points of view."

A review committee of school employees noted that *The Progressive* "would have to be of little value as a library source or be incendiary in nature to warrant a recommendation for its removal. There is no support for either conclusion."

The review committee also pointed out that the magazine had been part of the media center collection for ten years, and it would stay there. "We do students a disservice," said the committee, "if we feel they will succumb to every enticement they encounter. They are fully capable of ignoring the advertisements [the student] cites as objectionable."

Sooner or later, however, a very careful reader may come across the numbers 666 in an issue of *The Progressive* or in some book. That is the Devil's number, and in some other town, another review committee may be formed to banish the devil from the school library. In Wilton Manors, Florida, an elementary school play—with the number 666 in it—was denounced by parents and a local minister. The play was then revised, but by then, it was too late in the school year for it to be produced.

There once was a school—the Mowat Middle School in Florida—where everybody was an exultant reader. The school had become so lively a center of learning—where kids actually read books they didn't have to—that in 1985 it was one of 150 American and Canadian secondary schools designated a Center of Excellence by the National Council of Teachers of English.

In each classroom, there were libraries from which students could choose what they wanted—though no one had to read anything, including in class, that he or his parents objected to. By 1986, the ninth-graders at Mowat were scoring on the high-twelfth-grade reading level. As a parent said, "I've caught my son reading sometimes on weekends. I also caught him writing a letter to his grandmother without my telling him to do it."

Then came the affair of *I Am the Cheese*, by Robert Cormier, one of the most honored of all young adult novels (and a 1977 Library of Congress Children's Book of the Year). A parent didn't like some of the language, and the district superintendent, Leonard Hall, didn't like its negative attitude toward government. (The boy in the book is part of a family in the not-always-caring Witness Protection Program.)

I Am the Cheese was immediately removed from the curriculum, the superintendent having ignored the usual review procedure when there is a complaint about a book. Other books began to be cast into darkness.

Superintendent Hall commanded teachers to examine classroom books closely and separate them into three categories. In the first would be books without "vulgar, obscene or sexually explicit material." In the second category would be those with "very limited vulgarity and no sexually explicit or obscene material." In the dread third category would be books with "quite a bit of vulgarity or obscene and/or sexually explicit material."

"Quite a bit" was not made more specific—nor were any of the other terms in the formula. Teachers in the district's two high schools pored over the books and presented Hall with sixty-four titles that were flagrantly impure by his standards and so belonged in category three. Hall removed them all from the reading lists. Among the titles:

The Red Badge of Courage, Intruders in the Dust, Oedipus Rex, Animal Farm, Twelfth Night, The Autobiography of Benjamin Franklin, The Canterbury Tales, John Ciardi's translation of *The Inferno, Hamlet*, and, of course, *Fahrenheit 451*, Ray Bradbury's novel about a future time when the only way to keep certain books alive is to go into hiding and memorize them, for otherwise they would be burned by the state.

At a crowded school board meeting to consider this remarkable new way of grading Western literature, students and teachers wore black armbands.

Outside the room, a number of kids held up posters: "Why Teach Us to Read and Then Say We Can't?"

The school board put most of the books back on the classroom lists (*I Am the Cheese* excepted). But the superintendent and the principals under him retained the power to remove "unclean" books.

Subsequently, a number of books were banished from the Mowat School by its principal, including a young-adult novel of mine, *The Day They Came to Arrest the Book*. It's about attempts in a high school by black parents, fundamentalist Christian parents, and feminists to ban *Huckleberry Finn*. My novel was exiled because it has a "goddamn" in it.

Gloria Pipkin, a brave teacher at the Mowat Middle School, told me, as the censorship went on, that "ten of the eleven women in the English department at its peak have bailed out." Why does she keep on? That's what she was asked by a school board member who could not understand why she kept appearing before the board to convince it to bring back *I Am the Cheese*, among other books.

"Because it's worth it," Pipkin said.

She was the school's teacher of the year in 1983. Before the place was cleaned up.

During the unsuccessful resistance of teachers and students to the purges of the school library and curriculum, the superintendent said publicly that he was very disturbed at the effect of this battle over censorship on the children.

"All this talk of their rights," he said, "has distracted them from their studies. It has confused them."

THE TEXTBOOK WARS

Stephen Bates

This excerpt from Bates's book Battleground: One Mother's Crusade, the Religious Right, and the Struggle for Control of Our Classrooms *was first published in* National Review *in 1993.*

It has become one of journalism's autumn perennials: Book-burners are conspiring to relegate our children to ignorance. Read a bit further in the articles and, almost invariably, the would-be censors turn out to be conservatives.

Most book protests do indeed originate with the Right. Contrary to censorship experts, however, that's not because conservatives alone seek to inject their views into the classroom. Liberals are no less eager to shape schoolbooks; they just go about it differently.

A fuller accounting of both sides' efforts and impacts is now possible, thanks to a unique trove of information: 2,261 pages of internal files from the schoolbook publisher Holt, Rinehart & Winston. Subpoenaed during the mid-1980s lawsuit

Mozert v. *Hawkins County Board of Education*, these documents chart the evolution of Holt Basic Reading, a kindergarten-through-eighth-grade textbook series.

The memos and reports (supplemented with interviews) offer an uncommonly revealing glimpse into the secretive world of textbook development. They show that activists from both sides inundated Holt editors with complaints—some valid, some preposterous, and most in between. The difference is in how their complaints were treated.

Though Holt Basic Reading became a rousing success, dominating the reading market for years, it had a rocky start. The first edition was barely off the presses in 1973 when a Texas group charged that it lacked sufficient "stories with heroines," and the self-styled Task Force on Sexism called for its prompt *"elimination."* As the date for California's textbook adoptions neared, a Holt sales representative predicted that "we may squeeze through this time with only a minimum amount of changes, but by the next adoption, we will not be so fortunate."

"There, of course, has been some criticism of *sexism*—and we are guilty to a point," senior author Bernard J. Weiss conceded in a 1974 memo. He and his co-authors, along with staff editors at Holt, had been working on the books since 1967—"before the strong emergence of the Women's Movement," as one memo noted. In the books and accompanying film-strips, consequently, women and girls were "generally relegated to the background."

In the background, moreover, females rarely strayed from stereotypic niches. The workbook for the first-grade reader declared that books called *Dolls* and *Dresses* were "for girls," and asked who should read *Trains* and *Planes;* the right answer, according to the teachers' edition, was boys. Illustrations showed boys running, playing rambunctiously, and working with tools, while girls baked cookies, drew pictures, and cut out paper dresses. During development and production of the series, former Holt executive Thomas J. Murphy recalls, "nobody thought about how sexist the damn stuff was. . . . Women designers, women editors, women authors—nobody."

The depiction of race and ethnicity raised hackles too. In California in 1974, the Standing Committee to Review Textbooks from a Multicultural Perspective (that's right: multiculturalism in 1974) detected racism in such phrases as "the afternoon turned black," "it's going to be a black winter," and "the deputy's face darkened."

The multicultural committee also discerned an offensive Christian bias in the books. "Generally, the story of creation as told according to the Judaeo-Christian teachings is serious and presented in a factual way," the group charged. "Other non-Christian teachings about the origin of man or creation are treated as being highly imaginative, strange, and consequently false. Religious holidays are exclusively Christian."

"In a revision we need to do all that is financially possible to correct this situation," wrote Barbara Theobald, a staff editor assigned to the series. Using materials borrowed from "one of our editors, Ms. Virginia Vida, [who] is active in the Women's Liberation movement," Miss Theobald drafted new guidelines for the 1977 edition of the series.

The 1977 changes, Mr. Murphy says now constituted "a very political revision. We were counting heads as to whether we had 50 per cent females, whether we had every minority group represented."

Subsequent guidelines grew more elaborate. Opening with an epigram from Walt Whitman—"The Female equally with the Male I sing"—one version said that men should not be "brutish, violent, crude, harsh, or insensitive," and women should not be "fearful, squeamish, passive, dependent, weepy, mechanically inept, frivolous, shrewish, nagging, [or] easily defeated by simple problems." Girls should work with electricity, study insects, and solve math problems. Boys should read poetry, chase butterflies, and pay "attention to personal appearance and hygiene." Forbidden words included *manmade* (use *synthetic*), *workmanlike* (use *competent*), *plainsman* (use *plainsdweller*), *statesman* (use *diplomat*), and *letterman* (use *student who has won a school letter*).

The guidelines were equally punctilious when it came to race, ethnicity, and age. Blacks must not be "in low-paying jobs, unemployed, or on welfare," but rather "in professions at all levels." American Indians should be "involved in the American mainstream" rather than on reservations, and they too mustn't be "in low-paying jobs, unemployed, or on welfare." ("Unfortunately," Miss Theobald noted in a memo, "the reality for the Indian in our society falls into all of the *avoids*.") Asian Americans and Hispanics must speak English. Jews must not work in "stereotypical occupations," such as "diamond cutters, doctors, dentists, lawyers, classical musicians, tailors, shopkeepers, etc." Older people should not be depicted as living in nursing homes, wearing glasses, using canes or wheelchairs, or "in rocking chairs, knitting, napping, and watching television."

"When selecting authors and stories and when writing art and photo specs," the guidelines directed, "be sure to familiarize yourself with the latest U.S. population figures so that our materials reflect current statistics." "Counting and chart-keeping," said the guidelines, "should not be regarded as a useless editorial exercise. Careful tallies and analysis of how people are represented will reduce the need for costly reprint corrections and may prevent the loss of an adoption." One memo reported soberly on a particular volume: "The in-house count shows 146 female and 146 male characters, or a ratio of 1:1. Animal characters were not included in this count."

Editors struggled to meet the quotas. They ransacked the archives in search of an illustration of frontier families in which women as well as men carried guns. With the authors' permission, they changed characters' gender and ethnicity in some stories. "Freddie in the Middle," featuring Mrs. Jay, became "Maggie in the Middle," featuring Mrs. Chang.

More often, editors dropped materials by or about white males in favor of new materials. But finding the replacements wasn't easy. One editor lamented: "We simply could not find a good story with an Asian-American female lead."

The Holt files indicate that gender and ethnicity sometimes trumped other considerations, including literary quality. Miss Theobald observed that a particular story was "not great literature" but "we gain two points—a female leading character and characters with Spanish-American names." Another editor concurred that the story had "very little literary merit," but "it does help us to achieve some ethnic balance in a very *unbalanced* book." "I agree that this is not the greatest 'Indian' selection," an editor wrote of another story, "but we were very hard pressed to find anything better." "Two girls may be featured," Mr. Weiss remarked of one selection, "but that's the only positive statement I can make about this play."

Weiss also dissented from some of the linguistic mandates. "I feel we are reflecting too much paranoia in eliminating a word like 'mankind,' " he wrote in one letter; in another, he impishly used *peoplekind* rather than the Holt-decreed *humankind*. He also resisted changing *man-eating shark* to *flesh-eating shark;* "being an hors d'oeuvre," he reasoned, "is not sexist." One staff member grumbled that Weiss's "attitude generally about the material we sent him by and about women and minorities ill befits the author of a modern reading series."

Just as stories won points for featuring females and minorities, they lost points for featuring religion. Barbara Theobald liked the "strong female character and Amish culture" in one story, but she worried that it contained "quite a few religious references that may be difficult to handle." She thought that another submission "might be more than we want to get involved with" because it "raises many sensitive controversial issues—drinking, religion, hard times."

As strenuously as Holt editors labored, though, the critics weren't placated. Seattle's Ethnic Bias Review Committee judged the 1977 revision "unacceptable" because "while blacks are emphasized, it is a narrow representation of those in athletics and music," and because the series contained an intolerable stereotype—a black waiter. At the Texas textbook hearings in 1980, feminists disputed Holt's claim that the readers manifested a perfect gender balance. With animals included in the count (Holt had omitted them), males outnumbered females nearly 2 to 1. "Children of this age," one woman testified, "are influenced by a story about Mr. Rabbit just as much as they are by a story about Mr. Jones."

During the same hearings, NOW representative Twiss Butler denounced a story in which a boy initially dislikes his new female teacher ("I don't want to go to any gal teacher"), but later, after seeing her hit a home run, excitedly announces that she "can play on my side anytime." The boy's initial hostility, Miss Butler testified, was "the same old story: A mere schoolboy can oppose a woman's right to hold a job if he feels threatened by her competence." His turnabout also connoted patriarchy: "Well, her credentials are worthless until she meets the standards that he sets for approval."

"Some of the selections which we perceive to be positive responses end up being criticized most severely," Barbara Theobold noted. "We obviously have to read every selection at least once from the point of view of some of these critics." She suggested that Holt ask Twiss Butler and the director of the far-left Council on Interracial Books for Children to review the company's anti-bias guidelines.

In other instances too, Holt deferred to outsiders. Explaining why a particular story was eliminated from a revision, an editor said that it "is the example used by many 'cultural' advisory councils of what *not* to do. We didn't *dare* leave this one in!" "With regard to the offensive portrayal of Negroid facial characteristics on page 22," another editor wrote, ". . . the artist is himself a Negro. When we questioned his interpretation, he was very vocal in defending what he did. We didn't think we could impose our white eyes on his artistic interpretation." In thanking a college professor for sending a student's analysis of sexism in the Holt readers, one Holt staff member confessed that "some of our prejudices are so ingrained it is difficult to recognize them."

In fact, out of the 2,261 pages of in-house documents, only one memo exhibits animosity toward the feminists and multiculturalists. In 1974, Japanese-American activist Jeanette Arakawa, who was associated with the California multicultural committee, criticized the Holt readers on TV. "We even met with [Miss Arakawa] in June," a Holt sales representative fumed. "We are trying to cooperate with these people—talking to them and getting their input, making changes, etc., and then they turn right around and pull a Pearl Harbor on us. It just goes to show you, you can't trust any of them."

Conservatives were also protesting Holt Basic Reading. Indianapolis parents faulted the books for excessively using the word *hate*, describing two boys sleeping together, and depicting children lying, disobeying, scheming, and starting a business without their parents' permission. In Minnesota, one group of parents blasted the books as "anti-white" for containing too many minorities; another group condemned one volume for being "anti-parental in many respects," portraying "alien" philosophies, and advancing the march of "Atheistic Humanism in the Schools." In Texas, textbook critics Mel and Norma Gabler criticized the series for slighting phonics, invading students' privacy, encouraging rebellion, and promoting evolution and situational ethics.

Holt editors sometimes acceded to conservative demands. In response to the Indianapolis protest, Barbara Theobald recommended getting rid of *hate* in most places, replacing the story that showed boys sleeping together, and eliminating some depictions of ill-behaved children. But she drew the line at having the children consult their parents before starting a business. This criticism, she declared, represented "an intrusion on an author's or publisher's prerogatives."

Conservative influences were evident elsewhere too. The in-house guidelines urged authors to avoid references to evolution, invasions of students' privacy, and "any subtle propagandizing for Communism." One memo warned that an illustration showing a mixed-race couple "would make some people very nervous." In 1980, Holt even brought in a prominent conservative critic to address the staff: Kris McGough of Columbia, Maryland, a Catholic mother who had testified before Congress, written a monthly column for the journal of the National Council for the Social Studies, and served on Maryland's Values Education Commission.

Still, Holt people had only so much patience for conservative complaints, as reactions to the McGough talk demonstrate. One staff member wrote: "The Kris McGoughs, the John Birch Society, and other such groups do not want children to learn to think independently, to question, to evaluate because such processes threaten their control." Another declared that Holt shouldn't be "intimidated" by Mrs. McGough's "reductionist, simplistic, and reactionary" argument. Still another wondered what possessed people to "feel threatened by a question or an idea in a textbook." The staff never penned such sentiments when liberal critics came calling.

Another Holt staff member vented his ire when a small Texas newspaper, evidently inspired by the Gablers, published a negative item about a Holt book. "Is this article grounds for a suit for misrepresentation?" a regional sales manager wrote. "It sure as heck cannot do us any good. And I am tired of sitting back and taking it. Maybe CBS could do a news report on the Educational Research Analysts (The Gablers) of Longview, Texas, and expose their true qualifications as educators?" At the time, CBS Inc. owned Holt. (*60 Minutes* did air a feature about the Gablers, but it was relatively innocuous, and it didn't appear until nearly seven years after the memo was written.)

Holt editors viewed Mel Gabler, Kris McGough, and other conservative critics as fundamentally different from Twiss Butler, Jeanette Arakawa, and other liberal critics. In a 1981 speech, Barbara Theobald denounced the conservatives as the sort of "censors" one finds in "totalitarian societies." In the next section of her speech—a section entitled "Positive Pressure Groups"—she said: "At the other end of the spectrum we have other groups . . . who seek to improve our educational institutions and textbooks in a positive manner." At Holt, critics who wanted books to feature more working women were "positive pressure groups"; those who wanted more homemakers were "censors."

Through the revisions, Holt Basic Reading increasingly reflected the views of its liberal critics. One essay in the 1983 edition approvingly described the 1848 Seneca Falls conference, including its declaration that "the history of mankind is the history of repeated injuries and usurpations practiced on the part of man toward woman." Girls or women broke into all-male preserves in such stories as "The Revolt of Mother," "Young Ladies Don't Slay Dragons," and "The Queen Who Wouldn't Make Spice Nuts." (The Holt readers aren't unique; according to a 1987 study, a woman depicted in a basal reader is less likely to be a stay-home mother than to be a spy.)

The Christian bias that the multiculturalists had detected in 1974 was no longer a problem. Paul Vitz, a New York University psychology professor, analyzed the 1983 Holt series for the plaintiffs in the *Mozert* case. Of approximately six hundred stories and poems in the readers, not one depicted Biblical Protestantism. "There are no stories about life in the Bible Belt," Vitz testified at trial, "no stories about churchgoers, families or individuals who pray to God"; indeed, an excerpt of Laura Ingalls Wilder's *Little House in the Big Woods* omitted a prayer.

In contrast, Vitz found, non-Christian religions received respectful attention. In "Cherry Ann and the Dragon Horse," a Chinese girl prays to a horse idol. Other materials positively depicted Buddhism. Many stories portrayed American Indians, frequently with reference to their religious beliefs. And 18 stories dealt with magic or the occult.

The series also excerpted the theatrical version of *The Diary of Anne Frank*, in which Anne tells her friend, "I wish you had a religion, Peter." "No, thanks! Not me!" he replies. Anne responds: "Oh, I don't mean you have to be Orthodox, or believe in heaven and hell and purgatory and things. I just mean some religion, it doesn't matter what. Just to believe in something!"

"The textbooks picked a very small piece of Anne Frank, and what piece did they pick?" says Marc Stern, a lawyer with the American Jewish Congress. "The piece that said it doesn't matter what religion you have." In Stern's view, "these textbooks aren't neutral."

The changes to the Holt series didn't stem from editors' brainstorming in serene isolation. The feminism, multiculturalism, and other approaches took root, as we have seen, largely in response to a subset of outside critics—those from the Left.

At Holt, these liberal activists were seen as sometimes nettlesome, occasionally perplexing, but unceasingly right-thinking. Conservative activists, in contrast, were (in the words of one response to Kris McGough's talk) a "dangerous" and "paranoid minority." Liberals were welcomed into Holt offices. Conservatives were usually kept at a distance; when they were brought in, they were viewed with a mix of wariness and contempt.

As the Holt books veered further leftward, conservatives complained about them more vehemently. Lacking the access of their left-wing counterparts, the right-wing activists had to resort to the political process—where they were vilified as censors.

Here is the point that the annual censorship articles usually overlook. Schoolbook protests most often come from conservatives, not because they are uniquely intolerant of ideas that differ from their own, but because liberals have found a far better way to influence books. While conservatives are noisily lobbying elected officials, liberals are collaborating with text-book editors. In large part, the clamorous, occasionally successful "censors" of the Right are reacting against the hushed, hugely successful "positive pressure groups" of the Left.

A BOOK IS READ AS BIASED AT WELLESLEY

Have there been any incidents that you know about that are similar to this one that occurred at Wellesley College in Massachusetts in 1993? Compare the outcomes.

Wellesley College [has been] known for the civility and seriousness of its discourse, its willingness to hear all sides of a debate.

But a professor's use of a 1991 book commissioned by Louis Farrakhan, leader of the Nation of Islam, has touched off a furor on campus, pitting two cherished values against each other: academic freedom and academic responsibility.

New York Times, April 28, 1993, p. B8.

The book, "The Secret Relationship Between Blacks and Jews" (it has no named author), maintains that Jews played a dominant role in the slave trade. That thesis is disputed by leading black-studies scholars. But the thesis, coupled with the book's overall tone, has led scholars, Jewish organizations and college officials to condemn the book as anti-Semitic.

Even so, Tony Martin, a black tenured professor in the Africana Studies Department at Wellesley, is using the book in his course on African-American history. "I have used the same standard in selecting this book for my course as I would have used for any other book," he said in an interview today. "I believe the book is substantially accurate and represents a serious attempt at historical scholarship."

Professor Martin, 51, who has a doctorate in history from Michigan State University, has taught at Wellesley for 20 years. This is the first time he has been accused of using anti-Semitic material.

College officials say that they disagree with Professor Martin's position but that he has a right to use the book. "Academic freedom, freedom of speech and all First Amendment rights must be guaranteed to members of our community even when that speech is hateful," said Nancy Harrison Kolodny, dean of the college. "We also have a responsibility to challenge people who misuse that freedom, and I believe Tony Martin is misusing his constitutional right."

It was a Jewish student, Molly Kaplowitz of Killingworth, Conn., who first questioned Professor Martin's choice of the text for his class of 30 students, half of them white and a third black. Miss Kaplowitz, a sophomore who is not a student of Professor Martin's, saw the book in a bookstore and sat in on the class in which the professor explained how it would be used.

"It wasn't that I wanted the book banned," Ms. Kaplowitz said. "I just wanted to find out why it was being used and how it was being used, and whether it was being presented as propaganda or fact."

The professor responded to the complaints with a four-page letter to the faculty and students assailing unnamed leaders of Jewish groups who he said were frustrated over their loss of influence in the black community.

"The predominant Jewish response has been all too predictable to denounce the book and those who use it (including myself) as 'anti-Semitic,' " he wrote.

Some of his critics said Professor Martin's response was anti-Semitic and they found it more offensive than his choice of text. "He expanded the issue away from the book and he made it a Black-Jewish issue," said Adena Katz, a member of the campus chapter of Hillel, a national Jewish group. That is particularly dangerous, she said, on a campus where both groups are minorities; each make up about 7 percent of the 2,136 students.

But other students noted that the book was one of eight books on the reading list and that they spent less than an hour discussing it in class. "This is just another example of white arrogance, the habit of white people thinking that they have a right to dictate, develop and define how we interpret history," said La Trese Adkins, a black student in the class.

Jennifer Vanasco, the former editor of The Wellesley News, provided this perspective: "Everyone is so respectful here that a lot of times Wellesley students feel impotent in expressing their rage. This is a debate that affects everyone because it deals with whether we listen to faculty members as our mentors or whether we think for ourselves."

QUESTIONS TO HELP YOU THINK AND WRITE
ABOUT FREEDOM OF SPEECH ISSUES

1. What, according to Lasch, is the main responsibility of the public press in a democracy? Are Lasch's views about the responsibility and role of the press consistent with those that Katz says exist in young people's media? Now consider Crichton's and Cadre's views about the role and influence of the media (see pp. 233–236). Make your own claim about the future role and responsibility of the media, including newspapers, magazines, television, and electronic media. What are your reasons for your views?

2. List Lasch's reasons for his proposition (claim), "What democracy requires is public debate, not information." Which in your view is his strongest reason? List additional support and evidence from your experience to develop this reason further.

3. Give evidence from your experience that either strengthens or rebuts Katz's argument about the new media that is emerging for young people.

4. Consider the contexts for the use of the word "nigger" described by Marriott on pp. 236–239. How do the contexts change the usual meaning of language? Can you think of other examples of words that might be acceptable in one context but not in another, or words that might be acceptable to one culture but not to another? Should controversial language of this nature be used or suppressed by the media? Consider that the media includes music, television, and film, as well as printed materials.

5. Read the five articles about whether reading material should or should not be screened to protect students. What are the major positions that people take on this issue? What are the underlying warrants for each position? Which of these warrants are most acceptable to you?

6. Should there be any limits on what schoolchildren and older students are allowed to read? What criteria would you use to decide what they should read and what they should not read? Frame your answer in terms of grade-school children, high school students, and college students.

7. If one of your professors assigned reading material that offended your sense of values, as in the case of the incident at Wellesley, how would you react and why? Compare your reactions with those of the Wellesley students described in the article.

SECTION V
Environmental Issues

WHAT ARE THE ISSUES?

1. What Is the Relationship between Human Civilization and the Earth?

Four different perspectives, ranging from the Bible to Vice President Al Gore, on the age-old relationship between human beings and the environment.

    See also "Malling of America Puts Planet in Peril," pp. 239–241, and "The Birds and the Trees," pp. 123–124.

2. Who Is to Blame for the Environmental Problem, and How Serious Is It?

Two views on the causes and relative seriousness of environmental problems and what can still be done to solve them.

3. How Does Increasing Population Affect the Environment?

One 18th-century and two 20th-century authors demonstrate that increasing population is an enduring issue that is not solved yet.

4. What Are Some of the Environmental Solutions?

Two authors describe some of the recent attempts and pitfalls involved with solving environmental problems. Passing laws doesn't always work, according to Schneider. Some of the solutions described in the interview with Lester Brown may help.

    See also "An Interview with Garrett Hardin," pp. 24–32; "The Great Alaska Wolf Kill," pp. 165–166; and "Alaskan Wolf Management," pp. 343–347.

THE RHETORICAL SITUATION

Environmental issues, including the increasing population issue, are risky and somewhat scary issues for most people for several reasons. First, the problems associated with these issues can become life-threatening. Furthermore, the warrants associated with them often originate in the basic value systems that guide people's lives, and these include religious values. Finally, there is a constant conflict between preserving the environment and making economic progress at the expense of natural resources. As a result, it is tempting for many people to deny the problems associated with environmental issues or to simply ignore them.

Still, environmental issues are enduring issues that have created sufficient concern to attract many people's attention at various times throughout history, and they certainly concern most people of our time. The common perception is that environmental problems are accelerating, and solutions cannot be postponed for future generations.

Books and articles about environmental issues now appear regularly. In the spring and summer of 1992, more than the usual number were written, because of the first international United Nations conference on the environment held in Brazil in June. Also, Al Gore made environmental issues important in the 1992 presidential campaign. Think about what is happening right now, as you read this, that is drawing people's attention to these issues. The exigence is always present, but certain events often intensify it.

The following articles will introduce you to some of the major voices in the conversation on environmental issues. Economists, scientists, business leaders, and environmentalists are particularly vocal on these issues. You can be, too. Environmental issues are not all too complicated or remote to think about. Many of them affect your daily lives, such as changing automobile coolants, recycling old newspapers, not using elaborately packaged goods, conserving energy, buying smaller cars, cutting down on water pollution, conserving water, and even deciding whether to cut down trees to make way for construction. Discover some environmental issues that are close and important to you.

1. What Is the Relationship Between Human Civilization and the Earth?

GENESIS, CHAPTER 1; VERSES 26–28

This excerpt from the first book of the Bible describes a relationship between humans and the Earth that has been influential for centuries in Western culture. As one student put it, however, does "dominion over" mean to exploit the environment or protect it?

26   And God said, Let us make man in our image, after our likeness: and let them have dominion over the fish of the sea, and over the fowl of the air, and over the cattle, and over all the earth, and over every creeping thing that creepeth upon the earth.

27   So God created man in his own image, in the image of God created he him; male and female created he them.

28   And God blessed them, and God said unto them, Be fruitful, and multiply, and replenish the earth, and subdue it: and have dominion over the

King James translation.

fish of the sea, and over the fowl of the air, and over every living thing that moveth upon the earth.

THE AMERICAN FORESTS

John Muir

In 1892 John Muir founded the Sierra Club, a group that devotes itself to the study and protection of the Earth's scenic and ecological resources. Muir also worked with President Theodore Roosevelt to establish several national parks in the late 19th and early 20th centuries. This is an excerpt from an article published by Muir in The Atlantic Monthly *in 1901.*

Notwithstanding all the waste and use which have been going on unchecked like a storm for more than two centuries, it is not yet too late—though it is high time—for the government to begin a rational administration of its forests. About seventy million acres it still owns—enough for all the country, if wisely used. These residual forests are generally on mountain slopes, just where they are doing the most good, and where their removal would be followed by the greatest number of evils; the lands they cover are too rocky and high for agriculture, and can never be made as valuable for any other crop as for the present crop of trees. It has been shown over and over again that if these mountains were to be stripped of their trees and underbrush, and kept bare and sodless by hordes of sheep and the innumerable fires the shepherds set, besides those of the mill-men, prospectors, shake-makers, and all sorts of adventurers, both lowlands and mountains would speedily become little better than deserts, compared with their present beneficent fertility. During heavy rainfalls and while the winter accumulations of snow were melting, the larger streams would swell into destructive torrents, cutting deep, rugged-edged gullies, carrying away the fertile humus and soil as well as sand and rocks, filling up and overflowing their lower channels, and covering the lowland fields with raw detritus. Drought and barrenness would follow.

In their natural condition, or under wise management, keeping out destructive sheep, preventing fires, selecting the trees that should be cut for lumber, and preserving the young ones and the shrubs and sod of herbaceous vegetation, these forests would be a never failing fountain of wealth and beauty. The cool shades of the forest give rise to moist beds and currents of air, and the sod of grasses and the various flowering plants and shrubs thus fostered, together with the network and sponge of tree roots, absorb and hold back the

John Muir, "The American Forests," originally published in *The Atlantic Monthly,* 1901. Reprinted in John Muir, *Our National Parks* (San Francisco: Sierra Club Books, 1991).

rain and the waters from melting snow, compelling them to ooze and perco-
late and flow gently through the soil in streams that never dry. All the pine
needles and rootlets and blades of grass, and the fallen, decaying trunks of
trees, are dams, storing the bounty of the clouds and dispensing it in perennial
life-giving streams, instead of allowing it to gather suddenly and rush head-
long in short-lived devastating floods. Everybody on the dry side of the continent is beginning to find this out, and, in view of the waste going on, is growing
more and more anxious for government protection. The outcries we hear
against forest reservations come mostly from thieves who are wealthy and steal
timber by wholesale. [. . .]

Emerson says that things refuse to be mismanaged long. An exception
would seem to be found in the case of our forests, which have been mismanaged rather long, and now come desperately near being like smashed eggs and
spilt milk. Still, in the long run the world does not move backward. The wonderful advance made in the last few years, in creating four national parks in
the West, and thirty forest reservations, embracing nearly forty million acres;
and in the planting of the borders of streets and highways and spacious parks
in all the great cities, to satisfy the natural taste and hunger for landscape beauty
and righteousness that God has put, in some measure, into every human being
and animal, shows the trend of awakening public opinion. The making of the
far-famed New York Central Park was opposed by even good men, with misguided pluck, perseverance, and ingenuity; but straight right won its way, and
now that park is appreciated. So we confidently believe it will be with our great
national parks and forest reservations. There will be a period of indifference
on the part of the rich, sleepy with wealth, and of the toiling millions, sleepy
with poverty, most of whom never saw a forest; a period of screaming protest
and objection from the plunderers, who are as unconscionable and enterprising as Satan. But light is surely coming, and the friends of destruction will
preach and bewail in vain.

The United States government has always been proud of the welcome it
has extended to good men of every nation, seeking freedom and homes and
bread. Let them be welcomed still as Nature welcomes them, to the woods as
well as to the prairies and plains. No place is too good for good men, and still
there is room. They are invited to heaven, and may well be allowed in America.
Every place is made better by them. Let them be as free to pick gold and gems
from the hills, to cut and hew, dig and plant, for homes and bread, as the birds
are to pick berries from the wild bushes, and moss and leaves for nests. The
ground will be glad to feed them, and the pines will come down from the mountains for their homes as willingly as the cedars came from Lebanon for
Solomon's temple. Nor will the woods be the worse for this use, or their benign influences be diminished any more than the sun is diminished by shining. Mere destroyers, however, tree-killers, wool and mutton men, spreading
death and confusion in the fairest groves and gardens ever planted—let the
government hasten to cast them out and make an end of them. For it must be
told again and again, and be burningly borne in mind, that just now, while protective measures are being deliberated languidly, destruction and use are

speeding on faster and farther every day. The axe and saw are insanely busy, chips are flying thick as snowflakes, and every summer thousands of acres of priceless forests, with their underbrush, soil, springs, climate, scenery, and religion, are vanishing away in clouds of smoke, while, except in the national parks, not one forest guard is employed.

All sorts of local laws and regulations have been tried and found wanting, and the costly lessons of our own experience, as well as that of every civilized nation, show conclusively that the fate of the remnant of our forests is in the hands of the federal government, and that if the remnant is to be saved at all, it must be saved quickly.

Any fool can destroy trees. They cannot run away; and if they could, they would still be destroyed—chased and hunted down as long as fun or a dollar could be got out of their bark hides, branching horns, or magnificent bole backbones. Few that fell trees plant them; nor would planting avail much towards getting back anything like the noble primeval forests. During a man's life only saplings can be grown, in the place of the old trees—tens of centuries old—that have been destroyed. It took more than three thousand years to make some of the trees in these Western woods—trees that are still standing in perfect strength and beauty, waving and singing in the mighty forests of the Sierra. Through all the wonderful, eventful centuries since Christ's time—and long before that—God has cared for these trees, saved them from drought, disease, avalanches, and a thousand straining, leveling tempests and floods; but he cannot save them from fools—only Uncle Sam can do that.

THE LAND

N. Scott Momaday

N. Scott Momaday is a Native American author who is best known for his book
The Way to Rainy Mountain. *He originally contributed the passage reproduced here to a handbook for environmental activists published by the Sierra Club.*

I am interested in the way that a man looks at a given landscape and takes possession of it in his blood and brain. For this happens, I am certain, in the ordinary motion of life. None of us lives apart from the land entirely; such an isolation is unimaginable. We have sooner or later to come to terms with the world around us—and I mean especially the physical world, not only as it is revealed to us immediately through our senses, but also as it is perceived more truly in the long turn of seasons and of years. And we must come to moral terms. There is no alternative, I believe, if we are to realize and maintain our humanity, for our humanity must consist in part in the ethical as well as the

N. Scott Momaday, "The Land." In *Ecostatics: The Sierra Club Handbook for Environmental Activists*, ed. John G. Mitchell with Constance L. Stallings (New York: Simon and Schuster, 1970). pp. 102–104.

practical ideal of preservation. And particularly here and now is that true. We Americans need now more than ever before—and indeed more than we know—to imagine who and what we are with respect to the earth and sky. I am talking about an act of the imagination essentially, and the concept of an American land ethic.

It is no doubt more difficult to imagine in 1970 the landscape of America than it was in, say, 1900. Our whole experience as a nation in this century has been a repudiation of the pastoral ideal which informs so much of the art and literature of the nineteenth century. One effect of the Technological Revolution has been to uproot us from the soil. We have become disoriented, I believe; we have suffered a kind of psychic dislocation of ourselves in time and space. We may be perfectly sure of where we are in relation to the supermarket and the next coffee break, but I doubt that any of us knows where he is in relation to the stars and to the solstices. Our sense of the natural order has become dull and unreliable. Like the wilderness itself, our sphere of instinct has diminished in proportion as we have failed to imagine truly what it is. And yet I believe that it is possible to formulate an ethical idea of the land—a notion of what it is and must be in our daily lives—and I believe moreover that it is absolutely necessary to do so.

It would seem on the surface of things that a land ethic is something that is alien to, or at least dormant in, most Americans. Most of us in general have developed an attitude of indifference toward the land. In terms of my own experience, it is difficult to see how such an attitude could ever have come about.

EARTH IN THE BALANCE

Al Gore

This passage comes from Vice President Al Gore's Earth in the Balance: Ecology and the Human Spirit, *published in 1992 when he was still a senator.*

At the heart of every human society is a web of stories that attempt to answer our most basic questions: Who are we, and why are we here? But as the destructive pattern of our relationship to the natural world becomes increasingly clear, we begin to wonder if our old stories still make sense and sometimes have gone so far as to devise entirely new stories about the meaning and purpose of human civilization.

One increasingly prominent group known as Deep Ecologists makes what I believe is the deep mistake of defining our relationship to the earth using the

From Al Gore, *Earth in the Balance: Ecology and the Human Spirit* (New York: Houghton Miflin, 1992).

metaphor of disease. According to this story, we humans play the role of pathogens, a kind of virus giving the earth a rash and a fever, threatening the planet's vital life functions. Deep Ecologists assign our species the role of a global cancer, spreading uncontrollably, metastasizing in our cities and taking for our own nourishment and expansion the resources needed by the planet to maintain its health. Alternatively, the Deep Ecology story considers human civilization a kind of planetary HIV virus, giving the earth a "Gaian" form of AIDS, rendering it incapable of maintaining its resistance and immunity to our many insults to its health and equilibrium. Global warming is, in this metaphor, the fever that accompanies a victim's desperate effort to fight the invading virus whose waste products have begun to contaminate the normal metabolic processes of its host organism. As the virus rapidly multiplies, the sufferer's fever signals the beginning of the "body's" struggle to mobilize antigens that will attack the invading pathogens in order to destroy them and save the host.

The obvious problem with this metaphor is that it defines human beings as inherently and contagiously destructive, the deadly carriers of a plague upon the earth. And the internal logic of the metaphor points toward only one possible cure: eliminate people from the face of the earth. As Mike Roselle, one of the leaders of Earth First!, a group espousing Deep Ecology, has said, "You hear about the death of nature and it's true, but nature will be able to reconstitute itself once the top of the food chain is lopped off—meaning us."

Some of those who adopt this story as their controlling metaphor are actually advocating a kind of war on the human race as a means of protecting the planet. They assume the role of antigens, to slow the spread of the disease, give the earth time to gather its forces to fight off and, if necessary, eliminate the intruders. In the words of Dave Foreman, a cofounder of Earth First!, "It's time for a warrior society to rise up out of the earth and throw itself in front of the juggernaut of destruction, to be antibodies against the human pox that's ravaging this precious, beautiful planet." (Some Deep Ecologists, it should be added, are more thoughtful.)

Beyond its moral unacceptability, another problem with this metaphor is its inability to explain—in a way that is either accurate or believable—who we are and how we can create solutions for the crisis it describes. Ironically, just as René Descartes, Francis Bacon, and the other architects of the scientific revolution defined human beings as disembodied intellects separate from the physical world, Arne Naess, the Norwegian philosopher who coined the term Deep Ecology in 1973, and many Deep Ecologists of today seem to define human beings as an alien presence on the earth. In a modern version of the Cartesian dénouement of a philosophical divorce between human beings and the earth, Deep Ecologists idealize a condition in which there is no connection between the two, but they arrive at their conclusion by means of a story that is curiously opposite to that of Descartes. Instead of seeing people as creatures of abstract thought relating to the earth only through logic and theory, the Deep Ecologists make the opposite mistake, of defining the relationship between human beings and the earth almost solely in physical terms—as if we were nothing more than humanoid bodies genetically programmed to play out our bubonic destiny, having no intellect or free will with which to understand and change the script we are following.

The Cartesian approach to the human story allows us to believe that we are separate from the earth, entitled to view it as nothing more than an inanimate collection of resources that we can exploit however we like; and this fundamental misperception has led us to our current crisis. But if the new story of the Deep Ecologists is dangerously wrong, it does at least provoke an essential question: What new story can explain the relationship between human civilization and the earth—and how we have come to a moment of such crisis? One part of the answer is clear: our new story must describe and foster the basis for a natural and healthy relationship between human beings and the earth. The old story of God's covenant with both the earth and humankind, and its assignment to human beings of the role of good stewards and faithful servants, was—before it was misinterpreted and twisted in the service of the Cartesian world view—a powerful, noble, and just explanation of who we are in relation to God's earth. What we need today is a fresh telling of our story with the distortions removed.

2. Who Is to Blame for the Environmental Problem, and How Serious Is It?

THE END IS NOT AT HAND

Robert J. Samuelson

This author is an economist who writes for Newsweek. *This essay appeared there in 1992.*

Whoever coined the phrase "save the planet" is a public-relations genius. It conveys the sense of impending catastrophe and high purpose that has wrapped environmentalism in an aura of moral urgency. It also typifies environmentalism's rhetorical excesses, which, in any other context, would be seen as wild exaggeration or simple dishonesty.

Up to a point, our environmental awareness has checked a mindless enthusiasm for unrestrained economic growth. We have sensibly curbed some of growth's harmful side effects. But environmentalism increasingly resembles a holy crusade addicted to hype and ignorant of history. Every environmental ill is depicted as an onrushing calamity that—if not stopped—will end life as we know it.

Take the latest scare: the greenhouse effect. We're presented with the horrifying specter of a world that incinerates itself. Act now, or sizzle later. Food supplies will wither. Glaciers will melt. Coastal areas will flood. In fact, the probable losses from any greenhouse warming are modest: 1 to 2 percent of our economy's output by the year 2050, estimates economist William Cline. The loss seems even smaller compared with the expected growth of the economy (a doubling) over the same period.

No environmental problem threatens the "planet" or rates with the danger of nuclear war. No oil spill ever caused suffering on a par with today's civil war in Yugoslavia, which is a minor episode in human misery. World War II left more than 35 million dead. Cambodia's civil war resulted in 1 million to 3 million deaths. The great scourges of humanity remain what they have always been: war, natural disaster, oppressive government, crushing poverty and hate. On any scale of tragedy, environmental distress is a featherweight.

This is not an argument for indifference or inaction. It is an argument for perspective and balance. You can believe (as I do) that the possibility of greenhouse warming enhances an already strong case for an energy tax. A tax would curb ordinary air pollution, limit oil imports, cut the budget deficit and promote energy-efficient investments that make economic sense.

But it does not follow that anyone who disagrees with me is evil or even wrong. On the greenhouse effect, for instance, there's ample scientific doubt over whether warming will occur and, if so, how much. Moreover, the warming would occur over decades. People and businesses could adjust. To take one example: farmers could shift to more heat-resistant seeds.

Unfortunately, the impulse of many environmentalists is to vilify and simplify. Critics of environmental restrictions are portrayed as selfish and ignorant creeps. Doomsday scenarios are developed to prove the seriousness of environmental dangers. Cline's recent greenhouse study projected warming 250 years into the future. Guess what, it increases sharply. This is an absurd exercise akin to predicting life in 1992 at the time of the French and Indian War (1754–63).

The rhetorical overkill is not just innocent excess. It clouds our understanding. For starters, it minimizes the great progress that has been made, especially in industrialized countries. In the United States, air and water pollution have dropped dramatically. Since 1960, particulate emissions (soot, cinders) are down by 65 percent. Lead emissions have fallen by 97 percent since 1970. Smog has declined in most cities.

What's also lost is the awkward necessity for choices. Your environmental benefit may be my job. Not every benefit is worth having at any cost. Economists estimate that environmental regulations depress the economy's output by 2.6 to 5 percent, or about $150 billion to $290 billion. (Note: this is larger than the estimated impact of global warming.) For that cost, we've lowered health risks and improved our surroundings. But some gains are small compared with the costs. And some costs are needlessly high because regulations are rigid.

BALANCE

The worst sin of environmental excess is its bias against economic growth. The cure for the immense problems of poor countries usually lies with economic growth. A recent report from the World Bank estimates that more than 1 billion people lack healthy water supplies and sanitary facilities. The result is hundreds of millions of cases of diarrhea annually and the deaths of 3 million children (2 million of which the World Bank judges avoidable). Only by becoming wealthier can countries correct these conditions.

Similarly, wealthier societies have both the desire and the income to clean their air and water. Advanced nations have urban-air-pollution levels only a sixth that of the poorest countries. Finally, economic growth tends to reduce high birthrates, as children survive longer and women escape traditional roles.

Yes, we have environmental problems. Reactors in the former Soviet Union pose safety risks. Economic growth and the environment can be at odds. Growth generates carbon-dioxide emissions and causes more waste. But these problems are not—as environmental rhetoric implies—the main obstacles to sustained development. The biggest hurdle is inept government. Inept government fostered unsafe Soviet reactors. Inept government hampers food production in poor countries by, say, preventing farmers from earning adequate returns on their crops.

By now, everyone is an environmentalist. But the label is increasingly meaningless, because not all environmental problems are equally serious and even the serious ones need to be balanced against other concerns. Environmentalism should hold the hype. It should inform us more and frighten us less.

THE WEST SETS A BAD EXAMPLE

Maneka Gandhi

The author is India's former minister for the environment and forests. This article appeared in the World Press Review *in June 1992.*

Practically all environmental degradation in the East is due to over-consumption in the West. Consumption has many facets. First is the excessive and wasteful use of resources by the West—resources that it extracts forcibly, using the new colonial weapons of the International Monetary Fund, the World Bank, and other aid to keep us permanently in debt and thereby make us more amenable to exporting our irreplaceable assets. Second, to keep Western industries going, inefficient, outdated, and harmful machinery and chemicals are forcibly dumped on the East.

World Press Review, June 1992, p. 11.

Most important, however, is the constant brainwashing to the effect that prosperity means the Western way of life—more of everything and bigger, faster, more waste-generating. This generates imitation and raises consumption levels of people and countries that cannot afford it. It also destroys nature-based economies without replacing them with anything better.

The generation and distribution of electricity are one example. India has bought Western-style thermal plants and dams (and now nuclear plants), and 90 percent of the machinery in both comes from the West. These thermal plants work at less than 50 percent of their capacity. Sixteen hundred dams provide only 2.5 percent of the country's power, and the damage they cause, by flooding during the monsoon, runs into millions of dollars.

Fewer than 10 percent of our villages are electrified, because the power system does not work. But that does not prevent the West from selling or giving us as aid, new power plants that will need new machinery after a few years, which can then be sold at double the normal price.

Seventy percent of our water is polluted. A large part of that is due to pesticides that have been sold to us by countries that have banned the use of such products for themselves. Look at the diversion of land for export crops to help pay our international debt—debt incurred by the cost of oil and machinery. In a country where people cannot afford staple foods, the best land goes into tea, coffee, sugar cane, tobacco, and spices. All of these use a heavy concentration of pesticides and enormous amounts of water and are sold on the international market at prices fixed by the West that are lower today than they were in 1980! The most amazing land use is for fodder and flowers. Every seventh pound of meat eaten in Europe is from animals raised on grain grown in the East. So our people grow grain for animals so that people in the West can eat meat.

Reorganization must take place. Is it essential to truck fruits from Italy to Sweden every day? Is it necessary to have a second car? Is it necessary to use disposable diapers? Is it necessary to use a non-renewable resource such as oil in such wasteful ways that the price goes up and the Third World's burden of debt increases even further? Was it necessary to sell us chlorofluorocarbon technology 10 years after the West had discovered that it was destroying the ozone layer?

The greatest harm done to the environment by the West is through the spread of an ideology about growth that has taken firm root among our Third World elite. The axioms of this ideology are simple: More growth is good; less growth is worrying; negative growth is disastrous.

Multi-national companies that open factories in the East should be monitored strictly for safety procedures. Hundreds of units in India spew poison into the waters daily. Of course, Union Carbide is a case in point, making a chemical in Bhopal, India, that it was not allowed to make in the U.S. and doing so in the most careless way possible.

The United Nations Environment Program (UNEP) should be strengthened and given sanction-making powers. It could act as a monitor for restraining environmentally inefficient machinery and harmful chemicals from being forced on the East. Where it is established that a developing country has been coerced into consumption, the debt should be written off. UNEP could be the channel to pass on the latest technologies that are suitable for Eastern land, water, and weather conditions. It could also enforce the "polluter pays" principle, which would in time have its effect on Western governments and companies. It could come up with solutions that sustain life, not destroy it.

The East is ready to listen. Is the West?

3. How Does Increasing Population Affect the Environment?

ESSAY ON THE PRINCIPLE OF POPULATION

Thomas Malthus

This is an excerpt from Malthus's classic work Essay on the Principle of Population, *published in 1798. It states his central argument.*

I think I may fairly make two postulata.

First, that food is necessary to the existence of man.

Secondly, that the passion between the sexes is necessary, and will remain nearly in its present state.

These two laws ever since we have had any knowledge of mankind, appear to have been fixed laws of our nature; and, as we have not hitherto seen any alteration in them, we have no right [. . .] to conclude that they will ever cease to be what they now are, without an immediate act of power in that Being who first arranged the system of the universe; and for the advantage of his creatures, still executes, according to fixed laws, all its various operations.

I do not know that any writer has supposed that on this earth man will ultimately be able to live without food. But Mr Godwin has conjectured that the passion between the sexes may in time be extinguished. As, however, he calls this part of his work, a deviation into the land of conjecture, I will not dwell longer upon it at present, than to say, that the best arguments for the perfectibility of man, are drawn from a contemplation of the great progress that he has already made from the savage state, and the difficulty of saying where [. . .] he is to stop. But towards the extinction of the passion between

Thomas R. Malthus, *Essay on the Principle of Population*. London: J. Johnson, 1798.

the sexes, no progress whatever has hitherto been made. It appears to exist in as much force at present as it did two thousand, or four thousand years ago. There are individual exceptions now as there always have been. But, as these exceptions do not appear to increase in number, it would surely be a very unphilosophical mode of arguing, to infer merely from the existence of an exception, that the exception would, in time, become the rule, and the rule the exception.

Assuming then, my postulata as granted, I say, that the power of population is indefinitely greater than the power in the earth to produce subsistence for man. [. . .]

Population, when unchecked, increases in a geometrical ratio. Subsistence increases only in an arithmetical ratio. A slight acquaintance with numbers will show the immensity of the first power in comparison of the second.

By that law of our nature which makes food necessary to the life of man, the effects of these two unequal powers must be kept equal.

This implies a strong and constantly operating check on population from the difficulty of subsistence. This difficulty must fall somewhere; and must necessarily be severely felt by a large portion of mankind.

Through the animal and vegetable kingdoms, nature has scattered the seeds [. . .] of life abroad with the most profuse and liberal hand. She has been comparatively sparing in the room, and the nourishment necessary to rear them. The germs of existence contained in this spot of earth, with ample food, and ample room to expand in, would fill millions of worlds in the course of a few thousand years. Necessity, that imperious all-pervading law of nature, restrains them within the prescribed bounds. The race of plants, and the race of animals shrink under this great restrictive law. And the race of man cannot, by any efforts of reason, escape from it. Among plants and animals its effects are waste of seed, sickness, and premature death. Among mankind, misery and vice. The former, misery, is an absolutely necessary consequence of it. Vice is a highly probable consequence, and we therefore see it abundantly [. . .] prevail; but it ought not, perhaps, to be called an absolutely necessary consequence. The ordeal of virtue is to resist all temptation to evil.

This natural inequality of the two powers of population, and of production in the earth, and that great law of our nature which must constantly keep their effects equal, form the great difficulty that to me appears insurmountable in the way to the perfectibility of society. All other arguments are of slight and subordinate consideration in comparison of this. I see no way by which man can escape from the weight of this law which pervades all animated nature. No fancied equality, no agrarian regulations in their utmost extent, could remove the pressure of it even for a single century. And it appears, therefore, to be decisive against the possible existence of [. . .] a society, all the members of which, should live in ease, happiness, and comparative leisure; and feel no anxiety about providing the means of subsistence for themselves and families.

Consequently, if the premises are just, the argument is conclusive against the perfectibility of the mass of mankind.

I have thus sketched the general outline of the argument; but I will examine it more particularly; and I think it will be found that experience, the true source and foundation of all knowledge, invariably confirms its truth. [. . .]

HOW MANY IS TOO MANY?

Charles C. Mann

This selection is part of a longer article that first appeared in The Atlantic Monthly *in 1993. It is an exploratory paper on the increasing population issue.*

How many people is too many? Over time, the debate has spread between two poles. On one side, according to Garrett Hardin, an ecologist at the University of California at Santa Barbara, are the Cassandras, who believe that continued population growth at the current rate will inevitably lead to catastrophe. On the other are the Pollyannas, who believe that humanity faces problems but has a good shot at coming out okay in the end. Cassandras, who tend to be biologists, look at each new birth as the arrival on the planet of another hungry mouth. Pollyannas, who tend to be economists, point out that along with each new mouth comes a pair of hands. Biologist or economist—is either one right? It is hard to think of a question more fundamental to our crowded world.

Cassandras and Pollyannas have spoken up throughout history. Philosophers in ancient China fretted about the need to shift the masses to underpopulated areas; meanwhile, in the Mideast, the Bible urged humanity to be fruitful and multiply. Plato said that cities with more than 5,040 landholders were too large; Martin Luther believed that it was impossible to breed too much, because God would always provide. And so on.

Early economists tended to be Pollyannas. People, they thought, are a resource—"the chiefest, most fundamental, and precious commodity" on earth, as William Petyt put it in 1680. Without a healthy population base, societies cannot afford to have their members specialize. In small villages almost everyone is involved with producing food; only as numbers grow can communities afford luxuries like surgeons, scientists, and stand-up comedians. The same increase lowers the cost of labor, and hence the cost of production—a notion that led at least one Enlightenment-era writer, J. F. Melon, to endorse slavery as an excellent source of a cheap work force.

The Atlantic Monthly, February 1993, pp. 47–52.

As proof of their theory, seventeenth-century Pollyannas pointed to the Netherlands, which was strong, prosperous, and thickly settled, and claimed that only such a populous place could be so rich. In contrast, the poor, sparsely inhabited British colonies in the New World were begging immigrants to come and swell the work force. One of the chief duties of a ruler, these savants thought, was to ensure population growth. A high birth rate, the scholar Bernard Mandeville wrote in 1732, is "the never-failing Nursery of Fleets and Armies."

Mandeville wrote when the Industrial Revolution was beginning to foster widespread urban unemployment and European cities swarmed with beggars. Hit by one bad harvest after another, Britain tottered through a series of economic crises, which led to food shortages and poverty on a frightful scale. By 1803 local parishes were handing out relief to about one out of every seven people in England and Wales. In such a climate it is unsurprising that the most famous Cassandra of them all should appear: the Reverend Thomas Robert Malthus.

"Right from the publication of the *Essay on Population* to this day," the great economic historian Joseph Schumpeter wrote in 1954, "Malthus has had the good fortune—for this *is* good fortune—to be the subject of equally unreasonable, contradictory appraisals." John Maynard Keynes regarded Malthus as the "beginning of systematic economic thinking." Percy Bysshe Shelley, on the other hand, derided him as "a eunuch and a tyrant." John Stuart Mill viewed Malthus as a great thinker. To Karl Marx he was a "plagiarist" and a "shameless sycophant of the ruling classes." "He was a benefactor of humanity," Schumpeter wrote. "He was a fiend. He was a profound thinker. He was a dunce."

The subject of the controversy was a shy, kindly fellow with a slight harelip. He was also the first person to hold a university position in economics—that is, the first professional economist—in Britain, and probably the world. Married late, he had few children, and he was never overburdened with money. He was impelled to write his treatise on population by a disagreement with his father, a well-heeled eccentric in the English style. The argument was over whether the human race could transform the world into a paradise. Malthus thought not, and said so at length—55,000 words, published as an unsigned broadside in 1798. Several longer, signed versions followed, as Malthus became more confident.

"The power of population," Malthus proclaimed, "is indefinitely greater than the power in the earth to produce subsistence for man." In modern textbooks this notion is often explained with a graph. One line on the graph represents the land's capacity to produce food; it slowly rises from left to right as people clear more land and learn to farm more efficiently. Another line starts out low, quickly climbs to meet the first, and then soars above it; that line represents human population. Eventually the gap between the two lines cannot be bridged and the Horsemen of the Apocalypse pay a call. Others had anticipated this idea. Giovanni Botero, an Italian scholar, described the basic relationship of population and resources in 1589, two centuries before Malthus.

But few read Malthus's predecessors, and nobody today seems inclined to replace the term "Malthusian" with "Boterian."

The *Essay* was a jolt. Simple and remorselessly logical, blessed with a perverse emotional appeal, it seemed to overturn centuries of Pollyanna-dom at a stroke. Forget Utopia, Malthus said. Humanity is doomed to exist, now and forever, at the edge of starvation. Forget charity, too: helping the poor only leads to more babies, which in turn produces increased hardship down the road. Little wonder that the essayist Thomas Carlyle found this theory so gloomy that he coined the phrase "dismal science" to describe it. Others were more vituperative, especially those who thought that the *Essay* implied that God would not provide for His children. "Is there no law in this kingdom for punishing a man for publishing a libel against the Almighty himself?" demanded one anonymous feuilleton. In all the tumult hardly anyone took the trouble to note that logical counterarguments were available.

The most important derived from the work of Marie-Jean-Antoine-Nicolas Caritat, Marquis de Condorcet, a French *philosophe* who is best known for his worship of Reason. Four years before Malthus, Condorcet observed that France was finite, the potential supply of French infinite. Unlike Malthus, though, Condorcet believed that technology could solve the problem. When hunger threatens, he wrote, "new instruments, machines, and looms" will continue to appear, and "a very small amount of ground will be able to produce a great quantity of supplies." Society changes so fast, in other words, that Malthusian scenarios are useless. Given the level of productivity of our distant ancestors, in other words, we should already have run out of food. But we know more than they, and are more prosperous, despite our greater numbers.

Malthus and Condorcet fixed the two extremes of a quarrel that endures today. The language has changed, to be sure. Modern Cassandras speak of "ecology," a concept that did not exist in Malthus's day, and worry about exceeding the world's "carrying capacity," the ecological ceiling beyond which the land cannot support life. Having seen the abrupt collapses that occur when populations of squirrels, gypsy moths, or Lapland reindeer exceed local carrying capacities, they foresee the same fate awaiting another species: *Homo sapiens*. Pollyannas note that no such collapse has occurred in recorded history. Evoking the "demographic transition"—the observed propensity for families in prosperous societies to have fewer children—they say that continued economic growth can both feed the world's billions and enrich the world enough to end the population boom. No! the Cassandras cry. Growth is the *problem*. We're growing by 100 million people every year! We can't keep doing that forever!

True, Pollyannas concede. If present-day trends continue for centuries, the earth will turn into a massive ball of human flesh. A few millennia more, Ansley Coale, of Princeton, calculates, and that ball of flesh will be expanding outward at the speed of light. But he sees little point in the exercise of projecting lines on a graph out to their absurdly horrible conclusion. "If you had asked someone in 1890 about today's population," Coale explains, "he'd say, 'There's no way the United States can support two hundred and fifty million people. Where are they going to pasture all their horses?' "

Just as the doomsayers feared, the world's population has risen by more than half since Paul Ehrlich wrote *The Population Bomb*. Twenty-five years ago 3.4 billion people lived on earth. Now the United Nations estimates that 5.3 billion do—the biggest, fastest increase in history. But food production increased faster still. According to the Food and Agricultural Organization of the UN, not only did farmers keep pace but per capita global food production actually rose more than 10 percent from 1968 to 1990. The number of chronically malnourished people fell by more than 16 percent. (All figures on global agriculture and population in the 1990s, including those in this article, mix empirical data with projections, because not enough time has elapsed to get hard numbers.)

"Much of the world *is* better fed than it was in 1950," concedes Lester R. Brown, the president of the Worldwatch Institute, an environmental-research group in Washington, D.C. "But that period of improvement is ending rather abruptly." Since 1984, he says, world grain production per capita has fallen one percent a year. In 1990, eighty-six nations grew less food per head than they had a decade before. Improvements are unlikely, in Brown's view. Our past success has brought us alarmingly close to the ecological ceiling. "There's a growing sense in the scientific community that it will be difficult to restore the rapid rise in agricultural yields we saw between 1950 and 1984," he says. "In agriculturally advanced nations there just isn't much more that farmers can do." Meanwhile, the number of mouths keeps up its frantic rate of increase. "My sense," Brown says, "is that we're going to be in trouble on the food front before this decade is out."

Social scientists disagree. An FAO study published in 1982 concluded that by using modern agricultural methods the Third World could support more than 30 billion people. Other technophiles see genetic engineering as a route to growth that is almost without end. Biologists greet such pronouncements with loud scoffs. One widely touted analysis by Ehrlich and others maintains that humanity already uses, destroys, or "co-opts" almost 40 percent of the potential output from terrestrial photosynthesis. Doubling the world's population will reduce us to fighting with insects over the last scraps of grass.

Neither side seems willing to listen to the other; indeed, the two are barely on speaking terms. The economist Julian Simon, of the University of Maryland, asserts that there is no evidence that the increase in land use associated with rising population has led to any increase in extinction rates—despite hundreds of biological reports to the contrary. The biologist Edward O. Wilson, of Harvard University, argues that contemporary economics is "bankrupt" and does not accommodate environmental calculations—despite the existence of a literature on the subject dating back to the First World War. A National Academy of Sciences panel dominated by economists argues in 1986 that the problems of population growth have been exaggerated. Six years later the academy issues a statement, dominated by biologists, claiming that continued population growth will lead to a global environmental catastrophe that "science and technology may not be able to prevent." Told in an exchange of academic gossip that an eminent ecologist has had himself sterilized, an equally eminent demographer says, "That's the best news I've heard all week!" Asking himself what "deep insights" professional demographers have contributed, Garrett Hardin answers, "None."

The difference in the forecasts—prosperity or penury, boundless increase or zero-sum game, a triumphant world with 30 billion or a despairing one with 10—is so extreme that one is tempted to dismiss the whole contretemps as foolish. If the experts can't even discuss the matter civilly, why should the average citizen try to figure it out? Ignoring the fracas might be the right thing to do if it weren't about the future of the human race.

NATURAL LIMITS

Lester R. Brown

This author is president of the Worldwatch Institute, an environmental research group. This article first appeared in 1993.

When the history of the last half of this century is written, population growth is likely to get far more attention than it does now. Those of us born before mid-century have witnessed unprecedented worldwide rises in incomes, steady gains in food consumption and a dramatic extension of life expectancy. But this golden age may be coming to an end for reasons that we do not well understand. And that is what will fascinate historians.

After mid-century, the world's farmers more than doubled the grain harvest, something no previous generation had done. Raising the harvest from 631 million tons in 1950 to 1,650 million tons in 1984, they increased grain production by 40 percent per person, reducing hunger and malnutrition around the world. Since 1984, however, grain production has fallen behind population growth, falling roughly 1 percent a year.

An even more abrupt slowdown is restricting supplies of seafood, the world's principal source of animal protein. Between 1950 and 1989, the world catch climbed from 22 million tons to 100 million tons. As a result, we have enjoyed a doubling of seafood consumption per person.

Since 1989, however, the catch has declined—to an estimated 97 million tons in 1992, or 8 percent per person. For some time, marine biologists at the United Nations Food and Agriculture Organization have warned that the oceans could not sustain a catch of more than 100 million tons a year.

New York Times, July 24, 1993, Op-Ed, p. 14.

With grasslands, the other natural system on which we depend heavily for animal protein, demands are also straining the limits on every continent. From 1950 to 1990, world production of beef, most of it from grasslands, went from 19 million to 53 million tons. But since 1990, production has dropped more than 2 percent. Mutton, the other grass-based meat, has followed a similar trend.

Marine biologists and rangeland agronomists had warned that these natural systems were being pushed ever closer to their limits. The slowing growth in grain output was somewhat less predictable, but growth in the area planted in grain came to a halt in 1981.

Two other trends are partly responsible. First, the growth of irrigated areas, after more than doubling between 1950 and 1978, fell behind population growth. Since 1978, the irrigated area per person has shrunk by 7 percent. Second, the growth of fertilizer use, the engine that drove the growth in food output, is slowing. Fertilizer use increased ninefold from 1950 to 1984, but since then has increased little. In agriculturally advanced countries, applying more fertilizer now does little to raise output.

As growth in fertilizer use has slowed, so has growth in the world grain harvest. More disturbing, there is no new technology in prospect that will enable farmers to restore the 3 percent annual growth in grain production that prevailed from 1950 to 1984.

This is a matter of deepening concern. Last year, the National Academy of Sciences and the Royal Society of London issued a report that warned: "If current predictions of population growth prove accurate and patterns of human activity on the planet remain unchanged, science and technology may not be able to prevent either irreversible degradation of the environment or continued poverty for much of the world."

The world has quietly entered a new era, one in which satisfying the food needs of 90 million more people each year is possible only by reducing consumption among those already here.

The only sensible option may now be an all-out effort to slow population growth. The first step is to fill the family-planning gap by expanding services. But unless the world can go beyond that and attack the conditions that foster rapid population growth—namely, discrimination against women and widespread poverty—reversing the decline may not be possible.

4. What Are Some of the Environmental Solutions?

STATE WITHOUT ACID RAIN IS DEALT ANOTHER BLOW

Keith Schneider

Another article published in 1993 demonstrates some of the problems with environmental legislation.

When Congress established strict rules in 1990 to control acid rain by ordering coal-burning power plants to reduce emissions of sulfur dioxide, the managers of the South Carolina Electric and Gas Company estimated they would have to spend up to $300 million over five years to comply.

To say they were aggravated understates their reaction. The reason: There is no acid rain in South Carolina because the state has no problem with sulfur dioxide. Winds generally blow anything in South Carolina's air out to sea, not to nearby states.

The problem, the utility's executives say, is not just the expense of the rules but their usefulness as well. And South Carolina's concerns come amid growing questions about how serious a problem acid rain really is nationwide.

After years of rising concern about acid rain, Congress enacted the strict limits on sulfur emissions. The idea was to protect thousands of lakes, miles of forests and hundreds of streams in the East, and many other lakes in Canada, that were believed to be heavily damaged by acid falling from the sky.

IGNORED ITS OWN STUDY

Since then, utilities have spent $5 billion a year to comply. But when Congress approved the law, it ignored the results of its own $540 million study, commissioned a decade earlier and completed in 1990.

In one of the most thorough analyses of an environmental problem ever conducted, researchers checked acidity levels in more than 4,000 lakes and thousands of miles of streams. Their tests showed that acid rain, while a problem, was certainly not a crisis for this country. While a few hundred lakes and streams were shown to have high levels of acids, the study also said that thousands of others had not been affected.

Senator Daniel Patrick Moynihan, the New York Democrat who voted

New York Times, March 22, 1993, p. C8.

for the clean-air law, said the Congressional study was ignored because it would have upset the delicate regional political alliances that had been formed to push through the acid-rain protections.

"That's the way it happened," Mr. Moynihan said in an interview. "It was not a pretty way to make policy."

CREATING NEW PROBLEMS?

In South Carolina, state officials say they have never detected high acidity levels in any lakes or streams, most of which teem with fish. And utility officials say complying with the acid-rain requirements may actually cause more environmental problems. They argue that the scrubbing equipment most utilities use also produces thousands of tons of powdery wastes that must be buried somewhere.

But the state's chief air-quality manager says he is bound to enforce the law as it is written.

"How this came out was decided by Congress, and it must be changed by Congress," said James A. Joy 3d, the director of air quality in the state Department of Health and Environmental Control. "What would make more sense is to look at the actual causes of pollution and determine what are the true sources."

Mr. Joy declined to discuss the utility's specific problem. But he did say: "What's happening is that we are not looking very carefully at where we should be spending our money to make the environment safer. The concept of protecting the environment makes sense. How we are doing it now may not make sense in some instances."

The managers at South Carolina Electric and Gas are not nearly as reticent.

"Industry is not against paying for measures that protect the environment," said John W. Preston, the utility's senior engineer for environmental services. "The big concern we have is for every dollar you spend, are you getting at least a dollar in benefits? No matter which way you look at this acid-rain rule, it's hard to see any measurable benefits for us or our customers."

WHAT THE STUDY FOUND

The 1990 Government study on acid rain found high acidity in 4.2 percent of 1,181 lakes that were assessed and in about 3 percent of the nearly 4,000 miles of streams. Most of the problem, it said, was confined to Upper Michigan, the Adirondack region of New York, the Green Mountains in Vermont, the Monongahela National Forest in West Virginia and parts of Florida. The study also found that in those lakes that were affected, even those in Canada, acidity levels were already dropping as a result of requirements of the 1970 Clean Air Act.

In short, the study undermined the conventional wisdom that acid rain affected thousands of lakes and tens of thousands of miles of streams in every region east of the Mississippi River.

According to several Congressional staff members, Congress ignored this data because the members were intent on establishing an acid-rain rule that could be uniformly applied. They wanted to be sure that states with clean air could not gain a competitive edge over others, where expensive controls would have to be installed, and thus attract industry by offering less expensive power.

Here in South Carolina, the result is that by the end of the decade homeowners will pay $60 more each year for their electricity.

Since the state began measuring air quality more than two decades ago, even the highest annual concentration of sulfur dioxide was less than Federal standards. That was in Columbia in 1980, when the level reached 22 millionths of a gram per cubic meter, as against the Federal standard of 80 millionths of a gram. Surrounding states are not affected by the low levels here, since prevailing winds blow the sulfur dioxide out to sea.

"If I had $300 million to spend to improve air quality in South Carolina, I wouldn't spend it on acid rain," Mr. Joy said. "Most of our problem is smog caused by cars and trucks, and that's where I'd look for improvements—not in controlling sulfur dioxide from power plants."

THE ENVIRONMENTAL REVOLUTION: AN INTERVIEW WITH LESTER BROWN

This interview appears in the book Environment *by Peter H. Raven, Linda R. Berg, and George B. Johnson, published in 1993. It is included here to provide you with a sense of what is being done in response to the environmental problem and what more needs to be done.*

In 1974, Lester Brown founded the Worldwatch Institute, a private, nonprofit research institute devoted to the analysis of global environmental issues. Based in Washington, D.C., the Institute is internationally recognized for its bimonthly magazine, World Watch, *and for its annual series assessing environmental affairs worldwide,* State of the World. *Hailed as the "guru of the global environmental movement," Mr. Brown received his undergraduate degree in agricultural science from Rutgers University, and has an M.S. in agricultural economics from the University of Maryland and an M.P.A. from Harvard. In 1964, he was a foreign agricultural policy advisor to the U.S. Secretary of Agriculture, and in 1966 was appointed Administrator of the International*

From Peter H. Raven, Linda R. Berg, and George B. Johnson, *Environment* (Fort Worth, TX: 1993), Saunders College Publishing, Harcourt Brace Jovanovich, pp. 2–3.

Agricultural Development Service. In 1969, he helped establish the Overseas Development Council. Winner of the United Nations' 1989 environment prize, Mr. Brown is the author of a dozen books, including Man, Land and Food; World Without Borders; By Bread Alone; *and* Building a Sustainable Society.

In *State of the World 1992*, you call for an "Environmental Revolution." What does this mean and how might it occur?

The health of our planet has deteriorated dangerously during the past twenty years. We have so far failed to stem the tide of continuing rapid human population growth leading to deforestation, loss of plant and animal habitats and ultimately species extinction, overgrazing, soil erosion, and loss of productive cropland, and of water and air pollution with their attendant health costs and potential for altering the entire ecosphere. The decline in living conditions once predicted by some ecologists has become a reality for one sixth of humanity. As a result, our world faces potentially convulsive change. The question is, what sort of change? Will we enact strong worldwide initiatives that reverse the degradation of the planet and restore hope for the future? Or will we suffer the economic decline and social instability that will result from continued environmental deterioration? The policy decisions we make in the years immediately ahead will determine whether our children live in a world of development or decline. Muddling through will not work. Either we turn things around quickly, or the deterioration-and-decline scenario will take over.

What will it take to reverse these trends?

Building an environmentally sustainable future depends on restructuring the global economy, major shifts in human reproductive behavior, and dramatic changes in values and lifestyles. These changes add up to a revolution. If this Environmental Revolution succeeds, it will rank with the Agricultural and Industrial Revolutions as one of the great economic and social transformations in human history. But, unlike these past events, the Environmental Revolution must be compressed into a few decades.

To what extent will the success of this revolution be in the hands of governments?

Some of the conditions of environmental sustainability can be satisfied by individual choices, such as deciding to have fewer children or to use energy more efficiently. But policy decisions, such as phasing out chlorofluorocarbons, replacing fossil fuels with solar energy, or protecting the planet's biodiversity depend on national governments and international agreements. And without clear policy guidance from governments, corporations—which control a large share of the world's finances—are not likely to change environmentally destructive business practices.

Internationally, what are some of the measures governments are taking to move their economies onto an environmentally sustainable path?

Germany has committed itself to a 25% reduction in carbon emissions by the year 2005. Australia, Austria, Denmark, and New Zealand have pledged to cut emissions by 20% in the same period. Some developing countries, particularly China, are committing themselves to stabilizing population size. Bangladesh hopes to decrease the average number of children per woman from 4.9 in 1990 to 2.3 in 2000. Nigeria's goal is to reduce this number from 6.2 in 1990 to 4 in 2000, and Mexico plans to cut its 1990 population growth rate in half by 2000. Denmark has completely banned the use of disposable beverage containers, and the Netherlands has adopted the most comprehensive plan, involving reductions of carbon, sulfur dioxide, and nitrous oxide emissions; nitrogen and phosphorus pollution; and a switch from cars to bicycles and trains. Even the most progressive countries, however, are still in the early stages of the transformation.

What kind of measures would you like to see governments use more often?

By far their most effective tool is to tax environmentally destructive activities, such as the generation of hazardous wastes and the use of virgin resources. Taxing carbon emissions, for instance, discourages the use of fossil fuels, while encouraging investment in renewable energy sources. Such taxes also can have a direct economic impact on corporations, which generally have been accustomed to passing on the expense of the environmental disruption they cause to society at large.

Can we then expect to see increasing resistance from the corporate sector to this kind of governmental action?

Some corporate leaders will welcome industry-wide regulations and taxes, which would permit them to reduce environmental damage without being put at a competitive disadvantage. Corporations are facing an enormous amount of change in the years ahead. Shifting to a reuse–recycle economy, protecting the ozone layer, reducing air pollution, acid rain, and hazardous wastes are among the environmental influences that will increasingly shape the global economy. The switch from fossil fuels to a solar–hydrogen system alone will affect every sector of the economy, from transportation to food. Corporate leaders will have to respond. California regulations will require 2% of all cars sold there after 1998 to have zero emissions, that is, to be electric. General Motors plans to market its new electric car there by the mid-1990s.

Certain types of industries will be able to respond to the new environmental priorities more easily than others, won't they?

For some, the prospective changes are relatively modest. Manufacturers of electrical appliances, for example, can concentrate on designing them to be more energy-efficient and more easily repaired and recycled. Automakers can shift to electric or hydrogen-powered models. Producers of incandescent light bulbs can easily switch to super-efficient compact fluorescents. Many products manufactured on a limited scale today have an enormous market potential in an environmentally sustainable world. Among them are refillable beverage containers, photovoltaic cells, thermally efficient building materials, wind electric generators, high-speed rail cars, rooftop solar water heaters, and water-efficient plumbing appliances.

Other companies will have to make more fundamental decisions, simply because there will no longer be a place for their products. For example, coal and oil companies can either continue to conduct business as usual and face a bleak future, or they can help develop renewable energy sources. Like everyone else, corporations have a stake in a sustainable future. It is difficult to sustain profits in a declining economy. Those who see the need for change and move to the forefront will fare better than those who attempt to maintain the status quo.

What can we do, as members of the general public, to help launch the Environmental Revolution?

Individuals can do many things independently, but the Environmental Revolution depends on systemic change, and that requires an organized means of exerting sustained pressure, like that now coming from the thousands of environmental groups worldwide. These range from large international organizations, such as Greenpeace, to local, single-issue groups, such as the rubber tappers trying to save the Amazonian rain forest, or the women's groups in Kenya planting trees. These groups research issues, educate the public, litigate when necessary, and organize citizens to press local and national governments to abandon environmentally destructive policies.

Could the news media do a better job at disseminating the information that these groups generate?

Environmental issues are quite complex, and news editors, like society at large, sometimes have difficulty immediately grasping their importance and sifting through the information. Because it is environmental trends that are increasingly shaping our future, it is time for media organizations to reassess the resources devoted to environmental coverage. Newspapers should consider adding a daily environment section, and featuring at least as many environmental columnists on the editorial page as there are political ones. TV news programs might have a daily environment report, as well as a business one.

What's the single most important ingredient needed for a successful Environmental Revolution?

If it is to succeed, the Environmental Revolution will need the support of far more people than it now has. Up until now it has been viewed by society much like a sporting event—one where thousands sit in the stands watching, while only a handful are on the playing field actively attempting to influence the outcome of the contest. Success in this case depends on erasing the imaginary sidelines that separate spectators from participants so we can all get involved. Saving the planet is not a spectator sport.

QUESTIONS TO HELP YOU THINK AND WRITE
ABOUT ENVIRONMENTAL ISSUES

1. What do you think "dominion over" means in the first chapter of Genesis? Defend your position.

2. Read "The American Forests" by Muir and "The Birds and the Trees" on pages 123–124. How has forest management changed and how has it remained the same in the past 90 years? Imagine John Muir being called in as a consultant to settle the current logging controversy. What would his perspective be? What is your perspective? Give reasons for both.

3. Read Momaday and make a claim that formulates your own "ethical idea of the land." Defend it with a list of reasons.

4. What do you think the relationship between humans and the Earth should be? If there are international students in your class, discuss with them what their cultures teach and practice on this subject. What historical relationships between humans and the environment does Gore describe in his aricle? What does he find unacceptable about them? What is his view concerning the proper relationship of humans and the environment?

5. What are some of the causes of environmental problems according to Samuelson and Maneka Gandhi? Think of the environmental problems that are closest to you. What causes them? What are their effects?

6. The excerpt from Malthus's classic work on population growth is included here because it is referred to so often in discussions of the subject. Summarize his argument. Why is it so compelling to many people?

7. Mann identifies two schools of opinion on the human prospect: the Cassandras and the Pollyannas. Draw a line down the middle of a piece of paper and list the arguments that support the Cassandras in the first column and the arguments that support the Pollyannas in the second. Which position do you think Mann holds himself? Which do you think Samuelson might hold? Which do you identify with yourself? Why?

8. What, according to Lester R. Brown in his article "Natural Limits," are the main conditions that foster rapid population growth? What, in your opinion, can be done to attack this problem?

9. The last two articles in this section on environment deal with some of the solutions to the problem. Schneider describes problems with one solution that has been tried, and the interview with Lester Brown offers perhaps more promising solutions. What do you conclude is necessary to solve the world's environmental problems? What can you do yourself to help solve these problems?

SECTION VI

Issues Concerning Racism in America

WHAT ARE THE ISSUES?

1. Are Racial Minorities in Crisis?

Cornel West says that African-Americans are the victims of nihilism, or a hopelessness and a sense of meaninglessness in life. Andrew Hacker claims white
Americans are intensely aware of racial discrimination. The last article describes
problems created by the disproportionately large Hispanic school dropout rate.
See also "Stolen Promise," pp. 63–65.

2. What Causes Prejudice?

One author interviews residents of both a black neighborhood and a white neighborhood in Chicago and compares their thoughts and feelings about race, prejudice, and stereotypes.
See also "Jobs Illuminate What Riots Hid: Young Ideals," pp. 95–98, and "A
Simple 'Hai' Won't Do," pp. 67–68.

3. What Should Be Done to Solve Racial Problems?

MacDonald reports on diversity consultants who are being paid by businesses to
solve racial problems at work and Winerip describes diversity classes designed to
solve these problems at school. Finally, Wilkins offers another perspective on solutions to the race problem.
See also "Victims of Both Races," pp. 66–67; "A Call for Unity," pp. 244–245;
and "Letter from Birmingham Jail," pp. 246–258.

THE RHETORICAL SITUATION

Issues associated with race are difficult for many people because of the strong emotions associated with them. You will discover more emotional proof in this collection of articles about race than you will in any of the other issue areas.
    The warrants associated with racial issues include racist values held by some
people who claim that one race is naturally superior to another. Hitler expressed
these values in the 11th chapter, "On Nation and Race," of *Mein Kampf* (My
Struggle), published in 1925. There, he claimed that the Aryan or German race is
superior to other races. "All the human culture, all the results of art, science, and
technology that we see before us today," he claimed, "are almost exclusively the
creative product of the Aryan." The Aryan, he wrote, "is the founder of all higher
humanity, therefore representing the prototype of all that we understand by the
word 'man.' " Hitler's plan, of course, was to keep the Aryan race pure and to elim-

inate other, "inferior" races in an effort to create a utopia of Aryans. The Ku Klux Klan and other white supremacist groups have similar goals. Other warrants associated with racial issues are the needs to belong, to be safe, and to become self-actualized. Consult the list of common needs and values on page 271 to discover additional warrants.

The issues related to race in this section include the fact issue, "Are racial minorities in crisis?" the cause issue, "What causes prejudice?" and the policy issue, "What should be done?" Six other articles on race are scattered throughout Parts One through Three. Read them, along with the eight essays in this section, and begin to generate some ideas of your own about racial issues.

1. Are Racial Minorities in Crisis?

NIHILISM IN BLACK AMERICA

Cornel West

> *These are excerpts from West's book* Race Matters, *published in 1993. West is a philosopher, theologian, and activist who is professor of religion and director of Afro-American studies at Princeton University.*

The proper starting point for the crucial debate about the prospects for black America is an examination of the nihilism that increasingly pervades black communities. *Nihilism is to be understood here not as a philosophic doctrine that there are no rational grounds for legitimate standards or authority; it is, far more, the lived experience of coping with a life of horrifying meaninglessness, hopelessness, and (most important) lovelessness.* The frightening result is a numbing detachment from others and a self-destructive disposition toward the world. Life without meaning, hope, and love breeds a coldhearted, mean-spirited outlook that destroys both the individual and others.

Nihilism is not new in black America. The first African encounter with the New World was an encounter with a distinctive form of the Absurd. The initial black struggle against degradation and devaluation in the enslaved circumstances of the New World was, in part, a struggle against nihilism. In fact, the major enemy of black survival in America has been and is neither oppression nor exploitation but rather the nihilistic threat—that is, loss of hope and absence of meaning. For as long as hope remains and meaning is preserved, the possibility of overcoming oppression stays alive. The self-fulfilling prophecy of the nihilistic threat is that without hope there can be no future, that without meaning there can be no struggle.

From Cornel West, *Race Matters* (Boston: Beacon Press, 1993), pp. 14–20.

The genius of our black foremothers and forefathers was to create powerful buffers to ward off the nihilistic threat, to equip black folk with cultural armor to beat back the demons of hopelessness, meaninglessness, and lovelessness. These buffers consisted of cultural structures of meaning and feeling that created and sustained communities; this armor constituted ways of life and struggle that embodied values of service and sacrifice, love and care, discipline and excellence. In other words, traditions for black surviving and thriving under usually adverse New World conditions were major barriers against the nihilistic threat. These traditions consist primarily of black religious and civic institutions that sustained familial and communal networks of support. If cultures are, in part, what human beings create (out of antecedent fragments of other cultures) in order to convince themselves not to commit suicide, then black foremothers and forefathers are to be applauded. In fact, until the early seventies black Americans had the lowest suicide rate in the United States. But now young black people lead the nation in suicides.

What has changed? What went wrong? The bitter irony of integration? The cumulative effects of a genocidal conspiracy? The virtual collapse of rising expectations after the optimistic sixties? None of us fully understands why the cultural structures that once sustained black life in America are no longer able to fend off the nihilistic threat. I believe that two significant reasons why the threat is more powerful now than ever before are the saturation of market forces and market moralities in black life and the present crisis in black leadership. The recent market-driven shattering of black civil society—black families, neighborhoods, schools, churches, mosques—leaves more and more black people vulnerable to daily lives endured with little sense of self and fragile existential moorings.

Black people have always been in America's wilderness in search of a promised land. Yet many black folk now reside in a jungle ruled by a cutthroat market morality devoid of any faith in deliverance or hope for freedom. Contrary to the superficial claims of conservative behaviorists, these jungles are not primarily the result of pathological behavior. Rather, this behavior is the tragic response of a people bereft of resources in confronting the workings of U.S. capitalist society. Saying this is not the same as asserting that individual black people are not responsible for their actions—black murderers and rapists should go to jail. But it must be recognized that the nihilistic threat contributes to criminal behavior. It is a threat that feeds on poverty and shattered cultural institutions and grows more powerful as the armors to ward against it are weakened.

But why is this shattering of black civil society occurring? What has led to the weakening of black cultural institutions in asphalt jungles? Corporate market institutions have contributed greatly to their collapse. By corporate market institutions I mean that complex set of interlocking enterprises that have a disproportionate amount of capital, power, and exercise a disproportionate influence on how our society is run and how our culture is shaped. Needless to say, the primary motivation of these institutions is to make profits, and their basic strategy is to convince the public to consume. These institutions have helped create a seductive way of life, a culture of consumption that capitalizes on every opportunity to make money. Market calculations and cost-benefit analyses hold sway in almost every sphere of U.S. society.

The common denominator of these calculations and analyses is usually the provision, expansion, and intensification of *pleasure*. Pleasure is a multivalent term; it means different things to many people. In the American way of life pleasure involves comfort, convenience, and sexual stimulation. Pleasure, so defined, has little to do with the past and views the future as no more than a repetition of a hedonistically driven present. This market morality stigmatizes others as objects for personal pleasure or bodily stimulation. Conservative behaviorists have alleged that traditional morality has been undermined by radical feminists and the cultural radicals of the sixties. But it is clear that corporate market institutions have greatly contributed to undermining traditional morality in order to stay in business and make a profit. The reduction of individuals to objects of pleasure is especially evident in the culture industries—television, radio, video, music—in which gestures of sexual foreplay and orgiastic pleasure flood the marketplace.

Like all Americans, African Americans are influenced greatly by the images of comfort, convenience, machismo, femininity, violence, and sexual stimulation that bombard consumers. These seductive images contribute to the predominance of the market-inspired way of life over all others and thereby edge out nonmarket values—love, care, service to others—handed down by preceding generations. The predominance of this way of life among those living in poverty-ridden conditions, with a limited capacity to ward off self-contempt and self-hatred, results in the possible triumph of the nihilistic threat in black America.

A major contemporary strategy for holding the nihilistic threat at bay is a direct attack on the sense of worthlessness and self-loathing in black America. This *angst* resembles a kind of collective clinical depression in significant pockets of black America. The eclipse of hope and collapse of meaning in much of black America is linked to the structural dynamics of corporate market institutions that affect all Americans. Under these circumstances black existential *angst* derives from the lived experience of ontological wounds and emotional scars inflicted by white supremacist beliefs and images permeating U.S. society and culture. These beliefs and images attack black intelligence, black ability, black beauty, and black character daily in subtle and not-so-subtle ways. Toni Morrison's novel, *The Bluest Eye*, for example, reveals the devastating effect of pervasive European ideals of beauty on the self-image of young black women. Morrison's exposure of the harmful extent to which these white ideals affect the black self-image is a first step toward rejecting these ideals and overcoming the nihilistic self-loathing they engender in blacks.

The accumulated effect of the black wounds and scars suffered in a white-dominated society is a deep-seated anger, a boiling sense of rage, and a passionate pessimism regarding America's will to justice. Under conditions of slavery and Jim Crow segregation, this anger, rage, and pessimism remained relatively muted because of a well-justified fear of brutal white retaliation. The major breakthroughs of the sixties—more psychically than politically—swept this fear away. Sadly, the combination of the market way of life, poverty-ridden conditions, black existential *angst,* and the lessening of fear of white authorities has directed most of the anger, rage, and despair toward fellow black citizens, especially toward black women who are the most vulnerable in our society and in black communities. Only recently has this nihilistic threat—and its ugly inhumane outlook and actions—surfaced in the larger American society. And its appearance surely reveals one of the many instances of cultural decay in a declining empire.

What is to be done about this nihilistic threat? Is there really any hope, given our shattered civil society, market-driven corporate enterprises, and white supremacism? If one begins with the threat of concrete nihilism, then one must talk about some kind of *politics of conversion.* New models of collective black leadership must promote a version of this politics. Like alcoholism and drug addiction, nihilism is a disease of the soul. It can never be completely cured, and there is always the possibility of relapse. But there is always a chance for conversion—a chance for people to believe that there is hope for the future and a meaning to struggle. This chance rests neither on an agreement about what justice consists of nor on an analysis of how racism, sexism, or class subordination operate. Such arguments and analyses are indispensable. But a politics of conversion requires more. Nihilism is not overcome by arguments or analyses; it is tamed by love and care. Any disease of the soul must be conquered by a turning of one's soul. This turning is done through one's own affirmation of one's worth—an affirmation fueled by the concern of others. A love ethic must be at the center of a politics of conversion.

A love ethic has nothing to do with sentimental feelings or tribal connections. Rather it is a last attempt at generating a sense of agency among a downtrodden people. The best exemplar of this love ethic is depicted on a number of levels in Toni Morrison's great novel *Beloved.* Self-love and love of others are both modes toward increasing self-valuation and encouraging political resistance in one's community. These modes of valuation and resistance are rooted in a subversive memory—the best of one's past without romantic nostalgia—and guided by a universal love ethic. For my purposes here, *Beloved* can be construed as bringing together the loving yet critical affirmation of black humanity found in the best of black nationalist movements, the perennial hope against hope for trans-racial coalition in progressive movements, and the painful struggle for self-affirming sanity in a history in which the nihilistic threat *seems* insurmountable.

The politics of conversion proceeds principally on the local level—in those institutions in civil society still vital enough to promote self-worth and self-affirmation. It surfaces on the state and national levels only when grassroots democratic organizations put forward a collective leadership that has earned the love and respect of and, most important, has proved itself *accountable* to these organizations. This collective leadership must exemplify moral integrity, character, and democratic statesmanship within itself and within its organizations.

Like liberal structuralists, the advocates of a politics of conversion never lose sight of the structural conditions that shape the sufferings and lives of people. Yet, unlike liberal structuralism, the politics of conversion meets the nihilistic threat head-on. Like conservative behaviorism, the politics of conversion openly confronts the self-destructive and inhumane actions of black people. Unlike conservative behaviorists, the politics of conversion situates these actions within inhumane circumstances (but does not thereby exonerate them). The politics of conversion shuns the limelight—a limelight that solicits status seekers and ingratiates egomaniacs. Instead, it stays on the ground among the toiling everyday people, ushering forth humble freedom fighters—both followers and leaders—who have the audacity to take the nihilistic threat by the neck and turn back its deadly assaults.

WHITE RESPONSES TO RACE AND RACISM

Andrew Hacker

This excerpt from Hacker's book Two Nations: Black and White, Separate, Hostile, Unequal, *published in 1992, was quoted or referred to by most of the reviewers who wrote about the book. It particularly caught their attention. Hacker is a political science professor who has written extensively about racial issues.*

Most white Americans will say that, all things considered, things aren't so bad for black people in the United States. Of course, they will grant that many problems remain. Still, whites feel there has been steady improvement, bringing blacks closer to parity, especially when compared with conditions in the past. Some have even been heard to muse that it's better to be black, since affirmative action policies make it a disadvantage to be white.

What white people seldom stop to ask is how they may benefit from belonging to their race. Nor is this surprising. People who can see do not regard their vision as a gift for which they should offer thanks. It may also be replied that having a white skin does not immunize a person from misfortune or failure. Yet even for those who fall to the bottom, being white has a worth. What could that value be?

Let us try to find out by means of a parable: suspend disbelief for a moment, and assume that what follows might actually happen:

THE VISIT

You will be visited tonight by an official you have never met. He begins by telling you that he is extremely embarrassed. The organization he represents has made a mistake, something that hardly ever happens.

From Andrew Hacker, *Two Nations: Black and White, Separate, Hostile, Unequal* (New York: Macmillan, 1992), pp. 31–32.

According to their records, he goes on, you were to have been born black: to another set of parents, far from where you were raised.

However, the rules being what they are, this error must be rectified, and as soon as possible. So at midnight tonight, you will become black. And this will mean not simply a darker skin, but the bodily and facial features associated with African ancestry. However, inside you will be the person you always were. Your knowledge and ideas will remain intact. But outwardly you will not be recognizable to anyone you now know.

Your visitor emphasizes that being born to the wrong parents was in no way your fault. Consequently, his organization is prepared to offer you some reasonable recompense. Would you, he asks, care to name a sum of money you might consider appropriate? He adds that his group is by no means poor. It can be quite generous when the circumstances warrant, as they seem to in your case. He finishes by saying that their records show you are scheduled to live another fifty years—as a black man or woman in America.

How much financial recompense would you request?

When this parable has been put to white students, most seemed to feel that it would not be out of place to ask for $50 million, or $1 million for each coming black year. And this calculation conveys, as well as anything, the value that white people place on their own skins. Indeed, to be white is to possess a gift whose value can be appreciated only after it has been taken away. And why ask so large a sum? Surely this needs no detailing. The money would be used, as best it could, to buy protections from the discriminations and dangers white people know they would face once they were perceived to be black.

HISPANIC RATE FOR DROPOUTS REMAINS HIGH

William Celis 3d

William Celis wrote this article in 1992. He attempts to give the reasons for the high dropout rate of Hispanic students.

Lydia Vera was only in the tenth grade when she dropped out of high school against the wishes of her unemployed father, who is a gardner, and her mother, a clerk in a grocery store. She began working at a fast-food restaurant for about $100 a week to help her parents.

"They didn't want me to drop out," said Ms. Vera, who is now 17 years and studying for her diploma in an independent study program in the Sweetwater, Calif., schools, which has started one of several recent efforts around the country to bring Hispanic dropouts back to school. "But I felt I needed to help them. I felt like the whole world was coming down on me because we were having a lot of economic problems."

New York Times, October 14, 1992, pp. A1, B8.

Recessions affect all families, but for Hispanic families a weak economy pushes more youngsters out of school, aggravating what educators call a problem of crisis proportions. In 1991, 35.3 percent of all Hispanics between the ages of 16 to 24 were high school dropouts, roughly the same percentage as in 1972, according to an annual high school completion survey issued last month by the United States Education Department.

By comparison, the rate for blacks in the same age group fell to 13.6 percent from 21.3 percent over the same time period. For whites, the rate for that age group declined to 8.9 percent from 12.3 percent.

"The scary thing is the gap is growing between Hispanics and blacks and whites," said Mary Jo Marion, a policy expert at the National of La Raza, an Hispanic policy organization based in Washington. "Part of the problem is economics, but that isn't the only problem."

Educators say the financial pressures combine with a culture that puts family first. Language barriers also contribute to the problem, as does the dearth of Hispanic teachers and counselors. Just 3 percent of all classroom teachers are Hispanic and the percentage of counselors is even smaller, leaving Hispanic students who have academic problems, and their parents, with few advocates they can comfortably confide in.

Students themselves assert school is unchallenging; some teachers agree, saying a preponderance of Hispanic students attend classes in poor school systems, which cannot afford the best teachers, up-to-date textbooks and technology.

The dropout rate among Hispanic students has improved during times of relative prosperity and has tended to spike upward in times of economic distress.

In 1991, Hispanic households earned an average of $22,691, according to the Census Bureau, compared with $30,126 for all households in the United States, prompting many young people to leave school to supplement their parents' wages.

DROPPING OUT TO WORK

"One of the major reasons our kids drop out is to get a job," said Robin Willner, executive director of strategic planning for the New York City public school system, the nation's largest with nearly one million students, 35 percent of them Hispanic.

Anthony J. Trujillo, the Superintendent of Schools for the Ysleta Independent School District in El Paso, said: "Hispanic culture has always valued education up to a point," but when a family's income is threatened by layoffs of one or both parents, "the youngster can become part of the earning power of the family. We've had problems with the other issues, but economics is the big problem."

Many of the same cultural and economic issues have been faced by blacks and, more recently, Asians. The dropout rate for black students, however, has been significantly reduced in large part by efforts by black community leaders and parents, who have pushed for more black teachers and counselors. There are more similarities between Asian and Hispanic people, both of whom face language barriers.

Although neither group is monolithic, American-born Asians tend to be better educated and tend to earn more money than United States–born Hispanic people—including Mexican-Americans, Puerto Ricans and Cuban-Americans, according to Federal income and census data, and thus are more likely to instill in their children the importance of education. Asian immigrants also tend to be better educated than Hispanic immigrants. And Asians have generally faced less discrimination than other minority groups, sociologists and anthropologists say, leaving their communities less scarred and giving Asian students a more stable family and community base.

While both groups tend to have strong family units, many Asian families also consider themselves to be members of a larger family, the community itself. As a result, Asian students tend to stay in school even when family finances are strained because to drop out brings dishonor not only to the immediate family but also to the community, say educators who work with both groups. They add that the notion of community as a sort of extended family is less common among Hispanic groups.

"What motivates the Latino to drop out of school to contribute to the general welfare of the family is love," said Dr. Robert Harrington, director of instructional services for the San Francisco Unified School District, where he has worked with both Hispanic and Asian students for 33 years. "What motivates the Asian to stay in school is also love for family. It's just a different view of the world by two different cultures."

And so schools in many places find themselves struggling with family finances and the Hispanic culture that sometimes combine to undermine students. Lydia Vera, the California student who left Sweetwater High School last year, is a case in point.

Now she is back in school, finishing her high school degree through an independent study program. The school has created eight learning centers, where up to 20 students come for two hours a day, which can be scheduled around jobs. The students work at their own pace to complete degree requirements.

The district has assigned many of its best teachers to the learning centers and installed the latest technology, and has given the centers virtually all of the $3,500 aid for each enrolled student that the district receives from the state.

"This is a great second chance for kids," said Patrick Judd, a teacher at the Del Ray High School learning center, where Ms. Vera attends school. "It's important that we provide them with an environment where they can be successful."

Other programs lean heavily on working to involve parents and to help solve family programs to keep students in school. In the Ysleta Independent School District, parents have been hired by the school system to help Spanish-speaking parents navigate school bureaucracies.

"These parents don't speak English, and they are afraid to come to school," said Rachel Gonzales, a 27-year-old who is the parent liaison at Cedar Grove Elementary School. "The language barrier hurts."

Mrs. Gonzales is part counselor, part social worker for Cedar Grove students and parents, many of whom live in substandard housing, often without telephones. She signed up one family for food stamps last year after a fifth-grade student complained about stomach pains from hunger. She persuaded a shoe store to donate new shoes for another young boy, who wore his older brother's hand-me-down shoes three sizes too large.

"I've seen progress," she said. "If I can help the children by getting the basic services their families need, the children will do better in school and will be less likely to drop out later on."

The Ysleta program has been adopted in some variation by the Los Angeles school system, which also has established special schools or classes to help at-risk students.

In Dade County, Fla., the Cuban American National Council with the Dade County Public Schools spent $20,000 to set up institutes in Little Havana and Hialeah, a Miami suburb, to pay special attention to students at risk of dropping out.

The school system absorbs the daily expenses for the institutes, each of which has about 100 students, with one teacher for every 17 to 25 students, far lower than the public schools in the area.

"There's no magic to what we're doing," said Javier Bray, coordinator of the institutes. "We give them support, and we nurture them in a loving, caring environment." The approach is paying off: for the first time since the school in Little Havana was founded five years ago, not one student dropped out last year.

2. What Causes Prejudice?

THE TALLEST FENCE: FEELINGS ON RACE IN A WHITE NEIGHBORHOOD

Isabel Wilkerson

Isabel Wilkerson wrote two articles, this and the next one, about two Chicago working-class neighborhoods that are two miles apart. One is black, and the other is white. She interviewed many of the residents and concludes that the two neighborhoods represent a society of two nations where the issue of race is always present but rarely spoken of. These articles were published in 1992.

CHICAGO, June 20—In a kind of simulcast version of blue-collar America, the mechanics and postal workers of Chicago's Mount Greenwood and Roseland sections emerge each weekend to start the sprinklers and trim the junipers outside prim houses with picture windows.

New York Times, June 21, 1992, p. A12.

The two are churchgoing, workaday neighborhoods made up of people who put in overtime to pay the bills, who curse drugs and dandelions with equal indignation and who dream of a better life and maybe even college for their children.

The chief difference between the two is that Mount Greenwood is white and Roseland is black. They are separated by two miles, a highway and fear and suspicion so deep that many people in one community would not dare set foot in the other.

Their worlds are set up so that the races rarely intersect, coming together only briefly in the white sections of town at public places like the mall or at work, where people may know little about each other beyond names and job descriptions.

"It's fine for them to live in their neighborhoods and us to live in ours," said Peggy O'Connor, a Mount Greenwood waitress. "I guess that's the way it's supposed to be. We don't need to mix."

"Blacks live in their section and we live in ours, and that's okay," said Elaine Pomper, who owns Bob's Service, an automobile repair shop in Mount Greenwood.

The races are left to see each other through the distorted lens of segregation, and the perspective is further warped by the competition for a shrinking supply of blue-collar jobs. Particularly for whites, it seems, what they learn about the other race often comes from television news or stereotypes passed down through the generations.

In many ways, social scientists say, the two neighborhoods represent a society that is still two nations in one, 24 years after the Kerner Commission first made its diagnosis, and as dramatized this spring by the Los Angeles riots.

"This is a country in perpetual civil war," said Andrew Hacker, a professor of political science at Queens College and author of *Two Nations* (Macmillan, 1992). "Whites are saying: 'Look at what we did for you. You let the team down.' It is as if black Americans are on probation and have to prove themselves. Blacks are saying, 'Don't expect us to be grateful just because we can sit on the bus with you.' "

More than 100 residents in these two South Side communities, interviewed by reporters of their own race, bore out this scenario, forming a picture of divided worlds where race and discrimination are defining facts of daily life for blacks and somebody else's problem for whites.

As similar as the two neighborhoods seem, their differences are telling. The gap in their median household incomes widened significantly in the 1980's. Essentially a working-class area, Roseland embraces a much greater range of incomes, including real poverty. One insurer estimates that the same policy for the same car, a 1990 Ford Taurus, would cost $1,445 a year in Roseland but $958 in Mount Greenwood, presumably because the crime rate is so much higher in Roseland.

Mount Greenwood is an insular, Leave-It-to-Beaver world where white people can live out entire lives without ever getting to know a black person, where people rarely venture beyond understood borders.

Roseland is hardscrabble and rough-edged, made up of black home-owners who watched their dreams of integration evaporate in the 1970's as white neighbors moved out to places like Mount Greenwood.

The very mention of race unlocked a torrent of painful accounts from blacks in Roseland, who told of lifelong attacks and indignities and who said they felt discrimination was in some ways worse now than it was 20 years ago.

"Wherever you go you see hatred," said Clemmie Raggs, a forklift operator who lives in Roseland. "You never know where racism is going to stick its head up."

"The institutions, the media, the politicians—the whole system keeps the races divided," said Robert Scott, a Roseland resident who is a sewer maintenance worker. "We got the opportunity to move out to white areas, but they don't want us there."

Despite frequent negative experiences with whites, most Roseland residents said they would still welcome a person of the other race into their home and would like to live in an integrated neighborhood.

The same questions drew either blank looks or impassioned diatribes about welfare and affirmative action from most whites in Mount Greenwood. Many said they would not want a black to live next door. And while many described the few blacks they knew from work as decent, they still harbored an almost instinctive animosity toward black people in general.

Some Mount Greenwood residents were at first visibly uncomfortable with the topic of race. Some declined to discuss the matter.

Their reaction suggests an even greater schism, social scientists say. "Being white in America means never having to think about it," said Joe R. Feagin, a professor of sociology at the University of Florida, who has written extensively on race relations. "The racist world is the real world for us. It's the dominant culture, the way we look at things. For blacks, whiteness is oppression."

The 1980's were much kinder to Mount Greenwood than to Roseland. The two started the decade at about the same place, with Mount Greenwood's median household income then at $21,996 and Roseland's at $18,540.

But as manufacturing jobs waned nationwide and service jobs predominated, Mount Greenwood profited. Its median income nearly doubled to $40,226 in 1990, according to Census Bureau figures. Roseland's rose at about half that rate to $28,601. When inflation is taken into account, Roseland's families were in effect making $2,700 less a year in 1990 than they were in 1980. Mount Greenwood's families were making $5,097 more.

Black people are hurt and resentful over these disparities. "Go into any white neighborhood, and you'll see businesses and parks and playgrounds with swings in different colors," said Myshawn Davis, a hairdresser in Roseland. "It's like Disneyland."

The differences can perhaps best be seen along 111th Street, the commercial strip that runs through both communities, changing personality as it goes. It is gritty and weather-beaten in Roseland, one liquor store and rib shack after another. It is fresh-scrubbed in Mount Greenwood with its appliance centers, denture clinics, drapery stores and taverns with names like Molly McGillicuddy's. [. . .]

It is places like Roseland that Mount Greenwood residents ran from in the 1960's. They have little patience for talk of discrimination. And many say it is fine by them if there are no blacks around.

"I don't mind them, but I don't want them living next to me," said Peggy O'Connor, a waitress and wife of a police officer. "I don't want to be too close to them. I think they've been whining too long, and I'm sick of it."

Like other Mount Greenwood residents, Mrs. O'Connor is rarely around black people to hear the "whining" personally or to see what the trouble might be. It infuriates her that "blacks buy porterhouse steaks with food stamps, while we eat hamburgers," she said. She said she has never actually seen any blacks do this. But she has heard and read stories, and that is enough.

Stories like that take on mythical proportions in a place like Mount Greenwood. Here there is great pride in the legends of forebears who came over from the old country.

"My grandparents, when they came here from Italy, didn't ask anyone to speak Italian for them," said Adeline Barrins, a homemaker who runs a small T-shirt business in Mount Greenwood. "They became American, and they never asked for anything."

Most whites said they saw nothing stopping blacks from doing the same thing. "They feel they worked hard for what they got," said Robert T. Carter, an associate professor of psychology at Columbia University Teachers College, who specializes in the study of white racial attitudes. "It's a disguised way of saying that blacks are not worthy."

Slavery, a painful topic for blacks, is a sensitive area in Mount Greenwood too. It comes up in conversation often as whites say that past and even current discrimination is irrelevant. "It's up to them to paddle their own canoe," said Catherine Nielsen, a long-time resident. "Don't always think about the fact that they were slaves."

The racial fear and suspicion work both ways. But the paradox, interviews show, is that black people were fearful because much of their contact with white people was negative; whites were fearful because they had little or no contact. Across this divide, stereotypes become reality.

"It's either a stabbing or a shooting," Bernadette Quinn, a hardware store clerk in Mount Greenwood, said of blacks. "Those people don't talk to each other."

ASSUMPTIONS WITHOUT EXPERIENCE

She has never spent much time around black people to know whether this is true. But she is as convinced of this as she is that the perennials will bloom next spring. The few blacks she knows are "lovely people," she said. But she is skeptical about the rest.

That is why she would not want to live next to any. "I'd be afraid they wouldn't keep up the property," she said. "Who's to say they wouldn't rob you, or what kind of people they'd bring around?"

The disadvantages for blacks of isolation and discrimination are well documented. What is less talked about, social scientists say, is the psychic toll that segregation can take on whites. "Whites have to use a tremendous amount of energy to maintain the distortion," Professor Carter said. "Time, energy and money are devoted to creating safe environments away from black people."

When blacks appear where they are not expected, it takes some whites here time to adjust. Several years ago, Mrs. Quinn's teenage son had a party and invited a black girl.

"She was a lovely girl when we met her," Mrs. Quinn said. "But our first impression was, 'What is she doing in our house?' We were shocked. Our son said, 'Don't worry, she's a nice girl.' And she was. She is a lovely girl. She has been back a couple times now."

But those positive feelings do not transfer to black people in general. Each time she meets a black person, she must be convinced all over again that this one is O.K.

"Where I work, we have some black people that shop there," Mrs. Quinn said. "I'm very apprehensive about it. But once you get to know them, they're very nice."

In many ways, William Knepper Jr. is the opposite of what the Rev. Dr. Martin Luther King Jr. had in mind in his "I Have a Dream" message. Mr. Knepper, a 23-year-old auto mechanic, is the product of an all-white world. His parochial school was white, his block is white, his friends are white. And television is his window to the other America.

All he knows about blacks, he said, is this: "They came from Africa, and they can get away with a lot of stuff because they're black, they're a minority."

Sometimes he has to drive to black neighborhoods to get auto parts for his job. When he does, he takes a baseball bat. His few direct contacts with blacks are mostly benign, and on his turf. "The one time I ever come in contact with them is in stores, and they seem all right," Mr. Knepper said.

He is aware that being white has its benefits. "I think we still have the upper hand," Mr. Knepper said. "If I was running a business and two qualified people apply for a job, one black and one white, I would probably go with the white guy. I'd feel safer."

To Mr. Knepper, that is the way the world should be. And attitudes like his are no excuse for blacks not to try. "We have the upper hand but they can go out and get a job," he said.

Mr. Knepper is not exactly against affirmative action: "You only need a certain percentage of them in jobs, and as long as you get that percentage, the rest can be white."

Mr. Knepper's father, William Sr., an eighth-grade teacher at St. Christina's, said he never had a bad experience with blacks, and feels sympathetic toward them. "From my experience with them, they're like us," the elder

Mr. Knepper said. "They have the same goals, the same aspirations, the same fears. When they blame something on racism, I tend to agree with them."

In raising his three children, he said he "never pushed race one way or the other." He said he let them form their own opinions of blacks, that he tried to correct his son when he could. "Any time he said something about race, I told him, 'You don't really know,' " Mr. Knepper said.

Most people said they had never had a friend of the other race.

Among the few who did, whites usually had a broader definition of "friend." Some were quick to say that blacks they met at work or in service roles were their friends. Some police officers called the blacks whose neighborhoods they patrol their friends. But they said they rarely, if ever, did the things that friends do, like having them over for dinner.

Blacks were more cynical. While white co-workers called them friends, blacks said they felt more like mascots than intimates. "On the job they will laugh and joke with you," said Sebron Jones, a postal worker who lives in Roseland. "When they get off work, they're through with you."

He remembers once seeing a white co-worker at a bus stop and walking over to say hello. The co-worker turned his back and refused to answer him, apparently afraid of what people would think. Another white co-worker told Mr. Jones that he wanted to invite him to his house but was worried about the neighbors.

"I told him, 'If I want to invite you to my house, I wouldn't give a dog-gone what the neighbors think,' " Mr. Jones said.

Neither relationship survived. And Mr. Jones is doubtful whether blacks and whites can ever be friends. "There's never been one I could trust," he said.

A FAMILY RADICAL

The few whites in Mount Greenwood who made friends across the color line became suddenly aware of the anti-black sentiment.

Mary Knepper, who works at a Kentucky Fried Chicken and is young William Knepper's sister, is considered a radical in her family. She made friends with a black girl at a public high school she attended. Some neighborhood children once yelled epithets at them as the two walked down a Mount Greenwood street. Since then, Ms. Knepper has been protective. "I worry about her when she comes over," Ms. Knepper said. "If she's coming over on the bus, and she's late, I go out and start looking for her."

What happens in places like Roseland and Mount Greenwood has resonance for the rest of the country, social scientists say. "Racial tension and hostility show up first and more intensely in the working class because this group is in the immediate line of fire," said William Julius Wilson, a professor of sociology at the University of Chicago and author of *The Truly Disadvantaged* (University of Chicago Press, 1987).

"Not enough attention is given to black and white working-class folks," he said. "If you could get these groups to recognize their common interests, it would go a long way toward alleviating racial hostility."

The elder Mr. Knepper wonders if that would ever happen. He figures that even if white hostility toward blacks ended tomorrow, "we'd still find someone to hate."

BLACK NEIGHBORHOOD FACES WHITE WORLD WITH BITTERNESS

Isabel Wilkerson

The second of Wilkerson's articles is about a black neighborhood in Chicago. She compares it to the nearby white neighborhood described in the preceding article. Both were published in 1992.

CHICAGO, June 21—Twenty years ago, black hopes and white fears were on a collision course in picket-fenced neighborhoods around the nation as blacks pursued the dream of integration and whites ran from it. What resulted were places like Mount Greenwood and Roseland, two working-class neighborhoods in Chicago two miles apart, one now as black as the other is white.

Sebron and Marian (Mother) Jones did not want it this way. For them, Roseland represented a ticket out of the ghetto, and a yard of their own. They were one of the first black families on their block and could not wait to plant the irises and invite company over to see the neighborhood.

"It was trees meeting trees," Mrs. Jones remembers wistfully.

INTEGRATION TO SEGREGATION

But in the end, integration meant watching white neighbors move out as fast as they could and services and businesses go with them. Twenty years later, without even moving, the Joneses are in a virtually all-black community again, back on the other side of the wall between the races now symbolized by the Los Angeles riot.

The white evacuation was so rapid that it left huge gaps in the neighborhood that have never been filled. Houses stayed vacant or were rented at rock-bottom prices set by absentee landlords. Department stores left and drug dealers moved in. Never seeming to get the money or attention they needed, the library, the schools, the parks went downhill.

Now the Joneses can hear gunshots from their dinner table and have seen drugs being sold next door. "You could sit in your kitchen and watch them selling drugs outside that back window," Mrs. Jones said. "They would look you due in the eye and keep stepping. It hurts your heart to pieces."

In many ways, people in Roseland and Mount Greenwood lead similar lives: blue-collar, bowling-on-Saturday, church-on-Sunday lives, passing each other only on street corners or in the produce line.

But it is Roseland residents who pay a high price for this segregation. They are rejected for mortgages at three times the rate of Mount Greenwood residents of the same income. They pay as much as twice the automobile insurance rates that people in Mount Greenwood do. They have to travel several miles, usually to white areas, to buy fresh meat and vegetables because there are no major grocery stores for Roseland's 56,000 people, while Mount Greenwood's 19,000 residents have two.

It is disparities like these that lead many in Roseland to regard whites with bitterness and distrust.

Even when the numbers look even, things still work against Roseland. The Chicago police assign the same number of officers to both communities. But because crime is so much higher in Roseland, Mount Greenwood gets more than twice as much protection—118 patrols per 1,000 crimes—than Roseland whose patrols number 51 per 1,000 crimes, a study by the University of Illinois found.

Many whites in Mount Greenwood say that blacks in Roseland could pull themselves up if they wanted to. They point with pride to the new branch library that opened in Mount Greenwood a year ago with the support of powerful officials in the state capital and City Hall to finance it.

People in Roseland say they do not have those connections. Both branches belong to the Chicago Public Library system. While Mount Greenwood's library has private typewriting booths and compact discs to borrow, there is not even toilet paper in the restrooms or doors on the stalls of Roseland's library.

Every week, Roseland residents come in asking if the branch has computers or typewriters or videotapes to borrow like other libraries. The answer is always no.

"The reason they're coming to us is because they don't have them at home," said Melnee Simmons, the head librarian there.

For the past year, half the shelves at Roseland's library have been empty. Books have been packed away in anticipation of a promised renovation that for 15 years was supposed to happen any minute. Now there is talk that it might really happen this summer. Mrs. Simmons has been telling staff members to believe it when they see it.

Most blacks in Roseland do not have a lot of formal education but feel they have earned graduate degrees in race relations.

For them, race is a daily topic of conversation. What whites do and think and want is a life obsession and a matter of survival. Most of them have to work for whites, shop with whites and venture into white neighborhoods for services they cannot get at home.

They say they confront the stereotypes that Mount Greenwood residents seem to live by every time they step over the wall. They say they have come to expect a negative reaction, but they never get used to it. No matter how many times they are called a name or stopped by the police, one resident said, "It's like a bomb drops inside of you."

Elsie Melvin, a registered nurse, said she has had white patients who have refused to let her touch them. "They don't care how sick they are," she said. "They'll say, 'I don't want any colored nurse working on me.' "

Christopher Jones, a bus driver who is not related to Sebron and Marian Jones, said white passengers have spit on him on his bus route through white neighborhoods. As a child, whites chased him out of their neighborhood as he rode his bicycle.

Now when he and his wife, Regina, have to drive through white neighborhoods, they make sure they have a full tank of gas and enough air in the tires. "We look at it as if we're going to another state," Mrs. Jones said.

A few years ago, Jeannette Raggs, a postal worker, and her husband, Clemmie, were invited a few years ago to the wedding reception of one white co-worker. They walked in to see that the party was all white.

"The music stopped playing, everyone turned to look at us," Mr. Raggs said. Then the father of the bride greeted them from across the room.

"'What youse people want?'" Mr. Raggs recalled the man shouting. "Then the bride came up and said she had invited us, that she worked with my wife. Only then did that ugly, hatred look leave his face."

As hard as Roseland residents work to keep the irises blooming, this is still a neighborhood defined in part by what it used to be.

Up and down Michigan Avenue and across 111th Street in Roseland, there are the ghosts of a once white neighborhood—the Rose Bowl bowling alley, the old Gately's department store, the empty theater plastered with posters of missing children, the old flower shops and hardware stores that now sell wigs and Stroh's beer.

"This strip was booming, a gold mine," said Willie Lomax, executive director of a community group. "There were shoe repair shops, fabric stores, five hardware stores. We had restaurants with valet parking and A-1 service. Those were the days."

A few blocks away, young men sit out on porch steps with nothing to do. The occasional spit-shiny Cadillac, trimmed in gold, cruises down the street. Drug dealers, the homeowners say under their breath, cursing them as they pass.

The fathers and grandfathers of many of these young men were the meatpackers and steelworkers who came to Roseland to be near the plants and make a better life for their families. Now the plants are gone and so are the jobs.

Just outside Roseland's borders, halfway between Roseland and Mount Greenwood, is the steel plant graveyard.

Next to it sits a parking lot as long as an airport landing strip, now overrun by bushes and weeds. "All this was employees," Mr. Lomax said. "Three shifts."

Across the street are some concrete beams and rubble surrounded by grassland. "You're looking at Dutch Boy paint factory," Mr. Lomax said. "The young men you see hanging out on the corner weren't even born when this closed."

That has left residents like 28-year-old Darryl Gibson at the economic margins. It used to take him two and a half hours on the bus to get to his last job earning $6 an hour as a forklift operator. He was laid off last August and has not found another job since. His family lives off his wife Linda's salary as a sales clerk.

"It's hard when you have a wife and family, and you want to do right, but don't have much education," Mr. Gibson said. "Everyone can't be a doctor or a lawyer. Everyone is not going to finish college. Everyone doesn't have connections. There should be something out there for people like us."

While many whites in Mount Greenwood look at race with detachment and broad-brush stereotypes, most blacks in Roseland see it is a very personal matter. They are convinced that whites neither know them nor care to.

Their attitudes are shaped by vivid, demoralizing encounters with whites from childhood to the present. For some, the wounds are so deep that seemingly harmless incidents can take on major significance.

Mr. Raggs once stood silently for several moments after a white cashier put his nickels and quarters on the counter. A line formed behind him. The cashier, flustered, asked what was wrong. "You give me my money in my hand like I gave it to you," Mr. Raggs said.

Whites in Mount Greenwood see that kind of reaction as hypersensitivity. They say that something like that could happen to anybody. Blacks in Roseland can see such an incident as a final straw after a lifetime of indignities and one chance where they can demand the respect they may not get elsewhere.

"They can't even imagine what it's like to be black," said Myshawn Davis, a 25-year-old hairdresser who was chased off the school bus growing up in an all-white suburb. "They don't know what we go through. You try not to let this stuff drive you crazy. You'd be trying to kill every white person in the world."

While the great-grandparents of people in Mount Greenwood were learning the ways of America and starting small businesses in Irish and Italian ghettos, the great-grandparents of people in Roseland were earning pennies as sharecroppers in Mississippi or scrubbing white people's floors in Chicago.

And so blacks in Roseland say they do not want to hear about bootstraps and the work ethic. "Their fathers and grandfathers came of their own free will," Sebron Jones said. "Even if they didn't own slaves themselves, they didn't work for free," Mr. Jones said. "They got paid all those years we didn't."

There is quiet pain in the voice of his wife, Marian, as she remembers being 11 years old and going to do housework for a white woman. At about noon, the woman ordered her to stop washing the dishes.

"She made me go down into the dark basement," Mrs. Jones said. "Her husband had come home for lunch, and he didn't want any blacks in his house. I had to sit on the stairway and not move until he finished eating. When he was gone, she let me back up, and I went back to washing the dishes."

It has been more than 50 years, and she says she can still see the steps. "It gave me low self-esteem," she said. "I'm just now coming out of it."

3. What Should Be Done to Solve Racial Problems?

THE DIVERSITY INDUSTRY

Heather MacDonald

Heather MacDonald, a writer who lives in New York, wrote this essay for The New Republic *in 1993. This is an example of an objective essay with a "hidden" argumentative intent. How would you describe the author's attitude toward her subject? What is your evidence?*

Affirmative action has spawned a multimillion-dollar business: "diversity management." In recent years hundreds of small firms and large corporations have hired "diversity" consultants to ease racial tensions and improve the "diversity profile" of their businesses. Through "diversity awareness" and "valuing differences" training, these consultants purport to teach firms how to "manage" employees hired under affirmative action programs, whose high attrition and low promotion rates have occasioned much hand-wringing in corporate boardrooms.

Supporters of the diversity industry have a simple explanation for the problems of minority retention and advancement: racism. Never mind the business world's widespread acceptance of affirmative action programs: affirmative action itself, it turns out, embodies racist assumptions. Bringing minorities into companies and training them to fit into the "value system of WASPs" merely puts them "at a disadvantage and sets them up to fail," explains Donna Gillotte, a diversity consultant based in Westport, Connecticut, whose clients have included General Foods, Avon and Pepsi. According to diversity boosters like Gillotte, it isn't the new minority employees who need training—it's the managers. And what managers need to be trained to do is "value differences."

The concept of "valuing differences" is the cornerstone of the managing diversity movement. It translates questions of competence into questions of culture. Proponents argue that "non-traditional" workers who fail to advance are not underqualified, just "differently" qualified. Ethnic, racial and sexual groups, the reasoning goes, each possess a unique management style that will enable businesses to succeed in the global marketplace. White male managers, how-

The New Republic, July 5, 1993, pp. 22–25.

ever, label such different cultural styles "as negative or resistant behavior, for lack of a more accurate explanation," says Tom Nelson, vice president of education and training at U.S. Bancorp in Portland, Oregon. To tap their employees' valuable differences firms therefore must first abandon "white male" management practices and renounce their ethic of conformity and assimilation.

Diversity management is flourishing at the highest reaches of American business. American Airlines, Coca-Cola, Goodyear and Procter & Gamble, among others, are all engaged in one form or another. Indeed, *The New York Times* (which has itself gone to great lengths to diversify) reports that 40 percent of American companies have instituted some form of diversity training, a number that grows each year. Barbara R. Deane, editor of the industry newsletter *Cultural Diversity at Work*, estimates that approximately half of the Fortune 500 companies have "someone with some responsibility" for diversity. Diversity conferences are held weekly across the country, attracting hundreds of managers from business and government. The top business schools have added diversity programs.

Diversity consultants don't come cheap. Fees average $2,000 a day; the most sought-after consultants can fetch four to five times that amount. Diversity guru R. Roosevelt Thomas Jr. of the American Institute for Managing Diversity in Atlanta reportedly nets $8,000 a day; according to Deborah Raupp of UCLA, some trainers charge $10,000 a day. Many consultants won't even talk to a company unless it agrees to a long-term relationship. The stunningly successful Elsie Cross Associates, for example, whose clients include Eastman Kodak, American Express, G.E. Silicones, Corning Glass and Ortho Pharmaceutical, requires a five-year commitment from companies—at a total cost of more than $2.5 million.

Not surprisingly, the field is growing rapidly. "Many consultants are wiping the dust off their old [Equal Employment Opportunity Commission compliance] presentations and rushing to the marketplace with 'diversity' programs," said one respondent in a recent poll conducted by *Cultural Diversity at Work*. (Participants in the poll, titled "Diversity and Cross-Cultural Trainers: Do They Know What They're Doing?" concluded that 50 percent didn't.) Traditional business consulting firms, such as the international Towers Perrin, are adding "diversity" specializations; others, such as Diversitas, Inc. of New York City, are springing up specifically to capitalize on the demand for diversity training. "'Diversity' is the buzzword paying the rent of countless consultants," says Burke Stinson, a spokesman for AT&T, which has an active diversity program.

For the money, diversity consultants promise corporations that they will increase their profits by "empowering their whole work force," in the words of Kim Cromwell, corporate diversity programs manager at the Digital Equipment Corporation. But before a company can "fully utilize its diverse population," says Cromwell, it must remove existing obstacles to minority empowerment. By universal agreement among diversity advocates, the most important step a company can take to eliminate those obstacles is to commission a "culture audit." It is also one of the most expensive. According to Geoffrey Atkins, president of Diversitas, an audit can run from $30,000 to $100,000.

Through employee interviews and surveys, the auditor determines which of the firm's "cultural roots" are blocking the progress of its "non-traditional" employees, to use diversity jargon. One such cultural root that particularly offends diversity adherents is the widespread notion that "fairness equals treating people the same." Managing diversity proposes instead that "fairness equals treating people appropriately"—in other words, different standards for different groups. According to Ann Morrison, a leading diversity booster and director of the Center for Creative Leadership in La Jolla, California, minorities and whites cannot be evaluated under the same criteria, because minorities face a host of barriers from which whites are freed:

> Some executives have concluded that if non-traditional managers have more difficulty in performing an assignment, it must be because they are not as capable as their white male counterparts. But . . . the "same" assignment given to a white male manager and a non-traditional manager is hardly the same at all.

Reliance on traditional job qualifications is also a suspect "cultural root." "'Qualifications' is a code word in the business world with very negative connotations," explains Andrea Cisco of Towers Perrin. If minorities do not meet existing employment criteria, then "corporations need to expand the definition of qualifications," says Alan Richter, creator of the board game called "Diversity Game," which is intended to educate managers about cultural differences. Adds Morrison: "The weight placed on math, science and engineering credentials may be considerably biased." Diversity consultants argue that expectations of literacy should be challenged as well. "We haven't started to ask what are expendable requirements, such as the two-page memo or a certain writing style," complains Thomas.

After the audit uncovers a company's "institutional racism," the next step toward managing diversity is eliminating these prejudices through "diversity awareness" or "valuing differences" training. Typically, a company will pack off its entire white-collar work force to multiday training sessions conducted either by its in-house diversity officers or by outside consultants. The sessions are billed by trainers as a "safe place" for employees to confront their racism. [. . .]

Diversity trainers use a variety of gimmicks to uncover prejudice. Trainees draw pictures, participate in role-playing exercises and interpret Rorschach-like images. In her training sessions, West Coast consultant LueRachelle Brim-Donahoe tapes five posters to a wall, each of which describes a cultural archetype, such as "light-complexioned black female factory line supervisor with GED" and "white homeless drug-addicted father living in a car with two small children." Trainees are instructed to sit under the poster and describe the person they would most like to be. Their choices, claims Brim-Donahoe, reveal the chooser's preconceived notions about various subgroups in society.

To drive their point home, diversity trainers sometimes make an example of one of the trainees: writing in the conservative political journal *Heterodoxy*, K. L. Billingsley describes a "sensitivity" session at the University of Cincinnati in which consultant Edwin J. Nichols ordered a female academic to stand up in front of her colleagues as an example of "the privileged white elite." Later in the session, he asked her to stand again. "We all know who the most beautiful woman in the room is," he said. "It's the woman with the three private [school] degrees and the blond hair and the blue eyes. Let's have her stand up so everybody can look at her. Look at the pearls she's wearing, her clothes, her shoes." This time the woman remained in her seat, sobbing.

Diversity trainers operate on the assumption that simulating narrow-mindedness proves the existence of the real thing. Consultant George Arteaga warms up his groups with the invitation: "Let's talk stereotypes." Participants dutifully furnish stereotypes of the Anglo-Saxon male, Jews, Asians, blacks and Hispanics. Participants in Elsie Cross Associates workshops prepare a skit containing examples of office racism and sexism. The trainer then divides the group into distinct "cultures" and encourages them to denounce each other. At a recent diversity conference for businesses in New York City, consultant Nancy R. Hamlin asked the audience to guess her marital status, the number and ages of her children, if any, the type and color of her car, her hobbies, her ethnicity and her religion. Though all of the answers were wrong, Hamlin informed the audience that it had just engaged in "stereotyping."

Of course, one five-day stretch of diversity awareness training alone is rarely enough to overcome employees' prejudices. The Digital Equipment Corporation has "empowered" a set of thirty to sixty employee "core groups" that meet on a monthly basis with a company facilitator to "break down stereotypes about difference," according to Cromwell. Many firms establish "diversity councils" to ensure that company policies meet diversity standards and to set "strategic diversity goals"—i.e., hiring and promotion quotas. Thomas recommends a five-year plan for managing diversity that calls for seven "reeducation" programs, three "planning initiatives" and the appointment of four task forces and subcommittees.

The mandate that ultimately emerges from diversity training is contradictory. On one hand, managers learn that they must judge individual behavior as an expression of racial, sexual and cultural difference; on the other, they are told that they must not "base their behavior on how they think members of a particular cultural group will react." If this is too confusing, here is a simpler rule of thumb: it's fine to stereotype, as long as the stereotypes are of the right sort. According to Terry West, corporate media relations manager at Texas Instruments, minorities are "more nimble, entrepreneurial and innovative." Cle Jackson, former director of human services at Wang Laboratories, says that "blacks and Hispanics approach situations in a 'man-to-man' or 'feeling, caring' manner, whereas white males function primarily on a 'man-to-object' style based on power." Other "diversity approved" stereotypes are uncomfortably close, if not identical, to common sexism and bigotry. Shaunna Sowell, the environmental operations manager at Texas Instruments, enthuses that "women communicate to build relationships and understand the problem; men, to build power and authority within a hierarchy and to arrive at an immediate solution." Morrison reports approvingly a trainer's comment that blacks "react quickly to changing situations . . . as evidence[d] [by] the so-called black style of 'hot dogging' in playing basketball or running a football." [. . .]

Despite the grand rhetoric of its advocates, there is little evidence that diversity management can solve the problems it purports to address. In fact, it may make them worse. As diversity programs proliferate across corporate America, group infighting has become a problem second only to "backlash" by white men. "More and more groups are going at each other," says Morrison. "The women's group vies with the black group for promotions."

Nor will converting the workplace into an arena for the practice of identity politics do much to improve competitiveness or help minorities advance in the business world, where a deficit of business skills, not a proliferation of racism, is the overwhelming reason many minorities fail to advance. Diversity managers address this gap by making race and ethnicity qualifications in their own right. But the resources spent maintaining the fiction of equal preparedness would be better used to assist minorities lacking the business skills to compete on merit alone.

Indeed, diversity adherents acknowledge that they are unable to document the advantages of diversity training or even describe what managing-diversity heaven would look like. Though Thomas, for example, presents himself as a hardheaded businessman, he admits that "it is difficult to talk about how [diversity management] plays out in operation." He suggests that it entails "mindset shifts," and offers a clarifying analogy: "If you have a jar of red jelly beans and add some pink and green ones, diversity is not the pink and green beans, but the resulting mixture."

The preferred solution to the problems of measurement and description is to declare them irrelevant and proceed on faith alone. "One of the problems corporations have with diversity is that they like things in boxes," says Gillotte. This, she says, reflects a misunderstanding of the nature of diversity management. It "is not a program," she explains, "but an evolutionary process that is very difficult to be specific about. It is not about getting from point A to point B."

In fact, one never *does* get to "point B." Gillotte says that "you need to work five or ten years before you can say you're into the diversity process. It never ends." And at two grand a day, there's no reason to think it will.

A CULTURAL DIVERSITY COURSE REQUIREMENT

Michael Winerip

Michael Winerip wrote this essay about faculty and student attitudes towards diversity classes in a special education section of the New York Times.

It has taken years of work for professors to put into place a cultural diversity course requirement for University of Massachusetts/Boston students.

"The Diversity Subcommittee of the Academic Affairs Committee is re-

New York Times, May 4, 1994, p. A13.

sponsible for approving whether courses meet cultural diversity content standards," said Prof. Estelle Disch, the college's coordinator for diversity awareness.

Beginning with the class of '96, students in the College of Arts and Sciences must take at least two courses that have been approved as meeting the cultural diversity guidelines.

"If a professor submits a course for approval that deals with gender one week and social class another, but these issues are not infused, we'd have to say no," said Professor Disch. "We'd want the issues of diversity addressed every week."

The diversity push began in 1989 when several professors formed the Diversity Awareness Working Group and held 20 Diversity Awareness Workshops. There was much debate on how strict diversity guidelines should be. "Some of us wanted a central committee to certify which teachers were qualified to teach cultural diversity," said Professor Disch. "Totally nixed."

There was a proposal that all certified diversity courses would have to deal with seven formally identified diversity areas: race, class, sex, age, sexual orientation, physical ability and culture. "That was nixed, too," said Professor Disch.

"We were constantly amazed at the number of meetings we had to attend in order to get the diversity requirement passed," she said. "The usual governance meetings were the tip of the iceberg. Lobbying individual faculty members over long lunches or phone calls became a way of life."

Supporters got a boost from the Ford Foundation, which gave $150,000 to train faculty to teach these issues.

Some professors still resisted, including Peter Ittig, a business teacher who called the requirement "part of the political correctness party line." But the Diversity Awareness Working Group's advance work paid off. The requirement passed faculty and university governing bodies and took effect in the fall of '92.

And the reaction on campus today? "Doesn't seem to come up," concedes Professor Ittig.

While the cultural diversity/political correctness debate is usually written about in the context of flare-ups at elite schools, that is probably not typical. About a quarter of all colleges now have diversity requirements, according to the American Council on Education. UMass/Boston, a working-class, commuter university with 29 percent minority enrollment may be more typical. Here most students work to put themselves through college. Students take a practical view of education.

"This diversity thing is good," said Tim Weineck, a white junior. "You need it to function. You at least have to know where they're coming from, their mindset so you don't insult—whatever. Here it's in your face; you have to deal with it."

"I came from white-bread America," said Dennis Gilson, who works for the City of Boston. "My boss is an African-American woman. I'm conservative, but I believe these courses are great. Out in the work area, if you can't get along, you won't do well."

Esther Kingston-Mann, a history professor who teaches one of the 80 approved diversity courses in the College of Arts and Sciences, says the requirement makes for better teachers. "When I was in college we used this textbook, 'The History of the Modern World,' and it was really a history of Europe," she recalls.

She teaches modern world history, and says it took four years to teach herself the material she needed to incorporate Africa, Asia and South America into the course. "I feel it's dishonest to teach a modern world history course that's only about Europe," she says. "I don't want to do it. I don't think it has anything to do with political correctness to say you want a more complete, accurate view of the world."

The professors say they are constantly amazed by how differently their students see the world. The other day in Peter Kiang's "Asian Minorities in America" class, the topic was media stereotypes, and Danielle Ngo, who was born in Vietnam, said: "In the old Vietnam war movies, you'd watch and there weren't Vietnamese—they'd have any Asians playing Vietnamese. Now they're a little better about getting Vietnamese to play Vietnamese. It's better for our race."

In music history, Prof. Reebee Garofalo teaches the strengths and weaknesses of each musical form, and the dangers of being too quick to say one takes more talent than another. In one case study, he showed a tape of Pat Boone singing "Ain't That a Shame," the song Fats Domino made famous. "Notice Pat Boone snapping his fingers," said Prof. Garofalo. "He gets the wrong beat. He's got it backwards."

For his philosophy course on multiculturalism, Prof. Larry Blum took students to see "Schindler's List." Evonti Anderson, who is black, saw it a second time, with two friends from the Nation of Islam. "Afterwards we talked about seeing how the Jews caught hell," said Mr. Anderson. "We weren't the only ones being done to in the world."

"Sometimes you only look at your own struggles," said James Paschall, another black student taking the philosophy course. "I wish we could take what we learn in Professor Blum's class and let it cover the world."

"Maybe I'm being idealistic," said Michelle Berrong, who is paying for college by working as a dental assistant. "But these courses might reduce some of the hate and tension in the world. That does sound too idealistic, doesn't it?"

FREE AT LAST?

Roger Wilkins

Roger Wilkins is Clarence J. Robinson Professor of History and American Culture at George Mason University in Fairfax, Virginia, and a regular commentator for National Public Radio. This essay was published in 1994.

It is both odd and sad that 40 years after the Supreme Court of the United States ruled in Brown v. Board of Education, African-Americans are facing what historian John Hope Franklin describes as their greatest peril since slavery: a socioeconomic devastation that affects 40 percent of them and contributes to the continuing disintegration of the black family.

During the next 40 years we must make a sustained effort to rebuild the black family—especially in that besieged part of society. But before I sketch out my prescription, let me give a brief overview of the problem and a glimpse at how we arrived at this catastrophe.

A third of America's black population lives below the official poverty line, as opposed to 11 percent of whites. More than 60 percent of all black births are to single women, and almost 50 percent of black children are being raised in poverty. According to William Spriggs, Ph.D., of the National Commission for Employment Policy, the unemployment rate for black males (*excluding* those who've become so discouraged they've given up looking for work) has been above 10 percent since the late 1970s. During the 1980s it averaged almost 12 percent. Those are figures white Americans absolutely would not tolerate for themselves.

This economic devastation has resulted in hideous social disintegration. Murder is now the leading cause of death among black males ages 15 through 24. Our innercities and the schools in them are so dangerous that the majority of law-abiding people who live there and the children who want to learn lead lives of sheer terror.

The rest of the nation sees the crime and the family disintegration and recoils. The political manifestation of this revulsion is a precipitous drop in federal support for cities from 11.5 percent in 1980 to 3.8 percent in 1990, according to the Census Bureau. Our national leaders respond with loud cries about getting people off welfare and being tougher on crime. They give precious little emphasis to jobs and community-development programs in the devastated ghettos.

The idealists—both black and white—who fashioned the legal strategy that cracked segregation did not foresee the economic and social disasters that have befallen the most vulnerable blacks in our society. Had they contemplated

Modern Maturity, April–May 1994, pp. 27, 31, 33.

the trajectory of blacks coming out of slavery, they might have had some inkling of the problems that face the country today.

The masses of blacks who were at the bottom of society when the Brown case was evolving (and whom Richard Kluger described so well in *Simple Justice*, his masterful recapitulation of Brown) were trapped in the post-Civil War semislavery of the South. They had never been integrated into the mainstream of the economy. Kluger described conditions among the rural blacks of Clarendon County, South Carolina, in the late 1940s this way:

"It was nothing short of economic slavery, an unbreakable cycle of poverty and ignorance breeding more poverty and a bit less ignorance, generation upon generation. 'We had to take what was given us,' says a Clarendon farmer, 'or leave.' And a lot of them did leave, for urban ghettos. . . . But wherever they went and whatever they tried to do with their lives they were badly disabled, irreparably so for the most part, by the malnourishment the poverty and meanness their Clarendon birthright had inflicted upon [their childhood years]."

The boom economy of the 1960s and the attitudes fostered by the Civil Rights Movement permitted some poor blacks to break out of that vicious cycle. But in 1973 the boom ended. Income growth began to decline and the subsequent deindustrialization and globalization of the economy meant that those who had not escaped the pull of their slave history had nothing to offer America but unskilled labor.

The problem of integrating those African-Americans most damaged by history into the rest of society has troubled some of the best minds this country has ever produced. Jefferson, Madison, Monroe and Lincoln all thought former slaves should be deported. Ralph Bunche, the first black winner of the Nobel Peace Prize, thought that only a coalition of black and white workers could save the poorest blacks from being excess labor. W. E. B. Du Bois, who struggled for equality for three-quarters of a century, concluded that poor blacks would always be condemned to the expendable fringe of the labor pool.

So the problem of the undigested black masses still confronts us. Not only is it destroying black lives, it is also destroying our cities, dividing our country, and warping our political priorities.

The only adequate response is to develop and nurture healthier black families. Families are transmitters of values, discipline, a sense of connection to the economy, and, ultimately, hope and self-respect.

But it is almost impossible for families to function effectively or even exist when people live in ghetto conditions with no jobs. Just as lack of work is the most destructive force in the innercity, jobs are the central organizing principles of families. They provide a positive connection to the outside world; they offer self-respect; they force the household to develop discipline, and they give children a reason to believe study and hard work will give them a future. Government and industry should form councils that would place as many unemployed people as possible in private employment. Then government—at the federal, state, and local levels—should develop coordinated plans to offer employment as a last resort to those who cannot find work in the private sector.

But, important as it is, work alone cannot undo the damage. The children who live in these devastated communities need better parents than they now have, better schools than they now attend. Innercity schools should be physically connected to multipurpose service centers that meet the welfare, child- and health-care needs of parents and children. Most important, these centers should provide parenting classes for immature young people so they can support their children's education, and job-counseling services for those seeking work.

The final arm of this strategy is to support the many effective grassroots organizations that exist in our communities. These groups know the problems intimately and could provide superb assistance if they only had the resources.

Many white Americans believe that contemporary racial problems stem from a lack of black leadership. Nothing could be further from the truth. There is a broader, richer, abler array of black leadership in this country than at any time in our history. What is missing is white leadership. The black leaders of the '60s could not have changed the country by themselves. Whites in Congress, in city halls and statehouses, in pulpits, and ultimately in the White House provided leadership to white Americans that made it possible to destroy some of the shackles history had placed on us all.

Now, many white political leaders and opinionmakers push to marginalize the strongest black voices and condemn the behavior of those blacks most damaged by history and our current economic conditions.

Condemnation misses the point. People and families of all backgrounds fall apart under severe economic stress. Black America has been in a depression for 20 years, but white America rushes past obvious economic answers to settle on an ugly and persistent fretting about the wretched behavior patterns of the black poor. In fact, vast numbers of poor black people desperately want to work. Last November, when there was a strong hint of a new enterprise in Detroit, 10,000 people, mostly black, lined up in the cold to apply.

Neither, however, should white leaders embrace the fantasy that all poor blacks are saintly victims. They are not. Poverty and isolation have produced some very bad and some very reckless people. But many more people want law, order, and opportunity.

In any event, the black poor are part of us; a part of America that will have an enormous impact on our common future.

White politicians will not respond to this need until white opinion leaders join black leaders in demanding that we begin the final push to repair the deep and ugly racial damage our history has done to us all. But this will take time. Blacks arrived on the North American continent in 1619. For almost 250 of the ensuing 375 years we had slavery or something very close to it. And for a century after that we had Constitutionally sanctioned racial subordination. We have had something other than slavery or legal racial subordination for only 29 years.

The question for white leaders is simple: Would you rather spend our treasure on police and prisons or on programs that promote families and put people to work? Both are very expensive. It's just that the family program works a whole lot better for the people who are targeted—and for America's future as well.

QUESTIONS TO HELP YOU THINK AND WRITE ABOUT RACISM IN AMERICA

1. What does West mean by nihilism? What are the causes for nihilism in contemporary black culture? Is this a problem in other cultures? How great and pervasive a problem do you think it is? What can be done to solve the problems it creates?

2. Hacker's parable received a lot of attention when it was first published in 1992. What do you think of it? What does it suggest about the long-term success of the civil rights movement?

3. What, according to Celis, motivates Hispanic students to drop out of school? What evidence does he give? What solutions are there for the dropout problem that have either worked in the past or that could work in the future?

4. What do you think causes prejudice? Read the article about the black and white neighborhoods by Wilkerson to see if you can get additional insight into the causes of prejudice and list some of the causes. What are the author's attitudes on this subject? What ideas and information struck you as particularly convincing in these articles? What use could you make of the information? Did anything cause you to change your original attitudes or opinions about prejudice or segregation?

5. Read the articles by MacDonald and Winerip together. In your opinion, will the policy described in MacDonald's and Winerip's articles help solve racial problems? Why or why not? What policies to solve racial problems have worked? What might work in the future? Reread Martin Luther King, Jr.'s "Letter from Birmingham Jail" (pp. 246–258) to help you think about your answer.

6. What are your experiences, if any, with diversity classes? Based on Winerip's article, make a list of criteria to evaluate diversity classes, and write a value argument in which you defend or condemn these classes using your list of criteria (refer to p. 315 to help you do this).

7. Wilkins's article follows a problem-solution pattern. What is the problem, as he identifies it, and what is his solution? Think of another problem related to race, analyze what caused it, and list one or more solutions for it.

SECTION VII
Issues in Modern Science and Technology

WHAT ARE THE ISSUES?

1. What Effect Does Television Have on Its Viewers?

Three authors take positions on the benefits and harms of television. How it changes or influences the ideas and behavior of its viewers is a major facet of the issue.

2. Will Virtual Reality Have a Significant Social Impact?

Four articles examine the benefits and potential harms of a new technology that could, they claim, significantly change ideas about human behavior.

3. Will Genetic Engineering Require New Public Policy?

Five authors look at the pros and cons of the biotechnology revolution and the potential implications for the future of human beings.

THE RHETORICAL SITUATION

As you will learn from reading these essays, anxieties and concerns about emerging technologies and new scientific capabilities generate issues and argument. They have always done so. Pimentel and Teixeria speculate about the effect that the first written manuscripts might have had on early societies, and Rifkin wonders about early people's attitudes toward fire. In our own time, many people wonder about the changes in society that emerging technologies and modern science might eventually bring about. Particularly controversial in the 1990s are the technologies represented here: television, virtual reality (some people predict it is the future for computers), and biotechnology.

The authors who write about science and technology issues are often popularizers of science, and they organize most of their arguments around four of the five types of claims identified in Chapter 7: definition, cause (including effects), value, and policy. Definition articles help the layman understand an unfamiliar science or technology in the first place. In this section, Mander defines the nature of television, Rheingold defines virtual reality, and Rifkin defines genetic engineering. Hamill, Kolata, and Wilson, on the other hand, are interested in the effects that television, virtual reality, and genetic engineering will have on society. Thinking about effects leads many authors to evaluate science and technology and to argue how they may be either good or bad for society. Cooke and Greenough contribute value arguments. Finally, the possibility of change leads some authors to propose policies to manage the change. Stephens and Wuethrich write about policy issues.

Scientists who are busy "doing" science, unlike popularizers of science, tend to write for their colleagues rather than for the general public. Some of them caution that popularizers can slip into the realm of science fiction and exaggerate the speed of development or the eventual outcomes of certain technologies. The authors who are accused of this practice will reply that much that was once science fiction is now science fact. Pimentel and Teixeira point out that William Gibson's science fiction novel *Neuromancer*, published in 1984, has become an inspiration to young virtual reality builders and has also provided them with vocabulary. "Cyberspace" was first coined by Gibson. It is now used to describe the place where people are when they enter virtual reality. As you read, separate fact from fiction, but also notice the fiction that has now become fact.

1. What Effect Does Television Have on Its Viewers?

THE ILLUSION OF NEUTRAL TECHNOLOGY

Gerry Mander

This is an excerpt from Mander's book Four Arguments for the Elimination of Television, *published in 1978. Mander draws on Marshal McLuhan's idea that the medium (television) itself has significant social and psychological effects regardless of content.*

Most Americans, whether on the political left, center, or right, will argue that technology is neutral, that any technology is merely a benign instrument, a tool, and depending upon the hands into which it falls, it may be used one way or another. There is nothing that prevents a technology from being used well or badly; nothing intrinsic in the technology itself or the circumstances of its emergence which can predetermine its use, its control or its effects upon individual human lives or the social and political forms around us.

The argument goes that television is merely a window or a conduit through which any perception, any argument or reality may pass. It therefore has the potential to be enlightening to people who watch it and is potentially useful to democratic processes.

It will be [my] central point [. . .] that these assumptions about television, as about other technologies, are totally wrong.

If you once accept the principle of an army—a collection of military technologies and people to run them—all gathered together for the purpose of fighting, overpowering, killing and winning, then it is obvious that the supervisors of armies will be the sort of people who desire to fight, overpower, kill and

From Gerry Mander, *Four Arguments for the Elimination of Television* (New York: Morrow Quill Paperbacks, 1978), pp. 43–45.

win, and who are also good at these assignments: generals. The fact of generals, then, is predictable by the creation of armies. The kinds of generals are also predetermined. Humanistic, loving, pacifistic generals, though they may exist from time to time, are extremely rare in armies. It is useless to advocate that we have more of them.

If you accept the existence of automobiles, you also accept the existence of roads laid upon the landscape, oil to run the cars, and huge institutions to find the oil, pump it and distribute it. In addition you accept a sped-up style of life and the movement of humans through the terrain at speeds that make it impossible to pay attention to whatever is growing there. Humans who use cars sit in fixed positions for long hours following a narrow strip of gray pavement, with eyes fixed forward, engaged in the task of driving. As long as they are driving, they are living within what we might call "roadform." Slowly they evolve into car-people. McLuhan told us that cars "extended" the human feet, but he put it the wrong way. Cars *replaced* human feet.

If you accept nuclear power plants, you also accept a techno-scientific-industrial-military elite. Without these people in charge, you could not have nuclear power. You and I getting together with a few friends could not make use of nuclear power. We could not build such a plant, nor could we make personal use of its output, nor handle or store the radioactive waste products which remain dangerous to life for thousands of years. The wastes, in turn, determine that *future* societies will have to maintain a technological capacity to deal with the problem, and the military capability to protect the wastes. So the existence of the technology determines many aspects of the society.

If you accept mass production, you accept that a small number of people will supervise the daily existence of a much larger number of people. You accept that human beings will spend long hours, every day, engaged in repetitive work, while suppressing any desires for experience or activity beyond this work. The workers' behavior becomes subject to the machine. With mass production, you also accept that huge numbers of identical items will need to be efficiently distributed to huge numbers of people and that institutions such as advertising will arise to do this. One technological process cannot exist without the other, creating symbiotic relationships among technologies themselves.

If you accept the existence of advertising, you accept a system designed to persuade and to dominate minds by interfering in people's thinking patterns. You also accept that the system will be used by the sorts of people who like to influence people and are good at it. No person who did not wish to dominate others would choose to use advertising, or choosing it, succeed in it. So the basic nature of advertising and all technologies created to serve it will be consistent with this purpose, will encourage this behavior in society, and will tend to push social evolution in this direction.

In all of these instances, the basic form of the institution and the technology determines its interaction with the world, the way it will be used, the kind of people who use it, and to what ends.

And so it is with television.

Far from being "neutral," television itself predetermines who shall use it, how they will use it, what effects it will have on individual lives, and, if it continues to be widely used, what sorts of political forms will inevitably emerge.

CRACK AND THE BOX

Pete Hamill

Pete Hamill wrote this essay for Esquire *magazine in 1990. It was reprinted in the* Networker *later that year.*

One sad, rainy morning last winter I talked to a woman who was addicted to crack cocaine. She was 22, stiletto-thin, with eyes as old as tombs. She was living in two rooms in a welfare hotel with her children, who were two, three, and five years of age. Her story was the usual tangle of human woe: early pregnancy, dropping out of school, vanished men, smack and then crack, tricks with johns in parked cars to pay for the dope. I asked her why she did drugs. She shrugged in an empty way and couldn't really answer beyond "makes me feel good." While we talked and she told her tale of squalor, the children ignored us. They were watching television.

Walking back to my office in the rain, I brooded about the woman, her zombie-like children, and my own callous indifference. I'd heard so many versions of the same story that I almost never wrote them anymore; the sons of similar women, glimpsed a dozen years ago, are now in Dannemora or Soledad or Joliet; in a hundred cities, their daughters are moving into the same loveless rooms. As I walked, a series of homeless men approached me for change, most of them junkies. Others sat in doorways, staring at nothing. They were additional casualties of our time of plague, demoralized reminders that although this country holds only two percent of the world's population, it consumes 65 percent of the world's supply of hard drugs.

Why, for God's sake? Why do so many millions of Americans of all ages, races, and classes choose to spend all or part of their lives stupefied? I've talked to hundreds of addicts over the years; some were my friends. But none could give sensible answers. They stutter about the pain of the world, about despair or boredom, the urgent need for magic or pleasure in a society empty of both. But then they just shrug. Americans have the money to buy drugs; the supply is plentiful. But almost nobody in power asks, *Why?* Least of all, George Bush and his drug warriors.

Networker, November/December 1990, pp. 28, 29.

William Bennett talks vaguely about the heritage of '60s permissiveness, the collapse of Traditional Values, and all that. But he and Bush offer the traditional American excuse: It Is Somebody Else's Fault. This posture sets the stage for the self-righteous invasion of Panama, the bloodiest drug arrest in world history. Bush even accused Manuel Noriega of "poisoning our children." But he never asked *why* so many Americans demand the poison.

And then, on that rainy morning in New York, I saw another one of those ragged men staring out at the rain from a doorway. I suddenly remembered the inert postures of the children in that welfare hotel, and I thought: *television.*

Ah, no, I muttered to myself: too simple. Something as complicated as drug addiction can't be blamed on television. Come on . . . But I remembered all those desperate places I'd visited as a reporter, where there were no books and a TV set was always playing and the older kids had gone off somewhere to shoot smack, except for the kid who was at the mortuary in a coffin. I also remembered when I was a boy in the '40s and early '50s, and drugs were a minor sideshow, a kind of dark little rumor. And there was one major difference between that time and this: television.

We had unemployment then; illiteracy, poor living conditions, racism, governmental stupidity, a gap between rich and poor. We didn't have the all-consuming presence of television in our lives. Now two generations of Americans have grown up with television from their earliest moments of consciousness. Those same American generations are afflicted by the pox of drug addiction.

Only 35 years ago, drug addiction was not a major problem in this country. There were drug addicts. We had some at the end of the 19th century, hooked on the cocaine in patent medicines. During the placid '50s, Commissioner Harry Anslinger pumped up the budget of the old Bureau of Narcotics with fantasies of reefer madness. Heroin was sold and used in most major American cities, while the bebop generation of jazz musicians got jammed up with horse.

But until the early '60s, narcotics were still marginal to American life, they weren't the $120 billion market they make up today. If anything, those years have an eerie innocence. In 1955, there were 31,700,000 TV sets in use in the country (the number is now past 184 million). But the majority of the audience had grown up without the dazzling new medium. They embraced it, were diverted by it, perhaps even loved it, but they weren't *formed* by it. That year, the New York police made a mere 1,234 felony drug arrests; in 1988, it was 43,901. They confiscated 97 *ounces* of cocaine for the entire year, last year it was hundreds of pounds. During each year of the '50s in New York, there were only about a hundred narcotics-related deaths. But by the end of the '60s, when the first generation of children *formed* by television had come to maturity (and thus to the marketplace), the number of such deaths had risen to 1,200. The same phenomenon was true in every major American city.

In the last Nielsen survey of American viewers, the average family was watching television seven hours a day. This has never happened before in history. No people has ever been entertained for seven hours a *day*. The Elizabethans didn't go to the theater seven hours a day. The pre-TV generation did not go to the movies seven hours a day. Common sense tells us that this all-pervasive diet of instant imagery, sustained now for 40 years, must have changed us in profound ways.

Television, like drugs, dominates the lives of its addicts. And though some lonely Americans leave their sets on without watching them, using them as electronic companions, television usually absorbs its viewers the way drugs absorb their users. Viewers can't work or play while watching television; they can't read; they can't be out on the streets, falling in love with the wrong people, learning how to quarrel and compromise with other human beings. In short, they are asocial. So are drug addicts.

One Michigan State University study in the early '80s offered a group of four- and five-year-olds the choice of giving up television or giving up their fathers. Fully one third said they would give up Daddy. Given a similar choice (between cocaine or heroin and father, mother, brother, sister, wife, husband, children, job), almost every stone junkie would do the same.

There are other disturbing similarities. Television itself is a consciousness-altering instrument. With the touch of a button, it takes you out of the "real" world in which you reside and can place you at a basketball game, the back alleys of Miami, the streets of Bucharest, or the cartoony living rooms of Sitcom Land. Each move from channel to channel alters mood, usually with music or a laugh track. On any given evening, you can laugh, be frightened, feel tension, thump with excitement. You can even tune in "MacNeil/Lehrer" and feel sober.

But none of these abrupt shifts in mood is *earned*. They are attained as easily as popping a pill. Getting news from television, for example, is simply not the same experience as reading it in a newspaper. Reading is *active*. The reader must decode little symbols called words, then create images or ideas and make them connect; at its most basic level, reading is an act of the imagination. But the television viewer doesn't go through that process. The words are spoken to him or her by Dan Rather or Tom Brokaw or Peter Jennings. There isn't much decoding to do when watching television, no time to think or ponder before the next set of images and spoken words appears to displace the present one. The reader, being active, works at his or her own pace; the viewer, being passive, proceeds at a pace determined by the show. Except at the highest levels, television never demands that its audience take part in an act of imagination. Reading always does.

In short, television works on the same imaginative and intellectual level as psychoactive drugs. If prolonged television viewing makes the young passive (dozens of studies indicate that it does), then moving to drugs has a certain coherence. Drugs provide an unearned high (in contrast to the earned rush that comes from a feat accomplished, a human breakthrough earned by sweat or thought or love).

And because the television addict and the drug addict are alienated from the hard and scary world, they also feel they make no difference in its complicated events. For the junkie, the world is reduced to him or her and the needle, pipe, or vial; the self is absolutely isolated, with no desire for choice. The television addict lives the same way. Many Americans who fail to vote in presidential elections must believe they have no more control over such a choice than they do over the casting of "L.A. Law."

The drug plague also coincides with the unspoken assumption of most television shows: Life should be *easy*. The most complicated events are summarized on TV news in a minute or less. Cops confront murder, chase the criminals, and bring them to justice (usually violently) within an hour. In commercials, you drink the right beer and you get the girl. *Easy!* So why should real life be a grind? Why should any American have to spend years mastering a skill or craft, or work eight hours a day at an unpleasant job, or endure the compromises and crises of a marriage?

The doper always whines about how he or she *feels*; drugs are used to enhance feelings or obliterate them, and in this the doper is very American. No other people on earth spend so much time talking about their feelings; hundreds of thousands go to shrinks, they buy self-help books by the millions, they pour out intimate confessions to virtual strangers in bars or discos. Our political campaigns are about emotional issues now, stated in the simplicities of adolescence. Even alleged statesmen can start a sentence, "I feel that the Sandinistas should . . ." when they once might have said, "I *think* . . ." I'm convinced that this exaltation of cheap emotions over logic and reason is one by-product of hundreds of thousands of hours of television.

Most Americans under the age of 50 have now spent their lives absorbing television; that is, they've had the structures of drama pounded into them. Drama is always about conflict. So news shows, politics, and advertising are now all shaped by those structures. Nobody will pay attention to anything as complicated as the part played by Third World debt in the expanding production of cocaine; it's much easier to focus on Manuel Noriega, a character right out of "Miami Vice," and believe that even in real life there's a Mister Big.

What is to be done? Television is certainly not going away, but its addictive qualities can be controlled. It's a lot easier to "just say no" to television than to heroin or crack. As a beginning, parents must take immediate control of the sets, teaching children to watch specific television *programs*, not "television," to get out of the house and play with other kids. Elementary and high schools must begin teaching television as a subject, the way literature is taught, showing children how shows are made, how to distinguish between the true and the false, how to recognize cheap emotional manipulation. All Americans should spend more time reading. And thinking.

For years, the defenders of television have argued that the networks are only giving the people what they want. That might be true. But so is the Medellin Cartel.

TV CAUSES VIOLENCE? SAYS WHO?

Patrick Cooke

Patrick Cooke is a writer and television viewer who wrote this essay in 1993.

As the Beverly Hills conference on violence on television showed this month, academia's dire warnings about the dangers of watching the tube have always been an easy sell. But with Senator Paul Simon hinting darkly at Government censorship unless the industry does a better job of policing itself, the ante has been raised. The question is: do TV researchers know what they're talking about?

Since the late 1940's, there have been more than 3,000 reports on the effect on viewers of watching television, and TV research itself has become a cottage industry. Most of the conclusions have been grim; many have been baffling. Here are some of the findings of the past few decades: TV leads to hyperactivity in children; TV makes children passive. TV isolates viewers; TV comforts the lonely. TV drives families apart; TV brings families together.

Not even the Public Broadcasting Service has been spared. In 1975, when researchers noticed 2-year-old children obsessively reciting numbers and letters, one study cautioned parents about a new disorder called the "Sesame Street Hazard."

Four years ago, the Department of Education financed the most extensive survey to date of the research on childhood development and TV. It concluded that a disturbing amount of scholarship had been slipshod or influenced by a prevailing attitude that TV is harmful.

Despite the difficulty of obtaining reliable information on how television influences people, some beliefs, particularly about violence, are as persistent as "Cheers" reruns. The National Coalition on Television Violence, for example, has for years asserted that murders and rapes are more likely to occur because of TV violence. According to the organization, "It increases the chances that you will be mugged in the street or have your belongings stolen."

Many Americans agree with this conclusion; the link between mayhem on TV and a real-life violent society, after all, seems to make sense. But consider this possible area for research: Why doesn't anyone ever talk about the many occasions when people are nice to one another on TV? What effect has that had?

Much of the hand-wringing at the Beverly Hills conference centered on the sheer volume of brutality young people witness on TV and how, at the very least, such incidents desensitize them to real violence. But if teenagers have seen 18,000 TV murders by the age of 16, as one study estimated, isn't it possible, given the popularity of shows like "Fresh Prince of Bel Air," "Brooklyn Bridge" and "Beverly Hills 90210," that they also have seen many more incidents of kindness?

From "Little House on the Prairie" to "The Golden Girls" there is no end

New York Times, August 14, 1993, Op-Ed.

of people discovering their love for one another. Singles, marrieds, siblings, punks and homeboys share so much peace, tolerance and understanding that you might even call it gratuitous harmony.

It is tempting to conclude that a young person bombarded with hours of dramas in which characters are good-hearted becomes more sensitized to niceness. The conclusion might be wrong, but it's just as plausible as arguing that TV encourages evil.

These issues have been around longer than television has, of course. In the 1930's and 40's, studies warned of the harmful effects radio was having on children's school performance and their ability to distinguish fantasy from reality. "This new invader of the privacy of the home has brought many a disturbing influence in its wake," a psychologist wrote in 1936. "Parents have become aware of a puzzling change in the behavior of their children."

Socrates cautioned that writing would destroy people's memories. Plato's *Republic* warned about the danger of storytellers: "Children cannot distinguish between what is allegory and what isn't, and opinions formed at that age are difficult to change." Comic books were once blamed for young people's poor reading ability, and the early days of film prompted books like *Movies, Delinquency, and Crime.*

Today, of course, we lament that no one writes anymore. And whatever happened to those old-time storytellers? Comic books? Films? Those comics and films are classics now. And it's a shame many of us weren't around to hear those wonderful shoot-'em-up "Gangbusters" in the golden days of radio.

It is possible that today's kids will survive the effects of new technology as well as earlier generations did—provided they aren't forced to watch panel discussions by the TV experts.

2. Will Virtual Reality Have a Significant Social Impact?

VIRTUAL REALITY

Howard Rheingold

These are excerpts from Rheingold's book Virtual Reality, *published in 1991. Rheingold has written many books and articles about creativity and cognition, and has been a consultant to the U.S. Congress on technology. He edits the* Whole Earth Review.

Imagine a wraparound television with three-dimensional programs, including three-dimensional sound, and solid objects that you can pick up and manipulate, even feel with your fingers and hands. Imagine immersing yourself in an artificial world and actively exploring it, rather than peering in at it from a fixed

From Howard Rheingold, *Virtual Reality* (New York: Simon and Schuster, 1991), pp. 16–17, 19, 46, 386–389.

perspective through a flat screen in a movie theater, on a television set, or on a computer display. Imagine that you are the creator as well as the consumer of your artificial experience, with the power to use a gesture or word to remold the world you see and hear and feel. That part is not fiction. The head-mounted displays (HMDs) and three-dimensional computer graphics, input/output devices, computer models that constitute a VR system make it possible, today, to immerse yourself in an artificial world and to reach in and reshape it.

If you had to choose one old-fashioned word to describe the general category of what this new thing might be, "simulator" would be my candidate. VR technology resembles, and is partially derived from, the flight simulators that the Air Force and commercial airlines use to train pilots. In conventional flight simulators, pilots learn something about flying an aircraft without leaving the ground, by practicing with a replica of airplane controls; the "windshield" of a flight simulator is a computer graphics display screen upon which changing scenery is presented according to the course the pilot steers. The entire simulated cockpit is mounted on a motion platform that moves in accord with the motions of the simulated airplane. Virtual reality is also a simulator, but instead of looking at a flat, two-dimensional screen and operating a joystick, the person who experiences VR is surrounded by a three-dimensional computer-generated representation, and is able to move around in the virtual world and see it from different angles, to reach into it, grab it, and reshape it.

Right now, it is necessary to put a high-tech helmet on your head or don a pair of electronic-shutter glasses, the way I did, to see that world, and slide a special glove on your hand or grasp a mechanical input device in order to manipulate the objects you see there. [. . .]

One way to see VR is as a magical window onto other worlds, from molecules to minds. Another way to see VR is to recognize that in the closing decades of the twentieth century, reality is disappearing behind a screen. Is the mass marketing of artificial reality experiences going to result in the kind of world we would want our grandchildren to live in? What are the most powerful, most troubling, least predictable potentials of VR? If we could discern a clear view of the potentials and pitfalls of VR, how would we go about optimizing one and avoiding the other? The genie is out of the bottle, and there is no way to reverse the momentum of VR research; but these are young jinn, and still partially trainable. We can't stop VR, even if that is what we discover is the best thing to do. But we might be able to guide it, if we start thinking about it now.

The most lurid implications of VR have already been trumpeted in the mass media, via reports of what it just might make possible—such as "teledildonics" (simulated sex at a distance) or "electronic LSD" (simulations so powerfully addictive that they replace reality). And many of the reports in the popular press give the impression that the technology is "the latest thing to come out of California." But laboratories at places like the University of North Carolina have been conducting solid scientific research and developing potentially lifesaving applications for more than twenty years: anticancer medicines that already have been created with the VR molecular docking system that I tried out, and VR-based radiology treatment planning that is alleviating the suffering of real patients right now. [. . .]

Better medicines, new thinking tools, more intelligent robots, safer buildings, improved communications systems, marvelously effective educational media, and unprecedented wealth could result from intelligent application of VR. And a number of social effects, less pleasant to late-twentieth-century sensibilities, might also result from the same technologies.

Our most intimate and heretofore most stable personal characteristics—our sense of where we are in space, who we are personally, and how we define "human" attributes—are now open to redefinition. The technology that can replicate the human mind's fanciest trick—weaving sense-mediated signal streams into the fine-grained, three-dimensional, full-color, more-or-less consistent model we call "reality"—is in its infancy today. But technologies evolve more quickly these days than ever before. What will we think of each other, and ourselves, when we begin to live in computer-created worlds for large portions of our waking hours?

The early days of any technological revolution are filled with uncertainties. For a brief period, before industries, infrastructures, and belief systems grow out of and around a communication technology, the course of the technology is unknown. VR represents a unique historical opportunity. In retrospect, we now understand something about the way telephones, television, and computers expanded far beyond the expectations of their inventors and changed the way humans live. We can begin to see how better decisions might have been made twenty and fifty years ago, knowing what we know now about the social impact of new technologies. The ten to twenty years we still have to wait before the full impact of virtual reality technology begins to hit affords a chance to apply foresight—our only tool for getting a grip on runaway technologies. [. . .]

Virtual reality brings with it a set of questions about the industries and scientific capabilities it makes possible. It also brings with it a set of questions about human uses of technology, particularly the technologies that don't yet exist but are visible on the horizon. VR vividly demonstrates that our social contract with our own tools has brought us to a point where *we have to decide fairly soon what it is we as humans ought to become,* because we are on the brink of having the power of creating any experience we desire. The first cybernauts realized very early that the power to create experience is also the power to redefine such basic concepts as identity, community, and reality. VR represents a kind of new contract between humans and computers, an arrangement that could grant us great power, and perhaps change us irrevocably in the process.

The looming Faustian bargain involves certain changes in the partnership we have enjoyed with our machines. We might decide that we wouldn't mind becoming a little or a lot more machinelike in exchange for laborsaving devices, lifesaving tools, attractive conveniences and seductive entertainments. Such a decision would be a radical change, but not an abrupt one. Our minds, our senses, our consensual reality has been shaped for a century, to the point where billions of us are trained and ready to embrace our silicon partners more intimately than ever before. Trillions of human-hours have been logged so far in the virtual worlds of *I Love Lucy* and *Dallas*, FORTRAN and fax, computer networks, comsats, and mobile telephones. The transformations in our psyches triggered by the electronic media thus far may have been mere preparation for bigger things to come. The hinge of change seems to be connected with these machines we've created and the kind of partnership we are coevolving with our information tools.

VR is an important threshold in the evolution of human-computer symbiosis. But symbiosis is a two-way exchange; when one organism exists at the expense of another, without contributing something vital to the partnership, the relationship is parasitic. Two questions that emerge from an examination of VR are closely interrelated: How will cyberspace tools and environments affect the way we live, think and work? And how will cyberspace affect the way we apprehend the world, the way we define ourselves as sensing, thinking, communicating beings?

"Electronic media alter the ratios between the senses," was one of Marshall McLuhan's key epigrams: The ratios and amount of audio and visual input to the dominant reality recipe were altered by radio and telephones and then altered again by television; we see and hear and thus apprehend the world differently as a result. Those effects are taken for granted by now, three decades after *Understanding Media*. The cyberspace experience is destined to transform us in other ways because it is an undeniable reminder of a fact we are hypnotized since birth to ignore and deny—that our normal state of consciousness is itself a hyperrealistic simulation. We build models of the world in our mind, using the data from our sense organs and the information-processing capabilities of our brain. We habitually think of the world we see as "out there," but what we are seeing is really a mental model, a perceptual simulation that exists only in our brain. That simulation capability is where human minds and digital computers share a potential for synergy. Give the hyperrealistic simulator in our head a handle on computerized hyperrealistic simulators, and something very big might happen.

Cognitive simulation, mental model-making, is one of the things humans do best. We do it so well that we tend to become locked into our own models of the world by a seamless web of unconscious beliefs and subtly molded perceptions. And computers are model-making tools par excellence, although they are only beginning to approach the point where people might confuse simulations with reality. Computation and display technology are converging on hyperreal simulation capability. That point of convergence is important enough to contemplate in advance of its arrival. The day computer simulations become so realistic that people cannot distinguish them from nonsimulated reality we are in for major changes. [. . .]

If humans and computers are poised on the verge of a symbiotic relationship, as computer pioneer J. C. R. Licklider prophesied more than three decades ago, shouldn't we take the time to discuss what we are getting into, before we get any farther into it? If we get a handle on what we are changing into, what should we *want* to change into, what should we *not* want to change into, and how do we gain the power to make that decision? After a year and a half wrestling with the issues raised by the emergence of virtual reality technology, I still find myself asking questions I thought I had left back in philosophy class in college.

A NEW LITERACY

Ken Pimentel and Kevin Teixeira

These are excerpts from Pimentel and Teixeira's book Virtual Reality: Through the New Looking Glass, *published in 1993. The authors develop, design, and teach about virtual reality and other computer technology.*

The alphabet was created as a coding system to allow people to share their internal thoughts and realities without having to meet. Reading and writing created a form of external, nonperishable memory, one that retained its original information despite additional events. It became much easier to go back and compare new ideas to previous ones, to shape and refine an idea over time. Ideas could be quickly communicated, and copies could be made and distributed across boundaries, time zones, and cultures.

What we don't have from the early days of writing is a good record of the resistance or the social upheaval caused by the appearance of this new technology. How did Homer and the other Greek bards feel about having their stories written down? They depended on memory to store their sagas, and interaction with the audience to influence the telling. Did they argue that writing was destroying their culture?

What about the average merchant—did he change the way he did business? It took many generations for the use of writing to spread, and even in modern times there are vast numbers of people who never learn to read or write. But it has changed the world by changing the way people think even without everyone using it. What will VR's impact be?

Literacy means more than the ability to read and write, though these are its most basic requirements. Reading allows for reflection and contemplation about the ideas on a page. What does the writer mean? What is he trying to convince me of? What are the implications of these ideas to other ideas, institutions, and people—to me and my life? Do I agree or disagree?

Meredith Bricken, a research scientist with the HIT lab in Seattle,

From Ken Pimentel and Kevin Teixeira, *Virtual Reality: Through the New Looking Glass* (New York: McGraw-Hill, 1993), pp. 250–251.

Washington, points out that reading and writing are basically cognitive functions, but virtual reality is both cognitive and behavioral. The act of participating in a simulated world involves us physically, visually, emotionally, magically, and rationally in organized and spontaneous events.

Learning and understanding in a virtual environment involves you very differently than in an alphabet-based curriculum. The educational theorist S. Papert expressed the value of visual mental experience to learning in his 1980 book *Mindstorms*.

> If you can *be* a gear, you can understand how it turns by projecting yourself into its place and turning with it. . . . As well as connecting with the formal knowledge of mathematics, it also connects with the body knowledge, the sensory motor schemata of a child. It is this double relationship—both abstract and sensory—that gives a transitional object the power to carry mathematics into the mind.

Every virtual environment is an educational environment. VR was originally nurtured and developed by the military as an evolution of flight simulators, to train pilots and help them manage the information required to fly today's complex aircraft. Every simulation steps the user through a series of activities with rewards and penalties of various degrees—we learn by doing.

Someday teachers will be able to take students to the bottom of the ocean without leaving their classroom. Students will play with atoms and make their own molecules in VR to experience chemistry, instead of just reading about it. The development and widespread use of VR raises valid concerns about what we will teach ourselves and our children in these simulations. Optimistically, it will lead to a revolution in teaching and learning. Students will acquire a sense of control over knowledge.

But what about the violence of video games? Will home VR systems teach children to all be Mutant Ninja Turtles? There's a striking difference between the passive viewing of violence on television and being invited to spend hours hunting and shooting opponents in a virtual game.

When the context is a simulation it might be that adults are able to make the moral distinction between reality and fantasy, but what about children? How old is old enough to appreciate the difference when you're immersed in a world of 3-D sound and color and the enemy is attacking? Ray Bradbury asked this question allegorically over 30 years ago in his horror tale of a future virtual reality-like media room, *The Veldt*.

Will the military's use of VR lead to desensitized soldiers who fight video game wars, never seeing the enemy? The use of VR, computers, and telepresence in war could shield people from the disturbing consequences of their actions. It could also save lives by removing people from the battlefield.

It's dangerous, of course, to jump to conclusions too quickly, to look at the individual isolated from home, family, society and work, as if he is devoid of free will and easily influenced by every media message. More study and debate is needed in this area.

Some critics are ready to denounce virtual reality as a mind-numbing, brainwashing technology that will homogenize culture. The same fears were raised forty years ago with the emergence of television. These are valid concerns—even after 40 years the public debate continues over the numbing and conditioning effects of violence on television—but this is a debate over content, not technology.

As the debate on TV focuses on the negative, the global impact of television is often overlooked. TV has also lived up to its early promise of linking and communicating with vast areas of the world formerly isolated from each other.

Rather than homogenization, televised international communication seems to have lead to an increase in democratic institutions and individuality as demonstrated by the upheaval in Eastern Europe and the recent events in China.

Just as reading and writing can be used for propaganda, pleasure, or critical analysis, so too can VR. VR can be used to educate, train, and make us more aware of our own behavior. The alphabet allows writers and readers to carefully study thoughts and ideas, and virtual reality will allow the same critical analysis of behavior.

SILENCE OF THE RAMS: A CLEAN AND WELL-LIGHTED VIRTUAL REALITY

Tom Dworetzky

Tom Dworetzky wrote this short fictional account of a virtual reality experience for Omni *magazine in 1993. It is included here to provide you with an imaginary sense of this new technology. However, there is also an implicit claim in this story.*

Jacked into the net and surfed and rippled into the infotime continuum, I looked for a byte. The infomalls with their virtual-reality mannequins did nothing for me, so I floated to the DC server and killed the president. Mine was the three millionth assassination of the day . . . not enough to trash his directory, so he kept on ticking.

Since global VR went online a decade ago, all real-world problems, like getting killed or finding parking, are solved. Everyone stays in their homes and goes to work, to party, to live and die in VR. But the grand social experiment didn't work out exactly the way it was planned.

One day I surf over to a holocafé in the corner of a rundown virtual strip mall. It's pretty free of other virtual wanderers, clean and well lighted. I float my holo in and settle it on a chair by a round brown table in a corner and order a double juice to give my bits a lift. In the corner is an old man, a strange enough sight these days, since you can be whomever you want, and most opt for Cindy

Crawford or Richard Gere defaults. This can be confusing since everybody looks pretty much the same. And if experience builds character, and we all get the same experience on the net, then character, too, might as well be a default.

The old man is way into his juice, barely moving except from time to time to take another drink. The waiter, a classic Frenchman, gray and thin, comes over. I order another juice. "The old one," I ask. "Why is he so old?"

"Because he is," replies the waiter. "Because he wants to feel death."

"Why doesn't he just go out and get crashed in a bad neighborhood, then?" I ask. "Anyone can feel death in VR."

"No. Everyone cannot feel death by merely surfing the black. You must go old to do it, perhaps. But who knows? I'm just a waiter. I know he comes here each night and juices until we close."

I sit for a long time, but finally float over. "May I sit?" I ask him.

"If you must." He takes another drink.

"Why do you sit in this empty part of the grid?" I ask.

"It is empty."

"Yes, but boring."

"More boring than out there where everyone looks and acts the same—just like you?"

"I am just like them to you?"

"You are here; they are not."

"So I'm not like them?"

"In virtual reality, we are all alike. I am not me; you are not you. We are all like who we are but not who we are."

I hear him and suddenly realize that I am a million miles away—quite literally, that I'm not sitting in a café with an old man, but somewhere else, jacked in. I grow confused. I guess I panic after that, putting my gloved hand on the Esc button, pulling out of the routine. What in the world has VR come to? What is the point of all this stuff if it's the same and there's nothing on? The old man is right, I think, sitting in my jack box, the one room I call home. That's enough networking for awhile. I'm thinking I'll just sit like the old man in the café and spend time by myself, getting real, when a shadow reaches out and touches my shoulder. As I turn, I recognize two of my old schoolmates: John from L.A. and Peter who's been living in Tokyo for the last 16 years. I haven't seen them forever.

"Hey mates," I cry. "What are you doing here in this vast cyber-wasteland?"

"It's Captain Negativity," says John, flashing me a holosmile. "Isn't it great that we can run into each other now that there's no there there?"

"But look what they've done to it. It's full of virtual boredom and virtual evil."

"We know," says John, and Peter starts to laugh. "Is that Hemingway segment we ran on you some great new sim or what?"

"Maybe next time," says Peter, "we should drop him in one with a happier ending."

RESEARCHERS HOPE TO LEAD STUDENTS INTO "VIRTUAL REALITY"

David L. Wilson

David Wilson wrote this article for The Chronicle of Higher Education *about the possible educational benefits of virtual reality.*

Stephen C. Gibson, a graduate student in architecture, felt as though he were standing on the steps of the Parthenon. He was really in the middle of a classroom at Rensselaer Polytechnic Institute, wearing a helmet that enveloped him in computer-generated images that citizens of ancient Athens would have recognized.

Mr. Gibson could "move" into an animated image of the Parthenon, examining its columns and the roof. "It was exhilarating," he says. "It gave you a real sense of the space and the light."

Mr. Gibson was able to stroll through the Parthenon during experiments at RPI with a technique called "virtual reality." His helmet was connected to a computer that displayed images on screens inside the helmet so vividly that he seemed actually to be seeing one of the architectural masterpieces of ancient Greece.

Educators say virtual-reality systems offer a dramatic alternative to the way students learn. By the end of this decade, some say, students will be able to enter computer-created universes to perform chemistry experiments, examine rare manuscripts, and study objects and cultures that are otherwise inaccessible. Those with disabilities will be able to enter an artificial universe and interact with other people, giving no hint as to their handicap.

Researchers working on virtual-reality systems say they will be particularly useful for helping students understand abstract concepts by giving them concrete metaphors that can be manipulated in the computer.

For instance, William Bricken, principal scientist with the Human Interface Technology Laboratory at the University of Washington, is developing a virtual-reality universe in which the objects are controlled by algebraic, rather than physical, laws. Objects would ignore gravity, for example, but would react to an integer that was positive or negative. Students would move blocks around in the artificial universe, and those blocks could be aligned in various configurations, provided they did not violate the laws of algebra.

Its experiments make Rensselaer one of the few institutions in the country to attempt to use the technology with students in classes. While many scholars are enthusiastic about the applications of virtual reality, few have access to

The Chronicle of Higher Education, April 22, 1992, p. A23. These are excerpts from the article as it appeared in *The Chronicle of Higher Education*.

virtual-reality systems. Much of the work that is being done with virtual reality is confined to research laboratories.

Many problems will have to be overcome before the technology can be used widely in the classroom, experts say. The equipment costs too much—hundreds of thousands of dollars for a top-of-the-line system—to permit widespread use. Hardware and software must be improved. And scholars need to develop new methods of pedagogy to take advantage of the nearly limitless possibilities offered by virtual reality.

BLOCKING OUT SENSORY DATA

In addition, a debate over how complete the virtual-reality experience must be for students is continuing in the scholarly community. Some argue that the fundamental requirements of virtual reality—the ability to interact with others in an artificially created world—can be obtained using standard computer equipment at a relatively modest cost.

Some people insist that the key to virtual reality lies in largely blocking outside sensory data received through the eyes and ears and flooding the user with sights and sounds created by the computer. Most experimenters achieve that level of realism by using helmet-like devices like the one used at Rensselaer. The helmets contain two tiny television screens and stereo earphones.

One television screen is directly in front of each eye, blocking out views of the real world. The computer generates images of the engineered world that are slightly different for each eye, giving a three-dimensional effect, like an old-fashioned stereopticon.

Today's virtual-reality systems offer images that are mere cartoons, not at all like the high-quality images that can be seen on many computer screens.

Stereo sounds also are generated to match the pictures. Sensors in the helmet track the position of the user's head, altering the pictures as the head is moved. If the wearer looks up, for instance, the scene immediately shifts perspective. While the effect is startlingly realistic, it is not indistinguishable from reality. Users notice a momentary delay between moving their heads and seeing the scene move, as the computer rapidly calculates the new perspective. Researchers say this small delay can be very disconcerting over time, and is one of the major problems that must be overcome before the technology can become commonplace.

Users generally manipulate a device with their hands to move about in the computer-generated world. They say moving through the artificial universe feels like "flying."

The helmet, called a "head-mounted display," allows the user to be immersed entirely in the artificial world, but a similar effect can be obtained at a lower cost if the user stands in a sealed booth containing a computer monitor. With that type of system, the booth represents a cabin or cockpit, and the monitor represents a porthole or windshield. All of the systems have a goal of cutting the user off from other stimuli. [. . .]

BIG IMPACT FROM IMMERSION

Mr. Bricken of the University of Washington acknowledges some of the flaws of head-mounted displays, but he argues that the problems will be corrected. Simply looking at a computer monitor and doing the same sorts of tasks one can do in a virtual-reality environment is not the same thing as being inside the system, he says.

"This lab feels strongly, based on research, that the essential component in virtual reality is a feeling that you're dealing with an environment rather than an object in an environment," he says. "Monitor-based approaches can only approximate that feeling." Immersing the user in the virtual environment provides a much bigger impact than simply looking at an animated character on a screen that is supposed to represent the user, he says. "If you stick your hand in a bucket of water, that's not swimming."

Part of the point of virtual reality, says Mr. Bricken, is to eliminate the need to learn how to operate a keyboard or a mouse, which separates the user from the activity on the computer screen. Virtual reality, he says, allows users direct access to the software environment itself, and tasks in the environment can be set up so that users can perform them intuitively, with little or no training.

William D. Wynn, a professor of education at the University of Washington, is working with Mr. Bricken to develop educational uses for virtual reality, preparing for a day when use of virtual reality in the classroom could become widespread. Academe, he says, largely ignored the potential of computers to revolutionize pedagogy, meaning that scientists designed computers with little advice from the education community.

"For the first time, I think, educators are in on the ground floor of a new technology," he says of virtual reality.

Peter R. Theis, who is in his second year studying architecture at Rensselaer Polytechnic, says he hopes virtual-reality systems will soon come to the classroom permanently. Using standard computer-modeling techniques, he built the model of the Parthenon that was used in the virtual-reality experiment at RPI. Bill Glennie, director of the Computer Aided Architectural Design Laboratory and assistant professor of architecture at RPI, persuaded a California software company called Autodesk to lend the college a sophisticated computer and a head-mounted display to perform the experiments.

Mr. Theis says that, from an architect's standpoint, virtual reality is invaluable. "There are things I noticed in the virtual-reality model that I just had no grasp of when I was building the model on the regular computer. The scale is all blown out on the computer screen," he says. "When you're in virtual reality, bam, it's real-sized, and you're saying, 'Wow.' "

3. Will Genetic Engineering Require New Public Policy?

THE AGE OF BIOTECHNOLOGY

Jeremy Rifkin

> *Jeremy Rifkin is a populizer of science and is considered by some scientists to be too critical of their field. He does his homework, however. Here he both reports on the status of biotechnology and evaluates its implications for the future of society. These are excerpts from his book* From Alchemy to Algeny: A New Metaphor for the Coming Age, *published in 1983.*

For thousands of years humanity used fire to convert the earth's crust into new shapes and forms that never existed in nature. Now, for the first time in history, humanity has found a way to convert living material into new shapes and forms that never existed in nature. In 1973, American scientists performed a feat in the world of living matter to rival the importance of fire itself. Biologists Stanley Cohen of Stanford University and Herbert Boyer of the University of California reported that they had taken two unrelated organisms that would not mate in nature, isolated a piece of DNA from each, and then hooked the two pieces of genetic material together. The result was literally a new form of life, one that had never before existed on the face of the earth.

A product of nearly thirty years of investigation, climaxed by a series of rapid discoveries in the late 1960s and 1970s, recombinant DNA is a kind of biological sewing machine that can be used to stitch together the genetic fabric of unrelated organisms. Dr. Cohen divides recombinant DNA surgery into four stages. To begin with, a chemical scalpel, called a restriction enzyme, is used to split apart the DNA molecules from one source—a human, for example. Once the DNA has been cut into pieces, a small segment of genetic material—a gene, perhaps, or a few genes in length—is separated out. Next, the restriction enzyme is used to slice out a segment from the body of a plasmid, a short length of DNA found in bacteria. Both the piece of human DNA and the body of the plasmid develop "sticky ends" as a result of the slicing process. The ends of both segments of DNA are then hooked together, forming a genetic whole composed of material from the two original sources. Finally, the modified plasmid is used as a vector, or vehicle, to move the DNA into a host cell, usually a bacterium. Absorbing the plasmid, the bacterium proceeds to duplicate it endlessly, producing identical copies of the new chimera. These are called clones.

From Jeremy Rifkin, *From Alchemy to Algeny: A New Metaphor for the Coming Age* (New York: Viking, 1983), pp. 7–19.

The recombinant DNA process is the most dramatic technological tool to date in the growing biotechnological arsenal. The biologist is learning how to manipulate, recombine, and reorganize living tissue into new forms and shapes, just as his craftsmen ancestors did by firing inanimate matter. The speed of the discoveries is truly phenomenal. It is estimated that biological knowledge is currently doubling every five years, and in the field of genetics, the quantity of information is doubling every twenty-four months. We are virtually hurling ourselves into the age of biotechnology. [. . .]

In the pharmaceutical industry, those in the know predict that bioengineering will revolutionize the production of antibiotics, enzymes, antibodies, vaccines, and hormones.

In the mining industry, there is experimentation going on with the development of new microorganisms that can replace the miner and his machine in the extraction of ores. Tests are being conducted with organisms that will eat metals like cobalt, iron, nickel, and manganese. One company reports that it has already successfully blown a certain bacterium "into low-grade copper ores where it produces an enzyme that eats away salts in the ore, leaving behind an almost pure form of copper."[1] For low-grade ores that are difficult to tap with conventional mining techniques, microorganisms will provide a more economical approach to extraction and processing.

In the energy industry, the oil companies are beginning to experiment with renewable resources as a substitute for oil and gas. Scientists hope to improve on existing crops, like sugar cane, which is already producing alcohol for automobile consumption. The future is likely to see the emergence of biologically engineered "fuel crops," whose sole function will be to produce usable energy for society.

In the chemical industry, scientists are talking about replacing petroleum, which for years has been the primary raw material for the production of chemicals, with biomass, a renewable resource made up of plant and animal material.

In agriculture, bioengineering is being looked to as a substitute for petrochemical farming. Scientists are busy at work engineering new food crops that can take in nitrogen directly from the air, rather than having to rely on the more costly petrochemical-based fertilizers presently in use. There are also efforts under way to increase the photosynthetic capability of selective plants in order to increase yield. In addition, experiments are under way to transfer desirable genetic characteristics from one species to another in order to increase productive performance. Scientists are trying to locate genes that help ward off viruses and pests, and that can adapt a plant to salty or dry terrains, all in an effort to upgrade the flow of living material into economic utilities.

In the field of animal husbandry, new bioengineering technologies allow man to bypass the slow, often unpredictable process of natural breeding. New genetic traits can now be programmed directly into the fetus. Nor are scientists any longer constrained by species boundaries. In the future the transfer of genetic characteristics between species will be commonplace. The goal will be to engineer new forms of animals that can meet specific economic demands. For example, Dr. Thomas Wagner suggests that it might be cost-effective to engineer cattle that can grow as well on grass or hay as on the more expensive feed grains. Since the buffalo is already adapted to a roughage cuisine, Wagner suggests that "you might transfer this trait alone of a buffalo to a cow, and leave all the rest of the buffalo behind."[2] Cloning offers still another possibility. Many scientists believe that by the end of the current decade, entire herds of domestic livestock will be cloned in order to ensure a uniform high-quality yield of meat and meat by-products.

Finally, there is the question of engineering the human anatomy. Many of the bioengineering techniques that prove successful in animals and plants can be adapted to some degree to the human frame. Scientists are already looking to the day when "harmful" genetic traits can be eliminated from the fetus at conception. Eliminating the specific genes that are the cause of many dreaded diseases only scratches the surface of the possibilities that lie ahead. Researchers believe that when today's babies are old enough to have children of their own, they may be able to select from a wide range of beneficial gene traits they would like to have programmed directly into their offspring at the fetal stage, from manual dexterity skills to improved memory retention capability.

Meanwhile, gene surgery is also likely to be a medical reality within a matter of a few years. Scientists predict that specially engineered genes will be introduced directly into the human body in order to produce agents that will immunize against specific diseases. Other genes will be inserted that can help facilitate or retard growth, regenerate limbs, and perform a host of other medically useful activities.

The thought of recombining living material into an infinite number of new combinations is so extraordinary that the human imagination is barely able to grasp the immensity of the transition at hand. These first few processes and products are the biotechnical equivalent of the first pots and bins forged by our ancestors tens of thousands of years ago when they began experimenting with the pyrotechnical arts for the first time. From the moment our Neolithic kin first fired up the earth's material, transforming it into new forms, humanity locked itself into an irreversible journey that finally culminated in the Industrial Age. Our world, the world of twentieth-century man, is forged in fire. Its skyscrapers and satellites and sewers and electrical lines and highways and homes and virtually every other economic convenience are the final fruits of the pyrotechnical revolution begun eons ago when a few enterprising ancestors decided to torch a piece of ore with a hot flame.

Now humanity has set its sights on the living world, determined to reshape it into new combinations, and the far-distant consequences of this new journey are as unfathomable to today's biotechnologists as the specter of industrial society would have been to the first pyrotechnologists.

Accompanying this great technological transformation is a philosophical transformation of monumental proportions. Humanity is about to fundamentally reshape its view of existence to coincide with its new organizational relationship with the earth. [. . .]

Up to this point in history, humanity's ability to manipulate living things has always been dependent on its ability to alter their environments. People could decide where plants, animals, and other human beings were to live, what they were to eat and how much, and even whom they were to mate with. People could domesticate living things, including themselves, and they could even vary looks, weight, and other secondary characteristics through careful breeding. What they couldn't do was either fundamentally change the existing structure of plants, animals, and people or create wholly new structures. Human beings have had to live with the constraints imposed by existing biological forms. People could cultivate but they could not engineer or create.

In all of humanity's past experience, living things enjoyed a separate, unique, and identifiable place in the order of nature. There were always rabbits and robins, oaks and ostriches, and while human beings could tinker with the surface of each, they couldn't penetrate to the interior of any. Now, as we move from the age of pyrotechnology to the age of biotechnology, people are beginning to learn how to reorganize living things from the inside out. The redesign of existing organisms and the engineering of wholly new ones mark a qualitative break with humanity's entire past relationship to the living world. People's reconception of nature is going to change just as radically as their organization of it.

Engineering new forms of life requires a wholesale transformation of our thought patterns. It should be remembered that the entire way we formulate our conception of the world is etched in the fires of the age of pyrotechnology. We are dousing the Promethean flame, and the new world we are entering is alien to the vision of all the great theologians, philosophers, and metaphysicians of the past. As we move from firing dead ores to penetrating living tissues, as we invade the interior of living organisms with engineering tools, as we begin to plot new designs for the reconstruction of life itself, the voices of past seers fall silent. Their words were never meant to extend to this new epoch, were never meant to explain this emergent reality.

NOTES

1. Thomas O'Toole, "In the Lab: Bugs to Grow Wheat, Eat Metal," *Washington Post* (June 18, 1980), page A1.
2. Quoted in Victor Cohn, "Biologists Report Transfer of Gene from Rabbit to Mouse to Offspring," *Washington Post* (September 8, 1981), page A12.

BREAKING THE GENETIC CODE

Beverly Sills Greenough

This author is the former opera star Beverly Sills. She now donates time to the March of Dimes and is a managing director of the Metropolitan Opera. She had personal reasons, as you will see, for writing this essay for Newsweek *in 1993.*

Some people recoil when they hear the phrase "gene therapy." It conjures frightening images of scientists trying to play God. But the words actually hold great promise for doctors fighting to conquer crippling and lethal diseases.

Genes, units of DNA housed in human chromosomes, are the keys to heredity. They hold the codes that control individual characteristics like our eye color and blood type. Genes can also determine our long-term health. Persons with damaged or missing genes are vulnerable to a wide range of serious illnesses. Through gene therapy, scientists have begun to restore or replace faulty or missing genes with healthy ones.

Obviously, all of this isn't as simple as it sounds. Before researchers can replace a damaged gene, they have to locate it and determine its function. Thirty years ago, scientists knew the location of fewer than 100 of the estimated 100,000 genes that humans carry. By 1990, the number had risen to 1,850. That same year researchers began a massive effort to map the rest. The Human Genome Project, funded by the Department of Energy and the National Institutes of Health, is the largest biological research effort ever undertaken. The work is painstaking. It could take 15 to 20 years to complete a genetic blueprint of the human body.

But there have already been breakthroughs. One involves a 4-year-old girl who, because of a missing gene, had been ill from birth with an inherited deficiency of her immune system. Like the "bubble boy" in Texas who suffered from a similar ailment, any minor infection could have been life threatening. The condition made both the girl and her family virtual prisoners. Her mother and siblings seldom left home for fear they might bring back a potentially lethal infection.

In September 1990, doctors removed some of the girl's white blood cells, treated them with copies of the missing gene and reintroduced them into her body. Within a year, the child's immune system began to respond. She was well enough to take dancing lessons, swim, even go to a shopping mall. While the results are not conclusive, her prognosis is very promising. More than a happy ending for one little girl, the case marked the beginning of a new medical era. She was the world's first recipient of gene therapy.

Scientists have identified genes responsible for cystic fibrosis, Duchenne muscular dystrophy, Marfan syndrome, fragile X syndrome and certain cancers. The next step is the development of successful techniques to deliver corrected versions of genes to the cells of patients suffering from such disorders. Alzheimer's, diabetes and some forms of heart disease may be conquered by this technology.

Why should I care about all of this? One reason is that I am national chairman of the March of Dimes Birth Defects Foundation. We know that a large number of birth defects have a genetic origin. That's why the foundation devotes a sizable amount of its annual research budget to grants for the study of gene therapy.

There's a personal side for me as well.

My daughter was born profoundly deaf. And my son, soon after birth, was found to be autistic, epileptic *and* deaf. Unless you've been there, you cannot imagine how all this feels. Yet, during my pregnancies, I had the very best of prenatal care. I didn't smoke, drink or use any sort of drugs. It didn't matter.

PUBLIC IGNORANCE

We still do not know all of the reasons why babies are born sick or with major disabilities. But we *do* know some. One baby, maybe more, out of one hundred is born with a serious *genetic* problem. Gene therapy offers a very real possibility of correcting many of these disorders. It could transform—indeed, it already has—lives that are doomed to the pain and anguish of chronic illness.

But scientific advances can also generate misunderstanding and fear. The Salk polio vaccine, so closely identified with the March of Dimes, was one of the most important medical gains of our time. It was safe. It worked. But because earlier vaccines used "live" viruses that caused fatalities, researchers had to overcome public apprehension. (The Salk vaccine used a benign, "dead" virus.)

Some critics are concerned that gene therapy will be abused to create "super" humans. Others are disturbed about possible disclosures of personally sensitive medical history. Still, the public seems to be giving this new technology the benefit of the doubt. A recent survey conducted for the foundation revealed that 89 percent of Americans support gene therapy and favor continued research. Curiously, this same poll showed widespread public ignorance about this form of treatment. So the need for public education on a broad scale is self-evident. There is much yet for both scientists and lay people to learn.

The main thing is this: we *cannot* let our fears destroy our hopes. We cannot let myth and misinterpretation prevent us from seeking treatment for the thousands who suffer from genetic diseases. Let's continue to resolve the issues while moving onward to intensify the research effort.

From my own viewpoint, if gene therapy can spare *one* mother the anguish of knowing that her newborn will suffer throughout its whole life—if it can help sick little girls get well enough to dance—can we afford *not* to make the effort?

CLONING HUMAN EMBRYOS: DEBATE ERUPTS OVER ETHICS

Gina Kolata

*This article explores a variety of perspectives on the ethics of cloning human em-
bryos. The exigence for this article was a scientific experiment in 1993 that suggested this may soon become a viable technology.*

A day after the world learned that scientists at George Washington University
Medical Center had cloned human embryos, ethicists and fertility specialists
were already engaged in a vociferous debate yesterday.

While some ethicists foresee a nightmare scenario that should be stopped
before it is started, others say, "Why not?" Some ethicists argue that peoples'
embryos are their own and that if they want them cloned, it is not society's role
to stop them. Several ethicists said that rarely had they seen an issue so provocative and so divisive.

While some doctors who do in vitro fertilization said they would never
clone human embryos, others said they would offer it to their patients as soon
as the technology was ready. At least one clinic director said he expected to do
research to make it a practical possibility in the near future.

FAMILY OF TWINS?

The cloning procedure was devised as a means for helping infertile couples
conceive artificially, by producing extra embryos. But the technique would
make possible various unusual strategies, since parents could grow one embryo to term and store the others indefinitely. A spare embryo could be grown
to term later, being born as the identical but younger twin of the first. Or the
parents might decide to produce a family of identical twins all of different ages.

The spare embryos could also be sold, as sperm and eggs are now, to couples who could see from the already born child how the purchased embryo
might turn out.

The possibility of such developments raises awkward questions, from
those centering on the uniqueness of human beings to the rights of parents to
control their own embryos.

The American Fertility Society, in a statement yesterday, said that "this
subject is of such grave importance that relevant guidelines should be established at the national level."

INCREASING SUPPLY OF EMBRYOS

Clones are genetically identical individuals, a phenomenon that happens naturally in humans with the birth of identical twins or triplets. In a cloning procedure that has long been applied to cattle, an embryo is divided into separate

New York Times, October 26, 1993, pp. A1, B7.

clusters of cells, each of which is then implanted in the womb and develops in the normal way.

But until now the technique was not known to have been applied to humans. The doctor who performed the cloning, Dr. Jerry L. Hall, said he felt the technique would be a useful way to increase the supply of embryos in fertility clinics. As he reported at a meeting of the American Fertility Society in Montreal this month, Dr. Hall subdivided 17 human embryos into 48. Each of the 17 was genetically abnormal and would not have been brought to term. All the embryos were discarded six days after fertilization.

Dr. Robert Stillman, who directs the in vitro fertilization program at George Washington University where Dr. Hall works, said the method needed to be improved and tested before it could be offered to infertile couples. In the meantime, he added, he and his colleagues have no intention of going any further. It is time, he said, to step back and think about what science has wrought. "I believe that what can come from this is a debate in the science, medical and ethics community," Dr. Stillman said.

Dr. Norman Fost, a medical ethicist at the University of Wisconsin, said he believed it was the parents' prerogative to decide what to do with their embryos. He said he started "with a presumption of privacy and liberty, that people should be able to live their lives the way they want and to make babies the way they want."

Dr. Fost added that although some people say it is chilling to think of identical twins born years apart, "it strikes me as better to have twins born years apart than to have them born together," since the duties of child-raising would be more spread out.

MAKING "100 DAN QUAYLES"

Dr. Fost gave little credence to the fear that couples might buy cloned embryos and populate the world with identical individuals. It's the notion, Dr. Fost said, that "we'll make 100 Jimmy Carters or 100 Dan Quayles." He added: "Environment plays too large a role. You could take 100 Hitler embryos and raise them and never get Hitler again."

Dr. Albert Jonsen, an ethicist at the University of Washington in Seattle and chairman of the National Advisory Board on Ethics and Reproduction, said that he agreed with Dr. Fost and that his main concern with cloning was to develop it as an effective tool.

"The first attempts to clone leave us with the possibility that we will create a lot of monstrosities along the way," he said. But once the technique is perfected, he added, "I don't see any reason why it is morally wrong." The debate over cloning, he said, shows how "every odd question that one can ask about a new science becomes an ethical question. And that's dumb."

But Dr. Arthur Caplan, director of the Center for Bioethics at the University of Minnesota, said he found cloning morally suspect.

"One of the things we treasure about ourselves is our individuality," Dr. Caplan said. "Obviously, we have twins and triplets in the world, but they are there by accident. You begin to worry that when you deliberately set out to make copies of something, you lessen its worth."

SEEING EMBRYO'S FUTURE

Then there is the Dorian Gray scenario of identical twins born years apart. "Twins that become twins separated by years or decades let us see things about our future that we don't want to," Dr. Caplan said. "You may not want to know, at 40, what you will look like at 60. And parents should not be looking at a baby and seeing the infant 20 years later in an older sibling.

"Suppose someone said, 'I've got 10 embryos stored, here's what they will become. You can look at the 20-year-old and see what you've got.' Is that fair to the child? What expectations will you put on them?"

Dr. Caplan added, "I think that marketplace ethics and pounding the autonomy drum are not sufficient when it comes to decisions of how to make future generations of children and their descendants."

Taking issue with Dr. Fost, Dr. Caplan added the implications raised by cloning were more than just a matter of privacy. "I don't care how people behave in their bedrooms or what sort of clothes they wear," he said. Because cloning raised social issues, he added, "there is room for governmental and societal debate and, perhaps, prohibitions and control and restraints."

Dr. Ruth Macklin, a professor of bioethics at Albert Einstein College of Medicine in the Bronx, said that although it was hard to argue that ethical principles would be violated by cloning, the technique could provide "an opportunity for mischief." And, she added, that places a burden on those who would develop and offer the technique.

For example, what would happen to sibling rivalries between twins born years apart? Would children be hurt by being viewed as products of a scientist's tinkering in a laboratory. "We cannot accurately predict what the consequences would be," Dr. Macklin said. "We can only surmise. And, in general, people are rather poor predictors."

CLONING AS BUSINESS?

But in vitro fertilization is a business, developed and advanced without Federal money or oversight. And with the multitude of clinics that offer these very expensive services, the business has become highly competitive. Some questioned whether clinics might not seize on cloning to attract new clients.

Doctors who work at in vitro fertilization clinics, however, had mixed reactions to the possibility of cloning embryos.

Dr. Edward L. Marut, the medical director of the in vitro fertilization center at Michael Reese Hospital in Chicago, said he could not imagine offering cloning. "You have to draw a line at some point," he said. "It's a dangerous turn, trying to create the perfect child and then duplicating it. What do you do if you don't like the first child? Throw the cloned embryo away?"

Dr. Marut added that some clinics, however, might see a reason to offer cloning. "It will have a huge price tag, I'm sure," he said.

Dr. Mark Sauer of the in vitro fertilization program at the University of Southern California, said, "I'm sure it will be done in the future."

Dr. Sauer said he feared that some clinics would use the technique for publicity. "People who are looking for headlines or to sensationalize programs will do something of this nature without thinking it through," he said. "It's a competitive environment out there."

Dr. Sauer agreed with the researchers at George Washington University that cloning could be a real boon to couples who produce too few embryos for in vitro fertilization. Asked what he would do if a couple wanted to have twins born years apart, Dr. Sauer said: "I would have no problem with that as long as I understood what the couple's real motivation was. I've always been one to agree with reproductive choice."

Dr. Mark D. Hornstein, who directs the in vitro fertilization program at the Brigham and Women's Hospital in Boston, was more hesitant. "The ethical concerns are considerable," he said. "We've had a bad experience in this century with attempts to breed human beings."

While not saying he would rule out cloning, even for a couple that wants twins born years apart, Dr. Hornstein said he was let off the hook, in a way, because any requests like that would have to be approved by a hospital ethics board. And if the board agreed? Dr. Hornstein said he was still uncertain. "I have to sleep at night, too," he said.

But now that the group at George Washington University has taken the first step, Dr. Sauer said: "You'll see people go ahead with it. People may have been too timid before" to be the first to clone a human embryo. He added, "We and others who do micromanipulation will play a part in initiating it."

CRIME AND THE BIOTECH REVOLUTION

Gene Stephens

Stephens is a professor of criminal justice at the University of South Carolina. He is also the criminal justice editor for The Futurist, *and he wrote this article in 1992 for that magazine. Stephens examines the effects of both actual and possible future technologies for the criminal justice system. Parts of this article are still science fiction.*

An android with a human brain goes berserk. Should it be sent to a mental institution for treatment—or back to the factory for disassembly?

A clone is convicted as a psychopathic killer. Should it be sentenced as an individual, or should all of its fellow clones be sentenced as well?

A human being who has been altered with horse genes commits a crime. Would the criminal courts handle the case, or the Society for the Prevention of

The Futurist, November–December 1992, pp 28–42.

Cruelty to Animals? If that horse-human has committed murder, would we put it on trial, with full due process? Or would we simply have it "put to sleep"?

These and scores of other ethical and procedural questions could plague societies in the future, as the biotech revolution—the age of "participatory evolution"—hurtles forward at breakneck speed.

Because it will mean a reexamination of what is "human," the new era is more revolutionary than evolutionary. New biotechnology will force a reexamination of all aspects of human society, from family and lifestyles to law and justice. Indeed, even relationships among plants and animals will be altered.

Human genes may soon be mixed with plant genes, so that people might be capable of photosynthesis—converting light into chemical energy usable by the human body. Would these "little green men" still be classed as human, or would they be placed in some new category of creature? Add a few fish genes to the equation, and the creature is suddenly green and gilled. Suppose the creature decides to violate a human law: Now you have on your hands a little green criminal with gills.

And what if a human genetically altered with bird genes swoops down and swallows a little green man with gills? Is it murder—or just lunch?

POTENTIAL OUTCOMES OF RESEARCH

What started with the decoding of DNA in the late 1950s snowballed as geneticists made one amazing discovery after another over the next three decades. But the current Human Genome Project, which will map every gene in the human genome, will escalate the pace at which biotechnology advances. The project has already deciphered several thousand genetic codes, and it may complete its mission by the end of this decade.

New technologies are frequently adopted by creative criminals, as well as by the criminal-justice system. The new biotechnologies are no exception. Consider these possibilities:

• **Impacts of immortality.** Biotechnology researchers are almost certain to unlock the genetic passage to immortality. Current efforts to extend life 20 or 30 years pale in comparison to the probability that a genetic clock will be discovered in each of us and that ways will be found to slow down, speed up, or stop that clock. Old age might never take another life, though people (or semi-people!) could still die from disease, accident, or murder.

Among the issues that the prospect of immortality raises is how to punish someone who murders or negligently kills an "immortal." And if an immortal commits a murder, could society afford to sentence him to life imprisonment?

Age-control drugs present interesting dilemmas. For instance, a black market may form for anti-aging and aging drugs. Such products could also be used by the criminal-justice system. One form of punishment might be to speed up a person's aging process. A hot-headed 25-year-old could be "sentenced" to being turned into a more sedate 50-year-old. Older criminals might be punished by being deprived of anti-aging drugs.

• **Parts to spare?** Today, there are about three dozen body parts that can be replaced bionically, and certainly there will be more in the future. If the demand for body parts exceeds supply, laws may be enacted to deal with rich people who want to barter with poor people for their "spare parts."

Stealing organs—"organ legging"—may become a major issue. Recently, news accounts told of a man who woke up on a park bench after a night of drinking; noticing a pain in his side, he went to a clinic, where doctors found that his kidney had been surgically removed while he was intoxicated.

Parents might try to sell their children's body parts. Already, parents have produced additional children as a source of bone marrow for transplants for themselves or their other children. One possible solution would be to allow people to clone themselves and use their clones for spare parts. If governments outlaw the practice, an international black market in spare parts could develop.

Other dilemmas may arise from cryonics—freezing the bodies of people who die in the hope that someday medical science can thaw them, cure the disease they died of, and restore them to life. What will happen to a frozen person's assets while he or she awaits revival? If there is a power outage and the body thaws prematurely, deteriorating beyond repair, would the responsible person be charged with murder? [. . .]

JUSTICE AND "HUMAN" RIGHTS

The knowledge and the technology to correct genetic abnormalities and change undesirable traits are coming fast. Can it be much longer before we can create new semi-human creatures, thereby actively participating in the evolutionary process?

The "tinkering" has been under way for some time. Fish and plant genes have been mixed to create frost-resistant potato and tobacco crops. New life-forms—such as bacteria that eat oil—have been created in test tubes and marketed to industry. More recently, a new plant has been genetically engineered for use as biodegradable plastic. The U.S. government permits the patenting of new life-forms, thus protecting the developers' profits.

Mixing human and nonhuman genetic material once was banned in the United States, but recently human genes were implanted in pigs in order to provide humanlike kidneys for organ transplants. There is no ban on human—animal gene mixing in most countries. Clones, chimeras, cyborgs, and other bioengineering wonders are almost certain to appear in the twenty-first century. What impacts will these developments have on justice and social order?

The current difficulty of maintaining peace and order in a heterogeneous society of black and white, yellow and brown human beings will pale in comparison to trying to maintain a semblance of harmony among gilled, winged, multicolored, "mutated" humanoids.

The increasingly aggressive animal-rights movement will surely find new followers among the largely or partially human creations of biotechnology.

The pro-life and pro-choice movements will face massive confusion as procreation moves from the bedroom to the fertilization room. Choices will involve questions of what forms of life may be created; as an issue, abortion will seem trivial in comparison.

How will new semi-human life-forms be ranked on the "participatory evolutionary scale"? Will a catwoman have more rights than a dogman? Would a semi-human with animal genes, such as a fishman, have more rights than a semi-human with plant genes, say, an oak-woman? When the inevitable conflicts for food, housing, jobs, political appointments, etc., occur, who will get preference?

Will the protections of the U.S. Bill of Rights and the United Nations Declaration on Human Rights be granted to semi-humans? How "human" does a semi-human creation have to be in order to enjoy basic human rights and privileges under the law?

BIOCOMPUTERIZED CRIME-FIGHTING

The next big step in the technological revolution will be the merging of biological and information technologies. Computers will ultimately be implanted into the human body to improve organic functioning and to simulate, increase, and enhance the capacity and capabilities of the brain.

These developments will have dramatic impacts on crime and criminal justice. Criminals soon may carry all the information they need for computer theft in database implants in their brains. A police officer of the next century will walk down the street and identify everyone he sees: Complete birth-to-death dossiers of all citizens, including criminal records and "wanted" alerts, will be stored in the officer's computer-enhanced brain, and the officer will scan his implanted nanocomputer databank in fractions of a second.

A further development might be to use these organic nanocomputer implants to control human behavior. The Human Genome Project will not only unlock the secrets of the body, but also shed light on how body chemicals and electrical circuitry control mental functions and emotions. Adding or subtracting a few chemicals or altering synapses could control an individual's thoughts and emotions.

An organic nanocomputer in a person's brain could thus regulate chemical production and electrical impulses in the body and create whatever behavior was deemed appropriate. In the future, courts might sentence criminals to receiving a five-year behavioral-control implant rather than sending [them] to jail. Criminals may be sentenced to biochemical implants to keep them under control, or [to] implanted subliminal messages that constantly remind them to "obey the law" and "do the right thing."

As the biotech and information revolutions move forward, many more such procedural and ethical issues will arise for "human" society—particularly in the legal arena. How we resolve these policy issues will determine the quality of life in the future.

ALL RIGHTS RESERVED

Bernice Wuethrich

Bernice Wuethrich wrote this article for Science News *in late 1993. It is an exploratory article that describes some of the perspectives on the gene-patenting race and how it is affecting science. This article is not science fiction.*

Since the National Institutes of Health first filed for patents on thousands of fragments of human genes in 1992, a sense of unease has permeated much of the international community of human geneticists. Perhaps it is just the disquiet that comes with sudden change and its unknown consequences—unrest that will dissipate as they work through ethical and legal questions now entwined with their research.

But many researchers are waving red flags. They are confronting difficult problems arising at the complex intersection of science, private enterprise, and the law.

C. Thomas Caskey, a Howard Hughes Medical Institute geneticist at the Baylor College of Medicine in Houston, offers a case in point. Last October, his team cloned the human gene responsible for creating wrinkles on the surface of the brain. These wrinkles are initiated during the first nine to 14 weeks of fetal development. If a mutation in the gene blocks their formation, a newborn will suffer from a severe form of mental retardation caused by lissencephaly, or "smooth brain" disease. The Caskey team is seeking a patent on the discovery. They hope to create a diagnostic test for detecting defective genes in the fetus.

Since filing for the patent, however, Caskey says he has learned that NIH scientists had serendipitously cloned at least six tiny fragments of that same gene in 1991. NIH included these anonymous genetic scraps in its massive gene-patent filing in 1992. If NIH's patents are approved, a legal battle may ensue, potentially delaying diagnostic use of the gene.

This scenario, says Caskey, is "going to happen time and time again" if the patent office rules that human gene fragments of unknown biological function can be "owned."

Geneticist Diane Wilson Cox tells of how codiscoverers of the gene for dystrophin—a structural component of muscle—have come to face a similar imbroglio.

Mutations in this gene cause Duchenne muscular dystrophy. In the late 1980s, two research groups found and began to sequence the huge dystrophin gene, with each group concentrating on a different section. Later, each group—one at Toronto's Hospital for Sick Children, the other at Children's Hospital in Boston—applied for a U.S. patent on its section, says Cox, a geneticist at the Toronto hospital.

The Boston group, anticipating approval, licensed patent rights to Genica Pharmaceuticals Corp., a biotechnology firm in Worcester, Mass. The Toronto group had to drop its application because it could not afford the $20,000-plus cost of pursuing the patent. Nonetheless, the Toronto researchers continued their work with the gene and with their young patients. Part of that work involves producing antibodies that correspond to the patented sections of the gene and then using those antibodies to diagnose dystrophin dysfunction. Genica patent lawyers claimed this was a commercial use of their product and threatened to file a lawsuit for patent infringement, Cox says.

The Toronto doctors had three choices: stop their work, pay royalties, or await a lawsuit. The situation remains unresolved. "This is one of the issues you get into when patenting gene fragments," Cox laments.

At the crux of the controversy are the pending patents filed by NIH on 6,122 gene fragments. Although lawyers at the patent office may argue for years before deciding whether these genetic scraps can be owned, Congress has meanwhile mounted its own investigation, mandating that the Office of Technology Assessment (OTA) report on policy options by next spring. In July, OTA sought out the opinions of an international group of scientists as part of that effort. They deliberated whether the U.S. Patent and Trademark Office should approve patents on genetic fragments and, if it does, how such decisions might affect genetic research and medical progress.

"We heard person after person, from virtually every country, saying that fragments and genes of unknown function are not patentable," says Cox. While their reasons ranged from the moral to the pragmatic, almost all participants at the meeting agreed on this point.

No similar consensus exists in the United States, however. Here, two contrasting perspectives frame the debate. One view asserts that the patenting of human DNA—including anonymous fragments—will stimulate further research, spur the development of new medical diagnostics, and generate life-saving therapies. The other holds that such patents will stifle research, sow suspicion and secrecy among scientists, and slow medical progress.

Some U.S. researchers and companies—as well as NIH—are not idly awaiting the legal outcome of NIH's patent applications. Rather, they are filing their own patents, positioning themselves to have as much of a corner on the human gene market as possible. Their actions may reflect the reality of science and the marketplace in the United States. "The American practice is that we file for patents on these things," says Daniel Drell, a biologist at the Department of Energy (DOE).

So fast and furious is the race to identify human genes that within several years, patents may have been filed for every one of the estimated 100,000 genes nestled in human cells—the entire human genome. Thus, a small number of corporations, universities, and governments may soon "own" life's genetic code.

QUESTIONS TO HELP YOU THINK AND WRITE ABOUT ISSUES IN MODERN TECHNOLOGY

1. What is Mander's argument about the nature of television? What type of proof does he use to develop his argument? Is it effective? Why?

2. What types of proof does Hamill use to develop his argument about the effect of television? Are they effective? Why?

3. Compare the views of Hamill and Cooke on the effect of television on its viewers. Which do you agree with more? Frame a rebuttal for the essay you disagree with.

4. Read the articles by Rheingold and by Pimentel and Teixeira and the short story by Dworetzky. Speculate about the good effects of virtual reality. Also consider some of the potentially dangerous effects, according to your system of values. What are your reasons for considering them valuable or dangerous for the future development of the human race?

5. Read Wilson's article about the potential use of virtual reality in teaching. If it were available right now, what classroom material would you most like to experience through virtual reality? Why? How do you think it would help you learn? Would it be better for some subjects than others? Which ones? What type of virtual reality program would you create to use in the classroom if you had the means to do that? Why would you consider it to be valuable?

6. Read the four articles by Rifkin, Greenough, Kolata, and Stephens about the possibilities of biotechnology. Draw a line down the middle of a piece of paper to form two columns. In the first column, write all of the potential benefits of biotechnology. In the second column, write all of the potential harms. Use your own system of values to help you make these judgments. What value warrants are implicit in the judgments you made? Compare them with the judgments of others in your class. Are there some variations in the value warrants in your class?

7. Evaluate the policy of patenting genes. According to your value system, is this good or bad? Why do you think so?

SECTION VIII
Two Forums for Argument: Debate and Academic Inquiry

A PRO AND CON ISSUE FOR DEBATE: LEGALIZED ABORTION

1. What Are the Arguments on the Legal Abortion Issue?

Pro: What Are the Affirmative Arguments? Hardy's account of her experiences as an infiltrator of a prolife group (p. 599) will provide you with a sense of the intensity of this issue as well as with some arguments on both sides. Quindlen's article (p. 606) will provide you with some of the usual arguments in favor of abortion. See also "An Interview with Garrett Hardin," pp. 24–30.

Con: What Are the Negative Arguments? Heaphy (p. 608) provides arguments opposing abortion from a medical doctor's perspective.

Common Ground: What Are Some Areas for Common Ground? Banisky (p. 610) describes what prolife and prochoice groups have in common if they decide to seek common ground. See also "We're Good Republicans—and Pro-Choice," pp. 22–23.

OTHER PRO AND CON ISSUES IN "THE READER"

Capital Punishment

Pro: "Statements in Favor of the Death Penalty," pp. 463–467.
Con: "Why Capital Punishment?" pp. 459–463.

Tough Drug Sentencing

Pro: "Don't Let Judges Set Crooks Free," pp. 439–441.
Con: "The War on Drugs Is Self-Defeating," pp. 442–444.

Handgun Control

Pro: "Go Ahead Crooks, Make My Day," pp. 756–757.
Con: "A Pistol-Whipped Nation," pp. 453–456.

Controlling Textbook Content

Pro: "What Should Be Done About Bias in Our Children's Textbooks?" pp. 489–492.
Con: "Why Teach Us to Read and Then Say We Can't?" pp. 492–496.

Television

Pro: "TV Causes Violence? Says Who?" pp. 568–569.
Con: "Crack and the Box," pp. 564–567.

Men's and Women's Groups

Pro: "Ending the Battle between the Sexes," pp. 379–386 and "Breaking the Spell: Men and Men's Groups," pp. 403–405.
Con: "The Men's Movement," pp. 222–224.

THE RHETORICAL SITUATION

The issues motivated by the value we place on life are inflammatory, emotional issues, and some individuals take extreme positions on them. Consequently, it can be difficult to argue about them. Still, since you will encounter such issues along with the people who take extreme positions, you will need to learn ways to argue in these situations. Practicing in the relatively safe and controlled environment of the argument class will provide you with some strategies for arguing productively.

Issues in this category, at least for some people, include legalized abortion, assisted suicides (euthanasia), animal rights (including protecting endangered species), the adequacy of research resources for AIDS and breast cancer, the draft in time of war, capital punishment, handgun control, and child or wife abuse. All of these issues deal with life and death, and, as a result, many people respond to them with strong feelings. Furthermore, the press and some religious, political, and special interest groups frequently encourage people to polarize these issues and view them as pro or con, black or white.

Social-judgment theorists, who study the positions that individuals take on issues, plot positions on a continuum that ranges from extremely positive to extremely negative. They then describe these positions in terms of latitudes of acceptance. Individuals at the extremes of the continuum have narrow latitudes of acceptance and can usually only tolerate positions that are either the same as or very close to their own. Somewhere in the middle is a latitude of noncommitment. People in this area, who are close to the middle and who are not strongly ego-involved with the issue, have comparatively wide latitudes of acceptance and can tolerate a wide range of positions.

We draw on this basic theory to set up the debate in this section. Two groups are encouraged to take strong affirmative and negative positions and to argue from those points of view with presumably narrow latitudes of acceptance. A third, middle group with a wider latitude of acceptance is to look for common ground in the extreme positions and attempt to create a more productive argument with give and take and the possibility of better understanding or even a change of views.

Articles to help you invent pro and con arguments and also establish common ground are provided here for the abortion issue. If your class would prefer to argue another issue, a list of other possibilities is provided along with the articles in this book that provide pro and con viewpoints. Not all of these additional topics deal with life and death issues, but they will still provide opportunities for lively exchange. The class debate format will work equally well for any one of them.

Your final goals in arguing these issues are to learn ways to minimize or eliminate the conditions that cause argument to fail and to learn how to create the conditions that make it work. The objective is to learn to avoid a standoff.

HOW TO SET UP A CLASS DEBATE: ASSIGNMENT

The articles about the issue in this section have been organized to facilitate a class debate. The procedure for the debate assignment is that two groups of students will present pro and con arguments, and a third group will present suggestions for re- solving some of the conflict. The object is both to understand extreme positions and to contemplate ways to create common ground and reduce conflict.

Preparing for the Debates

1. *Select an issue.* The class votes to debate on either abortion or an alternate topic; see list, pp. 596–597.

2. *Create three groups.* The instructor helps the class divide itself into three groups: Group 1, the affirmative group that is in favor of the subject for debate; Group 2, the negative group that is against it; and Group 3, the critics/respondents who will attempt to resolve the conflict. The groups should be equal in size. To achieve this equality, some students may have to role-play positions that they do not, in fact, actually hold.

3. *Read essays.* Affirmative and negative groups should read both the essays in favor of their side of the issue to get ideas for their arguments and the opposing essays to anticipate the opposition's arguments. The critics/respondents should read essays on both sides to understand the opposing positions.

All three groups should also read the common-ground essay, but from three perspectives: the affirmative and negative groups read for ideas and evidence to strengthen their positions, and the critics/respondents read to discover common ground and ways to minimize the differences and resolve the conflict. (If the class is working with a topic other than abortion, everyone should read the common- ground essay on the topic of abortion and apply the ideas for achieving common ground to the issue for debate.)

4. *Assign papers.* Students in Groups 1 and 2 write one-page, 250-word pa- pers outside of class that present some arguments to support their positions. Two students from the affirmative group and two from the negative group agree to start debate by reading their papers.

Conducting the Debate

Day One

1. *Begin with the opening papers* (10 minutes). The first affirmative, first nega- tive, second affirmative, and second negative read their papers in that order.

2. *Others join in* (20 minutes). Students may now raise their hands to be rec- ognized by the instructor to give additional arguments from their papers. Each per- son should stand to speak. The speakers should represent each side in turn. The class should decide whether everyone should first be allowed to speak before any-

one is permitted to speak a second time. The instructor should cut off speakers who are going on too long.

3. *Caucus and closing remarks* (15 minutes). The affirmative and negative groups caucus for 5 minutes to prepare their closing arguments. Each group selects a spokesperson who then presents their final, strongest arguments in a 2-minute closing presentation.

4. *Critics/respondents prepare responses.* The critics write one-page, 250-word responses outside of class that answer the following question: Now that you have heard both sides, how would you resolve the conflict?

Day Two

1. *Critics read* (20 minutes). All critics/respondents read their papers. Each paper should take about 2 minutes to read.

2. *Analyze outcomes* (30 minutes). The class should now discuss the outcomes of the debate by addressing the following questions:

a. What, in general, were some of the outcomes?
b. Who changed their opinions? Which ones? Why?
c. Who did not change? Why?
d. What are some of the outcomes of the attempts to reduce conflict and establish common ground?
e. What strategies have you learned from participating in debate that can help you in real-life arguments on inflammatory topics?

1. What Are the Arguments on the Legal Abortion Issue?

IN GOD'S COUNTRY

Alexandra Hardy

Alexandra Hardy is a freelance writer who published this article in Texas Observer *in 1992. This article is included here to provide a sense of the emotional commitment some people have for this issue.*

Patricia had a revelation while protesting outside a southwest Houston abortion clinic.

"Suddenly I had the vision of red," she said. "It was the blood of Jesus and the aborted children, and then it went black. I knew I was in the womb of one of the women in the mill."

"Mill" is how people like Patricia and her fellow Operation Rescue members refer to abortion clinics.

Texas Observer, September 4, 1992, pp. 16–18, 23.

When I decided to infiltrate Operation Rescue just before the Republican National Convention in Houston, I had a few visions of my own: being discovered as a non-believer among a group of "rescuers," someone suddenly standing up and pointing to me screaming "traitor, spy, devil worshipper." Or worse.

The stern woman's voice on the recorded message wasn't what I expected from an organization trying to entice local residents into fighting for its cause.

"Thank you for calling Operation GOP: Guard-Our-Preborn. Four Christians were arrested today," the recorded voice said. It went on to inform callers of a rally that would take place that night at Liberty Revival Church.

Getting to the church was a test of faith in itself. The white aluminum building was 15 miles out in the suburbs off Highway 290, northwest of Houston, and I got there late. New converts are required to register and cough up a $10 "donation." This entitled me to attend all of the rallies. A young man who looked like he was home from college asked to see my driver's license. He compared that information with the form I'd filled out at the door. The form required my name and address, as well as home and work phone numbers. It also asked for the name of my church. I answered as truthfully as I could without giving away that I was a journalist. However, Episcopalians aren't noted for their involvement in the anti-abortion movement, nor are they particularly trusted by the overwhelmingly fundamentalist O.R. membership, so I wrote that I attended a Catholic church I was familiar with.

The young man at the door asked me to read the back of the form and sign it. It turned out to be a sort of loyalty oath, restricting the signer from talking to the media. It also included an understanding that I would allow myself to be arrested for the cause if it came to that. This was the first of many times I thought about backing out. This time, the young man interrupted my apprehension. "Don't worry," he assured me, "only the rescuers get arrested."

A wholesome young woman next to him snatched my driver's license and looked me over to make sure that I was the same person. After I passed her inspection I entered the church while the faithful were in the middle of a hymn. The 200 members of the congregation, all waving their hands toward God, reminded me of the fundamentalist Christian services I'd seen on television. After the song ended, Keith Tucci, an O.R. leader, began to whip the crowd up, implored them to get on their hands and knees and pray for the "dead babies."

Many in the congregation got down on the ground and prayed, looking like Muslims paying their daily homage to Allah, while others went to their knees and put their faces in the seats of their chairs. I began to get uncomfortable as I noticed people in the crowd crying, something I was unable to affect. So I got to my knees and pretended to pray, hands clasped together like a child at bedtime.

The atmosphere intensified as Tucci stepped up his rhetoric, invoking dead babies until the entire congregation was filled with the wrath of an angry Lord. I imagined terrified women going into the clinics that week, remembered how I and my friends who had made the decision to have an abortion felt in the past, running that gauntlet of hatred present every week at Houston clinics, if on a smaller scale. I thought of how frightened those women would be at having to face these people, whose numbers were multiplied tenfold during convention week. Women who would have to face these zealots as well as deal with the fear of the procedure itself.

While others were praying and I was simulating praying, these things went through my mind and finally did bring tears to my eyes, which in a cynical way was perfect because I began to fit in with the rest of the congregation.

After the prayer ended, Tucci asked all of the leaders of O.R. to come up to the front. Of the 10 or more leaders who came forward, not one was a woman. One of the leaders then asked for all of the women who could not have children to come forward, so that the leaders could "lay their hands on them." One woman came up and the leader asked for others to join her but he joked "only married women, after all this is a Christian rally."

Later Tucci introduced Randall Terry, the national leader of O.R. Terry worked the crowd, more like a lounge singer than a preacher. He got the faithful revved up by talking about the hated "pro-abort feminists."

Terry then sat down at a piano and randomly banged on the keys, creating an irritating cacophony. "I'm Judge O'Neill, I can't sing; I'm Ann Richards, I can't think," Terry said. (Prior to the convention, state District Judge Eileen O'Neill issued a restraining order restricting the anti-abortion protesters from coming within 100 feet of the clinics. Several O.R. leaders were arrested for violating the order. In retaliation, the O.R. members prayed all week for God to strike the judge down. So far, the prayers have not been answered.)

Terry then delighted his devoted audience by crooning "a song I wrote." He settled down to play his song, a recorded version of which, Terry said, "can be bought in the church store after the service."

Fundamentalist Barry Manilow is the only way to describe Terry's song. It began with Terry asking the musical question, "Grandpa, what did you do when all the babies were dying?" Later in the piece, he passionately howled, "Babies are dying while we're watching our TVs."

The next morning I made my first attempt to join O.R. protesters outside a clinic. I dressed conservatively and had listened carefully the night before to the other O.R. members so I could learn their terminology. Abortion clinics I now called "mills" or "abortuaries." There was no such thing as a "pro-choice" person to O.R. members, only "pro-abortionists" or "pro-aborts." I went to a "mill" in Southwest Houston where I'd already heard from my sister, a clinic defender privy to intelligence reports from pro-choice infiltrators, O.R. had scheduled a disturbance. My stomach became queasy as I approached an older man holding a sign with the familiar mutilated fetus on it. A fair-haired man in his 30s, who identified himself as Taylor, stood next to him carrying a picture of his 18-month-old daughter. Taylor told me he and the other man were showing passersby "the before and after pictures of babies."

"Where are our people?" I asked them. They pointed to a group of about 30 people, most of whom were on the ground in front of the clinic, praying. I left the two of them standing on the corner. The older man was telling Taylor, "If I was married I would have lots of children. I would name them Mary and Joseph—all of them would have names from the Bible."

Walking over to the anti-abortionists, I was followed by another woman who had just arrived. She looked like the stereotypical fundamentalist: bleached blond hair that seemed overstyled for a protest and a demure white smock-type dress. Patricia introduced herself, and when I informed her it was my first time she immediately took me under her wing. This was her first week out with the protesters. "Before, my husband told me I should just pray," she said. "He didn't want me to get involved because he's worried about me going to jail."

We crossed a white line on the sidewalk that marked the 100 feet from the clinic we were not allowed to cross. Fear tugged at my stomach again as I imagined getting arrested for violating the restraining order. I would later learn that the police did not automatically enforce the injunction. Patricia and I knelt on the sidewalk and prayed with the others. Patricia got up to buy a sign depicting David, O.R.'s name for this particular mutilated fetus. O.R. frequently names the fetuses. The sight of this angelic-looking woman buying the grotesque sign was unnerving, but there were many more moments like this to come in my week with O.R.

Shortly after Patricia purchased the sign she was interviewed by an Associated Press reporter. She patiently answered his questions and then asked him one of her own: "Is Christ your savior?" The young reporter looked around and squirmed a little before giving a half-earnest "yes." For a second I felt smug seeing a fellow reporter saying anything to get a good quote. Then I remembered what I was doing.

Patricia was delighted to have found a Christian among the heathen press. For me, suffering the contemptuous stares of my colleagues was unsettling and would become more so during the week. At one point as I knelt on the ground praying, I looked up at the pro-choice side to see a group of photographers laughing at us. I was fortunate that most of the press covering the clinic demonstrations were from out of town, so I was not recognized.

We prayed in the sun for about an hour before being told that we should go get some water. Standing by the cooler, I recognized more people from the rally; most of them were the hard core rescuers who had come from Georgia, Ohio and Southern California. I sat down next to Ronald, a small, oddly petite man in his 40s, with short gray hair. He wore a white T-shirt and stone-colored baggy pants and around his neck dangled a cross fashioned from yarn. I told him it was my first time out here. "Praise God," he smiled beatifically. After sharing with him my fear of getting arrested, Ronald began to open up to me.

Ronald, like most of the national O.R. people, travels around the country trying to close clinics. Ronald tried to give me guidance by sharing something he had heard Randall Terry say "Courage is not the lack of fear. Courage is what you do with that fear." I thanked him and told him I feared I was simply a coward. "No, don't say coward," he scolded. "The Bible says bad things about cowards."

About that time one of the national O.R. women asked me to hold her sign while she took a break. It read, "Abortionists lie to women to make money." I stood on the side of the street holding the sign in front of my face so no one passing by would recognize me. The pro-choice people had signs reading, "Honk if you're pro-choice." Every seventh car would honk and drivers would wave. No one waved at me.

The message on the O.R.-GOP hotline told me where "all Christians" were to meet the next morning. I was overwhelmed by the turnout on both sides. The Houston police had set up a long barricade separating the anti-abortionists from the pro-choice side. There was a sense of triumph within our group because the police had arrested a clinic defender who was accused of shoving an O.R. woman the previous day.

Becky, a young Hispanic anti-abortionist asked if I knew where we were going next. We tried to find out from the national O.R. people, but got answers like, "We don't know; the Lord will guide us." Finally, after about an hour of praying and singing hymns, we were given a flyer with the target clinic printed on it.

Becky, who had come on the O.R. bus, accepted my offer of a ride to the next site. On our way to the car she stopped to tell a young man that she was riding with me. He wore an O.R. T-shirt with "Baton Rouge, La." printed on it and the dates that he had protested there. "How do you know her?" he said, pointing at me. Becky smiled at him as if she thought he was being overly paranoid. "I know her," she said. "She's one of us." I tried to be friendly to him as we walked away but he didn't seem reassured.

Many anti-abortionists brought their children to the clinic in Southwest Houston. Newborn babies were kept in the sun for hours as their parents did "God's work." By now, the clinic defenders had prepared better chants, which they shouted at us endlessly. "It's my body and I'll breed if I want to, breed if I want to," they sang. "You can choose too if it happens to you." The O.R. side had songs as well, though I didn't know the tunes. One woman gathered all the children on the anti-abortion side and played her portable organ while the children held hands and sang as they walked in a circle. I was thrilled to finally recognize the tune: "Jesus loves the little children, all the children of the world." I sang enthusiastically.

Things heated up a bit when Keith Tucci walked across the street close to the front entrance of the clinic, where National Organization for Women President Patricia Ireland met him with a copy of Judge O'Neill's injunction. Tucci took the document, tore it up and dropped the pieces on Ireland's head. A woman next to me started crying hysterically. "Don't they realize they're going to hell?" she sobbed, pointing to the clinic defenders. The distraught anti-abortionist asked that I hold her sign while she collected herself. The sign was a picture of David, the mutilated fetus, which I had trouble looking at, much less holding. As I held the sign I spotted my father and sister on the other side. They had their arms linked with other defenders and appeared to be having a good time doing what they felt was worthwhile. I felt ashamed of my sign. I didn't see how carrying it was respecting life. An anti-abortionist cheerfully

604 • *The Reader*

passed around pictures in a flimsy plastic album like they give you with your prints at the drug store. The man behaved as though he were showing off his family vacation snapshots.

One of the photos showed a fetus which had its head severed from its body and was laid out on a white sheet on this man's dining room table. In one picture the man and his young child stood by the table glancing at the remains. From what I could determine from the photos, it appeared that the fetus was the result of a miscarriage, because of its size and the fact that it was mostly intact. The man claimed that the fetus came from "a mill I went to close down."

"When I went in, no one was there, only buckets full of dead babies," he said. He claimed he took the contents home and photographed them for the record.

One woman, looking over the pictures, asked if she could show them to her friend. I didn't know what made me more uneasy, the pictures themselves or the delight the "pro-lifers" took in looking at them.

The following Tuesday I put on my recently purchased "Save the Baby Humans" T-shirt and went to Planned Parenthood. I stood next to a group of O.R. leaders and local ministers and tried to listen as they plotted the day's events. There were no women in the group and I soon sensed that I was not welcome. The rest of the anti-abortion protesters were standing right across the street from the entrance to the building. I joined the others as we sang "We exhalt thee, we exhalt thee O Lord." Like those around me I stretched my hands toward God. Shortly after that the O.R. leaders and ministers crossed the street and exhorted us to "pray for the pro-aborts."

Randall Terry used a bullhorn to let the crowd know how pleased he was with President Bush's stance on the issue, but added that "We don't need any more Supreme Court justices like David Souter." As the all-male leadership got up to speak, they were drowned out by chants of "4, 6, 8, 10, why are all your leaders men?"

Half of our group was asked to go to the courthouse where the leaders were to appear—so that we could protest "the unjust persecution of Christians." I rode with Patricia. "The Lord has been opening up many doors for me," she said. Patricia told me of how she was miraculously put in touch with a group of GOP delegates from Colorado. She had made 1,000 copies of an anti-abortion poem, which, with the aid of the Colorado delegates, she passed out on the floor on the convention.

Then, Patricia said, "The Lord put me in touch with someone who was good friends with Pat Buchanan." The highlight of her evening came when she personally handed the poems to Buchanan. Patricia's ankle had been sprained during her strenuous activities on behalf of the anti-abortion movement, but she was able to find relief at the courthouse when her O.R. comrades laid their hands on her stricken ankle and prayed for it.

The next morning we met at Planned Parenthood. The past few days had been draining and I didn't feel up to the charade any longer. One of the national O.R. men asked me to point out people I knew within the organization before he would trust me with a flyer with directions to the next mill. Our group was greatly outnumbered by the pro-choicers, and for some reason the chants and their looks of scorn brought me close to tears. "Don't worry," the previously suspicious O.R. man said to me, "No woman is going to have an abortion while all of this is going on." Tears welled in my eyes as I thought of those women. "They don't hate you," he further consoled me, "they hate God."

The O.R. bus carrying "rescuers" left Planned Parenthood and hit several clinics. Two of the clinics were near downtown and I went to the wrong one. I finally reached the right clinic but the bus had already left. Fortunately, Patricia was there and she had a map to the next clinic, where the bus would stop. The midtown clinic was protected by the most radical group of clinic defenders I had seen, but the busload of rescuers was successful in surrounding the entrance to the clinic. The defenders kept the anti-abortionists from entering the clinic, and soon after our arrival the police arrived. The O.R. faction backed off when police threatened to arrest them. Getting arrested when there was no hope of shutting down the clinic wasn't worth it to the anti-abortionists, who proceeded to another mission. As I tried to find Patricia I was surrounded by a crowd of pro-choicers trying to isolate me from the rest of my group. Patricia, encircled by a group of angry clinic defenders, was treated worse. "Where is your God now?" the pro-choicers demanded as they closed their circle around the terrified anti-abortion protester.

During the convention I heard politicians talk of "middle ground." The past week has taught me that there is no middle ground. People like Patricia and others that I met taught me that there are kind and compassionate people who believe that abortion is wrong. Ironically, however by sharing her own story of being abandoned by an abusive husband who left her with two small children, Patricia unwittingly illustrated whose choice an abortion ultimately is.

And although both factions seemed to believe God was on their sides, I felt no divine presence at any of the confrontations between pro-choice supporters and anti-abortionists. I only sensed hatred.

HEARTS AND MINDS

Anna Quindlen

*The exigence for this article was a law concerning abortion that was being consid-
ered in Pennsylvania in 1992. Quindlen opposes the law, as you will discover in
reading her essay. In the process of refuting the law, she provides a number of the
usual arguments that are given in favor of allowing abortion as a choice.*

Today the Supreme Court will hear arguments on a Pennsylvania law that
would restrict access to abortion in that state. Today demonstrators from both
sides of the question will face each other across the unbridgeable moat of their
disparate beliefs outside clinics in Buffalo.

What about tomorrow?

With all this activity, in the courts and in the streets, it is important to remember that we have taken this debate exactly nowhere in the last 20 years.
The great social issues of this country are settled, not with placards or legal
briefs finally, but in hearts and minds. While the standard-bearers on both sides
posit from the margins of perfect certainty, the great majority learn nothing
that they didn't already know about abortion.

There has been a lot of talk that the Pennsylvania statute is a kind of abortion rights Armageddon. It includes parental consent and spousal notification,
a 24-hour waiting period and medical counseling about other available options,
the procedure and the gestational age of the fetus.

I do not like this law. It has as its subtext the assumption, prevalent among
anti-abortion zealots, that women decide to have abortions in the same way
they decide to have manicures. But it does not serve our credibility to inflate
its provisions. When we squander our rhetoric on restrictions in Pennsylvania,
what does that leave for the law in Louisiana, a slam-dunk of legal abortion
that allows it only in limited cases of rape and incest or to save the life of a
mother?

More important, when we excoriate waiting periods and parental consent we dismiss the ambivalence of many Americans and we miss an opportunity to communicate beyond the slogans. Waiting periods sound reasonable—until you evoke the impoverished mother of three who has driv-
en 600 miles and has only one day's worth of baby-sitting money in her pocket.

Parental consent is constantly justified with the aspirin analogy, the idea
that a girl who cannot get Tylenol in school without a parent's permission
should not be able to have an abortion without it. That's because the judicial
bypass that is a required alternative to consent is little more than a phrase. You
have only to describe a 15-year-old pleading her case before a judge to make

some people understand that this alleged attempt to legislate communication is designed to intimidate instead.

The spousal notification provision is supposed to send the message that husbands have rights, too. But common sense tells us all that a woman who can't discuss this with her husband probably has a reason so potent that no law is going to change her mind.

In short, there are many talking points. It is simply that we have not talked. We have taken stands, and stood.

I understand the positioning that is taking place here, to drum up support by evoking an imminent threat to legal abortion. And I understand the frustration at an issue that it seems will never be settled, and the temptation to meet zealotry with zealotry.

But it saddens me to see some of those who support abortion rights in Buffalo using language as ugly as that of the people who send me anonymous postcards filled with vitriol and photographs of fetuses. I imagined we were better than that. I picture folks seeing this on television and thinking that both groups are lousy with lunatics.

Most Americans, the poll tells us, feel truly represented by neither side. They are the people who say they simultaneously believe abortion is wrong and a private matter. While the demonstrators see black and white, they see gray.

In 1990, Archbishop Rembert G. Weakland of Milwaukee held six "listening sessions" to hear what Catholic women were saying about abortion. I wish in every town in America someone would do what the honorable Archbishop did: bring people together to talk, to disagree, and above all to acknowledge the gray areas.

If we rely on elections and legislation, those of us who believe abortion should be legal, our fortunes will vary with the personnel. If we make people feel their ambivalence is unacceptable, then we've lost them. But if we have reached out to, and reached, the hearts and minds of average Americans with honest discussion, that will drive so much of the rest.

Or we can continue moving from legal argument to legal argument, confrontation to confrontation, as we will today.

But what about tomorrow?

DISMEMBERMENT AND CHOICE

Michael R. Heaphy

Michael Heaphy is a physician who practices in Ohio. He is against abortion. This article was first published in National Review *in 1992.*

For the last few years, it has been commonplace to hear conventionally enlightened people soberly and confidently announce that they are not pro-abortion but, rather, pro-choice. Because of the generality that is implicit in the unqualified word "choice," it is logical to examine the pro-choice argument from a broad perspective.

To make a *pro-choice* argument is to assert a liberty to perform an action, X, without bothering to explain why X should be legal, without acknowledging the nature of X, and, sometimes, without permitting the name for X to cross one's lips. Illogically, "choice" is both the premise and the conclusion. The pro-choice argument for abortion is that abortion should be legal because women have a *right to choose*. The problem with this argument is that an unqualified right purely and simply to *choose* could be used to advocate legal status for drunk driving, cannibalism, insider trading, or anything else. Unless one believes that all conceivable actions should be legal, it is not reasonable to base advocacy of legality for a particular action on *unqualified* choice.

To understand what abortion is all about, it is useful to re-direct our attention from the abstract plane down to a more practical level. Such a real-world viewpoint can be achieved by considering the day-to-day work of a physician who does little else with his professional life except abortions. For example, in my own state of Ohio, there is the practice of W. Martin Haskell, M.D.

Depending on the size of the unborn child (or should I use one of the sanitized terms—like the "conceptus"?), Dr. Haskell employs various techniques. If the fetus isn't too far along, Haskell can probably use the suction curettage method in which a sharp curette is used to reduce the fetus into chunks small enough to be sucked out of the uterus.

Later in pregnancy the fetus is too large for this method. Such cases provide Dr. Haskell with many of his referrals. He is an expert at killing human fetuses at five and six months' gestation. He uses laminaria to dilate the cervix in a three-day procedure, then simply goes in, makes a direct instrument attack on the fetus, kills it, and takes it out.

Of course, the head is usually crushed in this D&E (dilation and evacuation) procedure. An unripened cervix just doesn't expand enough to pass a five- or six-month head. If the unborn baby is big enough, then the arms and legs may have to go too. The fetus is typically dismembered and removed piece by piece in a D&E abortion. The parts are often inspected to make sure an arm or a leg hasn't been left in the mother.

National Review, November 2, 1992, pp. 44, 45.

The news organizations' reticence about mentioning the actual nature of abortion may arise in part from a chink in the gleaming semantic armor that otherwise encases the subject: *The abortion advocates forgot to re-name the body parts encountered in abortion.*

Presumably the "conscientious practitioners" of abortion (as the AMA now calls them—in slight departure from its own earlier description of them as "modern day Herods"), would be loath to admit to killing unborn children. They would rather say that they *terminate pregnancies,* an odd assistance for a process that invariably terminates itself.

As long as the discussion is couched in such genteel terms, there isn't much room for primitive, natural words like "arm" and "leg." They are gaucheries. On the other hand, if we could simply introduce a few Choice words into the vocabulary, then our mass media would no longer need to shy away from the topic of abortion techniques. The unborn child won't be called a child but just a "fetus" (Latin for "offspring"), and the arm is only a "potential arm" or, say, a *"brachium."*

Dr. Haskell operates abortion facilities in Cincinnati and suburban Dayton. When Yvonne Brower, a University of Cincinnati student, called to enquire if she could observe abortions to gather information for a term paper, the clinic manager was magnanimous. On September 21, 1989, Miss Brower observed Dr. Haskell killing fetuses at the Women's Med Center, which he owns, in Kettering, Ohio. The events of that morning prompted Miss Brower to file a complaint with the police.

The following excerpt from the police report is of interest:

> She stated that by 11 o'clock she had already observed two "D&E" three-day procedures on two patients. She stated on the third patient, however, the abortion was different. . . . The patient's water was already broken and she spontaneously gave birth prematurely before the proper D&E procedure could be done. She stated that the baby was delivered feet first very quickly through the birth canal. The head was on its way out when Dr. Haskell reached over and got his scissors and snipped the right side of the baby's common carotid artery.

Even then, Miss Brower stated, the newborn infant was not exactly dead. The police report again:

> The complainant stated that the baby was still moving when she looked at it once again. . . . it was breathing shallow breaths, as was evidenced by the chest moving up and down. She stated that she could also observe the baby's hand having slow, controlled, muscular movements, unlike the short jerky twitchy motions she had seen and learned to expect when the baby was already dead before it came out of the birth canal.

The *Dayton Daily News* reported this story on Sunday, December 10, 1989. In the *Daily News* Dr. Haskell described the event in question in this way: "it came out very quickly after I put the scissors up in the cervical canal and pierced the skull and spread the scissors apart. It popped right on out. . . . the previous two, I had to use the suction to collapse the skull."

Haskell also said Miss Brower "quite possibly" misinterpreted what happened in the abortion. Miss Brower, however, said she saw Dr. Haskell perform 15 abortions the day before and two others that morning. "So it's not like I hadn't seen any before," she said.

Dr. Haskell was questioned by the police. He maintains that when he does abortions he always causes the death of the fetus to occur just before delivery rather than after. The prosecutor did not bring charges.

Of course, if killing the unborn, at the moment when Haskell *openly admits* to the act, is not merely *not illegal* but rather a "fundamental right," it would be remarkable for virtually the same act to constitute legal homicide a few seconds later. *Legal* homicide or not, however, it would seem clear that a direct, intentional, and lethal assault on a human fetus must constitute a *homicide-in-fact* in that old-fashioned, as-long-as-words-have-meanings sense that even our federal judges are not quite able to change. It would be rather surprising if, here or there, some abortionist did not proceed to act on the logical basis that the result is the same whether one kills the fetus and then takes it out or takes it out and then kills it.

At present, good people in America are working to undo a decree that has transformed an entire class of human beings into constitutional outlaws suitable for discretionary killing. The idea that something so grandiose and Platonic as "choice" will be lost to our people if this killing is prohibited is as ludicrous as suggesting that the American people are already deprived of the same ideal by the prohibition of burglary or rape. The abortion struggle is of pivotal importance for humanity because it is about the value of human life and the value of truth. If that seems too abstract, then consider a more concrete approach: Recall that it is also about crushing unborn babies' skulls and ask whether or not it is OK to do that.

ADVERSARIES ON ABORTION BEGIN REACHING FOR COMMON GROUND

Sandy Banisky

This article first appeared in the Baltimore Sun *and was syndicated across the United States in 1992.*

After 20 years of shouting at each other across barricades, some leaders in local abortion battles are trying something revolutionary: They're talking, away from the heat of politics, in an effort to find common ground.

The movement, still tiny and tentative, is growing in a country that finds itself exhausted by two decades of ceaseless conflict over abortion. Common-ground efforts are embraced by people wearied by the name-calling and frustrated by a political process unlikely to yield a clear victory to one side.

Baltimore Sun, January 14, 1992.

"I'm tired of the fight," says Frederica Mathewes-Green, a devoted abortion opponent who worked this summer on the campaign to defeat an abortion-rights law on the Maryland ballot. "This whole field is dominated by people who like a good fight. Searching for common ground means letting go of our enjoyment of a good fight."

In most of the groups, people who disagree profoundly about abortion agree to simply put the argument aside. That done, they find much to agree on. They care about women and children, about preventing unwanted pregnancies, about child support, day-care programs, health, birth control.

"Pro-life and pro-choice people were putting vast amounts of resources, passion and money into fighting each other, when we should be putting our money and our resources into other causes," says B. J. Isaacson-Jones, whose St. Louis clinic includes abortion services.

"We have been guilty of demonizing our opposition and they us," says the Rev. David Kunselman of Buffalo, N.Y., who objects to abortion. "It's high time we give our opponents dignity."

The common-ground efforts have no formal structure. They are whatever the organizers decide will work in their community. No one is asked to compromise on abortion. But everyone is urged to try to see beyond the stereotypes, the labels that deem one side "baby killers" and the other "oppressors of women."

The idea is delicate, its supporters say. But it can work.

In St. Louis, abortion opponents and abortion-rights activists agreed to support legislation that helps crack-addicted pregnant women. In Austin, Catholics who differ on abortion have joined to discuss women's issues. In Buffalo, leaders are working to help bring together a community rent by last spring's protracted abortion protests.

Frances Kissling, head of Catholics for a Free Choice in Washington, says the movement has emerged because "the general public has come to see the ugliness of the debate as unacceptable."

Both sides, she says, know the public's tolerance for intractable positions has waned. In response, the groups have subtly softened their positions in recent years. Abortion-rights groups now talk about reducing the numbers of abortions. Some anti-abortion groups talk about restricting abortion instead of outlawing it entirely.

But the common-ground movement is not for everyone.

Roger Stenson, head of Maryland Right to Life, sees little reason to talk with abortion-rights advocates. "I'd feel like taking a shower every time I left those people," he says. "Right to Life's job is to be for the right to life."

In St. Louis, where the common-ground movement began, the time to begin discussion came after the 1989 Supreme Court decision in *Webster* vs. *Reproductive Health Services*. In that case, the Supreme Court upheld a Missouri law that allowed the state to restrict abortions in public hospitals and clinics.

Six months later, Andrew Puzder, the lawyer who helped write the Missouri law, wrote a newspaper commentary that called for cooperation. "If we can put aside for a moment our simple win-lose attitudes and approach this issue sensibly and calmly, perhaps we can jointly accomplish some good for those we all seek to protect," he wrote.

Ms. Isaacson-Jones, the director of Reproductive Health Services in St. Louis, read the column and decided to call her legal adversary.

"It was a gutsy move on her part," says Mr. Puzder, now a lawyer in Southern California.

Ms. Isaacson-Jones, a veteran of clinic invasions, a firebombing, death threats and picket lines, invited him to come to the clinic. He agreed—but only after hours, when he was sure no abortions were being performed.

They met in her office.

"We both agreed," he recalls. "I'm not going to convince you to be pro-life, and you're not going to convince me to be pro-choice. Now, having said that, what can we do?"

They found that he was involved with a home for pregnant women, and she had set up an adoption agency in her clinic. "So we had a little common ground right there," he says.

From that first talk came many more—some just between Ms. Isaacson-Jones and Mr. Puzder, some in larger groups. The two sides work on issues in which they share an interest: preventing unwanted pregnancy, teaching abstinence to teen-agers, lowering rates of infant mortality, financing school-breakfast programs.

Then there are specific problems that they had faced together: When a 10-year-old girl turned up pregnant in the clinic and decided to have the baby, Ms. Isaacson-Jones worked together with Missouri Right to Life to find a sitter to stay with the girl when she was confined to bed.

But not everyone in the abortion fight was ready to embrace the enemy.

"I was accused of making the other side sound reasonable," Ms. Isaacson-Jones says. "And I said, 'Well, I'm talking with reasonable people.' "

Mr. Puzder says that some abortion opponents asked how he could talk with people who kill babies. "I said, 'Look, if I can do something that might save the life of a child, are you going to tell me not to, so you can protect your moral or ethical purity? If that's what you're telling me, I'm telling you to get the hell out.' "

Not all efforts to find common ground succeed. Patty Brous, executive director of Planned Parenthood of Greater Kansas City, Mo. says that she spent two hours with one of the leaders of the city's anti-abortion movement. But the discussion got stuck on the conflict between a woman's rights and a fetus's rights. "I can tell you from my short experience we did not find common ground," she says.

DISCOVERING ISSUES FOR ACADEMIC INQUIRY

Some issues lend themselves to inquiry much more readily than to debate. Recall from Chapter 1 that the purpose of inquiry is to discover new views, knowledge, and truths about a complex issue. There are no clear-cut pro and con positions, no judges, and no emphasis on winning, as there often are in debate. Instead, there are potentially as many views as there are participants, and each participant contributes new insights, new reasons, new examples, or new perspectives that the other participants may or may not have considered. Everyone achieves better understanding of the issue through mutual feedback, and sometimes individuals are even persuaded to change their minds. One way to display a variety of perspectives on an issue of common concern is in the symposium format.

How to Set Up a Class Symposium: Assignment

The procedure for this assignment is (1) to select an issue, (2) to identify different perspectives on it, (3) to form groups of students who will brainstorm ideas about each of the different perspectives; (4) to assign all students to write one-page, 250-word papers on the perspective that their group has discussed, and (5) to select one member from each group to read his or her paper in a symposium, which is followed by a class question-and-answer session. The object is to cooperate in discovering new views and knowledge on a difficult question that is still open to inquiry.

Day One: Preparing for the Symposium.

1. *Select an issue.* The class should vote on an issue for inquiry. Some suggestions for issues and accompanying essays that would invite a variety of perspectives for a symposium topic include:

Do People in Their Twenties Have Unrealistic Expectations?

See "The Whiny Generation," pp. 199–201.

How Can People Better Set Priorities and Manage Their Time?

See "We're Too Busy for Ideas," pp. 231–233.

Do Men Argue Better Than Women?

See "Are Opinions Male?" pp. 371–379.

Should Freedom of Speech Be Limited on College Campuses?

See "A Political Correction," pp. 285–286.

Any of the issue questions that are related to the seven issue areas in "The Reader" would provide productive topics for a symposium. Read through the table of contents to see which of these questions and groups of essays would be of interest to your class.

2. *Read.* Read the essay(s) relevant to the selected issue. Mark the passages that suggest original perspectives on the issue to you.

3. *Brainstorm ideas.* Class members as a whole group should brainstorm the different perspectives on the issue and list them on the board. They can refer to their reading notes to help them.

4. *Form groups, select topics, and invent ideas.* Students should work in groups of three or four. Each group selects a different perspective on the issue from the list on the board, makes a claim about it, and brainstorms ideas and support. Each group member makes notes for the one-page, 250-word paper that each student will write outside of class. Each group also selects one of its members to read his or her paper in the symposium.

Day Two: The Symposium.

1. *Conduct the symposium.* The class selects a moderator to sit with the speakers in the front of the room, preferably at a table. The moderator introduces the speakers and gives the titles of their papers. The speakers read their papers.

2. *Question-and-answer session.* Class members who have functioned as the audience ask the speakers questions and also contribute their own views on the subject.

3. *Conclusions.* Students spend 10 minutes writing their own conclusions about the symposium.

An Alternate Symposium Assignment

1. Present one set of argument papers written during the semester by members of the class in a symposium format. Each student writes a 250-word abstract of his or her paper, which states the claim, the main points made about it, and some of the evidence. Each paper will take about 2 minutes to read.

2. Organize groups around the same or related topics. The best group size is six or seven students with a moderator. The moderator calls on each student who in turn presents a paper. Each set of papers is followed by a 5–10-minute question-and-answer period. Two sets of papers can usually be presented in a class period. Thus, most classes can complete the symposium activity in two class periods.

Credits (*continued from page ii*)

Topic Index

*Note: Type in **boldface** identifies issues in the readings.*

Author–Title Index